THE WILLIAM STALLINGS BOOKS ON COMPUTER AND DATA COMMUNICATIONS TECHNOLOGY

OPERATING SYSTEMS

A state-of-the art survey of operating system principles. Covers fundamental technology as well as contemporary design issues, such as threads, real-time systems, multiprocessor scheduling, distributed systems, and security.

HANDBOOK OF COMPUTER-COMMUNICATIONS STANDARDS VOLUME 1
THE OPEN SYSTEMS INTERCONNECTION (OSI) MODEL AND OSI-RELATED STANDARDS, SECOND EDITION

A description of the master plan for all computer-communications standards: the OSI model. The book also provides a detailed presentation of OSI-related standards at all 7 layers, including HDLC, X.25, ISO internet, ISO transport, ISO session, ISO presentation, Abstract Syntax ONE (ASN.1), and common application service elements (CASE).

HANDBOOK OF COMPUTER-COMMUNICATIONS STANDARDS VOLUME 2
LOCAL AREA NETWORK STANDARDS, SECOND EDITION

A detailed examination of all current local network standards, including logical link control (LLC, IEEE 802.2), CSMA/CD (IEEE 802.3), token bus (IEEE 802.4), token ring (IEEE 802.5), and fiber distributed data interface (FDDI, ANS X3T9.5).

HANDBOOK OF COMPUTER-COMMUNICATIONS STANDARDS VOLUME 3
THE TCP/IP PROTOCOL SUITE, SECOND EDITION

A description of the protocol standards that are mandated on all DOD computer procurements and are becoming increasingly popular on commercial local network products, including TCP, IP, FTP, SMTP, and TELNET. The network management standards, SNMP and CMOT, are also presented.

Anne H. Duong

Falls 1992

ISDN and Broadband ISDN

SECOND EDITION

ISDN and Broadband ISDN

William Stallings

MACMILLAN PUBLISHING COMPANY
New York

MAXWELL MACMILLAN CANADA
Toronto

MAXWELL MACMILLAN INTERNATIONAL
New York   Oxford   Singapore   Sydney

Editor: John Griffin
Production Supervisor: John Travis
Production Manager: Valerie A. Sawyer
Text and Cover Designer: Natasha Sylvester
Illustrations and cover illustration by Precision Graphics

This book was set in Palatino by Ruttle, Shaw & Wetherill, and printed and bound by
Book Press. The cover was printed by Lehigh Press.

Macmillan Publishing Company is part
of the Maxwell Communication Group of Companies.

Macmillan Publishing Company
866 Third Avenue, New York, New York 10022

Maxwell Macmillan Canada, Inc.
1200 Eglinton Avenue East
Suite 200
Don Mills, Ontario M3C 3N1

Library of Congress Cataloging in Publication Data
Stallings, William
     ISDN : an introduction / William Stallings. — 2nd ed.
         p.   cm.
     Includes bibliographical references and index.
     ISBN 0-02-415475-X
     1. Integrated services digital networks. I. Title.
TK5103.7.S73   1992
004.6—dc20   91-17635
                                                                          CIP

Printing: 1 2 3 4 5 6 7 8   Year: 2 3 4 5 6 7 8 9 0 1

Again, for my loving wife Tricia Antigone

Preface

Perhaps the most important development in the computer-communications industry in the 1990s will be the evolution of the integrated services digital network (ISDN) and its follow-on, the broadband ISDN (B-ISDN). The ISDN and B-ISDN will have a dramatic effect of communications providers, component manufacturers, and both residential and business telecommunications users. Although the technology and standards for ISDN and B-ISDN are still evolving, a clear picture of the architecture, design approaches, and services of these networks is emerging.

Objective

The objective of this book is to provide a comprehensive introduction to the underlying technology and user-visible architecture of ISDN and B-ISDN. The book explores key topics related to ISDN and B-ISDN in the following general categories:

- *Underlying technology:* The ISDN is based on the development of digital transmission and switching technologies and their use to construct an integrated digital network (IDN) for telecommunications. In addition, the technologies of packet-switching and common-channel signaling are essential ingredients of an IDN.
- *Architecture:* The architecture of the ISDN exploits the emerging application of digital technology to integrate voice and data trans-

mission and to provide structured interfaces and transmission services for the end user.

- *Standards:* A massive effort is underway to develop standards covering the broad spectrum of ISDN protocols, architecture, and services.
- *Services:* The ISDN supports a wide variety of current and new digital services, including facsimile, Teletex, and videotex.

Intended Audience

This book is intended for a broad range of readers who will benefit from an understanding of ISDN and B-ISDN concepts. This includes students and professionals in the fields of data processing and data communications, designers and implementers, and data communication and networking customers and managers. The book is intended to be self-contained. For the reader with little or no background in data communications, a number of basic topics are covered in appendices.

Plan of the Text

The book is organized in such a way that new material is seen to fit into the context of the material already presented. The book divides into three major parts. Part I deals with the technology of the integrated digital network (IDN), which is the essential foundation of the integrated services digital network (ISDN). Part II is devoted to the ISDN, and Part III is devoted to B-ISDN. The organization of the chapters is as follows:

1. *Introduction:* Introduces the concept of ISDN and discusses the evolution towards ISDN.
2. *Circuit switching:* Discusses circuit-switching mechanisms, network design, and common-channel signaling.
3. *Packet-switching:* Examines the mechanisms of packet switched networking, including routing and congestion control. X.25 and fast packet switching are also examined.
4. *IDN technology:* Presents the technology of integrated digital networks, including digital subscriber loops.
5. *ISDN overview:* Provides a general introduction to ISDN, plus a look at the structure of the ISDN standards.
6. *ISDN services:* Presents the basic framework for specifying services for ISDN. This is followed by a look at specific services (Teletex, facsimile, X.400) supported by ISDN.
7. *ISDN Interfaces and Functions:* Looks at issues relating to the architecture of ISDN, including transmission structure, physical configuration, protocol architecture, terminal adaptation, addressing, and interworking.

8. *ISDN Physical Layer:* Presents the technical details for the physical layer of ISDN at the user-network interface.
9. *ISDN Data Link Layer:* Examines LAPD, which is the primary link control protocol for ISDN, and frame relay, which is an innovative new approach to packet-switching that is quickly becoming one of the most significant contributions of the ISDN effort.
10. *ISDN Network Layer:* Presents the call control protocol by which users can request connections across ISDN.
11. *Signaling System Number 7:* Examines the set of Recommendations that define an internal network management and control system for ISDN.
12. *Broadband ISDN:* Introduces the latest development in ISDN technology and standards, and examines the services and architecture of broadband ISDN.
13. *ATM and SONET/SDH:* Examines the fundamental mechanism of broadband ISDN, the asynchronous transfer mode (ATM), together with a look at the related SONET/SDH synchronous transmission standard.

In addition, the book includes an extensive glossary, a list of frequently-used acronyms, and a bibliography. Each chapter includes problems and suggestions for further reading.

A final note: a considerable portion of Part II and Part III of this book is devoted to a set of standards for ISDN, broadband ISDN, and Signaling System Number 7, produced by CCITT. All ISDN development is being done with a view to the need for conformance to the CCITT standards. Thus, these standards are of central importance to any discussion of ISDN and broadband ISDN. The standards for ISDN were initially published, in incomplete form, in 1984. A revised and more complete and internally consistent set were published in 1988. In 1990, additional revisions to the ISDN standards were made and the first set of broadband ISDN standards were published. This text reflects the 1988 and 1990 standards.

Related Materials

The author has produced other material that may be of interest to students and professionals. *Integrated Services Digital Networks (ISDN) and Broadband ISDN* (1992, IEEE Computer Society Press, 10662 Los Vaqueros Circle, P.O. Box 3014, Los Alamitos, CA 90720; telephone 800-272-6657) is a companion to this text. It contains reprints of many of the key references used herein.

Two videotape courses, one on ISDN and one on broadband ISDN, prepared by the author are available from the Media Group, Boston University, 565 Commonwealth Avenue, Boston, MA 02215; telephone 617-353-3217.

The Second Edition

The three years since the publication of the first edition of this book, which was entitled simply *ISDN*, has seen a number of major developments:

1. The 1988 edition of the CCITT Recommendations on ISDN and Signaling System Number 7 have been digested by industry, and products and services based on these standards have emerged.
2. Frame relay, a major innovation of the ISDN work, has achieved widespread acceptance as the technique that will replace X.25 packet switching, and is now being used in many ISDN and non-ISDN contexts.
3. The 1990 set of interim Recommendations for ISDN have clarified and expanded some areas of ISDN and provided much more detail on frame relay.
4. The 1990 set of interim Recommendations for broadband ISDN (B-ISDN) provide the first definitive specification of B-ISDN services and protocols.

Accordingly, an early second edition of this book was required and its expanded scope is suggested by the new title. This second edition is a major revision and expansion of the first. To give some feel for the scope of the revision, approximately 45% of the figures (93 out of 198), 65% of the tables (65 out of 100), and 40% of the references (86 out of 215) in the bibliography are new to this edition. The most significant new topics are the following:

- *Frame Relay:* This new technology is perhaps the most important innovation to come out of the work on ISDN. This edition provides an up-to-date treatment of frame relay protocols and services.
- *Asynchronous transfer mode (ATM):* This technique is at the heart of broadband ISDN. ATM and the requirements for ATM adaptation are covered.
- *U Interface:* Although the interface between the subscriber location and the local loop has still not been standardized by CCITT for ISDN, there now exists an ANSI standard plus some material on the subject in the 1988 and 1990 CCITT Recommendations. The line coding and framing defined for the U interface are described in this edition.

In addition, coverage of the following topics has been significantly expanded:

- *Signaling System No. 7 (SS7):* An entire chapter is now devoted to SS7, with much expanded coverage of the Signaling Connection Control Part (SCCP) and updated discussion of the ISDN User Part.

- *Terminal Adaptation:* A much more detailed presentation of this important topic is provided, including treatment of the important I.465/V.120 data link control protocol, which provides adaptation and multiplexing capabilities.
- *Broadband ISDN:* In addition to the introduction of ATM into this edition, the overall discussion of B-ISDN services and architecture has been expanded from one chapter to two.

With these additions and revisions, together with a number of other lesser revisions, the book provides an up-to-date and comprehensive survey of ISDN and Broadband ISDN.

W.S.

Contents

ISDN and Broadband ISDN

CHAPTER 1

Introduction

Ruth Jones was originally seen by Dr. Farnsworth at the Northern Virginia Hospital for an emergency ear trauma. She returned several times to his office at the hospital complex for follow-up. She is calling today to describe some new symptoms. Today, Dr. Farnsworth is at his suburban McLean office. The call that Mrs. Jones places to the hospital is automatically forwarded to Dr. Farnsworth's other office. The incoming call causes the phone of the physician's assistant in McLean to ring. At the same time, the name and phone number of the caller are displayed on a small screen that is part of the telephone. While the call is ringing, a message is automatically sent back to the hospital to search for any records associated with this call. A database search reveals that the caller is a patient of Dr. Farnsworth. The medical record is transmitted to the McLean office, and the first page of that record is displayed on a terminal screen next to the phone by the time the receiver is picked up.

The technology for this type of service is available today. What is needed to make it available in a practical, affordable fashion is to integrate existing services and new technologies into a network that can handle telephone, data, and other services for residential and business users, both locally and around the world. This integration, with the tongue-twisting name of Integrated Services Digital Network (ISDN), is already being developed and has begun to appear. It is truly a supernetwork, providing universal, accessible, flexible telephone and information services.

This book is an introduction to ISDN. It will explore the technology, applications, and standards of ISDN. The technology underlying ISDN has been driven by market pressures to reduce the cost of voice and data telecommunications. This **technology** consists of the digital transmission and switching architecture being used to build a new all-digital telecommunications infrastructure. Although driven by the need for low-cost voice and data transmission, this technology opens the way to a host of new information-related **applications.** Because a variety of providers will be involved in supplying both the underlying transmission and switching facilities as well as the applications, universal and flexible access can only be achieved with the imposition of **standards.** In this chapter, we give an overview of ISDN and some of the key factors driving the nature and pace of ISDN evolution. The remainder of the book explores these topics in depth.

1.1

THE ARRIVAL OF ISDN

Rapid advances in computer and communication technologies have resulted in the increasing merger of these two fields. The lines have blurred among computing, switching, and digital transmission equipment, and the same digital techniques are being used for data, voice, and image transmission. Merging and evolving technologies, coupled with increasing demands for efficient and timely collection, processing, and dissemination of information, are leading to the development of integrated systems that transmit and process all types of data. The ultimate goal of this evolution is something its proponents—some of the most powerful forces in the computing and telecommunications industries—call the integrated services digital network (ISDN).

The ISDN will be a worldwide public telecommunications network that will deliver a wide variety of services. The ISDN will be defined by the standardization of user interfaces and will be implemented as a set of digital switches and paths supporting a broad range of traffic types and providing value-added processing services. In practice, there will be multiple networks, implemented within national boundaries, but from the user's point of view there will be a single, uniformly accessible worldwide network.

The impact of ISDN on both users and vendors will be profound. To control ISDN evolution and impact, a massive effort at standardization is under way. Although ISDN standards are still evolving, both the technology and the emerging implementation strategy are well understood.

There are two key aspects to ISDN: universal access and user services. By standardizing the interfaces to ISDN, all ISDN-compatible equipment (e.g., telephones, computer terminals, personal computers) will be able to attach to the network anywhere in the world and connect to any other attached system. This can lead to extraordinary flexibility. For example, telephone numbers could be assigned in the same fashion as U.S. social security numbers, good for a lifetime. No matter where you lived, or how often you moved, dialing the number permanently assigned to you would always ring your telephone. Or it would be possible to assign names that connect to the nearest user of that name. Wherever you were, you could reach, say, the nearest Holiday Inn by tapping the telephone buttons marked H-O-L-I-D-A-Y-I-N-N.

The other aspect of ISDN is services. We have already mentioned one example, the medical record retrieval associated with a patient. As another example, consider the banking industry. Bank-by-phone services will depend on automatic identification of the calling party. Transaction privacy and security must be guaranteed. Other features that ISDN will support are increased and increasingly easy-to-use electronic funds transfer facilities and rapid check clearing.

A sample of the trends that are driving ISDN and that will be accelerated by ISDN:

- *Computers are joining together instead of standing alone.* An estimated 30 percent of today's personal computers have communications capability, and the percentage is rising. While yesterday's corporate computer was a stand-alone device, businesses today rely on a mix of small, medium, and large computers that can share resources (e.g., printers), share data, and exchange messages. Our analytical tools have sprouted wires; more and better wires are coming, and the wires will extend everywhere.

- *Cellular radio is making communications mobile.* Automobiles, taxis, and boats are becoming workstations. People can not only talk via cellular radio phones; they can also transmit data by linking up their portable computers. Look for the development of cellular phone/computer combinations. In time, automobiles will provide communication/computer systems as options. Any vehicle, then, will be a unit that can link up to the global information network.

- *Computers for personal use will be ubiquitous.* This will be especially so for students (from elementary school on up) and "knowledge workers," who deal primarily with paper—documents, reports, numbers. Soon many office workers will have at least one workstation at the office and one at home. In fact, many people already have such workstations. Furthermore, most people will own a powerful portable and possibly a wearable model—a very personal computer (VPC). The hotels you stay at in the future may have personal computers in their rooms as amentities; some hotels already do. Computing power will be at every hand; and, most important, each computer will tap into the network.

- *The volume and richness of data are increasing dramatically.* The first-generation personal computers have given way to the latest IBM PSs and MAC-IIs with color and high-quality graphics. New applications in the office environment are being developed that require much higher networking capacity, and desktop image processors will soon increase network data flow by an unprecedented rate. Examples of these applications include digital fax machines, document image processors, and graphics programs on personal computers. Resolutions as high as 400 × 400 per page are typical for these applications. Even with compression techniques, this will generate a tremendous data communications load. Table 1.1 compares the load generated by image processing and some other office applications. In addition, optical disks are beginning to reach technical maturity and are being developed toward realistic desktop capacities exceeding 1 Gbyte.

- *Voice recognition and natural language processing technology will increase the intelligence of systems and networks.* These have been two of the most difficult applications to develop, but they are now gradually emerging from artificial-intelligence laboratories. Voice recognition is the ability to recognize spoken words. Natural language processing is the ability to extract the meaning of words and sentences. As these two applications develop, access to information banks and data bases will become increasingly easier and therefore will create a greater demand. A user will be able to perform a transaction or access information with simple spoken or keyed commands. Interfacing with the worldwide network will be like talking with a very knowledgeable telephone operator, librarian, and universal expert rolled into one.

- *Government use of computer systems will become more efficient.* The government is the most prodigious producer and user of information in our society. ISDN will improve and disperse access and help to remove incompatibilities between different systems so that more can be done with less effort.

- *National and global business activities will become easier to promote.* The brokerage business has become almost a computer network in itself, depending upon instant transmission of information and automated buy–sell orders. Banking today relies upon more than automatic tellers and computerized accounting; money itself is becoming akin to information as fund transfers take place over growing data networks. And banks are beginning to sell online information services as adjuncts to electronic banking. Companies of all sizes are coming to depend upon telecommunications for their daily business activities. Remote data entry, electronic mail, facsimile

TABLE 1.1   Network Load Component Comparison

Traffic Type	Size in Bits
Compressed page image (400 × 400)	600,000
Compressed page image (200 × 200)	250,000
Word-processing page	20,000
Typical memo	3,500
Data processing transaction	500

Source: [BEVA86]

transmission, and decision support systems are just some of the operations that rely upon communications. Multinational corporations and joint ventures between American and foreign firms depend upon quick interchange of information. Communication networks are absolutely essential for the continued globalization of trade and industry.

- *Office buildings are being wired for intelligence.* The so-called "smart building" is beginning to appear. Such a building contains a network for voice, data, environmental control (heat, humidity, air conditioning), security (burglar, fire), and closed-circuit TV. Many of these services generate out-of-building transmission requirements.

- *Person-to-person interaction will increase.* Business is responding to the need for employees to interact and to avoid "telephone tag" with electronic mail, voice mail, file transfer, document exchange, and video teleconferencing facilities. All of these generate large data communications requirements.

- *The fiber revolution will bring enormous capacity that will generate its own demand.* In developed countries, fiber is rapidly replacing microwave and coaxial cable transmission paths. Fiber, together with satellite, is appearing more gradually elsewhere. The resulting quantum jump in capacity has permitted the planning and deployment of new applications on public and private networks.

These trends, and others, are part of the evolution to ISDN. In this book, we will relate these trends and the requirements they generate to the solution that ISDN represents.

1.2

THE COMPUTER–COMMUNICATIONS REVOLUTION

Ours has been called the postindustrial era. By that is meant that industrialization, which was the dominating factor and engine of change for over a century, no longer fulfills that role. To those societies that have experienced the industrial revolution, the social and economic changes have been profound. The postindustrial era is producing even greater and more rapid changes. Many trends are visible as threads making up the rope that is dragging mankind into a life and life-style dictated not by politicians and economists, but by the technologists. All of these threads, at bottom, depend on two major technologies: computers and communications.

Consider one example: biotechnology. One of the youngest technologies, biotechnology has already brought with it a number of firms in the business of producing commercially available products and some of the hottest action in the stock market in the 1980s. Biotechnology firms are doing research on substances that can combat cancer, eat oil spills, and solve many other problems facing society. It has been repeatedly alleged that biotechnology is also being applied in the Soviet Union to the development of biological weapons of immense potency. All of the goods, and ills, of this technology are impossible without sophisticated use of computers. Computers are used to monitor and control the fabrication of new biological entities and to model the process of creating new substances so that the most likely direction of research can be followed. Extremely fast and powerful computer systems are needed for this purpose.

Another example is what is known as factory automation. General Motors, in particular, is convinced that the only way to compete with Japanese automakers is to drastically reduce the labor cost of producing cars. To do this, the factory environment must increasingly include microcomputers, programmable controllers, and robots. Computer technology must replace human labor on the assembly line. For the automated factory to work, sophisticated computer-controlled devices are required. Equally important, all of these devices must be interconnected with a local area network (LAN). The LAN ties together all of the equipment in the factory so that control signs can be sent to the automated devices on the assembly line, and data and alarm signals can be sent by these devices to computers that act in the role of foreman and supervisor.

As a final example, consider office automation, which can be defined as the incorporation of appropriate technology in the office to help people manage information. The key motivation for the move to office automation is, again, productivity. As the percentage of white-collar workers has increased, the information and paperwork volume has grown. In most installations, secretarial and other support functions are heavily labor intensive. Increased labor costs combined with low productivity and increasing work load have caused employers to seek effective ways of increasing their rather low capital investment in office-related work. At the same time principals (managers, skilled information workers) are faced with their own productivity bind. Work needs to be done faster with less wait time and less waste time between segments of a job. This requires better access to information and better communication and coordination with others. As in the factory environment, the solution is a collection of computer-based equipment interconnected with a LAN.

It has become commonplace to talk about the dramatic pace of change in these two technologies, computers and communications. Rapid technological change has been characteristic of these two areas since the 1960s. What is new is that there has been a merger of these two technologies. This merger has been called the computer–communications revolution. It has had a profound impact on the providing industries and on the users—businesses and individuals. That merger, or revolution, was substantially accomplished by the late 1970s and early 1980s. We are now on the threshold of the aftermath and logical conclusion of that revolution: ISDN.

1.3

FROM COMMUNICATIONS TO COMPUTERS

The communications facilities that provide voice, data, and video transmission services are increasingly relying on digital technology and computerized systems. The two driving forces here are the changing economics and regulatory focus of telephone networks and the increasing demand for terminal user services.

The Evolving Telephone Network

The U.S. public telephone network, once the almost exclusive property of AT&T, and now fragmented among a number of companies, was originally an analog network. It is now in the slow process of evolving to what is being referred to as the integrated digital network (IDN), which is the subject of Part I of this book.

Increasingly, the choice of network designers is to use digital technology for transmission and switching. Despite its massive investment in analog equipment, AT&T is gradually converting to an all-digital network. Other long-distance transmission providers, such as MCI, are doing the same. The major reasons for this trend:

- *Component cost:* While the cost of analog components has remained fairly stable, the cost of digital components continues to drop. The use of large-scale integration (LSI) and very-large-scale integration (VLSI) decreases not only the size, but also the cost of virtually all equipment used to process digital signals.

- *Line sharing:* Over long distance, the signals from many telephone calls will share common transmission paths by means of multiplexing. Time–division multiplexing, using digital techniques, is more efficient than the analog-based frequency–division multiplexing. Thus, the voice input from the telephone is converted to digital for the long-distance links.
- *Network control:* Control signals that monitor the status and control the operation of networks are inherently digital. They can be more easily incorporated into an all-digital network.

Thus, more and more, digital technology is being applied to the telephone network. The techniques used are the same as those used in computer systems. So, increasingly, the major components of the telephone network are either computers themselves or computer-controlled.

Teleprocessing and Telematics

Historically, and still-today, telephone traffic has been the major reason for, and the major user of, long-distance communications facilities. Over the past 25 years, however, there has been a growing use of these facilities to transmit digital data. By far, the major component of this digital data requirement has been for communication between a user at a terminal and a computer remote from that user. The communications function that provides this remote terminal access is known as teleprocessing. More recently, additional services built on the basic teleprocessing function, known as telematics, have appeared.

To understand these trends, we need to say something about the way in which computer usage has evolved (see [STAL87a] for a lengthier discussion). In the 1950s, the typical computer was large and expensive. It was a limited resource that needed to be used efficiently. For this purpose, operating systems were developed. The original operating systems were batch, which controlled the execution of a sequence of user programs, called jobs. A user could submit a job, and that job would be queued up, waiting for the use of the computer. As soon as one job finished, the operating system would fetch the next job in line for execution.

As computers became more powerful and the demand for their use grew, batch operating systems became obsolete. The problem was that if only one program is executing, many of the system's resources are idle at any given time. For example, while data to be processed are being read in, those portions of the system that can perform arithmetic and logical functions are unused. To overcome this inefficiency, the time-sharing operating system was developed. With time sharing, many jobs can be active at any one time. The operating system orchestrates matters so that various resources are applied to particular jobs at any given time. And, whereas the user of a batch-oriented system would typically submit a job to a computer operator and come back some time later for the results, the time-sharing user interacts directly with the operating system from a terminal.

The first time-sharing users used terminals that were in close proximity to the computer. But soon the demand for remote terminal access, known as **teleprocessing,** developed. A large organization (e.g., a bank or an insurance company) might have a central data processing facility but potential users in a number of satellite offices. Time-sharing services sprang up. Such a service "rented time" on its computer to users who could not afford their own system. More recently, transaction-processing systems have appeared. Point-of-sale systems, airline reservation systems, and so forth involve many terminal users who perform transactions that are recorded in a data base on a remote computer.

Remote terminal access can be and is handled by the public telephone network. The digital data are converted to analog signals and transmitted just as the voice signals in an ordinary telephone call. But this is inefficient. When a call is placed, resources within the network are dedicated to setting up and maintaining the call. In effect, a circuit through the network is dedicated for the duration. Now, with a telephone call, generally one party or the other is talking most of the time, and good use is made of the circuit. But with a terminal-to-computer connection, much of the time the circuit is idle, when neither side is transmitting.

To improve efficiency, packet switching was developed. Terminal and computer data are sent out in small blocks, known as packets. These packets are routed through the network using paths and resources that are shared among a number of users sending packets. Thus the network must know how to handle and process packets—another example of computerization of communications.

The demand for data communications and the use of packet switching continue to grow. In addition to the more traditional teleprocessing services, new **telematic** services are appearing. Telematic facilities provide a user at a terminal with access to a specific application or data base. An example is a catalog-ordering service. The user is connected to the service and may select various items for viewing. Each catalog item is described on the user's terminal screen, and the user may place an order.

U.S. Regulatory Implications

Thus we see the increasing incorporation of computer technology into the public telecommunications networks, due to two driving forces. First, it has become more economical to use digital transmission and switching techniques in the network, and these require the use of computer technology. Second, there is an increased use of data communications services (teleprocessing and telematics), and the provision of these services by communication providers blurs the distinction between computer and communication technologies. This incorporation of computer technology into communications is reflected clearly by the history of communications regulation in the United States, the highlights of which are now recounted.

With the Communications Act of 1934, Congress established universal and affordable telephone service as a national goal. The Federal Communications Commission (FCC) was created to regulate and promote telecommunications. The FCC had primary responsibility for regulating the rates and conditions of interstate telephone service. Soon after its formation, the FCC began an investigation of the Bell Telephone System, which resulted in the development of a major antitrust suit against AT&T by the Department of Justice. Delayed by World War II, the suit was filed in 1949 and was settled by the **1956 Consent Decree.** For the present discussion, the key element of the Consent Decree was that Bell confine its activities to providing telecommunications services under regulation and refrain from providing commercial data processing services.

The Consent Decree proved inadequate in the face of advances in data communications and data processing. In the late 1960s, there was an increasing use of centralized mainframe computers with distributed terminals and increasing use of the telecommunications network for data transmission. This prompted the FCC to begin the first of three "computer inquiries": The first, known as **Computer Inquiry I,** asked for public and industry comments on the impact of data processing on communications. Two key issues:

1. The nature and extent of FCC regulation that should be applied along the continuum from pure data processing to pure data communications.
2. Whether, and if so, under what circumstances and subject to what conditions and safeguards should common carriers be allowed to provide data processing services.

The inquiry, completed in 1971, distinguished between telecommunications and data processing service, with the former to be regulated and the latter unregulated and open to competition. Hybrid services were to be dealt with on an ad hoc basis.

The 1971 definitions also proved to be inadequate as technology marched on. With the increased use of digital transmission and switching technology, and the development of packet switching, the distinctions between data processing and communications blurred. Data processing became increasingly distributed, with the attendant reliance on data communications and networks. Computer hardware and software were increasingly incorporated into telephone network equipment and private branch exchanges (PBXs). The FCC tried again in 1980 with the final report of **Computer Inquiry II.** The decision distinguished between basic and enhanced services. Basic services were the offering of transmission capacity for the transport of data. Enhanced services were defined as

> . . . services offered over common carrier facilities used in interstate communications, which employ computer processing applications that act on format, content, code, protocol or similar aspects of the subscriber's transmitted information; provide the subscriber additional, different, or restructured information; or involve subscriber interaction with stored information.

Again, the basic services were to be subject to regulation, while enhanced services were to be deregulated. Computer Inquiry II also specified that basic services would be provided to enhanced service providers with a fair rate structure. In addition, the Bell System was required to set up a separate corporate entity to offer enhanced services and customer premises equipment so that cross subsidization would be avoided.

A final noteworthy event is **Computer Inquiry III,** the latest chapter in the FCC's 20-year struggle to deal with the increasing integration of computers and transmission systems in telecommunications. The inquiry was begun in 1985, and a first Report and Order was issued in 1986. The most important part of the report is the decision to rest the future regulation of integrated telecommunication and information networks upon a new mandate for an **Open Network Architecture (ONA)** for equal access to basic telecommunication services:

> We consider Open Network Architecture to be the overall design of a carrier's basic network facilities and services to permit all users, including the enhanced service operations of the carrier and its competitors, to interconnect to specific basic network functions and interfaces on an unbundled and "equal access" basis. A carrier providing enhanced services through Open Network Architecture must unbundle key components of its basic service and offer them to the public under tarriff, regardless of whether its enhanced services utilize the unbundled components. These components, such as trunking interconnections, may utilize subcomponents that themselves are offered on an unbundled basis, such as separate channel signaling and called or calling signal identification. Such unbundling will ensure that competitors for the carrier's enhanced services operations can develop enhanced services that utilize the carrier's network on an economical basis.

The commission has so far not described in any significant detail what is meant by open network architecture. Indeed, with the increasing software component of telecommunication networks, which makes them increasingly virtual and "soft," and the evolution toward ISDN, any technical definition is working against a moving target. What can be said is that the concept of ONA is in the spirit of both deregulation and reliance on standardized interfaces and that it reflects the essential unity of data communications and computing.

1.4
FROM COMPUTERS TO COMMUNICATIONS

While communications facilities have increasingly made use of computer technology, the opposite is also true. The hardware and software within a computer specifically devoted to the communications function have grown in size and importance. The reason for this is that, increasingly, data processing facilities are being implemented as a collection of cooperating computers rather than a single large computer. This is known as distributed processing, since the processing function is distributed among a number of computers. To follow what has happened, we need to look at three aspects:

- The economic forces that have made distributed processing possible;
- The potential benefits of distributed processing that have encouraged its development;
- The implications in terms of the communications function.

Economic Forces and Potential Benefits

Two trends have combined to change the economic equation for distributed processing: the dramatic and continuing decrease in computer hardware costs, accompanied by an increase in computer hardware capability.

Today's microprocessors have speeds, instruction sets, and memory capacities comparable to those of minicomputers and even mainframes of just a few years ago. In general terms, this phenomenon is illustrated in Figure 1.1. By almost any measure of computer power, each class has grown in power over time. Going up the chart diagonally, one sees that a class of computers becomes more powerful as time goes on. Going across the chart horizontally, one sees that, over time, the same computing power can be provided by smaller, cheaper computers. This trend has spawned a number of changes in the way information is collected, processed, and used in organizations. There is an increasing use of small, single-function systems, such as word processors and small business computers, and of general-purpose microcomputers,

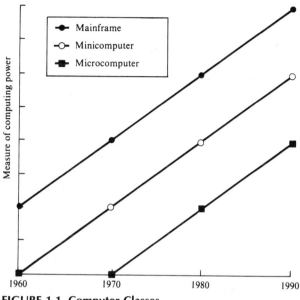

FIGURE 1.1 Computer Classes

such as personal computers and Unix workstations. These small, dispersed systems are more accessible to the user, more responsive, and easier to use than large central time-sharing systems. This explosion of small systems is shown in Figures 1.2 and 1.3. Note especially that, while large and medium-size systems continue to represent the majority of shipments in terms of installed value, the sheer number of microcomputers is overwhelming.

As the number of systems increases, there is likely to be a desire to interconnect these systems for a variety of reasons, including

- Sharing expensive resources, and
- Exchanging data between systems.

Sharing expensive resources, such as bulk storage and laser printers, is an important measure of cost containment. Although the cost of data processing hardware has dropped, the cost of such essential electromechanical equipment remains high. Even in the case of data that can be uniquely associated with a small system, economies of scale encourage the storage of those data on some sort of centralized server system. The cost per bit for storage on a microcomputer's floppy disk is orders of magnitude higher than that for a large disk or tape.

The ability to exchange data is an equally compelling reason for interconnection. Individual users of computer systems do not work in isolation and will want to retain some of the benefits provided by a central system, including the ability to exchange messages with other

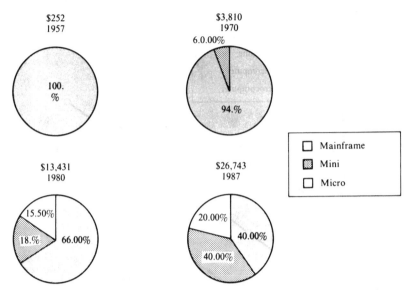

FIGURE 1.2 U.S. Consumption of Micros, Minis, and Mainframes (value in millions of 1986 dollars) [HODG87]

users and the ability to access data and programs from several sources in the preparation of a document or the analysis of data.

In addition to these benefits, several others are worth mentioning. A distributed system can be more reliable, more available to the user, and more able to survive failures. The loss of any one component should have minimal impact, and key components can be made redundant so that other systems can quickly take up the load after a failure. Finally, a distributed system provides the potential to connect devices from multiple vendors, which gives the cutomer greater flexibility and bargaining power.

The Computer's Communication Function

Distributed processing relies upon a communications facility for interconnecting the computers that make up the distributed processing system. But more is involved. In order to achieve cooperative action, the computers themselves must incorporate functions traditionally thought of as communications functions.

Consider, for example, the transfer of a file between two computers. There must be a data path between the two computers, either directly or via a communication network. In addition, a number of functions must be provided, such as

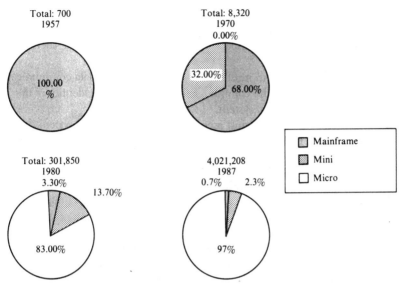

FIGURE 1.3 U.S. Shipments of Micros, Minis, and Mainframes [HODG87]

1. The source system must either activate the direct data communication path or inform the communication network of the identity of the desired destination system.
2. The source system must ascertain that the destination system is prepared to receive data.
3. The file transfer application in the source system must ascertain that the file management program in the destination system is prepared to accept and store the file.
4. If the file formats used on the two systems are incompatible, one or the other system must perform a format translation function.

It is clear that there must be a high degree of cooperation between the two computer systems. The exchange of information between computers for the purpose of cooperative action is generally referred to as computer communications. Similarly, when two or more computers are interconnected via a communication network, the set of computers is referred to as a computer network. Since a similar level of cooperation is required between a user at a terminal and a computer, these terms are often used when some of the communicating entities are terminals.

These functions, which deal with control and cooperation, have been developed for use within the telephone network and are now finding application in the computers that make up a distributed processing system. Thus, just as the communications providers are increasingly using computer technology, the opposite is also occurring.

1.5

OUTLINE OF THE BOOK

This chapter, of course, serves as an introduction to the entire book. A brief synopsis of the remaining chapters follows.

Circuit Switching

The first part of the book, after the introductory chapter, deals with the concept of the integrated digital network (IDN). The key technology of today's telecommunications, and the dominant technology of the evolving IDN, is circuit switching. Chapter 2 looks at the principles of circuit switching. In the digital realm, circuit switching is based on the use of time-division techniques, and these are examined. The chapter then looks at the way in which wide-area circuit-switched networks are constructed, examining multiplexing, routing, and signaling.

Packet Switching

The other key technology in wide-area networking is packet switching. In Chapter 3, the operational principles of packet switching are examined. The key technical issues of routing and congestion control are discussed. The common standard for interfacing to packet-switched networks, X.25, is also examined. Finally, the new technology of fast packet switching, which is expected to play an important role in ISDN, is introduced.

Integrated Digital Networks

The evolution of the existing telecommunication networks, specialized carrier facilities, and value-added data communication networks to an ISDN is based on two technological developments: digital transmission and digital switching. One outcome of the migration to digital techniques is that it allows the functions of transmission and switching to be integrated in a way that reduces cost, enhances reliability, and provides a base for ISDN. This integration of transmission and switching is referred to as an integrated digital network (IDN). Chapter 4 examines the key technologies and features of the IDN, including the use of Signaling System Number 7 for common channel signaling, thus setting the stage for the discussion in Part II.

ISDN Overview

With many of the technical underpinnings dealt with in Part I, Part II turns to a discussion of ISDN. Chapter 5 serves as an overview. The relationship between IDN and ISDN is examined, and key issues, such as standards, applications. ISDN-specific technology, and status are introduced.

ISDN Services

The reason for the existence of ISDN is the set of services that it will provide. These services define the requirements for ISDN. In Chapter 6, we look first at the general specification of services found in the ISDN standards. In these standards, services are defined in terms of a set of attributes that can take on a range of values. The chapter then examines three services that will be used extensively over ISDN: teletex, facsimile, and X.400 electronic mail.

ISDN Architecture

Chapter 7 describes the architecture of ISDN. ISDN includes a small set of standardized interfaces for users that support a wide variety of services. These services are available through a transmission structure that provides various data rates over a multiplexed line. Two related issues are the addressing of subscribers over ISDN and the need for interworking between ISDNs and between an ISDN and a non-ISDN network.

ISDN Physical Layer

Chapter 8 discusses the CCITT specifications for the physical layer of ISDN. These include a basic rate access at 192 kbps and a primary rate access at either 1.544 Mbps or 2.048 Mbps. All of these specifications deal with the interface between the subscriber's equipment and a network termination device on the subscriber's premises. In addition, Chapter 8 looks at a standard issued by the American National Standards Institute (ANSI) that covers the transmission from the subscriber's premises to the local ISDN exchange.

ISDN Data Link Layer

Chapter 9 discusses the CCITT specifications for the data link layer of ISDN. The fundamental standard at this layer is LAPD, which is used to support call control signaling and user packet switching on the D channel. Another standard, I.465/V.120, has been defined for use on B channels to support non-ISDN devices and to provide a simple multiplexing capability. Finally, the chapter looks at one of the most important innovations to come out of the work on ISDN: frame relay. Frame relay provides a more efficient means of supporting packet switching than X.25 and is finding wide use, not only for ISDN but in other networking contexts.

ISDN Network Layer

Chapter 10 discusses the CCITT specifications for the network layer of ISDN. The principal concern here is I.451/Q.931, which specifies a user-network call control protocol. This protocol is used for setting up, maintaining, and terminating connections on user channels. In addition, the chapter examines the call control protocol for support of frame relay.

Signaling System Number 7

Signaling System Number 7 (SS7) is an elaborate set of recommendations that defines the protocols and mechanisms for the internal management of ISDN and other integrated digital networks. Chapter 11 introduces the overall architecture of SS7 and then examines the protocols at each layer of the SS7 protocol reference model.

Broadband ISDN

Although the original version of ISDN, defined in a preliminary way in 1984 and more fully in 1988, is still in the process of being implemented, attention in the standards community has already shifted to a "second-generation" ISDN, known as broadband ISDN (B-ISDN). A B-ISDN will have significantly greater capacity than the current "narrowband" ISDN. Chapter 12 examines some of the key technical developments that are driving the B-ISDN effort. The chapter then looks at the services that B-ISDN will support and the overall architecture of B-ISDN.

ATM and SONET/SDH

The basic transmission mechanism for B-ISDN is known as the asynchronous transfer mode (ATM). Chapter 13 is devoted to a discussion of ATM and related issues. First, the details of the ATM mechanism are examined. Then, the way in which B-ISDN services are adapted to operate over ATM is examined. Then, a new synchronous digital transmission scheme, known as synchronous optical network (SONET) or synchronous digital hierarchy (SDH), is introduced. Finally, the chapter examines the alternative mechanisms for structuring ATM transmission, one of which is the use of SONET/SDH.

Flow Control, Error Detection, and Error Control

A number of the protocols discussed in this book make use of some basic techniques for flow control, error detection, and error control. These include X.25 level 3, LAP-B, the Signaling Link layer of Signaling System Number 7, and LAP-D. For the reader unfamiliar with these widely used techniques, Appendix A provides a brief description.

The OSI Model

Throughout this book, repeated reference is made to the open systems interconnection (OSI) model, and the structure of ISDN protocols is often compared to this model. The OSI model is of fundamental importance in the study of data and computer communications. It provides an architecture within which protocol standards can be developed. Furthermore, because of its universal acceptance, it provides a terminology and frame of reference that are commonly used in networking discourses. For the reader unfamiliar with this model, Appendix B provides a brief description.

Integrated Digital Networks

The evolution of existing public telecommunications networks, specialized carrier facilities, and value-added telecommunication networks to an ISDN is based on the development and integration of digital transmission and switching technologies. The integration of these technologies has been termed the **integrated digital network** (IDN). The term *integrated* in IDN has been used to refer to

- The integration of transmission and switching equipment;
- The integration of voice and data communications;
- The integration of circuit-switching and packet-switching facilities.

The IDN is the foundation and prerequisite for ISDN. Accordingly, the first part of this book is devoted to the study of IDN. The two major technologies underlying the development of IDN, circuit switching, and packet switching are examined in separate chapters. Integrated digital networks are evolving from today's circuit-switching networks, and this technology is examined in Chapter 2. The chapter examines the basic mechanism used in digital circuit switches, time-division switching. The chapter also looks at a number of issues related to the operation and control of circuit-switching networks, including routing and control signaling. Then packet switching is examined in Chapter 3. Although the increasing availability of digital circuit-switched networks in some sense offers competition to packet-switched networks, the latter will continue to play a key role in both IDN and ISDN. The technology and operation of such networks is examined, together with the standard interface to such networks, X.25.

Finally, Chapter 4 looks at other aspects of IDN beyond the basic technologies of circuit switching and packet switching. Following an overview of the IDN concept, there is a discussion of digital carrier systems. Then the essential issue of bringing digital service to the end subscriber is examined. Finally, software-defined networks, which may be viewed as a precursor to ISDN, are introduced.

CHAPTER 2

Circuit Switching

2.1

OVERVIEW

Circuit switching is the dominant technology for both voice and data communications today and will remain so into the ISDN era. Communication via circuit switching implies that there is a dedicated communication path between two stations. That path is a connected sequence of links between network nodes. On each physical link, a channel is dedicated to the connection. Communication via circuit switching involves three phases, which can be explained with reference to Figure 2.1.

1. Circuit establishment. Before any signals can be transmitted, an end-to-end (station-to-station) circuit must be established. For example, station A sends a request to node 4, requesting a connection to station E. Typically, the link from A to 4 is a dedicated line, so that part of the connection already exists. Node 4 must find the next leg in a route leading to node 6. Based on routing information and measures of availability and perhaps cost, node 4 selects the link to node 5, allocates a free channel (using frequency-division multiplexing, FDM, or time-division multiplexing, TDM) on that link and sends a message requesting connection to E. So far, a dedicated path has been established from A through 4 to 5. Since a number of stations may attach to 4, it must be able

23

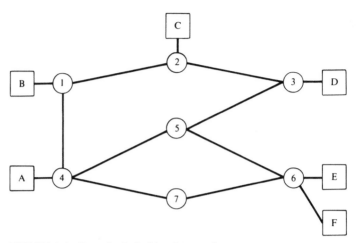

FIGURE 2.1 Generic Switching Network

to establish internal paths from multiple stations to multiple nodes. How this is done is the main topic of this chapter. The remainder of the process proceeds similarly. Node 5 dedicates a channel to node 6 and internally ties that channel to the channel from node 4. Node 6 completes the connection to E. In completing the connection, a test is made to determine if E is busy or is prepared to accept the connection.

2. Signal transfer. Signals can now be transmitted from A through the network to E. The transmitted signals may be analog voice, digitized voice, or binary data, depending on the nature of the network. As the carriers evolve to fully integrated digital networks, the use of digital (binary) transmission for both voice and data is becoming the dominant method. The path is: A-4 link, internal switching through 4, 4-5 channel, internal switching through 5, 5-6 channel, internal switching through 6, 6-E link. Generally, the connection is full duplex, and data may be transmitted in both directions simultaneously.

3. Circuit disconnect. After some period of data transfer, the connection is terminated, usually by the action of one of the two stations. Signals must be propagated to nodes 4, 5, and 6 to deallocate the dedicated resources.

Note that the connection path is established before data transmission begins. Thus channel capacity must be reserved between each pair of nodes in the path and each node must have available internal switching capacity to handle the requested connection. The switches must have the intelligence to make these allocations and to devise a route through the network.

Circuit switching can be rather inefficient. Channel capacity is dedicated for the duration of a connection, even if no data are being transferred. For a voice connection, utilization may be rather high, but it still does not approach 100 percent. For a terminal-to-computer connection, the capacity may be idle during most of the time of the connection. In terms of performance, there is a delay prior to data transfer for call establishment. However, once the circuit is established, the network is effectively transparent to the users. Data are transmitted at a fixed data rate with no delay other than the propagation delay through the transmission links. The delay at each node is negligible.

Some of the key characteristics of circuit switching are summarized in Box 2.1. In terms of applications, circuit switching was developed to handle voice traffic but is now also used for data traffic. The best-known example of a circuit-switching network is the public telephone network. This is actually a collection of national networks interconnected to form the international service. Although originally designed and implemented to service analog telephone subscribers, it handles substantial data traffic via modem and is gradually being converted to a digital network. Within the United States, the network is primarily provided by AT&T and the Bell Operating Companies (BOCs) that split off from AT&T in 1984. Another well-known application of circuit switching is the private branch exchange (PBX), used to interconnect telephones within a building or office. Circuit switching is also used in private networks. Typically, such a network is set up by a corporation or other large organization to interconnect its various sites. Such a network usually consists of PBX systems at each site interconnected by dedicated, leased lines obtained from one of the carriers, such as AT&T. A final common example of the application of circuit switching is the data switch. The data switch is similar to the PBX, but is designed to interconnect digital data processing devices, such as terminals and computers. The more recent generations of the PBX, known as digital PBXs, are able to easily handle both voice and data attachments.

Figure 2.2 illustrates the basic concepts of a circuit-switched telephone network. The most common switching function involves a direct connection between two subscribers connected to the same switch. One example of this is two telephones in the same building connected to the same PBX. Another example is two subscribers in the same metropolitan area connected to the same local telephone exchange, referred to as an end office. Transit switching involves setting up a path from a specific incoming line or channel to an outgoing channel on a trunk. Typically, an end office will be connected to a number of other switching centers by trunks and will perform transit switching as well as local

BOX 2.1

Circuit Switching

APPLICATIONS

Voice

Public Telephone Network

Provide interconnection for two-way voice signal exchange between attached telephones. Calls can be placed between any two subscribers on a national and international basis. This network is evolving to handle an increasing amount of data traffic.

Private Branch Exchange (PBX)

Provide a telephone exchange capability within a single building or cluster of buildings. Calls can be placed between any two subscribers within the local site; interconnection is also provided to public or private wide-area circuit-switched networks.

Private Wide-Area Network

Provide interconnection among a number of sites. Generally used to interconnect PBXs that are part of the same organization.

Data

Data Switch

Provide for the interconnection of terminals and computers within a local site.

REQUIREMENTS

1. Establish, maintain, and terminate call on subscriber request.
2. Provide transparent, full-duplex signal transmission.
3. Limit delay to that acceptable for voice connection (≤ 0.5 s).
4. Provide quality adequate for voice connection.
5. Limit blocking probability.

TECHNOLOGY

Switching Techniques

Space-division
Time-division
  TDM bus switching

Time-slot interchange (TSI)
Time-multiplexed switching (TMS)

Transmission

Multiplexed carrier
Routing algorithm
Control signals

switching. In addition, the network will include a number of switching centers that support only trunks to other switching centers. These tandem or toll switching centers perform transit switching between channels on different trunks.

Circuit-switching technology has been driven by those applications that handle voice traffic. This is reflected in the list of key requirements listed in Box 2.1. Voice signals must be transmitted with virtually no delay and certainly with no variation in delay. A constant signal transmission rate must be maintained since transmission and reception occur at the same signal rate. These requirements are necessary to allow normal human conversation. Further, the quality of the received signal must be sufficiently high to provide, at a minimum, intelligibility. The last requirement, on blocking probability, refers to the capacity of a switch and is defined subsequently.

Circuit switching achieved its widespread, dominant position be-

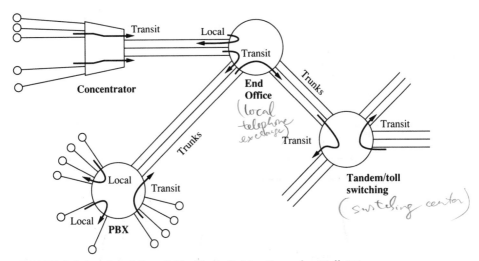

FIGURE 2.2 Local and Transit Traffic Switching Examples [Bell 91]

cause it is well suited to the analog transmission of voice signals. In today's digital world, its inefficiencies are more apparent. However, despite the inefficiency, circuit switching is and will remain an attractive choice for both local-area and wide-area networking. One of its key strengths is that it is transparent. Once a circuit is established, it appears like a direct connection to the two attached stations; no special networking logic is needed at the station. In addition, circuit switching avoids the complex routing, flow control, and error control requirements that we will see for packet-switched networks.

In the remainder of this chapter, we examine the basic technology of circuit switching. As we shall see, any treatment of the technology and architecture of circuit-switched networks must of necessity focus on the internal operation of a single switch. This is in contrast to packet switching, discussed in the next chapter, which is best explained by the collective behavior of the set of switches that make up the network.

2.2
ONE-NODE NETWORKS

A network built around a single circuit-switching node consists of a collection of devices or stations attached to a central switching unit. The central switch established a dedicated path between any two devices that wish to communicate. Figure 2.3 depicts the major elements of such a one-node network.

The heart of a modern system is a **digital switch.** The function of

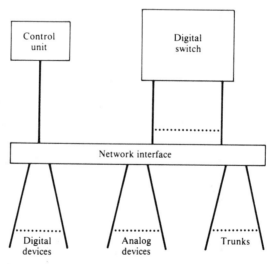

FIGURE 2.3 Elements of a Circuit-switching Node

the digital switch is to provide a transparent signal path between any pair of attached devices. The path is transparent in the sense that it appears to the attached pair of devices that there is a direct connection between them. Typically, the connection must allow full-duplex transmission. Figure 2.4 depicts a switch with 20 attached lines. The dotted lines inside the switch symbolize the connections that are currently active. Later in this chapter, we will discuss various techniques that may be used to establish and maintain such connections.

The advent of digital switching technology has dramatically improved the cost, performance, and capability of circuit-switched networks. Key to the operation of such a system are that (1) all signals are represented digitally, and (2) synchronous time-division multiplexing (TDM) techniques are used.

The **network interface** element represents the functions and hardware needed to connect digital devices, such as data processing devices and digital telephones, to the network. Analog telephones can also be attached if the network interface contains the logic for converting to digital signals. Trunks to other digital switches carry TDM signals and provide the links for constructing multiple-node networks.

The **control unit** performs three general tasks. First, it establishes connections. This is generally done on demand, that is, at the request of an attached device. To establish the connection, the control unit must handle and acknowledge the request, determine if the intended desti-

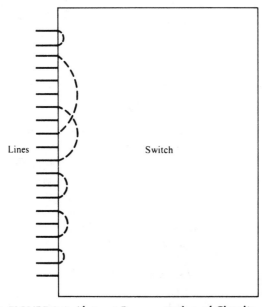

FIGURE 2.4 Abstract Representation of Circuits

nation is free, and construct a path through the switch. Second, the control unit must maintain the connection. Since the digital switch uses time-division principles, this may require ongoing manipulation of the switching elements. However, the bits of the communication are transferred transparently (from the point of view of the attached devices). Third, the control unit must tear down the connection, either in response to a request from one of the parties or for its own reasons.

An important characteristic of a circuit-switching device is whether it is blocking or nonblocking. Blocking occurs when the network is unable to connect two stations because all possible paths between them are already in use. A blocking network is one in which such blocking is possible. Hence a nonblocking network permits all stations to be connected (in pairs) at once and grants all possible connection requests as long as the called party is free. When a network is supporting only voice traffic, a blocking configuration is generally acceptable, since it is expected that most phone calls are of short duration and that therefore only a fraction of the telephones will be engaged at any time. However, when data processing devices are involved, these assumptions may be invalid. For example, for a data entry application, a terminal may be continuously connected to a computer for hours at a time. [BHUS85] reports that typical voice connections on a private branch exchange (PBX) have a duration of 120 to 180 seconds, whereas data calls have a range of from 8 seconds to 15 hours. Hence, for data applications, there is a requirement for a nonblocking or "nearly nonblocking" (very low probability of blocking) configuration.

We turn now to an examination of the switching techniques internal to a single circuit-switching node.

2.3

SPACE-DIVISION SWITCHING

Space-division switching was originally developed for the analog environment and has been carried over into digital technology. The fundamental principles are the same, whether the switch is used to carry analog or digital signals. As its name implies, a space-division switch is one in which the signal paths that are set up are physically separate from one another (divided in space). Each connection requires the establishment of a physical path through the switch that is dedicated solely to the transfer of signals between the two endpoints. The basic building block of the switch is a metallic crosspoint or semiconductor gate [ABBO84] that can be enabled and disabled by a control unit.

Figure 2.5 shows a simple crossbar matrix with N full-duplex I/O lines. The matrix has N inputs and N outputs; each device attaches to

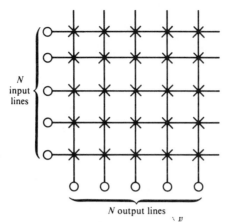

FIGURE 2.5 Single-stage Space-division Switch

the matrix via one input and one output line. Interconnection is possible between any two lines by enabling the appropriate crosspoint. Note that a total of N^2 crosspoints is required. The crossbar switch has a number of limitations:

- The number of crosspoints grows with N^2. This is costly for large N and results in high capacitive loading on any message path.
- The loss of a crosspoint prevents connection between the two devices involved.
- The crosspoints are inefficiently utilized (at most N out of N^2).

To overcome these limitations, multiple-stage switches are employed. N input lines are broken up into N/n groups of n lines. Each group of lines goes into a first-stage matrix. The outputs of the first-stage matrices become inputs to a group of second-stage matrices, and so on. The last stage has N outputs; thus, each device attaches its input line to the first stage and its output line to the last stage. Figure 2.6 depicts a three-stage network of switches. There are k second-stage matrices, each with N/n inputs and N/n outputs. The exact number of second-stage matrices is a design decision, as discussed subsequently. Each first-stage matrix has k outlets, so that it connects to all second-stage matrices. Each second-stage matrix has N/n outputs so that it connects to all third-stage matrices.

This type of arrangement has several advantages over a single-stage crossbar matrix:

- The number of crosspoints is reduced (see following), increasing crossbar utilization.
- There is more than one path through the network to connect two endpoints, increasing reliability.

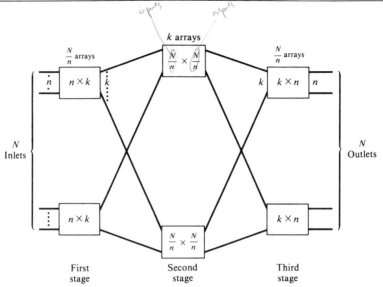

FIGURE 2.6 Three-stage Space-division Switch

Of course, a multistage network requires a more complex control scheme. To establish a path in a single-stage network, it is only necessary to enable a single gate. In a multistage network, a free path through the stages must be determined and the appropriate gates enabled.

A consideration with a multistage space-division switch is that it may be blocking. It should be clear from Figure 2.5 that a crossbar matrix is nonblocking; that is, a path is always available to connect an input to an output. That this may not be the case with a multiple-stage switch can be seen in Figure 2.7. The figure shows a three-stage switch with $N = 9$, $n = 3$, and $k = 3$. The heavier lines indicate lines that are

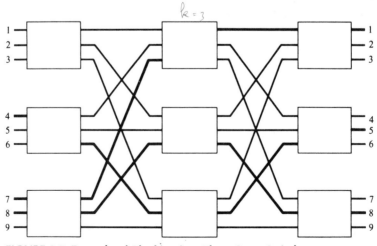

FIGURE 2.7 Example of Blocking in a Three-Stage Switch

already in use. In this state, input line 9 cannot be connected to either output line 4 or 6, even though both of these output lines are available.

It should also be clear that by increasing the value of k (the number of outputs from each first-stage switch and the number of second-stage switches), the probability of blocking is reduced. Figure 2.8 illustrates the value of k required to eliminate blocking. Consider that we wish to establish a path from input line a to output line b. The worst-case situation for blocking occurs if all of the remaining $n - 1$ input lines and $n - 1$ output lines are busy and are connected to different center-stage switches. Thus a total of $(n - 1) + (n - 1) = 2n - 2$ center switches is unavailable for creating a path from a to b. However, if one more center-stage switch exists, the appropriate links must be available for the connection. Thus, a three-stage network will be nonblocking if

$$k = 2n - 1$$

We now return to the claim that a multiple-stage switch requires fewer crosspoints than a single-stage switch. From Figure 2.6, the total number of crosspoints N in a three-stage switch is

$$Nx = 2Nk + k(N/n)^2$$

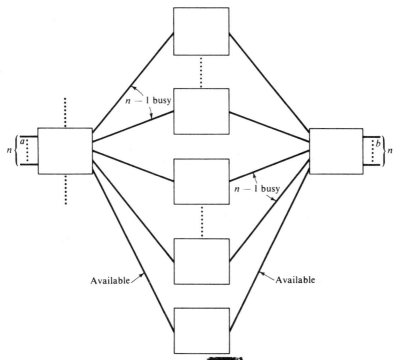

FIGURE 2.8 Nonblocking Three-stage Switch

Substituting the first equation above into the second,

$$Nx = 2N(2n - 1) + (2n - 1)(N/n)^2$$

for a nonblocking switch. The actual value as a function of N depends on the number of switches (N/n) in the first and third stages. To optimize, differentiate Nx with respect to n and set the result to zero. For large N, the result converges to $n = (N/2)^{1/2}$. Substituting into the last equation given previously,

$$Nx = 4N(\sqrt{2N} - 1)$$

Table 2.1 compares this value with the number of crosspoints in a single-stage switch. As can be seen, there is a savings that grows with the number of lines.

2.4

TIME-DIVISION SWITCHING

The technology of switching has a long history, most of it covering an era when analog signal switching predominated. With the advent of digitized voice and synchronous time-division multiplexing techniques, both voice and data can be transmitted via digital signals. This has led to a fundamental change in the design and technology of switching systems. Instead of relatively dumb space-division systems, modern digital systems rely on intelligent control of space- and time-division elements.

Virtually all modern circuit switches use digital time-division techniques for establishing and maintaining "circuits." Time-division switching involves the partitioning of a lower-speed bit stream into pieces that share a higher-speed stream with other bit streams. The individual pieces, or slots, are manipulated by control logic to route

TABLE 2.1   Number of Crosspoints in a Nonblocking Switch

Number of Lines	Number of Crosspoints for Three-stage Switch	Number of Crosspoints for Single-stage Switch
128	7,680	16,384
512	63,488	262,144
3,048	516,096	4.2×10^6
8,192	4.2×10^6	6.7×10^7
32,768	3.3×10^7	1×10^9
131,072	2.6×10^8	1.7×10^{10}

data from input to output. Three concepts comprise the technique of time-division switching:

- TDM bus switching.
- Time-slot interchange (TSI).
- Time-multiplex switching (TMS).

Table 2.2 briefly describes these forms of switching, as well as space-division switching.

TDM Bus Switching

TDM bus switching, and indeed all digital switching techniques, are based on the use of synchronous time-division multiplexing (TDM). As

TABLE 2.2   Circuit-Switching Techniques

Technique	Description	Comments
Space Division	Uses an interconnection matrix. Each connection through the switch takes a physically distinct path.	Inefficient use of cross-points. Can be used for either analog or digital switching. Less complex than time-division switching.
TDM Bus	All lines are connected to a bus. Time on the bus is divided into slots. A circuit is created between two lines by assigning repetitive time slots, as in synchronous TDM.	Simplest form of time-division switching. Size of switch is limited by the data rate on the bus. This architecture is common for small and medium-sized data switches and PBXs.
Time-Slot Interchange	All lines are connected to a synchronous TDM multiplexer and a synchronous TDM demultiplexer. A circuit is created by the interchange of time slots within a time-division multiplexed frame.	Size of switch is limited by the speed of the control memory. Can be used as a building block in multistage switches.
Time-Multiplexed	A form of space-division switching in which each input line is a TDM stream. The switching configuration may change for each time slot.	Used in conjunction with TSI unit to form multistage switches. There is a small increase in delay by the use of multiple stages, but this allows much larger capacity.

shown in Figure 2.9, synchronous TDM permits multiple low-speed bit streams to share a high-speed line. A set of inputs is sampled in turn. The samples are organized serially into slots (channels) to form a recurring frame of N slots. A slot may be a bit, a byte, or some longer block. An important point to note is that with synchronous TDM, the source and destination of the data in each time slot are known. Hence there is no need for address bits in each slot.

The mechanism for synchronous TDM may be quite simple. For example, each input line deposits data in a buffer; the multiplexer scans these buffers sequentially, taking fixed-size chunks of data from each buffer and sending them out on the line. One complete scan produces one frame of data. For output to the lines, the reverse operation is performed, with the multiplexer filling the output line buffers one by one. The I/O lines attached to the multiplexer may be synchronous or asynchronous; the multiplexed line between the two multiplexers is synchronous and must have a data rate equal to the sum of the data rates of the attached lines. Actually, the multiplexed line must have a slightly higher data rate, since each frame will include some overhead bits for synchronization. The time slots in a frame are assigned to the I/O lines on a fixed, predetermined basis. If a device has no data to send, the multiplexer must send empty slots. Thus the actual data transfer rate may be less than the capacity of the system.

Figure 2.10 shows a simple way in which this technique can be adapted to achieve switching. Each device attaches to the switch through two buffered lines, one for input and one for output. These lines are connected through controlled gates to a high-speed digital bus. Each input line is assigned a time slot. For the duration of the slot, that line's gate is enabled, allowing a small burst of data onto the bus. For that same time slot, one of the output line gates is also enabled. Thus, during that time slot, data are switched from the enabled input line to the enabled output line. During successive time slots, different input/ output pairings are enabled, allowing a number of connections to be carried over the shared bus. An attached device achieves full-duplex

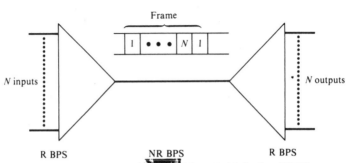

FIGURE 2.9 Synchronous Time-division Multiplexing (TDM)

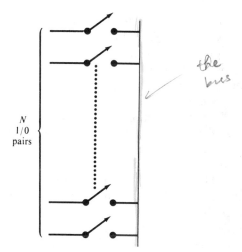

FIGURE 2.10 TDM Bus Switching

operation by transmitting during one assigned time slot and receiving during another. The other end of the connection is an I/O pair for which these time slots have the opposite meanings. We will refer to this technique as **TDM bus switching**.

Let us look at the timing involved more closely. First, consider a nonblocking implementation of Figure 2.10. For a switch that supports N devices, there must be N repetitively occurring time slots, each one assigned to an input and an output line. One iteration for all time slots is referred to as a *frame*. The input assignment may be fixed; the output assignments vary to allow various connections. When a time slot begins, the designated (enabled) input line may insert a burst of data onto the line, where it will propagate to both ends past all other lines. The designated (enabled) output line, during that time, copies the data, if present, as they go by. The time slot, therefore, must equal the transmission time of the input plus the propagation delay between input and output across the bus. In order to keep successive time slots uniform, time-slot length is defined as transmission time plus the end-to-end bus propagation delay. For efficiency, the propagation delay must be much less than the transmission time.

To keep up with the input lines, the data rate on the bus must be high enough that the slots recur sufficiently frequently. For example, consider a system connecting 100 full-duplex lines at 19.2 kbps. Input data on each line are buffered at the gate. Each buffer must be cleared by enabling the gate fast enough to avoid overrun. Thus the data rate on the bus in this example must be greater than 1.92 Mbps. The actual data rate must be high enough to also account for the wasted time due to propagation delay.

These considerations determine the traffic-carrying capacity of a blocking switch as well. For a blocking switch, there is no fixed assignment of input lines to time slots; they are allocated on demand. The data rate on the bus dictates how many connections can be made at a time. For a system with 200 devices at 19.2 kbps and a bus at 2 Mbps, about half of the devices can be connected at any one time.

The TDM bus-switching scheme can accommodate lines of varying data rates. For example, if a 9600-bps line gets one slot per frame, a 19.2-kbps line would get two slots per frame. Of course, only lines of the same data rate can be connected.

Figure 2.11 is an example that suggests how the control for a TDM bus switch can be implemented. Let us assume that the propagation time on the bus is 0.01 μsec. Time on the bus is organized into 30.06-μsec frames of six 5.01-μsec time slots each. A control memory indicates which gates are to be enabled during each time slot. In this example, 6 words of memory are needed. A controller cycles through the memory at a rate of one cycle every 30.06 μsec. During the first time slot of each cycle, the input gate from device 1 and the output gate to device 3 are enabled, allowing data to pass from device 1 to device 3 over the bus. The remaining words are accessed in succeeding time slots and treated accordingly. As long as the control memory contains the contents de-

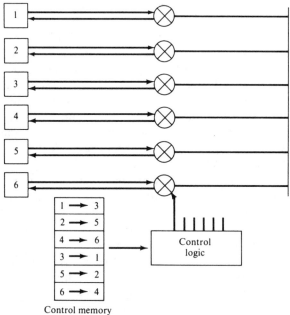

FIGURE 2.11 Control of a TDM Bus Switch

picted in Figure 2.11, connections are maintained between 1 and 3, 2 and 5, and 4 and 6.

Time-Slot Interchange

The basic building block of many time-division switches is the **time-slot interchange** (TSI) mechanism. A TSI unit operates on a synchronous TDM stream of time slots, or channels, by interchanging pairs of slots to achieve full-duplex operation. Figure 2.12a shows how the input line of a device I is connected to the output line of device J, and vice versa. In this figure, the input lines of N devices are passed through a synchronous time-division multiplexer to produce a TDM stream with N slots. To achieve the interconnection of two devices, the slots corresponding to the two inputs are interchanged; the resulting stream is demultiplexed to the outputs of the N devices. This results in a full-duplex connection between pairs of lines.

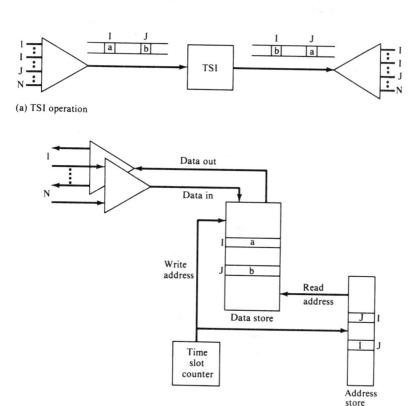

(a) TSI operation

(b) TSI mechanism

FIGURE 2.12 Time-slot Interchange (TSI)

Figure 2.12b depicts a mechanism for TSI. Individual I/O lines are multiplexed and demultiplexed. A random-access data store whose width equals one time slot of data and whose length equals the number of slots in a frame is used. An incoming TDM frame is written sequentially, slot by slot, into the data store. An outgoing TDM frame is created by reading slots from memory in an order dictated by an address store that reflect the existing connections. In the figure, the data in channels I and J are interchanged, creating a full-duplex connection between the corresponding stations.

We can see that, to allow the interchange of any two slots, the incoming data in a slot must be stored until they can be sent out on the right channel in the next frame cycle. Hence, the TSI introduces a delay and produces output slots in the desired order. Since each channel is provided a time slot in the frame, whether or not it transmits data, the size of the TSI unit must be chosen for the capacity of the TDM line, not the actual data transfer rate at any given time.

Let us look more closely at the operation of the data store; in particular, we need to view it as a function of time. As an example [DAVI73], consider a system with eight I/O lines, in which the following connections exist: 1-2, 3-7, and 5-8; the other two stations are not in use. Figure 2.13 depicts the contents of the data store over the course of one frame (eight slots). During the first time slot, data are stored in location 1 and read from location 2. During the second time slot, data are stored in location 2 and read from location 1, and so on.

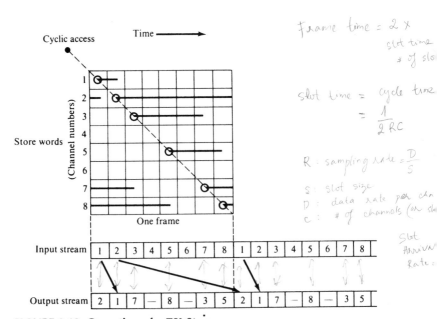

FIGURE 2.13 Operation of a TSI Store

As can be seen, the write accesses to the data store are cyclic, that is, accessing successive locations in sequential order, whereas the read accesses are acyclic, requiring the use of an address store. The figure also depicts two frames of the input and output sequences and indicates the transfer of data between channels 1 and 2. Note that in half the cases, data slots move into the next frame.

As with the TDM bus switch, the TSI unit can handle inputs of various data rates. Figure 2.14 suggests a way in which this may be done. Instead of presenting the input lines to a synchronous multiplexer, they are presented to a selector device. This device will select an input line based on a channel assignment provided from a store controlled by the time slot counter. Instead of sampling equally from each input, it may gather more slots from some channels than others.

Time-multiplexed Switching

TSI is a simple, effective way of switching TDM data. However, the size of such a switch, in terms of number of connections, is limited by the memory access speed. It is clear that, in order to keep pace with the input, data must be read into and out of memory as fast as they arrive. So, for example, if we have 24 sources operating at 64 kbps each, and a slot size of 8 bits, we would have an arrival rate of 192,000 slots

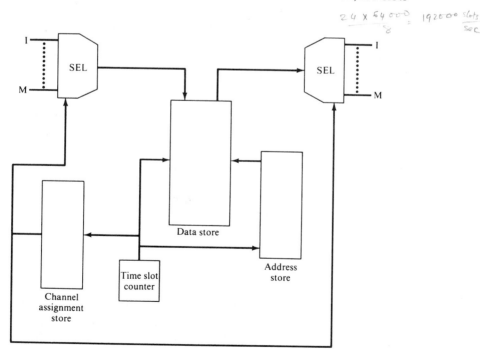

FIGURE 2.14 TSI Operation with a Variable-rate Input

per second. For each time slot, both a read and a write are required. In this example, memory access time would need to be $1/(192{,}000 \times 2)$, or about 2.6 μsec.

We can see, then, that a TSI unit can support only a limited number of connections. Further, as the size of the unit grows, for a fixed access speed, the delay at the TSI unit grows. To overcome both of these problems, multiple TSI units are used. Now, to connect two channels entering a single TSI unit, their time slots can be interchanged. However, to connect a channel on one TDM stream (going into one TSI) to a channel on another TDM stream (going into another TSI), some form of interconnection of the TSI units is needed. This interconnection must allow a slot in one TDM stream to be interchanged with a slot in another TDM stream. Naturally, we do not wish to switch all of the time slots from one stream to another; we would like to do it one slot at a time. This technique is known as **time-multiplexed switching** (TMS).

Multiple-stage networks can be built up by concatenating TMS and TSI stages. TMS stages, which move slots from one stream to another, are referred to as S (space), and TSI stages are referred to as T (time). Systems are generally described by an enumeration of their stages from input to output, using the symbols T and S. Figure 2.15 shows examples of both STS and TST three-stage architectures. In both cases, the TMS stages are implemented by digital selectors (SEL), which select one input at a time on a time-slot basis. These SEL devices provide the same function as those described in the preceding section, except that here each of their inputs is a TDM stream rather than a single line.

In an STS architecture, the path between an incoming and an outgoing channel has multiple possible physical routes equal to the number of TSI units, but only one time route. For a fully nonblocking switch, the number of TSI units must be double the number of incoming and outgoing TDM streams. On the other hand, the multiple routes between two channels in a TST network are all in the time domain; there is only one physical path possible. Here, too, blocking can occur. One way to avoid blocking is by expanding the number of time slots in the space stage. In all multistage switches, a path-search algorithm is needed to determine the route from input to output.

2.5

ROUTING

In a large circuit-switched network, such as the AT&T long-distance telephone network, many of the circuit connections will require a path through more than one switch. When a call is placed, the network must devise a route through the network from calling subscriber to called

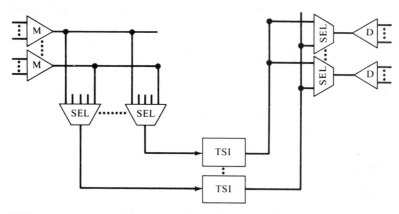

(a) Space-time-space network

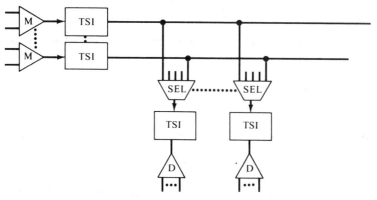

(b) Time-Space-Time network

FIGURE 2.15 Three-stage TDM Switches

subscriber that passes through some number of switches and trunks. As Box 2.2 indicates, there are two main requirements for the network's architecture that bear on the routing strategy. First, it is desirable to minimize the amount of equipment (switches and trunks) in the network, subject to the ability to handle the expected load. The load requirement is usually expressed in terms of a *busy-hour traffic load*. This is simply the average load expected over the course of the busiest hour of use during the course of a day. From a functional point of view, it is necessary to handle that amount of load. From a cost point of view, we would like to handle that load with minimum equipment. However, there is another requirement, namely resilience. Although the network may be sized for the busy-hour load, it is possible for the traffic to temporarily surge above that level (e.g., during a major storm). It will also be the case that, from time to time, switches and trunks will fail

---

BOX 2.2

Routing for Circuit-Switched Networks

FUNCTION

Define a path from calling subscriber to called subscriber through a series of switches and trunks.

REQUIREMENTS

Efficiency

The measure of how few facilities are required to carry the steady busy-hour traffic load of the network.

Resilience

The measure of the level of service maintained when either a traffic surge or equipment failure is experienced by the network.

APPROACHES

Direct

A fixed, preestablished route is followed for any pair of subscribers.

Alternate Hierarchical

Switches are arranged in a hierarchy with additional trunks beyond those required for the tree structure. The additional trunks provide alternate routes that may be taken to compensate for load or unavailability.

Dynamic Nonhierarchical

A more complex peer network architecture is used. The route between subscribers is dynamically chosen at call setup time, based on traffic load and availability.

---

and be temporarily unavailable (unfortunately, maybe during the same storm). We would like the network to provide a reasonable level of service under such conditions.

In the past, the two requirements of efficiency and resilience have been competing. That is, there has been a trade-off between the two. Network efficiency was achieved by minimizing switching and transmission capacity, whereas resilience was achieved by increasing that capacity, in the form of small trunk sections and high inter-exchange connectivity. This situation is rapidly changing with the availability of high-bandwidth fiber trunks and high-capacity digital switches, capable of handling tens of thousands of trunks. As we will see, all of this is tied to the routing strategy. Traditional routing strategies that have been common in telephone networks are unable to adapt to major network perturbations. Newer, dynamic routing strategies can take advantage of evolving technology to simultaneously improve both network efficiency and network resilience [HURL87].

These concepts are best explained with an example. In the remainder of this section, we look at the evolution of the AT&T network.

Architecture of a Public Telephone Network

The public telecommunications network in the United States consists primarily of the local service offered by the Bell Operating Companies (BOCs) that used to be part of AT&T and the long-distance service still offered by AT&T. There are, of course, a growing number of other providers, particularly of long-distance service. In this section, we look at the architecture of the BOC/AT&T network, which still handles the bulk of telephone traffic in the United States. Although both the routing and the architecture of this network have and are evolving since divestiture, the overall architecture can still be described as follows.

As with any network, the public telephone network can be described using four generic architectural components:

- *Stations:* generally denoted as *subscribers*, these are the devices that attach to the network.
- *Interfaces:* the interface between the stations and the network, referred to in the phone system as the *local loop.*
- *Nodes:* the *switching centers* in the network.
- *Links:* the branches between nodes, referred to as *trunks.*

Most of the **subscribers** on the network are telephones. The telephone contains a transmitter and receiver for converting back and forth between analog voice (sound waves) and analog electrical (voice frequency) signals. Some subscribers that transmit digital signals are being incorporated into the network.

The **local loop** is a pair of wires, generally twisted pair, that connects a subscriber to one of the nodes in the network. It is a direct-current (dc) loop that supplies a metallic path for the following [FREE89]:

- Voltage potential for the telephone transmitter. This is supplied over the line from the switching center and is used to convert acoustic energy into electric energy.

- An ac ringing voltage for the bell on the telephone instrument supplied from the switching center.
- Current to flow through the loop when the telephone instrument is taken out of its cradle (off hook), telling the serving switch that it requires access.
- Signals generated by the telephone dial or keypad used to communicate to the switch the number of the called subscriber.

The local loop generally covers a distance of a few kilometers to a few tens of kilometers at most. More detail on telephone transmission over the local loop can be found in [ATT61].

Each subscriber connects via local loop to a **switching center,** known as an end office. Typically, an end office will support many thousands of subscribers in a localized area. There are over 19,000 end offices in the United States, so it is clearly impractical for each end office to have a direct link to each of the other end offices; this would require on the order of 2×10^8 links. Rather, intermediate switching nodes are used. The function of these intermediate nodes and the manner in which they are interconnected determine the routing mechanism that is used.

The switching centers are linked together by **trunks.** These trunks are designed to carry multiple voice-frequency circuits using either FDM or synchronous TDM. Earlier, these were referred to as carrier systems.

Alternate Hierarchical Routing

Until recently, the organization of the end offices into a network has involved the use of a hierarchical or tree structure (Figure 2.16), consisting of five classes of switching centers or nodes [REY83]:

- *Class 1:* regional center.
- *Class 2:* sectional center.
- *Class 3:* primary center.
- *Class 4:* toll center.
- *Class 5:* end office.

Subscribers connect directly to an end office, which must perform the same functions listed earlier for a one-node network. The remaining centers simply serve the function of concentrating traffic so as to reduce transmission facility equipment. This distinction is shown in Figure 2.17. To connect two subscribers attached to the same end office, a circuit is set up between them in the same fashion as described before. If two subscribers connect to different end offices, a circuit between them consists of a concatenation of circuits through one or more intermediate offices. In the figure, a connection is established between lines *a* and *b* by simply setting up the connection through the end office. The connection between *c* and *d* is more complex. In *c*'s end office, a con-

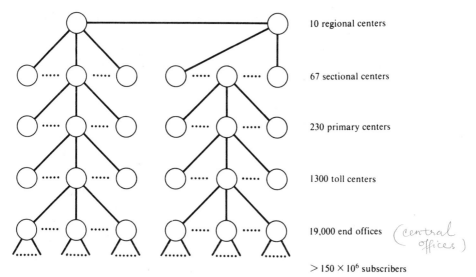

FIGURE 2.16 U.S. Public Circuit-switched Network Organization

nection is established between line c and one channel on a TDM or FDM trunk to the intermediate switch. In the intermediate switch, that channel is connected to a channel on a trunk to a's end office. In that end office, the channel is connected to line d.

The hierarchical structure depicted in Figure 2.16 is actually a set of 10 trees, each rooted in a regional center. The 10 regional centers are

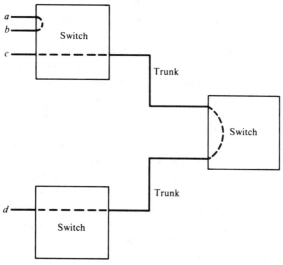

FIGURE 2.17 Circuit Establishment in a Multiple-switch Network

meshed together (45 full-duplex links) to provide full connectivity. In the early days of the telephone network, this was the extent of the architecture, and a very simple form of routing, known as **direct routing,** was used. With direct routing, connection establishment follows these rules:

1. If both subscribers attach to the same end office, that end office makes the connection.
2. If the two subscribers attach to different end offices that are attached to the same toll center, a connection is established between the end offices via that toll center.

And so on. The search continues up the hierarchy until a common node is reached. If the two subscribers are under the aegis of different regional centers, the circuit will involve a trunk between regional centers, for a total of nine trunks in the path between the two subscribers.

This architecture and routing strategy has several drawbacks. First, during peak hours, a tremendous amount of traffic must be carried at the upper levels of the hierarchy; accordingly, the facilities at these levels will be inefficiently used most of the time. Second, the loss or saturation of a single switching center decouples the network into isolated subnetworks. Finally, signal quality degrades as the number of switches and trunks increases (for analog transmission).

To compensate for these problems, two additional elements are added to the basic architecture. In addition to the five classes of switching centers, the network is augmented with additional switching nodes called *tandem switches.* These are used to interconnect adjacent end offices. Also, a large number of *high-usage trunks* are used for direct connection between switching centers with high volumes of internode traffic.

With these additions, an **alternate hierarchical routing** algorithm can be used. Traffic is always routed through the lowest available level of the network. Figure 2.18 shows the basic order of selection for alternate routes. The high-usage trunks are depicted as dashed lines, and the backbone hierarchical network is shown with solid lines. With alternate hierarchical routing, connection establishment is as follows. The basic rule is to complete the connection at the lowest possible level of the hierarchy, thus using the fewest trunks in sequence. In the figure, a call placed from telephone 1 to telephone 2 is first handled by the end office of telephone 1. Since telephone 2 is not served by the same end office and is not reachable via a tandem office, the call is routed to toll center A. Toll center A searches for an available high-usage (HU) trunk, first in the HU1 group and then in the HU2 group. If all trunks in these groups are busy, the call overflows to the final trunk group, which moves the call up one level in the hierarchy to primary center B. The

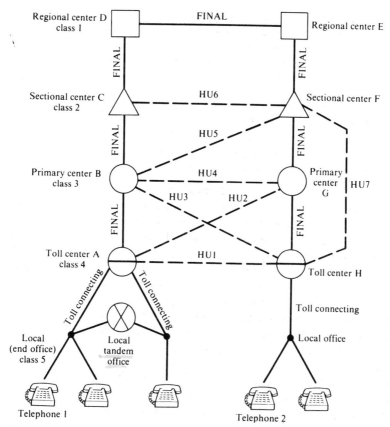

FIGURE 2.18 Alternate Hierarchical Routing [REY83]

primary center again searches for an available HU trunk in the order indicated. This process is dynamic and depends on the availability of high-usage trunks at the time the call is placed. Thus calls between two subscribers might follow different routes at different times. The routing algorithm is driven by the seven- or ten-digit telephone number, which uniquely identifies a subscriber and the centers in its direct hierarchy [FREE89,REY83].

Beginning in the 1940s, when it became possible for an exchange to choose a route based on trunk loading status, alternate hierarchical routing was gradually introduced until it reached the level of complexity just described. The high-usage trunks are sized based on cost in the following way. The requirement to be satisfied is that the probability of blocking during the average busy hour on any of the final paths (see Figure 2.18) is no more than 0.01 [REY83]. For any given high-usage trunk, the capacity of that trunk is optimized by increasing its capacity until the incremental cost of adding further capacity on the high-usage trunk would exceed the cost of carrying the incremental traffic on the final route. Figure 2.19 suggests the analysis involved. For a particular high-usage trunk, the cost of that trunk is a linearly increasing function of capacity. As the capacity of the high-usage trunk increases, the capacity of the final trunks needed to guarantee the 0.01 blocking measure decreases, and accordingly the cost of the final trunks decreases. As shown, there is a unique minimum that dictates the size of the high-usage trunk.

The alternate hierarchical routing approach provided significant gains in efficiency over the direct routing approach. More of the traffic is carried at lower levels of the hierarchy. Thus the average length of a connection (number of exchanges and trunks) is decreased for a given level of traffic. Furthermore, the way in which high-usage capacity is determined means that all trunk groups except the final ones are virtually fully loaded.

There are, however, remaining limitations. These limitations are in both the area of efficiency and of resilience. The single measure of an average busy hour is not powerful enough to permit a design that is optimum from the point of view of efficiency. For example, the busy hours for east/west traffic and north/south traffic do not coincide. It is difficult to analyze the effects of this, which leads to oversizing. In terms of resilience, the shortcoming of alternate hierarchical routing is that it is rigid and assumes no equipment or trunk failure. A major failure will cause a major local congestion near the site of the failure. Over time, various automatic and manual network control procedures have been added to the network, but the basic problem of a rigid hierarchical structure remained.

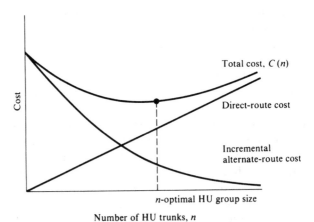

FIGURE 2.19 Cost Function for Alternate Routing [REY83]

Dynamic Routing

What is required is a more flexible scheme with a greater ability to adapt to changing conditions in the network. To achieve this, it is necessary to move away from a hierarchical architecture and to make use of a dynamic routing policy. A nonhierarchical architecture is one in which the circuit-switching nodes have a peer relationship with each other. All nodes are capable of performing the same functions. In such an architecture, routing is both more complex and more flexible. It is more complex because the architecture does not provide a "natural" path or set of paths based on hierarchical structure. But it is also more flexible, since more alternative routes are available.

With a network of peer switches, the opportunity for effective dynamic routing exists. Although the basic principles of dynamic routing have been known for over twenty-five years, they have only been applied in the last decade. All currently implemented dynamic routing systems share the following characteristics [REGN90]:

- Switches apply different routing tables at different times for calls to a given destination, depending on network and traffic conditions.
- The changes in routing tables are based on current measurements of offered traffic and network performance and are determined automatically rather than by human calculation.
- Global network and traffic information is used (either directly or indirectly) to determine the routing tables applied locally by each switch.
- The routing tables permit mutual overflow among links at each switch so that, in principle, every link may carry calls overflowing from other links.

With a peer network with a relatively large number of interconnections, dynamic routing enables very effective load sharing. For example, if a direct path between two switches is fully loaded, blocking new calls, alternate paths may be taken for additional calls, reducing the blocking probability. On the other hand, at times when the load on this direct path is lighter, it may be used as an alternate path or part of an alternate path for other calls, to help reduce blocking. Therefore, calls with different source/destination pairs share a larger pool of transmission and switching capacity for connection.

Dynamic routing results in increased efficiency and resiliency. Because there is more potential for sharing temporarily unused resources in a network that uses dynamic routing, fewer trunks are required in such a network than in an equivalent hierarchical network. Because the interconnection structure and routing alternatives are richer, a network that uses dynamic routing is more resilient than an equivalent nonhier-

archical network. As we move toward ISDN, which will place a greatly
increased burden on public circuit-switched networks, the nonhierarchical, dynamic-routing approach will become more prevalent. *Common*

Dynamic routing methods can be divided into two major categories
[WATA90]:

- *Time-dependent routing:* This approach exploits regular variations in
  demand (time of day, day of week, seasonal). Preplanned routing
  patterns are altered at fixed points in time to allocate network
  capacity to forecasted changes in traffic demand.
- *State-dependent routing:* This approach exploits random traffic variations to periodically make routing changes. Routing patterns vary
  automatically, depending on the state of the network. For this
  approach, it is necessary to collect appropriate information about
  network status, such as records of successful calls and outgoing
  trunk group occupancies. Selection of alternate paths is done at
  either each switch (distributed approach) or at a network management processor serving all switches (centralized approach).

Most routing systems that have been implemented are based on some
combination of these two approaches. In the remainder of this section
we look at two examples, AT&T's dynamic nonhierarchical routing
(DNHR), which is primarily time-dependent, and Northern Telecom's
dynamic traffic management (DTM), which is primarily state-dependent.

Dynamic Nonhierarchical Routing.   Dynamic nonhierarchical routing
(DNHR) is a routing capability developed by AT&T for the U.S. public
telephone network [GLEN86, ASH89, ASH90]. DNHR was conceived
as an evolution from the existing alternate hierarchical routing scheme.
Conversion began in 1984 and was completed by the end of 1987,
making it the first national dynamic routing network in the world.

With DNHR, the network contains a large number (about 100) of
regional centers. These centers are peer to each other and make up the
DNHR part of the total network. Any call that makes use of the DNHR
switches will pass through no more than three switches and two trunks.
Routing is based on known historical traffic patterns and on current
traffic status.

Figure 2.20 illustrates the DNHR scheme. There are two or three
switches involved in each route. The originating switch is responsible
for making the routing decision. The terminating switch is the intended
destination. Finally, in some cases, there is an intermediate switch that
is part of the route. Each switch is given a set of preplanned routes for
each destination, in order of preference. Usually, the first preference is
a direct trunk connection from the originating switch to the terminating
switch. These routing sequences reflect the optimal routes for a partic-

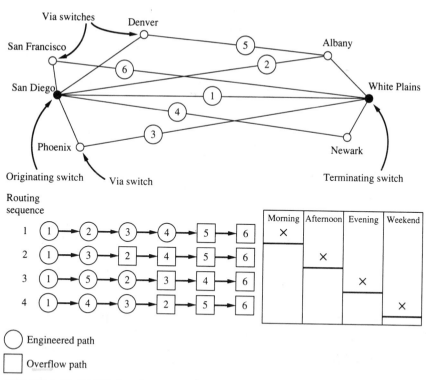

FIGURE 2.20 DNHR Routing [ASH90]

ular call, based on extensive operational measurement data, which are periodically provided by each participating switch to the central network planning system. To take advantage of the differing traffic patterns in different time zones and at different times of day, the day is divided into ten time periods, with a different set of preplanned routes for each time period. In addition to the preplanned routes, additional overflow paths may be assigned. These paths are assigned by a network management center, but the ability to use them depends on the current load. For example, if utilization on a given trunk group is high, no overflow traffic will be allowed on that trunk so that its limited remaining capacity stays available for preplanned routes.

In Figure 2.20, the originating switch has six possible routes to the terminating switch. The direct route (1) will always be tried first. If this trunk is unavailable (busy or out of service), the other routes will be tried in a particular order, depending on the time of day. For example, during the morning, route (2) is tried next. If the intermediate switch on a route is unable to complete a requested call, it sends a control message back to the originating switch so that it may try another route. After all preplanned routes have been tried, additional routes (overflow routes), which are not engineered to handle the specific origination-termination traffic, may be used if sufficient capacity is available. The distinction between the preplanned and overflow routes is that the capacity of the network (switch and trunk size) is engineered to handle the preplanned traffic at a particular probability of blocking (1 percent).

Control signaling is used to allow the switches to provide traffic information to a network management center. If the network management center determines that an overflow condition exists, it may dynamically change the route sets of any of the switches. The routing updates are communicated back to the switches by control signals.

Below the DNHR network, the remainder of the network is still hierarchical, much as in Figure 2.16. Calls within a particular hierarchy are still handled by alternate hierarchical routing. Each hierarchy attaches to a single regional switch, by which it enters the DNHR network to reach a switch in another hierarchy. This somewhat awkward arrangement is dictated by the need to migrate gradually and with minimum cost and network impact from a hierarchical to a nonhierarchical structure.

Dynamic Traffic Management. Dynamic traffic management (DTM) is a routing capability developed by Northern Telecom and is currently being implemented in the Canadian national and local telephone networks [REGN90]. In its planning stages, the capability was referred to as dynamically controlled routing (DCR).

DCR uses a central controller to find the best alternate route choices, depending on congestion in the network. The central controller collects status data from each switch in the network every ten seconds to determine preferred alternate routes. Each call is first attempted on the direct path, if any, between source and destination switches. If the call is blocked, it is attempted on a two-link alternate path.

Each switch i communicates the following traffic measurements to the central controller:

I_{ij} = The number of idle trunks on the link to switch j, for all switches in the network.

CPU_i = The CPU utilization of switch i.

O_{ij} = A measure of the traffic sent by i to j that overflowed the direct route.

Based on this information, the central controller periodically returns to each switch i, for each possible destination switch j:

r_{ij} = The identifier of the switch through which i should direct its calls to j when the direct link is full.

The selection of r_{ij} depends on whether or not a direct link exists between i and j. If a direct link exists, which is the case for the vast majority of the calls, then r_{ij} is determined as that switch t that achieves the maximum in

$$\text{MAX}\{A_t \times \text{Min}[I_{it} - PA_{it}, I_{tj} - PA_{tj}]\} \qquad t \neq i,j$$

If there is no direct link between i and j, then r_{ij} is determined as that switch t that achieves the maximum in

$$\text{MAX}\{A_t \times \text{Min}[I_{it}, I_{tj}]\} \qquad t \neq i,j$$

where

A_t = Parameter in the range [0,1] that reflects the availability of switch t. It is 1 if t functions normally, but it is less if t is overloaded. Its role is to make alternative routes transiting through overloaded switches less attractive and hence less likely to be chosen by the network controller.

PA_{xy} = Protective allowance parameter for the direct traffic on link x-y. Its role is to divert traffic away from the link when it is nearly fully occupied.

The second equation is the same as the first, except that protective allowances are not considered. The rationale is the following: If there is no direct link between switches i and j, then traffic from i to j should not concede priority to direct traffic over links on potential alternate routes.

Figure 2.21 illustrates the selection process. If the link from i to j is saturated, the recommended alternate route is i-y-j. Although route i-x-j has the largest idle capacity, it is not recommended because switch x is overloaded.

The use of a set of parameters based on network status provides a powerful routing capability. Furthermore, as indicated in [REGN90], it becomes an easy matter to experiment with various ways of determining the values of parameters and assessing their effect on performance. For example, the parameter PA_{xy} can be set to a fixed value in a relatively stable network, or the overflow measurement O_{xy} can be used.

2.6

CONTROL SIGNALING

In a circuit-switched network, control signals are the means by which the network is managed and by which calls are established, maintained, and terminated. Both call management and overall network management require that information be exchanged between subscriber and switch, among switches, and between switch and network management center. For a large public telecommunications network, a relatively com-

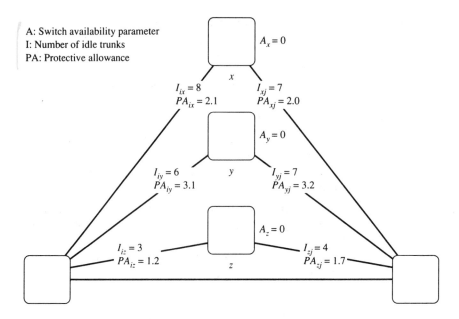

FIGURE 2.21 Alternate Route Selection in DTM [REGN 90]

plex control-signaling scheme is required. In this section, we provide a brief overview of control-signal functionality and then look at the technique that is the basis of modern integrated digital networks, common channel signaling.

Signaling Functions

Control signals are necessary for the operation of a circuit-switched network and involve every aspect of network behavior, including both network services visible to the subscriber and internal mechanisms. As networks become more complex, the number of functions performed by control signaling necessarily grows. The following functions, listed in [MART90], are among the most important:

1. Audible communication with the subscriber, including dial tone, ringing tone, busy signal, and so on.
2. Transmission of the number dialed to switching offices, which will attempt to complete a connection.
3. Transmission of information between switches indicating that a call cannot be completed.
4. Transmission of information between switches indicating that a call has ended and that the path can be disconnected.
5. A signal to make a telephone ring.

6. Transmission of information used for billing purposes.
7. Transmission of information giving the status of equipment or trunks in the network. This information may be used for routing and maintenance purposes.
8. Transmission of information used in diagnosing and isolating system failures.
9. Control of special equipment such as satellite channel equipment.

An example of the use of control signaling is shown in Figure 2.22 [REY83], which illustrates a typical telephone connection sequence from one line to another in the same central office. The steps involved appear as circled numbers in the figure:

1. Prior to the call, both telephones are not in use (on-hook). The call begins when one subscriber lifts the receiver (off-hook), which is automatically signaled to switch.
2. The switch responds with an audible dial tone, signaling the subscriber that the number may be dialed.

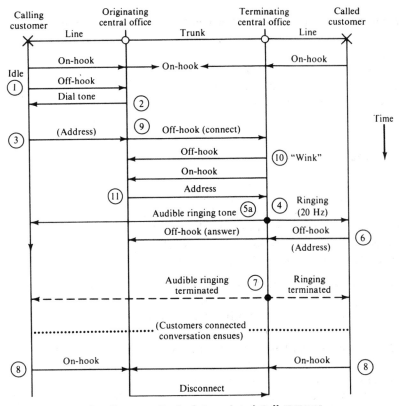

FIGURE 2.22 Signaling on a Typical Completed Call [REY83]

3. The caller dials the number, which is communicated as a destination address to the switch.
4. If the called subscriber is not busy, the switch alerts that subscriber to an incoming call by sending a ringing signal, which causes the telephone to ring.
5. Feedback is provided to the calling subscriber by the switch:
    a) If the called subscriber is not busy, the switch returns an audible ringing tone to the caller while the ringing signal is being sent to the called subscriber.
    b) If the called subscriber is busy, the switch sends an audible busy signal to the caller (not shown in the figure).
    c) If the call cannot be completed through the switch, the switch sends an audible "reorder" message to the caller (not shown in the figure).
6. The called party accepts the call by lifting the receiver (off-hook), which is automatically signaled to the switch.
7. The switch terminates the ringing signal and the audible ringing tone, and establishes a connection between the two subscribers.
8. The connection is released when either subscriber hangs up.

When the called subscriber is attached to a different switch than the calling subscriber, the following switch-to-switch trunk signaling functions are required:

9. The originating switch seizes an idle interswitch trunk, sends an off-hook indication on the trunk, and requests a digit register at the far end, so that the address may be communicated.
10. The terminating switch sends an off-hook followed by an on-hook signal, known as a "wink." This indicates a register-ready status.
11. The originating switch sends the address digits to the terminating switch.

This example gives some idea of the functions that are performed using control signals. A somewhat more detailed overview is given in Box 2.3. The functions performed by control signals can be roughly grouped into the categories of supervisory, address, call information, and network management.

The term **supervisory** is generally used to refer to control functions that have a binary character (true/false; on/off), such as request for service, answer, alerting, and return to idle. They deal with the availability of the called subscriber and of the needed network resources. Supervisory control signals are used to determine if a needed resource is available and, if so, to seize it. They are also used to communicate the status of requested resources.

Address signals identify a subscriber. Initially, an address signal is

BOX 2.3

Signaling Functions

SUPERVISORY

Supervisory signaling provides the mechanism for obtaining the resources to establish a call. It is used to initiate a call request, to hold or release an established connection, to initiate or terminate charging, to recall an operator on an established connection, to alert a subscriber, and to initiate custom calling. It involves the recognition of busy or idle states on subscriber lines and interoffice trunks, and the transmission of that information to the caller and switching system. This form of signaling involves both control and status functions.

Control

Supervisory signaling is used to control the use of resources. Switch and trunk capacity is assigned to a connection with supervisory signals. These resources, once seized, are held for the duration of the call and released upon call termination.

Status

Supervisory signaling also encompasses information concerning the status of a call or attempted call. This information is sent back through the network to the subscriber's switch.

ADDRESS

Address signaling provides the mechanism for identifying the subscribers participating in a call or call attempt. It conveys such information as the calling or called subscriber's telephone number and an area or country code or PBX trunk access code. It involves the transmission of digits of a called telephone number to a switching system from a subscriber or by one switching system to another. Address signaling includes both station-related and routing-related signals.

Station-Related

Address signaling originates with the calling subscriber. From a telephone the signal is generated as a sequence of pulses (rotary dial) or a sequence of two-frequency tones (push button). For digital subscribers, a digital control signal may be used.   *Cont.*

Routing-Related

If more than one switch is involved in the call setup, signaling is required between switches. This includes address signaling, which supports the routing function, and supervisory signaling, which is involved in allocating resources.

CALL INFORMATION

Call information signals are transmitted to a caller to provide information to callers and operators relative to the establishment of a connection through a telephone network. A variety of audible tones is used for this purpose. These signals can be categorized as alerting and progress.

Alerting

Alerting signals are provided to a subscriber who is not placing a call. These include ringing a called telephone and alerting the subscriber that the phone is off the hook.

Progress

Call progress signals indicate the status of the call to the calling subscriber.

NETWORK MANAGEMENT

Network management signals include all those signals related to the ongoing operation and management of the network. They include signals that cause control to be exerted and signals that provide status.

Control

Network management control signals are used to control the overall routing selection process (e.g., to change the preplanned routes of a switch) and to modify the operating characteristics of the network in response to overload and failure conditions.

Status

Network management status signals are used by a switch to provide status information to network management centers and to other switches. Status information includes traffic volume, overload conditions, persistent error conditions, and failures.

generated by a calling subscriber when dialing a telephone number. The resulting address may be propagated through the network to support the routing function and to locate and ring the called subscriber's phone.

The term **call information** refers to those signals that provide information to the subscriber about the status of a call. This is in contrast to internal control signals between switches used in call establishment and termination. Such internal signals are analog or digital electrical messages. In contrast, call information signals are audible tones that can be heard by the caller or an operator with the proper phone set.

Supervisory, address, and call information control signals are directly involved in the establishment and termination of a call. In contrast, **network management** signals are used for the maintenance, troubleshooting, and overall operation of the network. Such signals may be in the form of messages, such as a list of preplanned routes being sent to a station to update its routing tables. These signals cover a broad scope, and it is this category that will expand most with the increasing complexity of switched networks.

Location of Signaling

Control signaling needs to be considered in two contexts: (1) signaling between a subscriber and the network and (2) signaling within the network. Typically, signaling operates differently within these two contexts.

The signaling between a telephone or other subscriber device and the switching office to which it attaches is, to a large extent, determined by the characteristics of the subscriber device and the needs of the human user. Signals within the network are entirely computer-to-computer. The internal signaling is concerned not only with the management of subscriber calls but with the management of the network itself. Thus, for this internal signaling, a more complex repertoire of commands, responses, and set of parameters is needed.

Because two different signaling techniques are used, the local switching office to which the subscriber is attached must provide a mapping between the relatively less complex signaling technique used by the subscriber and the more complex technique used within the network. In Part II, we will see a specific example of each technique as part of ISDN, namely I.451 for subscriber-to-network signaling and Signaling System No. 7 for internal network signaling.

Common Channel Signaling

Traditional control signaling in circuit-switched networks has been on a per-trunk or inchannel basis. With **inchannel signaling,** the same channel is used to carry control signals as is used to carry the call to which the control signals relate. Such signaling begins at the originating subscriber and follows the same path as the call itself. This has the merit that no additional transmission facilities are needed for signaling; the facilities for voice transmission are shared with control signaling.

Two forms of inchannel signaling are in use: inband and out-of-band. **Inband signaling** uses not only the same physical path as the call it serves, it also uses the same frequency band as the voice signals that are carried. This form of signaling has several advantages. Because the control signals have the same electromagnetic properties as the voice signals, they can go anywhere that the voice signals go. Thus there are no limits on the use of inband signaling anywhere in the network, including places where analog-to-digital or digital-to-analog conversion takes place. In addition, it is impossible to set up a call on a faulty speech path, since the control signals that are used to set up that path would have to follow the same path.

Out-of-band signaling takes advantage of the fact that voice signals do not use the full 4 kHz bandwidth allotted to them. A separate narrow signaling band, within the 4 kHZ is used to send control signals. The major advantage of this approach is that the control signals can be sent whether or not voice signals are on the line, thus allowing continuous supervision and control of a call. However, an out-of-band scheme needs extra electronics to handle the signaling band.

The information transfer rate is quite limited with inchannel signaling. With inband signals, the channel is only available for control signals when there are no voice signals on the circuit. With out-of-band signals, a very narrow bandwidth is available. With such limits, it is difficult to accommodate, in a timely fashion, any but the simplest form of control messages. However, to take advantage of the potential services and to cope with the increasing complexity of evolving network technology, a richer and more powerful control signal repertoire is needed.

A second drawback of inchannel signaling is the amount of delay from the time a subscriber enters an address (dials a number) and the time the connection is established. The requirement to reduce this delay is becoming more important as the network is used in new ways. For example, computer-controlled calls, such as with transaction processing, use relatively short messages; therefore, the call setup time represents an appreciable part of the total transaction time.

Both of these problems can be addressed with **common channel signaling,** in which control signals are carried over paths completely independent of the voice channels (Table 2.3). One independent control signal path can carry the signals for a number of subscriber channels, and hence is a common control channel for these subscriber channels.

The principle of common channel signaling is illustrated and contrasted with inchannel signaling in Figure 2.23. As can be seen, the

TABLE 2.3   Signaling Techniques for Circuit-switched Networks

Technique	Description	Comment
Inchannel		
Inband	Transmit control signals in the same band of frequencies used by the voice signals.	The simplest technique. It is necessary for call information signals and may be used for other signals. Inband can be used over any type of line plant.
Out-of-band	Transmit control signals using the same facilities as the voice signal but a different part of the frequency band.	In contrast to inband, provides continuous supervision during the life of a connection.
Common channel	Transmit control signals over signaling links that are dedicated to control signals and are common to a number of voice channels.	Reduces call setup time compared to inchannel methods. It is also more adaptable to evolving functional needs.

signal path for common channel signaling is physically separate from the path for voice or other subscriber signals. The common channel can be configured with the bandwidth required to carry control signals for a rich variety of functions. Thus, both the signaling protocol and the network architecture to support that protocol are more complex than

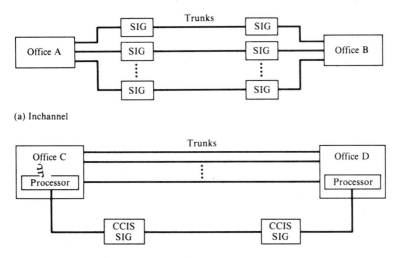

(a) Inchannel

(b) Common channel

CCIS SIG: common-channel interoffice signaling equipment
SIG: per-trunk signaling equipment

FIGURE 2.23 Inchannel and Common-channel Signaling

inchannel signaling. However, the continuing drop in computer hardware costs makes common channel signaling increasingly attractive. The control signals are messages that are passed between switches and between a switch and the network management center. Thus, the control signaling portion of the network is in effect a distributed computer network carrying short messages.

Box 2.4 lists some of the requirements that common-channel signaling is intended to address. These and other functions require that the control signals be independent of the subscriber signals and that quite elaborate control messages be used in some instances.

Two modes of operation are used in common-channel signaling (Figure 2.24). In the **associated mode**, the common channel closely tracks along its entire length the interswitch trunk groups that are served between endpoints. The control signals are on different channels from the subscriber signals, and inside the switch, the control signals are routed directly to a control signal processor. A more complex, but more powerful, mode is the **nonassociated mode**. With this mode, the network is augmented by additional nodes, known as signal transfer points. There is now no close or simple assignment of control channels to trunk groups. In effect, there are now two separate networks, with links between them so that the control portion of the network can exercise control over the switching nodes that are servicing the subscriber calls. Network management is more easily exerted in the nonassociated mode since control channels can be assigned to tasks in a more flexible manner. The nonassociated mode is likely to be the mode used in ISDN.

Box 2.4 also summarizes the merits of common-channel signaling relative to inchannel signaling. Some of the points listed bear elaboration. With inchannel signaling, control signals from one switch are originated by a control processor and switched onto the outgoing channel. On the receiving end, the control signals must be switched from the voice channel into the control processor. With common-channel signaling, the control signals are transferred directly from one control processor to another, without being tied to a voice signal. This is a simpler procedure, and one that is less susceptible to accidental or intentional interference between subscriber and control signals. This is one of the main motivations for common-channel signaling. Another key motivation for common-channel signaling is that call setup time is reduced. Consider the sequence of events for call setup with inchannel signaling when more than one switch is involved. A control signal will be sent from one switch to the next in the intended path. At each switch, the control signal cannot be transferred through the switch to the next leg of the route until the associated circuit is established through that switch. With common-channel signaling, forwarding of control information can overlap the circuit-setup process.

BOX 2.4

Common-Channel Signaling

REQUIREMENTS [REY 83]

- Transfer of network management signals.
- Combining different types of traffic on one trunk group but retaining their identity at the far end.
- Far-end make-busy of trunks for maintenance purposes.
- Return of busy signal from originating rather than terminating station, so that the intermediate trunk(s) can immediately be made available to other calls.
- Increased transparency for the network (such as removal of constraints imposed on customer data transmissions to prevent harmful interaction with inband signaling equipment).
- Call tracing.
- Elimination or improved handling of simultaneous seizure of both ends of two-way trunks.
- Reduction of fraud.

MODES OF OPERATION

Associated

A separate voice channel or channels carry signaling information, and the channel or channels are routed with the speech channels being served.

Nonassociated

Signaling information traverses a completely separate route from the voice paths that it controls. Signals are routed through signal transfer points.

COMPARISON WITH INCHANNEL SIGNALING [BELL82b]

Avantages

- Only one set of signaling facilities is needed for each trunk group instead of separate facilities for each individual circuit.
- Control information is transferred directly between control elements of switches with-

Disadvantages

- Control information pertaining to an established circuit (e.g., disconnect) must be relayed from one switch to the next. An inchannel signal automatically propagates through the network on the route of the circuit.

out going through the voice-channel processing equipment.

- There is no chance of interference between voice and control signals.
- The control channel is inaccessible to users, eliminating a potential means of fraud.
- Connections involving multiple switches can be set up more rapidly, since the control signals do not need to wait for circuit setup.
- The signaling channel does not have to be associated with any particular trunk group, allowing centralized control.

- If one node fails to relay the control signal, facilities downstream from the failure will not receive the control information. Thus reliability is more critical with common-channel signaling.
- There is no automatic test of the voice circuit.

With nonassociated signaling, a further advantage emerges: One or more central control points can be established. All control information can be routed to a network control center where requests are processed and from which control signals are sent to switches that handle subscriber traffic. In this way, requests can be processed with a more global view of network conditions.

Of course, there are disadvantages to common-channel signaling, as suggested in Box 2.4. These primarily have to do with the complexity of the technique. However, the dropping cost of digital hardware and the increasingly digital nature of telecommunication networks make common-channel signaling the appropriate technology.

All of the discussion in this section has dealt with the use of common-channel signaling inside the network, that is, to control switches. Even in a network that is completely controlled by common-channel signaling, inchannel signaling is needed for at least some of the communication with the subscriber. For example, dial tone, ringback, and busy signals must be inchannel to reach the user. In general, the subscriber does not have access to the common-channel signaling portion of the network and does not employ the common-channel signaling protocol. However, we will see in Part II that this statement will not be true for ISDN.

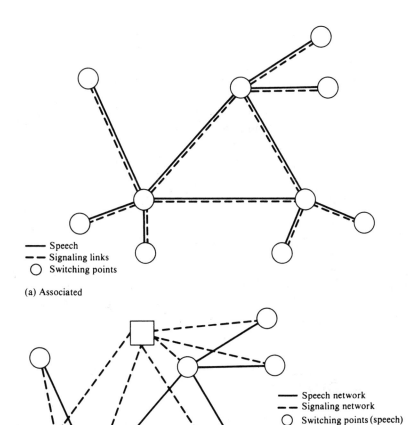

— Speech
– – Signaling links
○ Switching points

(a) Associated

— Speech network
– – Signaling network
○ Switching points (speech)
☐ Switching points (signal—
—transfer points)

(b) Nonassociated

FIGURE 2.24 Common-channel Signaling Modes [FREE89]

2.7
SUMMARY

Circuit switching was primarily designed to provide an efficient and high-quality facility for voice traffic. Key distinguishing features of circuit switching are that a circuit, once established, is transparent to the subscribers (equivalent to a direct connection) and that the delay across the circuit is nonvariable and small (the propagation delay of the transmission path).

Increasingly, digital switching and transmission techniques are being used. Digital switching involves the manipulation of time-division multiplexed streams of bits, representing either data or digitized voice. Several time-division switching techniques are in common use. The increasing use of both digital switching and digital transmission has paved the way for integrated digital networks, which are described in Chapter 4.

Several important aspects of circuit-switched networks are changing dramatically in the wake of the increasing complexity and digitalization of public telecommunication networks. Simple hierarchical routing schemes are being replaced with more flexible and powerful nonhierarchical schemes. This reflects a corresponding change in the underlying architecture, which leads to increased efficiency and resilience. Simple inchannel control signaling methods are being replaced with more complex and higher-speed common-channel signaling. Again, this has implications for the architecture of the network.

2.8

RECOMMENDED READING

As befits its age, circuit switching has inspired a voluminous literature. Two good books on the subject are [BELL91] and [KEIS85]. The first of these is particularly lucid and comprehensive. Worthwhile accounts may also be found in [MART90] and [DAVI73]. [BROO83] discusses alternative internal organizations for a switch.

The October 1990 issue of *IEEE Communications* magazine is devoted to the topic of routing in circuit-switched networks. Surveys of the subject can also be found in [MITR91], [ASH89], [HURL87], and [YUM87]. Discussions of control signaling can be found in [FREE89], [REY83], and [KEIS85].

2.9

PROBLEMS

2.1. Consider a nonblocking three-stage space-division switch with 1000 inputs and 1000 outputs (2048 full-duplex ports). For an optimum design, what is the total number of crosspoints required? How many arrays are needed for each stage and how many input and output lines are there per stage?

2.2. Repeat problem 2.1 using 2048 as the number of input and output lines.

2.3. How many crosspoints would be required for a three-stage space division switch to serve 500 ports
(a) in a nonblocking configuration? *optimized ?*
(b) in a blocking configuration that has 20 ports in each concentration and an expansion array with 15 center-stage arrays?

$M = 20$
$k = 15$

2.4. For the system of problem 2.1, how many switch points would be needed if a TDM bus were used?

2.5. What is the magnitude of delay through a TSI stage? $\frac{1}{R}$

2.6. Consider a simple TSI switch whose memory has a 50-nsec cycle time. The memory is organized into 16-bit words. Frames are 1024 bits. What is the maximum data rate per channel? What is the data rate of the trunk lines to and from the switch?

2.7. For STS, give an example of blocking when the numberr of TSI units equals the number of incoming channels. What is the minimum number of TSI units for proper functioning (even in blocking mode)?

2.8. Assume tht the velocity of propagation on a TDM bus is 0.7 *c*, its length is 10 m, and the data rate is 500 Mbps. How many bits should be transmitted in a time slot to achieve a bus efficiency of 99 percent?

2.9. Demonstrate that in a TSI store at most only half of the memory is usefully occupied at any one time. Devise a means of reducing the TSI memory requirement while maintaining its nonblocking property.

2.10. Consider the use of a 500-ns memory in a TSI device. Assume that voice signals are digitized for transmission at 64 kpbs. How many full-duplex voice channels can be supported by a TSI switch?

2.11. Justify the assertion in Section 2.4 that, for an STS network, the number of TSI units must be double the number of incoming and outgoing lines for nonblocking.

2.12. Determine the number of crosspoints and the total number of memory bits required for a TST switch defined as follows:
- Number of voice lines = 32.
- Single-stage space switch.
- Number of channels per frame = 30.
- Time expansion = 2.

2.13. How many bits of memory are needed in a TSI unit for a 60-channel signal with nine bits per time slot?

2.14. If one examines the rate structure of the long distance telephone services, it would appear that distance, while important, is not the major factor in determining cost. Speculate on the reason for this.

CHAPTER 3

Packet Switching

Around 1970, research began on a new form of architecture for long-distance digital data communications: packet switching. Although the technology of packet switching has evolved substantially since that time, it is remarkable that: (1) the basic technology of packet switching is fundamentally the same today as it was in the early-1970s networks, and (2) packet switching remains one of the few effective technologies for long-distance data communications. Even with the continuing evolution and increasing digital capability of long-haul circuit-switched networks, packet switching will continue to play an important role in integrated digital networks (IDNs).

This chapter provides an overview of packet-switching technology. We will see that many of the advantages of packet switching (flexibility, resource sharing, robustness, responsiveness) come with a cost. The packet-switched network is a distributed collection of packet-switched nodes. In the ideal, all packet-switched nodes would always know the state of the entire network. Unfortunately, because the nodes are distributed, there is always a time delay between a change in status in one portion of the network and the knowledge of that change elsewhere. Furthermore, there is overhead involved in communicating status information. As a result, a packet-switched network can never perform "perfectly," and elaborate algorithms are used to cope with the time delay and overhead penalties of network operation.

The chapter begins with an introduction to packet-switched network operation. Next, we look at the internal operation of these networks, introducing the concepts of virtual circuits and datagrams. Following this, the key technologies of routing and flow control are examined. The chapter concludes with an introduction to fast packet switching, which is one of the few genuine recent advances in packet-switching technology and will be important in the evolution of the IDN and ISDN networks.

3.1

OVERVIEW

The long-haul circuit-switched telecommunications network was originally designed to handle voice traffic, and the majority of traffic on these networks continues to be voice. A key characteristic of circuit-switched networks is that resources within the network are dedicated to a particular call. For voice connections, the resulting circuit will enjoy a high percentage of utilization since, most of the time, one party or the other is talking. However, as the circuit-switched network began to be used increasingly for data connections, two shortcomings became apparent:

- In a typical terminal-to-host data connection, much of the time the line is idle. Thus, with data connections, a circuit-switched approach is inefficient.
- In a circuit-switched network, the connection provides for transmission at constant data rate. Thus both devices that are connected must transmit and receive at the same data rate. This limits the utility of the network in interconnecting a variety of host computers and terminals.

To understand how packet switching addresses these problems, let us briefly summarize packet-switching operation. Data are transmitted in short packets. A typical upper bound on packet length is 1000 octets (bytes). If a source has a longer message to send, the message is broken up into a series of packets (Figure 3.1). Each packet contains a portion (or all for a short message) of the user's data plus some control information. The control information, at a minimum, includes the information that the network requires in order to be able to route the packet through the network and deliver it to the intended destination. At each node en route, the packet is received, stored briefly, and passed on to the next node.

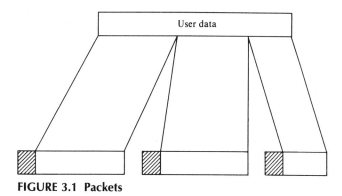

FIGURE 3.1 Packets

Let us return to Figure 2.1, but now consider that this is a simple packet-switched network. Consider a packet to be sent from station *A* to station *E*. The packet will include control information that indicates that the intended destination is *E*. The packet is sent from *A* to node 4. Node 4 stores the packet, determines the next leg of the route (say 5), and queues the packet to go out on that link (the 4-5 link). When the link is available, the packet is transmitted to node 5, which will forward the packet to node 6 and finally to *E*. This approach has a number of advantages over circuit switching:

- Line efficiency is greater, since a single node-to-node link can be dynamically shared by many packets over time. The packets are queued up and transmitted as rapidly as possible over the link. By contrast, with circuit switching, time on a node-to-node link is preallocated using synchronous time-division multiplexing. Much of the time, such a link may be idle because a portion of its time is dedicated to a connection that is idle.
- A packet-switched network can carry out data-rate conversion. Two stations of different data rates can exchange packets, since each connects to its node at its proper data rate.
- When traffic becomes heavy on a circuit-switched network, some calls are blocked; that is, the network refuses to accept additional connection requests until the load on the network decreases. On a packet-switched network, packets are still accepted, but delivery delay increases.
- Priorities can be used. Thus, if a node has a number of packets queued for transmission, it can transmit the higher-priority packets first. These packets will therefore experience less delay than lower-priority packets.

3.2

INTERNAL OPERATION

Switching Technique

A station has a message to send through a packet-switched network that is of length greater than the maximum packet size. It therefore breaks the message up into packets and sends these packets, one at a time, to the network. A question arises as to how the network will handle this stream of packets as it attempts to route them through the network and deliver them to the intended destination. There are two approaches that are used in contemporary networks: datagram and virtual circuit.

In the **datagram** approach, each packet is treated independently, with no reference to packets that have gone before. Let us consider the implication of this approach. Suppose that station A in Figure 2.1 has a three-packet message to send to E. It transmits the packets, 1-2-3, to node 4. On *each* packet, node 4 must make a routing decision. Packet 1 arrives for delivery to E. Node 4 could plausibly forward this packet to either node 5 or node 7 as the next step in the route. In this case, node 4 determines that its queue of packets for node 5 is shorter than for node 7, so it queues the packet for node 5. Ditto for packet 2. But for packet 3, node 4 finds that its queue for node 7 is now shorter and so queues packet 3 for that node. So the packets, each with the same destination address, do not all follow the same route. Because of this, it is just possible that packet 3 will beat packet 2 to node 6. Thus it is possible that the packets will be delivered to E in a different sequence from the one in which they were sent. It is up to E to figure out how to reorder them. Also, it is possible for a packet to be destroyed in the network. For example, if a packet-switched node crashes momentarily, all of its queued packets may be lost. If this were to happen to one of the packets in our example, node 6 has no way of knowing that one of the packets in the sequence of packets has been lost. Again, it is up to E to detect the loss of a packet and figure out how to recover it. In this technique, each packet, treated independently, is referred to as a datagram.

In the **virtual circuit** approach, a preplanned route is established before any packets are sent. For example, suppose that A has one or more messages to send to E. It first sends a special control packet, referred to as a Call Request packet, to 4, requesting a logical connection to E. Node 4 decides to route the request and all subsequent packets to 5, which decides to route the request and all subsequent packets to 6, which finally delivers the Call Request packet to E. If E is prepared to accept the connection, it sends a Call Accept packet to 6. This packet is passed back through nodes 5 and 4 to A. Stations A and E may now exchange data over the route that has been established. Because the route is fixed for the duration of the logical connection, it is somewhat similar to a circuit in a circuit-switching network and is referred to as a virtual circuit. Each packet now contains a virtual circuit identifier as well as data. Each node on the preestablished route knows where to direct such packets; no routing decisions are required. Thus every data packet from A intended for E traverses nodes 4, 5, and 6; every data packet from E intended for A traverses nodes, 6, 5, and 4. Eventually, one of the stations terminates the connection with a Clear Request packet. At any time, each station can have more than one virtual circuit to any other station and can have virtual circuits to more than one station.

So, the main characteristic of the virtual-circuit technique is that a route between stations is set up prior to data transfer. Note that this does not mean that this is a dedicated path, as in circuit switching. A packet is still buffered at each node and queued for output over a line. The difference from the datagram approach is that, with virtual circuits, the node need not make a routing decision for each packet. It is made only once for all packets using that virtual circuit.

If two stations wish to exchange data over an extended period of time, there are certain advantages to virtual circuits. First, the network may provide services related to the virtual circuit, including sequencing and error control. *Sequencing* refers to the fact that, since all packets follow the same route, they arrive in the original order. *Error control* is a service that assures not only that packets arrive in proper sequence, but that all packets arrive correctly. For example, if a packet in a sequence from node 4 to node 6 fails to arrive at node 6, or arrives with an error, node 6 can request a retransmission of that packet from node 4. Another advantage is that packets should transit the network more rapidly with a virtual circuit; it is not necessary to make a routing decision for each packet at each node.

One advantage of the datagram approach is that the call setup phase is avoided. Thus, if a station wishes to send only one or a few packets, datagram delivery will be quicker. Another advantage of the datagram service is that, because it is more primitive, it is more flexible. For example, if congestion develops in one part of the network, incoming datagrams can be routed away from the congestion. With the use of virtual circuits, packets follow a predefined route, and thus it is more difficult for the network to adapt to congestion. A third advantage is that datagram delivery is inherently more reliable. With the use of virtual circuits, if a node fails, all virtual circuits that pass through that node are lost. With datagram delivery, if a node fails, subsequent packets may find an alternate route that bypasses that node.

Box 3.1 summarizes the relative merits of the two approaches. Most currently available packet-switched networks make use of virtual cir-

---

BOX 3.1

Comparison of Virtual Circuits and Datagrams

INTERNAL OPERATION

Virtual Circuit Advantages

- Connection-oriented services, such as sequencing, and error control may be provided.
- Routing decisions are not required for each packet for each node, but only once at setup time. Thus packet transmission and delivery may take less time.

Datagram Advantages

- Call setup time is avoided. This is an advantage for short transactions.
- Network congestion can be bypassed, improving delivery performance.
- Network failures can be bypassed, improving reliability.

EXTERNAL SERVICE

Virtual Circuit Advantages

- Provides the user with connection-oriented services, such as sequencing and error control.

Datagram Advantages

- Supports connectionless applications.
- Avoids call setup time.

---

cuits for their internal operation. To some degree, this reflects a historical motivation to provide a network that presents a service as reliable (in terms of sequencing) as a circuit-switched network. There are, however, several providers of private packet-switched networks that make use of datagram operation. From the user's point of view, there should be very little difference in the external behavior based on the use of datagrams or virtual circuits. If a manager is faced with a choice, other factors such as cost and performance should probably take precedence over whether the internal network operation is datagram or virtual circuit.

Packet Size

One important design issue is the packet size to be used in the network. There is a significant relationship between packet size and transmission time, as shown in Figure 3.2. In this example, it is assumed that there is a virtual circuit from station X through nodes a and b to station Y. The message to be sent comprises 30 octets, and each packet contains

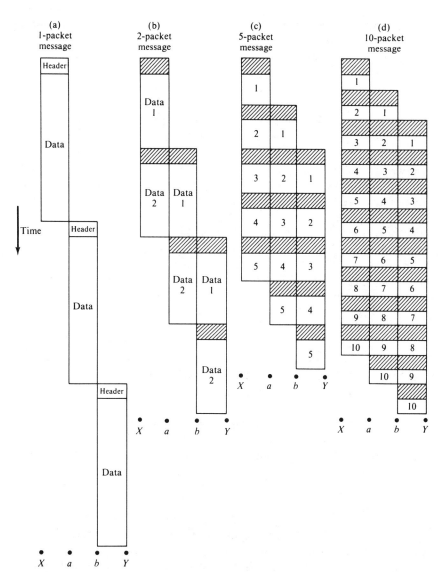

FIGURE 3.2 Effect of Packet Size on Transmission Time

3 octets of control information, which is placed at the beginning of each packet and is referred to as a *header*. If the entire message is sent as a single packet of 33 octets (3 octets of header plus 30 octets of data), then the packet is first transmitted from station X to node a (Figure 3.2a). When the entire packet is received, it can then be transmitted from a to b. When the entire packet is received at node b, it is then

transferred to station *Y*. The total transmission time is 99 octet-times (33 octets × 3 packet transmissions).

Suppose now that we break the message up into two packets, each containing 15 octets of the message and, of course, 3 octets each of header or control information. In this case, node *a* can begin transmitting the first packet as soon as it has arrived from *X*, without waiting for the second packet. Because of this overlap in transmission, the total transmission time drops to 72 octet-times. By breaking the message up into 5 packets, each intermediate node can begin transmission even sooner and the savings in time is greater, with a total of 63 octet-times. However, this process of using more and smaller packets eventually results in increased, rather than reduced delay, as illustrated in Figure 3.2d. This is because each packet contains a fixed amount of header, and more packets mean more of these headers. Furthermore, the example does not show the processing and queuing delays at each node. These delays are also greater when more packets are handled for a single message. Thus, packet-switched network designers must consider these factors in attempting to find an optimum packet size.

3.3

COMPARISON OF CIRCUIT SWITCHING AND PACKET SWITCHING

Having looked at the internal operation of packet switching, we can now return to a comparison of this technique with circuit switching. We first look at the important issue of performance and then examine other characteristics.

Performance

A simple comparison of circuit switching and the two forms of packet switching is provided in Figure 3.3. The figure depicts the transmission of a message across four nodes, from a source station attached to node 1 to a destination station attached to node 4.

For circuit switching, there is a certain amount of delay before the message can be sent. First, a call request signal is sent through the network, to set up a connection to the destination. If the destination station is not busy, a call-accepted signal returns. Note that a processing delay is incurred at each node during the call request; this time is spent at each node setting up the route of the connection. One the return, this processing is not needed since the connection is already set up. After the connection is set up, the message is sent as a single block, with no noticeable delay at the switching nodes.

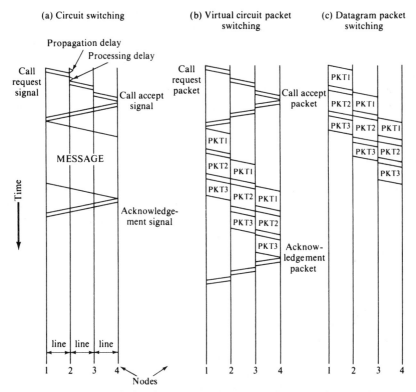

FIGURE 3.3 Event Timing for Various Communication Switching Techniques

Virtual-circuit packet switching appears quite similar to circuit switching. A virtual circuit is requested using a call request packet, which incurs a delay at each node. The virtual circuit is accepted with a call-accept packet. In contrast to the circuit-switching case, the call acceptance also experiences node delays, even though the virtual circuit route is now established. The reason is that this packet is queued at each node and must wait its turn for retransmission. Once the virtual circuit is established, the message is transmitted in packets. It should be clear that this phase of the operation can be no faster than circuit switching, for comparable networks. This is because circuit switching is an essentially transparent process, providing a constant data rate across the network. Packet switching requires some node delay at each node in the path. Worse, this delay is variable and will increase with increased load.

Datagram packet switching does not require a call setup. Thus, for short messages, it will be faster than virtual-circuit packet switching and perhaps circuit switching. However, since each individual datagram is routed independently, the processing for each datagram at each node may be longer than for virtual-circuit packets. Thus, for long messages, the virtual-circuit technique may be superior.

Figure 3.4 is intended only to suggest what the relative performance of the techniques might be; however, actual performance depends on a host of factors, including the size of the network, its topology, the pattern of load, and the characteristics of typical exchanges. The interested reader may pursue these topics in [KLEI76], [ROSN82], [SAND80], [KUMM80], [MIYA75], and [STUC85].

Other Characteristics

Besides performance, there are a number of other characteristics that may be considered in comparing the techniques we have been discussing. Table 3.1 summarizes the most important of these. Box 3.2 attempts to summarize some of the key relative merits of circuit switching and packet switching.

3.4
APPLICATION OF PACKET SWITCHING

Although we will later in this chapter explore some of the details of packet-switching technology, we are already in a position to comment on the applicability of this networking approach (Box 3.3). Recall that we said that packet switching held certain advantages over circuit switching for data communications. In particular, packet switching may make more efficient use of internal (to the network) communications resources and allow devices of differing data rates to interconnect.

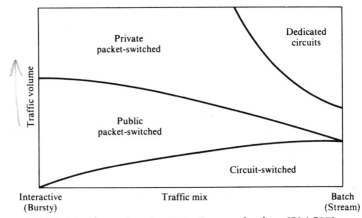

FIGURE 3.4 Alternatives for Data Communications [BLAC87]

TABLE 3.1 Comparison of Communication Switching Techniques

Circuit Switching	Datagram Packet Switching	Virtual-circuit Packet Switching
Dedicated transmission path	No dedicated path	No dedicated path
Continuous transmission of data	Transmission of packets	Transmission of packets
Fast enough for interactive	Fast enough for interactive	Fast enough for interactive
Messages are not stored	Packets may be stored until delivered	Packets stored until delivered
The path is established for entire conversation	Route established for each packet	Route established for entire conversation
Call setup delay; negligible transmission delay	Packet transmission delay	Call setup delay; packet transmission delay
Busy signal if called party busy	Sender may be notified if packet not delivered	Sender notified of connection denial
Overload may block call setup; no delay for established calls	Overload increases packet delay	Overload may block call setup; increases packet delay
Electromechanical or computerized switching nodes	Small switching nodes	Small switching nodes
User responsible for message loss protection	Network may be responsible for individual packets	Network may be responsible for packet sequences
Usually no speed or code conversion	Speed and code conversion	Speed and code conversion
Fixed bandwidth transmission	Dynamic use of bandwidth	Dynamic use of bandwidth
No overhead bits after call setup	Overhead bits in each packet	Overhead bits in each packet

However, in order to be more specific about the applicability of packet switching, we need to examine in more detail the nature of the data communications traffic.

Data communications traffic can be roughly classified into two categories: stream and bursty. **Stream traffic** is characterized by lengthy and fairly continuous transmission. Examples are file transfer, telemetry, other sorts of batch data processing applications, and digitized voice communication. **Bursty traffic** is characterized by short, sporadic transmissions. Interactive terminal-host traffic, such as transaction processing, data entry, and time-sharing, fits this description.

Figure 3.4 shows the relative applicability of four alternative networking approaches. The **circuit-switched network** approach makes use

BOX 3.2

Relative Merits of Circuit Switching and Packet Switching of Data

CIRCUIT SWITCHING
Advantages
- Compatible with voice. Economies of scale can be realized by using the same network for voice and data.
- Commonality of calling procedures for voice and data. No special user training or communication protocols are needed to handle data traffic.

Disadvantages
- Subject to blocking. This makes it difficult to size the network properly. The problem is less severe with the use of dynamic nonhierarchical routing techniques.
- Requires subscriber compatibility. The devices at each end of a circuit must be compatible in terms of protocol and data rate, since the circuit is a transparent connection. Furthermore, for each terminal connected to a host, a separate physical line into the host is required.
- Large processing and signal burden. For transaction-type applications, data calls are of short duration and need to be set up rapidly. This proportionally increases the overhead burden on the network.

PACKET SWITCHING
Advantages
- Provides speed conversion. Two attached devices with different data rates may exchange data; the network buffers the data and delivers it at the appropriate data rate.

Disadvantages
- Complex routing and control. To achieve efficiency and resilience, a packet-switched network must employ a complex set of routing and control algorithms.

- Appears nonblocking. As the network load increases, the delay increases, but new exchanges are usually permitted.
- Efficient utilization. Switches and trunks are used on demand rather than dedicating capacity to a particular call.
- Logical multiplexing. A host system can have simultaneous conversations with a number of terminals over a single line.

- Delay. Delay is a function of load. It can be long and it is variable.

of dial-up lines. The cost is based on data rate, connection time, and distance. As we have said, this is quite ineffecient for bursty traffic. However, for occasional stream-oriented requirements, this may be the most appropriate choice. For example, a corporation may have distributed offices. At the close of the day, each office transfers a file to headquarters summarizing the activities for that day. A dial-up line used for the single transfer from each office appears to be the most cost-effective solution. When there is a high volume of stream traffic between a few sites, the most economical solution is to obtain **dedicated circuits** between sites. These circuits, also known as leased lines or semipermanent circuits, may be leased from a telecommunications provider, such as a telephone company, or from a satellite provider. The dedicated circuit carries a constant fixed cost based on data rate and, in some cases, distance. If the traffic volume is high enough, then the utilization will be high enough to make this approach the most attractive.

On the other hand, if the traffic is primarily bursty, then packet switching has the advantage. Furthermore, packet switching permits terminals and computer ports of various data rates to be interconnected. If the traffic is primarily bursty, but is of relatively modest volume for an organization, then a **public packet-switched network** provides the best solution. A public packet-switched network works much like a public telephone network. In this case, the network provides a packet transmission service to a variety of subscribers, each of which has moderate traffic requirements. If there are a number of different sub-

---

BOX 3.3

Packet Switching

APPLICATIONS

Data

Public Data Network (PDN)/Value-added Network (VAN)

Provides a wide-area data communications facility for computers and terminals. The network is a shared resource, owned by a provider who sells the capacity to others. Thus it functions as a utility service for a number of subscriber communities.

Private Packet-switched Network

Provides a shared resource for one organization's computers and terminals. A private packet-switched network is justified if there are a substantial number of devices with a substantial amount of traffic in one organization.

Voice

Packetized Voice Network

Provides a communications facility for real-time voice traffic. This application requires the capability to transmit voice signals with very low delay and with virtually no delay variability.

TECHNOLOGY

Internal Operation

Datagram
Virtual circuit

External Interface

Connection-oriented (virtual circuit)
Connectionless (datagram)

---

scribers, then the total traffic should be great enough to result in high utilization. Hence, the public network is cost-effective from the provider's point of view. The subscriber gets the advantages of packet switching without the fixed cost of implementing and maintaining the network. The cost to the subscriber is based on both connection time and traffic volume, but not distance. Such a network is called a value-added network (VAN), reflecting the fact that the network adds value to the underlying transmission facilities. In most countries other than the United States, there is a single public network owned or controlled by the government and referred to as a public data network (PDN).

If the volume of an organization's bursty traffic is high and concentrated among a small number of sites, then a **private packet-switched network** is the best solution. This is a network in which the organization that owns the data communicating equipment (terminals, hosts) also owns the packet-switching nodes. The nodes are interconnected by dedicated circuits. With a lot of bursty traffic between sites, the private network provides much better utilization and hence lower cost than using circuit switching or simple dedicated lines. The cost of a private network (other than the initial fixed cost of the packet-switching nodes) is based solely on distance. Thus, it combines the efficiencies of public packet switching with the time and volume independence of dedicated circuits.

3.5

ROUTING

Requirements

The primary function of a packet-switched network is to accept packets from a source station and deliver them to a destination station. To accomplish this, a path or route through the network must be determined. To provide good performance and robustness, packet-switched networks typically have many interconnected nodes. Between any pair of stations, there will be a number of possible routes and a routing function must be performed. The requirements for this function include

- Correctness.
- Simplicity.
- Robustness.
- Stability.
- Fairness.
- Optimality.

The first two items on the list are self-explanatory. Robustness has to do with the ability of the network to deliver packets via some route in the face of localized failures and overloads. Ideally, the network can react to such contingencies without loss of packets or the breaking of virtual circuits. The designer who seeks robustness must cope with the competing requirement for stability. Techniques that react to changing conditions have an unfortunate tendency either to react too slowly to events or to experience unstable swings from one extreme to another. For example, the network may react to congestion in one area by shifting most of the load to a second area. Now the second area is overloaded and the first is underutilized, causing a second shift. During these shifts, packets may travel in loops through the network.

A trade-off also exists between fairness and optimality. Some performance criteria may give higher priority to the exchange of packets between nearby stations compared to an exchange between distant stations. This policy may maximize average throughput but will appear unfair to the station that primarily needs to communicate with distant stations. Finally, any routing technique involves some processing overhead at each node and often a transmission overhead as well. The penalty of such overhead needs to be less than the benefit accrued based on some reasonable metric, such as increased robustness or fairness.

Routing Techniques

In this section, our objective is to give the reader a feel for the complexity of the routing function and for some of the trade-offs involved in assessing alternate approaches. For a more complete treatment, the reader is referred to [STAL91a] or to one of the many survey articles on the subject, including [HSIE84a], [BELL86], [GERL84], [GERL81], and [SCHW80].

Before examining some typical routing algorithms, we need to specify the design criterion that is to be used. The selection of a route is generally based on some performance criterion. The simplest criterion is to choose the minimum-hop route (one that passes through the least number of nodes) through the network. This is an easily measured criterion and should minimize the consumption of network resources. A generalization of the minimum-hop criterion is least-cost routing. In this case, a cost is associated with each link and, for any pair of attached stations, the route through the network that accumulates the least cost is sought. For example, the costs in the network of Figure 3.5 are shown as numeric labels on the links. The shortest path (fewest hops) from node 1 to node 6 is 1-3-6 (cost = 5 + 5 = 10), but the least-cost path is 1-4-5-6 (cost = 1 + 1 + 2 = 4). Costs are assigned to links to support one or more design objectives. For example, the cost could be inversely related to the data rate (i.e., the higher the data rate on a link, the lower the assigned cost of the link) or the current queuing delay on the link. In the first case, the least-cost route should provide the highest throughput, since higher-rate links are preferred to lower-rate links. In the second case, the least-cost route should minimize delay, since less busy links are preferred to more busy links.

In either the minimum-hop or least-cost approach, the algorithm for

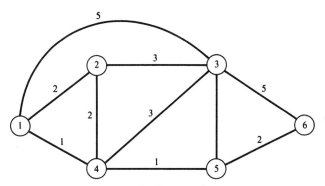

FIGURE 3.5 Packet-switched Network

determining the optimum route for any pair of stations is relatively straightforward [STAL91a], and the processing time would be about the same for either computation. Because the least-cost criterion is more flexible, this is more common than the minimum-hop criterion.

With this background, we now look at some of the important alternative routing techniques (Table 3.2).

Fixed Routing One of the simplest routing strategies is fixed routing. In this case, a route is selected for each source-destination pair of nodes in the network. The routes are fixed, or at least changed only when there is a change in the topology of the network. Thus the link costs used in designing routes cannot be based on any dynamic variable, such as traffic. They could, however, be based on actual transmission cost or expected traffic.

Figure 3.6 suggests how fixed routing might be implemented. A central routing directory is created, to be stored perhaps at a network control center. Note that it is not necessary to store the route for each possible pair of nodes. Rather, it is sufficient to know, for each pair of nodes, the identity of the first node on the route. To see that this is sufficient, consider the least-cost route between a pair of nodes i and n. Suppose that the least-cost route begins with the link from node i to node k. Let us use the label R_1 to refer to the remainder of the route, which is the part from k to n. Now, define the least-cost route from k to n to be R_2. If the cost of R_1 is greater than the cost of R_2, then the i-n route can be improved by using R_2 instead. If the cost of R_1 is less than the cost of R_2, then R_2 is not the least-cost route from k to n. Therefore, R_1 and R_2 are the same route. This line of reasoning demonstrates that, at each point along a route, it is only necessary to know the identity of the next node, not the entire route. Because of this, each node need only store a single row of the routing directory; the node's directory shows the next node to take for each destination.

TABLE 3.2   Routing for Packet-switched Networks

Technique	Description	Comment
Fixed	All routes through the network are preplanned and do not change with changing conditions.	A simple algorithm that might be useful in a very stable network.
Flooding	A packet to be sent from one station to another is replicated as required so that all possible routes through the network are followed. A hop-count limit is used to terminate the process.	An extremely wasteful procedure and not useful for general-purpose routing. Because it is highly reliable, this technique could be used for occasional important network control packets.
Adaptive		
Isolated	Each node makes a routing decision based only on some predefined preferences and the current state of queuing delays on outgoing links.	The simplest form of adaptive routing. In a small and relatively stable network, this technique might be attractive.
Distributed	Routing decisions are based on knowledge of network topology and delay conditions. This information is shared among the packet-switching nodes, and each node makes its own routing decisions.	A flexible and robust approach. There is a trade-off between the amount of information provided to the nodes and the need to minimize overhead so as to avoid degrading performance.
Centralized	Routing decisions are based on knowledge of network topology and delay conditions. This information is provided to a central controller by all the nodes. The central controller then issues routing instructions back to the nodes.	A relatively efficient adaptive approach. There is a risk that the controller will become a bottleneck. Also, failure of the controller disables the routing mechanism.

With fixed routing, there is no difference between routing for datagrams and virtual circuits. All packets from a given source to a given destination follow the same route. The advantage of fixed routing is its simplicity, and it should work well in a reliable network with a steady load. Its disadvantage is its lack of flexibility. It does not react to network congestion or failures. Thus, fixed routing is typically not used in large networks. However, the method is worth presenting, since the use of a next-node directory is to be found in many more sophisticated routing techniques.

		\multicolumn{6}{c}{To node}				
		1	2	3	4	5	6
From node	1	—	2	4	4	4	4
	2	1	—	3	4	4	4
	3	5	2	—	5	5	5
	4	1	2	5	—	5	5
	5	4	4	3	4	—	6
	6	5	5	5	5	5	—

FIGURE 3.6 Fixed Routing

Flooding Another simple routing technique is flooding. This technique requires no network information whatsoever and works as follows. A packet is sent by a source node to every one of its neighbors. At each node, an incoming packet is retransmitted on all outgoing links except for the link upon which it arrived. This technique is illustrated in Figure 3.7, which shows a packet transmission from node 1 to node 6. If node 1 has a packet to send to node 6, it sends a copy of that packet to nodes 2, 3, and 4. Node 2 will send a copy to nodes 3 and 4. Node 4 will send a copy to nodes 2, 3, and 5. And so it goes. Eventually, a number of copies of the packet will arrive at node 6. The packet must have some unique identifier (e.g., sequence number) so that node 6 knows to discard all but the first copy.

It is clear that unless something is done to stop the incessant retransmission of packets, the number of packets in circulation just from a single source packet grows without bound. A simple solution is to limit the number of hops, or times, that a packet can be forward, by the inclusion of a *hop count* field in each packet. The count is initially set by the source node to some positive integer value. Each time a node receives a packet to be passed on, it decreases the hop count by one. If the count reaches zero, the packet is discarded.

One interesting property of the flooding technique is that all possible routes between source and destination are tried. Thus, no matter what link or node outages have occurred, a packet will always get through so long as at least one path between source and destination exists. As a result, the technique is highly robust and could be used to send high-priority messages. An example application is for a military network that

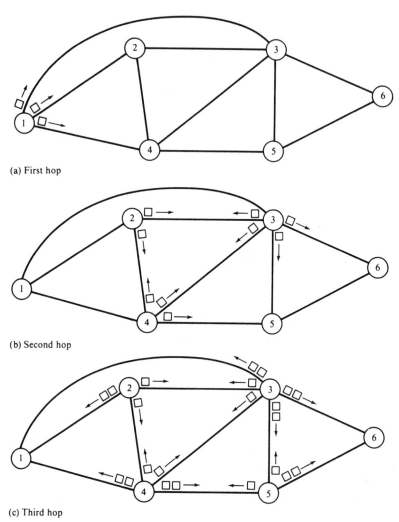

(a) First hop

(b) Second hop

(c) Third hop

FIGURE 3.7 Flooding Example

is subject to extensive damage. Flooding could also be used to broadcast a message to all nodes. Broadcasting is sometimes used in adaptive routing, which is described next.

Adaptive Routing   The routing strategies discussed so far do not react to changing conditions within the network, or at most react infrequently as the result of some system operator action. This characteristic is not necessarily a bad one. Consider these drawbacks of an adaptive strategy, one in which the routing decision depends on the changing conditions of the network:

- The routing decision is more complex; therefore, the processing burden on the network increases.
- In most cases, adaptive strategies depend on status information that is collected at one place but used at another; therefore, the traffic burden on the network increases.
- An adaptive strategy may react too quickly, causing congestion-producing oscillation, or too slowly, being irrelevant.

Despite these real dangers, adaptive routing strategies are by far the most prevalent, for two reasons:

- From the user's point of view, an adaptive routing strategy can improve performance, since packets are routed by the best route available at the time of the routing decision.
- From the network's point of view, an adaptive strategy aids in congestion control by smoothing out the network load. That is, when some areas of the network experience relatively heavy load, subsequent traffic will favor the lightly loaded portions of the network.

These benefits may or may not be realized, depending on the soundness of design and the nature of the load. By and large, it is an extraordinarily complex task to perform properly.

All adaptive routing strategies, by definition, produce routing decisions that adapt to changing conditions in the network. Two parameters that serve to differentiate adaptive routing strategies are the place at which the routing design is made and the amount of information used to make the decision. Based on these two parameters, virtually all strategies are in one or a hybrid combination of the following categories:

- *Isolated adaptive:* local information, distributed control.
- *Distributed adaptive:* information from adjacent nodes or all nodes, distributed control.
- *Centralized adaptive:* information from all nodes, centralized control.

A simple **isolated adaptive** scheme is for a node to route each packet to the outgoing link with the shortest queue length, Q, regardless of destination. This would have the effect of balancing the load on outgoing links. However, some outgoing links may not be headed in the correct general direction. An improvement can be obtained by also taking into account preferred directions. Each link emanating from a node can be assigned a bias B_{ij} for each neighbor node i and each destination node j. For each incoming packet headed for node j, the node would choose the link that has the minimum $Q_i + B_{ij}$ for all neighbors i, where Q_i is the current queue length for the link to node i. Thus a node would tend to send packets in the right direction with concession made to current traffic delays.

As an example, Figure 3.8 shows the status of node 4 of Figure 3.5 at a certain point in time. Node 4 has links to four other nodes. A fair number of packets have been arriving and a backlog has built up, with a queue of packets waiting for each of the outgoing links. A packet arrives from node 1, destined for node 6. Based on current queue lengths and the values of the biases ($B_{i,6}$) for each outgoing link, the minimum value of $Q + B$ is four, on the link to node 3. Thus the packet is routed through node 3.

Isolated adaptive schemes are not in general use. Since they make little use of available information, they do not adapt well to changing conditions. The other two adaptive (distributed, centralized) strategies are more commonly found. Both take advantage of the information that other nodes have about the link delays and outages that they experience.

An example of a **distributed adaptive** algorithm is that used in the Defense Data Network (DDN). This algorithm was developed on ARPANET, which is one of the components of DDN [MCQU80]. For this algorithm, each node maintains two data structures. First, there is a delay matrix, which shows, for each directly connected pair of nodes, this node's current estimate of the delay on the intervening link in both directions (for a pair of nodes not directly connected, the corresponding matrix entry has the value infinity). With this information, the node can calculate a least-cost route to each of the other nodes and develop a routing matrix, such as was seen in Figure 3.6. The vector shows, for each possible destination node, the identity of the next node on the route.

The key design issue for this algorithm is the manner in which the values for the delay matrix are obtained. Every ten seconds, each node

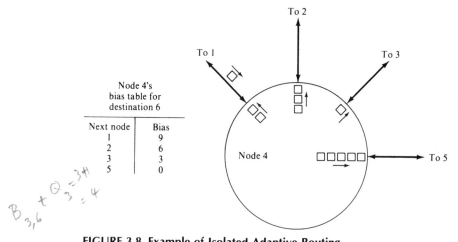

FIGURE 3.8 Example of Isolated Adaptive Routing

computes the average delay on each of its outgoing links. If there are any significant changes in any of the delay values since the last computation, or if there is any change in connectivity, the information is sent to all other nodes using flooding. Each node updates its delay matrix every time one of these flooded packets arrives. Experience with this algorithm indicates that it is responsive and stable. The overhead induced by flooding is moderate, since each node does this at most once every ten seconds.

An example of a **centralized adaptive** algorithm is that used in TYMNET [TYME81]. In TYMNET, one node is designed as supervisor (with a backup for reliability). The supervisor performs the routing function on a virtual-circuit basis. When a virtual circuit is requested, the supervisor determines the least-cost route and passes the necessary routing information for this virtual circuit to each node on the route. When the virtual circuit terminates, the supervisor informs each node on the route.

There are two key design issues with this algorithm: how costs are assigned to each link and how the route is communicated to the nodes that will form a virtual circuit. Link cost is based on data rate, satellite versus land-based link, traffic type, and load condition. For example, if a virtual circuit is requested by a low-speed interactive terminal, a 9600-bps land link is assigned a lower cost than a 56-kbps satellite, because of the longer delay of the satellite. If the virtual circuit is to be used for host-to-host file transfer, the satellite link has the lower cost; throughput is more important than response time. The load component of cost also depends on the traffic type. For stream-oriented traffic, a link is assigned additional cost if it has reached "high-speed overload." This condition occurs when the link cannot support all of its current virtual circuits at the desired data rates. For interactive traffic, a link is assigned additional cost if it has reached "low-speed overload." This condition occurs when the average delay on a link exceeds 0.5 seconds several times in a four-minute period. When either form of overload occurs or ceases to occur, the affected node reports this to the supervisor.

When a virtual circuit is requested, the request is sent to the supervisor, which computes the least-cost route based on the costs appropriate for the traffic type. The supervisor then sends a "needle" to the source node, containing the route as an ordered list of nodes. The needle threads its way along the designated route, depositing routing information as it goes. If an outage is encountered, the needle retraces to the origin and the supervisor is informed.

There are several problems with a centralized adaptive routing strategy compared to a distributed one. Most important is a problem of reliability. The loss of the supervisor disables the entire network with respect to new virtual circuits. This problem can be fixed at the cost of redundant supervisors. Also related to reliability is that the centralized approach is practical only for virtual-circuit operation, and as we have mentioned, a datagram network is inherently more robust. Finally, there is a potential congestion problem in the proximity of the supervisor, since it receives all routing requests and link status information and transmits all routing information.

There are also some advantages of centralized compared to distributed routing. The computation requirements at individual nodes are reduced. Centralized routing permits a more accurate optimization of the routes, eliminating loops and oscillations that may occur when routing decisions are made collectively by nodes acting independently. Finally, with centralized routing, the supervisor has a reasonably accurate and reasonably current picture of the network load distribution. This permits the supervisor to limit new virtual circuits in an effort to control congestion.

3.6

CONGESTION CONTROL

The Need for Congestion Control

In addition to routing, the other main function of a packet-switched network is congestion control. The objective of congestion control is to maintain the number of packets within the network or a region of the network below the level at which queuing delays become excessive. In essence, a packet-switched network is a network of queues. At each node, there is a queue of packets for each outgoing link. If the rate at which packets arrive and queue up exceeds the rate at which packets are transmitted, the queue size grows without bounds, and the delay experienced by a packet goes to infinity. Even if the packet arrival rate is less than the packet transmission rate, queue length will grow dramatically as the arrival rate approaches the transmission rate. As a rule of thumb, when the line for which packets are queuing becomes more than 80 percent utilized, the queue length grows at an alarming rate.

Figure 3.9 shows the effects of congestion in general terms. Figure 3.9a plots the throughput of a network (number of packets delivered to destination stations) versus the offered load (number of packets transmitted by source stations). Both axes are normalized to the theoretical capacity of the network, which can be expressed as the rate at which the network is theoretically capable of handling packets, based on the data rates of the network links. In the ideal case, throughput and hence network utilization increase to accommodate an offered load up to the capacity of the network. Utilization then remains at 100 percent if the load is increased further. The ideal case, of course, requires that all stations somehow know the timing and rate of packets that can be

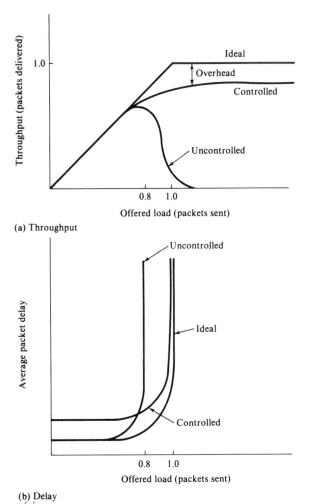

(a) Throughput

(b) Delay

FIGURE 3.9 The Effects of Congestion

presented to the network with no overhead and no time delay in acquiring this information, which is impossible. If no congestion control
is exercised, we have the curve labeled "uncontrolled." For this case,
as the load increases, utilization increases for a while. Then, as the
queue lengths at the various nodes begin to grow, throughput actually
drops. The reason for this is that the buffers at each node are of finite
size. When a node's buffers are full, it must discard additional incoming
packets. Thus the source stations must retransmit the discarded packets
in addition to new packets. This only exacerbates the situation: As more
and more packets are retransmitted, the load on the system grows, and
more buffers become saturated. While the system is trying desperately

to clear the backlog, stations are pumping old (retransmitted) and new packets into the system. Even a successfully delivered packet may be retransmitted because it takes so long for the receiver to acknowledge it that the sender assumes the packet was lost and tries again. Under these circumstances, the effective capacity of the system is virtually zero.

It is clear that these catastrophic events must be avoided, which is the task of congestion control. The object of all congestion-control techniques is to limit queue lengths at the nodes so as to avoid throughput collapse. This control involves some unavoidable overhead. Thus a congestion-control technique cannot perform as well as the theoretical ideal. However, a good congestion-control strategy will avoid throughput collapse and maintain a throughput that differs from the ideal by an amount roughly equal to the overhead of the control (Figure 3.9a).

Figure 3.9b points out that no matter what technique is used, the average delay experienced by packets grows without bounds as the load approaches the capacity of the system. Note that initially the uncontrolled policy results in less delay than a controlled policy because of its lack of overhead. However, the uncontrolled policy will saturate at a lower load.

Techniques

A key tool in most congestion-control techniques is flow control. **Flow control** is used to regulate the flow of data between two points. The receiver limits the rate at which data can be transmitted by the sender. This technique is used on point-to-point configurations in data link control protocols, such as HDLC and LAP-D (see Chapter 8). Flow control can also be used between indirectly connected points, such as two stations that are attached to a packet-switched network and are the endpoints of a virtual circuit. One application of this latter technique is in the X.25 standard, discussed later in this chapter.

As with routing, the techniques used for congestion control will be addressed only briefly. For a more complete treatment, the reader is referred to [STAL91a] or one of the survey articles on the subject, including [GERL84], [GERL81], [HSIE84b], [GERL80], and [POUZ81].

Congestion-control techniques can be categorized along two dimensions:

- Datagram versus virtual circuit.
- Hop versus entry-to-exit versus network access.

Box 3.4 defines these terms, and Figure 3.10 [GERL84] illustrates the distinction between hop, entry-to-exit, and network access control. These various techniques are used alone or in combination on different packet-switched networks. As with routing, congestion control involves a trade-off between the power of the congestion control capability and the need to minimize overhead.

BOX 3.4

Congestion Control for Packet-switched Networks

FUNCTION

Control the number and distribution of packets within the network in order to minimize delays in the network as a whole and in regions of the network.

REQUIREMENT

Limit the length of queues of packets at each node, so that the queuing delay is limited. Specifically, this requires that overall and local traffic loads should be limited to no more than 80 percent of theoretical capacity.

TECHNIQUES

Scope of Control

Packet

Concerned with the movement of individual packets at various points in the network. Such techniques are localized and primarily concerned with the loading on a single node. These techniques are used in datagram networks but may also find application in a virtual-circuit network.

Virtual Circuit

Concerned with controlling the flow of packets through a virtual circuit. By controlling activity on all the virtual circuits that are currently active in a network, the packets moving through that network are controlled.

Level of Control

Hop

Deals with controls exerted between adjacent nodes. These controls can be used to avoid local buffer congestion.

Entry-to-Exit

Concerned with the flow of packets between two endpoints. These controls are generally exerted on a virtual-circuit basis and prevent buffer congestion at the exit switch.

Cont.

BOX 3.4 continued

Network Access

Limits the number of packets transmitted by a particular attached station. These controls limit external inputs based on internal congestion.

ARPANET, which is a datagram network, provides an example of an entry-to-exit technique. The network enforces a limit of eight messages in transit between any pair of hosts. Each message may in turn consist of up to eight packets per message. The source node is required to reserve buffer space at the destination node for each message to be sent, up to the limit of eight. If the destination node is experiencing buffer congestion, it may withhold allocation in order to limit the flow of incoming packets. In addition, ARPANET uses hop-level flow control to prevent buffer congestion in individual nodes.

Another interesting example is afforded by TYMNET, which operates on a virtual-circuit basis and includes both network access and hop-level mechanisms [RIND79, TYME81]. The route for an individual virtual circuit is, of course, defined as a series of hops from node to node. On each node-to-node hop, each current virtual circuit that uses that hop is assigned a quota by the receiving node to the sending node. As a node becomes congested, it reduces the quota for the incoming hops. This controls congestion at the node. Furthermore, this hop-level technique produces a backpressure phenomenon: When one node reduces quotas, adjacent nodes are unable to transmit as fast and must therefore exert flow control on their incoming traffic. For each virtual circuit, these restrictions work their way backward to the node to which the source station is attached. This node then restricts the flow of traffic coming from the source station by means of the X.25 network access protocol, described next.

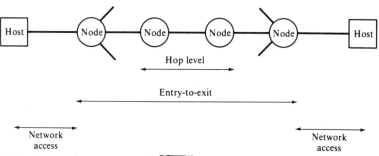

FIGURE 3.10 Flow Control Levels

3.7 $\mathcal{S} \not\vdash \mathcal{P}$

X.25

Perhaps the best known and most widely used protocol standard is X.25, which was originally approved in 1976 and subsequently revised in 1980, 1984, and 1988. The standard specifies an interface between a host system and a packet-switched network. This standard is almost universally used for interfacing to packet-switched networks and will be employed for packet switching in ISDN. In this section, a brief overview of the standard is provided. Greater detail can be found in [STAL90b] and in a number of survey articles, including [DHAS86], [SIRB85], and [ERDE86].

The standard specifically calls out three levels of protocols:

- Physical level. $\left(X.21 \quad or \quad RS \; 232 \right)$
- Link level. $\left(LAP\text{-}B \right)$
- Packet level. $\left(X.25 \right)$

These three levels correspond to the lowest three layers of the OSI model (see Appendix B). The physical level deals with the physical interface between an attached station (computer, terminal) and the link that attaches that station to the packet-switching node. It makes use of the physical-level specification in a standard known as X.21, but in many cases other standards, such as RS-232-C, are substituted. The link level provides for the reliable transfer of data across the physical link, by transmitting the data as a sequence of frames. The link-level standard is referred to as LAP-B (Link Access Protocol-Balanced). LAP-B is a subset of a well-known data link control protocol, HDLC (high-level data link control). LAP-B is very similar to the more recent LAP-D, which is described in Chapter 8. The packet level provides a virtual-circuit service and is described briefly in this section.

Figure 3.11 illustrates the relationship between the levels of X.25. User data are passed down to X.25 level 3, which appends control information as a header, creating a packet. This control information is used in the operation of the protocol, as we shall see. The entire X.25

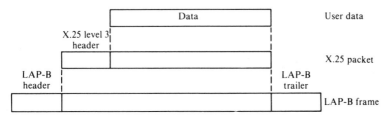

FIGURE 3.11 User Data and X.25 Protocol Control Information

packet is then passed down to the LAP-B entity, which appends control information at the front and back of the packet, forming a LAP-B frame. Again, the control information in the frame is needed for the operation of the LAP-B protocol.

Before examining the details of the packet level of X.25, it would be well to distinguish the concepts of internal operation and external service.

Internal Operation and External Service

One of the most important characteristics of a packet-switched network is whether it uses datagrams or virtual circuits. Actually, there are two dimensions of this characteristic, as illustrated in Figure 3.12. At the interface between a station and a network node, a network may provide either a connection-oriented or connectionless service. With a connection-oriented service, a station performs a call request to set up a logical connection to another station. All packets presented to the network are identified as belonging to a particular logical connection and are numbered sequentially. The network undertakes to deliver packets in sequence-number order. The logical connection is usually referred to as a virtual circuit, and the connection-oriented service is referred to as an **external virtual-circuit service;** unfortunately, this external service is distinct from the concept of **internal virtual-circuit operation,** as we shall see. With connectionless service, the network only agrees to handle packets independently and may not deliver them in order or reliably. This type of service is sometimes known as an **external datagram service;** again, this is a distinct concept from that of **internal datagram operation.** Internally, the network may actually construct a fixed route beween endpoints (virtual circuit) or not (datagram). These internal and external design decisions need not coincide:

- *External virtual circuit, internal virtual circuit:* When the user requests a virtual circuit, a dedicated route through the network is constructed. All packets follow that same route.
- *External virtual circuit, internal datagram:* The network handles each packet separately. Thus, different packets for the same external virtual circuit may take different routes. However, the network buffers packets at the destination node, if necessary, so that they are delivered to the destination station in the proper order.
- *External datagram, internal datagram:* Each packet is treated independently from both user's and the network's point of view.
- *External datagram, internal virtual circuit:* This combination makes little sense, since one incurs the cost of a virtual-circuit implementation but gets none of the benefits.

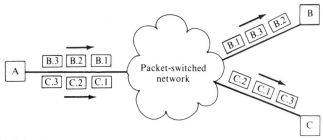

(a) External datagram

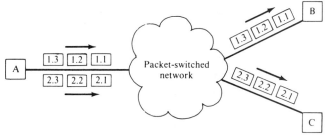

(b) External virtual circuit

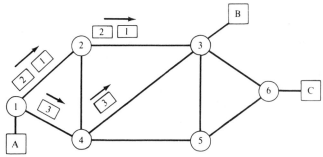

(c) Internal datagram

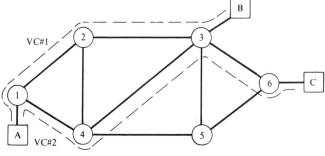

(d) Internal virtual circuit

FIGURE 3.12 External and Internal Virtual Circuits and Datagrams

The question arises as to the choice of virtual circuits or datagrams, both internally and externally. This will depend on the specific design objectives for the communication network and the cost factors that prevail. We have already made some comments concerning the relative merits of internal-datagram versus virtual-circuit operation. With respect to external service (Box 3.1), we can make the following observations. The datagram service, coupled with internal datagram operation, allows for efficient use of the network; no call setup and no need to hold up packets while a packet in error is retransmitted. This latter feature is desirable in some real-time applications. The virtual-circuit service can provide end-to-end sequencing and error control. This service is attractive for supporting connection-oriented applications, such as file transfer and remote terminal access. In practice, the virtual-circuit service is much more common than the datagram service and will remain so for ISDN-related packet-switched networks. The reliability and convenience of a connection-oriented service is seen as more attractive than the benefits of the datagram service.

X.25 Packet Level

With the X.25 packet level, data are transmitted in packets over external virtual circuits. A variety of packet types is used (Table 3.3), all using the same basic format, with variations (Figure 3.13). The standard refers to user machines as Data Terminal Equipment (DTE) and to a packet-switching node to which a DTE is attached as Data Circuit-terminating Equipment (DCE).

The virtual-circuit service of X.25 provides for two types of virtual circuit: virtual call and permanent virtual circuit. A *virtual call* is a dynamically established virtual circuit using a call setup and call-clearing procedure, explained subsequently. A *permanent virtual circuit* is a permanent, network-assigned virtual circuit. Data transfer occurs as with virtual calls, but no call setup or clearing is required.

Virtual Calls   Figure 3.14 shows a typical sequence of events in a virtual call. The left-hand part of the figure shows the packets exchanged between user machine *A* and the packet-switching node to which it attaches; the right-hand part shows the packets exchanged between user machine *B* and its node. The routing of packets inside the network is not visible to the user.

The sequence of events is as follows:

1. *A* requests a virtual circuit to *B* by sending a Call Request packet to *A*'s DCE. The packet includes the source and destination addresses, as well as the virtual-circuit number to be used for this new virtual circuit. Future incoming and outgoing transfers will

TABLE 3.3 X.25 Packet Types

Packet Type		Service	
From DCE to DTE	From DTE to DCE	VC	PVC
Call Setup and Clearing			
Incoming call	Call request	X	
Call connected	Call accepted	X	
Clear indication	Clear request	X	
DCE clear confirmation	DTE clear confirmation	X	
Data and Interrupt			
DCE data	DTE data	X	X
DCE interrupt	DTE interrupt	X	X
DCE interrupt confirmation	DTE interrupt confirmation	X	X
Flow Control and Reset			
DCE RR	DTE RR	X	X
DCE RNR	DTE RNR	X	X
	DTE REJ	X	X
Reset indication	Reset request	X	X
DCE reset confirmation	DTE reset confirmation	X	X
Restart			
Restart indication	Restart request	X	X
DCE restart confirmation	DTE restart confirmation	X	X
Diagnostic			
Diagnostic		X	X
Registration			
Registration confirmation	Registration request	X	X

be identified by this virtual-circuit number.

2. The network routes this call request to *B*'s DCE.
3. *B*'s DCE receives the call request and sends a Call Indication packet to *B*. This packet has the same format as the Call Request packet but a different virtual-circuit number, selected by *B*'s DCE from the set of locally unused numbers.
4. *B* indicates acceptance of the call by sending a Call Accepted packet specifying the same virtual-circuit number as that of the Call Indication packet.
5. *A* receives a Call Connected packet with the same virtual-circuit number as that of the Call Request packet.
6. *A* and *B* send data and control packets to each other using their respective virtual-circuit numbers.
7. *A* (or *B*) sends a Clear Request packet to terminate the virtual circuit and receives a Clear Confirmation packet.
8. *B* (or *A*) receives a Clear indication packet and transmits a Clear Confirmation packet.

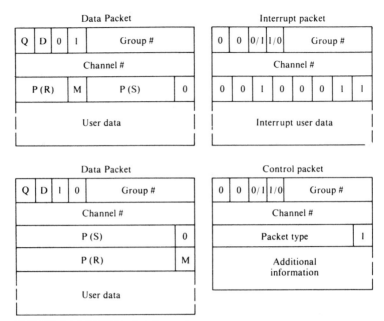

FIGURE 3.13 X.25 Packet Formats

We now turn to some of the details of the standard.

Packet Format   Figure 3.13 shows the packet formats used in the standard. For user data, the data are broken up into blocks of some maximum size, and a 24-bit header is appended to each block to form a **data packet.** The header includes a 12-bit virtual-circuit number (expressed as a 4-bit group number and an 8-bit channel number). The P(S) and P(R) fields support the functions of flow control and error control on a virtual-circuit basis, as explained subsequently. The M, D, and Q bits support specialized functions, which will not be explored here (see [STAL90b]), or one of the other references cited earlier.

In addition to transmitting user data, X.25 must transmit control information related to the establishment, maintenance, and termination of virtual circuits. Control information is transmitted in a **control packet.** Each control packet includes the virtual-circuit number; the packet type, which identifies the particular control function; and additional control information related to that function. For example, a Call Request packet includes the following additional fields:

- Calling DTE address length (4 bits): Length of the corresponding address field in 4-bit units.

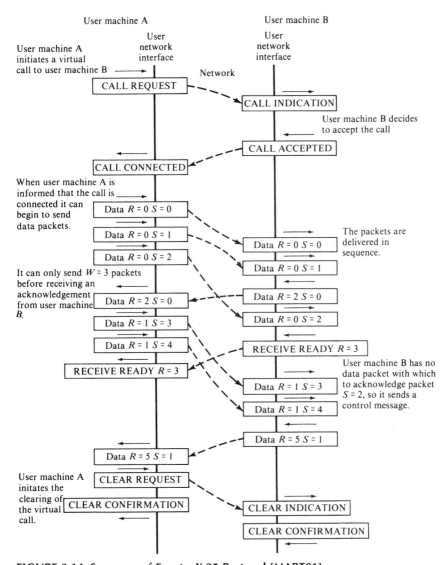

FIGURE 3.14 Sequence of Events: X.25 Protocol [MART81]

- Called DTE address length (4 bits): Length of the corresponding address field in 4-bit units.
- DTE addresses (variable): The calling and called DTE addresses.
- Facility length: Length of the facility field in octets.
- Facilities: A sequence of facility specifications. Each specification consists of an 8-bit facility code and zero or more parameter codes. Facilities are discussed subsequently.

The way in which user data are encapsulated is as follows. The transmitting DTE must break its data up into units of some maximum length. X.25 specifies that the network must support a maximum user field length of at least 128 octets (i.e., the user data field may be some number of bits up to the maximum). In addition, the network may allow selection of some other maximum field length in the range 16 to 4096 octets. The DTE constructs control packets and encapsulates user data in data packets. These are then transmitted to the DCE via LAP-B. Thus the packet is encapsulated in a layer 2 frame (one packet per frame). The DCE strips off the layer 2 control fields and may encapsulate the packet according to some internal network protocol. The reader unfamiliar with the concept of encapsulation should consult Appendix B.

Multiplexing   Perhaps the most important service provided by X.25 is multiplexing. A DTE is allowed to establish up to 4095 simultaneous virtual circuits with other DTEs over a single physical DTE-DCE link. The DTE can internally assign these circuits in any way it pleases. Individual virtual circuits could correspond to applications, processes, or terminals, for example. The DTE-DCE link provides full-duplex multiplexing. That is, at any time, a packet associated with a given virtual circuit can be transmitted in either direction.

To sort out which packets belong to which virtual circuits, each packet contains a 12-bit virtual-circuit number (expressed as a 4-bit logical group number plus an 8-bit logical channel number). The assignment of virtual-circuit numbers follows the convention depicted in Figure 3.15. Number zero is always reserved for diagnostic packets common to all virtual circuits. Then, contiguous ranges of numbers are allocated for four categories of virtual circuits. Permanent virtual circuits are assigned numbers beginning with 1. The next category is one-way incoming virtual calls. This means that only incoming calls from the network can be assigned these numbers; the virtual circuit, however, is two-way (full duplex). When a call request comes in, the DCE selects an unused number from this category.

One-way outgoing calls are those initiated by the DTE. In this case, the DTE selects an unused number from among those allocated for these calls. This separation of categories is intended to avoid the simultaneous selection of the same number for two different virtual circuits by the DTE and DCE.

The two-way virtual call category provides an overflow for allocation shared by DTE and DCE. This allows for peak differences in traffic flow.

Flow and Error Control   Flow control and error control in X.25 are implemented using sequence numbers. The flow control is the sliding-window mechanism, and error control is the go-back-N automatic-re-

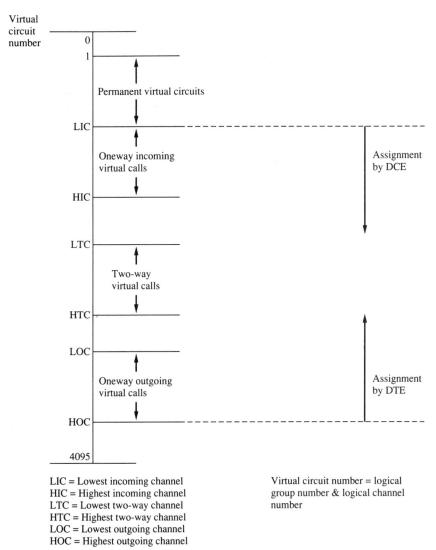

LIC = Lowest incoming channel
HIC = Highest incoming channel
LTC = Lowest two-way channel
HTC = Highest two-way channel
LOC = Lowest outgoing channel
HOC = Highest outgoing channel

Virtual circuit number = logical
group number & logical channel
number

FIGURE 3.15 Virtual Circuit Number Assignment

peat-request (ARQ) mechanism. The basic operation of these mechanisms is explained in Appendix A. The **send sequence number,** P(S), is used to uniquely number packets. As a default, 3-bit sequence numbers are used, and P(S) of each new packet on a virtual circuit is one more than that of the preceding packet, modulo 8. Optionally, a DTE may request, via the user facility mechanism described subsequently, the use of extended 7-bit sequence numbers.

The **receive sequence number,** P(R), contains the number of the next packet expected from the other side of a virtual circuit; this is known as piggybacked acknowledgment. If one side has no data to send, it may acknowledge incoming packets with the Receive Ready (RR) control packet, which contains the number of the next packet expected from the other side.

Flow control is provided by means of the Receive Not Ready (RNR) control packet; this packet acknowledges receipt of previous packets but indicates that the issuer is unable to receive additional packets. When such an indication is received, all transmission of data packets must cease; the busy side will notify the other side that it can resume transmission by means of an RR packet.

The basic form of **error control** is go-back-N ARQ (see Appendix A). Negative acknowledgment is in the form of a Reject (REJ) control packet. If a node receives a negative acknowledgment, it will retransmit the specified packet and all subsequent packets. Figure 3.16 illustrates this algorithm.

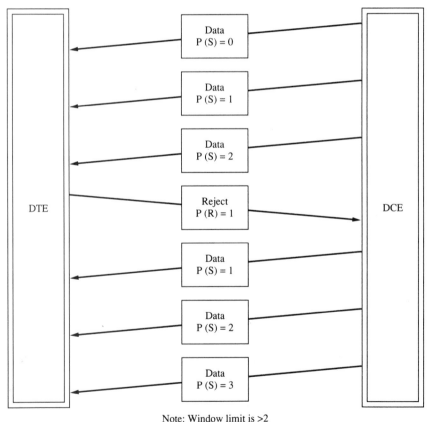

Note: Window limit is >2

FIGURE 3.16 X.25 Packet Exchange

Reset and Restart X.25 provides two facilities for recovering from errors. The reset facility is used to reinitialize a virtual circuit. This means that the sequence numbers on both ends are set to zero. Any data or interrupt packets in transit are lost. It is up to a higher-level protocol to recover from the loss of packets. A reset can be triggered by a number of error conditions, including loss of a packet, sequence number error, congestion, or loss of the network's internal virtual circuit. In this latter case, the two DCEs must rebuild the internal virtual circuit to support the still-existing X.25 DTE-DTE external virtual circuit. Either a DTE or DCE can initiate a reset, with a Reset Request or Reset Indication. The recipient responds with a Reset Confirmation. Regardless of who initiates the reset, the DCE involved is responsible for informing the other end.

A more serious error condition calls for a restart. The issuance of a Restart Request packet is equivalent to sending a Clear Request on all virtual calls and a Reset Request on all permanent virtual circuits. Again, either a DTE or DCE may initiate the action. An example of a condition warranting restart is temporary loss of access to the network.

Interrupt Packets A DTE may send an interrupt packet that bypasses the flow control procedures used for data packets. The packet does not contain send and receive sequence numbers and is not blocked by an RNR or a closed window. The interrupt packet carries up to 32 octets of user data and is to be delivered to the destination DTE by the network at a higher priority than data packets in transit. A DTE may not send another interrupt packet on any virtual circuit until delivery of the outstanding interrupt packet is confirmed. This prevents flooding the network with packets that are not flow controlled. An example of the use of this service is to transmit a terminal break character.

Call Progress Signals X.25 includes provision for call progress signals, and these are defined by X.96 (Table 3.4). These signals fall into two overlapping categories. **Clearing call progress signals** are used to indicate the reason why a Call Request is denied; they are also used to indicate the reason for a Clear Request. In both cases the signal is carried in a Clear Indication Packet. **Resetting call progress signals** are used to indicate the reason why a virtual circuit is being reset or why a restart takes place. The appropriate code is contained in a Reset Request, Reset Indication, Restart Request, or Restart Indication packet.

User Facilities X.25 provides for the use of optional user facilities. These are facilities that may be provided by the network and that may be employed at the user's option. Some facilities are selectable for use for an agreed period of time and are arranged ahead of time between subscriber and network provider. Other facilities are requested on a

TABLE 3.4   Packet-switched Call Progress Signals (X.96)

Signal	Applicable to[a] VC	PVC	Usage[b]	Description
Local Procedure Error	X	X	C, R	Procedure error caused by local DTE
Network Congestion	X	X	C, R	Temporary network congestion or fault
Invalid Facility Request	X		C	Requested user facility not valid
RPOA Out of Order	X		C	Recognized private operating agency unable to forward call
Not Obtainable	X		C	Called DTE address unassigned or unknown
Access Barred	X			
Reverse Charging Acceptance Not Subscribed	X		C	Called DTE will not accept charges on collect call
Fast Select Acceptance Not Subscribed	X		C	Called DTE does not support fast select
Incompatible Destination	X		C, R	The remote DTE does not have a function used or a facility requested
Out of Order	X	X	C, R	Remote DTE out of order
Number Busy	X		C	Called DTE is busy
Remote Procedure Error	X	X	C, R	Procedure error caused by remote DTE
Network Operational	X	X	R	Network ready to resume after temporary failure or congestion
Remote DTE Operational		X	R	Remote DTE ready after temporary failure
DTE Originated	X	X	C, R	Remote DTE has refused call or requested reset
Ship Absent	X		C	Called ship absent (used with mobile maritime service)
Network Out of Order		X	R	Network temporarily unable to handle data traffic
Registration/Cancellation Confirmed	X	X	R	Facility request confirmed.

[a] VC, virtual call; PVC, permanent virtual circuit.
[b] C, clearing call progress signal; R, resetting or restarting call progress signal.

per-virtual-call basis, as part of the Call Request packet; with these facilities, the capability or value applies only to the one virtual call.

The facilities that may be provided are defined in X.2, which contains a rather long list. Some of these are termed "essential." Essential facilities must be offered by the network, although their use is optional (Table 3.5). The remaining facilities are termed "additional" and need not be offered by the network.

3.8
FAST PACKET SWITCHING

Packet switching was developed to operate in an environment characterized primarily by relatively low-speed transmission facilities (≤ 64 kbps) and relatively high bit error rates. In today's era of integrated digital networks, high-speed transmission facilities (> 1 Mbps) with very low error rates are becoming increasingly important. This evolution has led to the development of the concept of *fast packet switching*, which refers to the exploitation of packet switching in a high-speed technology environment [RAHN88, BAUW87, GREE87, NOJI86, TURN86, HOBE83]. Fast packet switching is an attractive technology for incorporation in an ISDN facility. In this section, we begin by looking at the requirements that have driven the development of this technology, and then briefly introduce the technology itself.

Requirements

The technology of packet switching was developed to provide an efficient data-rate-independent facility for wide-area data communication. Figure 3.4 illustrates its area of applicability. A broader area of application is that of providing a wide-area facility that can support both voice and data communication. For this application, the following requirements can be identified:

- Availability.
- Message integrity.
- End-to-end delay limit.
- Voice connections.
- Trunk utilization.
- Data-rate independence.
- Fast connection/disconnect.

There are two aspects to the requirement for **availability:** call setup and call maintenance. The first can be expressed as the probability that

TABLE 3.5 Essential Optional Packet-switched User Facilities (X.2)

Assigned for an Agreed Contractual Period

Flow Control Parameter Negotiation

This facility permits negotiation on a per-call basis of the window size and maximum user data field length to be used on that call in each direction.

Throughput Class Negotiation

This facility permits negotiation on a per-call basis of the number of bits of data that can be transferred on a virtual circuit. The range of values is 75 bps to 48 Kbps.

Closed User Group

This enables the DTE to belong to one or more closed user groups. A closed user group permits the DTEs belonging to the group to communicate with each other but precludes communication with all other DTEs. Thus members are protected by the network from unauthorized access. A DTE may belong to one or more closed user groups.

Fast Select Acceptance

This facility authorizes the DCE to transit to the DTE incoming Fast Select calls. Without such authorization, the DCE blocks such incoming calls. This is useful to prevent the enlarged Fast Select packets from being delivered to a DTE that has not implemented Fast Select.

Incoming Calls Barred

This facilty prevents incoming calls from being presented to the DTE.

Outgoing Calls Barred

This facility prevents the DCE from accepting outgoing virtual calls.

One-way Logical Channel Outgoing

This facility reserves a block of virtual circuit numbers for outgoing calls. A subscriber reserves a number of logical channels in this fashion to match an expected or desired pattern of calls.

Requested on a Per-Virtual-Call Basis

Flow Control Parameter Negotiation

When a DTE has subscribed to this facility, it may, in a CALL REQUEST packet, separately request user data-field sizes and window sizes. The DCE indicates its acceptance or modification of these values in the CALL CONNECTED packet. The DCE may modify window size requests in the direction of $W = 2$ and may modify user data-field size requests in the direction of 128 octets.

Throughput Class Negotiation

Operates in a manner similar to Flow Control Parameter Negotiation. The DCE may revise the proposed values in either direction to values smaller than those requested.

Closed User Group Selection

When a DTE has subscribed to this facility, it may, in a CALL REQUEST packet, indicate the closed user group applicable to this call: Similarly, the DCE can indicate the closed user group applicable to an incoming call in an INCOMING CALL packet.

Fast Select
The DTE may employ the fast select facility.

Transit Delay Selection and Identification
The DTE may request a particular transit delay that the network will attempt to meet.

---

the network can support a connection request. This simply requires that the capacity of the network be sufficiently great to handle the anticipated peak load. With the use of high-speed trunks, the key design issues here are ensuring that there is sufficient connectivity in the network and ensuring that the packet-switching nodes are sufficiently numerous and of sufficient capacity. Once the call is set up, the second aspect of availability has to do with maintaining the virtual circuit. If a node or trunk failure occurs after a call is established, then the network must be able to switch to an alternate route quickly enough so that the two end users are unaffected. For a data connection, this means that there should be no loss of packets or only the loss of a few packets. If there is a long delay in route switching, and/or if a large number of packets are lost, it is likely that a higher layer of software will break the connection, requiring the user to set up a new connection. In the case of packetized voice, the loss of voice packets should be so small that there is no serious disruption of the voice signal.

The requirement for **message integrity** places a limit on the number of packets that may be lost. In the case of data packets and a virtual-circuit service, we would like to guarantee that no data are lost. This requires, at a minimum, that there be end-to-end error control within the network. For packetized voice, voice users can tolerate occasional short dropouts of the speech signal as long as the probability of such loss stays within prescribed limits.

The requirement for an **end-to-end delay limit** is dependent on the application. In the case of data connections, it will depend on whether the connection is for stream or interactive traffic. For interactive traffic, there is evidence that productivity is greatly enhanced if the response time is less than one second [THAD81, SHNE84]. Since part of this delay is host software and part is network delay, a delay budget of 0.5 seconds for the network might be reasonable. This implies a one-way delay of less than a quarter of a second. Thus, satellite links, which involve a one-way delay of a quarter of a second, become questionable for interactive traffic. in the case of a **voice connection,** there are two aspects. First, the overall delay should be small. Again, this suggests that satellite links may be inappropriate. A second aspect is that the delay should not be variable. The speech signal must emerge at a smooth rate matching the rate at which it is generated. This implies that voice packets cannot be buffered waiting for the retransmision of a packet that suffers an error.

Trunk utilization remains a requirement, as in an ordinary packet-switching network. With the tremendous capacities of the fiber systems now installed and in the pipeline, there is some question of the degree of importance of this requirement. However, past experience indicates that workload always expands to fill the available capacity. Consequently, utilization should remain an important issue, and the potential efficiency gains of packet switching compared to circuit switching remain attractive in a high-capacity environment.

Data-rate independence will also remain a requirement. Terminals and compressed voice digitizers of varying data rates will continue to compete in the marketplace, and full interoperability requires that the network be able to cope with a variety of data rates.

Finally, **fast connect/disconnect** will be expected by customers who are paying for the use of a high-speed network. If internal virtual circuits are used, which seems likely in a high-speed environment, then the techniques for setting up virtual circuits must be designed to provide for rapid route selection.

Characteristics of Fast Packet-switching Networks

In reviewing the requirements for high-speed wide-area networks listed previously, traditional packet-switching technology has a number of strengths. Its key strengths include

- *Data rate independence:* Because of the dynamic allocation of trunk capacity and the use of buffering, it is not necessary that source and destination systems operate at the same data rate.
- *Accommodation of bursty traffic:* As was discussed, packet switching is more efficient than circuit switching for bursty traffic.
- *Flexibility:* Packet switching can handle devices of a variety of data rates, can respond easily to load changes, and lends itself to dynamic route reconfiguration.

However, traditional packet switching has some weaknesses in the context of high-speed networking:

- *Large delay:* This is because of packet processing and queuing time at each node and packet retransmissions due to errors.
- *Variable delay:* Because capacity is not dedicated to a given call, the queuing time experienced through the various hops from source

to destination may vary from packet to packet, even on the same internal virtual circuit.

- *Throughput bottlenecks:* Despite the use of sophisticated adaptive routing and congestion-control algorithms, bottlenecks can develop in a large, complex network.

An attempt to retain the advantages of packet switching while overcoming its weaknesses has led to ongoing research in fast packet switching. The key characteristics of this approach are

- No link-by-link error control.
- No link-by-link flow control.
- End-to-end error control if necessary.
- The use of internal virtual circuits.
- Hardware switching.

The first two points have to do with the nature of the processing on each packet hop through the network. In a traditional packet-switched network, a packet is passed from one node to the next using a data link control protocol such as HDLC, which provides both error control and flow control (see Appendix A). As each packet is transmitted on each hop from one node to the next, the packet is encapsulated with a link-level header and trailer. The trailer includes a frame check sequence (FCS), used for error detection. If an error is detected, then the frame is discarded by the receiver and must be transmitted over the link. Each header includes a sequence number, and the receiving node can regulate the rate at which frames are received from adjacent nodes. These techniques are useful in an environment in which errors are reasonably common and in which the hop-by-hop delay introduced by such processing is tolerable.

With fast packet switching, this hop-by-hop processing is eliminated. Figure 3.17 gives an example of the kind of format that is used in fast packet switching for hop-level transmission, compared to the X.25-HDLC combination. In traditional packet switching, there are two levels of processing at each node: the packet level and the data link level. In fast packet switching, there is only one level of processing. The use of flags for delimiting and the use of an FCS for error detection are retained from HDLC. However, if an error is detected, the packet is simply discarded; there is no attempt to provide for hop-level retransmission. Flow control and error control are dispensed with; hence there is no need for sequence numbers. The only other field required (other than the data field) is for the virtual circuit number, which is used for routing.

The high quality and speed of modern digital transmission trunks, such as optical fiber links, eliminate the need for error control on a per-

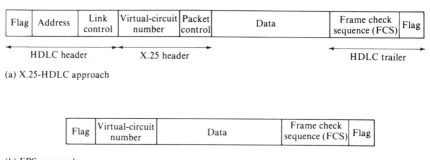

(a) X.25-HDLC approach

(b) FPS approach

FIGURE 3.17 Packet-switching Formats

link basis. Services that require completely error-free transmission and that do not employ some higher-level error-recovery protocol can use a network-provided end-to-end error-recovery mechanism. Thus, end-to-end error control can be incorporated within the network, but its use will be decided on a virtual-circuit basis. For example, it will not be provided for a packetized voice connection.

To complete the picture, a fast packet-switching facility requires that there be little or no time spent on routing decision once an external virtual circuit is set up. To accomplish this, internal virtual circuits are used, and the packet-switch nodes implement the routing function in hardware or firmware. Thus, the information required to map from a virtual circuit number to a next-node decision must be organized in some sort of simple table format.

Application

We have outlined the major features of a fast packet-switched network. To conclude, let us briefly describe the application of such an architecture to both voice and data communication.

Voice Communication   Voice signals can be digitized and transmitted as a stream of small packets. The key requirements, recall, are that the delay be short and that the rate of delivery be constant. The architecture that has just been discussed assures that the delay will be short. Nevertheless, even with very fast packet-switching nodes and high-speed trunks, there is a queuing delay at each node, which is variable and which is cumulative across a virtual-circuit route. Several measures can be taken. First, voice packets can be given higher priority than data packets. This will cut down on the queuing delay and hence its variability. Second, end-to-end error control is not employed. If an error is detected, the packet is discarded. Finally, corrective means must be employed to ensure that the packet delivery rate is constant.

One procedure for achieving near-constant data rate is illustrated in Figure 3.18. Each voice packet includes an additional field in the header that is used to measure the accumulated queuing and node processing delay along a route. The field in the ith packet, $D(i)$, is initialized to zero. At each node en route, the node measures, with a local clock, the intranode delay and adds this to $D(i)$. At the destination node, an amount C is added to the accumulated $D(i)$. C is an estimate of the transmission delay contributed by all of the trunks along the route. Since the route for a given virtual circuit is fixed, this will not vary during the call and can be estimated from the topology of the network. Finally, at the destination node, prior to delivery of each packet, the packet is delayed a variable amount $V(i)$ so that

$$D(i) + C + V(i) = T$$

The observed accumulated delay is increased to produce a constant total delay of T, so that the delay experienced by voice packets is constant. If a packet arrives for which $D(i) + C$ already exceeds T, then that packet is discarded. Periodically, based on the observed performance of a given virtual circuit, T is adjusted. The competing objectives are to minimize end-to-end delay (make T smaller) and to minimize packet discard (make T bigger).

Data Communication   With voice packets, a detected error results in packet discard. In general, the user expects a reliable service for data packets, and so a discard strategy is not acceptable. However, hop-by-hop flow and error control are likely to lead to unacceptable delays. Accordingly, an end-to-end strategy is used both for congestion control

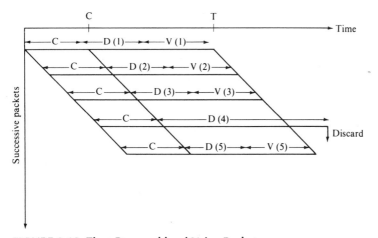

FIGURE 3.18 Time Reassembly of Voice Packets

and error control. On each virtual circuit, incoming packets are numbered, and the destination node maintains a buffer that allows it to retain packets while requesting a retransmission of a damaged packet.

Data packets are of lower priority than voice packets. In addition, several levels of priority may be used for data packets. For example, interactive traffic may be given higher priority than batch traffic.

3.9
SUMMARY

Packet switching was designed to provide a more efficient facility than circuit switching for bursty data traffic. Key distinguishing elements of packet-switched networks are whether the internal operation is datagram or virtual circuit and whether the external service is datagram or virtual circuit. The virtual-circuit service, using the X.25 network access protocol, is by far the most common, but this may be supported by either a datagram or virtual-circuit operation.

With traditional packet switching, the key technical problems are routing and congestion control. Adaptive routing techniques are typically employed. These allow the network to continue to function in the face of lost nodes or trunks and also provide a degree of load leveling. Congestion control is intended to avoid the buildup of excessive queuing delays.

Current research in packet switching is focused on the development of fast packet switching. This technology adapts the techniques of packet switching to the high-speed digital environment of the IDN and appears to offer considerable promise as a component service for ISDN.

3.10
RECOMMENDED READING

The literature on packet switching is enormous. Only a few of the worthwhile references are mentioned here. A number of survey articles were written in the early days of packet switching; among the most interesting are [KIMB75], [GREE77], and [KLEI78]. Surveys of specific networks include [WOOD85], [ROBE78], [QUAR86], and [AMAN86]. Books with good treatments of this subject include [BERT87], [ROSN82], and [DAVI79]. There is also a large body of literature on performance. Good summaries are to be found in [KLEI76] and [SCHW77]. [AHUJ83] provides a mathematical analysis of performance and reliability aspects of traffic control and routing. [MARU83] is an exhaustive analysis of the performance of virtual-circuit-based routing algorithms.

There is a large literature on X.25. [DHAS86], [SIRB85], and [ERDE86] are recommended. [BURG83] is a discussion of the practical application of X.25.

3.11

PROBLEMS

3.1. Consider a packet-switched network of N nodes connected by the following topologies:

a. Star: one central node with no attached station; all other nodes attach to the central node.

b. Loop: each node connects to two other nodes to form a closed loop.

c. Fully connected: each node is directly connected to all other nodes.

For each case, give the average number of hops between stations.

3.2. Consider a binary tree topology for a packet-switched network. The root node connects to two other nodes. All intermediate nodes connect to one node in the direction toward the root, and two in the direction away from the root. At the bottom are nodes with just one link back toward the root. If there are $2^N - 1$ nodes, derive an expression for the mean number of hops per packet for large N, assuming that trips between all node pairs are equally likely.

3.3. In Figure 3.5, node 1 sends a packet to node 6 using flooding. Counting the transmission of one packet across one link as a load of one, what is the total load generated if

a. Each node discards duplicate incoming packets?

b. A hope count field is used and is initially set to 4?

3.4. With the flooding technique, because all routes are followed, at least one copy of the packet follows the minimum-hop route; therefore, flooding could be used to initially determine all minimum-hop routes. Can flooding be used to determine the minimum-delay route?

3.5. How does the inclusion of a second criterion, bias, improve an isolated adaptive routing strategy based on queue length? What is the basis for the bias? Is bias static or dynamic?

3.6. Another adaptive routing technique is known as *backward learning*. As a packet is routed through the network, it carries not only the destination address, but the source address plus a running hop count that is incremented for each hop. Each node builds a routing table that gives the next node and hop count for each destination. How is the packet information used to build the table? What are the advantages and disadvantages of this technique?

3.7. A proposed congestion-control measure is known as *isarithmic* *control*. In this method, the total number of packets in transit is fixed by inserting a fixed number of permits into the network. These permits circulate through the network at random. Whenever a node wants to send a packet just given to it by an attached station, it must first capture and destroy a permit. When a packet reaches the destination node, that node reissues the permit. List three potential problems with this technique.

3.8. Assuming no malfunction in any of the stations or nodes of a network, is it possible for a packet to be delivered to the wrong destination?

3.9. Define the following parameters for a switching network:

- N: number of hops between two given stations.
- L: message length in bits.
- B: data rate, in bps, on all links.
- P: packet size in bits
- H: overhead (header) bits per packet.
- S: call setup time (circuit-switched or virtual circuit) in seconds.
- D: propagation delay per hop, in seconds.

a. For $N = 4$, $L = 3200$, $B = 9600$, $P = 1024$, $H = 16$, $S = 0.2$, $D = 0.001$, compute the end-to-end delay for circuit switching, virtual-circuit packet switching, and datagram packet switching. Assume that there is no node delay.

b. Derive general expressions for the three techniques, taken two at a time (three expressions in all), showing the conditions under which delays are equal.

3.10. What value of P, as a function of N, B, and H, results in minimum end-to-end delay in a datagram network? Assume that L is much larger than P and that D is zero.

3.11. Flow-control mechanisms are used at both levels 2 and 3 of X.25. Are both necessary or is this redundant? Explain.

3.12. There is no error-detection mechanism (frame-check sequence) in X.25. Isn't this needed to assure that all of the packets are delivered properly?

3.13. When an X.25 DTE and the DCE to which it attaches both decide to put a call through at the same time, a call collision occurs and the incoming call is canceled. When both sides try to clear the same virtual circuit simultaneously, the clear collision is resolved without canceling either request; the virtual circuit in question is cleared. Do you think that simultaneous resets are handled like call collisions or clear collisions? Why?

3.14. In X.25, why is the virtual-circuit number used by one station of two communicating stations different from the virtual-circuit number used by the other station? After all, it is the same full-duplex virtual circuit.

CHAPTER 4

IDN
Technology

Public telephone and telecommunications networks are rapidly evolving to the exclusive use of digital technology. The ways in which these networks employ digital technology are listed in Box 4.1.

The movement toward digital technology has been "pushed" by the competitive desire to lower cost and improve quality of voice transmission and networking services. As the use of distributed processing and data communications has grown, this evolution of an all-digital network has been "pulled" by the need to provide a framework for ISDN.

This chapter focuses on the technology of IDN. We begin with an overview of the evolution of integrated digital networks. The remainder of the chapter looks at some of the most important elements of IDN technology:

- *Digital carriers:* the digital backbone of IDN.
- *Digital subscriber loops:* the most difficult technical requirement for IDN is the provision of a digital interface to the subscriber.
- *Virtual networks:* this technology provides a preview of the type of services that will be available to users with fully digital networks.

4.1

THE EVOLUTION OF IDN

The evolution of the existing telecommunications networks and specialized carrier facilities to integrated digital networks is based on two

121

BOX 4.1

Use of Digital Technology in Public Telecommunications Networks

SWITCHING

The circuit-switching nodes of the network make use of digital time-division switching techniques rather than analog space-division switching techniques.

TRUNK (CARRIER) TRANSMISSION

Digital transmission technology is used on the multiplexed trunks between switches, although either analog or digital signaling may be used. Each trunk carries multiple voice and/or data channels using synchronous time-division multiplexing.

SUBSCRIBER LOOP

Digital transmission technology may also be used between the subscriber and the switch to which the subscriber attaches over the "subscriber loop." This implies that digitized voice is employed and that full-duplex digital transmission over the subscriber loop is used.

CONTROL SIGNALING

Common-channel signaling over a packet-switched network embedded into the public telecommunications network is used. Packets contain messages used for routing, monitoring, and control.

---

technological developments: digital switching and digital transmission. The technology of digital switching was discussed in Chapter 2. Digital transmission, in essence, means that the signals being transmitted are interpreted as a stream of binary digits. At each switching or relay point, the binary data are recovered from the signal and a new signal is generated. Such handling results in higher-quality (lower-error) transmission compared to analog transmission.[1]

Both digital switching and digital transmission are, of course, well

---

[1] The concept of digital transmission is distinct from that of digital signal. Digital transmission techniques can be applied to both digital and analog signals. This topic is explored in Appendix 4A. For voice traffic, both digital transmission and digital switching require the use of digitized voice input. This topic is briefly summarized in Appendix 4B.

established. The first T-carrier system was introduced into commercial service by AT&T in 1962, and the first large-scale time-division digital switch, the Western Electric 4ESS, was introduced in 1976. More important than the benefits of either of these two technologies, however, was the revolutionary idea that the functions of transmission and switching could be integrated to form an **integrated digital network** (IDN). The idea was proposed as early as 1959 [VAUG59] and is in the process of being implemented worldwide [DORR83, COOK84].

To understand the implications of an IDN, consider Figure 4.1. Traditionally, the transmission and switching systems of an analog telephone network have been designed and administered by functionally separate organizations. The two systems are referred to by the operating telephone companies as outside plant and inside plant, respectively. In an analog network, incoming voice lines are modulated and multiplexed at the end office and sent out over a frequency-division multiplexed (FDM) line. As you know, the constituent signals may pass through one or more intermediate switching centers before reaching the destination end office (Figure 2.17). At each switching center, the incoming FDM carrier has to be demultiplexed and demodulated by an *FDM channel bank*, before being switched by a space-division switch (Figure 4.1a). After switching, the signals have to be multiplexed and modulated again to be transmitted. This repeated process results in an accumulation of noise, as well as cost.

When both the transmission and switching systems are digital, integration as in Figure 4.1b can be achieved. Incoming voice signals are digitized using pulse-code modulation (PCM) and multiplexed using

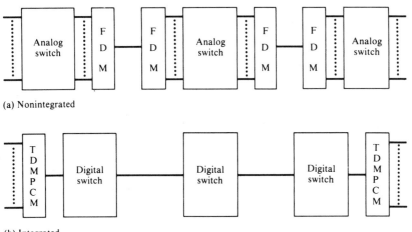

(a) Nonintegrated

(b) Integrated

FIGURE 4.1 The Integration of Transmission and Switching

time-division multiplexing (TDM). Time-division digital switches along the way can switch the individual signals without decoding them. Furthermore, separate multiplex/demultiplex channel banks are not needed at the intermediate offices, since that function is incorporated into the switching system.

Figure 4.2 gives a simple example that suggests the architectures that are involved in the two approaches. Consider an intermediate switch in a circuit-switched network that has six voice channels (labeled A, B, C, D, E, F) of data coming in on one trunk (Figure 4.2a). Based on the calls that are currently established, three of the channels are to be switched out on one trunk (A, B, E) and three channels on another

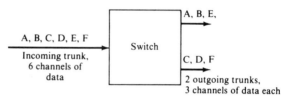

(a) General block diagram

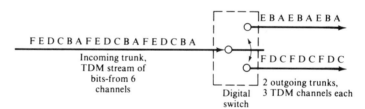

(b) Digital time division switch

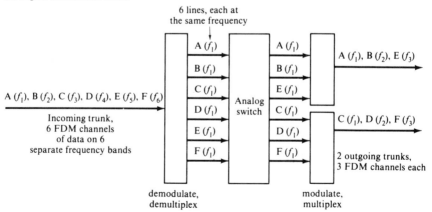

FIGURE 4.2 Example of Digital Versus Analog Switching

trunk (C, D, F). All three trunks link to other switches and are multiplexed to carry multiple channels of data. In the case of a digital system (Figure 4.2b), the voice signals are digitized and transmitted as a stream of bits. On a multiplexed trunk, bits from various voice signals are interleaved using time-division multiplexing (TDM). Thus, the incoming trunk has bits from six different voice channels interleaved in time. Inside the digital switch, one or more of the techniques discussed in Chapter 2 are employed to extract the slots of data from the incoming stream and route them to the appropriate outgoing stream.

The architecture for the equivalent analog system is considerably more complex. Each voice signal occupies a frequency band of about 4 kHz. The incoming trunk requires a bandwidth of at least 24 kHz, and each voice signal occupies one channel centered on a unique frequency (f_1 for channel A, f_2 for channel B, etc.). These channels must be fed into a space-division analog switch. However, such a switch is only capable of switching signals from a collection of input lines to a collection of output lines. For general operation, any input line must be connectable to any output line; therefore, all inputs and outputs must be at the same frequency. Thus, the frequency-division multiplexed (FDM) input must be demultiplexed and each signal must be returned to the base voice frequency (f_1) to provide input to the switch. The switch routes the incoming data to the appropriate output lines, with each output line dedicated to a particular output trunk. For each trunk, the associated lines must pass through a modulator/multiplexer to produce an FDM signal for transmission over the outgoing trunk.

The conversion of telecommunications networks to digital transmission and digital switching is well under way. Much less well developed is the extension of digital service to the end user. Telephones are still sending analog voice signals to the end office where they must be digitized. Lower-speed (< 56 kbps) end-user digital service is commonly available via leased lines at present, and higher-speed leased services are being introduced [HOLM83]. The provision of switched digital service over the local loop [KELC83, HARR86, ERIK86] will eventually lead to an end-to-end switched digital telecommunications network.

A number of advantages to the use of digital rather than analog techniques in wide-area circuit-switched networks can be cited (Box 4.2). However, the evolution from analog to digital has been driven primarily by the need to provide economic voice communications. The resulting network is also well suited to meet the growing variety of digital data service needs. Thus, the IDN will combine the coverage of the geographically extensive telephone network with the data-carrying capacity of digital data networks in a structure called the **integrated services digital network** (ISDN). In this latter context, the "integrated" of ISDN refers to the simultaneous carrying of digitized voice and a variety of data traffic on the same digital transmission links and by the same digital exchanges. The key to ISDN is the small marginal cost for offering data services on the digital telephone network, with no cost or performance penalty for voice services already carried on the IDN.

4.2

DIGITAL CARRIER SYSTEMS

In Chapter 2, we examined the internal switching mechanisms of a circuit-switched node. Of course, a wide-area circuit-switched network will involve a number of interconnected nodes. A link between a pair of nodes, referred to as a *trunk*, uses multiplexing to carry the traffic on a number of channels, or circuits. This multiplexing may be in the form of frequency-division multiplexing (FDM) or synchronous time-division multiplexing (TDM). Table 4.1 briefly compares the two techniques. As wide-area telecommunication networks evolve toward an

TABLE 4.1 Multiplexing Techniques for Carrier Systems

Technique	Description	Comments
Frequency-division multiplexing	The division of a transmission facility into two or more channels by splitting the transmitted frequency band into narrower bands, each of which is used to carry a separate channel.	Traditional scheme used in telephone networks. Each analog voice signal is assigned its own channel. This technique requires considerable signal processing, which reduces signal quality and increases cost compared to TDM.
Synchronous time-division multiplexing	The division of a transmission facility into two or more channels by dividing the transmission capacity into time slots and assigning time slots on a fixed, predetermined basis to various attached devices. The repetitive sequence of time slots allocated to a device constitutes the channel for that device.	This technique is preferred to FDM for digital signals, including digital data and digitized voice. It is more efficient and results in higher-quality received signals than FDM.

TABLE 4.2   North American and International TDM Carrier Standards

(a) North American			(b) International (CCITT)		
Digital Signal Number	Number of Voice Channels	Data Rate (Mbps)	Level Number	Number of Voice Channels	Data Rate (Mbps)
DS-1	24	1.544	1	30	2.048
DS-1C	48	3.152	2	120	8.448
DS-2	96	6.312	3	480	34.368
DS-3	672	44.736	4	1920	139.264
DS-4	4032	274.176	5	7680	565.148

integrated digital network, synchronous TDM techniques are becoming dominant.

The long-distance carrier system provided in the United States and throughout the world was designed to transmit voice signals over high-capacity transmission links, such as optical fiber, coaxial cable, and microwave. Part of the evolution of these telecommunications networks to digital technology has been the adoption of synchronous TDM transmission structures. In the United States, AT&T developed a hierarchy of TDM structures of various capacities; this structure is used in Canada and Japan, as well as the United States. A similar, but unfortunately not identical, hierarchy has been adopted internationally under the auspices of CCITT[2] (Table 4.2). As we shall see, this dichotomy remains unresolved in the ISDN standards.

The basis of the TDM hierarchy is the DS-1 transmission format (Figure 4.3), which multiplexes 24 channels. Each frame contains eight bits per channel plus a framing bit for $24 \times 8 + 1 = 193$ bits. For voice transmission, the following rules apply. Each channel contains one word of digitized voice data. The original analog voice signal is digitized using pulse-code modulation (PCM) at a rate of 8000 samples per second. Therefore, each channel slot and hence each frame must repeat 8000 times per second. With a frame length of 193 bits, we have a data rate of $8000 \times 193 = 1.544$ Mbps. For five of every six frames, 8-bit PCM samples are used. For every sixth frame, each channel contains a 7-bit PCM word plus a signaling bit. The eight bits form a stream for each voice channel that contains network control and routing information. For example, control signals are used to establish a connection or terminate a call.

The same DS-1 format is used to provide digital data service. For compatibility with voice, the same 1.544-Mbps data rate is used. In this

---

[2] The International Telegraph and Telephone Consultative Committee is an international standards-making organization. It is described in Appendix 5A, page 189.

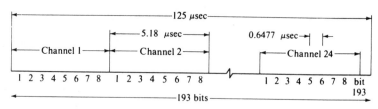

Notes:
1. Bit 193 is a framing bit, used for synchronization.
2. Voice channels:
   . 8-bit PCM used on five of six frames.
   . 7-bit PCM used on every sixth frame, bit 8
     of each channel is a signalling bit.
3. Data channels:
   . Channel 24 used for signaling only in some schemes.
   . Bit 8 is a control bit.
   . Bits 1-7 used for 56 kbps service.
   . Bits 2-7 used for 9.6 kbps, 4.8 kbps, and 2.4 kbps service.

FIGURE 4.3 DS-1 Transmission Frame

case, 23 channels of data are provided. The twenty-fourth channel position is reserved for a special sync byte, which allows faster and more reliable reframing following a framing error. Within each channel, seven bits per frame are used for data, with the eighth bit used to indicate whether the channel, for that frame, contains user data or system control data. With seven bits per channel, and since each frame is repeated 8000 times per second, a data rate of 56 kbps can be provided per channel. Lower data rates are provided using a technique known as **subrate multiplexing**. For this technique, an additional bit is robbed from each channel to indicate which subrate multiplexing rate is being provided. This leaves a total capacity per channel of $6 \times 8000 = 48$ kbps. This capacity is used to multiplex five 9.6-kbps channels, ten 4.8-kbps channels, or twenty 2.4-kbps channels. For example, if channel 2 is used to provide 9.6-kpbs service, then up to five data subchannels share this channel. The data for each subchannel appear as six bits in channel 2 every fifth frame.

Finally, the DS-1 format can be used to carry a mixture of voice and data channels. In this case, all 24 channels are utilized; no sync byte is provided.

Above this basic data rate of 1.544 Mbps, higher-level multiplexing is achieved by interleaving bits from DS-1 inputs. For example, the DS-2 transmission system combines four DS-1 inputs into a 6.312-Mbps stream. Data from the four sources are interleaved 12 bits at a time. Note that $1.544 \times 4 = 6.176$ Mbps. The remaining capacity is used for framing and control bits.

Each higher level of the TDM hierarchy is formed by multiplexing signals from the next lower level or by combination of those signals

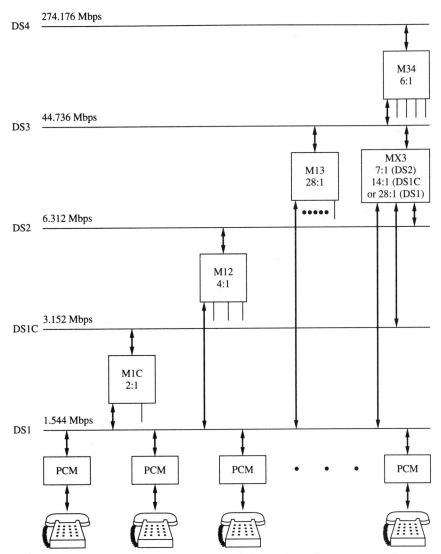

FIGURE 4.4 North American (AT&T) Digital TDM Hierarchy

plus input at the appropriate data rate from other sources. Figure 4.4 illustrates this hierarchy. First, the DS-1 transmission rate is used to provide both a voice and data service. The data service is known as the Dataphone Digital Service (DDS). The DDS provides digital transmission service between customer data devices at data rates of from 2.4 to 56 kbps. The service is available at customer premises over two twisted-pair lines.

Various standardized multiplexers are employed to create higher-

TABLE 4.3   Capacity of Some Communication Carriers

Carrier Designation	Number of Voice Channels	Data Rate (Mbps)	Combinations		
T-1	24	1.544	—	—	—
T-1C	48	3.152	2 T-1	—	—
T-2	96	6.312	4 T-1	2 T1-C	—
T-3	672	44.736	28 T-1	14 T1-C	7 T-2
T-4	4032	274.176	168 T-1	84 T-1C	42 T-2

capacity transmission facilities. The most commonly used ones are shown in Figure 4.4. The designations DS1, DS1C, and so on refer to the multiplexing scheme used for carrying information. AT&T and other carriers supply transmission facilities that support these various multiplexed signals, referred to as **carrier systems**. These are designated with a "T" label. Thus, the T-1 carrier provides a data rate of 1.544 Mbps and is capable of supporting the DS-1 multiplex format and so on for higher data rates. Table 4.3 lists some of these TDM facilities for various transmission media.

4.3

DIGITAL LOCAL LOOPS

The extension of the digital links to network subscribers is an essential part of IDN evolution. It is not sufficient that the internal transmission and switching facilities of the network be digital. To provide the wide range of digital services planned for IDN and ISDN, the link between the network subscriber and the network switch, known as the **subscriber loop**, or **local loop**, must be digital.

Currently, most of the local loop to businesses and virtually all of the local loop to homes makes use of twisted-pair cable. With the increasing demand for services that require high data rates, there is increasing interest in the use of optical fiber. We look at these two media for the local loop in turn.

Twisted Pair in the Local Loop

The simplest approach to providing digital service is the use of two twisted-pair wires between each subscriber and the local office or switch to which the subscriber attaches. One twisted-pair link would be used for transmission in each direction. However, the existing telephone network plant installed worldwide is based on the use of a single twisted-pair link between each subscriber and the local office. Thus, this approach would require the installation of a tremendous amount of new cable. Because of the economic impracticality of this approch, interest has focused on schemes that would allow full-duplex digital transmission over a single twisted-pair connection.

Approaches to Full-duplex Transmission.   The installed twisted-pair local loop system was intended for analog transmission. A simple means of achieving full-duplex transmission, then, is to use modems to convert the digital data into analog signals and to use a different frequency band in each direction.

An example of this approach is the 300-bps Bell 108 modem specification (Figure 4.5), which uses frequency-shift keying (FSK) to transmit digital data over an analog system. In FSK, the two binary values are represented by signals at two different frequencies. For transmission in one direction, the frequencies used to represent 1 and 0 are centered on 100 Hz, with a shift of 100 Hz on either side. The effect of alternating between these two frequencies is to produce a signal spectrum, as indicated in the shaded area on the left of Figure 4.5. Similarly, for transmission in the other direction, the modem uses frequencies shifted to 100 Hz to each side of a center frequency of 2125 Hz. The spectrum of this signal is indicated in the shaded area on the right of Figure 4.5. Note that there is little overlap and thus little interference.

A difficulty with this approach is that only half of the bandwidth of the line is available for transmission in either direction. To satisfy ISDN requirements, the minimum data rate in each direction is 144 kbps. It

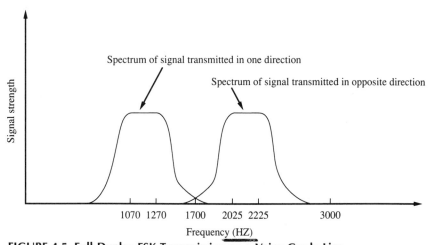

FIGURE 4.5 Full-Duplex FSK Transmission on a Voice-Grade Line

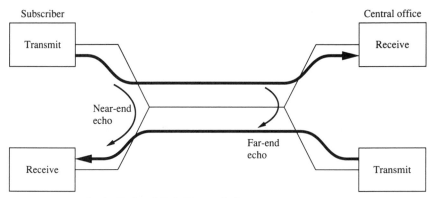

FIGURE 4.6 Echo in Twisted-Pair Transmission

is difficult to achieve these data rates with existing modem technology and with the installed twisted-pair plant.

The alternative is to dispense with modems and to transmit digital signals directly. For full-duplex operation, both stations transmit digital signals at the same time. In principle, the originating station is capable of sorting out an incoming signal from its own outgoing signal because the signal magnitude of its originating signal is known. Unfortunately, due to irregularities in the electrical characteristics of the loop, some portion of the originator's signal returns in the form of an echo.

Figure 4.6 illustrates the problem. Both transmitter and receiver are connected to the subscriber line through a hybrid, which is a device that allows signals to pass in both directions simultaneously. The echo is a reflection of the transmitted signal back to the sender, either from the sender's hybrid and the cable (near-end echo) or from the receiver's hybrid (far-end echo). The relative magnitude of the echo, compared to the true signal arriving from the other side, may be significant. This is because of the considerable difference in amplitude between transmitted and received signals at the ends of the wire pair, which may be as much as three orders of magnitude.

To overcome the problems associated with full-duplex digital transmission over a single twisted pair, two techniques have been developed: time-compression multiplexing and echo cancellation. Both techniques have been seriously considered for use in IDNs. At present, the consensus is that echo cancellation is the superior system. For example, this approach is favored in the U.S.; there is an American National Standard[3] for the local loop that uses echo cancellation (ANSI T1.601). Nevertheless, it is instructive to examine both approaches.

---

[3] American National Standards are issued by the American National Standards Institute (ANSI) and are widely used in the United States. Many ANSI standards subsequently become international standards.

BOX 4.2

Advantages of Digital Networking

COST

The advent of large-scale integration (LSI) and very-large-scale integration (VLSI) has caused a continuing drop in the cost and size of digital circuitry. Analog equipment has not shown a similar drop. Further, maintenance costs for digital circuitry are a fraction of those for analog circuitry.

DATA INTEGRITY

With the use of digital repeaters rather than analog amplifiers, the effects of noise and other signal impairments are not cumulative. Thus it is possible to transmit data longer distances and over lesser-quality lines by digital means while maintaining the integrity of the data.

CAPACITY UTILIZATION

It has become economical to build transmission links of very high bandwidth, including satellite channels and optical fiber. A high degree of multiplexing is needed to effectively utilize such capacity, and this is more easily and cheaply achieved with digital (time-division) rather than analog (frequency-division) techniques.

SECURITY AND PRIVACY

Encryption techniques can be readily applied to digital data and to analog data that have been digitized.

INTEGRATION

By treating both analog and digital data digitally, all signals have the same form and can be treated similarly. Thus economies of scale and convenience can be achieved by integrating voice, video, and digital data.

Time-compression Multiplexing.   In the technique of time-compression multiplexing (TCM), also known as the ping-pong method, data are transmitted in one direction at a time, with transmission alternating between the two directions. To achieve the desired subscriber data rate, the subscriber's bit stream is divided into equal segments, compressed

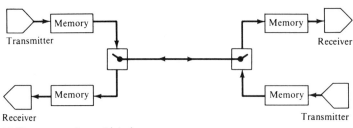

(a) Time compression multiplexing

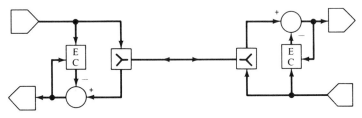

(b) Echo cancellation

FIGURE 4.7 Techniques for Full-duplex Transmission Over the Sub-scriber Loop

in time to a higher transmission rate, and transmitted in bursts, which are expanded at the other end to the original rate. A short quiescent period is used between bursts going in opposite directions to allow the line to settle down. Thus the actual data rate on the line must be greater than twice the data rate required by the subscriber and local office.

The timing implications are shown in Figure 4.8. The two sides alternate in the transmission of data. Each side sends blocks of some fixed length, which take a time T_b to transmit; this time is a linear function of the number of bits in a block. In addition, a time T_p is required for the propagation of a signal from one end to the other; this time is a linear function of the length of the subscriber loop. Finally, a guard time T_g is introduced to turn the line around. Thus we can see that the time to send one block is $(T_p + T_b + T_g)$. However, since the two sides must alternate transmissions, the rate at which blocks can be transmitted is only $1/2(T_p + T_b + T_g)$. We can relate this to the effective data rate, R, as seen by the two endpoints as follows. Let B be the size of a block in bits and R be the desired data rate in bits per second. Then the effective number of bits transmitted per second is

$$R = \frac{B}{2(T_p + T_b + T_g)}$$

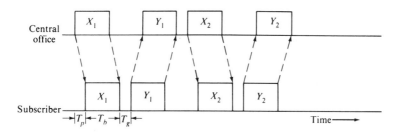

T_p = Propagation delay
T_b = Burst transmission time
T_g = Guard time

FIGURE 4.8 Transmission Using Time Compression Multiplexing

The actual data rate, A, on the medium can easily be seen to be

$$A = \frac{B}{T_b}$$

Combining the two, we have

$$A = 2R\left(1 + \frac{T_p + T_g}{T_b}\right)$$

Thus, the actual data rate on the link is more than double the effective data rate seen by the two sides. We will see that one of the basic data rates offered by ISDN is 144 kbps. To achieve this, it is necessary to transmit at over twice this rate, which would be something greater than 288 kbps. The actual value is in the neighborhood of 350 kbps. This is quite difficult to achieve on an ordinary twisted pair.

The choice of block size, B, is a compromise between competing requirements. If B is increased, there is a decrease in the actual data rate, A. This makes the task of implementation easier. On the other hand, this is accompanied by an increase in the signal delay due to buffering that is undesirable for voice traffic. A block size of 16 to 24 bits seems reasonable [KADE81].

Figure 4.9 depicts the internal structure of a TCM unit. In both directions (transmit and receive) a buffer is needed that is equal to the block size, B. Data to be transmitted are entering into the buffer at a data rate of $R = B/2(T_p + T_b + T_g)$. The data are subsequently transmitted at a rate $A = B/T_b$. The reverse process occurs for reception. Transmission and reception alternate under a central timing control.

Echo Cancellation. With the echo cancellation method, digital transmission is allowed to proceed in both directions within the same band-

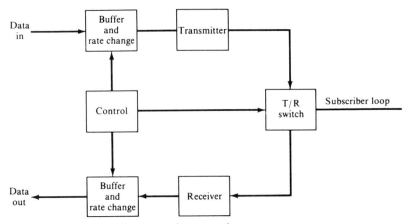

FIGURE 4.9 Internal Structure of TCM Unit

width simultaneously. An estimate of the echo signal is generated at the transmitting end and is subtracted from the incoming signal. This effectively cancels the echo. Because the transmitted signal is known, the echo canceller can estimate the echo characteristics and produce an approximation. However, the exact behavior of the echo will depend on the physical characteristics and configuration of the copper wire. Not only is it difficult to measure these characteristics precisely, but they will vary over time. To enable more accurate approximation, a feedback circuit is included.

A typical approach to echo cancellation is illustrated in Figure 4.10

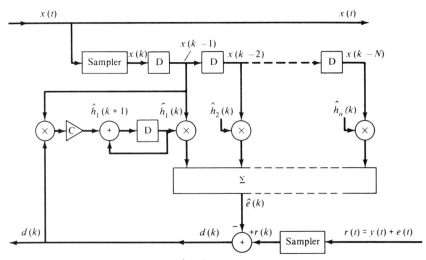

FIGURE 4.10 Internal Structure of Echo Canceller

[BELL82, TAO84]. Because the transmitted signal will be reflected at various points in the system, a number of signal elements, each delayed by a different amount, will contribute to the echo at any point in time. Furthermore, since the different contributing signal elements have traveled different distances, they will suffer different amounts of attenuation. This can be expressed in discrete time notation as follows:

$$e(k) = \sum_{n=1}^{\infty} h_n x(k - n)$$

where

$e(k)$ = echo signal sampled at time k

$x(k - n)$ = signal transmitted at time $k - n$

h_n = weighting factor for signal delayed by a time n

This echo signal can be estimated with

$$\hat{e}(k) = \sum_{n=1}^{N} \hat{h}_n(k) x(k - n)$$

where

$\hat{h}_n(k)$ = estimate of h_n at time k

If signal elements delayed longer than a time N make no measurable contribution to the echo, and if the $\hat{h}_n$ are exactly equal to the h_n, then the estimate will be equal to the actual echo. Of course, the $\hat{h}_n$ can only be approximations. In any case, this approximation is subtracted from the received signal to attempt to cancel the echo:

$$d(k) = r(k) - \hat{e}(k) = y(k) + e(k) - \hat{e}(k)$$

where

$d(k)$ = signal resulting after cancellation
$r(k)$ = received signal
$y(k)$ = component of received signal due to transmission from other side

Again, assuming that only the first N components of the transmitted signal are significant, we can rewrite this as

$$d(k) = y(k) + \sum_{n=1}^{N} (h_n - \hat{h}_n(k)) x(k - n)$$

As Figure 4.10 illustrates, the outgoing signal, $x(t)$, is sampled periodically to produce $x(k)$ for various sampling times $k(k = 1,2,3, \ldots)$. This sample is passed through a series of delays to retain delayed versions of the signal, $x(k - n)$. These delayed samples are then available at time k to produce the estimate $\hat{e}(k)$. The weighting factors, $\hat{h}_n(k)$, are updated at each sampling time by means of feedback:

$$\hat{h}_n(k + 1) = \hat{h}_n(k) + Cx(k - n)d(k)$$

where C is a scaling factor. This equation is somewhat easier to appreciate if we consider the case when there is no signal from the other side. In that case, we have

$$d(k) = \Sigma(h_n - \hat{h}_n(k))x(k - n)$$

In this case, the value of $d(k)$ would be zero if the echo estimate were exact. If the estimate is not exact, then each weighting factor, $\hat{h}_n(k)$ is adjusted by an amount proportional to $x(k - n)d(k)$. This procedure will result in a convergence of the weighting factors to the true values. Even in the presence of an actual signal, $y(t)$, the weighting factors converge, although more slowly [GERW84, FALC82].

The technique of echo cancellation avoids the necessity, found in TCM, of transmitting at more than double the subscriber rate. At the 144-kbps rate recommended by CCITT for ISDN, this gives echo cancellation a distinct advantage over TCM. A careful analysis of the two systems indicates that for typical twisted-pair installations at a subscriber data rate of 144 kbps, a range of 2 km is practical for TCM, compared to a range of 4 km for echo cancellation [SZEC86]. Thus, the introduction of TCM into the subscriber loop would require the extensive use of equipment such as concentrators and repeaters to overcome the poor range of the technique. Echo cancellation systems would require such equipment in far fewer cases.

Echo cancellation has the disadvantage of requiring complex digital signal processing circuitry. However, with the continuing advances in VLSI technology, the cost of echo cancellation is dropping, and it has become the preferred technique to achieve digital subscriber loops [MESS86, LECH86].

Optical Fiber in the Local Loop

Although optical fiber has enjoyed increased usage in the interexchange trunk portion of telecommunication networks, so far there has been little use of it in the local loop. As part of the planning for broadband ISDN, however, there has been significant effort devoted to design alternatives for bringing fiber to business and residential subscribers. Fiber local loop will be necessary to support the high data rates offered by broadband ISDN.

There has been a wide range of alternatives suggested for providing fiber in the local loop (e.g., see [LIN89, SHUM89, BARR90]). Fundamentally, all of these alternatives fall into two broad categories: those in which the subscriber interface appears as a simple direct link and those in which the subscriber interface must implement multiple-access logic.

To gain an understanding of these two approaches, let us begin with a simplified view of the existing twisted-pair arrangement, which is illustrated in Figure 4.11a. In this configuration, each subscriber accesses its central office (local switching center) via a single twisted pair. That

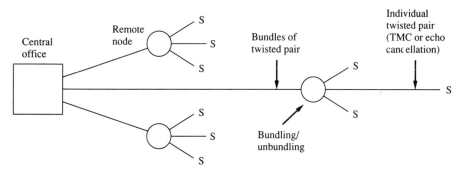

(a) Wire-based local loop

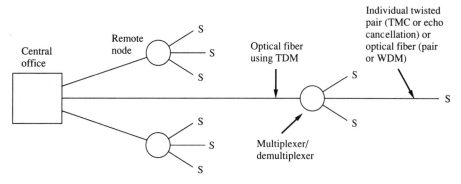

(b) Fiber-based active star

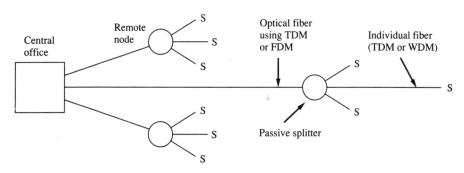

(c) Fiber-based passive star

FIGURE 4.11 Digital Local Loop Approaches

is, there is a direct, point-to-point, twisted-pair link between each subscriber and the central office. In the U.S., the average length of subscriber loops is about 3 km [REY83].

The physical layout of the collection of twisted pair from the central office to all subscribers, referred to as the **distribution network**, is a star topology, with one link from the central office to each subscriber. For convenience, the actual installation involves collecting individual pairs into bundles that are encased in a cable. At various points in the distribution network, the wires are unbundled for the final run to the subscriber.

The same installation layout can be used for a fiber-based digital local loop. Perhaps the simplest approach is illustrated in Figure 4.11b. In this layout, the central office is connected to a set of remote nodes by **feeder cables**. The feeder cable uses digital time-division multiplexing (TDM) to support multiple channels. A number of subscribers may be connected to a remote node, each with a single direct link. Thus, the remote node is a multiplexer that multiplexes traffic from a number of subscribers onto the feeder cable and demultiplexes traffic from the feeder cable to the subscribers. This approach is referred to as an **active star**, since each remote node serves as the base for a star layout, and each remote node is active, performing a multiplexing/demultiplexing function.

To provide full-duplex digital transmission on the feeder cable, two approaches are possible:

- *Two-fiber:* One optical fiber is used for transmission in each direction.
- *Wavelength-division multiplexing (WDM):* Two different signals are carried on the fiber at two different nonoverlapping frequency bands, one in each direction. In non-fiber systems, this would be referred to as frequency-division multiplexing (FDM), but the term WDM is preferred for fiber transmission.

This approach lends itself to a gradual evolution of the network. Typically, an initial deployment will involve optical fiber only for the feeder cables, with twisted pair used from the remote node to the subscriber. Either echo cancellation or time-compression multiplexing, as just discussed, can be used for this final link to the subscriber. Later on, the twisted pair can be replaced with fiber. To provide full-duplex digital transmission to the subscriber, either two-fiber or WDM is used in the final run to the subscriber.

The layout is not limited to a single layer of remote nodes but may actually involve a cascade of multiplexers, as illustrated in Figure 4.12. Here, the feeder cable from the central office supports N channels using a TDM structure. For example, a T-1 cable would support 24 channels.

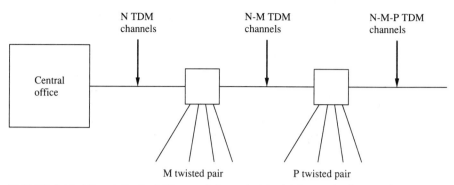

FIGURE 4.12 Use of Optical Fiber and Cascaded Multiplexers in the Local Loop

At the first multiplexer, M lines are run to subscribers, and the remaining N-M channels continue on to a second multiplexer. This arrangement allows the network to support many subscribers over a large area with minimum of cable.

With the active star approach, the subscriber is not aware of the details of the implementation of the feeder and distribution network. In particular, the TDM structure of the feeder cable is of no concern to the subscriber equipment. An alternative structure, known as passive star, simplifies the remote nodes at the cost of additional logic at the subscriber equipment (Figure 4.11c).

With passive star, the feeder cable carries multiple channels as before. At the remote node, the signal is optically split onto a number of fibers going to the individual subscribers. Thus, all subscribers receive the same signal.

Two approaches to multiplexing are possible with the passive star arrangement:

- *Dense WDM:* Each subscriber is provided with a dedication downstream (central office to subscriber) and dedicated upstream (subscriber to central office) wavelength [WAGN89]. The term *dense* refers to the number of wavelengths supported. As many as 40 to 50 wavelengths may be possible with existing technology and components [LIN90], allowing the support of 20 to 25 subscribers per feeder cable.
- *TDM:* Capacity on the fiber is shared using time-division multiplexing. In the downstream direction, the TDM signal from the central office is broadcast to all of the subscribers on a feeder cable; each subscriber equipment copies the time slots assigned to it from the incoming signal. In the upstream direction, each subscriber is assigned time slots based on some fixed or dynamic multiple-access technique. British Telecom has developed a system that uses a 20-

Mbps signal, splitting it 128 ways to provide 144 kbps per subscriber [FINN89].

The passive star approach has the advantage that it does not require power at the remote node. Its disadvantage is that it requires more complex equipment at the subscriber end. Of the two multiplexing techniques considered for passive star, the TDM approach is less expensive at the present time. However, WDM component prices are falling, and this approach may soon be competitive with TDM techniques.

4.4
VIRTUAL NETWORKS

A relatively recent offering from a number of telecommunications providers is a capability referred to as a software defined network (SDN), or a virtual network [GILH87, GAWD86, COCH85]. A number of providers are offering services that fit into this category. In general terms, a virtual network is a facility based on a public circuit-switched network that gives the user the appearance of a private network. The network is "software defined" in the sense that the user provides the service supplier with entries to a database used by the supplier to configure, manage, monitor, and report on the operation of the network.

Virtual networks are the first offering of a new wave of networking services characterized by flexibility, a rich set of features, a high degree of user control, and an ability to be changed quickly based on user needs. In this respect, they may be viewed as precursors to ISDNs. Thus, a brief review of the virtual network will give us some idea of the kinds of capabilities that will become available with ISDN.

Private Networks

The use of private networks by subscribers with large traffic demands has been commonplace for decades. A typical example is a private voice network. Such a network supports telephone connections in a number of sites belonging to the same organization and consists of the following ingredients:

- Subscriber telephones.
- PBX.
- Network trunks.
- Access lines to a public switched telecommunications network.

Typically, the network trunks are lines leased from a telecommunications provider. Each subscriber is provided with a unique on-network telephone number. One user may dial another user anywhere on the network simply by dialing the on-net number. In addition, each PBX is equipped with an access line to a public telecommunications network so that off-network calls can be sent and received.

These private networks have evolved both in scope and sophistication. With the use of digital technology, a private network can support both data devices and telephones. This requires the use of digital PBXs and digital trunks, typically T1 (1.544 Mbps) trunks in the United States. Such a private network supports a number of features, including

- Uniform numbering plans for all users, regardless of specific location.
- Alternate routing of calls around the network based on load factors, resulting in fewer on-net calls being blocked.
- End-user authorization codes and charge-back mechanisms.
- Call detail reporting and traffic reports.

In general, this sort of private network allows an organization to reduce costs by concentrating traffic from a number of corporate locations and funneling it onto a limited number of long-distance circuits.

Although a private network, particularly a private digital network, can afford the user savings plus a greater degree of network control, there are a number of shortcomings:

- The network may not be economically extendable to all the remote points the user might want. For example, the user may have one or more small offices with only a limited number of telephones that generate a small amount of traffic to the remainder of the organization. This may not be sufficient to justify a leased network line to the nearest network switch. Such offices must be reached by ordinary dial service. Thus, there is a nonuniform numbering scheme, and advanced network services are limited to on-net subscribers.
- Changes are often difficult to implement when requirements change. The acquisition of a new PBX or additional leased line is a significant rather than a small incremental step.
- Similarly, the economic viability of any network configuration may depend on idiosyncratic tariffs that, when changed, may drastically alter the configuration's cost-effectiveness.

With the increasing use of common-channel signaling, and the increasingly digital nature of the public circuit-switched networks, an alternative to the private network becomes possible. That alternative is to provide the types of services and user control available on a private network by means of public-network services tailored to a particular user by means of software.

Virtual Network Architecture

The virtual network concept involves substituting a long-distance circuit-switched network for the leased trunks customarily used in private networks, while giving the user a special set of interfaces to that network that make it seem to the user as if it is an actual private network. For the most part, these special interfaces have to do with the ways calls are processed and with the monitoring and reporting functions involved.

A simple example of a virtual network is the Advanced 800 Service that has been available from AT&T since 1982 [RAAC84], which is illustrated in Figure 4.13. The figure illustrates a customer with two locations, one on the West Coast and one on the East Coast. A single toll-free number is used by customers. A database is maintained at a network control point (NCP) that shows the destination for each call based on the area code of the originating call. A portion of that database is shown. Thus, calls originating in area code 717 (Pennsylvania) are always routed to the East Coast location, with the terminating number of 919-567-7000. Calls coming in from the 602 area (Arizona) are routed to the West Coast during business hours and to the East Coast at other times. These events are illustrated in parts b through d of the figure. A call is placed by dialing the 800 number. This triggers a query from a switch in the network to the NCP, which directs the call to the appropriate destination number. These control messages are communicated using common-channel signaling. The switches, which are part of the AT&T network, are referred to as Action Points (ACP) to reflect the fact that the switches now have sufficient intelligence to work with the NCP to provide tailored customer service.

The Advanced 800 Service allows incoming 800 calls to be routed based on

- Originating area code.
- Time of day.
- Day of week.
- Caller-entered digits: Callers hear a recorded message that will help them route their calls to the department or service of their choice by dialing additional digits.
- Percentage allocation: A customer can apportion calls to two or more call-answering locations by specifying the percentage of calls each location should receive.
- Customer-preplanned special situations: Allows customers to respond to spontaneous needs, such as emergencies, by preestablishing alternate routes for handling incoming calls.

This service is a relatively primitive form of software-defined network but gives an indication of the kinds of things that can be done with

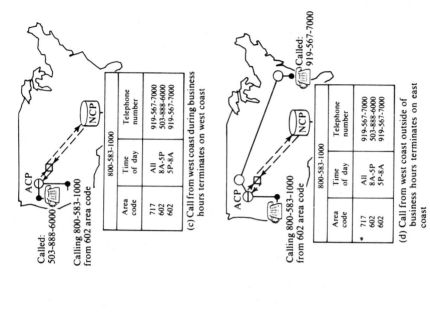

FIGURE 4.13 Example Use of AT&T Advanced 800 Service

(a) AT & T advanced 800 service: the terminating numbers are determined by originating NPA and time of day

800-583-1000		
Area code	Time of day	Telephone number
717	All	919-567-7000
602	8A-5P	503-888-6000
602	5P-8A	919-567-7000

Called: 503-888-6000

Called: 919-567-7000

(b) Call from east coast terminates on east coast

800-583-1000		
Area code	Time of day	Telephone number
717	All	919-567-7000
602	8A-5P	503-888-6000
602	5P-8A	919-567-7000

Calling 800-583-1000 from 717 area code

Called: 919-567-7000

(c) Call from west coast during business hours terminates on west coast

800-583-1000		
Area code	Time of day	Telephone number
717	All	919-567-7000
602	8A-5P	503-888-6000
602	5P-8A	919-567-7000

Called: 503-888-6000

Calling 800-583-1000 from 602 area code

(d) Call from west coast outside of business hours terminates on east coast

800-583-1000		
Area code	Time of day	Telephone number
717	All	919-567-7000
602	8A-5P	503-888-6000
602	5P-8A	919-567-7000

Called: 919-567-7000

Calling 800-583-1000 from 602 area code

digital networks controlled by a common-channel signaling protocol such as Signaling System Number 7.

Figure 4.14 illustrates, in general terms, the key ingredients of a software-defined network [GILH87]. These are

- A set of switches (service switching points) interconnectd to provide both a public dial-up circuit-switched capability and the intelligence to provide software-defined private network capability.
- A central network management location (service control point) that maintains a centralized database with algorithms and customer instructions for routing the information to be transported.
- An operations-support center that provides features such as planning, engineering, ordering, provisioning, maintenance, and repair, offering greatly enhanced network management and increased customer control.
- An SS7 packet-switched network that interconnects the service control point, the operations-support center, and the service switching points.

Box 4.3 lists the types of services that can be provided by a virtual network. The advantages of such networks, compared to a private network, are [COOL87]

- The use of the public telecommunications facilities means that the circuits may be shared among many users, providing for greater efficiency at lower cost.
- The overall flexibility is greater and its reliability is enhanced, since the user is no longer constrained to a particular physical private line.
- Because the network is implemented in software, it is able to support network-based services not normally provided by dedicated special-service circuits.

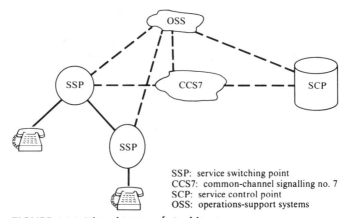

SSP: service switching point
CCS7: common-channel signalling no. 7
SCP: service control point
OSS: operations-support systems

FIGURE 4.14 Virtual Network Architecture

BOX 4.3

Typical Features of a Software-Defined Network

CALL PROCESSING

Uniform Numbering Plan

Each subscriber in the network has a unique number.

Access to Switched Network

Call may be placed from an on-net subscriber to a number off-net, off-net callers can directly dial on-net subscribers. Frequently called off-net numbers can be incorporated into the uniform numbering plan.

Off-Net Overflow

SDN calls automatically overflow off-net for completion when all dedicated SDN direct lines are busy.

Private Network Interface

A uniform numbering plan can be provided to encompass an SDN and a private network. Callers need not know whether the called subscriber is an SDN location or a private network location. The resulting hybrid network is beneficial to an organization that is migrating from private to SDN and to an organization for which the private network is the most economical for part of its needs.

Routing

Routing incoming off-net calls to different locations specified by the customer based on location of the calling party, time of day, day of week, additional digits dialed by caller in response to prompt, and busy-idle status of customer's destination numbers.

CALL MANAGEMENT

Originating Screening

Allows the SDN customer to define a list of numbers that may not be called from a given number or group of numbers (caller group). Individual numbers may be assigned to one or more caller groups. The list of numbers that may not be called can vary by time of day or week. Also, authorization codes may be required to call particular

Cont.

BOX 4.3 continued

numbers. The requirement to enter an authorization code may also vary by time and day.

Location Screening

Allows the SDN customer to define a list of numbers that may not be called from a given location

Queuing

Calls may be queued to a particular number or called group (rotary group).

MANAGEMENT AND CONTROL

Update

Customers can update their own database on-line. This includes changes to routing, authorization codes, and group membership.

Reports

Detailed reports on network activity are provided, including database definition reports, summary traffic, and call detail.

- The software that supports such a network allows enhanced user management and control of the communications facility.

Of course, as with any technology, there are disadvantages to SDN, and it is not the right solution for every organization [MCQU85]. In particular, if the traffic patterns of an organization are relatively stable and not subject to significant fluctuations, the extra expense of implementing the interfaces to an SDN may not be justified. Also, for smaller networking needs, the expense of incorporating the new SDN interfaces may be too much.

4.5

SUMMARY

Public telephone and telecommunications networks have evolved from an all-analog technology to one that is increasingly digital. In the U.S., the switching and interexchange transmission facilities are virtually all digital. Digital carrier standards specify a time-division multiplexed structure for transmission within the network.

The last portion of such networks to convert to digital is the portion between the network and the business and residential subscribers, referred to as the local loop. With the existing twisted-pair facility, full-duplex digital transmission requires the use of either time-compression multiplexing or echo cancellation. The latter approach has proved the most popular. Ultimately, to support the higher data rates that will be demanded by customers, twisted pair will be replaced by optical fiber in the local loop. Various techniques involving multiplexing, TDM, and WDM are being explored.

A natural outgrowth of IDN technology has been the introduction of virtual networks. Such networks present the appearance of a private network to the user. In fact, the virtual network uses existing public facilities, with usage structured and controlled by software. These offerings exploit the flexibility and power of digital networks and are a precursor of ISDN offerings.

4.6
RECOMMENDED READINGS

Books that provide good overall coverage of IDN concepts are [KEIS85], [BELL91], and [INOS79].

[STAI90] and [DAYT89] provide good coverage of digital carrier systems.

There is not a great deal of literature on the digital subscriber loop. [WYND82] is a special issue devoted to the topic; however, this issue predates recent advances in echo cancellation and concentrates on time-compression multiplexing. Significant portions of [MESS84b] and [DECI86a] are devoted to echo cancellation. [LIN88, LIN90, and MURA90] are good recent references on echo cancellation. The August 1990 issue of *IEEE LCS* is devoted to fiber in the local loop. [LU90] provides a comparative analysis of various optical-fiber approaches.

[GILH87], [GAWD86], [BROW86], and [COOL87] present aspects of virtual networks. [BRIE90] is a thorough discussion of virtual network services and current commercial offerings.

4.7
PROBLEMS

4.1. Bit 193 in the DS-1 transmission format is used for frame synchronization. Explain its use.

4.2. In the DS-1 transmission format, what is the control signal data rate for each voice channel?

4.3. Find the number of the following devices that could be accommodated by a T1-type TDM line if 1% of the line capacity is reserved for synchronization purposes.
   a. 110-bps teleprinter terminals.
   b. 300-bps computer terminals.
   c. 1200-bps computer terminals.
   d. 9600-bps computer terminals.
   e. 64-kbps PCM voice-frequency lines.
   How would these numbers change if each of the sources were operational an average of 10% of the time?

4.4. Assume that a digital subscriber line is to be used for 64-kbps PCM voice plus 8-kbps data in each direction plus one additional bit for every nine to be used for framing and synchronization. Let each burst in each direction have a length of 20 bits. For a typical cable, the propagation delay is 5 μs/km. Assume a guard time of 25 μs. What is the maximum length of cable that can be accommodated?

4.5. Are the modem and the codec functional inverses (i.e., could an inverted modem function as a codec, and vice versa)?

APPENDIX 4A

ANALOG AND DIGITAL DATA TRANSMISSION

The terms **analog** and **digital** correspond, roughly, to continuous and discrete, respectively. These two terms are used frequently in data communications in at least three contexts:

- Data.
- Signaling.
- Transmission.

Very briefly, we define data as entities that convey meaning. A useful distinction is that data have to do with the form of something; information has to do with the content or interpretation of those data. Signals are electric or electromagnetic encoding of data. Signaling is the act of propagating the signal along some suitable medium. Finally, transmission is the communication of data by the propagation and processing of signals. In what follows, we try to make these abstract concepts clear by discussing the terms *analog* and *digital* in these three contexts.

The concepts of analog and digital data are simple enough. **Analog data** take on continuous values on some interval. For example, voice and video are continuously varying patterns of intensity. Most data collected by sensors, such as temperature and pressure, are continuous-valued. **Digital data** take on discrete values; examples are text and integers.

In a communications system, data are propagated from one point to another by means of electric signals. An **analog signal** is a continuously varying electromagnetic wave that may be propagated over a variety of media, depending on frequency; examples are wire media, such as twisted pair and coaxial cable, fiber optic cable, and atmosphere or space propagation. A **digital signal** is a sequence of voltage pulses that may be transmitted over a wire medium; for example, a constant positive voltage level may represent binary 1 and a constant negative voltage level may represent binary 0.

The principal advantages of digital signaling are that it is generally cheaper than analog signaling and is less susceptible to noise interference. The principal disadvantage is that digital signals suffer more from attenuation than do analog signals. Figure 4.15 shows a sequence of voltage pulses, generated by a source using two voltage levels, and the received voltage some distance down a conducting medium. Because of the attenuation or reduction of signal strength at higher frequencies, the pulses become rounded and smaller. It should be clear that this attenuation can rather quickly lead to the loss of the information contained in the propagated signal.

Both analog and digital data can be represented, and hence propagated, by either analog or digital signals. This is illustrated in Figure 4.16. Generally, analog data are a function of time and occupy a limited frequency spectrum. Such data can be directly represented by an electromagnetic signal occupying the same spectrum. The best example of this is voice data. As sound waves, voice data have frequency components in the range 20 Hz to 20 kHz. However, most of the speech energy is in a much narrower range. The standard spectrum of voice signals is 300 to 3400 Hz, and this is quite adequate to propagate speech intelligibly and clearly. The telephone instrument does just that. For all sound input in the range of 300 to 3400 Hz, an electromagnetic signal with the same frequency-amplitude pattern is produced. The process is performed in reverse to convert the electromagnetic energy back into sound.

Digital data can also be represented by analog signals by use of a *modem* (modulator-demodulator). The modem converts a series of binary

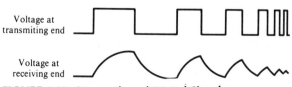

Voltage at transmiting end

Voltage at receiving end

FIGURE 4.15   Attenuation of Digital Signals

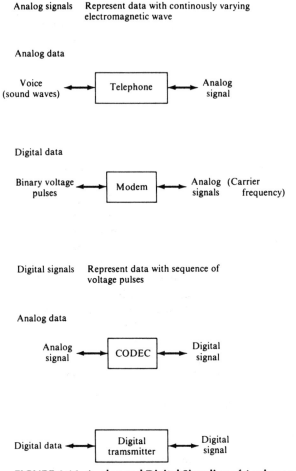

FIGURE 4.16 Analog and Digital Signaling of Analog and Digital Data

(two-valued) voltage pulses into an analog signal by modulating a *carrier frequency*. The resulting signal occupies a certain spectrum of frequency centered about the carrier and may be propagated across a medium suitable for that carrier. The most common modems represent digital data in the voice spectrum and hence allow those data to be propagated over ordinary voice-grade telephone lines. At the other end of the line, a modem demodulates the signal to recover the original data.

In an operation very similar to that performed by a modem, analog data can be represented by digital signals. The device that performs this function for voice data is a *codec* (coder-decoder). In essence, the codec takes an analog signal that directly represents the voice data and approximates that signal by a bit stream. At the other end of the line, the bit stream is used to reconstruct the analog data. This topic is explored in Appendix 4B.

Finally, digital data can be represented directly, in binary form, by two voltage levels. To improve propagation characteristics, however, the binary data are often encoded into a more complex form of digital signal [STAL88a].

A final distinction remains to be made. Analog and digital signals may be transmitted on suitable transmission media. The way these signals are treated is a function of the transmission system. Table 4.4 summarizes the methods of data transmission. **Analog transmission** is a means of transmitting analog signals without regard to their content; the signals may represent analog data (e.g., voice) or digital data (e.g., data that pass through a modem). In either case, the analog signal will suffer attenuation that limits the length of the transmission link. To achieve longer distances, the analog transmission system includes amplifiers that boost the energy in the signal. Unfortunately, the amplifier also boosts the noise components. With amplifiers cascaded to achieve long distance, the signal becomes more and more distorted. For analog data, such as voice, quite a bit of distortion can be tolerated and the data remain intelligible. However, for digital data transmitted as analog signals, cascaded amplifiers will introduce errors.

Digital transmission, in contrast, is concerned with the content of the signal. We have mentioned that a digital signal can be propagated only a limited distance before attenuation endangers the integrity of

TABLE 4.4   Analog and Digital Transmission

(a) Treatment of Signals		
	Analog Transmission	**Digital Transmission**
Analog Signal	Is propagated through amplifiers; same treatment for both analog and digital data	Assumes digital data; at propagation points, data in signal are recovered and new analog signal is generated
Digital Signal	Not used	Repeaters retransmit new signal; same treatment for both analog and digital data

(b) Possible Combinations		
	Analog Transmission	**Digital Transmission**
Analog Data	Analog signal	Digital signal
Digital Data	Analog signal	Digital signal
		Analog signal

the data. To achieve greater distances, repeaters are used. A repeater receives the digital signal, recovers the pattern of ones and zeros, and retransmits a new signal. Thus the attenuation is overcome.

The same technique may be used with an analog signal if it is assumed that the signal carries digital data. At appropriately spaced points, the transmission system has retransmission devices rather than amplifiers. The retransmission device recovers the digital data from the analog signal and generates a new, clean analog signal. Thus noise is not cumulative.

For long-haul communications, digital signaling is not as versatile and practical as analog signaling. For example, digital signaling is impossible for satellite, microwave, and optical fiber systems. However, digital transmission is superior to analog, both in terms of cost and quality (see Box 4.2), and the long-haul communications systems are gradually converting to digital transmission for both voice and digital data.

APPENDIX 4B

DIGITAL ENCODING OF ANALOG DATA

The evolution of public telecommunications networks to digital transmission requires that voice data be represented in digital form. It is important to note that this does not necessarily imply that the voice data be transmitted using digital signals. Figure 4.17 illustrates a common situation. Analog voice signals are digitized to produce a pattern of ones and zeros. As a digital signal, this pattern of ones and zeros may be fed into a modem so that an analog signal may be transmitted. However, this new analog signal differs significantly from the orginal voice signal, in that it represents an encoding of a binary stream. Hence, the digital transmission techniques discussed in Appendix 4A can be applied. In particular, retransmission devices rather than amplifiers are used to extend the length of a transmission link. Ultimately, of course, the new analog signal must be converted back to analog data that approximate the original voice input. For the remainder of this appendix, we can safely ignore the step of converting the digital data back into analog form and concentrate on the voice digitization process.

FIGURE 4.17 Digitizing Analog Data

The best-known technique for voice digitization is **pulse-code mod-ulation** (PCM). PCM is based on the sampling theorem, which states:

If a signal $f(t)$ is sampled at regular intervals of time and at a rate higher than twice the highest significant signal frequency, then the samples contain all the information of the original signal. The function $f(t)$ may be reconstructed from these samples by the use of a low-pass filter.

A proof of this theorem can be found in [STAL88a].

If voice data are limited to frequencies below 4000 Hz, a conservative procedure for intelligibility, then 8000 samples per second would be sufficient to completely characterize the voice signal. Note, however,

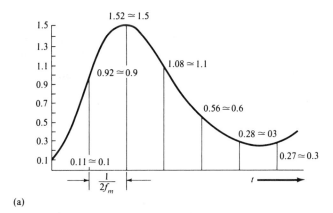

(a)

Digit	Binary equivalent	Pulse-code waveform
0	0000	
1	0001	
2	0010	
3	0011	
4	0100	
5	0101	
6	0110	
7	0111	
8	1000	
9	1001	
10	1010	
11	1011	
12	1100	
13	1101	
14	1110	
15	1111	

(b)

FIGURE 4.18 Pulse Code Modulation

that these are analog samples. To convert to digital, each of these analog samples must be assigned a binary code. Figure 4.18 shows an example in which each sample is approximated by being "quantized" into one of 16 different levels. Each sample can then be represented by four bits. Of course, it is now impossible to recover the original signal exactly. By using an 8-bit sample, which allows 256 quantizing levels, the quantity of the recovered voice signal is comparable to that achieved via analog transmission. Note that this implies that a data rate of 8000 samples per second × 8 bits per sample = 64 kbps is needed for a single voice signal.

Typically, the PCM scheme is refined using a technique known as *nonlinear encoding,* which means, in effect, that the 256 quantization levels are not equally spaced. The problem with equal spacing is that the mean absolute error for each sample is the same, regardless of signal level. Consequently, lower-amplitude values are relatively more distorted. By using a greater number of quantizing steps for signals of low amplitude, and a smaller number of quantizing steps for signals of large amplitude, a marked reduction in overall signal distortion is achieved.

PCM can, of course, be used for other than voice signals. For example, a color TV signal has a useful bandwidth of 4.6 MHz, and reasonable quality can be achieved with 10-bit samples for a data rate of 92 Mbps.

In recent times, variations on the PCM technique, as well as other encoding techniques, have been used to reduce the digital data rate required to carry voice [AOYA88]. Good-quality voice transmission can be achieved with data rates of 32 kbps and 16 kbps [MULL87]. A reasonable long-term goal appears to be in the neighborhood of 4 kbps [ROB186, JAYA86, HASK81]. With video, advantage can be taken of the fact that from frame to frame most picture elements will not change. Interframe coding techniques should allow the video requirement to be reduced to about 15 Mpbs [MURA87], and for slowly changing scenes, such as found in a video teleconference, down to 1.5 Mbps or less [SABR84, NETR80, KANE80]. Indeed, recent advances have resulted in commercial videoconference products with data rates as low as 64 kbps [HASK87].

Integrated Services Digital Networks

In Part One of this book, we looked at the underlying technology that supports the ISDN, that is, the technology of integrated digital networks (IDN). We are now in a position to turn to the ISDN itself. We begin, in Chapter 5, with an overview that provides a general description of the architecture of ISDN and looks at the standards that define ISDN.

Chapter 6 examines the services to be provided by ISDN. These services, in effect, are the requirements that ISDN must satisfy. This chapter looks at the general service capabilities defined for ISDN and then examines three specific applications: Teletex, facsimile, and electronic mail.

Chapter 7 begins our detailed examination of ISDN architecture and protocols. The chapter includes a consideration of the multiplexed transmission structure, the possible configurations of ISDN at the user-network interface, the protocol architecture, and issues relating to addressing and interworking.

The next three chapters look at the protocols at the user-network interface for ISDN. Chapter 8 deals with the physical layer. After a review of line-coding techniques, the two principal physical interfaces, basic and primary, are explored. The chapter also looks at details of the subscriber loop needed to support ISDN. Chapter 9 deals with the data link layer. The most important protocol at this level is LAPD. In addition, an important new technique, known as frame relay, is being introduced to ISDN. Chapter 10 deals with the network layer. The concern here is call control, which is provided by I.451/Q.931. Call control for frame relay is also examined.

Part Two closes with a discussion of Signaling System Number 7 (SS7) in Chapter 11. This system is an elaborate set of recommendations that define protocols for the internal management of an ISDN.

CHAPTER 5

ISDN OVERVIEW

5.1
A CONCEPTUAL VIEW OF ISDN

ISDN is a massive undertaking in many ways, and it is difficult to provide a concise description of it. To begin to understand ISDN, we look in this section at the concept of ISDN from several different viewpoints:

- Principles of ISDN.
- Evolution of the ISDN.
- The user interface.
- Objectives
- Benefits.
- Services.
- Architecture.

Principles of ISDN

Standards for ISDN are being defined by CCITT, a topic that we explore later in this chapter. Box 5.1, which is the complete text of one of the ISDN-related standards, states the principles of ISDN from the point of view of CCITT. Let us look at each of these points in turn.

159

BOX 5.1

CCITT Recommendation 1.120 (1988)

INTEGRATED SERVICE DIGITAL NETWORKS (ISDNs)

1 Principles of ISDN

1.1   The main feature of the ISDN concept is the support of a wide range of voice and non-voice applications in the same network. A key element of service integration for an ISDN is the provision of a range of services (see Part II of the I-series of Recommendations) using a limited set of connection types and multipurpose user-network interface arrangements (see parts III and IV of the I-series of Recommendations).

1.2   ISDNs support a variety of applications including both switched and non-switched connections. Switched connections in an ISDN include both circuit-switched and packet-switched connections and their concatenations.

1.3   As far as practicable, new services introduced into an ISDN should be arranged to be compatible with 64 kbit/s switched digital connections.

1.4   An ISDN will contain intelligence for the purpose of providing service features, maintenance and network management functions. This intelligence may not be sufficient for some new services and may have to be supplemented by either additional intelligence within the network, or possibly compatible intelligence in the user terminals.

1.5   A layered protocol structure should be used for the specification of the access to an ISDN. Access from a user to ISDN resources may vary depending upon the service required and upon the status of implementation of national ISDNs.

1.6   It is recognized that ISDNs may be implemented in a variety of configurations according to specific national situations.

2   Evolution of ISDNs

2.1   ISDNs will be based on the concepts developed for telephone IDNs and may evolve by progressively incorporating additional functions and network features including those of any other dedicated networks such as circuit switching and packet switching for data so as to provide for existing and new services.

2.2   The transition from an existing network to a comprehensive ISDN may require a period of time extending over one or more decades. During this period arrangements must be developed for the interworking of services on ISDNs and services on other networks (see Part I, Section 4 of the I-series).

2.3   In the evolution toward an ISDN, digital end-to-end connectivity will be obtained via plant and equipment used in existing networks, such as digital transmission, time-division multiplex switching and/or space-division multiplex switching. Existing relevant Recommendations for these constituent elements of an ISDN are contained in the appropriate series of Recommendations of CCITT and of CCIR.

2.4   In the early stages of the evolution of ISDNs, some interim user-network arrangements may need to be adopted in certain countries to facilitate early penetration of digital service capabilities.

   i)   Some of those interim arrangements are recommended by CCITT, such as hybrid access arrangements.

   ii)   Other arrangements corresponding to national variants may comply partly or wholly with I-Series Recommendations. However, the intention is that they are not specifically included in the I-series.

2.5   An evolving ISDN may also include at later stages switched connections at bit rates higher and lower than 64 kbit/s.

---

1. *Support of voice and nonvoice applications using a limited set of standardized facilities.* This principle defines both the purpose of ISDN and the means of achieving it. The ISDN will support a variety of services related to voice communications (telephone calls) and non-voice communications (digital data exchange). These services are to be provided in conformance with standards (CCITT Recommendations) that specify a small number of interfaces and data transmission facilities. The benefit of standards will be explored later in this chapter. For now, we simply state that without such a limitation, a global interconnected ISDN is virtually impossible.

2. *Support for switched and nonswitched applications.* ISDN will support both circuit switching and packet switching. As we discussed in Part I, there is a place for both technologies. In addition, ISDN will support nonswitched services in the form of dedicated lines.

3. *Reliance on 64-kbps connections.* ISDN is intended to provide circuit-switched and packet-switched connections at 64 kbps. This is the fundamental building block of ISDN. This rate was chosen because, at the time, it was the standard rate for digitized voice, and hence was being introduced into the evolving IDNs. Although this data rate is useful, it is unfortunately restrictive to rely solely on it. Future developments in ISDN will permit greater flexibility.

4. *Intelligence in the network.* An ISDN is expected to be able to provide sophisticated services beyond the simple setup of a circuit-switched call. In addition, network management and maintenance capabilities need to be more sophisticated than in the past. All of this is to be achieved by the use of Signaling System Number 7 and by the use of intelligent switching nodes in the network.

5. *Layered protocol architecture.* The protocols being developed for user access to ISDN exhibit a layered architecture and can be mapped into the OSI model. This has a number of advantages:

   • Standards already developed for OSI-related applications may be used on ISDN. An example is X.25 level 3 for access to packet-switching services in ISDN.
   • New ISDN-related standards can be based on existing standards, reducing the cost of new implementations. An example is LAP-D, which is based on LAP-B.
   • Standards can be developed and implemented independently for various layers and for various functions within a layer. This allows for the gradual implementation of ISDN services at a pace appropriate for a given provider or a given customer base.

6. *Variety of configurations.* More than one physical configuration is possible for implementing ISDN. This allows for differences in national policy (single-source versus competition), in the state of technology, and in the needs and existing equipment of the customer base.

Evolution of ISDN

As we discussed in Chapter 4, ISDN evolves from and with the integrated digital network (IDN). The evolution of the IDN has been driven by the need to provide economic voice communications. The resulting network, however, is also well suited to meet the growing variety of digital data service needs. Whereas the "I" in IDN refers to the integration of digital transmission and switching facilities, the "I" in ISDN refers to the integration of a variety of voice and data transmission services.

The second part of Box 5.1 gives the CCITT view of the way in which ISDN will evolve. Let us look at each of these points in turn.

1. *Evolution from telephone IDNs.* The intent is that the ISDN evolve from the existing telephone networks. Two conclusions can be drawn from this point. First, the IDN technology developed for and evolving within existing telephone networks forms the foundation for the services to be provided by ISDN. Second, although other facilities, such as third-party (not the telephone provider)

packet-switched networks and satellite links, will play a role in ISDN, the telephone networks will have the dominant role. Although packet switching and satellite providers may be less than happy with this interpretation, the overwhelming prevalence of telephone networks dictates that these networks form the basis for ISDN.

2. *Transition of one or more decades.* The evolution to ISDN will be a slow process. This is true of any migration of a complex application or set of applications from one technical base to a newer one. The introduction of ISDN services will be done in the context of existing digital facilities and existing services. There will be a period of coexistence in which connections and perhaps protocol conversion will be needed between alternative facilities and/or services.

3. *Use of existing networks.* This point is simply an elaboration of point 2. For example, ISDN will provide a packet-switched service. For the time being, the interface to that service will be X.25. With the introduction of fast packet switching and more sophisticated virtual call control, there may need to be a new interface in the future.

4. *Interim user-network arrangements.* Primarily, the concern here is that the lack of digital subscriber loops might delay introduction of digital services, particularly in developing countries. With the use of modems and other equipment, existing analog facilities can support at least some ISDN services.

5. *Connections at other than 64 kbps.* The 64-kbps data rate was chosen as the basic channel for circuit switching. With improvements in voice digitizing technology, this rate is unnecessarily high. On the other hand, this rate is too low for many digital data applications. Thus, other data rates will be needed.

The details of the evolution of ISDN facilities and services will vary from one nation to another, and indeed from one provider to another in the same country. These points simply provide a general description, from CCITT's point of view, of the process.

The User Interface

Figure 5.1 is a conceptual view of the ISDN from a user or customer point of view. The user has access to the ISDN by means of a local interface to a digital "pipe" of a certain bit rate. Pipes of various sizes will be available to satisfy differing needs. For example, a residential customer may require only sufficient capacity to handle a telephone and a videotex terminal. An office will typically wish to connect to the ISDN via an on-premise digital PBX and will require a much higher-capacity pipe.

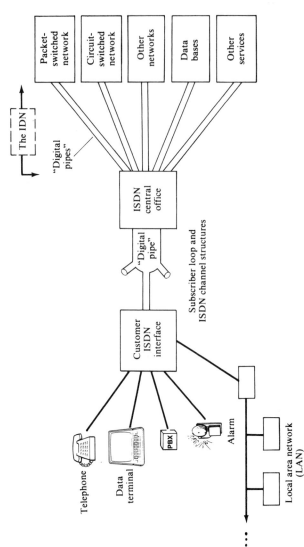

FIGURE 5.1 Conceptual View of ISDN Connection Features

That more than one size of pipe will be needed is emphasized in Figure 5.2, taken from Recommendation I.410. At the low end of demand would be a single terminal (e.g., a residential telephone) or multiple terminals in some sort of multidrop arrangement (e.g., a residential telephone, personal computer, and alarm system). Offices are more likely to contain a network of devices attached to a LAN or PBX, with an attachment from that network acting as a gateway to the ISDN.

At any given point in time, the pipe to the user's premises has a fixed capacity, but the traffic on the pipe may be a variable mix up to the capacity limit. Thus a user may access circuit-switched and packet-switched services, as well as other services, in a dynamic mix of signal types and bit rates. The ISDN will require rather complex control signals to instruct it how to sort out the time-multiplexed data and provide the required services. These control signals will also be multiplexed onto the same digital pipe.

An important aspect of the interface is that the user may, at any time, employ less than the maximum capacity of the pipe and will be charged according to the capacity used rather than "connect time." This characteristic significantly diminishes the value of current user design efforts that are geared to optimize circuit utilization by use of concentrators, multiplexers, packet switches, and other line sharing arrangements.

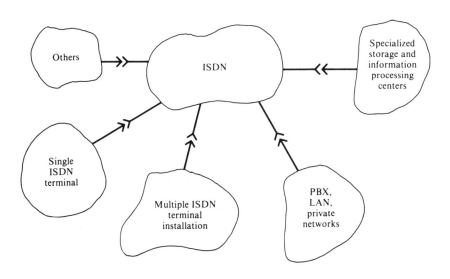

——◄◄——— ISDN user-network interface

FIGURE 5.2 ISDN User-Network Interface Examples

Objectives

Activities currently under way are leading to the development of a worldwide ISDN. This effort involves national governments, data processing and communication companies, standards organizations, and others. Certain common objectives are, by and large, shared by this disparate group. We list here key objectives.

- Standardization.
- Transparency.
- Separation of competitive functions.
- Leased and switched services.
- Cost-related tariffs.
- Smooth migration.
- Multiplexed support.

Standardization is essential to the success of ISDN. Standards will provide for universal access to the network. ISDN-standard equipment can be moved from one location to another, indeed from one country to another, and be plugged into the network. The cost of such equipment will be minimized because of the competition among many vendors to provide the same type of functionality. In addition, the use of a layered protocol architecture and standardized interfaces allows users to select equipment from multiple suppliers and allows changes to be made to a configuration in a gradual, piece-by-piece fashion.

It is also important that the digital transmission service have the property of **transparency;** that is, the service is independent of, and does not affect, the content of the user data to be transmitted. This permits users to develop applications and protocols with the confidence that they will not be affected by the underlying ISDN. Once a circuit or virtual circuit is set up, the user should be able to send information without the provider being aware of the type of information being carried. In addition, user-provided encryption techniques can be employed to provide security of user information.

The ISDN must be defined in a way that does not preclude the **separation of competitive functions** from the basic digital transmission services. It must be possible to separate out functions that could be provided competitively as opposed to those that are fundamentally part of the ISDN. In many countries, a single, government-owned entity will provide all services. Some countries desire (in the case of the United States, require) that certain enhanced services be offered competitively (e.g., videotex, electronic mail). These alternative views are depicted in Figures 5.3 and 5.4 [RUTK82]. Competition promotes innovation and the ability to respond to and satisfy a wide range of user requirements.

The ISDN should provide both **leased and switched services.** This will give the user the greatest range of options in configuring network

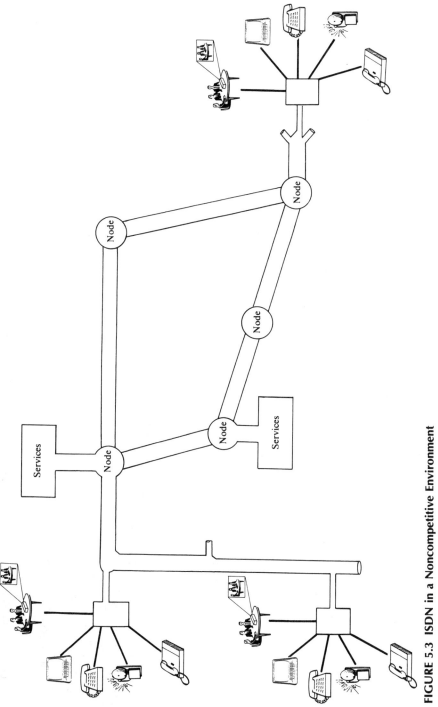

FIGURE 5.3 ISDN in a Noncompetitive Environment

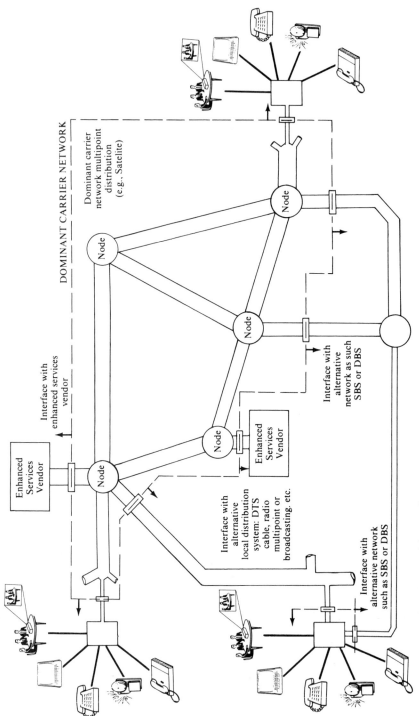

FIGURE 5.4 ISDN in a Competitive Environment

services and allow the user to optimize on the basis of cost and performance.

The price for ISDN service should be related to cost and indpendent
of the type of data being carried. Such a **cost-related tariff** will assure
that one type of service is not in the position of subsidizing others.
Price distinctions should be related to the cost of providing specific
performance and functional characteristics of a service. In this way,
distortions are avoided and providers can be driven by customer need
rather than some artificial tariff structure.

Because of the large installed base of telecommunications equipment
in the networks, and because of customer equipment with interfaces
designed for those networks, the conversion to ISDN will be gradual.
Thus, for an extended period of time, the evolving ISDN must coexist
with existing equipment and services. To provide for a **smooth migration** to ISDN, ISDN interfaces should evolve from existing interfaces,
and interworking arrangements must be designed. Specific capabilities
that will be needed include adapter equipment that allows pre-ISDN
terminal equipment to interface to ISDN, internetwork protocols that
allow data to be routed through a mixed ISDN/non-ISDN network
complex, and protocol converters to allow interoperation of ISDN services and similar non-ISDN services.

In addition to providing low-capacity support to individual users,
multiplexed support must be provided to accommodate user-owned
PBX and local area network (LAN) equipment.

There are, of course, other objectives that could be named. Those
just listed are certainly among the most important and widely acepted,
and they help to define the character of the ISDN.

Benefits

The principal benefits of ISDN to the **customer** can be expressed in
terms of cost savings and flexibility. The integration of voice and a
variety of data on a single transport system means that the user does
not have to buy multiple services to meet multiple needs. The efficiencies and economies of scale of an integrated network allow these services to be offered at lower cost than if they were provided separately.
Further, the user needs to bear the expense of just a single access line
to these multiple services. The requirements of various users can differ
greatly in a number of ways: for example, in information volume, traffic
pattern, response time, and interface types. The ISDN will allow the
user to tailor the service purchased to actual needs to a degree not
possible at present. In addition, customers enjoy the advantages of
competition among equipment vendors. These advantages include
product diversity, low price, and wide availability of services. Interface
standards permit selection of terminal equipment and transport and

other services from a range of competitors without changes in equipment or use of special adapters. Finally, because the offerings to the customer are based on the ISDN recommendations, which of necessity are slow to change, the risk of obsolescence is reduced.

Network providers, on a larger scale but in a similar way, profit from the advantages of competition, including the areas of digital switches and digital transmission equipment. Also, standards support universality and a larger potential market for services. Interface standards permit flexibility in selection of suppliers, consistent control signaling procedures, and technical innovation and evolution within the network without customer involvement.

Manufacturers can focus research and development on technical applications and be assured that a broad potential demand exists. In particular, the cost of developing VLSI implementations is justified by the potential market. Specialized niches in the market create opportunities for competitive, smaller manufacturers. Significant economies of scale can be realized by manufacturers of all sizes. Interface standards assure that the manufacturer's equipment will be compatible with the equipment across the interface.

Finally, **enhanced service providers** of, for instance, information-retrieval or transaction-based services, will benefit from simplified user access. End users will not be required to buy special arrangements or terminal devices in order to gain access to particular services.

Of course, any technical innovation comes with penalties as well as benefits. The main penalty here is the cost of migration. This cost, however, must be seen in the context of evolving customer needs. There will be changes in the telecommunications offerings available to customers, with or without ISDN. It is hoped that the ISDN framework will at least control the cost and reduce the confusion of migration. Another potential penalty of ISDN is that it will retard technical innovation. The process of adopting a standard is a long and complex one. The result is that by the time a standard is adopted and products are available, more advanced technical solutions have appeared. This is always a problem with standards. By and large, the benefits of standards outweigh the fact that they are always at least a little way behind the state of the art.

Services

The ISDN will provide a variety of services, supporting existing voice and data applications as well as providing for applications now being developed. Some of the most important applications are

- *Facsimile:* service for the transmission and reproduction of graphics, handwritten and printed material. This type of service has been available for many years but has suffered from a lack of standardization and the limitations of the analog telephone network. Digital facsimile standards are now available and can be used to transmit a page of data at 64 kbps in 5 seconds.

- *Teletex:* service that enables subscriber terminals to exchange correspondence. Communicating terminals are used to prepare, edit, transmit, and print messages. Transmission is at a rate of one page in 2 seconds at 9.6 kbps.
- *Videotex:* An interactive information retrieval service. A page of data can be transmitted in 1 second at 9.6 kbps.

Table 5.1 shows the types of services that could be supported by ISDN. These services fall into the broad categories of voice, digital data, text, and image. Most of these services can be provided with a transmission capacity of 64 kbps or less. This rate, as we have mentioned, is the standard rate offered to the user. Some services require considerably higher data rates and may be provided by high-speed facilities outside the ISDN (e.g., cable TV distribution plants) or in future enhancements to ISDN (see Chapter 9 on broadband ISDN).

One of the key aspects of the ISDN will be that it is an "intelligent network." By use of a flexible signaling protocol, the ISDN will provide a variety of network facilities for each service. Table 5.2 gives some examples of planned facilities.

Architecture

Figure 5.5, based on a figure in CCITT Recommendation I.325, is an architectural depiction of ISDN. The ISDN will support a completely new physical connecter for users, a digital subscriber loop, and a variety of transmission services.

The common physical interface provides a standardized means of attaching to the network. The same interface should be usable for telephone, computer terminal, and videotex terminal. Protocols are required to define the exchange of control information between user device and the network. Provision must be made for high-speed interfaces to, for example, a digital PBX or a LAN. The interface supports a *basic* service consisting of three time-multiplexed channels, two at 64 kbps and one at 16 kbps. In addition, there is a *primary* service that provides multiple 64-kbps channels.

The subscriber loop provides the physical signal path from subscriber to ISDN central office. This loop must support full-duplex digital transmission for both basic and primary data rates. Initially, much of the subscriber loop plant will be twisted pair. As the network evolves and grows, optical fiber will be increasingly used.

The ISDN central office connects the numerous subscriber loops to the digital network. This provides access to a variety of lower-layer (OSI layers 1–3) transmission functions, including circuit-switched, packet-

TABLE 5.1   Candidate Services for Integration

| Bandwidth | | Service | | |
	Telephony	Data	Text	Image
Digital voice (64 kbps)	Telephone	Packet-switched data	Telex	
		Circuit-switched data	Teletex	
	Leased circuits	Leased circuits	Leased circuits	
	Information retrieval (by voice analysis and synthesis)	Telemetry	Videotex	
		Funds transfer		Facsimile
		Information retrieval	Information retrieval	Information retrieval
		Mailbox	Mailbox	Surveillance
		Electronic mail	Electronic mail	
		Alarms		
Wide band (> 64 kbps)	Music	High-speed computer communication		TV conferencing
				Teletex
				Videophone
				Cable TV distribution

TABLE 5.2   Basic and Additional Facilities for ISDN Services

Telephony	Data	Teletex	Videotex	Facsimile
		Basic		
National toll access	Automatic dialed call	Incoming call not disturbing local mode	Information retrieval by dialog with a database	Automatic dialed call
International toll access	Manual dialed call	Message printed on operator demand		Manual dialed call
Malicious call blocking	Automatic answer	Message presentation as in the original		Automatic answer
		Day and hour automatic indication		
		Additional		
Transfer call	Direct call	Delayed messages	Transactions (e.g., reservation, shopping)	Delayed delivery
Abbreviated dialing	Closed user group	Abbreviated address		Multiple destination
Rerouting to verbal announcements	Closed user group with outgoing access	Multiple address		
Intermediate call	Calling line identification	Charging indication	Message box service between users	Code, speed, and format conversion for different terminals
Conference call	Called line identification	Telex access		
Camp-on busy	Abbreviated address calling	Graphic mode	Loading of software from a database to a terminal	
Barring outgoing toll traffic	Barred incoming call		Loading of special character set	
	Multiaddress calling			
Hot line	Detailed billing			
Detailed billing	Transfer call			
Automatic wake-up	Call charging indication			

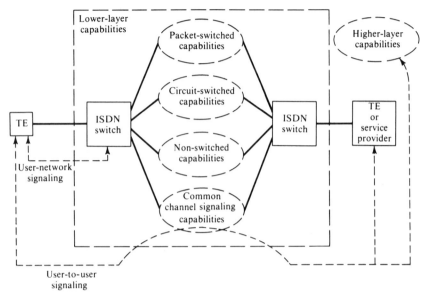

FIGURE 5.5 ISDN Architecture

switched, and dedicated facilities. In addition, common-channel signaling, used to control the network and provide call management, will be accessible to the user. This signaling will allow user-network control dialogue. The use of these control signaling protocols for user-to-user dialogue is a subject for further study within CCITT. By and large, these lower-layer functions will be implemented within the ISDN. In some countries with a competitive climate, some of these lower-layer functions (e.g., packet switching) may be provided by separate networks that may be reached by a subscriber through ISDN.

There will also be higher-layer (OSI layers 4–7) functions to support applications such as teletex, facsimile, and transaction processing. These functions may be implemented within ISDN or provided by separate networks, or a mixture of the two.

5.2

ISDN STANDARDS

Although a number of standards organizations are involved in various aspects of ISDN, the controlling body is the International Telegraph and Telephone Consultative Committee (CCITT). In this section, we first look at the rationale for standards and then examine the ISDN-related standards from CCITT. An appendix to this chapter looks at CCITT itself.

The Importance of Standards

It has long been accepted in the telecommunications industry that standards are required to govern the physical, electrical, and procedural characteristics of communication equipment. With the increasingly digital character of telecommunication networks, and with the increasing prevalence of digital transmission and processing services, the scope of what should be standardized has broadened. As we shall see, the functions, interfaces, and services embodied in ISDN that are subject to standardization cover an extremely broad range.

Although there is no widely accepted and quoted definition of the term *standard,* the following definition from the 1979 National Policy on Standards for the United States encompasses the essential concept [NSPA79]:

> A prescribed set of rules, conditions, or requirements concerning definition of terms; classification of components; specification of materials, performance, or operation; delineation of procedures; or measurement of quantity and quality in describing materials, product, systems, services, or practices.

[CERN84] lists the following advantages of standards:

- Increased productivity and efficiency in industry because of larger-scale, lost-cost production.
- Increased competition by allowing smaller firms to market products, readily acceptable by the consumer, without the need for a massive advertising budget.
- Dissemination of information and the transfer of technology.
- Expansion of international trade because of the feasibility of exchange of products among countries.
- Conservation of resources.
- Increased opportunity for worldwide exchange of information, both voice and data.

In the case of ISDN, because of the complexity of ISDN, and because its success depends on the capability of providing true interconnectivity and interoperability, standards are not only advantageous but essential in the introduction of such a network.

Historical Background

The development of ISDN is governed by a set of recommendations issued by CCITT, called the I-series of recommendations. These recommendations, or standards, were first issued in 1984. A more complete set was issued in 1988.

It is enlightening to look at the history of CCITT's interest in ISDN. In 1968, CCITT established Special Study Group D (forerunner of today's Study Group XVIII, which has ISDN responsibility within CCITT) to look at a variety of issues related to the use of digital technology in the telephone network. At each Plenary Assembly, the study group was given assignments for the next four-year study period. The first and principal question assigned over this period is shown in Table 5.3. The titles of the first question reflect the evolution of CCITT interest. The focus shifts from digital technology, to integrated digital networks (IDN), to ISDN.

In 1968, Study Group D was set up to study all questions related to the standardization of transmission of pulse-code-modulated (PCM) voice and to coordinate work going on in other groups relating to digital networking. Even at this early stage, there was a vision of an ISDN. Recommendation G.702, issued in 1972, contained the following definition of an integrated services digital network:

> An integrated digital network in which the same digital switches and digital paths are used to establish for different services, for example, telephony, data.

At this point, there was no information on the type of network that could integrate digital switches and paths, or how the network could integrate various services. Nevertheless, it was a recognition of the path that could be followed with digital technology.

During the next study period (1973–1976), there were continuing advances in digital transmission technology. In addition, digital switching equipment began to emerge from the laboratory. Thus the construction of integrated digital networks became a real possibility. Accordingly, the 1976 set of recommendations included specifications dealing with digital switching as well as the specification of a new signaling system (Number 7) designed for use in the forthcoming digital networks. The first question for this period also specifically deals with the integration of services.

In planning for the 1977–1980 study period, CCITT recognized that the evolution toward a digital network was under way and was more important than the standardization of individual digital systems and equipment. Thus the focus was on the integration aspects of the digital network and on the integration of services on an IDN. Two key developments that emerged during this study period were the following:

- The integration of services is based on providing a standardized user-network interface that allows the user to request various services through a uniform set of protocols.
- ISDN will evolve from the digital telephone network.

TABLE 5.3   Question 1 As Assigned to Special Study Group D (1969–1976) and to Study Group XVIII (1977–1992)

Study Period	Title of Question 1
1969–1972	Planning of digital systems
1973–1976	Planning of digital systems and integration of services
1977–1980	Overall aspects of integrated digital networks and integration of services.
1981–1984	General network aspects of an integrated services digital network (ISDN)
1985–1988	General question on ISDN
1989–1992	General aspects of ISDN

At the end of this period, the first ISDN standard emerged, entitled Integrated Services Digital Network (ISDN), G.705 (Box 5.2). No other standards on ISDN were issued in 1980; at this point, only the general concept of an ISDN had been developed.

As the next period began (1981–1984), ISDN was declared the major concern of CCITT for the upcoming study period. A set of recommendations, called the I-Series, was published at the end of this period. This initial set of specifications was incomplete and, in some cases, internally inconsistent. Nevertheless, the specification of ISDN by 1984 was sufficient for manufacturers and service providers to begin to develop ISDN-related equipment and to demonstrate ISDN-related services and networking configurations. The 1984 series included this definition of ISDN, retained in the 1988 documents:

> An ISDN is a network, in general evolving from a telephony IDN, that provides end-to-end digital connectivity to support a wide range of services, including voice and non-voice services, to which users have access by a limited set of standard multi-purpose user-network interfaces.

Work on the I-series and related recommendations continued in the 1985–1988 period. At the beginning of this period, CCITT was significantly restructured to give a number of its study groups a part of future ISDN work. The dominant function of CCITT became the study of ISDN matters. The 1988 version of the I-series recommendations was sufficiently detailed to make preliminary ISDN implementations possible in the late 1980s.

The 1988 I-Series Recommendations

The bulk of the description of ISDN is contained in the I-series of Recommendations,[1] with some related topics covered in other Recom-

---

[1] Some Recommendations have two designations. For example, I.450 is also designated as Q.930. When such standards are referenced in this book, both designations are supplied (e.g., I.450/Q.930).

BOX 5.2

CCITT Recommendation G.705 (1980)

INTEGRATED SERVICES DIGITAL NETWORK (ISDN)

The CCITT,
considering

(a) the measure of agreement that has so far been reached in the studies of Integrated Digital Networks (IDNs) dedicated to specific services such as telephony, data and also of an Integrated Services Digital Network (ISDN),

(b) the need for a common basis for the future studies necessary for the evolution towards an ISDN,

recommends

that the ISDN should be based on the following conceptual principles:

(1) The ISDN will be based on and evolve from the telephony IDN by progressively incorporating additional functions and network features including those of any other dedicated networks so as to provide for existing and new services.

(2) New services introduced into the ISDN should be arranged to be compatible with 64-kbit/s switched digital connections.

(3) The transition from the existing networks to a comprehensive ISDN may require a period of time extending over one or two decades.

(4) During the transition period arrangements must be developed for the interworking of services on ISDNs and services on other networks.

(5) The ISDN will contain intelligence for the purposes of providing service features, maintenance and network management functions. This intelligence may not be sufficient for some new services and may have to be supplemented by either additional intelligence within the network, or possibly compatible intelligence in the customer terminals.

(6) A layered functional set of protocols appear desirable for the various access arrangements to the ISDN. Access from the customer to ISDN resources may vary depending upon the service required and on the status of evolution of national ISDNs.

Note—Existing relevant Recommendations for some of the constituent elements of the ISDN are contained in Series G, O, Q, and X Recommendations and also in relevant volumes of the CCIR.

mendations. The characterization of ISDN contained in these recommendations is centered on three main areas:

1. The standardization of services offered to users, so as to enable services to be internationally compatible.
2. The standardization of user-network interfaces, so as to enable terminal equipment to be portable, and to assist in (1).
3. The standardization of ISDN capabilities to the degree necessary to allow user-network and network-network interworking, and thus to achieve (1) and (2).

The structure of the 1988 I-series Recommendations is shown in Table 5.4; Appendix 5B provides a brief description of each recommendation. Figure 5.6 illustrates the relationship among the various I-series standards. The 1984 set contained recommendations in series I.100 through I.400. Some updates and expansions occurred in these series in the 1985–1988 study period. The I.500 and I.600 series were left for further study in 1984, and a preliminary set of specifications was ready for 1988, with additional work to be done in the 1989–1992 study period.

I.1100 Series—General Concepts The I.100 series serves as a general introduction to ISDN. The general structure of the ISDN recommendations is presented as well as a glossary of terms. I.120, reproduced as Box 5.1, provides an overall description of ISDN and the expected evolution of ISDNs. Recommendation I.130 introduces terminology and concepts that are used in the I.200 series to specify services.

This chapter has covered much of what is in the I.100 series.

I.200 Series—Service Capabilities The I.200 series is in a sense the most important part of the CCITT ISDN recommendations. Here, the services to be provided to users are specified. We may look on this as a set of requirements that the ISDN must satisfy. In the ISDN glossary (I.112), the term *service* is defined as

> That which is offered by an Administration or RPOA to its customers in order to satisfy a specific telecommunication requirement.

Although this is a very general definition, the term *service* has come to have a very specific meaning in CCITT, a meaning that is somewhat different from the use of that term in an OSI content. For CCITT, a standardized service is characterized by [CERN84]

- Complete, guaranteed end-to-end compability.
- CCITT-standardized terminals, including procedures.
- Listing of the service subscribers in an international directory.
- CCITT-standardized testing and maintenance procedures.
- Charging and accounting rules.

TABLE 5.4 Structure of the 1988 CCITT I-Series Recommendations

Part I—General Structure

Section 1—Framework of I-Series Recommendations

I.110   Preamble and General Structure of the I-Series Recommendations

I.111   Relationship with Other Recommendations Relevant to ISDNs

I.112   Vocabulary of Terms for ISDNs

I.113   Vocabulary of Terms for Broadband Aspects of ISDN

Section 2—Description of ISDNs

I.120   Integrated Services Digital Networks

I.121   Broadband Aspects of ISDN

I.122   Framework for Providing Additional Packet-Mode Bearer Services

Section 3—General Modeling Methods

I.130   Method for the Characterization of Telecommunication Services Supported By an ISDN and Network Capabilities of an ISDN

Section 4—Telecommunication Network and Service Attributes

I.140   Attribute Technique for the Characterization of Telecommunication Services Supported By an ISDN and Network Capabilities of an ISDN

I.141   ISDN Network Charging Capabilities Attributes

Part II—Service Recommendations

I.200   Guidance to the I.200 Series of Recommendations

Section 1—General Aspects of Service in ISDN

I.210   Principles of Telecommunication Services Supported by an ISDN and the Means to Describe Them

Section 2—Common Aspects of Services in the ISDN

I.220   Common Dynamic Description of Basic Telecommunication Services

I.221   Common Specific Characteristics of Services

Section 3—Bearer Services Supported by an ISDN

I.230   Definition of Bearer Service Categories

I.231   Circuit-Mode Bearer Service Categories

I.232   Packet-Mode Bearer Service Categories

Section 4—Teleservices Supported by an ISDN

I.240   Definition of Teleservices

I.241   Teleservices Supported by an ISDN

Section 5—Supplementary Services in ISDN

I.250   Definition of Supplementary Services

I.251   Number Identification Supplementary Services

I.252   Call Offering Supplementary Services

I.253   Call Completion Supplementary Services

I.254   Multiparty Supplementary Services

I.255   Community of Interest Supplementary Services

I.256   Charging Supplementary Services

I.257   Additional Information Transfer

Part III—Overall Network Aspects and Functions

Section 1—Network Functional Principles
I.310   ISDN—Network Functional Principles

Section 2—Reference Models
I.320   ISDN Protocol Reference Model
I.324   ISDN Network Architecture
I.325   Reference Configurations for ISDN Connection Types
I.326   Reference Configurations for Relative Network Resource Requirements

Section 3—Numbering, Addressing, and Routing
I.330   ISDN Numbering and Addressing Principles
I.331   Number Plan for the ISDN Era
I.332   Numbering Principles for Interworking Between ISDNs and Dedicated
         Networks with Different Numbering Plans
I.333   Terminal Selection in ISDN
I.334   Principles Relating ISDN Numbers/Subaddresses to the OSI Reference
         Model Network Layer Addresses
I.335   ISDN Routing Principles

Section 4—Connection Types
I.340   ISDN Connection Types

Section 5—Performance Objectives
I.350   General Aspects of Quality of Service and Network Performance in Dig-
         ital Networks, Including ISDN
I.351   Recommendations in Other Series Concerning Network Performance
         Objectives That Apply at Reference Point T of an ISDN
I.352   Network Performance Objectives for Connection Processing Delays in
         an ISDN

Part IV—ISDN User-Network Interfaces

Section 1—ISDN User-Network Interfaces
I.410   General Aspects and Principles Relating to ISDN User-Network Inter-
         faces
I.411   ISDN User-Network Interfaces—Reference Configurations
I.412   ISDN User-Network Interfaces—Interface Structures and Access Capabil-
         ities

Section 2—Application of I-Series Recommendations to ISDN User-Network
I.420   Basic User-Network Interface
I.421   Primary Rate User-Network Interface

Section 3—ISDN User-Network Interfaces: Layer 1 Recommendations
I.430   Basic User-Network Interface—Layer 1 Specification
I.431   Primary Rate User-Network Interface—Layer 1 Specification

Section 4—ISDN User-Network Interfaces: Layer 2 Recommendations
I.440   ISDN User-Network Interface Data Link Layer—General Aspects
I.441   ISDN User-Network Interface Data Link Layer Specification

Cont.

TABLE 5.4   Structure of the 1988 CCITT I-Series Recommendations
(continued)

Part IV—ISDN User-Network Interfaces

Section 5—ISDN User-Network Interfaces: Layer 3 Recommendations
I.450   ISDN User-Network Interface Layer 3—General Aspects
I.451   ISDN User-Network Interface Layer 3 Specification for Basic Call Control
I.452   Generic Procedures for the Control of ISDN Supplementary Services

Section 6—Multiplexing, Rate Adaptation, and Support of Existing Interfaces
I.460   Multiplexing, Rate Adaptation, and Support of Existing Interfaces
I.461   Support of X.21-, X.21 *bis*-, and X.20 *bis*-Based DTEs By an ISDN
I.462   Support of Packet Mode Terminal Equipment by an ISDN
I.463   Support of DTEs with V-Series Type Interfaces by an ISDN
I.464   Multiplexing, Rate Adaptation, and Support of Existing Interfaces for Restricted 64-kbps Transfer Capability
I.465   Support by an ISDN of DTEs with V-Series Type Interfaces with Provisions for Statistical Multiplexing

Section 7—Aspects of ISDN Affecting Terminal Requirements
I.470   Relationship of Terminal Functions to ISDN

Part V—Internetwork Interfaces

I.500   General Structure of ISDN Interworking Recommendations
I.510   Definitions and General Principles of ISDN Interworking
I.511   ISDN-to-ISDN Layer 1 Internetwork Interface
I.515   Parameter Exchange for ISDN Interworking
I.520   General Arrangements for Network Interworking Between ISDNs
I.530   Network Interworking Between an ISDN and a PSTN
I.540   General Arrangements for Interworking Between CSPDNs and ISDNs for the Provision of Data Transmission
I.550   General Arrangements for Interworking Between PSPDNs and ISDNs for the Provision of Data Transmission
I.560   Requirements to Be Met in Providing the Telex Service Within the ISDN

Part VI—Maintenance Principles

I.601   General Maintenance Principles of ISDN Subscriber Access and Subscriber Installation
I.602   Application of Maintenance Principles to ISDN Subscriber Installation
I.603   Application of Maintenance Principles to ISDN Basic Accesses
I.604   Application of Maintenance Principles to ISDN Primary Rate Accesses
I.605   Application of Maintenance Principles to Static Multiplexed ISDN Basic Accesses

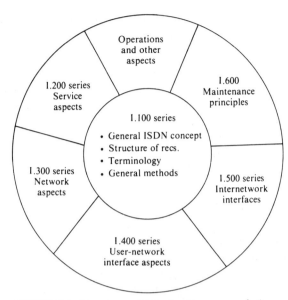

FIGURE 5.6 Structure of I-Series Recommendations

There are three fully standardized CCITT services: telegraphy, telephony, and data. There are four newer CCITT *telematic services* in process of standardization: teletex, facsimile, videotex, and message handling. The goal with all of these services is to ensure high-quality international telecommunications for the end user, regardless of the make of the terminal equipment and the type of network used nationally to support the service.

The I.200 series classifies services into lower-level bearer services and higher-level teleservices. For each service, various attributes are defined, constituting a "laundry list" that is configured by agreement between the subscriber and the provider. Chapter 6 is devoted to the topic of ISDN services.

I.300 Series—Network Aspects Whereas the I.200 series focuses on the user, in terms of the services provided to the user, the I.300 series focuses on the network, in terms of how the network goes about providing those services. A protocol reference model is presented that, while based on the 7-layer OSI model, attempts to account for the complexity of a connection that may involve two or more users (e.g., a conference call) plus a related common-channel signaling dialogue. Issues such as numbering and addressing are addressed. There is also a discussion of ISDN connection types.

Chapter 7 includes a discussion of ISDN network aspects.

I.400 Series—User-Network Interfaces The I.400 series deals with the interface between the user and the network. Three major topics are addressed:

- Physical configurations: the issue of how ISDN functions are configured into equipment. The standards specify functional groupings and define reference points between those groupings.
- Transmission rates: the data rates and combinations of data rates to be offered to the user.
- Protocol specifications: the protocols at OSI layers 1 through 3 that specify the user-network interaction.

The first two of these topics are covered in Chapter 7. Chapters 8 through 10 deal with ISDN protocols.

I.500 Series—Internetwork Interfaces ISDN will support services that are also provided on older circuit-switched and packet-switched networks. Thus, it is necessary to provide interworking between an ISDN and other types of networks to allow communications between terminals belonging to equivalent services offered through different networks. The I.500 series deals with the various network issues that arise in attempting to define interfaces between ISDN and other types of networks. Chapter 7 includes a discussion of I.500 issues.

I.600 Series—Maintenance Principles This series provides guidance for maintenance of the ISDN subscriber installation, the network portion of the ISDN basic access, primary access, and higher data rate services. Maintenance principles and functions are related to the reference configuration and general architecture of ISDN. A key function that is identified in the series is loopback. In general, loopback testing is used for failure localization and verification.

Ongoing Work and the Interim 1990 Recommendations

With the publication of the 1988 set of ISDN Recommendations, much of the work on ISDN is complete. The focus for the 1989–1992 study period has shifted to broadband ISDN, a topic that we explore in Part Three of this book. However, a number of details on ISDN remain to be resolved, and these have been assigned to various working groups for the 1989–1992 study period.

As was mentioned, ISDN and its follow-on, broadband ISDN, are now the focus of CCITT activity. This is reflected in Table 5.5, which lists ISDN-related questions for the 1989–1992 study period. Study Group XVIII continues to have the lead role in the development of both

TABLE 5.5   Questions Relating to ISDN in the 1989–1992 Study Period

Study Group I (Services)

21/I	New services on the ISDN
22/I	Broadband services on the ISDN
23/I	Existing telematic and data transmission services on the ISDN
29/I	Customer control procedures in the PSTN and ISDN
30/I	User indications in the PSTN and ISDN

Study Group II (Network Operation)

5/II	Evolution of numbering and numbering plan interworking for ISDN era
6/II	Evolution of routing plan in the ISDN era
7/II	Non-voice aspects of networks during transition from PSTN to ISDN
8/II	Service quality of networks (PSTN/ISDN)
17/II	Traffic reference models for ISDN traffic engineering

Study Group III (Tariff and Accounting Principles)

21/III	Charging and accounting principles to be applied to the services offered by an ISDN
22/III	General charging and accounting principles for non-voice services provided by interworking between the ISDN and existing public data networks
23/III	Tariff and accounting principles to be applied to permanent and reserved services within the ISDN

Study Group IV (Maintenance)

21/IV	Maintenance of ISDN

Study Group V (Protection Against Electromagnetic Effects)
(None)

Study Group VI (Outside Plant)

6/VI	Copper networks for ISDN services

Study Group VII (Data Communications Networks)

1/VII	Standardization of the technical characteristics of user classes of service, international data transmission services, and optional user facilities in PDNs and ISDNs and the categories of access for DTEs to such services
13/VII	Interworking between public data networks (circuit-switched and packet-switched) and ISDNs and between ISDNs, for the provision of data services
30/VII	Support of X-Series interfaces in an ISDN and new interface aspects for data services in ISDNs
31/VII	Requirements and arrangements for the provision of data services in ISDNs

Study Group VIII (Terminals for Telematic Services)
(None)

Cont.

**TABLE 5.5   Questions Relating to ISDN in the 1989–1992 Study Period
(continued)**

Study Group IX (Telegraph Networks and Telegraph Terminal Equipment)

17/IX   Integration of the telex network with other networks that use com-
             mon-channel signaling, particularly ISDN

Study Group X (Languages for Telecommunications Applications)
(None)

Study Group XI (Switching and Signaling)

10/XI   Evolution of the ISDN user part
11/XI   Call control and bearer control protocols in Signaling System No. 7
             for the full range of ISDN telecommunication services
22/XI   ISDN user-network protocol conformance

**Study Group XII (Transmission Performance of Telephone Networks and
  Terminals)**

27/XII   Talker echo, propagation time, and stability in telephone networks,
             ISDN, and interconnection with ISDN

Study Group XV (Transmission Systems and Equipment)
(None)

Study Group XVII (Data Transmission Over the Telephone Network)

6/XVII   Characteristics of a device used to interface a DTE to digital channels
             other than ISDN
11/XVII   Support of DTEs (TE2) with V-Series type interfaces on an ISDN and
             interworking of DTEs with modems on PSTNs with TE2s and TE1s
             on ISDNs

Study Group XVIII (ISDN)

1/XVIII   General aspects of ISDN
2/XVIII   Asynchronous Transfer Mode (ATM)
3/XVIII   Network aspects of digital hierarchies
4/XVIII   Network application of SDH with reference to the Network Node
             Interface (NNI)
5/XVIII   General aspects of quality of service and network performance in
             digital networks including ISDNs
6/XVIII   Network performance objectives for ISDN circuit-mode information
             transfer
7/XVIII   Performance objectives for ISDN circuit-mode information transfer
8/XVIII   Network performance objectives for ISDN connection, processing,
             and packet-mode information transfer
9/XVIII   Performance objectives for ISDN availability
10/XVIII   Impact of signal processing on ISDN
11/XVIII   Interworking of ISDNs with other networks, including compatibility
             checking and terminal selection
12/XVIII   Interworking between networks using different digital hierarchies—
             Layer 1 functionality
13/XVIII   Network capabilities for the support of broadband services in ISDNs

14/XVIII	ISDN network capabilities for the support of additional and/or new services
15/XVIII	ISDN packet-mode bearer services—services and user-network interface aspects
16/XVIII	ISDN architecture and functional principles, characterization methods and reference configuration (including user-network interfaces)
17/XVIII	ISDN protocol reference model
18/XVIII	ISDN connection types
19/XVIII	Network capabilities for the integration of mobile network services into the ISDN
20/XVIII	Layer 1 characteristics of ISDN interfaces and ISDN access
21/XVIII	Vocabulary for ISDNs
22/XVIII	Broadband ISDN influence on principles for video encoding
23/XVIII	Guidelines for implementing ISDN field trials in developing countries

ISDN and broadband ISDN recommendations. The study group is organized as eight working parties, each with its own focus (Table 5.6).

Because of the pace of change of technology and the rapidity with which new products and services are being introduced into the telecommunications arena, CCITT is finding that the traditional four-year cycle is inadequate. This is especially so in the case of broadband ISDN, which is discussed in Part III. However, even in the ordinary ISDN area, there is a desire to produce results outside of the normal four-year schedule. Accordingly, a number of the CCITT working groups published interim new recommendations and interim revisions to existing recommendations in 1990. Those that relate to ISDN (as opposed to B-ISDN) are listed in Appendix 5C.

In this part of the book, our discussion of ISDN is based primarily on the 1988 standards. Where appropriate, the revisions and additions published in 1990 are also incorporated.

TABLE 5.6   Working Parties of CCITT Study Group XVIII for the 1989–1992 Study Period

Working Party XVIII/1	General aspects and coordination
Working Party XVIII/2	Interworking, frame-mode bearer services, and field trials
Working Party XVIII/3	Interfaces—layer 1 characteristics
Working Party XVIII/4	Architecture and models
Working Party XVIII/5	Network capabilities
Working Party XVIII/6	Performance
Working Party XVIII/7	Digital hierarchies
Working Party XVIII/8	General B-ISDN aspects

5.3

RECOMMENDED READING

The literature of ISDN is growing as rapidly as the field itself. [STAL91b] contains reprints of a number of the key papers. The April 1990 issue of *IEEE Communications* magazine and the February 1991 issue of the *Proceedings of the IEEE* are devoted to ISDN. In the Proceedings issue, [WU91] and [KANO91] provide an overview of the standardization efforts under way for ISDN.

A number of books on ISDN have been published in recent years. Perhaps the most useful are [HELG91], [VERM90], and [BECK88], all of which provide detailed technical coverage. The first two have the advantage of working from the final version of the 1988 Recommendations, while the last went to press while these recommendations were still not entirely stable. [KESS90] is also useful, though perhaps less detailed. [HARD90] is a short book aimed at the design or implementer; while it is less detailed technically, it does provide some useful tips. Another short book is [GRIF90], which provides a readable but technically uneven presentation.

5.4

PROBLEMS

5.1. Is an IDN necessary for an ISDN? Sufficient? Explain.

5.2. Elaborate on the statement in Section 5.1 that ISDN is virtually impossible without a limitation on the number of different user-ISDN interfaces and data transmission facilities.

5.3. In Chapter 4, we discussed the concept of a virtual network and pointed out some of its advantages compared to the traditional private network built on dedicated (leased) lines. With ISDN, the network will have a high degree of intelligence, will be controlled internally with common-channel signaling, and may be controlled externally with a common-channel signaling interface. Why, then, as stated in Principle 2 (Box 5.1) is there a need for non-switched support?

5.4. It was mentioned in Section 5.1 that user-implemented multidrop lines and multiplexers may disappear. Explain why.

5.5. Compare Recommendation G.705 (Box 5.2) of 1980 with I.120 (Box 5.1) of 1984. What do the differences reveal about the evolution of CCITT thinking with respect to ISDN?

APPENDIX 5A
CCITT

The International Telegraph and Telephone Consultative Committee (CCITT) is a committee of the International Telecommunications Union (ITU), which is itself a United Nations specialized agency [HUMM85]. Hence the members of CCITT are governments. The U.S. representation is housed in the Department of State. The charter of CCITT is "to study and issue recommendations on technical, operating, and tariff questions relating to telegraphy and telephony." Its primary objective is to standardize, to the extent necessary, techniques and operations in telecommunications to achieve end-to-end compatibility of international telecommunication connections, regardless of the countries of origin and destination.

CCITT is organized into 15 study groups that prepare standards, called Recommendations by CCITT. There are three areas of activity concerned with ISDN matters: data communications, telematic services, and integrated services digital networks (ISDN). Telematic services are user-oriented services that involve information transfer, query, and update.

Work within CCITT is conducted in four-year cycles [BELL84]. Every four years, a Plenary Assembly is held. The work program for the next four years is established at the assembly in the form of questions submitted by the various study groups, based on requests made to the study groups by their members. The assembly assesses the questions, reviews the scope of the study groups, creates new or abolishes existing study groups, and allocates questions to them.

Based on these questions, each study group prepares draft recommendations to be submitted to the next assembly, four years hence. After approval by the assembly, these are published as CCITT Recommendations. If a certain draft recommendation is very urgent, a study group may employ a balloting procedure to gain approval before the end of the four years. In general, however, the process of standardization within CCITT is a slow one.

APPENDIX 5B

1988 CCITT Recommendations on ISDN

Number	Title	Description
I.110	Preamble and General Structure of the I-Series Recommendations	Provides a broad outline of the structure of the I-Series Recommendations and their relationships to other Recommendations.
I.111	Relationship with Other Recommendations Relevant to ISDNs	Lists of other Recommendation relevant to ISDNs and/or used in developing I-Series Recommendations.
I.112	Vocabulary of Terms for ISDNs	Defines terms considered essential to the understanding and application of the principles of an ISDN.
I.113	Vocabulary of Terms for Broadband Aspects of ISDN	Defines terms considered essential to the understanding and application of the principles of B-ISDN.
I.120	Integrated Services Digital Networks	Defines the principles used to develop ISDNs; describes the evolutionary path to be taken.
I.121	Broadband Aspects of ISDN	Serves as a guideline for evolving Recommendations on B-ISDN during the study period 1989–1992. Includes principles, service aspects, and basic architectural model.
I.122	Framework for Providing Additional Packet Mode Bearer Services	Establishes an architectural framework that allows for the description of additional packet mode services. Also provides a general description on interworking requirements between I.122-based services and I.462 (X.31)-based services for PSPDNs.
I.130	Method for the Characterization of Telecommunication Services Supported by an ISDN and Network Capabilities of an ISDN	Defines an attribute method for characterizing ISDN services and capabilities. Methodology to be used to insure compatibility among all ISDN Recommendations.
I.140	Attribute Technique for the Characterization of Telecommunication Services Supported by an ISDN	Introduces the attribute technique, describes attributes, and lists attribute values. Attributes characterize services and network capabilities of

Number	Title	Description
	and Network Capabilities of an ISDN	an ISDN. Serves as a library of all attributes and attribute values used in other I-Series Recommendations.
I.141	ISDN Network Charging Capabilities Attributes	Discusses the method for identifying the network charging capabilities and provides a list of attributes.
I.200	Guidance to the I.200 Series of Recommendations	General introduction to the I.200 Series.
I.210	Principles of Telecommunication Services Supported by an ISDN and the Means to Describe Them	Provides classification and a descriptive method for the telecommunication services to be supported by an ISDN as defined in I.130. Gives a basis for defining network capabilities required by ISDNs.
I.220	Common Dynamic Description of Basic Telecommunication Services	Diagrams provide the dynamic description of basic telecommunication services. Provides terminology for user/network interactions.
I.221	Common Specific Characteristics of Services	Identifies and describes specific characteristics of services that are common to both individual services and form a relationship between services.
I.230	Definition of Bearer Service Categories	Defines a recommended set of bearer service categories that may be supported by an ISDN together with an overall provision.
I.231	Circuit Mode Bearer Service Categories	Identifies eight bearer service categories and defines their attributes, values, and dynamic descriptions.
I.232	Packet Mode Bearer Services Categories	Describes a recommended set of packet mode bearer service categories and their provision in ISDN.
I.240	Definition of Teleservices	Defines a recommended set of teleservices supported by an ISDN.
I.241	Teleservices Supported by an ISDN	Contains service descriptions for telephony, teletex, telefax 4, mixed mode, videotex, and telex.
I.250	Definition of Supplementary Services	Defines supplementary services to be used in association with basic bearer services and with basic teleservices.

Cont.

Number	Title	Description
I.251	Number Identification Supplementary Services	Describes supplementary number identification services.
I.252	Call Offering Supplementary Services	Describes and defines call offering supplementary services.
I.253	Call Completion Supplementary Services	Describes call completion supplementary services.
I.254	Multiparty Supplementary Services	Describes multiparty supplementary services.
I.255	Community of Interest Supplementary Services	Describes Community of Interest Supplementary Services.
I.256	Charging Supplementary Services	Describes Charging Supplementary Services.
I.257	Additional Information Transfer	Describes Additional Information Transfer services.
I.310	ISDN—Network Functional Principles	Outline of the functional principles of the network aspects of ISDNs.
I.320	ISDN Protocol Reference Model	Describes the reference model used to model the information flow within ISDN.
I.324	ISDN Network Architecture	Describes the components and capabilities of the basic architectural model of an ISDN.
I.325	Reference Configurations for ISDN Connection Types	Describes the development of reference configurations for ISDN connection types and what form reference configurations should take. Gives specific reference configurations for 64-kbps, packet, and broadband classes.
I.326	Reference Configurations for Relative Network Resource Requirements	Evaluates relative network resource requirements. Describes minimum requirements for international transit connection elements.
I.330	ISDN Numbering and Addressing Principles	Provides the concepts, principles, and requirements of the ISDN numbering plan.
I.331	Number Plan for the ISDN Era	The ISDN numbering plan and addressing principles.
I.332	Numbering Principles for Interworking Between	Represents a framework by which progress on numbering plans inter-

Number	Title	Description
	ISDNs and Dedicated Networks with Different Numbering Plans	working in Study Groups may be coordinated.
I.333	Terminal Selection in ISDN	Defines terminal selection and outlines selection procedures and responsibilities.
I.334	Principles Relating ISDN Numbers/Subaddresses to the OSI Reference Model Network Layer Addresses	Specifies concepts and terminology relating ISDN numbers and subaddresses to one another and to OSI reference model network layer addresses.
I.335	ISDN Routing Principles	Describes basic routing principles defining the relationship between ISDN telecommunication services and ISDN network capabilities.
I.340	ISDN Connection Types	Describes the set of connection types to be used to support ISDN services.
I.350	General Aspects of Quality of Service and Network Performance in Digital Networks, Including ISDN	Defines, describes, and states purpose of quality of service and network performance and how their concepts are applied in digital networks, including ISDN.
I.351	Recommendations in Other Series Concerning Network Performance Objectives That Apply at Reference Point T of an ISDN	Simply a reference to G.821 and G.822.
I.352	Network Performance Objectives for Connection Processing Delays in an ISDN	Provides network performance objectives and values for connection processing delays that can be used as design objectives in network planning and system design.
I.410	General Aspects and Principles Relating to ISDN User-Network Interfaces	Provides the general aspects and principles to be used in defining the user-network interfaces of ISDNs. Elaborates the concept of having a limited set of such interfaces.
I.411	ISDN User-Network Interfaces—Reference Configurations	Defines the various reference configurations to be found at the ISDN user-network interface.

Cont.

Number	Title	Description
I.412	ISDN User-Network Interfaces—Interface Structures and Access Capabilities	Defines limited set of channel types and interface structures for ISDN.
I.420	Basic User-Network Interface	Simply a list of I.400 Series Recommendations that specify the basic user-network interface.
I.421	Primary Rate User-Network Interface	Simply a list of I.400 Series Recommendations that specify the primary user-network interface.
I.430	Basic User-Network Interface—Layer 1 Specification	Defines the layer 1 characteristics of the basic user-network interface to be applied at the S or T reference points.
I.431	Primary Rate User-Network Interface—Layer 1 Specification	Defines the layer 1 characteristics of the primary user-network interface to be applied at the S or T reference points.
I.440	ISDN User-Network Interface Data Link Layer—General Aspects	A cross-reference to Q.920, which provides a service definition of the ISDN LAP-D data link layer.
I.441	ISDN User-Network Interface Data Link Layer Specification	A cross-reference to Q.921, which provides a specification of the LAP-D protocol.
I.450	ISDN User-Network Interface Layer 3—General Aspects	A cross-reference to Q.930, which provides a definition of the ISDN layer 3 signaling service.
I.451	ISDN User-Network Interface Layer 3 Specification for Basic Call Control	A cross-reference to Q.931, which provides a specification of the ISDN layer 3 user-network signaling protocol.
I.452	Generic Procedures for the Control of ISDN Supplementary Services	Defines the generic procedures applicable for the control of supplementary services at the user-network interface.
I.460	Multiplexing, Rate Adaptation, and Support of Existing Interfaces	A description of how ISDN will support older terminals by means of rate adaptation. Defines methods for multiplexing multiple lower-rate information streams onto a 64-kbps channel.
I.461	Support of X.21-, X.21 *bis*-, and X.20 *bis*-Based DTEs by an ISDN	Covers the connection of X.21, X.21 *bis*, and X.20 *bis* terminals to ISDN operating in accordance with cir-

Number	Title	Description
		cuit-switched or leased circuit services.
I.462	Support of Packet Mode Terminal Equipment By an ISDN	Defines the aspects of the packet-mode services provided to ISDN users in accordance with ISDN bearer services.
I.463	Support of DTEs with V-Series Type Interfaces By an ISDN	A description of the functions needed to support synchronous V-series terminals on an ISDN.
I.464	Multiplexing, Rate Adaptation, and Support of Existing Interfaces for Restricted 64 kbps Transfer Capability	A description of the method of supporting a 56-kbps rate on an ISDN.
I.465	Support By an ISDN of DTEs with V-Series Type Interfaces with Provisions for Statistical Multiplexing	A cross-reference to V.120, which covers the connection to ISDN of terminals with interfaces for V-series modems.
I.470	Relationship of Terminal Functions to ISDN	Provides direction to the potential functional requirements that may be necessary for any specific terminal to be compatible with ISDN.
I.500	General Structure of ISDN Interworking Recommendations	Explains the organization of the I.500 series of Recommendations.
I.510	Definitions and General Principles of ISDN Interworking	Establishes the definition and general principles for interworking between ISDNs, between ISDNs and other networks, and internal to an ISDN.
I.511	ISDN-to-ISDN Layer 1 Internetwork Interface	Defines the layer 1 aspects of the ISDN interworking, including reference configurations and interworking functions.
I.515	Parameter Exchange for ISDN Interworking	Provides parameter exchange principles and functional descriptions for ISDN interworking.
I.520	General Arrangements for Network Interworking Between ISDNs	Identifies the general arrangements for ISDN-ISDN interworking and defines the functions and other requirements for the ISDN-ISDN interface.

Cont.

Number	Title	Description
I.530	Network Interworking Between an ISDN and a PSTN	Identifies the interworking functions and requirements to support interworking between an ISDN and a PSTN.
I.540	General Arrangements for Interworking Between CSPDNs and ISDNs for the Provision of Data Transmission	Describes the general arrangements for interworking between CSPDNs and ISDNs.
I.550	General Arrangements for Interworking Between PSPDNs and ISDNs for the Provision of Data Transmission	Describes the general arrangements for interworking between PSPDNs and ISDNs.
I.560	Requirements to Be Met in Providing the Telex Service Within the ISDN	Outlines configuration models for the integration of the telex service into ISDN.
I.601	General Maintenance Principles of ISDN Subscriber Access and Subscriber Installation	Outlines general aspects and principles relating to reference configuration and general architecture.
I.602	Application of Maintenance Principles to ISDN Subscriber Installation	Presents the possible elementary functions for the maintenance of the subscriber installation.
I.603	Application of Maintenance Principles to ISDN Basic Accesses	Covers maintenance part of the ISDN subscriber basic access, controlled by the network.
I.604	Application of Maintenance Principles to ISDN Primary Rate Accesses	Describes the minimum functions required to maintain the subscriber primary access.
I.605	Application of Maintenance Principles to Static Multiplexed ISDN Basic Accesses	Covers the maintanence of the static multiplexed basic rate access and describes the operations and maintenance aspects of the V_4 interface defined in Q.512.

APPENDIX 5C
1990 CCITT Interim Recommendations on ISDN

Number	Title	Description
I.2xy	ISDN Frame Mode Bearer Services	Describes the frame mode bearer services for the order-preserving bi-directional transfer of LAP-D frames from one S or T reference point to another. The two services are frame-relay bearer service and frame-switching bearer services.
I.320	ISDN Protocol Reference Model	Revised version of I.320, to include a discussion of protocol blocks.
I.324	ISDN Network Architecture	Revised version of I.324, to include the aspects of private networks.
I.325	Reference Configurations for ISDN Connection Types	Revised version of I.325, to include the aspects of private networks and definitions of network fabric, por-tions, and boundaries.
I.333	Terminal Selection in ISDN	Revised version.
I.351	Recommendations in Other Series Concerning Net-work Performance Objec-tives That Apply at Refer-ence Point T of an ISDN	This revised recommendation now describes the relationships among the 14 existing or planned ISDN performance-related recommenda-tions.
I.352	Network Performance Ob-jectives for Connection Processing Delays in an ISDN	Revised version of I.352, to include consideration of national and inter-national network fabrics.
I.35a	Availability Performance for 64 kbps ISDN Connection Types	Specifies service availability perfor-mance parameters for circuit-mode and packet-mode ISDN bearer ser-vices.
I.35e	Reference Events for Defin-ing ISDN Performance Pa-rameters	Defines the performance model, consistent with I.325, to be used in the ISDN performance description.
I.35p	Network Performance Ob-jectives for Packet-Mode Communication in an ISDN	Defines speed, accuracy, and de-pendability performance parameters and performance objectives for packet-mode information transfer in an ISDN.

Cont.

Number	Title	Description
I.3xx	Congestion Management for the Frame-Relaying Bearer Service	Describes user-plane congestion management strategy and mechanisms for frame-relaying bearer service. It covers both network and end-user mechanisms and responsibilities to avoid or recover from periods of congestion.
I.464	Multiplexing, Rate Adaptation, and Support of Existing Interfaces for Restricted 64 kbps Transfer Capability	Adds an appendix to I.464 that describes an HDLC-based approach to rate adaptation.
I.515	Parameter Exchange for ISDN Interworking	Addition to I.515 that describes optional out-of-band protocol selection procedures for use by multiprotocol terminal adaptors.
I.520	General Arrangements for Network Interworking Between ISDNs	Minor revision to Table 4 of I.520.
I.530	Network Interworking Between an ISDN and a PSTN	Amendments to I.530 to include packet-mode interworking and the special requirements for the 7-kHz audio bearer service.
I.5xz	FMBS Interworking	Provides the guidelines and functional requirements across interfaces for interworking between the two frame mode bearer services and other services.

CHAPTER 6

ISDN
Services

The ISDN will provide a variety of services, supporting existing voice and data applications as well as providing for applications now being developed. In this chapter, we begin by looking at the service capabilities defined in the CCITT ISDN recommendations. We will find that these are somewhat general in nature and will focus on network capabilities needed to support anticipated user requirements. The remainder of the chapter is devoted to a look at three of the most important telecommunications services that ISDN will need to support: digital facsimile, teletex, and electronic mail. We will also examine some of the protocol implications of these services.

6.1

SERVICE CAPABILITIES

The I.200 series of CCITT recommendations, referred to as *service capabilities*, provides a classification and method of description of the telecommunication services supported by ISDN. These services encompass existing services and define additional ones. The purpose of the recommendations is to provide a unifying framework for viewing these services and to set forth the user requirements for ISDN. The series, however, does not impose implementation or configuration guidelines. That is, the way in which the service is to be provided is left open. For

199

example, the description of a teletex service does not presuppose which organization (user, private network, public network, information service provider, etc.) provides the various elements that make up a complete teletex service.

Three types of services are defined by CCITT: bearer services, teleservices, and supplementary services. **Bearer services** provide the means to convey information (speech, data, video, etc.) between users in real time and without alteration of the content of the message. These services correspond to the lower three layers of the OSI model. **Teleservices** combine the transportation function with the information-processing function. They employ bearer services to transport data and, in addition, provide a set of higher-layer functions. These higher-layer functions correspond to OSI layers 4 through 7. Whereas bearer services define requirements for, and are provided by, network functions, teleservices include terminal as well as network capabilities. Examples of teleservices are telephony, teletex, videotex, and message handling. Both bearer services and teleservices may be enhanced by **supplementary services.** A supplementary service is one that may be used in conjunction with one or more of the bearer or teleservices. It cannot be used alone. An example is reverse charging. This can be used to reverse charges on a circuit-switched call or a packet-switched virtual call. Reverse charging can also be used with a teleservice, such as the message-handling service, to create a "collect message."

In each of these three categories (bearer, teleservice, supplementary), there are a number of specific services defined by CCITT. To characterize and differentiate these various services, a collection of **attributes** has been defined. Each service is characterized by specific values assigned to each descriptive attribute. This method makes it easy to precisely define a service and to compare different services.

Table 6.1 lists the attributes that have so far been defined by CCITT (in I.140). Table 6.2 provides a brief definition together with the values that they can take on. Most of these terms are self-explanatory; some of the others will be discussed later in this section, in the context of a specific service. One additional comment may be useful. A distinction is made between a communication and a connection. These terms are defined as follows in I.112:

Communication: The transfer of information according to agreed conventions.

Connection: A concatenation of transmission channels or telecommunication circuits, switching, and other functional units set up to provide for the transfer of signals between two or more points in a telecommunication network, to support a single communication.

TABLE 6.1 Service and Network Attributes

Service Attributes	Network Attributes
Bearer Services	**Connection Types**
1 Information transfer mode	1 Information transfer mode
2 Information transfer rate	2 Information transfer rate
3 Information transfer capability	3 Information transfer susceptance
4 Structure	4 Establishment of connection
5 Establishment of communication	5 Symmetry
6 Symmetry	6 Connection configuration
7 Communication configuration	7 Structure
8 Access channel and rate	8 Channel (rate)
9-1 Signaling access protocol layer 1	9 Connection control protocol
9-2 Signaling access protocol layer 2	10 Information transfer coding/
9-3 Signaling access protocol layer 3	protocol
9-4 Information access protocol layer 1	11 Network performance
9-5 Information access protocol layer 2	12 Network interworking
9-6 Information access protocol layer 3	13 Operations and management
10 Supplementary services provided	**Connection Elements**
11 Quality of service	1 through 13, as above
12 Interworking possibilities	
13 Operational and commercial	
Teleservices	
1 through 9-6, as above	
10 Type of user information	
11 Layer 4 protocol	
12 Layer 5 protocol	
13 Layer 6 protocol	
14 Layer 7 protocol	
15 Supplementary services provided	
16 Quality of service	
17 Interworking possibilities	
18 Operational and commercial	

Thus, a communication is a user-oriented concept, and a connection is a network-oriented concept. Those attributes that refer to communication are used to characterize ISDN service, while those attributes that refer to connections are used to characterize ISDN connections. This latter topic will be discussed in the next chapter.

In addition to service attributes, I.140 defines associated network attributes. These attributes relate to connections. For a given communication over a given connection, the connection attributes must be such as to support the attributes of the communication.

TABLE 6.2   Attributes and Their Values

Attribute	Definition	Values
Information transfer mode	Mode for transferring user information	Circuit, packet
Information transfer rate	Bit rate (circuit mode) or throughput (packet mode) between two access points	Appropriate bit rate or throughput
Information transfer capability	Used to characterize the transfer of different types of information through ISDN	Unrestricted digital information: sequence of bits with specified bit rate without alteration Speech: digitized speech with a specific encoding rule 3.1-kHz audio: digitized audio with a bandwidth of 3.1 kHz with a specific encoding rule 7-kHz audio: as above, for 7 kHz 15-kHz audio: as above, for 15 kHz Video: digitized video with a specific encoding rule
Structure	Capability to deliver information retaining data integrity	8 kHz integrity: all bits transmitted in a single 125-µsec interval are delivered in a corresponding 125-µsec interval Service data unit integrity: all bits submitted as a block are delivered in a corresponding block Time-slot sequence integrity: information is delivered in the same order as sent Restricted differential time delay: information is delivered within 50 ms Unstructured: no structure is implied
Establishment of communication	Mode of establishing and releasing a communication	Demand: in response to user request Reserved: connection and release times reserved via user request Permanent: preestablished connection

Symmetry	Relationship of information flow between two or more access or reference points	Unidirectional: only one direction Bidirectional symmetric: flow characteristics are the same in both directions Bidirectional asymmetric: flow characteristics may differ in the two directions
Communication configuration	Spatial arrangement for transferring information between two or more access points	Point-to-point: only two access points Multipoint: more than two access points Broadcast: for further study
Access channel and rate	Channels and rates used to transfer user and/or signaling information	Name of channel and corresponding bit rate
Signaling access protocol layers 1–3	Protocols on the signaling channel	Appropriate protocols
Information access protocol layers 1–3	Protocols on the information transfer channel	Appropriate protocols
Supplementary services provided	Supplementary services associated with a given telecommunications service	Appropriate services
Quality of service	A group of specific subattributes, e.g., service reliability	For further study
Interworking possibilities	To be defined	
Operational and commercial	To be defined	
Type of user information	Type of user information	Speech, sound, text, facsimile, text-facsimile, videotex, video, text-interactive

Cont.

TABLE 6.2   Attributes and Their Values (*continued*)

Attribute	Definition	Values
Layers 4–7 protocol	Protocols on the information transfer channel	Appropriate protocols
Information transfer susceptance	Identifies equipment that may restrict types of information	Speech-processing equipment, echo suppression equipment, multi-satellite hops
Establishment of connection	Mode of establishment and release of a connection that supports a communication	Demand: set up on demand Semipermanent: provided for a definite period, pass through a switched network Permanent: preestablished connection
Connection configuration	Spatial arrangement for transferring information on a connection	Appropriate topology and timing of connection establishment and release
Network performance	Network performance that relates to a connection	Error and slip performance
Network interworking	To be defined	
Operation and management	To be defined	

Bearer Services

So far, a total of 11 different bearer services have been defined by ISDN; these are listed in Table 6.3; Table 6.4 is a list of the possible values for service attributes for these bearer services.

The first four defined services provide for the capability of 64-kbps data transfer. This data rate is the fundamental building block of ISDN services. The first of these, known as **64-kbps unrestricted, 8 kHz structured,** is the most general-purpose service at that data rate. The term *unrestricted* means that the information is transferred without alteration; this is also known as a transparent bearer service. Users may employ this service for any application that requires a data rate of 64 kbps. Figure 6.1 [SCAC86] illustrates two possible applications. In the first, the user is connecting digital PBX systems and using them to transport voice digitized at 32 kbps. Although 64 kbps in the ISDN standard data rate for digitized voice, sophisticated encoding algorithms make high-quality voice transmission possible at 32 kbps. Thus, the user is saving on data transmission capacity by employing a private encoding algorithm. However, the basic unit of switching within ISDN is 64 kbps; consequently, the two 32-kbps voice channels must be connected to the same pair of subscribers. That is, it is not possible to use this service to set up two 32-kbps circuits going to two different destinations. Figure 6.1b shows another use of this service. In this case, the

TABLE 6.3 ISDN Bearer Services (I.230)

Circuit-mode Bearer Services	Packet-mode Bearer Services
• 64-kbps unrestricted, 8-kHz structured • 64-kbps, 8-kHz structured, usable for speech information transfer • 64-kbps, 8-kHz structured, usable for 3.1-kHz audio information transfer • Alternate speech/unrestricted 64-kbps, 8-kHz structured • 2 × 64 kbps unrestricted, 8-kHz structured • 384-kbps unrestricted, 8-kHz structured • 1536-kbps unrestricted, 8-kHz structured • 1920-kbps unrestricted, 8-kHz structured	• Virtual call and permanent virtual circuit • Connectionless (further study) • User signaling (further study)

TABLE 6.4 Values for Each Bearer Service Attribute

Attributes[a]	Possible Values of Attributes					
Information transfer attributes						
1. Information transfer mode	Circuit					Packet
2. Information transfer rate	Bit rate (kbit/s): 64, 2 × 64, 384, 1536, 1920, Other values for further study					Throughput: Options for further study, Others for further study
3. Information transfer capability	Unrestricted digital information	Speech	3.1-kHz audio	7-kHz audio	15-kHz audio	Video
4. Structure	8-kHz integrity	Service data unit integrity[b]	Unstructured	TSSI[c]	RDTD[d]	
5. Establishment of communication[e]	Demand	Reserved	Permanent			
6. Symmetry	Unidirectional	Bidirectional symmetric	Bidirectional asymmetric			
7. Communication configuration	Point-to-point	Multipoint	Broadcast[f]			
Access attributes						
8. Access channel and rate	D (16)	D (64)	B	H₀	H₁₁	H₁₂, Others for further study
9.1. Signaling access protocol layer 1	Rec. I.430/Rec. I.431	Rec. I.461	Rec. I.462	Rec. I.463	(Rec. V.120) Rec. I.465	Others for further study
9.2. Signaling access protocol layer 2	Rec. I.440/Rec. I.441	Rec. I.462	Rec. X.25			Others for further study

9.3. Signaling access protocol layer 3	Rec. I.450/ Rec. I.451		Rec. I.461	Rec. I.462	Rec. X.25	Rec. I.463			Others for further study
9.4. Information access protocol layer 1	Rec. I.430/ Rec. I.431	Rec. I.460[g]	Rec. I.461	Rec. I.462	Rec. I.463	(Rec. V.120) Rec. I.465	Rec. G.711	Rec. G.722	Others for further study
9.5. Information access protocol layer 2	HDLC LAPB	I.440/ I.441	Rec. X.25	Rec. I.462	Rec. I.462	Others for further study			
9.6. Information access protocol layer 3[h]	T.70-3		Rec. X.25	Rec. I.462	Rec. I.462	Others for further study			
General attributes 10. Supplementary services provided 11. Quality of service 12. Interworking possibilities 13. Operational and commercial aspects	Under study								

[a] The attributes are intended to be independent of each other.
[b] The need for a "data sequence integrity" attribute is for further study.
[c] Time slot sequence integrity (TSSI).
[d] Restricted differential time delay (RDTD).
[e] A definition of the establishment of communication is given in Recommendation I.140.
[f] The characterization of the information transfer configuration attribute "broadcast" is for further study.
[g] The inclusion of Recommendation I.460 implies the support of non-ISDN CCITT standardized services (e.g., at X.1 rate). The necessary user-network signaling is provided in Recommendation I.451.
[h] The use of Recommendation I.451 as an information access protocol is for further study.

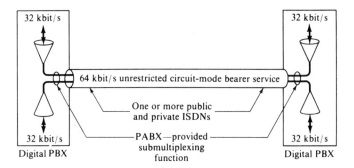

(a) Multiplexed 32-kbps voice channels

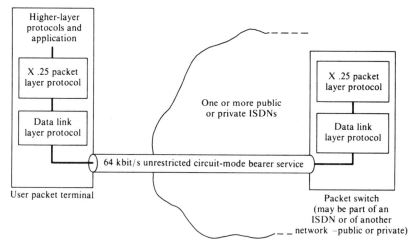

(b) Packet-switching network access

FIGURE 6.1 Example Uses of the 64-kbps, 8 kHz Structured, Unrestricted Service [SCAC86]

64-kbps circuit is used to connect a host system to a non-ISDN packet-switched network.

The term *8 kHz structured* means that, in addition to bit transmission, a structure is transferred between customers. When one user transmits information to another user, the transmission is accompanied by 8-kHz timing information, which delimits the data in 8-bit units. This 8-kHz structural integrity implies that octets are preserved within the corresponding time interval; that is, an octet is never split across a time-interval boundary. This applies in particular to speech, which requires the 8-kHz structure in addition to the 64-kbps information flow so as to be able to recognize the octets, which are formed by speech encoding, at the receiving side. In text transmission, character boundaries are preserved. Thus, there is no need for the user to provide an in-band, user-to-user synchronization scheme.

The service referred to as **64-kbps, 8 kHz structured, usable for speech information transfer** defines a specific structure for the digital signal, namely pulse-code modulation (PCM) as defined in CCITT Recommendation G.711. Because the network may assume that the encoded data are speech, it may use processing techniques appropriate for speech, such as analog transmission, echo cancellation, and low bit-rate voice encoding. Because these transformations may not be precisely reversible, bit integrity is not guaranteed. However, the received signal should produce a high-quality reproduction of the transmitted voice signal. In other respects, this service is the same as the unrestricted service. The restriction to speech allows the use of processing techniques in the network that may optimize the transmission. Furthermore, the network may perform conversions between digital encoding laws. For example, the G.711 standard specifies two versions of the PCM algorithm, μ-law and A-law. The former is used in North America and Japan; the latter is used in the rest of the world. Thus the voice signal on a connection that crosses these geographic boundaries is automatically converted.

The service referred to as **64-kbps, 8 kHz structured, usable for 3.1-kHz audio information transfer** assumes that digitized audio information is being transmitted. This permits routing over analog circuits using codecs, as in the previous service. However, other forms of processing peculiar to speech signals are prohibited. For example, a form of multiplexing known as time-assigned speech interpolation (TASI) exploits the bursty character of speech to multiplex speech channels: Thirty speech calls can be squeezed into a T1 24-channel system with no noticeable degradation. However, this technique is not appropriate for nonspeech signals that happen to occupy the voice frequency band, such as digital data that have been passed through a voice-grade modem.

The next service, **alternate speech/64-kbps unrestricted,** involves the alternate transfer of speech and unrestricted data. There is a requirement for a short (as yet undefined) changeover time when the user requests a change from one service to the alternate service.

The next circuit-mode bearer service is **2 × 64 kbps, 8-kHz structured, unrestricted.** This service provides for the use of two 64-kbps channels that bear some relationship to each other. The details of this service remain to be worked out.

The next three services provide for high-speed digital transfer, at rates of **384, 1536, and 1920 kbps.** These services could be used for a variety of applications, including video, private networking between PBXs, and links between other networks.

The remaining services are packet-switching types of services. The

virtual call and permanent virtual circuit service is the traditional packet-network interface allowing both types of virtual circuits; the user attaches to ISDN in the same manner as attaching to a packet-switched network, using X.25. The **connectionless** service provides for a datagram style of packet service. This service might be provided to support applications such as telemetry, alarm, and transaction services, which do not need the connection-oriented service. The access protocol would differ from X.25 and is a subject for further study. The final packet-mode bearer service, **user signaling,** provides for user-to-user control signaling in a packetized manner. The protocol for this signaling is a subject for further study.

More bearer services, especially at higher data rates, will be defined in the future. However, this mix of services so far defined provides the capability of meeting a wide variety of user requirements and is sufficient for initial implementations of ISDN.

Teleservices

The area of teleservices in ISDN is significantly less well developed than that of bearer services. Teleservices are intended to cover a wide variety of user applications over ISDN. The list of services so far defined in I.241 is shown in Box 6.1. In general, they cover applications that are in the nature of terminal-service applications, most of which have been defined by CCITT. This can be contrasted with what might be considered computer-to-computer applications. These latter applications have mostly been defined by ISO and include file transfer and document architecture.

Table 6.5 is a list of the possible values for service attributes for the teleservices. The lower-layer (OSI layers I–3) attributes are essentially the same as for the bearer services. This is because a teleservice relies on a bearer service for information transport across the ISDN. The upper-layer attributes form a protocol architecture that maps into OSI layers 4 through 7; this topic is addressed in the next section.

One service conspicuously absent from Box 6.1 is the message-handling service (MHS), defined by the X.400 series of recommendations. This is one of the most important and widely available of the CCITT-defined teleservices and will be included in future revisions to I.240. We examine this service later in this chapter. Two other important services are also examined: facsimile and teletex.

Supplementary Services

As was mentioned, supplementary services are always associated with a bearer service or teleservice. Each service is defined, and could be implemented, in a manner independent from the bearer services and

ISDN Teleservices

TELEPHONY

Provides 3.1-kHz speech communication. The digital signal follows the agreed encoding laws for speech, and the network may use digital signal processing techniques, such as echo cancellation. User information is provided over a B-channel; signaling is provided over the D-channel.

TELETEX

Provides end-to-end text communication using standardized character sets, presentation formats, and communication protocols. The high-layer attributes are based on those of the CCITT standardized teletex service (F.200). User information is provided over a B-channel; signaling is provided over the D-channel.

TELEFAX

Provides end-to-end facsimile communication using standardized picture coding, resolution, and communication protocols. The high-layer attributes are based on the facsimile Group 4 Recommendations of CCITT. User information is provided over a B-channel; signaling is provided over the D-channel.

MIXED MODE

Provides combined text and facsimile communication (mixed mode) for end-to-end transfer of documents containing mixed information of text and fixed images. The high-layer attributes are based on the CCITT Recommendation for the teletex service and facsimile Group 4, mixed mode (F.200, Annex C). User information is provided over a B-channel; signaling is provided over the D-channel.

VIDEOTEX

The videotex service in the ISDN is an enhancement of the existing videotex service with retrieval and mailbox functions for text (alpha) and graphic (mosaic, geometric, photographic) information.

TELEX

This service provides interactive text communication. The digital signal follows the internationally agreed Recommendations for telex above the ISDN physical layer. User information is transferred over circuit- or packet-mode bearer channels; signaling is provided over the D-channel.

TABLE 6.5 Possible Values for Each Teleservice Attribute

Attributes[a]	Possible Values of Attributes				
Information transfer attributes					
1. Information transfer mode	Circuit				Packet
2. Information transfer rate	Bit rate (kbit/s)				Throughput
	64	Other values for further study			Options for further study
3. Information transfer capability	Unrestricted digital information	Speech	3.1-kHz audio	7-kHz audio	Others for further study
4. Structure	8-kHz integrity	Service data unit integrity	Unstructured		Others for further study
5. Establishment of communication[b]	Demand	Reserved	Permanent		
6. Symmetry	Unidirectional	Bidirectional symmetric	Bidirectional asymmetric		
7. Communication configuration	Point-to-point	Multipoint	Broadcast[c]		
Access attributes					
8. Access channel and rate	D (16)	D (64)	B		Others for further study

	Speech (telephony)	Sound	Text (Teletex)	Fascimile (Telefax 4)	Text-facsimile (Mixed mode)	Videotex	Video	Text interactive (Telex)	Other
9.1. Signaling access protocol layer 1	Rec. I.430/Rec. I.431	Rec. I.461	Rec. I.462	Rec. I.463	Rec. I.465 (Rec. V.120)	Others for further study			
9.2. Signaling access protocol layer 2	Rec. I.440/Rec. I.441		Rec. I.462	Rec. X.25	Others for further study				
9.3. Signaling access protocol layer 3	Rec. I.450/Rec. I.451		Rec. I.461	Rec. I.462	Rec. X.25	Rec. I.463	Others for further study		
9.4. Information access protocol layer 1	Rec. I.430/Rec. I.431	Rec. I.460	Rec. I.461 (Rec. X.30)	Rec. I.462 (Rec. X.31)	Rec. I.463 (Rec. V.110)	Rec. I.465 (Rec. V.120)	Rec. G.711	Others for further study	
9.5. Information access protocol layer 2	HDLC LAPB		Rec. I.440/Rec. I.441	Rec. X.75 SLP	Rec. X.25 LAPB	Others for further study			
9.6. Information access protocol layer 3	ISO 8208[d] (Rec. X.25 PLP)			Rec. X.25 PLP		Others for further study			
10. Type of user information	Speech (telephony)	Sound	Text (Teletex)	Fascimile (Telefax 4)	Text-facsimile (Mixed mode)	Videotex	Video	Text interactive (Telex)	Other
11. Layer 4 protocol	Rec. X.224		Rec. T.70			Others for further study			
12. Layer 5 protocol	Rec. X.225		Rec. T.62			Others for further study			

Cont.

TABLE 6.5 Possible Values for Each Teleservice Attribute (*continued*)

Attributes[a]	Possible Values of Attributes				
13. Layer 6 protocol	T.400-Series	Rec. G.711	Rec. T.61	Rec. T.6	Others for further study
Resolution[e,f]	200 ppi	240 ppi	300 ppi	400 ppi	Others for further study
Graphic mode[f]	Alpha-mosaic	Geometric	Photographic		Others for further study
14. Layer 7 protocol	Rec. T.60		T.500-Series		Others for further study
General attributes	Under study				

SLP Single-link protocol
PLP Packet-layer protocol
ppi Picture elements per inch

[a] The attributes are intended to be independent of each other.
[b] A definition of the establishment of communication is given in Recommendation I.140.
[c] The characterization of the information transfer configuration attribute "broadcast" is for further study.
[d] For those teleservices that use circuit-mode bearer capability X.25 PLP, description is as per ISO 8208.
[e] These attribute values are mentioned in order to give an example of a specific presentation description of characteristics such as coding of the user information, resolution, and graphic mode. Attribute values for other presentation characteristics are for further study.
[f] If applicable.

teleservices with which it might be used. This allows each supplementary service to be used in a uniform fashion, regardless of the bearer service or teleservice that it supports. For example, the methods of requesting and authorizing reverse charging should be the same for a circuit-switched call or an MHS message.

Box 6.2 lists the supplementary services that have been defined so far. All of these originated in the telephone world. However, most of them can also be applied to packet-mode bearer services and to some teleservices. Table 6.6 indicates the relationship between supplementary services and the bearer and teleservices to which they apply.

6.2
Teleservice Protocol Architecture

So far, we have discussed teleservices in general and listed the key teleservices to be supported by ISDN (Box 6.1). In terms of the OSI model, these teleservices have primarily been defined at the presentation and application layers. However, the successful provision of a telecommunication service will require the lower layers as well. To some extent, general-purpose OSI-related standards can be employed to support ISDN teleservices. However, CCITT has found justification for issuing standards for some protocols that are specific to the teleservice requirement.

An overall picture of the protocol architecture for the support of CCITT teleservices is shown in Figure 6.2.

Lower-layer Protocols

Teleservices defined by CCITT are intended for use over a variety of networks. Recommendation T.70 specifies four types of networks:

- *Packet-switched public-data network (PSPDN):* a packet-switched network with the X.25 interface.
- *Circuit-switched public-data network (CSPDN):* a circuit-switched network intended for carrying data, usually with the X.21 interface.
- *Public-switched telephone network (PSTN):* the analog telephone network.
- *ISDN.*

With a **packet-switched public-data network (PSPDN),** the three-level X.25 standard discussed in Section 3.7 is employed. With this type of network, teletex messages and facsimile images are transmitted as a sequence of packets.

BOX 6.2

ISDN Supplementary Services (I.250)

NUMBER IDENTIFICATION

Direct dialing in
Enables a user to call directly to another user on an ISDN-compatible PBX or Centrex, without attendant intervention, or to call a terminal on a passive bus selectively.

Multiple subscriber number
Allows multiple ISDN numbers to be assigned to a single interface (e.g., multiple telephone numbers at the same residence).

Calling line identification presentation
Service offered to the called party that provides the ISDN number of the calling party.

Calling line identification restriction
Service offered to the calling party to restrict presentation of the calling party's ISDN number to the called party.

Connected line identification presentation
Service offered to the calling party that provides the ISDN number of the party to whom the caller is connected.

Connected line identification restriction
Service offered to the connected party to restrict presentation of the connected party's ISDN number to the calling party.

Malicious calls identificaton
For further study.

Subaddressing
For further study.

CALL OFFERING

Call transfer
Enables a user to transfer an established call to a third party. This service is different from the call forwarding service since, in this case, the call to be transferred must have an established end-to-end connection prior to the transfer.

Call forwarding busy
Permits a served user to have the network send incoming calls (or just those associated with a specified basic service) addressed to the served user's ISDN number to another number when this user's line is busy. The served user's originating service is unaffected.

Call forwarding no reply
Permits a served user to have the network send incoming calls (or just those associated with a specified basic service) addressed to

the served user's ISDN number to another number when there is no answer on this user's line. The served user's originating service is unaffected.

Call forwarding unconditional

Permits a served user to have the network send all incoming calls (or just those associated with a specified basic service) addressed to the served user's ISDN number to another number. The served user's originating service is unaffected.

Call deflection

For further study.

Line hunting

Enables incoming calls to a specific ISDN number (or numbers) to be distributed over a group of interfaces or terminals.

CALL COMPLETION

Call waiting

Enables a terminal equipment, which is already active in a communication, to notify its user of an incoming call. The user then has the choice of accepting, rejecting, or ignoring the waiting call.

Call hold

Allows a user to interrupt communications on an existing call and then subsequently reestablish the connection.

Completion of calls to busy subscribers

For further study.

MULTIPARTY

Conference calling

Allows multiple users to simultaneously communicate with one another.

Three-party service

Allows a subscriber to hold an existing call and make a call to a third party. The following arrangements may then be possible: the ability to switch between the two calls, the introduction of a common speech path between the three parties, and the connection of the other two parties.

COMMUNITY OF INTEREST

Closed user group

Allows a group of users to intercommunicate only among themselves or, as required, one or more users may be provided with incoming/outgoing access to users outside the group.

Private numbering plan

For further study.

Cont.

BOX 6.2 continued

CHARGING

Credit card calling
   For further study.
Advice of charge
   Provides the user paying for a call with usage-based charging in-formation. This service may be provided at call setup time, during the call, and/or at the completion of the call.
Reserve charging
   For further study.

ADDITIONAL INFORMATION TRANSFER

User-to-user signaling
   Allows an ISDN user to send/receive a limited amount of infor-mation to/from another ISDN user over the signaling channel in association with a call to the other ISDN user.

In the **circuit-switched public-data network (CSPDN),** the user ob-tains a high-speed digital data circuit between the two user endpoints. Two phases of operation need to be distinguished:

- *Call establishment phase:* The three-level X.21 standard is employed. This is an interface protocol between the subscriber device and the network, used to set up a connection and request network facilities (e.g., reverse charging).
- *Data transfer phase:* Once a circuit is set up between two subscribers, data are passed through the network in a transparent fashion. In effect, the circuit is an OSI layer 1 connection, and layers 2 and above are end-to-end protocols between users. The link layer is the level-2 single-link protocol of the X.75 standard, which in essence is LAPB (almost identical to the X.25 LAPB). The network layer is not really needed since we have, in effect, a direct connection. Accordingly, a very minimal network layer is defined in T.70, which employs a two-octet packet header. The header contains a length indicator and a packet-type identifier (only one type has been de-fined). No protocol functions are performed at this level in the current standard.

The third option specified in T.70 is a **public-switched telephone network (PSTN),** using an analog link. Thus, the physical layer is specified as a modem interface; either a half-duplex or full-duplex mo-dem may be used. If the link is full-duplex, then the data link layer is

TABLE 6.6 Association of Supplementary Services to Basic Bearer Services and to Basic Teleservices Supported by ISDN

Supplementary Services	Circuit-mode Bearer Services						Teleservices				
	64 kbit/s unrestricted demand	64 kbit/s speech demand	64 kbit/s, 3.1 kHz audio demand	64kbit/s unrestricted permanent	64 kbit/s, 3.1 kHz audio permanent	1920 kbit/s unrestricted permanent	Telephony	Teletex	Telefax 4	Videotex	Mixed mode
Direct dialing in	X	X	X				X	X	X	X	X
Multiple subscriber number	X	X	X				X	X	X	X	X
Calling line identification presentation	X	X	X	b	b	b	X	X	X	X	X
Calling line identification restriction	X	X	X	b	b	b	X	X	X	X	X
Connected line identification presentation	X	X	X	b	b	b	X	X	X	X	X
Connected line identification restriction	X	X	X	b	b	b	X	X	X	X	X
Malicious calls identification[a]											
Subaddressing[a]											
Call transfer	X	X	X				X				
Call forwarding busy	X	X	X				X				
Call forwarding no reply	X	X	X				X			X	

Cont.

TABLE 6.6   Association of Supplementary Services to Basic Bearer Services and to Basic Teleservices Supported by ISDN (continued)

Supplementary Services	Circuit-mode Bearer Services						Teleservices				
	64 kbit/s unrestricted demand	64 kbit/s speech demand	64 kbit/s, 3.1 kHz audio demand	64kbit/s unrestricted permanent	64 kbit/s, 3.1 kHz audio permanent	1920 kbit/s unrestricted permanent	Telephony	Teletex	Telefax 4	Videotex	Mixed mode
Call forwarding unconditional	X	X	X				X			X	
Call deflection[a]											
Line hunting	X	X	X				X				
Call waiting	X	X	X				X				
Call hold	X	X	X				X				
Completion of calls to busy subscribers[a]											
Conference calling	X	X	X				X				
Three-party service	X	X	X				X				
Closed user group	X	X	X				X	X	X	X	X
Private number-ing plan[a]											
Credit card calling[a]											
Advice of charge	X	X	X				X	X	X	X	X
Reserve charging[a]				b	b	b					
User-to-user signaling	X	X	X				X	X	X	X	X

X denotes applications of supplementary services identified within each supplementary service description; other associations are for further study.
[a] This supplementary service is not yet included in the descriptions.
[b] Further study is required on the association of this supplementary service to this circuit-mode bearer service.

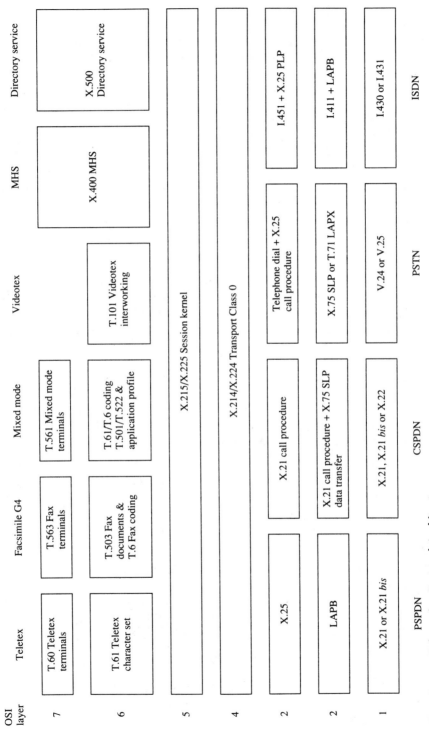

FIGURE 6.2 Teleservice Protocol Architecture

LAP-B, as defined in X.75. If the link is half-duplex, then LAP-X is used. LAP-X is an extension of LAP-B that enforces a half-duplex discipline. At the network layer, a two-stage selection process applies. First, the calling user establishes a physical-level circuit with the called user employing normal telephone procedures. Second, the X.25 call-control procedure is used to set up a logical connection between the two users. Strictly speaking, such a logical connection is not needed; however, it is specified to facilitate interworking with packet-switched networks. Once a virtual call is established, the X.25 data transfer capability is used.

In addition to these three types of networks, of course, teleservices will be supported over ISDN. Table 6.5 indicates the protocols that are involved in that context.

Transport and Session Layers

For the transport and session layers, CCITT has specified standards that are compatible with, and subsets of, more general-purpose OSI-related standards.[1] The transport-layer protocol is specified in T.70, and the session-layer standard, referred to as "Control Procedures for Teletex and Group 4 Facsimile Services," is specified in T.62.

The transport layer is specified in terms of a transport service, provided to the session layer, and a transport protocol that implements the transport service. The transport service definition is very similar to the OSI-based standard, issued by CCITT as X.214 (transport service) and X.224 (transport protocol). There are only two differences between the T.70 specification and the X.214 transport service specification:

- The OSI standard includes a service for expedited data, to be delivered as quickly as possible. For the teleservices, this service was not felt to be needed.
- The T.70 standard explicitly defines an optional error-reporting facility. This facility would normally also be present in an OSI service, but it is not specifically defined there.

The transport protocol that implements the transport service is also specified in T.70. This protocol is a subset of the OSI-based protocol defined in X.224. Specifically, the T.70 protocol is the same as the OSI transport protocol Class 0. This is the simplest type of transport protocol defined in X.224/ISO 8073. It assumes a reliable network service, and

---

[1] For a discussion of the transport and session standards referred to in this section, see [STAL90b] or [STAL91a].

transport connections are mapped one-to-one onto network connections. Flow control and error control are based on network-level flow control and error control, and transport connection release is based on the release of the network connection.

The session layer specification in T.62 is also structured in terms of a session service and session protocol. As with the transport layer, it is intended that the T.62 specification be compatible with the OSI-based standards, specifically, X.215 for the session service and X.225 for the session protocol. T.62 specifies the use of the basic activity subset (BAS) of the OSI standards. The key elements of T.62 are that it enforces a two-way alternate (half-duplex) form of interaction and that it provides a checkpointing mechanism by which the sender will retain a copy of any transmitted message or document until assured that it is successfully stored at the receiver.

T.62 defines the session connection and termination procedure and the control over the direction of document transfer. Session connection involves a transfer of reference parameters from document sender to document receiver, which become the source information for the Call Identification Line. These parameters define the document sender's terminal identification, the date and time of call origination, and an optional session identification to uniquely define each session. Session identification is used for session linkage if a document is prematurely terminated and then continued in a later session. Session connection may also include a negotiation between sender and receiver for optional terminal capabilities (e.g., line spacing), for session capabilities (e.g., number of pages, or checkpoints, that may be transmitted without waiting for a checkpoint response), and for optional private facilities. Document transfer direction control permits document transmission from the called terminal to the calling terminal. Session termination includes both normal and abnormal indications.

Upper-layer Protocols

Layer 6, the presentation layer, includes the functions and conventions for the presentation of information, including text and graphics character set, and the format and structure of a document.

Layer 7, the application layer, deals with the specific application or piece of equipment as seen by the user. Aspects include the protocols for the exchange of information and functions for editing and processing message contents for communication. Also at layer 7 are functions for the control of the communication process, such as the type of information, quality requirements, name or address of the communication partner, and authorizations and data protection (encryption).

6.3

FACSIMILE

A significant class of applications that make use of communications networks are those that involve the transmission of documents and messages. The most common techniques transmit character information and are suitable for transmitting documents consisting solely of text. Teletex and electronic mail, both discussed later in this chapter, fall into this category. Another technique is to electronically transmit a visual image of the original. A bit-map representation is created of the image, which can include text, graphics, or pictures. This is the approach taken with facsimile.

Facsimile has a number of advantages over other forms of document or message transmission. In addition to printed text, facsimile can transmit pictures, graphs, drawings, handwritten notes, and anything else that can be put on paper. Also, facsimile saves preparation time because information does not have to be entered into a message system through a keyboard. The paper itself is scanned for patterns of light and dark, which are transmitted to the receiving end.

Although facsimile was developed in 1843 (yes, 1843), it is only since the mid-1970s that the system has come into common use. That use is now growing rapidly, thanks to a number of factors:

- Until recently, there were legal restrictions in some countries inhibiting the use of the public telephone network for facsimile transmission.
- The development and widespread acceptance of CCITT standards are making compatible interworking of facsimile possible on an international scale.
- Facsimile technology has advanced, bringing higher speed, better quality, reduced machine size, reduced machine and transmission costs, and simpler machine operation.
- The advent of the digital facsimile allows a page of information to be easily manipulated by computer systems, stored on disk or tape, and encrypted for security.

With digital facsimile, the role of the facsimile has broadened. In digital form, pages can be transmitted between facsimile machines without ever going through the on-paper stage. A document can be prepared using a graphics package, drawing program, or word processor and handled in digital facsimile form. More sophisticated processing is possible by combining text and graphics capabilities. Thus, the user can easily create and edit text, combine it with charts, pictures, and other graphics, and subsequently treat the whole thing as an electronic or paper image.

Facsimile systems can be classified as either *photographic facsimile,* in which the original copy is reproduced with black, white, and intermediate gray scales, or *document facsimile,* in which only black and white are used. The primary interest in office and telecommunication applications has been in document facsimile, which is the subject of this section.

Traditionally, facsimile equipment operates by a local scan of a page, the transmission of an electronic version of the scanned information to a remote counterpart, and the printing of the same image at the remote location (Figure 6.3). In earlier designs, the scanning and printing processes are synchronized; there is little or no signal storage between the scanner and the printer. In more recent digital designs, buffered facsimile equipment has appeared on the market. And of course, as was mentioned, either the source or destination may be electronic instead of paper.

A variety of technologies have been used for both the scanning and printing processes. Since the focus of this work is communications, we will not examine these alternatives. A good survey on the topic is [KOBA85].

Facsimile Standards

CCITT has classified facsimile equipment for use over public networks into four categories, or groups:

- *Group 1:* The original low-speed analog facsimile technique. Transmission is in analog frequency modulation (FM), with several levels of gray supported as analog midpoints in the white-to-black spectrum. It is suitable for transmission of documents of ISO A4 size (210 × 297 mm; about 8.25 × 11.7 in) at about 4 lines per mm (about 100 lines per inch) in about 6 minutes.
- *Group 2:* An improved analog facsimile that employs bandwidth compression techniques to achieve a speed-up of a factor of 2 or more for the same resolution of Group 1. Transmission is duobinary phase modulation (PM), again supporting gray-scale values as well as black and white. Group 2 standards are still widely observed.
- *Group 3:* This is the first digital facsimile standard. This system provides only black-and-white values, with sampling densities of

FIGURE 6.3 Facsimile: Generic Block Diagram

200 spots per inch horizontally across the paper and 100 or 200 lines per inch vertically down the page. Group 3 uses a digital encoding scheme and incorporates a means of reducing the redundant information in the document signal prior to modulation. It is assumed that Group 3 transmission is via a modem over an analog telephone network. Transmission time is speeded up by a factor of 3 or more compared to Group 2.

- *Group 4:* Group 4 is also a black/white digital facsimile standard. It is intended for use over digital networks at speeds of up to 64 kbps and with provision for error-free reception. Resolutions of from 200 to 400 pels[2] per inch are specified. As with Group 3, compression techniques are used to reduce the number of bits transmitted. With Group 4, transmission times drop to a few seconds rather than the minutes of earlier standards.

Groups 1 and 2 were first standardized in 1976; Group 3 in 1980, and Group 4 in 1984. Table 6.7 compares key characteristics of the various CCITT standards. Note that Group 4 facsimile systems are further divided into three classes. Class 1 is a pure facsimile machine. Class 2 is capable of receiving and printing on a document a message transmitted via teletex. Class 3 is capable of transmitting and receiving in teletex and facsimile modes.

Figure 6.4 is a possible organization for a Group 4 facsimile system. The key elements are

- *Preprocessor:* This takes the input from an analog scanning device and applies a threshold to convert each scan position to black or white.
- *Compressor:* The bit matrix representing the picture is compressed to reduce redundant information.
- *Storage:* The source and destination systems must both buffer sufficient compressed data to accommodate uncertainties of the error-control system in the data network and terminal/network interface link.
- *Communication interface:* The Group 4 system can interface to a circuit-switched or packet-switched network, including ISDN.
- *Decompressor:* At the destination, the data stream is decompressed so that the original image can be reproduced.
- *Post-processor:* The decompressed bit matrix may be processed further to improve the image. For example, when the resolution of the printer is greater than that of the scanner, it is possible to interpolate in a manner to provide improved image quality.

---

[2] A *picture element,* or *pel,* is the smallest discrete scanning-line sample of a facsimile system, which contains only black–white information (no gray scales). A *pixel* is a picture element that contains gray-scale information.

TABLE 6.7 Characteristics of CCITT Facsimile Standards

Characteristic	Group 1	Group 2	Group 3	Group 4		
				Class 1	Class 2	Class 3
Recommendation	T.2	T.3	T.4	T.5	T.5	T.5
Signal	Analog	Analog	Digital	Digital	Digital	Digital
Horizontal Resolution	3.85 li/mm	3.85 li/mm	7.7 li/mm	200 pels/in	300 pels/in	300 pels/in
Vertical Resolution	3.85 li/mm	3.85 li/mm	7.7 li/mm	200 pels/in	300 pels/in	300 pels/in
Speed	6 min	3 min	<1 min	<10 s	<10 s	<10 s
Network	PSTN	PSTN	PSTN	ISDN	ISDN	ISDN
Data Encoding	N/A	2/3 level spectrum compression	MH, MR	MR	MR	MR
Equipment	Fax	Fax	Fax	Fax	Fax, receive from teletex	fax, teletex

PSTN = Public Switched Telephone Network
MH = Modified Huffman Code
MR = Modified Relative Element Address Designate

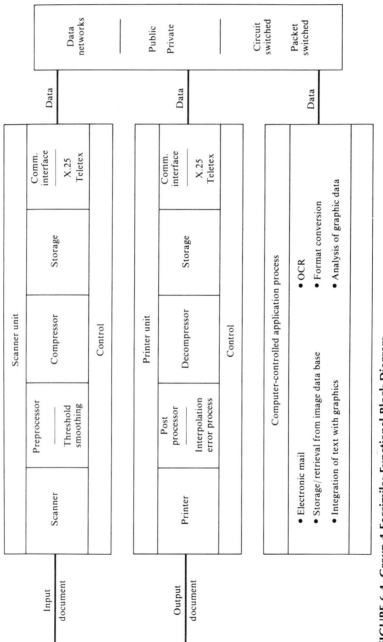

FIGURE 6.4 Group 4 Facsimile: Functional Block Diagram

The figure also indicates that a number of additional applications, beyond document scan and print, are possible. These include

- *Electronic mail:* As an alternative to traditional electronic mail systems.
- *Storage/retrieval from an image database:* Documents can be stored for later remote printing. Documents can be created using a graphics processor.
- *Format conversion:* from one facsimile standard to another.
- *OCR/analysis of graphic data:* Images could be transmitted in bit-map form for later processing using pattern recognition and other image-processing techniques.

Compression Techniques

Compression techniques are essential to the widespread use of digital facsimile machines. To see this, consider that an A4 page with 200-pel-per-inch resolution (which is adequate but not unnecessarily high resolution) generates 3,740,000 bits. At 64 kbps, the basic ISDN data rate, this page would take about one minute to transmit. Ultimately, users will expect their systems to operate at a rate similar to that of a copier, or one page every few seconds. To meet this requirement without an inordinately high data rate requires the use of data compression techniques.

There are two broad classes of black-white graphic coding techniques. *Information-preserving techniques* reproduce an exact replica of the original scanned and thresholded binary image. *Approximation techniques* approximate the original image. Both of the compression techniques standardized by CCITT are information-preserving techniques. The two techniques that have been standardized are the Modified Huffman (MH) and Modified READ (MR) algorithms. The MH technique is the default for Group 3, with MR as an option. Group 4 specifies MR. Both techniques are examined in the section. However, to clarify the discussion, we begin with a simpler technique, the Huffman code.

Huffman Encoding. The problem that is addressed by Huffman encoding is this. We wish to construct and transmit a message using N symbols. The simplest technique is to use binary numbers of equal length L to represent each symbol. L will be the smallest number such that

$$L \geq \log_2 N \text{ bits/symbol}$$

For example, if we wish to use the 26 letters of the alphabet, then $\log_2 (26) = 4.7$, and $L = 5$ bits.

Now, if all of the symbols to be transmitted were equally probable, then this encoding scheme cannot be improved upon. However, if this is not the case, then such a *fixed-length code* is not the most efficient. We would like to use an encoding scheme in which common symbols are assigned short codes and rare symbols are assigned long codes. In this way, the average code length, calculated over the actual transmission, should be reduced.

We can determine how good our *variable-length encoding* scheme is by using a result from information theory. If a source produces N different symbols, then the average information, or entropy, per symbol of the output is

$$H = \sum_{k=1}^{N} P_k \log_2 P_k$$

where P_k is the probability of occurrence of the kth symbol. As an example, consider an alphabet of 5 symbols, with respective probabilities of occurrence of 0.4, 0.3, 0.2, 0.04, and 0.02. The value of H for this source, using the preceding formula, is 1.999 bits per symbol. This value is the theoretical minimum value of the number of bits used to encode a source. Because each source symbol must be represented by an integral number of bits, this minimum usually cannot be met. However, the Huffman code produces an efficiency very close to the theoretical minimum.

A Huffman code can be constructed as follows. List the symbols in decreasing order of probability. Consider each symbol to be a leaf node in a binary tree to be constructed. Merge the two nodes of lowest probability into a node whose probability is the sum of the two constituent probabilities. At each step, repeat this procedure. The process stops when one unmerged node remains. The result is a binary tree. Label each pair of branches with a zero and a one. The codeword for any symbol is the string of labels from the root node back to the original symbol. Figure 6.5 is an example, using the symbol set defined earlier. Note that straightforward fixed-length encoding would require 3 bits per symbol, whereas Huffman coding is an average of just over 2 bits per symbol.

A Huffman code has the property that no codeword is the prefix of any other codeword. Thus, codewords of successive symbols can be concatenated with no punctuation. A proof that the Huffman code is optimum can be found in [GALL68].

Modified Huffman Code. In a typical document, the black and white areas of the image tend to cluster. If we view the document as a sequence of lines, and consider the pattern of black and white on a given line, we observe that there are long *runs* of black (B) and white (W) pels. This property is exploited in a family of techniques referred

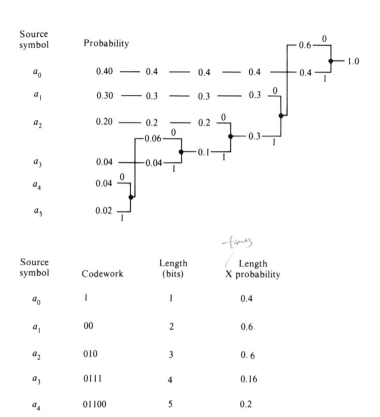

Source
symbol

Source symbol	Codework	Length (bits)	Length X probability
a_0	1	1	0.4
a_1	00	2	0.6
a_2	010	3	0.6
a_3	0111	4	0.16
a_4	01100	5	0.2
a_5	01101	5	0.1

2.06

Average codeword length = 2.06 bits/symbol
Entropy of source = 1.999 bits/symbol

FIGURE 6.5 Huffman Coding Example

to as *run-length encoding*. The two-valued input is converted to a many-valued run-length process, and this process is subsequently coded for transmission. In addition, because longer runs of black or white are in general less probable than shorter runs, variable-length coding can be employed to advantage.

The Huffman code, as just described, could be used for the purpose of facsimile encoding. It could be applied to an image one horizontal line at a time to encode the sequence of black and white pels. For example, in Figure 6.6, one scan of the image produces a sequence of W7, B7, W4, B8, W4, B7, W10. If we consider each of these elements as a symbol in a source alphabet, then Huffman encoding can be used to encode the source. However, since CCITT standards require at least 1728 pels per line, the number of different codes and hence the average length of code are very large.

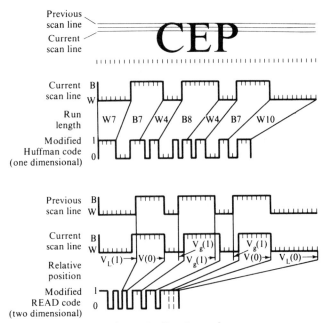

FIGURE 6.6 MH and MR Coding Examples

An alternative is the Modified Huffman (MH) encoding technique. MH regards a run-length N as the sum of two terms:

$$N = 64 m + n; \quad m = 0, 1, 2, \ldots, 27; \quad n = 0, 1, 2, \ldots, 63$$

Each run length can now be represented by two values, one for m and one for n, and these values can then be encoded using Huffman encoding. For this purpose, CCITT has defined eight representative documents and calculated the probabilities of the different run-length occurrences. As these probabilities are different for black and white, two sets of probabilities were calculated. From this information two code tables were developed, as shown in Table 6.8. The terminating code is used for run lengths of less than 64. For run lengths greater than 64, a combination of a terminating code (n) and a make-up code (m) is needed. Figure 6.6 shows an example of the application of this code.

There are several additional details concerning this code. Each line ends with a unique codeword for end of line (EOL). This is a codeword that can never be found in a valid line of data; it therefore facilitates resynchronization after an error burst. Within a line, codewords for black and white runs must alternate. However, note that different codes are used for the black and white runs; this provides an additional form of error checking. Finally, by convention, each line begins with a white run length. If the first pel is black, then a white run length of zero is used.

TABLE 6.8   Modified Huffman Code Table

Terminating Codewords

Run Length	White	Black	Run Length	Whte	Black
0	00110101	0000110111	32	00011011	000001101010
1	000111	010	33	00010010	000001101011
2	0111	11	34	00010011	000011010010
3	1000	10	35	00010100	000011010011
4	1011	011	36	00010101	000011010100
5	1100	0011	37	00010110	000011010101
6	1110	0010	38	00010111	000011010110
7	1111	00011	39	00101000	000011010111
8	10011	000101	40	00101001	000001101100
9	10100	000100	41	00101010	000001101101
10	00111	0000100	42	00101011	000011011010
11	01000	0000101	43	00101100	000011011011
12	001000	0000111	44	00101101	000001010100
13	000011	00000100	45	00000100	000001010101
14	110100	00000111	46	00000101	000001010110
15	110101	000011000	47	00001010	000001010111
16	101010	0000010111	48	00001011	000001100100
17	101011	0000011000	49	01010010	000001100101
18	0100111	0000001000	50	01010011	000001010010
19	0001100	00001100111	51	01010100	000001010011
20	0001000	00001101000	52	01010101	000000100100
21	0010111	00001101100	53	00100100	000000110111
22	0000011	00000110111	54	00100101	000000111000
23	0000100	00000101000	55	01011000	000000100111
24	0101000	00000010111	56	01011001	000000101000
25	0101011	00000011000	57	01011010	000001011000
26	0010011	000011001010	58	01011011	000001011001
27	0100100	000011001011	59	01001010	000000101011
28	0011000	000011001100	60	01001011	000000101100
29	00000010	000011001101	61	00110010	000001011010
30	00000011	000001101000	62	00110011	000001100110
31	00011010	000001101001	63	00110100	000001100111

Make-up Codewords

Run Length	White	Black	Run Length	White	Black
64	11011	0000001111	960	011010100	0000001110011
128	10010	000011001000	1024	011010101	0000001110100
192	010111	000011001001	1088	011010110	0000001110101
256	0110111	000001011011	1152	011010111	0000001110110
320	00110110	000000110011	1216	011011000	0000001110111
384	00110111	000000110100	1280	011011001	0000001010010

Cont.

TABLE 6.8   **Modified Huffman Code Table** *(continued)*

	Make-up Codewords				
Run Length	White	Black	Run Length	White	Black
448	01100100	000000110101	1344	011011010	0000001010011
512	01100101	0000001101100	1408	011011011	0000001010100
576	01101000	0000001101101	1472	010011000	0000001010101
640	01100111	0000001001010	1536	010011001	0000001011010
704	011001100	0000001001011	1600	010011010	0000001011011
768	011001101	0000001001100	1664	011000	0000001100100
832	011010010	0000001001101	1728	010011011	0000001100101
896	011010011	0000001110010	EOL	000000000001	000000000001

Modified READ Code.   The use of modified Huffman encoding significantly reduces the total number of bits that must be transmitted compared to a straightforward transmission of the bit-map image. Further gains in efficiency can be achieved by recognizing that there is a strong correlation between the black-white patterns of two adjacent lines. In fact, for typical facsimile documents, approximately 50 percent of all the B-W and W-B transitions are directly underneath a transition on the previous line, and an additional 25 percent differ by only one pel [SILV87]. Therefore, approximately 75 percent of all transitions can be defined by a relationship that is plus or minus at most one pel from the line above it. This is the underlying basis of the Modified Relative Element Address Designate (MR) Code.

In MR encoding, run lengths are encoded by encoding the position of changing elements, that is, elements that are of a different color than the immediately preceding element on the same line. A changing element a_1 is coded in terms of its distance to one of two reference pels: either a preceding changing element a_0 on the same line or a changing element b_1 on the previous line. The selection of a_0 or b_1 depends on the exact configuration, as explained subsequently.

Figure 6.7 illustrates the five changing elements that are defined for this scheme. The encoding procedure is summarized in Table 6.9 and can be defined as follows:

Step 1
   a. If the position of b_2 lies to the left of a_1, this is coded using the word 0001. After this encoding, the position of a_1 is shifted to lie under b_2. This is referred to as pass mode. The algorithm resumes at Step 1.
   b. If the condition in (a) is not satisfied, go to Step 2.

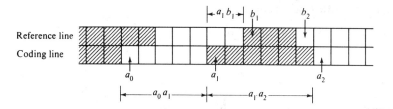

Definition of changing picture elements:

a_0 The reference or starting changing element on the coding line. At the start of the coding line, a_0 is set on an imaginary white changing element just to the left of the first element on the line. During the coding of a line, a_0 is redefined after every encoding.

a_1 The next changing element to the right of a_0 on the coding line.

a_2 The next changing element to the right of a_1 on the coding line.

b_1 The first changing element on the reference line to the right of a_0 and of opposite color to a_0.

b_2 The next changing element to the right of b_1 on the reference line.

FIGURE 6.7 Changing Picture Elements for the MR Technique

Step 2

a. If the position of a_1 is within three of the position of b_1 ($|a_1b_1| \leq 3$), then a_1 is coded in the vertical mode, after which the old position a_1 becomes the new position a_0, a_2 becomes a_1, and so on.

b. If the position of a_1 is not within three of the position of b_1, then a_1 is coded in the horizontal mode. Following the horizontal mode code 001, a_0a_1 and a_1a_2 are encoded by one-dimensional MH coding. After this, the old position a_2 becomes the new position a_0.

Step 1 is used to move the position of b_1 and b_2 along after the exercise of Step 2. Also, Step 1 has the effect of avoiding long run lengths. In Step 2, if the current changing element to be encoded is within three positions of the same transition in the previous line, then the position is encoded with one of seven possible values using MH. This situation will hold most of the time. In the few cases in which a transition in the current line is not within three positions of the same transition in the previous line, the next two runs are encoded using MH (Table 6.8).

The MR scheme is more sensitive to an error than the MH scheme; the effects of an error could propagate for unpredictable distances. To avoid this, MH encoding is used for every Kth scanning line. CCITT recommends a value of $K = 2$ for a resolution of 3.85 li/mm and $K = 4$ for 7.7 li/mm.

TABLE 6.9   MR Code Tables

Mode	Elements to Be Coded		Notation	Code Word
Pass	b_1, b_2		P	0001
Horizontal	a_0a_1, a_1a_2		H	$001 + M(a_0a_1) + M(a_1a_2)$ (see Note)
Vertical	a_1 just under b_1	$a_1b_1 = 0$	V(0)	1
	a_1 to the right of b_1	$a_1b_1 = 1$	$V_R(1)$	011
		$a_1b_1 = 2$	$V_R(2)$	000011
		$a_1b_1 = 3$	$V_R(3)$	0000011
	a_1 to the left of b_1	$a_1b_1 = 1$	$V_1(1)$	010
		$a_1b_1 = 2$	$V_1(2)$	000010
		$a_1b_1 = 3$	$V_1(3)$	0000010

Note — Code M( ) of the horizontal mode represents the code words in Table 6.8

Table 6.10 shows the performance of the MH and MR schemes against a representative set of pages [YASU80]. In both cases, considerable compression is achieved. The compression achieved by MR is clearly superior. Similar results are also reported in [PRAT80].

6.4

TELETEX

Teletex is a relatively new international telecommunication service that provides direct electronic document exchange between such office text

TABLE 6.10   Compression Ratios for MH and MR

CCITT Document Number	Normal Resolution (3.85 lines/mm)		Higher Resolution (7.7 lines/mm)	
	MH	MR	MH	MR
1	15.42	22.03	15.42	28.95
2	16.56	38.47	16.59	50.97
3	8.41	14.83	8.42	17.9
4	4.7	5.6	4.71	7.41
5	8.1	12.66	8.11	15.94
6	10.73	26.13	10.75	30.98
7	4.8	5.75	4.8	7.62
8	8.62	22.9	8.61	29.85
Average	8.02	12.27	8.02	15.84

machines as electronic typewriters, word processors, and personal computers that are equipped with transmitting and receiving storages. The document exchange occurs directly from the transmit storage of the sending text machine to the receive storage of the receiving machine, independently of concurrent operator text entry or editing. The system provides for a rich set of graphic (printable) and control characters to allow the preparation of text documents to satisfy almost all users of Latin-based alphabets. Teletex can be used with a wide variety of communication networks, including telephone, packet-switched, and ISDN networks.

Teletex is intended to replace the older telex capability. Whereas telex operates at a leisurely 50 bps, a rate of 2400 bps is the default for teletex. Furthermore, teletex offers a much greater selection of graphic and control characters to allow the exchange of text-based documents such as letters and memos, rather than simply the text stream allowed with telex.

Characteristics and Functions

The CCITT standards for teletex ensure that teletex terminals and software packages from different manufacturers will be compatible. Recommendation T.60 specifies not only the data rate, but the character set and document characteristics supported by teletex. The key characteristics and functions listed in the recommendation are

- *Equipment compatibility:* All equipment must implement a common basic set of functions. This assures that all terminals attached to a national or international teletex network can communicate with each other with regard to text and control characters, transmission error control procedures, determination of paper size, and automatic answerback.
- *Unattended operation:* When the receiving terminal is unattended or busy with local operations, it must store and safeguard incoming messages so that no information is lost before it is printed out.
- *Simultaneous terminal usage and document reception:* While the terminal is being used for local typing (e.g., teletex message preparation), it must be capable of receiving and acknowledging incoming messages without interrupting the local operation. Once the local typing is complete, the stored messages are printed out.
- *Compatibility with telex:* A teletex terminal must be capable of receiving and printing telex messages and of operating in telex mode so that it can send messages to a telex terminal. This capability is essential to a smooth migration from telex to teletex.
- *Sheet paper usable area:* In contrast to the typical telex terminal, which uses a continuous roll of paper, teletex terminals use individual

sheets of paper. Because both the ISO A4 (210 × 297 mm) and
North American (216 × 280 mm; 8.5 × 11 in.) paper sizes are in
widespread use, the teletex format restricts the usable print area to
the area common to both page sizes.

Teletex procedures call for the exchange of reference information
before sending a message. This includes call identification and its subset, terminal identification (Figure 6.8). The call identification line identifies the called and calling terminal, the data and time of call origination, and the document and page reference. Each teletex terminal has
a unique terminal identification, consisting of four fields. The first field
identifies the country and, if necessary, the network within the country.
Field 2 identifies the network address of the terminal and is assigned
by the network administration. Field 3, which was originally provided
to allow terminal subaddressing, is optional; its use is a subject for
further CCITT study. Field 4 is an abbreviated name used to identify
the owner of the terminal.

Teletex Character Set

Table 6.11 shows the 8-bit encoding of the basic repertoire of teletex
characters. Most of the character codes represent graphic, or printable
characters. In addition to the Latin alphabet, the graphic character set
includes accented letters and umlauts, and nonalphabetic characters,
such as decimal digits, punctuation marks, and arithmetic signs.

In addition to printable characters, the teletex standard defines a set
of control functions that enable a receiving terminal to produce a document that is identical in contents, layout, and format to that produced
by the sending terminal. Each control function is encoded as one or
more control characters. The basic repertoire of control characters is
listed and defined in Table 6.12. Control characters fall into four categories:

- *Format Effectors:* Control the positioning of the printing element.
- *Presentation Control:* Influences the following presentation attributes: page orientation, horizontal and vertical spacing, and use or
nonuse of underlining. Each of these functions includes a control
character followed by a parameter value.
- *Code Extension:* Used to provide coded representations for additional control functions.
- *Miscellaneous:* Other control functions.

Table 6.11 shows the codes for those control functions represented
by a single 8-bit character. The remainder of the control functions require multiple characters; each begins with the code extension character.

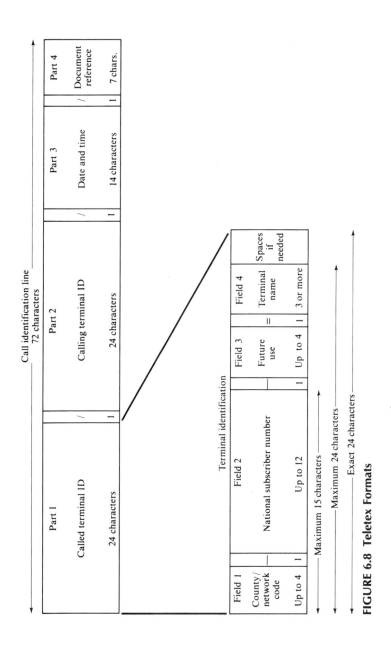

FIGURE 6.8 Teletex Formats

TABLE 6.11 Teletex Printable and Control Character Codes

b8 b7 b6 b5 →																
b8	0	0	0	0	0	0	0	0	1	1	1	1	1	1	1	1
b7	0	0	0	0	1	1	1	1	0	0	0	0	1	1	1	1
b6	0	0	1	1	0	0	1	1	0	0	1	1	0	0	1	1
b5	0	1	0	1	0	1	0	1	0	1	0	1	0	1	0	1
Column	0	1	2	3	4	5	6	7	8	9	10	11	12	13	14	15

b4 b3 b2 b1	Row	0	1	2	3	4	5	6	7	8	9	10	11	12	13	14	15
0 0 0 0	0			SP	0	@	P		p				°			Ω	ĸ
0 0 0 1	1			!	1	A	Q	a	q			¡	±	´		Æ	æ
0 0 1 0	2			"	2	B	R	b	r			¢	²	`		Đ	đ
0 0 1 1	3			④	3	C	S	c	s			£	³	^		ª	ð
0 1 0 0	4			④	4	D	T	d	t			$	×	¯		Ħ	ħ
0 1 0 1	5			%	5	E	U	e	u			¥	µ	˘			ı
0 1 1 0	6			&	6	F	V	f	v			#	¶	ʼ		IJ	ij

b4 b3 b2 b1	Row	0	1	2	3	4	5	6	7	8	9	10	11	12	13	14	15
0 1 1 1	7			'	7	G	W	g	w			§	·	˙		Ŀ	ŀ
1 0 0 0	8	BS		(	8	H	X	h	x			¤	÷	¨		Ł	ł
1 0 0 1	9			)	9	I	Y	i	y			'	'	②		Ø	ø
1 0 1 0	10	LF	SUB	*	:	J	Z	j	z			"	"	°		Œ	œ
1 0 1 1	11			+	;	K		k		PLD	CSI	«	»	¸		º	ß
1 1 0 0	12	FF		,	<	L		l		PLU			1/4	③		Þ	þ
1 1 0 1	13	CR		-	=	M		m					1/2	˝		Ŧ	ŧ
1 1 1 0	14			.	>	N		n					3/4'	˛		Ŋ	ŋ
1 1 1 1	15			/	?	O	①	o					¿	ˇ		'n	

Note 1—When interworking with videotex, this code shall have the meaning *delimiter*.

Note 2—In the 1980 version of this Recommendation code 12/9 was allocated to represent the umlaut mark. The use of this facility is discouraged. Its removal is foreseen in the future.

Note 3—Non-spacing underline is not a diacritical mark and may be combined with any graphic character of the teletex repertoire.

Note 4—Teletex terminals should send only the codes 10/6 and 10/8 for graphic characters # and ¤ respectively. When receiving codes 2/3 and 2/4, terminals should interpret them as # and ¤ .

TABLE 6.12   Teletex Basic Repertoire of Control Functions

Identifier	Name	Definition
	Format Effectors	
SP	Space	Advance one character position.
BS	Backspace	Move character position back by one.
LF	Line Feed	Advance to corresponding character position on next line.
FF	Form Feed	Advance to corresponding character position on next page.
CR	Carriage Return	Move to home position on same line.
PLD	Partial Line Down	Make partial vertical offset down. Used to begin subscript or to end superscript.
PLU	Partial Line Up	Make partial vertical offset up. Used to begin superscript or to end subscript.
	Presentation Control	
PFS	Page Format Selection	Select vertical or horizontal orientation.
SGR	Select Graphic Rendition	Select default or underlined.
SHS	Select Horizontal Spacing	Select character spacing.
SVS	Select Vertical Spacing	Select line spacing.
	Code Extension	
CSI	Control Sequence Introducer	Used to provide additional control functions.
	Miscellaneous	
SUB	Substitute Character	Used in the place of a character that has been found to be invalid or in error.
IGS	Identify Graphic Subrepertoire	Indicates that a particular subrepertoire of graphic characters is to be used.

In addition to the basic repertoire, additional application-oriented graphic and printable characters may be employed. Several different escape sequences are used to indicate that the teletex message is entering/leaving a nonbasic character set. The standard does not require that a teletex terminal be able to handle these additional characters. A teletex terminal must be able to accept all characters in the basic repertoire and be able to transmit all or a subset of the basic repertoire.

6.5

MESSAGE-HANDLING SYSTEMS

The final teleservice that we will examine in this chapter is referred to by CCITT as a message-handling system. It is essentially an electronic mail capability. Although teletex illustrates some of the aspects of an electronic mail system, it does not provide the full range of functions and services usually associated with electronic mail. In many cases, the teletex service will prove adequate. However, in other cases, a more complete electronic mail system is required. We begin this section with a discussion of electronic mail in general. We then look at the CCITT standards in this area.

Electronic Mail

One of the deadliest wasters of time in the office is a phenomenon known as "telephone tag." Mr. X calls Ms. Y, who is away from her desk. Some time later Y returns the call but X is out or on another line. X is now "it" and must return Y's return to X's call. And so on. . . . Independent studies have shown that over 70 percent of all business telephone calls do not reach the intended recipient on the first try [MAR179]. The problem is that the caller and callee must both be at their phones and available to answer at the same time. If the caller could simply write a note and leave it on the callee's desk, the problem could be avoided. Electronic mail provides a way to do this.

Electronic mail addresses another problem as well: the office paper explosion. Offices generate a tremendous amount of paperwork, most of it in the form of internal memos and reports: over 80 percent of all business documents are textual and/or numeric (no graphics) and originate and remain within the same organization [POTT77].

Electronic mail, also known as a computer-based message system (CBMS), is a facility that allows users at terminals to compose and exchange messages. The messages need never exist on paper unless the user (sender or recipient) desires a paper copy of the message. Some electronic mail systems serve only users on a single computer; others provide service across a network of computers. In this section, we briefly look at the functionality of single-system electronic mail, then turn our attention to the more interesting (for this book) case of network electronic mail. Finally, the CCITT X.400 family of standards is described.

Single-system Electronic Mail. The simplest, and by far the most common, form of electronic mail is the single-system facility. This facility allows all the users of a shared computer system to exchange messages. Each user is registered on the system and has a unique identifier, usually the person's last name. Associated with each user is a mailbox. The electronic mail facility is an application program available to any user logged on to the system. A user may invoke the electronic mail facility, prepare a message, and "send" it to any other user on the system. The act of sending simply involves putting the message in the recipient's mailbox. The mailbox is actually an entity maintained by the file management system and is in the nature of a file directory. One mailbox is associated with each user. Any "incoming" mail is simply stored as a file under that user's mailbox directory. The user may later go and fetch that file to read the message. The user reads messages by invoking the mail facility and "reading" rather than "sending." In most systems, when the user logs on, he or she is informed if there is any new mail in that user's mailbox.

A basic electronic mail system performs four functions:

- *Creation:* A user creates and edits a message, generally using a rudimentary editing capability. Most systems also allow the user to create a message using the system editor or a word processor and then incorporate the resulting file as the body of the message.
- *Sending:* The user designates the recipient (or recipients) of the message, and the facility stores the message in the appropriate mailbox(es).
- *Reception:* The intended recipient may invoke the electronic mail facility to access and read the delivered mail.
- *Storage:* Both sender and recipient may choose to save the message in a file for more permanent storage.

Because we are interested in the networking aspects of electronic mail, the topic of basic user services will not be further pursued here. More detail can be found in [HIRS85] and [BARC81].

Network Electronic Mail. With a single-system electronic mail facility, messages can only be exchanged among users of that particular system. Clearly, this is too limited. In a distributed environment, we would like to be able to exchange messages with users attached to other systems. Thus, we would like to treat electronic mail as an application-layer protocol that makes use of lower-layer protocols to transmit messages.

Figure 6.9 suggests the internal system architecture required. Let us refer to a single-system mail facility as a *native mail* facility. For native mail, three major modules are needed. Users will interact with native mail via terminals; hence, terminal-handling software is needed. Mail is stored as files in the file system, so file-handling software is needed.

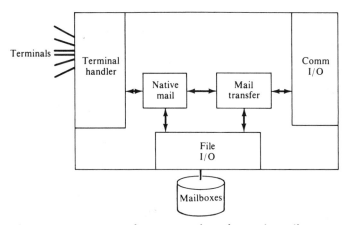

FIGURE 6.9 Conceptual Structure of an Electronic Mail System

Finally, there must be a native mail package that contains all the logic for providing mail-related services to users.

To extend this system to *network mail,* two more modules are needed. Since we are going to communicate across some sort of network or transmission system, communication I/O logic is needed; in the most general case, this would encompass layers 1 through 6 of the OSI model. Mail transfer logic is also needed, which knows how to invoke the communications function, to specify the network address of the recipient, and to request whatever communication services are needed (e.g., priority). Note in the figure that the user does not directly interact with the mail transfer module. Ideally, the user interface for local and remote mail should be the same. If the user designates a local recipient, the message is stored in a local mailbox. If a remote recipient is designated, the native mail module passes the message to the mail transfer module for transmission across the network. Incoming mail from the network is routed to the appropriate mailbox and henceforth treated the same as other messages in the mailbox.

Many vendors now offer a network version of their basic electronic mail facility. However, this will only allow the user to send mail to users on systems of the same vendor. As in other areas, standards are needed. It is to these standards that we now turn our attention.

The CCITT X.400 Family of Standards

In 1984, CCITT issued a family of standards for message-handling systems (MHS) that encompasses the requirements of what we have referred to as network electronic mail; the standards were substantially revised in 1988. The standards do not deal with the user interface or the services available directly to the user (what we have referred to as native mail). They do, however, specify what services are available for use in sending messages across the network and thus provide the base for building the user interface.

Table 6.13 lists the nine recommendations that comprise the X.400 family. All of the recommendations fit into the framework of an MHS model, which is described in X.400. We describe that model first and then look at some of the key aspects of the specifications of services and protocols.

MHS Functional Model. X.400 defines a functional model for the message-handling system, as shown in Figure 6.10. This model provides a framework for all of the other recommendations. The model defines a number of key components (Table 6.14).

The actual work of message transfer is done in the message transfer system, which consists of an interconnected set of message transfer agents (MTAs). The **message transfer agent** accepts messages from a user agent (UA) for delivery to other UAs or to a message store (MS). Sometimes the MTA that accepts submission of a message delivers it directly to the destination UA or MS. In other cases, it is necessary for the message to be relayed through a series of MTAs to the destination. For example, if only some MTAs have access to the proper long-distance communication paths, a message addressed to a distant UA might be relayed in several stages. Using relays also eliminates the need to have all UAs and MTAs available on a 24-hour basis. The store-and-forward action makes it feasible to treat electronic mail components like any other office equipment that gets turned off at night.

The other elements of the message-handling system are users of the message transfer system. The **user agent** operates on behalf of a user. The UA submits messages to an MTA for transmission across the network. The X.400 series specifies the interaction of the UA with MTA and other UA entities but does not specify the interaction between the UA and its user.

The **message store** is a concept that was introduced in the 1988 version of the standard. One of the drawbacks of the 1984 scheme, which had no message store, was that if a remote UA was off-line for a period of time, it could be flooded with messages at the log-on stage. Furthermore, a message delivered to the UA was "trapped" in that UA system; it caused problems for users on the move, who wanted to access their mailboxes from terminals at different locations or from a portable terminal. The MS concept is designed to alleviate these problems.

The functionality defined for the message store can be summarized as follows [CHIL90]:

TABLE 6.13   The CCITT X.400 Family of Standards for Message-handling Systems

Number	Title	Description
X.400	Message-handling System and Service Overview	Defines the message-handling system model consisting of user agents and message-transfer agents, discusses naming and addressing, defines interpersonal messaging and message transfer services, and discusses protocols for implementation.
X.402	Overall Architecture	Defines the overall architecture and serves as a technical introduction to it.
X.403	Conformance Testing	Specifies the criteria for acceptance of an implementation as conforming to the X.400 family of recommendations.
X.407	Abstract Service Definition Conventions	Defines techniques for formally specifying the distributed information-processing tasks that arise in message handling.
X.408	Encoded Information Type Conversion Rules	Specifies the conversion between different types of encoded information to allow dissimilar devices to exchange messages. The encoded information types that are handled include telex, teletex, ASCII terminals, facsimile, and videotex.
X.411	Message Transfer System: Abstract Service Definition and Procedures	Defines the conceptual layer service provided by the message-transfer layer and the message-transfer protocol.
X.413	Message Store: Abstract Service Definition	Defines the services provided by the message store.
X.419	Protocol Specifications	Defines the protocols for accessing the message transfer system and a message store, as well as those that are used between message transfer agents to provide for the distributed operation of the MTS.
X.420	Interpersonal Messaging System	Defines the services provided by interpersonal messaging and the procedures for providing those services.

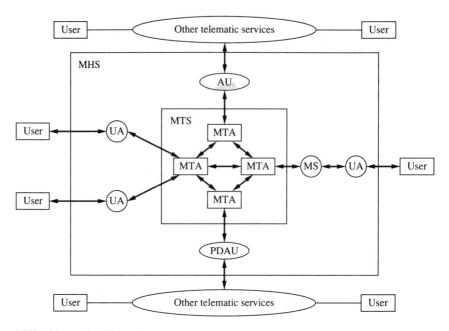

MHS = Message handling system
MTS = Message transfer system
MTA = Message transfer agent
MS = Message store
UA = User agent
AU = Access unit
PDUA = Physical delivery access unit

FIGURE 6.10 X.400 MHS Functional Model

- One MS acts on behalf of one user (i.e., one originator/response address).
- When a UA subscribes to an MS, all messages destined for the UA are delivered to the MS; when a message is delivered to an MS, the role of the message transfer system (MTS) in the transfer process is complete. Note that the MS does not store submitted messages, only delivered messages.
- It is possible to request an alert when a certain message arrives.
- Message submission from the UA to its MTA, via the MS, is transparent.
- Users are provided with general message-management facilities such as selective message retrieval, delete, and list.

In effect, the MS specification is just a standardized definition of how otherwise local UA functions have been taken over by a separate system and accessed via a protocol.

Finally, various **access units** (AUs) allow MHS users to communicate

TABLE 6.14 Basic Components of a Message-handling System (MHS)

Message-transfer Agent (MTA)
The MTA is a functional entity which, in cooperation with similar entities, conveys messages through the message-transfer system. When a message is submitted, the MTA validates the submission envelope and performs housekeeping functions, such as recording submission time and generating a message identifier.

User Agent (UA)
Operates on behalf of the user (person or application program that originates and receives messages). It interacts directly with the user and performs functions for preparing messages and submitting messages for routing to the destination(s). In the process, the source UA interacts with destination UAs, which perform the delivery function. The UAs also assist the user in dealing with other message functions, such as filing, replying, retrieving, and forwarding.

Message Store (MS)
The MS provides a mailbox facility. Messages may be delivered from the message-transfer system (MTS) into the MS to be picked up later by a UA.

Access Unit (AU)
An AU provides a gateway between the MHS and an external communications service, such as telex or teletex.

Physical Delivery Access Unit (PDAU)
A PDAU is an AU that provides access to a physical delivery system such as the postal system. It produces a hard copy of the message contents together with an envelope addressed using the electronic addressing information provided by the originator.

with other message-based systems. The rules for coded information conversion are defined, making it possible to standardize the conversion of message contents for transfer of messages between dissimilar systems.

Figure 6.11 suggests the way in which messages are constructed and transmitted. The user prepares the *body* of a message outside of the scope of X.400, using some sort of word processor or editor. The user presents this body to the user-agent software, together with a description, which might include recipient, subject, and priority. The user agent appends a *header* containing this qualifying information to the *message*, forming a complete message. This message is submitted to a message transfer agent. The MTA appends an *envelope* to the message; the envelope contains the source and destination addresses plus other control information needed for relaying the message through the network.

The X.400 Protocol Architecture. The message-handling protocols defined in the X.400 series are located in the application layer of the OSI

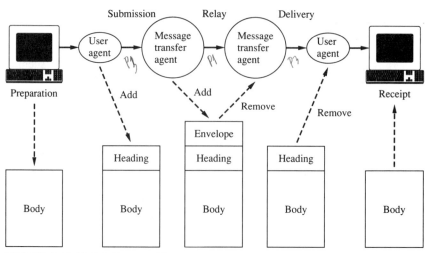

FIGURE 6.11 X.400 Message Flow

model. The MHS protocols are determined by application contexts that specify combinations of MHS-specific application service elements (ASEs) and other ASEs shared by a number of applications. Table 6.15 lists the ASEs relevant to X.400.

In order to observe how these ASEs interact, refer to Figure 6.12. The figure shows the permissible application contexts: a remote user accessing the MTS, a user accessing the MS, and the basic message-transfer operation. In each case, the overall interaction, which involves a number of ASEs, is designated by a particular protocol name (Table 6.16).

An example of the use of these protocols is shown in Figure 6.13. User A sends a message to User B and User C. The message is handed over to User A's UA, which *submits* the message after putting it in an envelope. The envelope is, in effect, the header of a P3 protocol data unit. The MTAs take over the *transfer* of the message until it reaches an MTA that can make a *delivery* of the message. The routing of the message among the MTAs is accomplished with the P1 protocol. The recipient, User B, gets delivery to B's UA, via protocol P3, where it can be directly read. For recipient User C, a copy of the message is delivered into C's MS, from where it can later be retrieved via protocol P7.

The P1 protocol is used to transfer a message from the originator's MTA to the recipient's MTA through zero or more intermediate MTAs. The protocol is also used, if the service has been requested, for transferring a notification of delivery or nondelivery back to the originator's MTA. Of course, if the originator and recipient share the same MTA, then this protocol is not needed.

TABLE 6.15   Application Service Elements Relevant to X.400

MHS ASEs

Message Administration Service Element (MASE)
The MASE provides protocol operations between MTA and UA and between MS and UA. It covers various administrative tasks, such as changing passwords and providing information about message status.

Message Delivery Service Element (MDSE)
The MDSE provides protocol operations between MTA and UA. It allows the MTA to deliver messages to the UA.

Message Retrieval Service Element (MRSE)
The MRSE provides protocol operations between MS and UA. It allows the UA to retrieve messages from the message store.

Message Submission Service Element (MSSE)
The MSSE provides protocol operations between MTA and UA and between MS and UA. It provides for the submission of complete messages by the UA and for submission of a probe, which is a limited envelope to verify delivery parameters.

Message Transfer Service Element (MTSE)
The only symmetric MHS service element. It provides a set of services to MTA for message transfer.

Common ASEs

Association Control Service Element (ACSE)
Supports the establishment and release of logical connections (called associations) between a pair of application entities. The ACSE contains the parameters that determine the use of the underlying presentation service and indirectly the session service.

Remote Operation Service Element (ROSE)
Supports interactive request/reply operation within the MHS model. It is used with the asymmetric MHS service elements (all but MTSE) to order the interactions between dissimilar open systems.

Remote Transfer Service Element (RTSE)
Supports the reliable transfer of application data. It ensures the reliable transfer of messages without duplication or loss.

Three types of protocol data units are defined: user, delivery report, and probe. The user PDU consists of the user-agent sublayer PDU plus a header, known as the envelope (Figure 6.14). The envelope contains the information needed for handling the message, including a network name for the recipient that will allow routing, a unique identifier, and information on how to process the PDU, such as the priority and whether a delivery report is required. The delivery report includes a header that consists of a unique identifier, the name of the originator that submitted the message to which this report refers, and trace infor-

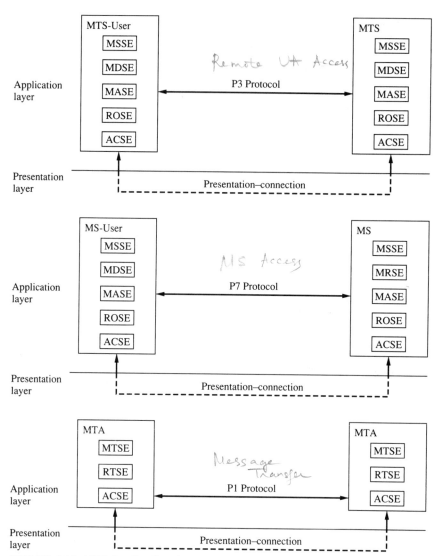

FIGURE 6.12 MHS Application Contexts

mation, which indicates the route that the delivery report followed. The body of the delivery report PDU includes the identifier of the original user PDU plus information about the delivery. This may include such items as the trace of the original user PDU, billing information, and, of course, whether delivery was successful.

The probe PDU is similar to the envelope protion of a user PDU. Its purpose is to determine if a particular delivery is possible without

TABLE 6.16   MHS Protocols (X.419)

Message Transfer Protocol (P1)

P1 provides for relaying messages and other interactions among the various message-transfer agents. It thus serves as the backbone switching protocol.

Remote UA Access Protocol (P3)

P3 enables a user agent (UA) that is remote from its message-transfer agent (MTA) to obtain access to the message-transfer service for submission from the US and retrieval from the MTA. In effect, P3 is a remote procedure call protocol.

MS Access Protocol (P7)

P7 enables a user agent to interact with a message store, providing in effect a mailbox facility.

actually sending a user message. Delivery reports will be returned on probe PDUs.

Figure 6.14 also indicates the presence of a message heading. The heading is transparent to the message transfer agent and to the various protocols (P1, P3, P7). However, the format of the message heading is specified for use by user agents. The heading contains the following fields:

- Message ID.
- Originator.
- Authorizing users.
- Primary recipients.

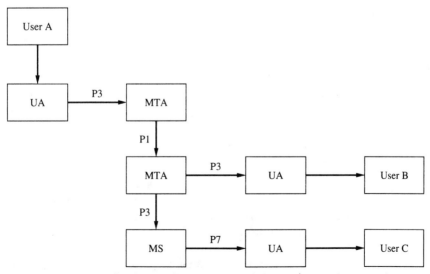

FIGURE 6.13 Example of How the X.400 Protocols Can Be Used [MANR89]

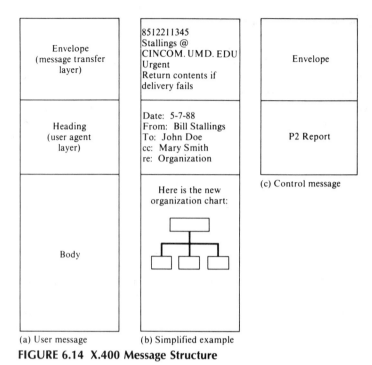

FIGURE 6.14 X.400 Message Structure

- Copy recipients.
- Blind copy recipients.
- Replies to message.
- Obsolete messages.
- Related messages.
- Subject.
- Expiry time.
- Reply time.
- Reply recipients.
- Importance.
- Sensitivity.
- Auto-forward.
- Extensions.

X.400 Services.   As with most communications standards, the X.400 series specifies not only protocols but the services to be provided to users. In this case the users are either terminal users who invoke electronic mail facilities or application programs that exchange messages. Corresponding to the two protocol sublayers discussed previously, the services are grouped into message transfer services and interpersonal messaging services.

For both sets of services, the services are divided into three categories: basic, essential optional, and additional optional. *Basic* services are inherent in the message-handling system and must be implemented. The remaining services are known as optional user facilities, which may be invoked at the option of the user, in some cases on a per-message basis and in others for an agreed contractual period. *Essential optional user facilities* must be offered by the service provider; that is, the provider

TABLE 6.17   Message Transfer Layer Services (X.401)

Basic Services	
Access management	Enables UA to submit and have messages delivered to it
Content type indication	Specified by originating UA
Converted indication	Specifies any conversions performed on message being delivered
Submission/delivery time stamp	Submission and delivery time are supplied with each message
Message identification	Unique identifier for each message
Nondelivery notification	Message cannot be delivered
Registered encoded information types	Allows UA to specify types that can be delivered to it
Original encoded information types	Specified by submitting UA and supplied to receiving UA

Essential Optional Services	
Alternate recipient allowed	Deliver to alternate if designated recipient cannot be found
Deferred delivery	Deliver no sooner than specified date and time
Deferred delivery cancellation	Abort delivery of deferred message
Delivery notification	Notify originator of successful delivery
Disclosure of other recipients	Disclose list of recipients to recipient
Grade of delivery selection	Request urgent, normal, or nonurgent
Multidestination delivery	Specify more than one recipient
Conversion prohibition	Prevents MTS from conversion
Probe	Determines if a message could be deliverable

Additional Optional Services	
Prevention of nondelivery notification	Supress potential nondelivery notice
Return of contents	Return message contents if nondelivery
Explicit conversion	Specifies particular conversion
Implicit conversion	Perform necessary conversion on all messages without explicit instruction
Alternate recipient assignment	Requests designation of requesting UA as alternate recipient
Hold for delivery	Requests that messages intended for this UA be held in MTS until later time

TABLE 6.18   Interpersonal Messaging Services

Basic Services	
IP-message identification	Assign reference identifier to each message content sent or received
Typed body	Allows nature and attributes of message body to be conveyed along with body

Essential Optional Services (for both origination and reception)	
Originator indication	Identifies the user that sent message
Primary and copy recipients indication	Allows UA to specify primary and secondary recipients
Replying IP-message indication	Specifies an earlier message to which this is a reply
Subject indication	Description of message

Additional (for origination) and Essential (for reception) Optional Services	
Blind copy recipient indication	List of recipients whose identities are not to be disclosed to primary or copy recipients
Autoforwarded indication	Marks a message as containing an automatically forwarded message
Authorizing users indication	Indicates one or more persons who authorized the message
Expiry date indication	Conveys a date and time after which the originator considers the message invalid
Cross-referencing indication	Specifies one or more other messages related to this one
Importance indication	Specifies low, normal, or high
Obsoleting indication	Specifies previous messages that are obsolete and superseded by this one
Sensitivity indication	Specifies personal, private, or company-confidential
Reply request indication	Asks for response; may also specify date and time and other recipients
Forwarded IP-message indication	Marks a message as containing a forwarded message
Body part encryption indication	Body part of message is encrypted
Multipart body	Enables sending message with multiple parts, each with its own attributes

Additional Optional Services (for both origination and reception)	
Nonreceipt notification	Requests that originator be informed if message is not received by its intended recipient
Receipt notification	Requests that originator be notified of receipt of message by intended recipient

must offer the option, but it is up to the user to select or not select the option. Finally, *additional optional user facilities* may or may not be offered by the provider.

Table 6.17 lists the services provided by the message transfer sub-layer. The layer attempts to deliver messages to one or more intended recipients and can be asked to notify the originator's UAE of the success or failure of each attempt. This layer may also invoke presentation-layer transformations on behalf of the user-agent sublayer. The originator may request that delivery take place no earlier than a specified time. The recipient may request that a message be temporarily held in the system prior to delivery. In addition, the originator may designate a message as urgent.

Interpersonal messaging services are provided at the user-agent sub-layer and listed in Table 6.18. In this case, optional services receive two designations, one for origination and one for reception. Note that many of the services that are additional (need not be offered) for origination are essential for reception. For example, UAs are not required to allow a user to mark a message as private but must be able to appropriately handle a received message marked private. There are many services at this sublayer. Among the most fundamental are specification of primary and secondary recipients and the subject of the message. Other services have to do with how to handle the message and instructions for notification.

6.6

SUMMARY

The requirements that guide the design and implementation of ISDN can be expressed in terms of telecommunications services. These services are the reason for the existence of ISDN or any network. Thus it is important to be clear about what services are to be provided and, in detail, what characteristics and attributes that the user expects to have associated with these services. Once this is known, the network capabilities needed to support the services can be determined.

CCITT has specified these services as part of the I-series of recommendations. Two types of services are defined: bearer services and teleservices. Bearer services are the lower-level functions responsible for transferring data between subscribers across ISDN. These services correspond to layers 1 through 3 of the OSI model. CCITT has defined these services quite explicitly. Teleservices are the actual user-visible services that are supported across ISDN. These services correspond to layers 4 through 7 of the OSI model and make use of the bearer services.

Strictly speaking, the protocols that are part of the teleservices are not part of and are not visible to a communications network, including ISDN. However, there are several reasons for addressing teleservices in the context of ISDN. First, both teleservices and bearer services make use of a common set of supplementary services (e.g., reverse charging), and a uniform means of specifying and invoking those services is useful. Second, the nature of a teleservice will determine the nature of the bearer service used, and standards on the interrelationships are useful.

In addition to a general description of teleservices, this chapter reviews three of the most important teleservices. *Teletex* is a message preparation and delivery service that is an upgrade to *telex*. *Group 4 facsimile* is a digital facsimile service that provides high-speed image transfer using sophisticated image-compression techniques. CCITT has also standardized mixed-mode terminals that can prepare and display/print images consisting of both text and images. Finally, the X.400 standards on *message-handling systems* define a sophisticated electronic mail facility.

6.7

RECOMMENDED READING

[KOBA85] is a good survey of facsimile technology and CCITT standardization of it. [RYAN87] is also a good discussion, with an emphasis on CCITT-compliant products. Good discussions of MH and MR compression techniques are provided in [JAYA84] and [FREE85]. [BODS86] looks at the throughput of Group 4 facsimile over ISDN and packet-switched networks. The teletex standard is presented in [HELM82] and [MOOR83]; a discussion can also be found in [BLAC87].

[HENS88] provides a good discussion of the 1988 X.400 standards; a somewhat briefer presentation is in [CHIL90]. [MANR89] and [CRAI88] explain the rather substantial differences between the 1984 and 1988 versions of X.400.

6.8

PROBLEMS

6.1. In the United States, there has been considerable thought given to the types of telecommunication services that should be subject to government regulation of price and quality and those that should be offered competitively with little or no regulation. Two important efforts in this regard are the Computer Inquiry II by the Federal

Communications Commission (FCC) and the Modification of Final Judgment (MFJ), which resulted in the break-up of AT&T. In Computer Inquiry II, the FCC defined the following terms:

Basic Service limited to the common-carrier offering of transmission capacity for the movement of information.

Enhanced Service any offering over the telecommunications network that is more than a basic transmission service. Such services employ computer processing applications that act on the format, content, code, protocol, or similar aspects of the subscriber's transmitted information; provide the subscriber additional, different, or restructured information; or involve subscriber interaction with stored information.

The MFJ produced the following definitions:

Telecommunication Service the transmissions, between or among points specified by the user, of information of the user's choosing, without change in the form or content of the information as seen and received, by means of electromagnetic transmission, with or without benefit of any closed transmission medium, including all instrumentalities, facilities, apparatus, and services (including the collection, storage, forwarding, switching, and delivery of such information) essential to such transmission.

Information Service a capability for generating, acquiring, storing, transforming, processing, retrieving, utilizing, or making available information that may be conveyed via telecommunications, except that such service does not include any use of such capability for the management, control, or operation of a telecommunications system or the management of a telecommunications service.

Compare these two pairs of definitons with these definitions from I.112:

Bearer Service a type of telecommunication service that provides the capability for the transmission of signals between user-network interfaces.

Teleservice a type of telecommunication service that provides the complete capability, including terminal equipment functions, for communication between users according to protocols established by agreement between Administrations and/or RPOAs.

6.2. Consider Figure 6.4. With the Group 4 recommendation, the compressor/decompressor and communication interface modules are standardized. Do you think that the preprocessor/postprocessor modules are also standardized? Justify your answer.

6.3. Consider a binary source that produces symbols $\times 1$ and $\times 2$ with probabilities 0.8 and 0.2 respectively.

a. What is the entropy H?

b. A simple binary code will produce an output of 1 bit per symbol, which is considerably above the entropy. A rate closer to H can be achieved by a combination of encoding delay and variable-length encoding. We look at all possible source sequences of length 2 and assign codewords to each of the four sequences. Show the Huffman code for this scheme and compute the average codeword length.

6.4. Consider a source with four symbols whose probabilities of occurrence are 0.5, 0.25, 0.125, and 0.125.

a. What is the entropy H?

b. Develop the Huffman code. What is the average codeword length?

6.5. Consider a high-resolution facsimile document of 2376 × 1728 two-level pels.

a. Without data compression, how long will it take to transmit this page over a 4800-bps line?

b. To transmit the message over a 4800-bps line in one minute, what compression ratio is required?

6.6. Suppose the document of Problem 6.5 is encoded using MR, achieving a compression ratio of 10 pels/bit. Assume that transmission errors do not propagate beyond one horizontal line. If there is to be no more than 1 degraded line per document on the average, what (approximately) is the acceptable value for the probability of a random bit error?

6.7. Suppose that a document has 150 × 200 mm of text with 0.5 char/mm and 0.24 lines of text per mm (not to be confused with scanning lines). Assume digitization of 400 × 400 pels per mm. If the document is transmitted as text, 8-bit teletex characters are used. Ignoring protocol overhead, compare the message transmission time of teletex, uncompressed facsimile, and facsimile compressed at a ratio of 10 pels/bit over a 64-kbps ISDN line.

6.8. Protocol P1 provides that a message envelope and its contents be transmitted from one MTAE to another. The standard specifies that the message envelope and the message content be transmitted as a single P1 PDU. Several other mechanisms are possible. The sending MTAE could transmit the message envelope first, wait for approval from the second MTAE, and then transmit the message content. A third method is to transmit the message envelope first, one parameter at a time, waiting for a positive acknowledgment after each parameter. For example, the recipient list might be transmitted first, then handling instructions, and so on. Discuss the relative advantages and disadvantages of each method.

6.9. Electronic mail systems differ in the manner in which multiple recipients are handled. In some systems, the originating UA or MTA makes all the necessary copies and these are sent out independently. An alternative approach is to determine the route for each destination first. Then a single message is sent out on a common portion of the route and copies are only made when the routes diverge; this process is referred to as *mail-bagging*. Discuss the relative advantages and disadvantages of the two methods.

CHAPTER 7

ISDN Interfaces and Functions

This chapter looks at a variety of issues related to ISDN architecture as seen by the user. On the whole, the user need not be concerned with the internal functioning or mechanisms of an ISDN. However, the user is concerned with the nature of the interface and the way in which services are requested and provided.

Seven technical areas are examined in this chapter:

- *Transmission structure:* the way in which logical channels providing bearer services are organized for transmission over the local loop.
- *User-network interface configurations:* the way in which user-ISDN interactions are organized functionally and how this guides the actual equipment configuration and the definition of the user-ISDN interface.
- *Protocol architecture:* the structure of user-network protocols and their relationship to the OSI model.
- *ISDN connections:* the types of end-to-end connections that are supported by ISDN.
- *Terminal adaption:* the way in which ISDN provides support for non-ISDN terminals and computers.
- *Addressing:* the way in which a calling user specifies the called user so that the network can perform routing and delivery functions.
- *Interworking:* the capability for an ISDN subscriber to establish a connection to a subscriber on a non-ISDN network.

7.1

TRANSMISSION STRUCTURE

The digital pipe between the central office and the ISDN subscriber will be used to carry a number of communication channels. The capacity of the pipe, and therefore the number of channels carried, may vary from user to user. The transmission structure of any access link will be constructed from the following types of channels:

- *B channel:* 64 kbps.
- *D channel:* 16 or 64 kbps.
- *H channel:* 384 (H0), 1536 (H11), or 1920 (H12) kbps.

The **B channel** is a user channel that can be used to carry digital data, PCM-encoded digital voice, or a mixture of lower-rate traffic, including digital data and digitized voice encoded at a fraction of 64 kbps. In the case of mixed traffic, all traffic of the B channel must be destined for the same endpoint; that is, the elemental unit of circuit switching is the B channel. If a B channel consists of two or more subchannels, all subchannels must be carried over the same circuit between the same subscribers. Three kinds of connections can be set up over a B channel:

- *Circuit-switched:* this is equivalent to switched digital service, available today. The user places a call and a circuit-switched connection is established with another network user. An interesting feature is that the call establishment does not take place over the B channel, but is done using common-channel signaling.
- *Packet-switched:* the user is connected to a packet-switching node, and data are exchanged with other users via X.25.
- *Semipermanent:* this is a connection to another user set up by prior arrangement and not requiring a call establishment protocol. This is equivalent to a leased line.

The designation of 64 kbps as the standard user channel rate highlights the fundamental disadvantage of standardization. The rate was chosen as the most effective for digitized voice, yet the technology has progressed to the point at which 32 kbps or even less will produce equally satisfactory voice reproduction. To be effective, a standard must freeze the technology at some defined point. Yet by the time the standard is approved, it may already be obsolete.

The **D channel** serves two main purposes. First, it carries common-channel signaling information to control circuit-switched calls on associated B channels at the user interface. In addition, the D channel may be used for packet-switching or low-speed (e.g., 100 bps) telemetry at times when no signaling information is waiting. Table 7.1 summarizes the types of data traffic to be supported on B and D channels.

H channels are provided for user information at higher bit rates. The user may use such a channel as a high-speed trunk or subdivide the channel according to the user's own TDM scheme. Examples of applications include fast facsimile, video, high-speed data, high-quality audio, and multiplexed information streams at lower data rates.

These channel types are grouped into transmission structures that are offered as a package to the user. The best-defined structures at this time (Figure 7.1) are the basic channel structure (basic access) and the primary channel structure (primary access).

Basic access consists of two full-duplex 64-kbps B channels and a full-duplex 16-kbps D channel. The total bit rate, by simple arithmetic, is 144 kbps. However, framing, synchronization, and other overhead bits bring the total bit rate on a basic access link to 192 kbps; the details of these overhead bits are presented in Chapter 8. The basic service is intended to meet the needs of most individual users, including residential subscribers and very small offices. It allows the simultaneous use of voice and several data applications, such as packet-switched access, a link to a central alarm service, facsimile, teletex, and so on. These services could be accessed through a single multifunction terminal or several separate terminals. In either case, a single physical interface is provided. Most existing two-wire local loops can support this interface [GIFF86].

In some cases, one or both of the B channels remain unused. This results in a $B + D$ or D interface, rather than the $2B + D$ interface. However, to simplify the network implementation, the data rate at the interface remains at 192 kbps. Nevertheless, for those subscribers with more modest transmission requirements, there may be a cost savings in using a reduced basic interface.

TABLE 7.1   ISDN Channel Functions

B Channel (64 kbps)	D Channel (16 kbps)
Digital voice	Signaling
64-kbps PCM	Basic
Low bit rate (32 kbps)	Enhanced
High-speed data	Low-speed data
Circuit-switched	Videotex
Packet-switched	Terminal
Other	Telemetry
Facsimile	Emergency services
Slow-scan video	Energy management

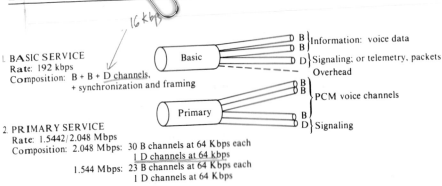

1. BASIC SERVICE
   Rate: 192 kbps
   Composition: B + B + D channels,
                 + synchronization and framing

2. PRIMARY SERVICE
   Rate: 1.5442/2.048 Mbps
   Composition: 2.048 Mbps: 30 B channels at 64 Kbps each
                            1 D channels at 64 kbps
                1.544 Mbps: 23 B channels at 64 Kbps each
                            1 D channels at 64 Kbps

FIGURE 7.1 ISDN Channel Structures

Primary access is intended for users with greater capacity requirements, such as offices with a digital PBX or a LAN. Because of differences in the digital transmission hierarchies used in different countries,
it was not possible to get agreement on a single data rate. The United
States, Canada, and Japan make use of a transmission structure based
on 1.544 Mbps; this corresponds to the T1 transmission facility of AT&T.
In Europe, 2.048 Mbps is the standard rate. Both of these data rates are
provided as a primary interface service. Typically, the channel structure
for the 1.544-Mbps rate will be 23 B channels plus one 64-kbps D channel
and, for the 2.048-Mbps rate, 30 B channels plus one 64-kbps D channel.
Again, it is possible for a customer with lesser requirements to employ
fewer B channels, in which case the channel structure is $nB + D$,
where n ranges from 1 to 23 or from 1 to 30 for the two primary services.
Also, a customer with high data rate demands may be provided with
more than one primary physical interface. In this case, a single D
channel on one of the interfaces may suffice for all signaling needs, and
the other interfaces may consist solely of B channels (24B or 31B).

The primary interface may also be used to support H channels. Some
of these structures include a 64-kbps D channel for control signaling.
When no D channel is present, it is assumed that a D channel on
another primary interface at the same subscriber location will provide
any required signaling. The following structures are recognized:

- *Primary rate interface H0 channel structures:* This interface supports
  multiple 384-kbps H0 channels. The structures are $3H0 + D$ and
  $4H0$ for the 1.544-Mbps interface and $5H0 + D$ for the 2.048-Mbps
  interface.
- *Primary rate interface H1 channel structures:* The H11 channel structure
  consists of one 1536-kbps H11 channel. The H12 channel structure
  consists of one 1920-kbps H12 channel and one D channel.
- *Primary rate interface structures for mixtures of B and H0 channels:*
  Consist of zero or one D channels plus any possible combination
  of B and H0 channels up to the capacity of the physical interface
  (e.g., $3H0 + 5B + D$ or $3H0 + 6B$ for the 1.544-Mbps interface).

7.2

USER-NETWORK INTERFACE CONFIGURATIONS

Reference Points and Functional Groupings

To define the requirements for ISDN user access, an understanding of the anticipated configuration of user premises equipment and of the necessary standard interfaces is critical. The first step is to group functions that may exist on the user's premises in ways that suggest actual physical configurations. Figure 7.2 shows the CCITT approach to this task, using

- *Functional groupings:* certain finite arrangements of physical equipment or combinations of equipment.
- *Reference points:* conceptual points used to separate groups of functions.

An analogy with the OSI model might be useful at this point. The principal motivation for the 7-layer OSI architecture is that it provides a framework for standardization. Once the functions to be performed in each layer are defined, protocol standards can be developed at each layer. This effectively organizes the standards work and provides guidance to software and equipment providers. Furthermore, by defining the services that each layer provides to the next higher layer, work in each layer can proceed independently. So long as the interface between two layers remains stable, new and different technical approaches can be provided within one layer without an impact on neighboring layers.

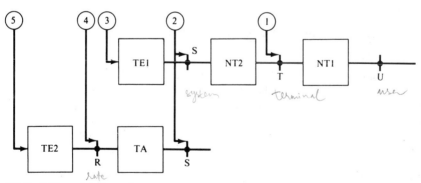

R,S,T = Reference interface points
TE1 = Terminal equipment type 1
TE2 = Terminal equipment type 2
TA = Terminal adaptor
NT1 = Network termination 1
NT2 = Network termination 2

FIGURE 7.2 ISDN Reference Points and Functional Groupings

In the case of ISDN, the architecture on the subscriber's premises is broken up functionally into groupings separated by reference points. This permits interface standards to be developed at each reference point. Again, this effectively organizes the standards work and provides guidance to the equipment providers. Once stable interface standards exist, technical improvements on either side of an interface can be made without impact on adjacent functional groupings. Finally, with stable interfaces, the subscriber is free to procure equipment from different suppliers for the various functional groupings, so long as the equipment conforms to the relevant interface standards.

Let us consider first the functional groupings. **Network termination 1** (NT1) includes functions that may be regarded as belonging to OSI layer 1, that is, functions associated with the physical and electrical termination of the ISDN on the user's premises (Table 7.2). The NT1 may be controlled by the ISDN provider and forms a boundary to the network. This boundary isolates the user from the transmission technology of the subscriber loop and presents a new physical connector interface for user device attachment. In addition, the NT1 will perform line maintenance functions such as loopback testing and performance monitoring. The NT1 supports multiple channels (e.g., 2B + D); at the physical level, the bit streams of these channels are multiplexed together, using synchronous time-division multiplexing. Finally, the NT1 interface might support multiple devices in a multidrop arrangement. For example, a residential interface might include a telephone, personal computer, and alarm system, all attached to a single NT1 interface via a multidrop line. For such a configuration, the NT1 includes a contention resolution algorithm to control access to the D channel; this algorithm is described in Chapter 8.

TABLE 7.2   Functions of ISDN Functional Groupings

NT1	NT2	TE
Line transmission termination	Layers 2 and 3 protocol handling	Protocol handling
Line maintenance and performance monitoring	Layers 2 and 3 multiplexing	Maintenance functions
Timing	Switching	Interface functions
Power transfer	Concentration	Connection functions to other equipment
Layer 1 multiplexing	Maintenance functions	
Interface termination, including multidrop termination employing layer 1 contention resolution	Interface termination and other layer 1 functions	

Network termination 2 (NT2) is an intelligent device that may include, depending on the requirement, up through OSI layer 3 functionality. NT2 can perform switching and concentration functions. Examples of NT2 are a digital PBX, a terminal controller, and a LAN. For example, a digital PBX can provide NT2 functions at layers 1, 2, and 3. A simple terminal controller can provide NT2 functions at only layers 1 and 2. A simple time-division multplexer can provide NT2 functions at only layer 1. An example of a switching function is the construction of a private network using semipermanent circuits among a number of sites. Each site could include a PBX that acts as a circuit switch or a host computer that acts as a packet switch. The concentration function simply means that multiple devices, attached to a digital PBX, LAN, or terminal controller, may transmit data across ISDN.

Terminal equipment refers to subscriber equipment that make use of ISDN. Two types are defined. **Terminal equipment type 1** (TE1) refers to devices that support the standard ISDN interface. Examples are digital telephone, integrated voice/data terminals, and digital facsimile equipment. **Terminal equipment type 2** (TE2) encompasses existing non-ISDN equipment. Examples are terminals with a physical interface, such as RS-232, and host computers with an X.25 interface. Such equipment requires a **terminal adaptor** (TA) to plug into an ISDN interface.

The definitions of the functional groupings also define, by implication, the reference points. **Reference point T** (terminal) corresponds to a minimal ISDN network termination at the customer's premises. It separates the network provider's equipment from the user's equipment. **Reference point S** (system) corresponds to the interface of individual ISDN terminals. It separates user terminal equipment from network-related communications functions. **Reference point R** (rate) provides a non-ISDN interface between user equipment that is not ISDN-compatible and adaptor equipment. Typically, this interface will comply with an X series or V series CCITT recommendation. The final reference point, illustrated in Figure 7.2, is **reference point U** (user). This interface describes the full-duplex data signal on the subscriber line. At the present time, this reference point is not defined in I.411, which states:

> There is no reference point assigned to the transmission line, since an ISDN user-network interface is not envisaged at this location.

Earlier drafts of I.411, up through 1981, defined such a reference point. In 1981, this definition was dropped without explanation, to be replaced by the flat assertion just noted, which survived into the 1984 final version of I.411 and has not subsequently been removed. Despite this statement, it is clear that, at least in the United States, the U interface will be present. The issue involved is one that clearly illustrates that a difference in philosophy concerning the degree of competitiveness in ISDN provision can have detailed technical impact. It is therefore worthy of a brief elaboration.

To begin, let us consider why the T reference point was defined by CCITT as occurring between an NT1 and an NT2, rather than combining these two functional groups and defining the loop transmission system as the standard user-network interface. It was felt that there must be a decoupling of customer premises equipment from network technology, configuration, and evolution. This would allow customers to preserve their investment in user equipment and software while the capabilities and performance characteristics of the network evolve. Because the subscriber loop transmission system is the most expensive single part of ISDN, continuing technical evolution in that area is essential to provide high-performance, low-cost network service. Furthermore, the technology in this area is changing rapidly, and there are a number of possible solutions to the technical challenges presented by the subscriber loop (e.g., echo cancellation versus time-compression multiplexing). Accordingly, it is not desirable to define an interface directly at the subscriber loop, which in turn defines the loop transmission technology.

Within the United States, however, the consequences of Computer Inquiry II (see Section 1-3) dictate an opposite conclusion. In addition to drawing a distinction between basic and enhanced services, Computer II defined a distinction between network equipment and customer premises equipment and mandated that the latter must be available to users independently of the network provider. Indeed, network services providers are forbidden from supplying customer premises equipment as a part of the basic network. The FCC determined that what it referred to as Network Channel Terminating Equipment (NCTE) is customer premises equipment. Accordingly, service providers must provide a standardized interface that allows the customer to procure NCTE devices from other vendors.

The problem for ISDN planning arises in that the NCTE and NT1 units are analogous if not identical. Therefore, the concept of the NT1 being part of the network is contrary to Computer II. The FCC commented on this issue in its first report on ISDN, issued in 1984:

> Our NCTE decision as applied to ISDN implicitly requires that an interface to the input of the NT1 be established. Stated alternatively, our NCTE decision requires that there be established an interface to the loop, to which customer-premises equipment may be connected.
>
> It appears clear that an interface to the loop facilities will be required to facilitate the provision of equipment or capabilities comparable to the NT1 by subscribers in the United States. Since ISDN hs been directed towards arriving at relatively uniform international recommendations governing ISDN, it may prove appropriate for the CCITT to arrive at a

suitable definition of a U interface to facilitate this. To avoid potential confusion and inconsistency of domestic implementations of ISDN with the international recommendations, it would be desirable for the international ISDN planning efforts to include sufficient flexibility as they evolve to accommodate the U interface concept. Therefore, we urge that this matter be pursued in the continuing ISDN planning efforts.

There has been considerable work within the U.S. standards groups affiliated with CCITT to develop a U interface standard based on echo cancellation techniques. This work has resulted in a U.S. standard. At this time, it is not clear whether this standard will be adopted by CCITT.

Service Support

The structure defined in Figure 7.2 can be related to the ISDN services. This helps to further clarify the distinction between bearer services and teleservice, while also clarifying the implications of the functional groupings and reference points.

Bearer services supported by ISDN are accessed at points 1 and/or 2 (reference points T and S). In both cases, the basic service concept is identical. Thus, for example, a bearer service of *circuit-mode 64-kbps 8 kHz-structure unrestricted* can be supplied at either reference point. The choice between access points 1 and 2 depends on the configuration of the communications equipment at the customer premises.

At access point 4 (reference point R), other standardized services (e.g., X series and V series interfaces) may be accessed. This allows terminals not conforming to the ISDN interface standards to be used in conjunction with the bearer services. For such terminals, a terminal adapter is required to adapt the existing standard to the ISDN standard. Such adaption can include data rate, analog-to-digital, or other interface characteristics.

Access points 3 and 5 provide access to teleservices. ISDN teleservices incorporating terminals that conform to ISDN standards are accessed at access point 3. Teleservices that make use of terminals based on existing non-ISDN standards are accessed at point 5. For these services, as with the bearer services, a terminal adapter may be required.

Access Configurations

Based on the definitions of functional groupings and reference points, various possible configurations for ISDN user-network interfaces have been proposed by CCITT. These are shown in Figure 7.3. Note that on the customer's premises there may be interfaces at S and T, at S but not T, at T but not S, or at a combined S-T interface. The first case (S and T) is the most straightforward; one or more pieces of equipment cor-

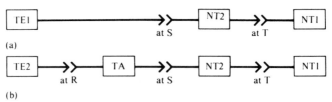

(a)

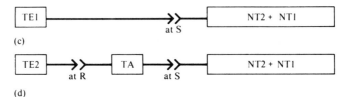

(b)

Configurations where ISDN physical interfaces occur at reference points S and T

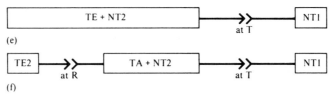

(c)

(d)

Configurations where ISDN physical interfaces occur at reference point S only

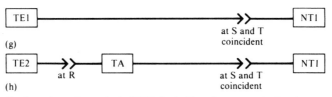

(e)

(f)

Configurations where ISDN physical interfaces occur at reference point T only

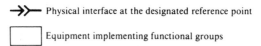

(g)

(h)

Configurations where a single ISDN physical interface occurs at a location where both reference points S and T coincide

──➤➤── Physical interface at the designated reference point

▢ Equipment implementing functional groups

FIGURE 7.3 Examples of Physical Configurations

respond to each functional grouping. Examples were given previously when the functional groupings were defined.

In the second case (S but not T), the functions of NT1 and NT2 are combined. In this case, the line termination function is combined with other ISDN interface functions. Two possible situations are reflected by this arrangement. In many countries without competitive provision of telecommunications services, the ISDN provider will provide the NT1 function. If that same provider also offers computer, local area network, and/or digital PBX equipment, the NT1 functions can be integrated into this other equipment. In the United States, the NT1 function is not an integral part of the ISDN offering and can be supplied by a number of vendors. In this case, a LAN or digital PBX vendor might integrate the NT1 function into its equipment.

In the third case (T but not S) the NT2 and terminal (TE) functions are combined. One possibility here is a host computer system that supports users but also acts as a packet switch in a private packet-switching network that uses ISDN for trunking. Another possibility is that terminal equipment is supported by non-ISDN-standard interfaces. This latter possibility is illustrated in Figure 7.3c and discussed subsequently.

The final configuration (combined S-T interface) illustrates a key feature of ISDN interface compatibility: An ISDN subscriber device, such as a telephone, can connect directly to the subscriber loop terminator or into a PBX or LAN, using the same interface specifications and thus ensuring portability.

Figure 7.4 provides examples of the ways in which a customer may implement the NT1 and NT2 functions. These examples illustrate that a given ISDN function can be implemented using various technologies and that different ISDN functions can be combined in a single device. For example: Figure 7.4c illustrates that a LAN can interface to ISDN using a primary or basic access interface, while the user devices make use of a very different interface (e.g., a token-ring LAN interface).

One additional set of configurations is suggested by CCITT. These cover cases in which the subscriber has more than one device at a particular interface point, but not so many devices that a separate PBX or LAN is warranted. In these cases, it is possible to have multiple physical interfaces at a single reference point. Examples are shown in Figure 7.5. Figure 7.5a and b show multiple terminals connected to the network, either through a multidrop line or through a multiport NT1. These cases are not intended to require that individual terminals can talk to each other, as in a LAN, but rather that each terminal can communicate with the network.

Figures 7.5c and d provide multiple connections between TE1s and NT2. The two figures more or less correspond to PBX and LAN, re-

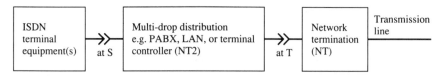

(a) An implementation (see Figure 7.5a) where ISDN physical interfaces occur at reference points S and T.

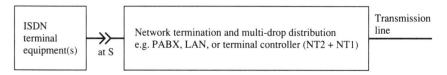

(b) An implementation (see Figure 7.5c) where an ISDN physical interface occurs at reference point S but not T.

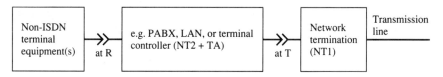

(c) An implementation (see Figure 7.5f) where an ISDN physical interface occurs at reference points T but not S.

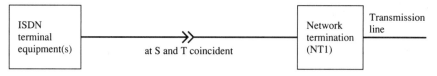

(d) An implementation (see Figure 7.5g) where a single ISDN physical interface occurs at a location where both reference points S and T coincide.

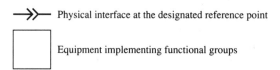

FIGURE 7.4 Examples of Implementation of NT1 and NT2 Functions

spectively. Figure 7.5e shows the case of multiple NT1 equipment, whereas Figure 7.5f shows a case in which NT1 provides a layer 1 multiplexing of multiple connections.

The final two configurations indicate that either S or T, but not both, need not correspond to a physical interface in a particular configuration. We have already referred to the combination of NT1 and NT2. In addition, an NT2 can be equipped with the capability to attach TE2 equipment directly.

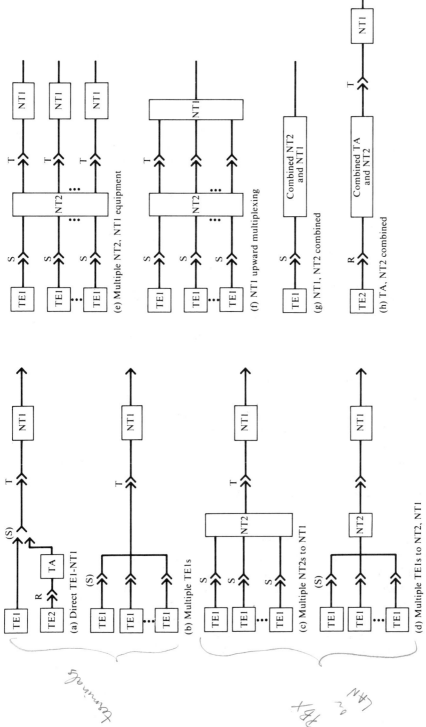

FIGURE 7.5 Possible Configurations for ISDN User-Network Interfaces

7.3

ISDN PROTOCOL ARCHITECTURE

The development of standards for ISDN includes, of course, the development of protocols for interaction between ISDN users and the network and for interaction between two ISDN users. It would be desirable to fit these new ISDN protocols into the OSI framework, and to a great extent this has been done. However, there are certain requirements for ISDN that are not met within the current structure of OSI. Examples of these are

- **Multiple related protocols:** The primary example of this is the use of a protocol on the D channel to set up, maintain, and terminate a connection on a B channel.
- **Multimedia calls:** ISDN will allow a call to be set up that allows information flow consisting of multiple types, such as voice, data, facsimile, and control signals.
- **Multipoint connections:** ISDN will allow conference calls.

These and other functions are not directly addressed in the current OSI specification. However, the basic 7-layer framework appears valid even in the ISDN context, and the issue is more one of specific functionality at the various layers. The issue of the exact relationship between ISDN and OSI remains one for further study.

Figure 7.6 suggests the relationship between OSI and ISDN. As a network, ISDN is essentially unconcerned with user layers 4–7. These are end-to-end layers employed by the user for the exchange of information. Network access is concerned only with layers 1–3. Layer 1, defined in I.430 and I.431, defines the physical interface for basic and primary access, respectively. Since the B and D channels are multiplexed over the same physical interface, these standards apply to both types of channels. Above this layer, the protocol structure differs for the two channels.

For the D channel, a new data link layer standard, LAP-D (Link Access Protocol, D Channel) has been defined. This standard is based on HDLC, modified to meet ISDN requirements. All transmission on the D channel is in the form of LAP-D frames that are exchanged between the subscriber equipment and an ISDN switching element. Three applications are supported: control signaling, packet switching, and telemetry. For **control signaling,** a call-control protocol has been defined (I.451/Q.931). This protocol is used to establish, maintain, and terminate connections on B channels. Thus, it is a protocol between the user and the network. Above layer 3, there is the possibility for higher-layer functions associated with user-to-user control signaling. These are a subject for further study. The D channel can also be used to provide

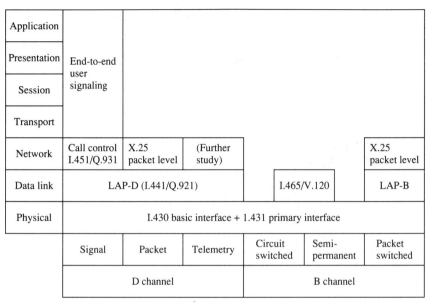

FIGURE 7.6 ISDN Protocol Architecture at the User-Network Interface

packet-switching services to the subscriber. In this case, the X.25 level 3 protocol is used, and X.25 packets are transmitted in LAP-D frames. The X.25 level 3 protocol is used to establish virtual circuits on the D channel to other users and to exchange packetized data. The final application area, **telemetry,** is a subject for further study.

The B channel can be used for circuit switching, semipermanent circuits, and packet switching. For **circuit switching,** a circuit is set up on a B channel on demand. The D channel call-control protocol is used for this purpose. Once the circuit is set up, it may be used for data transfer between the users. Recall from Chapter 2 that a circuit-switched network provides a transparent data path between communication stations.

A **semipermanent circuit** is a B channel circuit that is set up by prior agreement between the connected users and the network. As with a circuit-switched connection, it provides a transparent data path between end systems.

With either a circuit-switched connection or a semipermanent circuit, it appears to the connected stations that they have a direct full-duplex link with each other. They are free to use their own formats, protocols, and frame synchronization. Hence, from the point of view of ISDN, layers 2–7 are not visible or specified. In addition, however, CCITT has standardized I.465/V.120, which does provide a common link-control functionality for ISDN subscribers.

In the case of **packet switching,** a circuit-switched connection is set up on a B channel between the user and a packet-switched node using the D channel control protocol. Once the circuit is set up on the B channel, the user employs X.25 levels 2 and 3 to establish a virtual circuit to another user over that channel and to exchange packetized data.

7.4

ISDN CONNECTIONS

ISDN provides four types of service for end-to-end communication:

- Circuit-switched calls over a B channel.
- Semipermanent connections over a B channel.
- Packet-switched calls over a B channel.
- Packet-switched calls over a D channel.

Circuit Switching

The network configuration and protocols for circuit switching involve both the B and D channels. The B channel is used for the transparent exchange of user data. The communicating users may use any protocols they wish for end-to-end communication. The D channel is used to exchange control information between the user and the network for call establishment and termination and access to network facilities.

Figure 7.7 depicts the protocol architecture that implements circuit switching (see Table 7.3 for a key to Figures 7.7, 7.10, and 7.11). The B channel is serviced by an NT1 or NT2 using only layer 1 functions. The end users may employ any protocol, although generally layer 3 will be null. On the D channel, a three-layer network access protocol is used and is explained subsequently. Finally, the process of establishing a circuit through ISDN involves the cooperation of switches internal to ISDN to set up the connection. These switches interact using Signaling System Number 7.

Semipermanent Connections

A semipermanent connection between agreed points may be provided for an indefinite period of time after subscription, for a fixed period, or for agreed periods during a day, week, or other interval. The upper protocol structure depicted in Figure 7.7 is also valid in this case. That is, only layer 1 functionality is provided by the network interface; the call-control protocol is not needed, since the connection already exists.

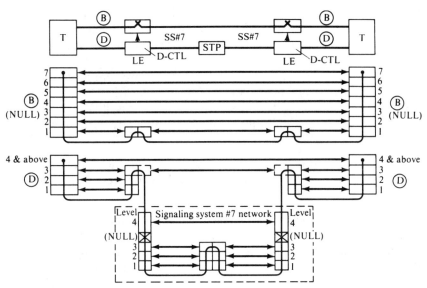

FIGURE 7.7 Network Configuration and Protocols for Circuit Switching

Packet Switching

The ISDN must also permit user access to packet-switched services for data traffic (e.g., interactive) that is best serviced by packet switching. There are two possibilities for implementing this service: Either the packet-switching capability is furnished by a separate network, referred to as a packet-switched public data network (PSPDN), or the packet-switching capability is integrated into ISDN.

TABLE 7.3   Key to Figures 7.7, 7.10, and 7.11

B = An ISDN B channel	
D = An ISDN D channel	
T = Terminal	
D-CTL = D channel controller	
SS 7 = CCITT Signaling System 7	
STP = Signaling transfer point	
(Null) = Channel not present	
7, 6, 5, 4, 3, 2, 1 = Layers in ISO basic reference model	
LEVEL = Levels in SS 7	
LE = Local exchange	
TE = Transit exchange	
PSF = Packet-switching facility	
Horizontal line = Peer-to-peer protocol	
Vertical line = Layer-to-layer data flow	

PSPDN Service.   When the packet-switching service is provided by a separate PSPDN, the access to that service is via a B channel. Both the user and the PSPDN must therefore be connected as subscribers to the ISDN. In the case of the PSPDN, one or more of the packet-switching network nodes, referred to as packet handlers, are connected to ISDN. We can think of each such node as a traditional X.25 DCE (see Figure 3.16), supplemented by the logic needed to access ISDN. Any ISDN subscriber can then communicate, via X.25, with any user connected to the PSPDN, including

- Users with a direct, permanent connection to the PSPDN.
- Users of the ISDN that currently enjoy a connection, through the ISDN, to the PSPDN.

The connection between the user (via a B channel) and the packet handler with which it communicates may be either semipermanent or circuit-switched. In the former case, the connection is always there, and the user may freely invoke X.25 to set up a virtual circuit to another user. In the latter case, the D channel is involved, and the following sequence of steps occurs (Figure 7.8):

- The user requests, via the D channel call-control protocol (I.451/Q.931), a circuit-switched connection on a B channel to a packet handler.

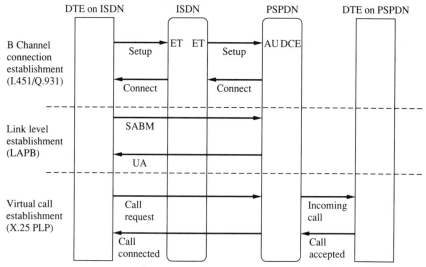

FIGURE 7.8 Virtual Call Setup

- The connection is set up by ISDN and the user is notified via the D channel call-control protocol.
- The user sets up a virtual circuit to another user via the X.25 call establishment procedure on the B channel (described in Chapter 3). This requires that first a data link connection, using LAP-B, must be set up between the user and the packet handler.
- The user terminates the virtual circuit using X.25 on the B channel.
- After one or more virtual calls on the B channel, the user is done and signals via the D channel to terminate the circuit-switched connection to the packet-switching node.
- The connection is terminated by ISDN.

Figure 7.9 shows the configuration involved in providing this service. In the figure, the user is shown to employ a DTE device that expects an interface to an X.25 DCE. Hence, a terminal adapter is required. Alternatively, the X.25 capability can be an integrated function of an ISDN TE1 device, dispensing with the need for a separate TA.

ISDN Service. When the packet-switching service is provided by ISDN, the packet-handling function is provided within the ISDN, either

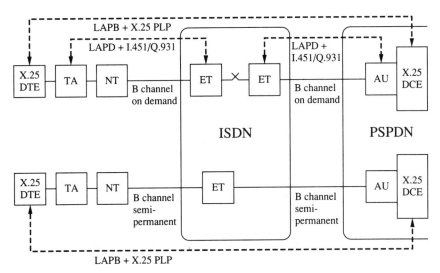

AU = ISDN access unit
TA = Terminal adapter
NT = Network termination 2 and/or 1
ET = Exchange termination
PLP = Packet-level procedure
PSPDN = Packet-switched public data network

FIGURE 7.9 Access to PSPDN for Packet-Mode Service

by separate equipment or as part of the exchange equipment. The user may connect to a packet handler either by a B channel or the D channel. On a B channel, the connection to the packet handler may be either switched or semipermanent, and the same procedures described previously apply for switched connections. In this case, rather than establish a B channel connection to another ISDN subscriber that is a PSPDN packet handler, the connection is to an internal element of ISDN that is a packet handler. Figure 7.10 illustrates the protocol implications.

In addition, packet-switching service can also be obtained on the **D channel.** For D channel access, ISDN provides a semipermanent connection to a packet-switching node within the ISDN. The user employs the X.25 level 3 protocol, as is done in the case of a B channel virtual call. Here, the level 3 protocol is carried by LAP-D frames. Since the D channel is also used for control signaling, some means is needed to distinguish between X.25 packet traffic and ISDN control traffic. This is accomplished by means of the link layer addressing scheme explained in Chapter 9. Figure 7.11 illustrates the protocol implications.

Figure 7.12 shows the configuration for providing packet switching within ISDN. Note that any ISDN user can engage in an X.25 virtual circuit with any other ISDN user over either the B or D channels. In addition, it will be typical to also provide access to X.25 users on other ISDNs and PSPDNs by appropriate interworking procedures. One common approach is the use of X.75, which specifies an interworking scheme between two public X.25 networks.

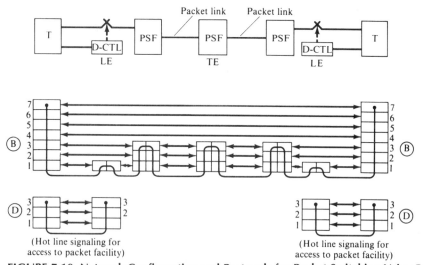

FIGURE 7.10 Network Configuration and Protocols for Packet Switching Using B Channel with Circuit-Switched Access

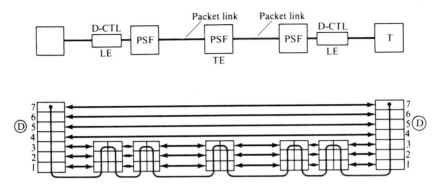

Note: There is another possibility: that LE is transparent to layer 3.

FIGURE 7.11 Network Configuration and Protocols for Packet Switching for D Channel

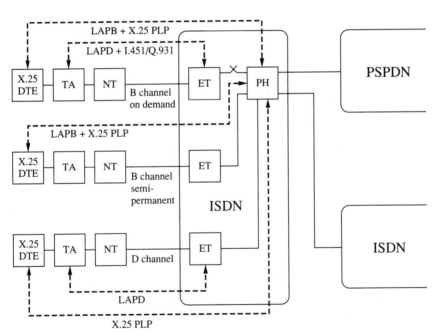

TA = Terminal adapter
NT = Network termination 2 and/or 1
ET = Exchange termination
PLP = Packet-level procedure
PSPDN = Packet-switched public data network
PH = Pacekt handling function

FIGURE 7.12 Access to ISDN for Packet-Mode Service

7.5

TERMINAL ADAPTION

Much of the existing data communications equipment is not compatible with the interfaces, protocols, and data rates of ISDN. In the long run, equipment will be built with ISDN interfaces, but this existing equipment must be accommodated during the transition period. This is the function of the terminal adapter (TA). In essence, a terminal adapter maps a non-ISDN terminal, personal computer, multiplexer, or modem into an ISDN interface. Analog telephones and facsimile machines can also be accommodated. In most cases, the adaption is to the basic rate (2B + D) interface.

There is actually a family of terminal adapters, one type for each type of non-ISDN interface. All of these devices map the characteristics and functions of a particular device to the ISDN characteristics and functions. In general terms, the following functions are performed:

- *Rate adaption:* A data stream of less than 64 kbps is mapped into a 64-kbps data stream.
- *Signaling conversion:* The signaling protocol of the device is mapped into the ISDN signaling protocol, I.451/Q.931. For example, many devices support interfaces, such as X.21 or EIA-232-D, which provide an in-band signaling protocol. These in-band messages must be converted to D channel I.451/Q.931 messages.
- *X.25 conversion:* The functions of non-ISDN X.25 devices are converted to operate on the B and/or D channels. This involves both rate adaption and signaling conversion.
- *Physical interface conversion:* The ISDN interface consists of two twisted pairs at the S or T interface. The non-ISDN interface must be mapped onto this physical interface.
- *Digitization:* In the case of analog devices, analog-to-digital conversion is required.

To accommodate the wide variety of existing equipment and the need to support both circuit-switching and packet-switching applications, CCITT has developed a complex set of capabilities that are defined primarily in the I.460 series of recommendations. Table 7.4 summarizes the procedures defined in the I.460 series, and Table 7.5 compares the features of the various approaches.

The terminal adapter may be either a standalone device or a personal computer circuit card. In either case, the TA supports D channel signaling (I.451/Q.931 and I.441/Q.921) and a procedure on the B channel that indicates the nature of the adaption. The TA allows the terminal equipment (TE2 in Figure 7.2) to communicate across ISDN with another TE2 attached to a TA. A TE2 may also communicate across ISDN with

TABLE 7.4   Summary of TA Procedures

ISDN Service	TA Procedures	R Interface(s)	ISDN Channel(s)
Circuit-Switched	I.465/V.120 (U.S.)	V.24, V.35	B, H
	I.463/V.110 (Europe, Japan)	V.24, V.35	B
	I.461/X.30	X.21	B
Packet-Switched	I.462/X.31 circuit mode	X.25	B
	I.462/X.31 packet mode	X.25	B, D, H

a TE1. In both cases, the two partners must use the same B channel procedure, such as V.110 or V.120, in order to communicate.

Rate Adaption

The principal means of transmitting user data is the B channel, which operates at a data rate of 64 kbps. However, it is desirable to be able to support subscriber devices on the B channel that operate at data rates of less than 64 kbps. There are two reasons for this. First, much existing equipment, such as terminals and personal computers, operates at data rates of less than 64 kbps.

TABLE 7.5   Comparison of TA Standards [WEIS89]

	I.463/V.110 and I.461/X.30	I.465/V.120	I.462/X.31
ISDN bearer service	Circuit	Circuit	Circuit/packet
Rate adaption	1–3 stages	Flag stuffing	Flag stuffing
Multiple destinations	No	No	Yes
HDLC-based	No	Yes	Yes
B channel multiplexing	No	Yes—LLI	Yes—VCN
D channel operation	No	No	Yes, with packet bearer service
Error detection	None	CRC—V.41	CRC—V.41
Error correction	None	Retransmission	Retransmission
Flow control	Limited (X bit)	Yes—sliding window	Yes—sliding window
Type of DTE at R	Async/sync (bit transparent)	Async/HDLC/bit transparent	X.25 sync

CRC   = cyclic redundancy check
DTE   = data terminal equipment
I field = information field
VCN   = virtual circuit number
LLI   = logical-link ID
PAD   = packet-assembler/disassembler
TA   = terminal adapter

The second reason has to do with the advantages of multiplexing. As we have pointed out, in the current version of the ISDN standards, the entire B channel is the fundamental unit of circuit switching. That is, even if a B channel is logically divided into a number of subchannels, all of the subchannels must be carried on a single circuit between the same pair of subscribers. Even so, a subscriber may have several devices attached to an ISDN interface and wish to connect two or more of them to the same destination. For example, a residential user might want to connect to his or her office and make use of a personal computer and a facsimile at the same time. It will be cheaper if all of this traffic can be carried on one B channel. Furthermore, if all of the data traffic to the office is multiplexed on one B channel, the other B channel of the resident's basic interface is free for sending and receiving telephone calls.

We examine rate adaption in this subsection and then look at multiplexing in the next subsection.

Rate adaption is the function of adapting a terminal with a data rate of less than 64 kbps to a data rate of 64 kbps. Figure 7.13 summarizes the techniques that are specified in I.460.

The initial distinction made in I.460 is whether the bit stream to be carried on the B channel is exactly 8, 16, 32 kbps or whether it is some other data rate.

Data Rate of 8, 16, or 32 kbps.   The first case is illustrated in Figure 7.14. Bits are transmitted on the B channel as a stream of octets at a rate of 64 kbps, or equivalently, 8000 octets per second. For an 8-kbps subscriber device, a terminal adapter (TA) works as follows. Data from the subscriber arrive at the TA at a rate of 8 kbps. Each incoming bit is transmitted in an octet in which the first bit of the octet is a user data bit and the remaining 7 bits are each set to binary one. For data arriving from the ISDN side, the first bit of each incoming octet is passed on to the terminal and the remaining 7 bits are discarded. A similar adaption procedure is followed for terminals operating at 16 kbps and 32 kbps. For 16-kbps streams, the first two bits of each octet are used, and for 32-kbps streams, the first four bits of each octet are used.

Synchronous Circuit-mode Devices.   The second case listed in I.460 (rates other than 8, 16, or 32 kbps) breaks down into a number of subcases, several of which are broken down even further. Let us consider next the case of a synchronous device using the B-channel circuit-mode service; procedures for this case are defined in I.461/X.30 (terminals that use the X.21, X.21 *bis*, and X.20 *bis* interfaces) and I.463/V.110 (terminals that use the V-series interfaces). If the terminal data rate is less than 32 kbps, then a two-stage adaption function is used; this is illustrated in Figure 7.15. The allowable input rates are all of the form

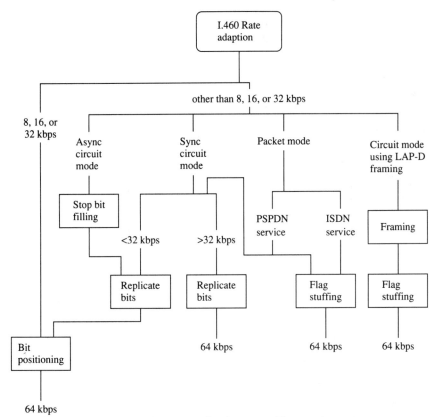

FIGURE 7.13 Alternatives for Rate Adaption to 64-kbps B-Channel

b	1	1	1	1	1	1	1

(a) 8-kbps stream

b	b	1	1	1	1	1	1

(b) 16-kbps stream

b	b	b	b	1	1	1	1

(c) 32-kbps stream

FIGURE 7.14 Allocation of Bits in B Channel Octet for Rate Adaption

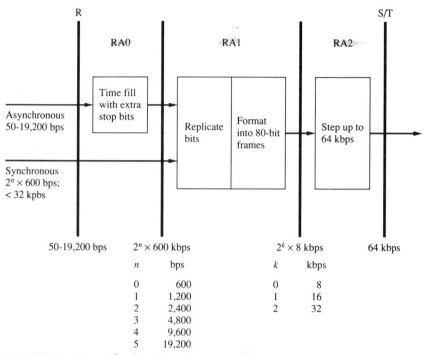

FIGURE 7.15 Rate Adaption (I.463/V.110)

$2^n \times 600$ bps, for $n = 1, 2, 3, 4, 5$. The user data rate is first converted to an intermediate rate of 8, 16, or 32 kbps and then converted from this intermediate rate to 64 kbps. The advantage of using a two-stage technique is that the second stage could be reversed (e.g., from 64 kbps to 8 kbps) somewhere in the network for the purpose of conserving loop or trunk capacity. As a service offering, this could carry a lower tariff rate [COLL83].

The second stage of the rate adaption, labeled RA2 in Figure 7.15, is the same as that just described for adapting 8, 16, or 32 kbps to 64 kbps. The first stage, labeled RA1, involves the creation of a frame, with only some of the bits in the frame carrying user data. As a specific example, consider the adaption of a user rate of 2400 bps to an intermediate ISDN rate of 8 kpbs, which is illustrated in Table 7.6. The conversion is implemented by means of an 80-bit frame structure. Although the data transmitted out of the RA1 module is a constant bit stream, it is considered to consist of a sequence of 80-bit frames. The bits of the frame are as follows:

1. The first octet is all zeros. The first bit of the remaining nine octets is one. These seventeen bits constitute a frame alignment pattern that provides a means of synchronization.

$$\frac{2400 \text{ bps}}{100 \text{ frames/sec}} = 24 \text{ bits} \quad f_n$$

TABLE 7.6 Adaption of 2400-bps User Rate to 8-kbps Intermediate Rate

Octet				Bits			
1	0	0	0	0	0	0	0	0
2	1	D1	D1	D2	D2	D3	D3	S
3	1	D4	D4	D5	D5	D6	D6	X
4	1	D7	D7	D8	D8	D9	D9	S
5	1	D10	D10	D11	D11	D12	D12	S
6	1	1	1	0	E4	E5	E6	E7
7	1	D13	D13	D14	D14	D15	D15	S
8	1	D16	D16	D17	D17	D18	D18	X
9	1	D19	D19	D20	D20	D21	D21	S
10	1	D22	D22	D23	D23	D24	D24	S

D = data bits
S = status bits
E = user data rate indication
X = reserved for future use

2. The sixth octet contains a one followed by a set of "E-bits," E1, E2, . . . , E7. These bits are used to indicate the user data rate. At present only the first three bits are used for this purpose; the remaining bits are reserved for future use. The code 110 for E1, E2, E3 indicates that the user data rate is 2400 bps.
3. The S bits are status bits that convey channel-associated status information. The exact nature of these bits depends on the physical interface between the subscriber terminal and the terminal adapter.
4. The X bits are unused and reserved for future use.
5. Each data bit is repeated. This repetition is not strictly necessary; it acts to fill in unneeded bit positions. These positions could also have been filled in with arbitrary bits.

Each frame contains 24 user data bits. Since we have an 8-kbps output data rate and 80-bit frames, the rate of transmission of frames is 100 frames per second; therefore, the rate of transmission of user data is 2400 bps, as required. In general, we can summarize the function of the RA1 module in Figure 7.15 as follows. Define

F = the number of bits in the frame.
F_u = the number of data bits in the frame.
R_u = the user data rate.
R_f = the desired rate of transmission, in frames per second.
R = the desired rate of transmission, in bits per second.

Two formulas must be satisfied:

$$F \times R_f = R$$

$\frac{R_u}{R_f} = F_u$

$80 \text{ bits/frame} \times 100 \text{ frames/sec} = 8 \text{ Kbps}$

and

$$\frac{R_u^{'}}{R_f} = F_u \quad \text{with no remainder}$$

When the data rate to be adapted is between 32 kbps and 64 kbps, only the RA1 stage of Figure 7.15 is needed.

So far, we have discussed the case of circuit-switched connections. With this type of connection, there is a transparent transmission of data between the two subscribers. With rate adaption, it is still necessary that the two subscribers operate at the same data rate. For example, a terminal operating at 2400 bps can be rate-adapted to 64 kbps. One could attempt to connect this terminal through ISDN to a 4800-bps computer port that is also rate-adapted to 64 kbps. However, the computer will transmit data at 4800 bps and the terminal's adapter expects and requires that the incoming 64-kbps stream contain only user data at a rate of 2400 bps. Thus, the traditional circuit-switching requirement, that the data rate of both users connected to the same circuit must be the same, applies in ISDN.

One final point about the circuit-switching rate adaption. The user data rate is identified during the call setup, which takes place via common-channel signaling on the D channel. During the call setup phase, the network will assure that the data rate of the two subscribers is the same; otherwise, the connection request is rejected.

Asynchronous Circuit-mode Devices.   I.463/V.110 also specifies TA functions for handling asynchronous devices (see Appendix 7B for a definition of asynchronous transmission). To accommodate these devices, a three-stage method is employed. The second and third stages are the RA1 and RA2 functional modules defined for the synchronous case. The first stage, labeled RA0, converts an asynchronous character stream to one of the acceptable synchronous data rates ($2^n \times 600$ bps, for $n = 1, 2, 3, 4, 5$).

The technique used in the RA0 stage is to simply add additional stop bits between characters to step up the data rate to the nearest intermediate rate that can be accepted by the RA1 module. Since asynchronous transmission allows multiple stop bits between characters, the asynchronous receiver can accept the padded character stream directly. If the receiver is to match the data rate of the asynchronous transmitter, then the additional stop bits can be stripped off by the TA at the receiving end.

Packet Mode Support.   As discussed earlier, Recommendation I.462/X.31 specifies the support of packet mode equipment over ISDN. Recall that there are two cases: packet switching done by an external network (Case A) and packet switching done within ISDN (Case B). In either case, the subscriber does not have a direct circuit to another subscriber. Rather, the subscriber has a circuit connection to a packet-switched node and communicates with other packet-switching subscribers via X.25. Here again, we may be faced with the case of a preexisting subscriber device that operates at a data rate of less than 64 kbps.

Consider first Case A, connection to an external packet-switching node via a circuit over a B channel. Recall from Figure 3.11 that X.25 packets are transmitted in LAP-B frames. If the data rate of the subscriber device is less than 64 kbps, then a terminal adaptor can function as follows. LAP-B frames are accepted from the subscriber at the subscriber's data rate and buffered in the TA. Each frame is then transmitted onto the B channel at 64 kbps. Since frames are being transmitted faster than they are generated, there will be gaps. These gaps are filled with additional flag octets (01111110). When frames are received from the network at 64 kbps, they are buffered and delivered to the subscriber at the subscriber's data rate. Excess flag octets between frames are discarded. This process is known as *interframe flag stuffing*. With this procedure, the network cannot distinguish between packet-mode devices operating at 64 kbps and those operating at less than 64 kbps. Therefore, the D channel signaling used to connect a device to a packet-switching node indicates a data rate of 64 kbps.

The alternative approach is the *two-stage rate adaption* of Figure 7.15 (RA1 and RA2). In this case, the bits transmitted by the subscriber are embedded into the 80-octet structure described earlier, and the D channel signaling indicates the user data rate. With this technique, the packet-switching node to which the subscriber is linked must match the data rate of the subscriber. This is clearly less flexible than the interframe flag stuffing approach, and the latter is recommended by CCITT.

In Case B, ISDN offers an internal packet-switching service over both the B channel and the D channel. X.25 packets are carried in LAP-B frames for the B channel and LAP-D frames for the D channel. Rate adaption to 64 kbps for the B channel and to 16 kbps for the D channel is accomplished via flag stuffing.

Circuit-mode Support Using LAP-D Framing.   An alternative method of supporting synchronous circuit-mode equipment is defined in I.465/V.120. In essence, an incoming synchronous bit stream is encapsulated into LAP-D frames and then adapted to 64 kbps by flag stuffing. Unlike the other techniques discussed so far, I.465/V.120 may also be used on H0 (384 kbps), H11 (1.536 Mbps), and H12 (1.92 Mbps) channels.

The terminal adaption function is based on a modification of LAP-D that supports connections between subscribers using the I.465/V.120 protocol. This protocol provides a consistent method for carrying different types of data streams. In this section, we provide a brief introduction to I.465/V.120 and focus on its rate adaption functions. The protocol is examined in more detail in Chapter 9.

I.465/V.120 provides support for three R-interface terminal types:

- Asynchronous protocol sensitive.
- HDLC synchronous protocol sensitive.
- Bit transparent.

The **asynchronous protocol sensitive** case refers to communication between an asynchronous terminal and a host that expects asynchronous input or between two asynchronous terminals. For transmission, the start and stop bits of each character are removed and the incoming characters are buffered in the terminal adapter. The length of the buffer equals the maximum information field size that may be transmitted in a frame. When the buffer is full, a LAP-D frame is created and transmitted. In addition, a partially full buffer of characters may be sent when a carriage return is received or when a timeout occurs. When a frame is received, the characters are recovered and sent to the destination TE with the appropriate start and stop bits.

The **HDLC synchronous protocol sensitive** case refers to communication between entities that are using HDLC as a link-control protocol for end-to-end operation. For transmission, most of the HDLC frame is encapsulated in a LAP-D frame. Several inessential fields are discarded. On reception, the HDLC frame is recovered, the missing fields are added, and the reconstituted frame is passed on to the destination entity. The details of this frame processing are examined in Chapter 9.

The **bit transparent** case will accommodate any synchronous device. The TA encapsulates the bits from the R interface into fixed-size LAP-D frames as they are received. The TA takes data from frames received and sends it to the TE2.

The advantage of the I.465/V.120 approach compared to the I.461/V.110 approach is that the data are transmitted in I.465/V.120 using a data link control protocol. This provides for the benefits of flow control and error control that are inherent in a link-control protocol (see Appendix A).

Multiplexing

Multiplexing, in the context of this section, is the function of combining traffic from multiple terminals, each with a data rate of less than 64 kbps, onto a single B channel at 64 kbps. Figure 7.16 summarizes the techniques that are specified in I.460. As in the case of rate adaption, the initial distinction made in I.460 is whether the bit stream to be carried on the B channel is exactly 8, 16, or 32 kbps or whether it is some other data rate.

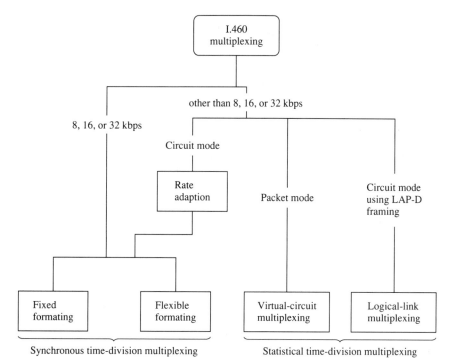

FIGURE 7.16 Alternatives for Multiplexing on a 64-kbps B-Channel

Data Rate of 8, 16, or 32 kbps. In this case, there are multiple bit streams of 8, 16, and/or 32 kbps with an aggregate data rate that is less than or equal to 64 kbps. For this case, bits from different streams, up to a total of 64 kbps, are interleaved within each octet.

Two approaches to multiplexing are defined, With **fixed-format multiplexing,** the following rules are observed:

- An 8-kbps bit stream may occupy any bit position; a 16-kbps bit stream may occupy bit positions (1, 2), (3, 4), (5, 6) or (7, 8); a 32-kbps bit stream may occupy bit positions (1, 2, 3, 4) or (5, 6, 7, 8).
- A subrate stream occupies the same bit position(s) in each successive B channel octet.
- All unused bit positions are set to binary one.

If this procedure is used and the data substreams are added one at a time, it is possible that the 64-kbps capacity will not be effectively utilized. For example, if bit positions 1 and 8 are used to support two 8-kbps substreams, then a 32-kbps substream cannot be added even though the capacity is available. An approach that avoids this is **flexible-format multiplexing.** The following rules are observed:

- An attempt is made to accommodate a new subrate stream using the fixed-format procedure.
- If this attempt fails, the new subrate stream is added by inserting each successive bit of the new stream into the earliest available bit position in the B channel octet.
- A subrate stream occupies the same bit position(s) in each successive B channel octet.
- All unused bit positions are set to binary one.

This procedure always allows subrate streams to be multiplexed up to the 64-kbps limit of the B channel. The fixed-format procedure is simpler to implement and should be used if the mixture of subrate streams is known in advance. When the mixture is dynamic, CCITT recommends the use of the more complex flexible format procedure.

Note that both of these approaches are examples of synchronous time-division multiplexing.

Circuit-mode Devices.   The second case listed in I.460 (rates other than 8, 16, or 32 kbps) breaks down into a number of subcases. Let us consider next the case of a device using the B channel circuit-mode service. In this case, a two-stage approach is used. First, each stream is rate-adapted to 8, 16, or 32 kbps. Second, the resulting streams are multiplexed as described previously.

As with the previous case, the approach described here is an example of synchronous time-division multiplexing.

Packet-mode Support.   For packet-mode devices, the multiplexing function is automatically provided by the layer 3 virtual circuit mechanism of X.25. Recall that in X.25, a DTE is allowed to establish up to 4095 simultaneous virtual circuits (Chapter 3). Thus, once a connection is made via a B channel or D channel to a packet-switching node, multiple virtual circuits can be set up across that connection. Furthermore, the virtual circuits need not all terminate at the same destination. A virtual circuit can be established with any subscriber to the same packet-switching network service.

Finally, this multiplexing capability exists whether the packet switching is provided by an external packet-switching network that is reached via a B channel circuit (Case A) or is supported internal to the ISDN (Case B).

Circuit-mode Support Using LAP-D Framing.   As described previously, I.465/V.120 specifies that all data be transmitted in modified LAP-D frames. One of the fields of the frame is a 13-bit logical link identifier (LLI). The LLI functions much as the X.25 virtual circuit number but operates in this case at the link layer. With the use of the LLI, the subscriber can simultaneously establish multiple logical links over a single B channel circuit. The LLI enables the recipient to sort out the incoming traffic and route it to the appropriate user.

One limitation of this approach, compared to the X.25 approach, is that all of the multiplexing occurs between the same two endpoints. That is, a single-channel circuit, defined between two subscribers, supports multiple logical channels between those two subscribers.

7.6

ADDRESSING

In the worldwide public telephone network, calls are placed based on the telephone number of the called party. For worldwide telephone connectivity, each subscriber must have a unique telephone number, and the network must be able to determine the location of the subscriber based on that number. A telephone number supports two important functions:

- It routes the call;
- It activates the necessary procedures for proper call charging.

Similarly, a numbering plan is needed for ISDN. The numbering scheme for ISDN should be based on the following requirements:

- It should be easily understood and used by the subscriber.
- It should be compatible with existing and planned switching equipment.
- It should allow for expansion of the size of the subscriber population.
- It should facilitate interworking with existing public network numbering schemes.

As work on ISDN proceeded through the early 1980s, there was considerable sentiment that ISDN numbering should be based on the current numbering plan for telephony, embodied in CCITT E.163. However, E.163 allows for only 12 decimal digits and was felt to be inadequate for the large number of subscribers anticipated for ISDN. ISDN must accommodate not only telephones but a large population of data devices. The result was the adoption of a numbering scheme that is an enhancement of E.163.

The ISDN numbering plan is presented in I.330 and I.331 and embodies the following principles:

- As mentioned, it is an enhancement of E.163. In particular, the telephone country code specified in E.163 is used to identify countries in the ISDN numbering plan.

- It is independent of the nature of the service (e.g., voice or data) or the performance characteristics of the connection.
- It is a sequence of decimal digits (not alphanumeric).
- Interworking between ISDNs requires only the use of the ISDN number.

ISDN Address Structure

CCITT makes a distinction between a number and an address. An **ISDN number** is one that relates to the ISDN network and ISDN numbering plan. It contains sufficient information for the network to route a call. Typically, but not always, an ISDN number corresponds to the subscriber attachment point to the ISDN, i.e., to the T reference point. An **ISDN address** comprises the ISDN number and any mandatory and/or optional additional addressing information. This additional information is not needed by the ISDN to route the call but is needed at the subscriber site to distribute the call to the appropriate party. Typically, but not always, an ISDN address corresponds to an individual terminal, i.e., to the S reference point. This situation is illustrated in Figure 7.17a, which shows a number of terminals connected to an NT2 (e.g., a PBX or LAN). The NT2 as a whole has a unique ISDN number, while each individual terminal has an ISDN address. Another way to express the distinction between ISDN numbers and addresses is that an ISDN number is associated with a D channel, which provides common-channel signaling for a number of subscribers, each of which has an ISDN address.

Other correspondences between reference points and ISDN numbers and addresses are possible; these are discussed subsequently.

Figure 7.18 shows the format of the ISDN address. An address in this format would appear in call setup messages communicated in common-channel signaling protocols such as Signaling System Number 7. The elements of the address are

- *Country code:* specifies the destination country (or geographic area) of the call. It is composed of a variable number of decimal digits (1 to 3) and is defined in Recommendation E.163 (existing telephony numbering plan).
- *National destination code:* is of variable length and a portion of the national ISDN number. If subscribers within a country are served by more than one ISDN and/or public switched telephone network (PSTN), it can be used to select a destination network within the specified country. It can also be used in a trunk code (area code) format to route the call over the destination network to a particular region of the network. The NDC code can, where required, provide a combination of both of these functions.

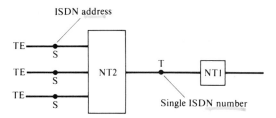

(a) Single ISDN number at T interface

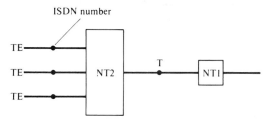

(b) Direct dialing-in

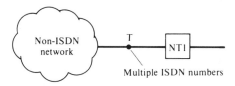

(c) Non-ISDN network

FIGURE 7.17 ISDN Addressing

Country code	National destination code	ISDN Subscriber number	ISDN subaddress (max 40 digits)

National ISDN number

International ISDN number (max 15 digits)

ISDN address (max 55 digits)

FIGURE 7.18 Structure of the ISDN Address

- *ISDN subscriber number:* is also of variable length and constitutes the remainder of the national ISDN number. Typically, the subscriber number is the number to be dialed to reach a subscriber in the same local network or numbering area.
- *ISDN subaddress:* provides additional addressing information and is a maximum of 40 digits in length. The subaddress is not considered part of the numbering plan but constitutes an intrinsic part of the ISDN addressing capability.

The national destination code plus the ISDN subscriber number form a unique national ISDN number within a country. This plus the country code form the international ISDN number, which is at present limited to a maximum of 15 digits. CCITT is considering expanding this to 16 or 17 digits. The ISDN subaddress is added to the international ISDN number to form an ISDN address with a maximum of 55 digits.

Address Information

Figure 7.17a shows the most straightforward way of employing ISDN numbers and addresses: Each T reference point is assigned an ISDN number, and each S reference point is assigned an ISDN address. The last field of the ISDN address, known as the subaddress, allows multiple subscribers to be discriminated at the subscriber site in a fashion that is transparent to the network. As an example, consider a site consisting of a digital PBX supporting some number of telephones. The national ISDN number for the PBX could be 617-543-7000. To address a local telephone with extension number 678, a remote caller would need to dial 617-543-7000-678. The ISDN would route the call based on the first 10 digits; the remaining 3 digits would be used by the PBX to connect the call to the appropriate extension.

An alternative use of numbers and addresses is suggested by Figure 7.17b. In this case, a number of terminals each have their own ISDN number. This feature is referred to as **direct dialing-in** (DDI). With DDI, the numbering scheme for local terminals is built into the national scheme. For example, again suppose a digital PBX with a main number of 543-7000, with an extension to that PBX of 678. To dial the extension directly from the outside, a user would dial 543-7678, and the 543-7XXX block would be lost for use except for 999 extension possibilities for that PBX. DDI is simpler for the subscriber than subaddressing, since fewer digits are needed to place a call. With DDI, the ISDN still routes on the basis of the ISDN number. In addition, the last few digits forming the end of the ISDN number are transferred to the called subscriber's installation. The number of digits used varies and depends upon the requirement of the called subscriber's equipment and the capacity of the numbering plan used. DDI must be used sparingly to assure that sufficient ISDN numbers are available to support all subscribers.

It is possible to combine DDI and subaddressing. This would allow direct dialing-in to certain intermediate equipment on site, such as terminal concentrators, with the subaddress used to discriminate devices attached to the intermediate equipment.

Another alternative is to assign multiple ISDN numbers to a single reference point. For example, at an ISDN interface, a user might have an attachment to a non-ISDN network, such as a private packet-switching network (Figure 7.17c). Although physically there is only a single attachment point to the ISDN, it might be desirable to provide visibility to ISDN of a number of the devices on the private network by assigning a unique ISDN number to each.

Numbering Interworking

For some extended transition period, there will be a number of public networks in addition to ISDN, including public switched telephone networks (PSTN) and public data networks, such as X.25 packet-switching networks and telex networks. A variety of standards have been issued that deal with the address structure and address assignment for these various networks. Unfortunately, although these standards have been developed with knowledge of the others, they are not compatible with each other or with the ISDN numbering plan. This creates the problem of how addressing can be performed between an ISDN subscriber and a subscriber on another network that has a connection to ISDN.

Other Address Structures.   Figure 7.19 illustrates the address structure for the major international public network standards. The international PSTN standard, E.163, makes use of a 12-digit number. The country code is the same as the country code used in ISDN. The national significant number of the PSTN corresponds to the national ISDN number, although the latter may contain three more digits. Thus, E.163 and the ISDN standard (I.330 and I.331) are reasonably compatible.

X.121 provides a standard for public data networks. As can be seen, there are a number of variations, depending on the network. If a data terminal is accessed through a public data network, then the E.163 number, prefixed by a 9, is used. For public data networks, a data country code is used, which unfortunately is not the same as a telephone country code. Nor is the national data number related in any way to the national telephone number. The telex numbering scheme also bears no relation to E.163 or I.33x.

Finally, ISO has developed an international numbering scheme in

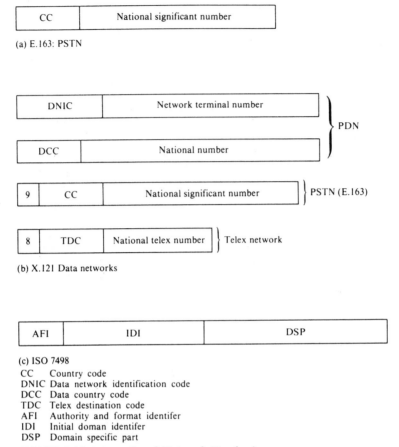

(a) E.163: PSTN

(b) X.121 Data networks

(c) ISO 7498
CC   Country code
DNIC   Data network identification code
DCC   Data country code
TDC   Telex destination code
AFI   Authority and format identifer
IDI   Initial doman identifer
DSP   Domain specific part

FIGURE 7.19 International Network Numbering

the context of the OSI model. The authority and format identifier (AFI) portion of the ISO address confines one of six subdomains of the global network addressing domain:

- A set of four domains, each of which corresponds to a type of public telecommunications network (i.e., packet-switched, telex, PSTN, and ISDN), all of which are administered by CCITT.
- An ISO geographic domain that is allocated and corresponds to individual countries. ISO member bodies within each country are responsible for assigning these addresses.
- An ISO international organization domain that is allocated and corresponds to different international organizations (e.g., NATO).

In addition, the AFI specifies the format of the IDI part and the structure of the DSP part. The initial domain identifier is the initial (and perhaps only) part of the actual address and is interpreted according to the value of the AFI. Finally, the DSP part, if any, provides additional addressing information.

For ISDN networks, the AFI has a value of 44 for ISDN numbers expressed as decimal digits and 45 for ISDN numbers expressed as binary numbers. The latter is not standard ISDN procedure, but may be employed by a user in an OSI context; in that case, the number would have to be converted to decimal for use by ISDN. In general, the international ISDN number is identical to the initial domain iden-tifier, and the ISDN subaddress is identical to the domain-specific part of the ISO address.

Interworking Strategies. From the point of view of ISDN addressing, interworking is defined as a procedure whereby an ISDN subscriber can set up a call to subscribers or services terminated on other public networks. Two general approaches are possible: single-stage and two-stage selection.

With the **single-stage approach,** the calling party designates the ad-dress of the called party in the call setup procedure. This address contains sufficient information for

- ISDN to route the call to a point at which the called network attaches to ISDN.
- The called network to route the call to the called party.

CCITT suggests two ways in which single-stage addresses could be constructed. In the first method, the address begins with a prefix that identifies the particular network to be accessed; the remainder of the address is in the format used by that network (Figure 7.20a). In this approach, the calling address would have to identify the called num-bering plan as part of the calling procedure. An example of such a prefix is the authority and format indicator of the ISO address structure. In the ISDN signaling protocol (I.451), to be discussed in Chapter 8, there is in fact a place in the call setup address field for such a code, known as the numbering plan identification field.

An alternative address structure for the single-stage approach is one that conforms to the ISDN address structure. In this case, some national destination codes (NDC; see Figure 7.18) could be specially assigned for interworking purposes. This is a less general solution than the prefix approach, as the number of available NDCs is limited.

With the **two-stage approach,** the first stage of selection provides the calling party access via ISDN to an interworking unit (IWU) associated with the point of attachment of the called network to the ISDN. The calling party uses an ISDN number to set up a connection to the IWU. When a connection is established, the IWU responds. The necessary address information for the called party on that particular network is

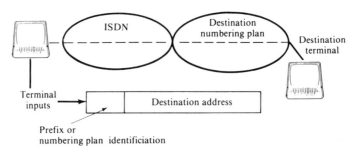

(a) Single-stage interworking

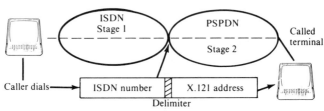

(b) Two-stage interworking (example)

FIGURE 7.20 Strategies for Numbering Interworking

then forwarded, as a second stage of selection, through the ISDN and the IWU to complete the call in the non-ISDN network ((Figure 7.20b).
The main disadvantages of the two-stage approach are

- Additional digits must be dialed by the caller.
- The caller must employ two numbering plans.
- A delimiter or pause is necessary between the two stages (e.g., a second dial tone).

For these reasons, CCITT prefers the one-stage approach but allows the two-stage approach.

7.7

INTERWORKING

It is clear that there is never likely to be a single, monolithic, worldwide ISDN. In the near term, there will be a variety of non-ISDN public networks operating, with the need for the subscribers on these networks to connect to subscribers on ISDN networks. Even in the case of different national ISDNs, differences in services or the attributes of services may persist indefinitely. Accordingly, CCITT has begun to address the issue of the interworking of other networks with ISDN.

One issue related to interworking, that of interworking between numbering plans, was discussed in the preceding section. The interworking of numbering plans allows an ISDN subscriber to identify a non-ISDN subscriber for the purpose of establishing a connection and using some service. However, for successful communication to take place there must be agreement on, and the capability to provide, a common set of services and mechanisms. To provide compatibility between ISDN and existing network components and terminals, a set of interworking functions must be implemented. Typical functions include

- Provide interworking of numbering plans.
- Match physical-layer characteristics at the point of interconnection between the two networks.
- Determine if network resources on the destination network side are adequate to meet the ISDN service demand.
- Map control signal messages such as services identification, channel identification, call status, and alerting between the ISDN's common-channel signaling protocol and the called network's signaling protocol, whether the latter is inchannel or common channel.
- Ensure service and connection compatibility.
- Provide transmission structure conversion, including information modulation technique and frame structure.
- Maintain synchronization (error control, flow control) across connections on different networks.
- Collect data required for proper billing.
- Coordinate operation and maintenance procedures to be able to isolate faults.

Thus interworking may require the implementation of a set of interworking functions, either in ISDN or the network attached to ISDN. The approach identified by CCITT for standardizing the interworking capability is to define additional reference points associated with interworking and to standardize the interface at that reference point. This is a sound strategy that should minimize the impact both on ISDN and on other networks. The inclusion of these additional reference points is illustrated in Figure 7.21. As before, ISDN-compatible customer equipment attaches to ISDN via the S or T reference point. The following additional reference points are defined:

- K: Interface with an existing telephone network or other non-ISDN network requiring interworking functions. The functions are performed by ISDN.
- L: As with K, but it is the responsibility of the other network to perform the interworking functions.
- M: A specialized network, such as teletex or MHS. In this case, an adaption function may be needed, to be performed in the specialized network.

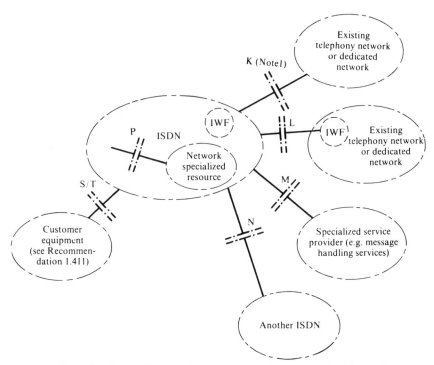

Note 1 — Different interface specifications will exist at the K reference point depending on the type of network.

Note 2 — The specification of interfaces at the K, L, M, N and P reference points need further study.

FIGURE 7.21 Reference Points Associated with the Interconnection of Customer Equipment and Other Networks to an ISDN

- N: Interface between two ISDNs. Some sort of protocol is needed to determine the degree of service compatibility.
- P: There may be some specialized resource that is provided by the ISDN provider but that is clearly identifiable as a separate component or set of components.

In I.510, CCITT identifies five other types of networks that support telecommunication services that are also supported by an ISDN and that are candidates, therefore, for interworking with an ISDN:

- Another ISDN.
- Public-switched telephone network (PSTN).
- Circuit-switched public data network (CSPDN).
- Packet-switched public data network (PSPDN).
- Telex.

Table 7.7, from I.510, depicts the type of interworking functions that may be required for each interworking configuration. Recall from Chap-

TABLE 7.7 ISDN Support of Telecommunication Services in an Interworking Configuration (I.510)

Telecommunication Services Supported by ISDN	ISDN Interconnected With					
	ISDN	PSTN	CSPDN	PSPDN	Telex	Other Dedi-cated Net-work
Telephony	0	N	—	—	—	N
Data transmission	(L)	N, L	N, (L)	N, (L)	—	N, (L)
Telex	0	—	—	—	N, L	N, L
Teletex	0	N, L	N, L	N, L	—	N, L, H
Facsimile	0	N, L	N, L	N, L	—	N, L, H

0   No interworking function foreseen
N   Connection-dependent interworking needed
L   Lower-layer communication-dependent interworking needed
H   Higher-layer communication-dependent interworking needed
( )   N/L/H may be needed

ter 6 that a connection is a network-oriented function relating to the establishment of an information transfer path through the network, while a communication is a user-oriented function, relating to the end-to-end protocols needed for the exchange of information between subscribers.

ISDN-ISDN Interworking

The simplest case of interworking involves two ISDNs. If the two ISDNs provide identical bearer services and teleservices, then no interworking capabilities are required. However, it may be the case that the two networks differ in the attribute values that they support for one or more services. In that case, interworking is needed. The interworking would occur in two phases. In the *control phase*, a service negotiation takes place in order to reach a service agreement. A service agreement can be reached if the maximum common service that can be provided across the two networks equals or exceeds the minimum service that the caller will accept. If agreement is reached, then the connection is established, which involves splicing together connections from the two ISDNs to form a single connection from the user's point of view. User-to-user communication can then take place in the *user phase*.

Figure 7.22 illustrates the call negotiation procedure used to reach service agreement. The following steps are involved:

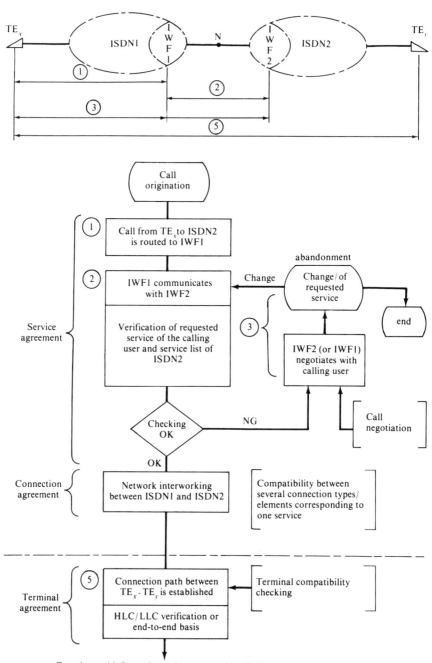

Function and information to be supported by IWF
i)   Service list of ISDN (I.200 conformed description)
ii) Service agreement
iii) Network interworking

FIGURE 7.22 Call Negotiation Procedure in ISDN-ISDN Interworking

1. A call from TEx to ISDN2 is routed to IWF1.
2. IWF1 communicates with IWF2 and determines whether the requested service (indicated by bearer capability) of the calling user
   is supported by ISDN2, using a service list in IWF2. If the compability is satisfied, network interworking between ISDN1 and
   ISDN2 begins.
3. If the service compatibility does not exist, IWF2 (or IWF1) nego-
   tiates with the calling user to change or abandon the service
   request.
4. With a changed service request, step 2 or 3 is repeated until service
   compatibility is satisfied or the effort abandoned.
5. When the connection between TEx and TEy is established, low-
   level compatibility (bearer) and high-level compatibility (teleservice) is examined on an end-to-end basis. The network does not
   participate in this procedure, but agreement between ISDNs concerning user-to-user information transfer method might be required.

Thus, it is first necessary to determine if the two ISDNs can support
the required attributes of the caller's requested bearer service. Then,
the end-to-end compatibility between the two users is determined.

ISDN-PSTN Interworking

In many countries, digitization of the existing public switched telephone
network (PSTN) has been ongoing for a number of years, including
implementation of digital transmission and switching facilities and the
introduction of common-channel signaling. The availability of digital
subscriber loops has lagged behind the introduction of these other
digital aspects. In any case, such networks exhibit some overlap with
the capabilities of a full ISDN but lack some of the services that an
ISDN will support. Thus, it will be necessary for some time to provide
interworking between ISDN and PSTN facilities.

Table 7.8 (from I.530) identifies the key characteristics of an ISDN
and a PSTN, indicating possible interworking functions to accommodate
dissimilar characteristics. Some sort of negotiation procedure, similar to
that depicted in Figure 7.22 will be needed to establish connections.

The interworking between an ISDN and PSTN is reasonably straightforward. The number plan of the telephone network is the same as that
used for ISDN, so no conversion is required. The interworking function
must include a mapping between the control signaling used in ISDN
and that used in the telephone network. Finally, a conversion is needed
between digital and analog forms of user information.

TABLE 7.8   Key ISDN and PSTN Characteristics

	ISDN	PSTN	Interworking Functions
Subscriber interface	Digital	Analog	a
User-network signaling	Out-of-band (I.441/I.451)	Mainly inband (e.g., DTMF)	b, e
User terminal equipment supported	Digital TE (ISDN NT, TE1 or TE2 + TA)	Analog TE (e.g., dial pulse telephones, PABXs modem-equipped DTEs)	c
Interexchange signaling	SS No. 7 ISDN user part (ISUP)	Inband (e.g., R1, R2, No. 4, No. 5) or out-of-band (e.g., No. 6, No. 7 TUP)	d, e
Transmission facilities	Digital	Analog/digital	a
Information transfer mode	Circuit/packet	Circuit	f
Information transfer capability	Speech, digital unrestricted, 3.1-kHz audio, video, etc.	3.1-kHz audio (voice/voiceband data)	f

where:
a. Analog-to-digital and digital-to-analog conversion on transmission facilities.
b. Mapping between PSTN signals in the subscriber access and I.451 messages for intra-exchange calls.
c. Support of communication between modem-equipped PSTN DTEs and ISDN terminals.
d. Conversion between the PSTN signaling system and Signaling System No. 7 ISDN user part.
e. Mapping between signals in the ISDN subscriber (I.441, I.451) access and PSTN in-band interexchange signaling (e.g., R1).
f. Further study required.

ISDN-CSPDN Interworking

A circuit-switched public data network, as the name implies, provides a digital transmission service using circuit switching. The interface for DTEs to this type of network is X.21. Like X.25, X.21 is actually a three-layer set of protocols that includes inband control signaling for setting up and terminating connections. In the case of X.21, the connections are actual rather than virtual circuits.

The interworking functions for this case have not been fully worked out; much has been left for further study. A mapping is required between the call-control protocol of X.21 and that used in ISDN. For addressing, ISDNs and CSPDNs utilize differing numbering plans (i.e., E.164 and X.121, respectively). A one-stage address translation, as described in the previous section, is specified. *should it be two-stage?*

ISDN-PSPDN Interworking

A packet-switched public data network provides a packet-switching service using an X.25 interface. There are two interworking cases:

- A circuit-mode bearer service is used on ISDN.
- A packet-mode bearer service is used on ISDN.

In the first case, interworking is achieved by means of a circuit-mode connection across ISDN from an ISDN subscriber to a packet handler in the PSPDN (see Figure 7.9). In the second case, the ISDN functions as a packet-switching network (Figure 7.12). For this case, there is an established interworking protocol to be used between two public packet-switching networks: X.75. In essence, X.75 acts as a splicing mechanism to tie together two virtual circuits in the two networks in such a way that it appears as a single virtual circuit to the two end DTEs.

7.8

SUMMARY

The functions performed by an ISDN can be defined by the services that it supports and the functions visible at the user-network interface. Among the most important defining characteristics of ISDN are the following:

- *Transmission stucture:* ISDN offers a service structured as a set of channels. The B channel is a user channel that supports circuit-switched, semipermanent, and packet-switched use. The D channel supports user-network control signaling and packet switching. The two standard transmission offerings are the basic service, consisting of two B channels and one D channel, and the primary service, consisting of 24 or 31 B channels and one D channel.
- *User-network interface configurations:* The user-network interface is defined in terms of reference points and functional groupings. This approach provides for standardized interfaces that facilitate the use of equipment from multiple vendors and that simplify access to ISDN.
- *Protocol architecture:* The interaction between ISDN and a subscriber can be described within the context of the OSI protocol reference

model. Essentially, the ISDN recommendations deal with layers 1 to 3 of that model. A physical layer specification covers both basic and primary access for all channels. For the D channel, LAP-D is defined at the data link layer, and I.451/Q.931 (call control) and the X.25 packet level (packet-mode service on the D channel) are specified for the network level. For the B channel, ISDN supports the use of X.25 and LAP-B for packet-mode service and also provides I.465/V.120 as a common optional data link mechanism.

- *ISDN connections:* ISDN provides four types of service for end-to-end communication: circuit-switched calls over a B channel, semi-permanent connections over a B channel, packet-switched calls over a B channel, and packet-switched calls over the D channel.
- *Terminal adaption:* ISDN must provide support for existing non-ISDN terminals and computers. Key functions of adaption are rate adaption and control-signaling adaption.
- *Addressing:* Addressing refers to the way in which a calling user specifies the called user so that the network can perform routing and delivery functions. ISDN makes use of a number scheme based on E.164 and can interwork with non-ISDN numbers to allow interworking of ISDN with other networks.
- *Interworking:* Interworking refers to the capability for an ISDN subscriber to establish a connection to a subscriber on a non-ISDN network. The most important such networks are public switched telephone networks (analog networks), circuit-switched public data networks (X.21 networks), and packet-switched public data networks (X.25 networks.)

7.9

RECOMMENDED READING

[BOCK88], [KESS90], and [VERM90] provide good coverage of most of the topics in this chapter. [TURM88a, b] is a clear discussion of the use of packet-mode terminals on ISDN, while [WEIS89] is an equally clear discussion of terminal adaption. [PAND90] looks at both terminal adaption and interworking issues, with an emphasis on ISDN-PSTN interworking.

7.10

PROBLEMS

7.1. List all of the approved interface structures for the primary rate interface. Don't forget combinations that include H channels.

7.2. An ISDN customer has offices at a number of sites. A typical office is served by two 1.544-Mbps digital pipes. One provides circuit-switched access to ISDN; the other is a semipermanent connection to another user site. The on-premises equipment consists of a digital PBX plus a host computer system with an X.25 capability. The user has three requirements:

- Telephone service.
- A private packet-switched network for data.
- Video teleconferencing at 1.544 Mbps.

How might the user allocate capacity optimally to meet these requirements?

7.3. What is the percentage overhead on the basic channel structure?

7.4. Construct tables similar to Table 7.2 for the following data rate adaptions:
   a. 600 bps to 8 kbps.
   b. 1200 bps to 8 kbps.
   c. 4800 bps to 8 kbps.
   d. 9600 bps to 16 kbps.
   e. 19.2 kbps to 64 kbps.
   f. 48 kbps to 64 kbps.
   g. 56 kbps to 64 kbps.

7.5. In the discussion of rate adaption, it was suggested that the two-stage procedure could save network capacity, since a conversion of, say, 8 kbps to 64 kbps could be reversed in the network. Since all of the subchannels of a single B channel must be carried on the same ISDN circuit between the same pair of subscribers, what opportunity for such savings is possible?

7.6. Subscriber X sets up a 64-kbps circuit-switched connection to subscriber Y over a B channel. Over time, various subchannels of traffic are carried between X and Y on the B channel. The pattern of traffic is: add 8 kbps; add 32 kbps; add 16 kbps; subtract 32 kbps; add 16 kbps; subtract 8 kbps; add 32 kbps. Using flexible format multiplexing, show the assignment of B channel octet bits over time.

7.7 In Figure 7.4, there is no access point defined for reference point U. One reason for this is that CCITT has not yet recognized this interface. However, if and when this interface is incorporated in the CCITT recommendations, is it appropriate to talk about accessing services (bearer or teleservices) at this reference point, or is this a primitive level of interfacing below the level at which services become available to the subscriber?

7.8 For each of the configurations of Figure 7.5, indicate the possible correspondences between ISDN numbers and ISDN addresses on the one hand and reference point on the other.

7.9 What is the difference between direct dialing in (Figure 7.17b), in which there are multiple ISDN numbers, one for each of multiple S reference points, and the use of multiple ISDN numbers at a single T reference point?

APPENDIX 7A

ASYNCHRONOUS ANI˜ SYNCHRONOUS TRANSMISSION

The reception of digital data involves sampling the incoming signal once per bit time to determine the binary value. One of the difficulties encountered in such a process is that various transmission impairments will corrupt the signal so that occasional errors will occur. This problem is compounded by a timing difficulty: In order for the receiver to sample the incoming bits properly, it must know the arrival time and duration of each bit that it receives.

Suppose that the sender simply transmits a stream of data bits. The sender has a clock that governs the timing of the transmitted bits. For example, if data are to be transmitted at 10,000 bits per second (bps), then one bit will be transmitted every 1/10,000 = 0.1 millisecond (ms), as measured by the sender's clock. Typically, the receiver will attempt to sample the medium at the center of each bit time. The receiver will time its samples at intervals of one bit time. In our example, the sampling would occur once every 0.1 ms. If the receiver times its samples based on its own clock, then there will be a problem if the transmitter's and receiver's clocks are not precisely aligned. If there is a drift of 1 percent (the receiver's clock is 1 percent faster or slower than the transmitter's clock), then the first sampling will be 0.01 of a bit time (0.001 ms) away from the center of the bit (center of bit is 0.05 ms from beginning and end of bit). After 50 or more samples, the receiver may be in error because it is sampling in the wrong bit time (50 × 0.001 = 0.05 ms). For smaller timing differences, the error would occur later, but eventually the receiver will be out of step with the transmitter if the transmitter sends a sufficiently long stream of bits and if no steps are taken to synchronize the transmitter and receiver.

Asynchronous Transmission

Two approaches are common for achieving the desired synchronization. The first is called, oddly enough, asynchronous transmission. The strategy with this scheme is to avoid the timing problem by not sending long, uninterrupted streams of bits. Instead, data are transmitted one character at a time, where each character is five to eight bits in length. Timing or synchronization must only be maintained within each character only; the receiver has the opportunity to resynchronize at the beginning of each new character.

The technique is easily explained with reference to Figure 7.23. When no character is being transmitted, the line between transmitter and receiver is in an "idle" state. The definition of idle is equivalent to the signaling element for binary 1. Typically, idle would be the presence of a negative voltage on the line. The beginning of a character is signaled by a *start bit* with a value of binary 0. This is followed by the five to eight bits that actually make up the character. Usually, this is followed by a *parity bit*. The parity bit is set by the transmitter such that the total number of ones in the character, including the parity bit, is even (even parity) or odd (odd parity), depending on the convention being used. The final element is a *stop*, which is a binary 1. A minimum length for the stop is specified, and this is usually 1, 1.5, or 2 times the duration of an ordinary bit. No maximum value is specified. Since the stop is the same as the idle state, the transmitter will continue to transmit the stop signal until it is ready to send the next character.

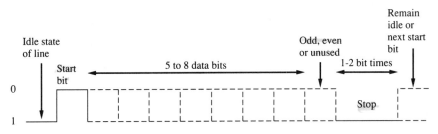

(a) Character format

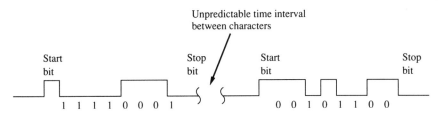

(b) 8-bit asynchronous character stream

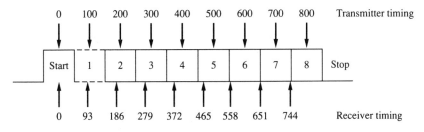

(c) Effect of timing error

FIGURE 7.23 Asynchronous Transmission

If a steady stream of characters is sent, the interval between two characters is uniform and equal to the stop element. The start bit (0) starts the timing sequence for the next character. In the idle state, the receiver looks for a transition from 1 to 0 to signal the beginning of the next character and then samples the input signal at one-bit intervals for seven intervals. It then looks for the next 1-to-0 transition, which will occur no sooner than one more bit time.

The timing requirements for this scheme are modest. For example, ASCII characters are typically sent as 8-bit units, including the parity bit. If the receiver is 5 percent slower or faster than the transmitter, the sampling of the eighth information bit will be displaced by 45 percent and still be correctly sampled. Figure 7.23c shows the effects of a timing error of sufficient magnitude to cause an error in reception. In this example we assume a data rate of 10,000 bits per second (10 kbps); therefore, each bit is of 0.1 millisecond (ms), or 100 nanoseconds (ns), duration. Assume that the receiver is off by 7 percent, or 7 nanoseconds per bit time. Thus, the receiver samples the incoming character every 93 ns (based on the transmitter's clock). As can be seen, the last sample is erroneous.

Asynchronous transmission is simple and cheap but requires an overhead of two to three bits per character. For example, for a 7-bit code, using a 1-bit-long stop bit and no parity bit, two out of every nine bits convey no information but are there merely for synchronization; thus the overhead is $2/9 \times 100\% = 22\%$. To achieve greater efficiency, a different form of synchronization, known as synchronous transmission, is used.

Synchronous Transmission

With synchronous transmission, a block of bits is transmitted in a steady stream without start and stop codes. The block may be many characters in length. To prevent timing drift between transmitter and receiver, their clocks must somehow be synchronized. One possibility is to provide a separate clock line between transmitter and receiver. One side (transmitter or receiver) pulses the line regularly with one short pulse per bit time. The other side uses these regular pulses as a clock. This technique works well over short distances, but over longer distances the clock pulses are subject to the same impairments as the data signal, and timing errors can occur. The other alternative is to embed the clocking information in the data signal. Techniques for doing this will be discussed in Chapter 8.

With synchronous transmission, there is another level of synchronization required to allow the receiver to determine the beginning and end of a block of data. To achieve this, each block begins with a *preamble* bit pattern and generally ends with a *postamble* bit pattern. In addition, other bits are added to the block that convey control information used in data link control procedures. The data plus preamble, postamble, and control information are called a **frame**. The exact format of the frame depends on which data link control procedure is being used.

For sizeable blocks of data, synchronous transmission is far more efficient than asynchronous. Asynchronous transmission requires 20 percent or more overhead. The control information, preamble, and postamble in synchronous transmission are typically less than 100 bits. For example, one of the more common schemes, HDLC, contains 48 bits of control, preamble, and postamble. Thus, for a 1000-character block of data, each frame consists of 48 bits of overhead and $1000 \times 8 = 8,000$ bits of data, for a percentage overhead of only $48/8048 \times 100\% = 0.6\%$.

For large systems and computer networks, the efficiency of synchronous transmission is needed, even though it introduces the technical problem of synchronizing the clocks of transmitter and receiver.

In addition to the requirement for efficiency, large transfers introduce a requirement for error checking. The interactive user checks his or her own input and output for errors by looking at the screen and rekeying or asking for retransmission of portions that contain errors. Such a procedure is clearly impractical for long file transfers that occur at fast rates and often without an operator present. As we will see, synchronous transmission involves the use of a data link control procedure, which will automatically detect transmission errors and cause a frame in error to be retransmitted.

APPENDIX 7B

ISDN ELEMENTARY FUNCTIONS

In I.310, CCITT specifies a set of elementary functions for ISDN. The objective is to provide a functional description of ISDN that lists those functions required to support ISDN services while at the same time leaving implementers free to implement and configure these functions in the network as they see fit. The functions required to support ISDN services are classified into the following categories:

- *Connection handling:* functions that enable the establishment, holding, and release of connections (e.g., user-to-network signaling).
- *Routing:* functions that determine a suitable connection for a particular call request (e.g., called number analysis).
- *Resources handling:* functions that enable the control of the resources necessary for the use of connections (e.g., transmission equipment, switching resources, data storage equipment).

- *Supervision:* functions that check the resources used to support the connections, to detect and signal possible problems, and to solve them if possible (e.g., transmission error detection and correction).
- *Operations and maintenance:* functions that control the correct working of the services/network as well for the subscriber as for the network administration.
- *Charging:* functions for charging subscribers.
- *Interworking:* functions that provide for both service and network interworking.

Table 7.9 lists the elementary functions defined in I.310.

TABLE 7.9   ISDN Elementary Functions (I.310)

Connection Handling
Characteristics of services-requested examination Determine the required service characteristics of a call by means of information sent by terminal.
Connection elements type determination Determine connection types and connection elements necessary to provide requested service.
User access resources reservation Determine type of user-network access (basic, primary) and channel availability; reserve needed channels.
Transit resources reservation Reserve transit connection element, based on the state of resources.
Communication references handling Assign a local reference to the call and in internal reference to the connection, and clear these references when the call/connection is cleared/released.
Establishment control Set up a connection.
Release control Release a connection.
Service-related authorization examination Determine the authorization (calling or called user) relating to basic and supplementary services that have been subscribed to.
User-network signaling handling Support layer 3 protocol of the user-network signaling system.
Interexchange signaling handling (user part) Support the user part of the interexchange signaling system.
Supplementary services compatibility checking Check the compatibility of requested supplementary services with requested bearer service or teleservice and with other requested supplementary services; verify coherence of associated parameters.

Building up and maintaining dynamic information related to the call/connection
Compile information related to the call/connection (e.g., resources needed, details of call in progress, supplementary services, and associated parameters).

Signaling interworking
Support interworking functions between signaling systems.

Priority
Handle specific calls with priority (e.g., in the case of overload or degraded mode of operation).

Queue handling
Store requests in a queue in order to handle request later in a predefined order.

Routing

ISDN number identification
Identify the ISDN number of the user-network interface.

Called number analysis
Analyze called ISDN number sent by the calling terminal in the call setup phase.

Routing information examination
Analyze routing information that may be sent by the calling terminals and that has an effect on path selection.

Predetermined specific routing
Select a specific routing according to the information received from the calling terminal (e.g., routing toward operators, access points, an interworking unit, and operational or maintenance unit).

Connection path selection
Select the transit outgoing part relating to connection types used and the overall path through the network.

Rerouting
Select a new connection path through the network depending on changed conditions during call setup or information transfer phases.

Resources Handling

Hold and release of channels
Hold channel(s) reserved to support a communication and release it at the end of this communication.

Hold and release of circuits
Hold the circuit(s) reserved to support a communication and release it at the end of this communication.

Insertion and suppression of specific equipment
Insert or remove specific equipments to satisfy the service request invoked by the user (e.g., echo suppressors, A-μ law conversion units, interworking unit, storage unit).

Cont.

TABLE 7.9   ISDN Elementary Functions (I.310) *(continued)*

Resources Handling

Tones, announcements, and display information
Provide call progress information as a tone, a recorded announcement, or visual display information

User-network signaling handling
Support layers 1 and 2 of the user-network signaling system.

Interexchange signaling handling (message transfer)
Support the message-transfer part of the interexchange signaling system.

Path search inside switching unit
Select an internal connection inside the switching unit.

Synchronization handling
Provide synchronization between different functional entities and provide internal synchronization.

Timing handling
Provide timing between time instances involved in calls.

Line service marking
Store for each customer information on the bearer services, teleservices, and supplementary services subscribed to.

Real-time clock
Provide real-time information.

Supervision

User-network access resources monitoring
Check the correct operation of subscriber access resources.

Transit resource monitoring
Check the correct operation of the transit resources.

Continuity checking
Check the correct operation of the transit resources.

Detection of congestion
Detect congestion during the selection of a connection path.

Semipermanent connection checking
Check the availability of a given semipermanent connection.

Operation and Maintenance

Management of subscriber data
Manage subscriber data related to services (e.g., in/out of service, number translation, changing of subscriber data).

Fault report
Register the cause if an attempt to set up a call fails.

Charging

Charging management
Determine the charging mode (free, ordinary, peak, reduced rate).

Charging registering
Register the details of the call.

Charging recording
Format the charging details in a standardized way.

Billing
Calculate the variable charges that depend on the use of a service and the fixed costs of the subscription.

Accounting
Analyze, store, and forward information relating to the use of inter-network resources between the different administrations involved in a call.

Charging information
Indicate to the user the amount of the charge involved in the use of a service.

Interworking

Rate adaption
Adapt the user/dedicated network bit rates to the ISDN bit rates.

Protocol conversion
Support mapping functions between interfaces.

Handling of signaling for interworking
Handle signaling information for interworking.

Numbering interworking
Support interworking functions between numbering plans.

CHAPTER 8

ISDN Physical Layer

The ISDN physical layer is presented to the user at either reference point S or T (Figure 7.2). In either case, the following functions are included as physical layer (OSI layer 1) functions:

- Encoding of digital data for transmission across the interface.
- Full-duplex transmission of B channel data.
- Full-duplex transmission of D channel data.
- Multiplexing of channels to form basic or primary access transmission structure.
- Activation and deactivation of physical circuit.
- Power feeding from network termination to the terminal.
- Terminal identification.
- Faulty terminal isolation.
- D channel contention access.

The last function is needed when there is a multipoint configuration for basic access; this is described subsequently.

The nature of the physical interface and functionality differs for basic and primary user-network interfaces. We begin with an examination of two aspects that are of importance to both interfaces: digital encoding and physical connection. Then we examine each interface in turn. Finally, we look at the U reference point, which is not standardized as part of the CCITT I series, but which is an ANSI standard.

321

8.1

LINE-CODING TECHNIQUES

In ISDN, both analog and digital data are transmitted using digital signals. A digital signal is a sequence of transmitted voltage pulses that is used to represent a stream of binary data. For example, a constant positive voltage level may represent binary 0, and a constant negative voltage level may represent binary 1. More complex encoding schemes may be used to improve performance or quality. In this section, we look at schemes that are used in ISDN; they are defined in Table 8.1 and depicted in Figure 8.1. First, we examine the criteria by which alternative schemes may be assessed.

Evaluation Criteria

There are two important tasks involved in interpreting digital signals at the receiver. First, the receiver must know the timing of each bit. That is, the receiver must know with some accuracy when a bit begins and ends. Second, the receiver must determine whether the signal level for each voltage pulse is high or low.

A number of factors determine how successful the receiver will be in interpreting the incoming signal: the signal-to-noise ratio (S/N), the data rate, and the bandwidth of the signal. With other factors held constant, the following statements are true:

- An increase in data rate increases bit error rate (the probability that a bit is received in error).

TABLE 8.1 Definition of Digital Signal-encoding Formats

Nonreturn to zero—level (NRZ-L)
   0 = high level
   1 = low level

Bipolar-AMI
   0 = no line signal
   1 = positive or negative level, alternating for successive ones

Pseudoternary
   0 = positive or negative level, alternating for successive zeros
   1 = no line signal

B8ZS
   Same as bipolar AMI, except that any string of eight zeros is replaced by a
   string with two code violations

HDB3
   Same as bipolar AMI, except that any string of four zeros is replaced by a string
   with one code violation

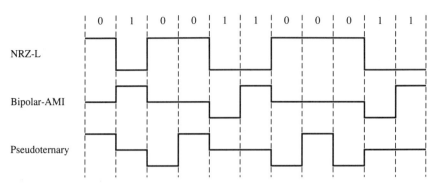

FIGURE 8.1 Digital Signal Encoding Formats

- An increase in S/N decreases bit error rate.
- Increased bandwidth allows increased data rate.

There is another factor that can be used to improve performance—the encoding scheme, which is simply the mapping from data bits to signal elements. A variety of approaches have been tried. Before describing some of these approaches, let us consider the ways of evaluating or comparing the various techniques. Among the important factors:

- Signal spectrum.
- Signal synchronization capability.
- Error-detection capability.
- Cost and complexity.

Several aspects of the **signal spectrum** are important. A lack of high-frequency components means that less bandwidth is required for transmission. On the other hand, lack of a direct-current (dc) component is also desirable. With a dc component to the signal, there must be direct physical attachment of transmission components; with no dc component, ac coupling via transformer is possible. This provides excellent electrical isolation, reducing interference. Finally, the magnitude of the effects of signal distortion and interference depend on the spectral properties of the transmitted signal. In practice, the transmission fidelity of a channel is usually worse near the band edges. Therefore, a good signal design should concentrate the transmitted power in the middle of the transmission bandwidth. In such a case, a smaller distortion should be present in the received signal. To meet this objective, codes can be designed with the aim of shaping the spectrum of the transmitted signal.

For successful reception of digital data, the receiver must know the timing of each bit. That is, the receiver must know with some accuracy when a bit begins and ends, so that the receiver may sample the incoming signal once per bit time to recognize the value of each bit.

Thus, there must be some **signal synchronization capability** between transmitter and receiver. It is inevitable that there will be some drift between the clocks of the transmitter and receiver, and so some separate synchronization mechanism is needed. One approach is to provide a separate clock lead to synchronize the transmitter and receiver. This approach is rather expensive, since it requires an extra line, plus an extra transmitter and receiver. The alternative is to provide some synchronization mechanism that is based on the transmitted signal. This can be achieved with suitable encoding.

Error detection is the responsibility of a data link protocol that is executed on top of the physical signaling level. However, it is useful to have some **error-detection capability** built in to the physical signaling scheme. This permits errors to be detected more quickly. Many signaling schemes have an inherent error-detection capability.

Finally, although digital logic continues to drop in price, the **cost and complexity** of the signaling scheme is a factor that should not be ignored.

Nonreturn to Zero (NRZ)

The most common, and easiest, way to transmit digital signals is to use two different voltage levels for the two binary digits. Codes that follow this strategy share the property that the voltage level is constant during a bit interval; there is no transition (no return to a zero voltage level). For example, the absence of voltage can be used to represent binary 0, with a constant positive voltage used to represent binary 1. More commonly, a negative voltage is used to represent one binary value and a positive voltage is used to represent the other. This latter code, known as **nonreturn-to-zero-level** (NRZ-L), is illustrated[1] in Figure 8.1. NRZ-L is generally the code used to generate or interpret digital data by terminals and other devices. If a different code is to be used for transmission, it is typically generated from an NRZ-L signal by the transmission system.

The NRZ codes are the easiest to engineer and, in addition, make efficient use of bandwidth. This latter property is illustrated in Figure 8.2, which compares the spectral density of various encoding schemes. In the figure, frequency is normalized to the data rate. As can be seen,

---

[1] In this figure, a negative voltage is equated with binary 1 and a positive voltage with binary 0. This is the opposite of the definition used in virtually all other textbooks. However, there is no "standard" definition of NRZ-L, and the definition here conforms to the use of NRZ-L in data communications interfaces and the standards that govern those interfaces.

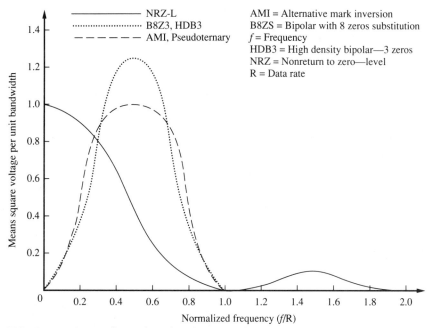

FIGURE 8.2 Spectral Density of Various Signal Encoding Schemes

most of the energy in an NRZ signal is between dc and half the bit rate. For example, if an NRZ code is used to generate a signal with a data rate of 9600 bps, most of the energy in the signal is concentrated between dc and 4800 Hz.

The main limitations of NRZ signals are the presence of a dc component and the lack of synchronization capability. To picture the latter problem, consider that with a long string of 1s or 0s for NRZ-L, the output is a constant voltage over a long period of time. Under these circumstances, any drift between the timing of transmitter and receiver will result in the loss of synchronization between the two.

Because of their simplicity and relatively low frequency response characteristics, NRZ codes are commonly used for digital magnetic recording. However, their limitations make these codes unattractive for signal transmission applications.

Multilevel Binary

A category of encoding techniques known as multilevel binary addresses some of the deficiencies of the NRZ codes. These codes use more than two signal levels. Two examples of this scheme are illustrated in Figure 8.1: bipolar-AMI (alternate mark inversion) and pseudoternary.[2]

In the case of the **bipolar-AMI** scheme, a binary 0 is represented by no line signal, and a binary 1 is represented by a positive or negative pulse. The binary 1 pulses must alternate in polarity. There are several advantages to this approach. First, there will be no loss of synchronization if a long string of 1s occurs. Each 1 introduces a transition, and the receiver can resynchronize on that transition. A long string of 0s would still be a problem. Second, since the 1 signals alternate in voltage from positive to negative, there is no net dc component. Also, the bandwidth of the resulting signal is considerably less than the bandwidth for NRZ (Figure 8.2). Finally, the pulse alternation property provides a simple means of error detection. Any isolated error, whether it deletes a pulse or adds a pulse, causes a violation of this property.

The comments of the previous paragraph also apply to **pseudoternary.** In this case, it is the binary 1 that is represented by the absence of a line signal, and the binary 0 by alternating positive and negative pulses. There is no particular advantage of one technique versus the other, and each is the basis of some applications.

Although a degree of synchronization is provided with these codes, a long string of 0s in the case of AMI or 1s in the case of pseudoternary still presents a problem. Several techniques have been used to address this deficiency. One approach is to insert additional bits that force transitions. We will see that this technique is used in ISDN for relatively low data rate transmission. Of course, at a high data rate, this scheme is expensive, since it results in an increase in an already high signal transmission rate. To deal with this problem at high data rates, a technique that involves scrambling the data is used. We examine two examples of this technique later in this section.

Thus, with suitable modification, multilevel binary schemes overcome the problems of NRZ codes. Of course, as with any engineering design decision, there is a tradeoff. With multilevel binary coding, the line signal may take on one of three levels, but each signal element, which could represent $\log_2 3 = 1.58$ bits of information, bears only one bit of information. Thus multilevel binary is not as efficient as NRZ coding. Another way to state this is that the receiver of multilevel binary signals has to distinguish between three levels ($+A$, $-A$, 0) instead of just two levels in the other signaling formats previously discussed. Because of this, the multilevel binary signal requires approximately 3 db more signal power than a two-valued signal for the same probability of bit error. This is illustrated in Figure 8.3. Put another way, the bit

---

[2] These terms are not consistently used in the literature. In some books, these two terms are used for different encoding schemes than those defined here, and a variety of terms have been used for the two schemes illustrated in Figure 8.1. The nomenclature used here corresponds to the usage in various CCITT standards documents.

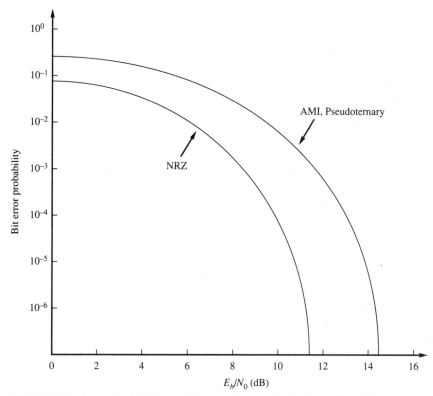

FIGURE 8.3 Theoretical Bit Error Rate for Various Digital Encoding Schemes

error rate for NRZ codes, at a given signal-to-noise ratio, is significantly less than that for multilevel binary.

Scrambling Techniques

As was mentioned, one way to deal with the synchronization deficiency of multilevel binary codes is to force transitions by including additional bits. This approach is not attractive at high data rates because of the many additional but superfluous bits that would need to be transmitted, reducing efficiency.

Another approach is to make use of some sort of scrambling scheme. The idea behind this approach is simple: Sequences that would result in a constant voltage level on the line are replaced by filling sequences that will provide sufficient transitions for the receiver's clock to maintain synchronization. The filling sequence must be recognized by the receiver and replaced with the original data sequence. The filling sequence is the same length as the original sequence, so there is no data rate increase. The design goals for this approach can be summarized as follows:

- No dc component.
- No long sequences of zero-level line signals.
- No reduction in data rate.
- Error-detection capability.

Two techniques are in use in ISDN; these are illustrated in Figure 8.4.

A coding scheme that is commonly used in North America is known as **bipolar with 8-zeros substitution (B8ZS).** The coding scheme is based on a bipolar AMI. We have seen that the drawback of the AMI code is that a long string of zeros may result in loss of synchronization. To overcome this problem, the encoding is amended with the following rules:

- If an octet of all zeros occurs and the last voltage pulse preceding this octet was positive, then the eight zeros of the octet are encoded as $000 + - 0 - +$.
- If an octet of all zeros occurs and the last voltage pulse preceding this octet was negative, then the eight zeros of the octet are encoded as $000 - + 0 + -$.

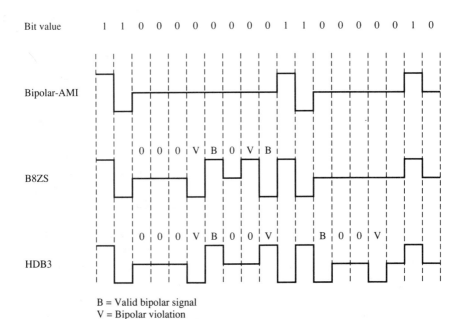

B = Valid bipolar signal
V = Bipolar violation

FIGURE 8.4 Encoding Rules for B8ZS and HDB3

This technique forces two code violations of the AMI code, an event unlikely to be caused by noise or other transmission impairment. The receiver recognizes the pattern and interprets the octet as consisting of all zeros.

A coding scheme that is commonly used in Europe and Japan is known as the **high-density bipolar–3 zeros (HDB3)** code (Table 8.2). As before, it is based on the use of AMI encoding. In this case, the scheme replaces strings of four zeros with sequences containing one or two pulses. In each case, the fourth zero is replaced with a code violation. In addition, a rule is needed to ensure that successive violations are of alternate polarity so that no dc component is introduced. Thus, if the last violation was positive, this violation must be negative and vice versa. The table shows that this condition is tested for by knowing whether the number of pulses since the last violation is even or odd and knowing the polarity of the last pulse before the occurrence of the four zeros.

Figure 8.2 shows the spectral properties of these two codes. As can be seen, neither has a dc component. Most of the energy is concentrated in a relatively sharp spectrum around a frequency equal to one-half the data rate. Thus, these codes are well suited to high data rate transmission.

8.2

BASIC USER-NETWORK INTERFACE

The layer 1 specification for the basic user-network interface is defined in Recommendation I.430. Recall that the basic interface supports a 2B + D channel structure at 192 kbps. In this section, we examine four key aspects of the basic interface:

- Line coding.
- Physical connector.
- Framing and multiplexing.
- Contention resolution for multidrop configurations.

TABLE 8.2   HDB3 Substitution Rules

Polarity of Preceding Pulse	Number of Bipolar Pulses (ones) Since Last Substitution	
	Odd	Even
−	000−	+00+
+	000+	−00−

Line Coding

At the interface between the subscriber and the network terminating equipment (T or S reference point), digital data are exchanged using full-duplex transmission. A separate physical line is used for the transmission in each direction. Hence, we need not concern ourselves with echo cancellation or time-compression multiplexing techniques to achieve full-duplex operation. Because the distances are relatively short, and because all of the equipment is on the subscriber's premises, it is far easier to use two separate physical circuits than to use any other technique for full-duplex operation.

The electrical specification for the interface dictates the use of a pseudoternary coding scheme (Figure 8.1 and Table 8.1). Binary one is represented by the absence of voltage; binary zero is represented by a positive or negative pulse of 750 mV ± 10%. The data rate is 192 kbps.

Basic Access Physical Connector

The actual physical connection between a TE and an NT at the S or T reference point for the basic access interface is specified not in a CCITT Recommendation but in an ISO standard (ISO 8877).[3] This standard specifies an 8-pin physical connector (Figure 8.5).

The physical connection terminates in matching plugs that provide for 4, 6, or 8 contacts. The number of contacts provided depends on usage, as is explained subsequently.

Table 8.3 lists the contact assignments for each of the 8 pins on both the NT and TE sides. Two pins each are needed to provide balanced transmission in each direction. These contact points are used to connect twisted-pair leads coming from the NT and TE devices.

The specification provides for the capability to transfer power across the interface. The direction of power transfer depends on the application. In a typical application, it may be desirable to provide for power transfer from the network side toward the terminals in order to, for example, maintain a basic telephony service in the event of failure of the locally provided power. Two possibilities are seen for the transfer of power from an NT to a TE (Figure 8.6):

- Using the same access leads used for the bidirectional transmission of the digital signal (power source and sink 1).
- On additional wires, using access leads g-h.

The remaining two leads are not used in the ISDN configuration but may be useful in other configurations. Thus, the ISDN physical interface consists of just six leads.

[3] ISO Standard ISO 8807, *Interface Connector and Contact Assignments for ISDN Basic Access Interface Located at Reference Points S and T*, 1987.

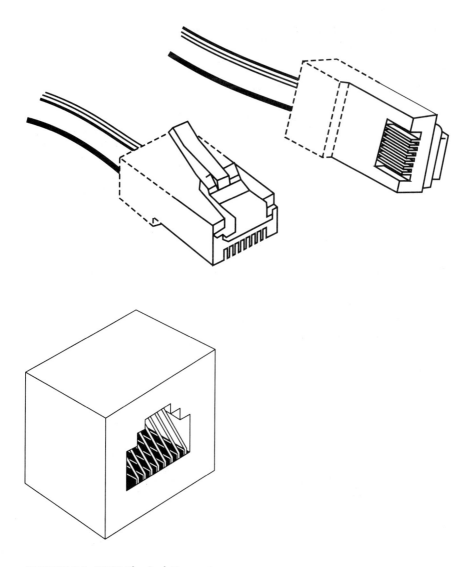

FIGURE 8.5 ISDN Physical Connector

Framing and Multiplexing

The basic access structure consists of two 64-kbps B channels and one 16-kbps D channel. These channels, which produce a load of 144 kbps, are multiplexed over a 192-kbps interface at the S or T reference point. The remaining capacity is used for various framing and synchronization purposes.

TABLE 8.3   Contact Assignments for Plugs and Jacks of ISDN Physical Connector (ISO 8877)

Contact Number	TE	NT
a	Power Source 3	Power Sink 3
b	Power Source 3	Power Sink 3
c	Transmit	Receive
d	Receive	Transmit
e	Receive	Transmit
f	Transmit	Receive
g	Power Sink 2	Power Source 2
h	Power Sink 2	Power Source 2

TE = terminal equipment
NT = network-terminating equipment

Frame Format.   As with any synchronous time-division multiplexed (TDM) scheme, basic access transmission is structured into repetitive, fixed-length frames. In this case, each frame is 48 bits long; at 192 kbps, frames must repeat at a rate of one frame every 250 μsec. Figure 8.7 shows the frame structure; the upper frame is transmitted by the network (NT1 or NT2) to the subscriber's terminal equipment (TE); the

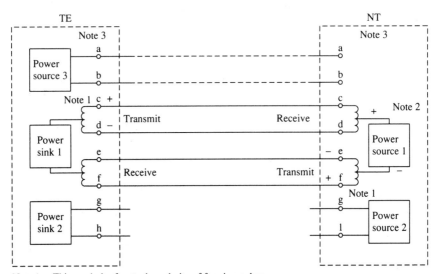

Note 1— This symbol refers to the polarity of framing pulses.
Note 2—This symbol refers to the polarity of power during normal power conditions (reversed for restricted conditions).
Note 3—The access lead assignments indicated in this figure are intended to provide for direct interface cable wiring, i.e., each interface pair is connected to a pair of access leads having the same two letters at TEs and NTs.

FIGURE 8.6 Reference Configuration for Signal Transmission and Power-Feeding in Normal Operating Mode

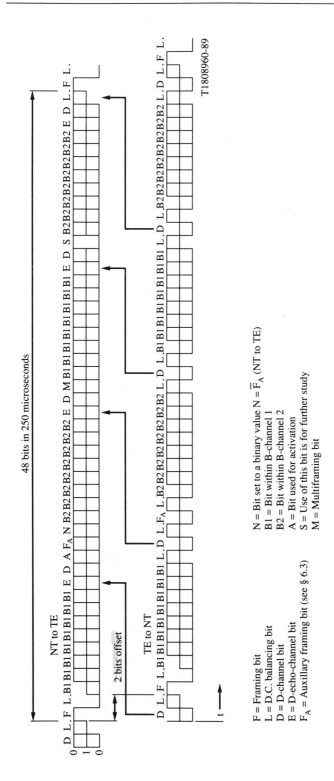

FIGURE 8.7 Frame Structure at Reference Points S and T for Basic Rate

lower frame is transmitted from the TE to the NT1 or NT2. The pseudoternary coding is illustrated with the interpretation shown in Figure 8.8. Frame synchronization is such that each frame transmitted from a TE toward the NT is later than the frame in the opposite direction by two bit-times.

Each frame of 48 bits includes 16 bits from each of the two B channels and 4 bits from the D channel. The remaining bits have the following interpretation. Let us first consider the frame structure in the TE-to-NT direction. Each frame begins with a framing bit (F) that is always transmitted as a positive pulse. This is followed by a dc balancing bit (L) that is set to a negative pulse to balance the voltage. The F-L pattern thus acts to synchronize the receiver on the beginning of the frame. The specification dictates that, following these first two bit positions, the first occurrence of a zero bit will be encoded as a negative pulse. After that, the pseudoternary rule is observed. The next eight bits (B1) are from the first B channel. This is followed by another dc balancing bit (L). Next comes a bit from the D channel, followed by its balancing bit. This is followed by the auxiliary framing bit (F_A), which is set to zero unless it is to be used in a multiframe structure, as explained subsequently. There follows another balancing bit (L), eight bits (B2) from the second B channel, and another balancing bit (L). This is followed by bits from the D channel, first B channel, D channel again, second B channel, and the D channel yet again, with each group of channel bits followed by a balancing bit.

The frame structure in the NT-to-TE direction is similar to the frame structure for transmission in the TE-to-NT direction. The following new bits replace some of the dc balancing bits. The D channel echo bit (E) is a retransmission by the NT of the most recently received D bit from the TE; the purpose of this echo is explained subsequently. The activation bit (A) is used to activate or deactivate a TE, allowing the device to come on line or, when there is no activity, to be placed in low power-

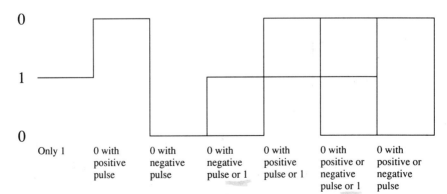

FIGURE 8.8 Interpretation of Figure 8.7

consumption mode. The N bit is normally set to binary one. The N and M bits may be used for multiframing, as explained subsequently. The S bit is reserved for other future standardization requirements.

Frame Alignment. To assure that the transmitter (NT or TE) and receiver (TE or NT) do not get out of alignment, the frame structure includes deliberate violations of the pseudoternary code. The receiver looks for these violations to assure that frame alignment is being maintained. Two violations are included:

- The first F bit: This bit is always a positive zero. The frame is structured so that the last zero bit of the frame is positive.
- The first zero bit after the first L bit: Both of these bits are negative polarity. This second violation occurs at the F_A bit at the latest.

Multiframe Structure. A recently added feature of the basic interface specification is the provision for an additional channel for traffic in the TE-to-NT direction, called the Q channel. At present, the use of the Q channel is for further study. However, the current version of I.430 provides the structure for the Q channel (Table 8.4). To implement the Q channel, a multiframe structure is established by setting the M bit (NT-to-TE direction) to binary 1 on every twentieth frame. In the TE-to-NT direction, the F_A bit in every fifth frame is a Q bit. Thus, in each 20-frame multiframe there are 4 Q bits.

Normally, in the NT-to-TE direction the F_A bit is set to binary zero, with the following N bit set to binary one. To identify the Q-bit positions in the TE-to-NT direction, the corresponding F_A/N bits in the NT-to-TE direction are inverted (F_A = binary one, N = binary zero).

Contention Resolution for Multidrop Configurations

Multidrop Configurations. With the basic access interface, it is possible to have more than one TE device in a passive-bus configuration. Figure 8.9 shows the allowable configurations. The simplest is a point-to-point configuration, with only one TE. In this configuration, the maximum distance between the NT equipment and the TE is on the order of 1 km. The second configuration is an ordinary passive bus, which has traditionally been referred to as a multidrop line. This kind of configuration imposes limitations on the distances involved. This has to do with the way in which signal strength is determined.

When two devices exchange data over a link, the signal strength of the transmitter must be adjusted to be within certain limits. The signal must be strong enough so that, after attenuation and signal impairment across the medium, it meets the receiver's minimum signal strength requirements and maintains an adequate signal-to-noise ratio. On the other hand, the signal must not be so strong as to overload the circuitry

TABLE 8.4   Q-bit Position Identification and Multiframe Structure

Frame Number	NT-to-TE F_A Bit Position	TE-to-NT F_A Bit Position (Notes 1 and 2)	NT-to-TE M Bit
1	ONE	Q1	ONE
2	ZERO	ZERO	ZERO
3	ZERO	ZERO	ZERO
4	ZERO	ZERO	ZERO
5	ZERO	ZERO	ZERO
6	ONE	Q2	ZERO
7	ZERO	ZERO	ZERO
8	ZERO	ZERO	ZERO
9	ZERO	ZERO	ZERO
10	ZERO	ZERO	ZERO
11	ONE	Q3	ZERO
12	ZERO	ZERO	ZERO
13	ZERO	ZERO	ZERO
14	ZERO	ZERO	ZERO
15	ZERO	ZERO	ZERO
16	ONE	Q4	ZERO
17	ZERO	ZERO	ZERO
18	ZERO	ZERO	ZERO
19	ZERO	ZERO	ZERO
20	ZERO	ZERO	ZERO
1	ONE	Q1	ONE
2	ZERO	ZERO	ZERO
etc.			

Note 1 — If the Q-bits are not used by a TE, the Q-bits shall be set to binary ONE.
Note 2 — Where multiframe identification is not provided with a binary ONE in an appropriate M bit, but where Q-bit positions are identified, Q-bits 1 through 4 are not distinguished.

of the transmitter, which creates harmonics and nonlinear effects. With a point-to-point link, the principal factor to take into account is the length of the medium. With a multidrop link, each tap into the bus creates losses and distortions. Accordingly, for a given data rate and transmission medium, a multidrop line will need to be shorter than a point-to-point line. In the case of the basic access interface, CCITT specifies a maximum distance of between 100 and 200 meters, with a maximum of 8 TEs connected at random points along the interface cable.

The length of the short passive bus is also limited by the differential round-trip delay in signal propagation. Because the devices are connected at various points, the NT receiver must cater to pulses arriving with different delays from various terminals. To maintain receiver synchronization, the limit of 100 to 200 meters is needed. A greater length

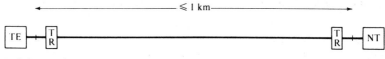

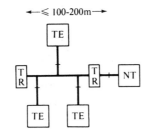

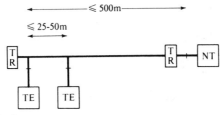

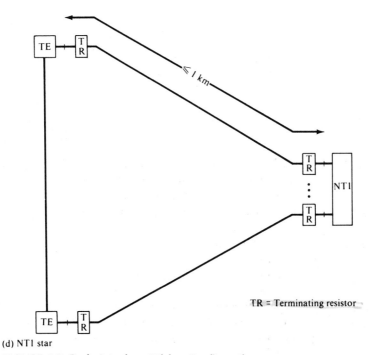

FIGURE 8.9 Basic Interface Wiring Configurations

can be achieved if all of the devices are clustered together at the far end of the line (Figure 8.9c). With this extended bus configuration, a maximum length of 500 meters, with a maximum differential distance between terminals of 25–50 meters, is possible.

The final configuration, illustrated in Figure 8.9d, is the star configuration. This configuration permits multiple TEs but requires only point-to-point wiring. In this configuration, the NT1 must include digital logic to provide for the operation of the D channel echo. The NT1 must transmit the same echo bit over all NT1-to-TE lines. The value of the echo bit is 0 if any of the incoming D bits is 0; otherwise, it is 1. On the network side, the NT1 must merge the transmissions from all of the TEs to form a single 192-kbps stream.

Contention Resolution.   With the configurations of Figure 8.9b and c, there is a contention problem. In the case of the two B channels, no additional functionality is needed, since each channel is dedicated to a particular TE at any given time. However, the D channel is shared by all TEs for control signaling and D channel packet transmission. For incoming data, we will see that the LAP-D addressing scheme is sufficient to sort out the proper destination TE for each frame. For outgoing data, some sort of contention-resolution protocol is needed to assure that only one device at a time attempts to transmit.

The D channel contention-resolution algorithm has the following elements:

1. When a subscriber device has no LAPD frames to transmit, it transmits a series of binary ones on the D channel. Using the pseudoternary encoding scheme, this corresponds to the absence of line signal.
2. The NT, on receipt of a D channel bit, reflects back the binary value as a D channel echo bit (Figure 8.10).
3. When a terminal is ready to transmit an LAPD frame, it listens to the stream of incoming D channel echo bits. If it detects a string of 1-bits of length equal to a threshold value X_i, then it may transmit. Otherwise, the terminal must assume that some other terminal is transmitting, and wait.
4. It may happen that several terminals are monitoring the echo stream and begin to transmit at the same time, causing a collision. To overcome this condition, a transmitting TE monitors the echo bits and compares them to its transmitted bits. If a discrepancy is detected, the terminal ceases to transmit and returns to a listen state.

The electrical characteristics of the interface (i.e., 1-bit = absence of signal) are such that any user equipment transmitting a 0-bit will override user equipment transmitting a 1-bit at the same instant. This ar-

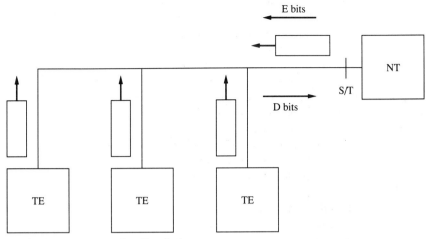

FIGURE 8.10 Contention Resolution

rangement ensures that one device will be guaranteed successful completion of its transmission.

The algorithm also includes a primitive priority mechanism based on the threshold value X_i. Signaling information is given priority over packet information. Within each of these two priority classes, a station begins at normal priority and then is reduced to lower priority after a transmission. It remains at the lower priority until all other terminals have had an opportunity to transmit. The values of X_i are as follows:

- Signaling information
    Normal priority $X_i = 8$
    Lower priority $X_i = 9$
- Signaling information
    Normal priority $X_i = 10$
    Lower priority $X_i = 11$

Figure 8.11 shows an example of contention resolution. Three TEs (A, B, and C) are all attempting to use the D channel. As long as all binary zeros and ones from all sources are identical, all continue to transmit. As soon as a source notes a binary zero on the E channel when it has transmitted a binary one on the D channel in the corresponding bit position, the source drops out.

8.3

PRIMARY RATE USER-NETWORK INTERFACE

The primary interface, like the basic interface, multiplexes multiple channels across a single transmission medium. In the case of the pri-

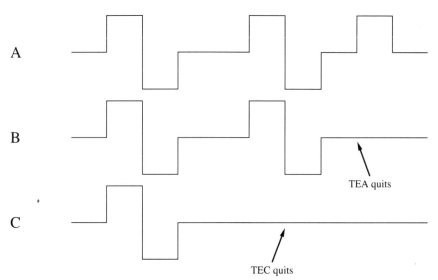

FIGURE 8.11 Example of Contention Resolution

mary interface, only a point-to-point configuration is allowed. Typically, the interface exists at the T reference point with a digital PBX or other concentration device controlling multiple TEs and providing a synchronous TDM facility for access to ISDN. Two data rates are defined for the primary interface: 1.544 Mbps and 2.048 Mbps.

Interface at 1.544 Mbps

The ISDN interface at 1.544 Mbps is based on the North American DS-1 transmission structure, which is used on the T1 transmission service. Figure 8.12a illustrates the frame format for this data rate. The bit stream is structured into repetitive 193-bit frames. Each frame consists of 24 8-bit time slots and a framing bit. The same time slot repeated over multiple frames constitutes a channel. At a data rate of 1.544 Mbps, frames repeat at a rate of one every 125 μsec, or 800 frames per second. Thus each channel supports 64 kbps. Typically, the transmission structure is used to support 23 B channels and 1 D channel. As discussed in Chapter 7, other assignments can be made, including 24 B channels and various combinations of H channels.

The framing bit is used for synchronization and other management purposes. A multiframe structure of 24 193-bit frames is imposed, and Table 8.5 shows the assignment of values to the 24 framing bits across the 24-frame multiframe. Six of the bits form a frame-alignment signal, with the code 001011, which repeats every multiframe. The purpose is to provide a form of synchronization. If for some reason the receiver becomes one or more bits out of alignment with the transmitter, it will

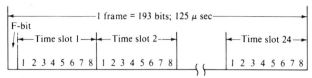

(a) Interface at 1.544 Mbps

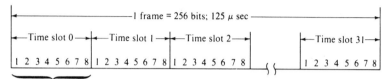

Framing channel

(b) Interface at 2.048 Mbps

FIGURE 8.12 Primary Access Frame Formats

fail to detect the alignment signal and hence will detect the misalignment.

The bits designated as e_i bits can be used as a 6-bit cyclic redundancy check (CRC) of the framing bits (see Appendix A for a discussion of CRC).

The remaining bits, labeled m bits, are currently not assigned in the standard, but they may possibly be used in the future.

The line coding for the 1.544-Mbps interface is AMI using B8ZS.

Interface at 2.048 Mbps

The ISDN interface at 2.048 Mbps is based on the European transmission structure of the same data rate. This scheme is defined in detail in G.704.[4]

Figure 8.12b illustrates the frame format for this data rate. The bit stream is structured into repetitive 256-bit frames. Each frame consists of 32 8-bit time slots. The first time slot is used for framing and synchronization purposes; the remaining 31 time slots support user channels. At a data rate of 2.048 Mbps, frames repeat at a rate of one every 125 μsec, or 800 frames per second. Thus each channel supports 64 kbps. Typically, the transmission structure is used to support 30 B channels and 1 D channel. As discussed in Chapter 7, other assignments can be made, such as 31 B channels and various combinations of H channels.

[4] CCITT Recommendation G.704, *Synchronous Frame Structures Used at Primary and Secondary Hierarchical Levels*, 1988.

TABLE 8.5   Multiframe Structure for 1.544-Mbps Interface

Multiframe Frame Number	F-Bits			
	Multiframe Bit Number	Assignments		
		FAS	See Note	See § 4.2.6
1	1	—	m	n
2	194	—	—	e_1
3	387	—	m	—
4	580	0	—	—
5	773	—	m	—
6	966	—	—	e_2
7	1159	—	m	—
8	1352	0	—	—
9	1545	—	m	—
10	1738	—	—	e_3
11	1931	—	m	—
12	2124	1	—	—
13	2317	—	m	—
14	2510	—	—	e_4
15	2703	—	m	—
16	2896	0	—	—
17	3089	—	m	—
18	3282	—	—	e_5
19	3475	—	m	—
20	3668	1	—	—
21	3861	—	m	—
22	4054	—	—	e_6
23	4247	—	m	—
24	4440	1	—	—

Table 8.6 shows the use of the bits in time slot 0. The frame-alignment signal occupies positions 2 to 8 in channel time slot 0 of every other frame. This signal, which is 0011011, is used for alignment in the same fashion as the frame-alignment signal on the 1.544-Mbps interface. The S_i bits may be used for a 4-bit CRC procedure, explained in the next paragraph. The A bit can be used for a remote alarm indication; in an alarm condition, it would be set to 1. The S_{ai} bits are spare bits with no current defined use.

Where there is a need for enhanced error-monitoring capability, a multiframe structure, illustrated in Table 8.7, may be used. The 4-bit CRC value is carried in the first bit position of alternate frames. The two E bits are used to signal back to the other side that a CRC error has been detected, by setting the binary value of one E-bit from 1 to 0 for each errored sub-multiframe.

The line coding for the 2.048-Mbps interface is AMI using HDB3.

TABLE 8.6 Allocation of Bits 1 to 8 of the Frame in 2.048-Mbps Interface

Bit Number / Alternate Frames	1	2	3	4	5	6	7	8
Frame containing the frame-alignment signal	S_i	0	0	1	1	0	1	1
	Note 1	Frame-alignment signal						
Frame not containing the frame-alignment signal	S_i	1	A	S_{a4}	S_{a5}	S_{a6}	S_{a7}	S_{a8}
	Note 1	Note 2	Note 3	Note 4				

Note 1 — S_i = bits reserved for international use. One specific use is for CRC. Other possible uses may be defined at a later stage. If no use is realized, these bits should be fixed at 1 on digital paths crossing an international border. However, they may be used nationally if the digital path does not cross a border.

Note 2 — This bit is fixed at 1 to assist in avoiding simulations of the frame-alignment signal.

Note 3 — A = Remote alarm indication. In undisturbed operation, set to 0; in alarm condition, set to 1.

Note 4 — S_{a4} to S_{a8} = Additional spare bits whose use may be as follows:

i.   Bits S_{a4} to S_{a8} may be recommended by CCITT for use in specific point-to-point applications (e.g., transcoder equipments conforming to Recommendation G.761).

ii. Bit S_{a4} may be recommended by CCITT as a message-based data link for operations, maintenance, and performance monitoring. This channel originates at the point where the frame is generated and terminates where the frame is split up. This requires further study.

iii. Bits S_{a5} to S_{a7} are for national usage where there is no demand on them for specific point-to-point applications [see (i) above].

Bits S_{a4} to S_{a8} (where these are not used) should be set to 1 on links crossing an international border.

8.4

U INTERFACE

Recommendation I.411 states that there is no reference point assigned to the transmission line (local loop) between the subscriber premises and the local exchange, since an ISDN user-network interface is not envisaged at this location. However, CCITT has issued Recommendation G.961,[5] which does address the interface between NT equipment and the local loop for basic rate access. This interface is often referred to as the U reference point.

G.961 is only a partial specification. It specifies the use of either echo cancellation or time-compression multiplexing over a single twisted pair. Several alternative line-coding techniques are defined in appendices. In

[5] CCITT Recommendation G.961, *Digital Transmission System on Metallic Local Lines for ISDN Basic Rate Access*, 1988.

TABLE 8.7 Multiframe Structure for 2.048-Mbps Interface

Sub-mul-tiframe (SMF)	Frame Number	Bits 1 to 8 of the Frame							
		1	2	3	4	5	6	7	8
	0	C_1	0	0	1	1	0	1	1
	1	0	1	A	S_{a4}	S_{a5}	S_{a6}	S_{a7}	S_{a8}
	2	C_2	0	0	1	1	0	1	1
I	3	0	1	A	S_{a4}	S_{a5}	S_{a6}	S_{a7}	S_{a8}
	4	C_3	0	0	1	1	0	1	1
	5	1	1	A	S_{a4}	S_{a5}	S_{a6}	S_{a7}	S_{a8}
	6	C_4	0	0	1	1	0	1	1
Multi-frame	7	0	1	A	S_{a4}	S_{a5}	S_{a6}	S_{a7}	S_{a8}
	8	C_1	0	0	1	1	0	1	1
	9	1	1	A	S_{a4}	S_{a5}	S_{a6}	S_{a7}	S_{a8}
	10	C_2	0	0	1	1	0	1	1
II	11	1	1	A	S_{a4}	S_{a5}	S_{a6}	S_{a7}	S_{a8}
	12	C_3	0	0	1	1	0	1	1
	13	E	1	A	S_{a4}	S_{a5}	S_{a6}	S_{a7}	S_{a8}
	14	C_4	0	0	1	1	0	1	1
	15	E	1	A	S_{a4}	S_{a5}	S_{a6}	S_{a7}	S_{a8}

Note 1: E = CRC-4 error indication bits.
Note 2: S_{a4} to S_{a8} = Spare bits.
Note 3: C_1 to C_4 = Cyclic Redundancy Check-4 (CRC-4) bits.
Note 4: A = Remote alarm indication.

the U.S., work in this area has progressed much further. ANSI has issued a complete standard, T1.601,[6] for the basic access interface to the local loop. We examine the ANSI standard in this section.

Line Coding

The line-coding technique specified in T1.601 is known as **two binary, one quaternary (2B1Q)** coding. This code provides for more efficient use of bandwidth by having each signaling element represent two bits instead of one. Four different voltage levels are used. Since each signal element can take on one of four possible values, two bits of information are conveyed.

Table 8.8 shows the definition of 2B1Q. Two positive and two negative voltage levels are used. Corresponding to each voltage level is a pair of bits. The first bit is one if the polarity of the pulse is positive and zero if the polarity is negative. The second bit is one if the magnitude of the pulse is 0.833 V and zero if the magnitude of the pulse is

[6] American National Standard ANSI T1.601, *Integrated Services Digital Network (ISDN)— Basic Access Interface for Use on Metallic Loops for Application on the Network Side of the NT (Layer 1 Specification),* 1988.

TABLE 8.8   Two Binary, One Quaternary (2B1Q) Signaling Levels

First Bit (Polarity)	Second Bit (Magnitude)	Quaternary Symbol	Voltage Level (Volts)
1	0	+3	2.5
1	1	+1	0.833
0	1	−1	−0.833
0	0	−3	−2.5

2.5 V. Each of the four combinations of two bits is assigned a symbol. The four values listed under "quaternary symbol" in the table should be understood as symbol names, not numerical values.

Figure 8.13 is an example of 2B1Q coding.

With 2B1Q, we see a distinction between data rate and modulation rate. The data rate, expressed in bits per second (bps) is the rate at which bit values are transmitted. The modulation rate, expressed in bauds, is the rate at which signal elements are generated. In general,

$$D = \frac{R}{b} = \frac{R}{\log_2 L}$$

where

D = modulation rate, bauds.
R = data rate, bps.
L = number of different signal elements.
b = number of bits per signal element.

In the case of T1.601, the data rate is 160 kbps, and the modulation rate is therefore 80 kbaud.

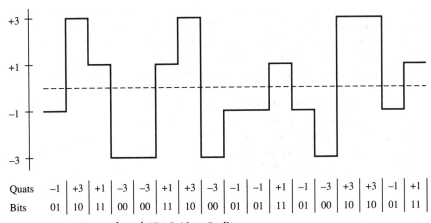

FIGURE 8.13 Examples of 2B1Q Line Coding

The advantage of this type of encoding is that, in general, the band-width of the corresponding signal, compared to NRZ-L, is equal to the bandwidth of NRZ-L divided by the number of bits per signal element [COUC90]. Thus, 2B1Q should require only about half the bandwidth of NRZ-L. This code was chosen over other codes with higher baud rates for the U interface primarily because the lower baud rate mini-mized the two dominant transmission limitations in this application: intersymbol interference and near-end echo [LECH89].

A final note about the 2B1Q coding scheme. Prior to transmission the data are scrambled and then are subsequently descrambled at re-ception. This gives the data a pseudorandom nature that helps the receiver extract bit-timing information. It also improves the spectral characteristics of the signal, giving it a more uniform power distribution, as opposed to the potentially strong discrete spectral lines in nonscram-bled data. See Appendix 8A for a discussion of scrambling.

Framing and Multiplexing

The basic access structure consists of two 64-kbps B channels and one 16-kbps D channel. These channels, which produce a load of 144 kbps, are multiplexed over a 160-kbps interface at the U reference point. The remaining capacity is used for various framing and synchronization purposes.

Frame Format.   As with any synchronous time-division multiplexed (TDM) scheme, basic access transmission is structured into repetitive, fixed-length frames. In this case, each frame is 240 bits long; at 160 kbps, frames must repeat at a rate of one frame every 1.5 msec. Figure 8.14a shows the frame structure; the structure consists of three parts:

- *Synchronization word:* The first nine symbols (18 bits) of the frame form a synchronization word, with the quaternary symbols in the sequence ($+3$ $+3$ -3 -3 -3 $+3$ -3 $+3$ $+3$), except as noted subsequently. This word allows the receiver to easily synchronize on the beginning of each frame.
- *User data:* The next twelve groups of 18 bits each carry B and D channel data, as illustrated in Figure 8.14b.
- *M channel:* The last 6 bits of the frame form a 4-kbps M channel for maintenance and other purposes.

Note that the interleaving of B and D bits is different at the U reference points (8 B1, 8 B2, 2 D) than at the S and T reference points (8 B1, D, 8 B2, D). Since the channel data rates are the same at all three reference points, this presents only a minor buffering problem. The NT1 is responsible for the conversion between the two different frame formats.

Function	SW/ISW	$12 \times (2B + D)$	M
	Synchronization word	Twelve groups of $2b_8 + D_2$	Overhead
Number of quats	9	108	3
Number of bits	18	216	6

(a) Overall 1.5-msec basic frame

Data	B_1				B_2				D
Bit pairs	$b_{11}b_{12}$	$b_{13}b_{14}$	$b_{15}b_{16}$	$b_{17}b_{18}$	$b_{21}b2_{22}$	$b_{23}b_{24}$	$b_{25}b_{26}$	$b_{27}b_{28}$	d_1d_2
# Bits	8				8				2
# Quats	4				4				1

(b) 2B1Q encoding of 2B+D Bit Fields

FIGURE 8.14 2B1Q Transmission Frame

Multiframe Structure. The basic frame structure is organized into superframes consisting of 8 frames each, as shown in Table 8.9. The first frame in the superframe is identified by inverting the polarity of the synchronization word in that frame, with the pattern (-3 -3 $+3$ $+3$ $+3$ -3 $+3$ -3 -3). Within the superframe, there are 48 M bits, and these are used for a variety of purposes. The most notable use is to form a 12-bit CRC for error checking.

Table 8.10 provides a comparison of the basic rate interface at the U and S/T reference points.

8.5

SUMMARY

The physical layer specification for ISDN is divided into two principal parts: one for basic access and one for primary access.

The basic-rate access supports 2 B channels and 1 D channel for a user data rate of 144 kbps. At the S and T reference points, the interface provides a frame structure operating at 192 kbps that supports the three user channels plus some overhead and maintenance bits. The pseudo-ternary coding scheme is used. An 8-pin physical connector is specified.

The primary rate operates at 1.544 and 2.048 Mbps. The 1.544-Mbps interface uses AMI coding with B8ZS. The 2.048-Mbps interface uses AMI coding with HDB3.

Although CCITT has not issued an ISDN recommendation for the so-called U interface, ANSI has issued a standard that uses echo cancellation and the 2B1Q line code at 160 kbps to support the basic rate interface.

TABLE 8.9   2B1Q Superframe Technique and Overhead Bit Assignments

		Framing	2B + D	Overhead Bits (M_1–M_6)					
Quat Positions		1–9	10–117	118s	118m	119s	119m	120s	120m
Bit Positions		1–18	19–234	235	236	237	238	239	240
Superframe #	Basic Frame #	Sync Word	2B + D	M_1	M_2	M_3	M_4	M_5	M_6
A	1	ISW	2B + D	eOC_{a1}	eOC_{a2}	eOC_{a3}	act	1	1
	2	SW	2B + D	eOC_{dm}	eOC_{i1}	eOC_{i2}	dea	1	febe
	3	SW	2B + D	eOC_{i3}	eOC_{i4}	eOC_{i5}	1	crc_1	crc_2
	4	SW	2B + D	eOC_{i6}	eOC_{i7}	eOC_{i8}	1	crc_3	crc_4
	5	SW	2B + D	eOC_{a1}	eOC_{a2}	eOC_{a3}	1	crc_5	crc_6
	6	SW	2B + D	eOC_{dm}	eOC_{i1}	eOC_{i2}	1	crc_7	crc_8
	7	SW	2B + D	eOC_{i3}	eOC_{i4}	eOC_{i5}	1	crc_9	crc_{10}
	8	SW	2B + D	eOC_{i6}	eOC_{i7}	eOC_{i8}	1	crc_{11}	crc_{12}
B, C, . . .									

(a) Network → NT

		Framing	2B + D	Overhead Bits (M_1–M_6)					
Quat Positions		1–9	10–117	118s	118m	119s	119m	120s	120m
Bit Positions		1–18	19–234	235	236	237	238	239	240
Superframe #	Basic Frame #	Sync Word	2B + D	M_1	M_2	M_3	M_4	M_5	M_6
1	1	ISW	2B + D	eOC_{a1}	eOC_{a2}	eOC_{a3}	act	1	1
	2	SW	2B + D	eOC_{dm}	eOC_{i1}	eOC_{i2}	ps_1	1	febe

	SW	2B+D	eoc$_{i3}$	eoc$_{i4}$	eoc$_{i5}$	ps$_2$	crc$_1$	crc$_2$
3	SW	2B+D	eoc$_{i3}$	eoc$_{i4}$	eoc$_{i5}$	ntm	crc$_1$	crc$_2$
4	SW	2B+D	eoc$_{i6}$	eoc$_{i7}$	eoc$_{i8}$	cso	crc$_3$	crc$_4$
5	SW	2B+D	eoc$_{a1}$	eoc$_{a2}$	eoc$_{a3}$	1	crc$_5$	crc$_6$
6	SW	2B+D	eoc$_{dm}$	eoc$_{i1}$	eoc$_{i2}$	1	crc$_7$	crc$_8$
7	SW	2B+D	eoc$_{i3}$	eoc$_{i4}$	eoc$_{i5}$	1	crc$_9$	crc$_{10}$
8	SW	2B+D	eoc$_{i6}$	eoc$_{i7}$	eoc$_{i8}$	1	crc$_{11}$	crc$_{12}$
2, 3, . . .								

(b) NT → Network

NOTE: 8 × 1.5 ms Basic Frames → 12 ms Superframe.
NT-to-Network superframe delay offset from Network-to-NT superframe by 60±2 quats (about 0.75 ms).
All bits other than the Sync Word are scrambled.

Symbols & Abbreviations:

act = activation bit (set = 1 during activation)
crc = cyclic redundancy check: covers 2B+D & M$_4$
  1 = most significant bit
  2 = next most significant bit
  etc.
cso = cold-start-only bit (set = 1 to indicate cold-start-only)
dea = deactivation bit (set = 0 to announce deactivation)
eoc = embedded operations channel
  a = address bit
  dm = data/message indicator (0 = data, 1 = message)
  i = information (data or message)

febe = far-end block error bit (set = 0 for errored superframe)
ntm = NT in test-mode bit (set = 0 to indicate test mode)
ps$_1$, ps$_2$ = power status bits (set = 0 to indicate power problems)
quat = pair of bits forming quaternary symbol
  s = sign bit (first in quat)
  m = magnitude bit (second in quat)
"1" = reserved bit for future standard (set = 1)
2B+D = user data, bits 19–234 in frame
M = M channel, bits 235–240 in frame
SW/ISW = synchronization word/inverted synchronization word, bits 1–18 in frame

TABLE 8.10   Comparison of Basic Rate Interface Physical Layer Standards [KESS90]

	CCITT I.430	ANSI T1.601
Reference point	S or T	U
Devices	TE1/TA to NT	NT1 to LE
Distance	1 km	5.5 km
Physical configuration	point-to-point or point-to-multipoint	point-to-point
Bit rate	192 kbps	160 kbps
User data rate	144 kbps	144 kbps
Line code	pseudoternary	2B1Q
Signaling rate	192 kbaud	80 kbaud
Maximum voltage	$\pm$ 750 mV	$\pm$ 2.5 V
Timing source	NT	LE
Number of wire pairs	2	1
Full-duplex method	One wire pair for each direction	Echo cancellation
Interleaving scheme*	$B1_8D_1B2_8D_1$ (twice per frame)	$B1_8B2_8D_2$ (12 time per frame)
Number of bits per frame	48	240
Number of bits user data	36	216
Number of bits overhead	12	24
Number of frames/sec	4,000	666.666 . . .

* Subscript indicates the number of contiguous bits that are sent on B1, B2, and D channels

8.6

RECOMMENDED READING

A good analysis of line-coding schemes can be found in [PEEB87]. [SKLA88] also provides some insights, while [LECH89] specifically looks at line-coding alternatives for the digital subscriber loop. [HUAN91] is a detailed survey of the technical issues to be addressed at the U interface.

8.7

PROBLEMS

8.1. Develop a state diagram (finite state machine) representation of pseudoternary coding.

8.2. Consider the following signal-encoding technique. Binary data are presented as input, a_m, $m = 1, 2, 3, \ldots$ Two levels of processing occur.

First, a new set of binary numbers is produced:

$$b_m = a_m + b_{m-1} \bmod 2$$

These are then encoded as

$$c_m = b_m - b_{m-1}$$

On reception, the original data are recovered by

$$a_m = c_m \bmod 2$$

a. Verify that the received values of a_m equal the transmitted values of a_m.

b. What sort of encoding is this?

8.3. Figure 8.7 indicates that, with the exception of the first occurrence of the L bit in a D channel frame, all subsequent L bits have either zero voltage or a positive voltage, but not a negative voltage. Why?

8.4. Demonstrate that the last nonzero pulse of a D channel frame is always positive. Note that the first pulse of the following frame is also positive. Is there an advantage to that?

8.5. What is the data rate on the Q channel?

8.6. In the discussion of D channel contention resolution, it was stated that a station remains at lower priority until all other terminals have had a chance to transmit. In the standard (I.430) it states that the value of the lower level of priority is changed back to the value of the higher level of priority when the TE observes a string of 1-bits on the echo stream of length equal to the value of the lower level of priority. Does this in fact guarantee that all other terminals have had a chance to transmit?

8.7. For the B8ZS coding scheme to be effective, the probability of occurrence of more than one code violation (two pulses in a row with the same polarity) due to an error must be quite small. What is the probability of the occurrence of more than one code violation in 8 bits for an error rate per bit of 10^{-6}? For an error rate of 10^{-3}?

8.8. What is the percentage overhead for each of the two primary rate interfaces?

APPENDIX 8A

SCRAMBLING AND DESCRAMBLING

For some digital data-encoding techniques, a long string of binary zeros or ones in a transmission can make it difficult for the receiver to maintain synchronization with the transmitter. Also, other transmission properties are enhanced if the data are more nearly of a random nature rather than constant or repetitive [BELL82a]. A technique commonly used to improve signal quality is scrambling and descrambling. The scrambling process tends to make the data appear more random.

The scrambling process consists of a feedback shift register, and the matching descrambler consists of a feedforward shift register. An example is shown in Figure 8.15. In this example, the scrambled data sequence may be expressed as follows:

$$B_m = A_m \oplus B_{m-3} \oplus B_{m-5}$$

where $\oplus$ indicates the exclusive or operation. The descrambled sequence is

$$
\begin{aligned}
C_m &= B_m + B_{m-3} \oplus B_{m-5} \\
&= (A_m \oplus B_{m-3} \oplus B_{m-5}) \oplus B_{m-3} \oplus B_{m-5} \\
&= A_m
\end{aligned}
$$

As can be seen, the descrambled output is the original sequence.

We can represent this process with the use of polynomials. Thus, for this example, the polynomial is $P = 1 \oplus X^{-3} \oplus X^{-5}$. The input is

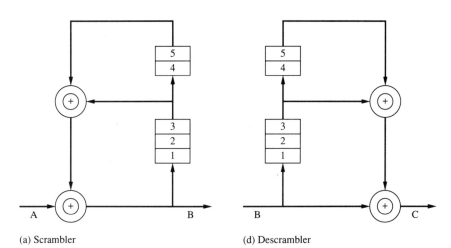

(a) Scrambler   (d) Descrambler

FIGURE 8.15 Scrambler and Descrambler

divided by this polynomial to produce the scrambled sequence. At the
receiver, the received scrambled signal is multiplied by the same polynomial to reproduce the original output. Figure 8.16 is an example using
the polynomial P and an input of 101010100000111. The scrambled
transmission, produced by dividing by P (100101), is 101110001101001.
When this number is multiplied by P, we get the original input. Note
that the input sequence c the periodic sequence 10101010 as well as a
long string of zeros. The scrambler effectively removes both patterns.

For the 2B1Q specification, in the network-NT direction, the polynomial is

$$1 \oplus X^{-5} \oplus X^{-23}$$

```
                              1 0 1 1 1 0 0 0 1 1 0 1 0 0 1 ←── B
P ──► 1 0 0 1 0 1 ) 1 0 1 0 1 0 1 0 0 0 0 0 1 1 1 - - - - - - ←── A
                    1 0 0 1 0 1
                    ─────────
                      1 1 1 1 1 0
                      1 0 0 1 0 1
                      ─────────
                        1 0 0 1 1 0
                        1 0 0 1 0 1
                        ─────────
                          1 1 0 0 1 0
                          1 0 0 1 0 1
                          ─────────
                            1 1 0 0 1 1
                            1 0 0 1 0 1
                            ─────────
                              1 0 1 1 0 1
                              1 0 0 1 0 1
                              ─────────
                                1 0 0 0 0 0
                                1 0 0 1 0 1
                                ─────────
                                  1 0 1 0 0 0
```

(a) Scrambling

```
              1 0 1 1 1 0 0 0 1 1 0 1 0 0 1 ←── B
                              1 0 0 1 0 1 ←── P
              ─────────────────────────────
              1 0 1 1 1 0 0 0 1 1 0 1 0 0 1
            1 0 1 1 1 0 0 0 1 1 0 1 0 0 1
        1 0 1 1 1 0 0 0 1 1 0 1 0 0 1
C = A ──► 1 0 1 0 1 0 1 0 0 0 0 0 1 1 1 - - - - - -
```

(b) Descrambling

FIGURE 8.16 Example of Scrambling with $P(X) = 1 + X^{-3} + X^{-5}$

and in the NT-network direction it is

$$1 \oplus X^{-18} \oplus X^{-23}$$

A shift register implementation is shown in Figure 8.17.

NT transmit scrambler (NT to LT):

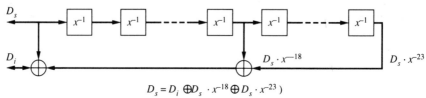

$$D_s = D_i \oplus D_s \cdot x^{-18} \oplus D_s \cdot x^{-23})$$

LT transmit scrambler (LT to NT):

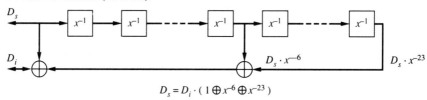

$$D_s = D_i \cdot (1 \oplus x^{-6} \oplus x^{-23})$$

LT receive descrambler (NT to LT):

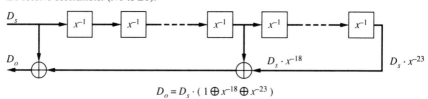

$$D_o = D_s \cdot (1 \oplus x^{-18} \oplus x^{-23})$$

NT receive descrambler (LT to NT):

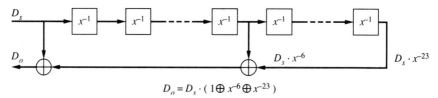

$$D_o = D_s \cdot (1 \oplus x^{-6} \oplus x^{-23})$$

FIGURE 8.17 Scrambler and Descrambler for 2B1Q Specification

CHAPTER 9

ISDN Data Link Layer

Above the physical layer, a data link control protocol is needed for communication. The principal emphasis by CCITT has been in defining a data link control protocol for the D channel. This protocol, known as LAPD, is used for communication between the subscriber and the network. All D channel traffic employs the LAPD protocol. For B channel traffic, the situation is somewhat different. For a packet-switched connection, LAPB is used to connect the subscriber to a packet-switching node. For a circuit-switched connection, there is an end-to-end circuit between two subscribers, and they are free to use any protocol at the link level for end-to-end data link control. However, two ISDN-related data link control protocols are available. I.465/V.120 is a 1988 Recommendation for terminal adaptation that is based on the use of a data link control protocol similar to LAPD. This protocol allows the multiplexing of multiple logical connections over a single B channel circuit between two end users. Since the publication of the 1988 standards, CCITT has been at work on a capability known as frame relaying, which takes the concept of I.465/V.120 a step further. Frame relaying is based on a data link control protocol that allows multiplexing of multiple logical connections over a single B channel but allows these connections to link with different end users. In effect, frame relay provides a packet-switching service that operates at the data link layer.

9.1

LAPD

All traffic over the D channel employs a link-layer protocol known as LAPD (link access protocol—D channel), defined in I.441/Q.921. We look first at the services that LAPD provides to the network layer, and then at various elements of the LAPD protocol.[1]

Services

The purpose of LAPD is to convey user information between layer 3 entities across ISDN using the D channel. The LAPD service will support:

- Multiple terminals at the user-network installation (e.g., see Figure 8.9).
- Multiple layer 3 entities (e.g., X.25 level 3, I.451/Q.931).

The LAPD standard provides two forms of service to LAPD users: the unacknowledged information-transfer service and the acknowledged information-transfer service. The **unacknowledged information-transfer service** simply provides for the transfer of frames containing user data with no acknowledgment. The service does not guarantee that data presented by one user will be delivered to another user, nor does it inform the sender if the delivery attempt fails. The service does not provide any flow-control or error-control mechanism. This service supports both point-to-point (deliver to one user) or broadcast (deliver to a number of users). This service allows for fast data transfer and is useful for management procedures such as alarm messages and messages that need to be broadcast to multiple users.

The **acknowledged information-transfer service** is the more common one and is similar to the service offered by LAPB and HDLC. With this service, a logical connection is established between two LAPD users. Three phases occur: connection establishment, data transfer, and connection termination. During the *connection establishment phase*, the two users agree to exchange acknowledged data. One user issues a connection request to the other. If the other is prepared to engage in a logical connection, then the request is acknowledged affirmatively, and a logical connection is established. In essence, the existence of a logical connection means that the LAPD service provider at each end of the connection will keep track of the frames being transmitted and those being received, for the purposes of error control and flow control.

---

[1] The basic link-control functions of flow control, error detection, and error control, which are part of the LAP-D protocol, are discussed in Appendix A.

During the *data transfer phase*, LAPD guarantees that all frames will be delivered in the order that they were transmitted. During the *connection termination phase*, one of the two users requests termination of the logical connection.

LAPD Protocol: Basic Characteristics

The LAPD protocol is modeled after the LAPB protocol used in X.25 and on HDLC. Both user information and protocol-control information and parameters are transmitted in frames. Corresponding to the two types of service offered by LAPD, there are two types of operation:

- *Unacknowledged operation:* Layer 3 information is tranferred in un-numbered frames. Error detection is used to discard damaged frames, but there is no error control or flow control.
- *Acknowledged operation:* Layer 3 information is transferred in frames that include sequence numbers and that are acknowledged. Error-control and flow-control procedures are included in the protocol. This type is also referred to in the standard as multiple-frame operation.[2]

These two types of operations may coexist on a single D channel. With the acknowledged operation, it is possible to simultaneously support multiple logical LAPD connections. This is analogous to the ability in X.25 level 3 to support multiple virtual circuits.

Frame Structure

All user information and protocol messages are transmitted in the form of frames. Figure 9.1 depicts the structure of the LAPD frame. Let us examine each of these fields in turn.

Flag Fields. Flag fields delimit the frame at both ends with the unique pattern 01111110. A single flag may be used as the closing flag for one frame and the opening flag for the next. On both sides of the user-network interface, receivers are continuously hunting for the flag sequence to synchronize on the start of a frame. While receiving a frame, a station continues to hunt for that sequence to determine the end of the frame. Since the protocol allows the presence of arbitrary bit patterns

---

[2] In the 1984 version of I.440, another form of acknowledged operation, known as *single-frame operation*, was also defined. With this form, the stop-and-wait flow-control technique was used, allowing only one frame to be outstanding at a time. In contrast, the multiple-frame form uses the sliding-window flow-control technique, which allows multiple frames to be outstanding at a time (see Appendix A for a discussion of these flow-control techniques). Because of lack of support, single-frame operation was subsequently dropped from the recommendation.

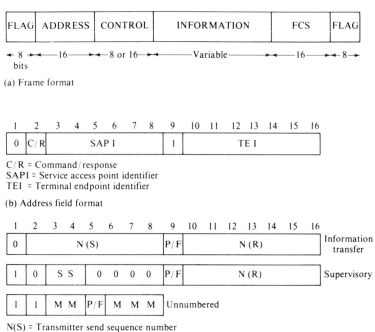

(a) Frame format

C/R = Command/response
SAPI = Service access point identifier
TEI = Terminal endpoint identifier

(b) Address field format

N(S) = Transmitter send sequence number
N(R) = Transmitter receive sequence number
S = Supervisory function bit
M = Modifier function bit
P/F = Poll/final bit

(c) Control field formats

FIGURE 9.1 LAPD Formats

(i.e., there are no restrictions on the content of the various fields imposed by the link protocol), there is no assurance that the pattern 01111110 will not appear somewhere inside the frame, thus destroying synchronization. To avoid this problem, a procedure known as _bit stuffing_ is used. Between the transmission of the starting and ending flags, the transmitter will always insert an extra 0-bit after each occurrence of five 1s in the signal unit. After detecting a starting flag, the receiver monitors the bit stream. When a pattern of five 1s appears, the sixth bit is examined. If this bit is 0, it is deleted. If the sixth bit is a 1 and the seventh bit is a 0, the combination is accepted as a flag. If the sixth and seventh bits are both 1, the sender is indicating an abort condition.

Because of the use of bit stuffing, arbitrary bit patterns can be inserted into the data field of the frame. This property is known as _data transparency_.

Figure 9.2 shows an example of bit stuffing. Note that in the first two cases, the extra 0 is not strictly necessary for avoiding a flag pattern but is necessary for the operation of the algorithm. The pitfalls of bit stuffing are also illustrated in this figure. When a flag is used as both

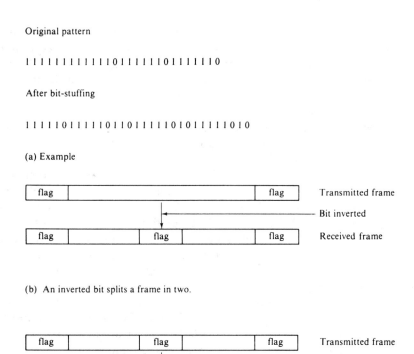

Original pattern

1 1 1 1 1 1 1 1 1 1 1 1 0 1 1 1 1 1 1 0 1 1 1 1 1 1 0

After bit-stuffing

1 1 1 1 1 0 1 1 1 1 1 0 1 1 0 1 1 1 1 1 0 1 0 1 1 1 1 1 0 1 0

(a) Example

(b) An inverted bit splits a frame in two.

(c) An inverted bit merges two frames.

FIGURE 9.2 Bit Stuffing

an ending and starting flag, a 1-bit error merges two frames into one. Conversely, a 1-bit error inside a frame could split it in two.

Address Field. LAPD has to deal with two levels of multiplexing. First, at a subscriber site, there may be multiple user devices sharing the same physical interface. Second, within each user device, there may be multiple types of traffic: specifically, packet-switched data and control signaling. To accommodate these levels of multiplexing, LAPD employs a two-part address, consisting of a terminal endpoint identifier (TEI) and a service access point identifier (SAPI).

Typically, each user device is given a unique **terminal endpoint identifier (TEI)**. It is also possible for a single device to be assigned more than one TEI. This might be the case for a terminal concentrator. TEI assignment occurs either automatically when the equipment first connects to the interface or manually by the user. In the latter case, care must be taken that multiple pieces of equipment attached to the same interface do not have the same TEI. The advantage of the automatic procedure is that it allows the user to change, add, or delete equipment at will without prior notification to the network administration. Without this feature, the network would be obliged to manage a database for each subscriber that would need to be updated manually. Table 9.lb shows the assignment of TEI numbers.

The **service access point identifier (SAPI)** identifies a layer 3 user of LAPD and thus corresponds to a layer 3 protocol entity within a user device. Four specific values have been assigned, as shown in Table 9.1a. A SAPI of 0 is used for call-control procedures for managing B channel circuits; the value 16 is reserved for packet-mode communication on the D channel using X.25 level 3; and a value of 63 is used for the exchange of layer 2 management information. The most recent assignment made since 1984 is the value of 1 for packet-mode communication using I.451/Q.931. This could be used for user-user signaling. Finally, values in the range 32 to 62 have tentatively been reserved to support frame relay connections, as described in Section 9.3.

The SAPI values are unique within a TEI. That is, for a given TEI, there is a unique layer 3 entity for a given SAPI. Thus the TEI and the SAPI together uniquely identify a layer 3 user at subscriber site. The TEI and SAPI together are also used to uniquely identify a logical connection; in this context, the combination of TEI and SAPI is referred to as **data link connection identifier** (DLCI). At any one time, LAPD may maintain multiple logical connections, each with a unique DLCI. Thus, at any one time, a layer 3 entity may have only one LAPD logical connection. Figure 9.3 provides an example. It shows five independent

TABLE 9.1   SAPI and TEI Assignments

(a) SAPI Assignments	
SAPI Value	**Related Protocol or Management Entity**
0	Call-control procedures
1	Reserved for packet-mode communication using I.451 call-control procedures
16	Packet communication conforming to X.25 level 3
32–62	Frame relay communication
63	Layer 2 management procedures
All others	Reserved for future standardization

(b) TEI Assignments

TEI Value	**User Type**
0–63	Nonautomatic TEI assignment user equipment
64–126	Automatic TEI assignment user equipment
127	Used during automatic TEI assignment

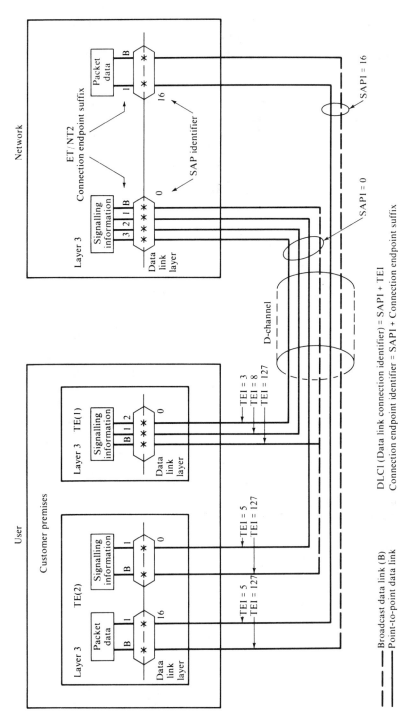

NOTE – The management entity is not shown in this figure.

FIGURE 9.3 Overview Description of the Relation Between SAPI, TEI, and Data Link Endpoint Identifier (I.440)

logical connections over a single D channel interface, terminating in two TEs on the user side of the interface.

The address field format is illustrated in Figure 9.1b. The SAPI and TEI fields refer to the address of the subscriber layer 3 entity. On transmission, the layer 3 entity includes this address in the frame. Frames arriving from the network have this address, and the LAPD entity uses the address to deliver the user data to the appropriate layer 3 entity. In addition, the address field includes a **command/response** (C/R) bit. As explained subsequently, all LAPD messages are categorized as either commands or responses, and this bit is used to indicate which type of message is contained in the frame.

Control Field.   LAPD defines three types of frames, each with a different control field format. **Information-transfer frames** (I-frames) carry the data to be transmitted for the user. Additionally, flow- and error-control data, using the go-back-N ARQ mechanism (see Appendix A), are piggybacked on an information frame. **Supervisory frames** (S-frames) also provide the ARQ mechanism. **Unnumbered frames** (U-frames) provide supplemental link-control functions and are also used to support unacknowledged operation. The first one or two bits of the control field serve to identify the frame type. The remaining bit positions are organized into subfields, as indicated in Figure 9.1c. Their use is explained in the subsequent discussion of LAPD operation.

All of the control field formats contain the poll/final (P/F). In command frames, it is referred to as the P bit and is set to 1 to solicit (poll) a response frame from the peer LAPD entity. In response frames, it is referred to as the F bit and is set to 1 to indicate the response frame transmitted as a result of a soliciting command.

Information Field.   The information field is present only in I-frames and some unnumbered frames. The field can contain any sequence of bits but must consist of an integral number of octets. The length of the information field is variable up to some system-defined maximum. In the case of both control signaling and packet information, I.441/Q.921 specifies a maximum length of 260 octets.

Frame-check Sequence Field.   The frame-check sequence (FCS) is an error-detecting code calculated from the remaining bits of the frame, exclusive of flags. The code used is the CRC-CCITT code defined in Appendix A.

Acknowledged Operation

The acknowledged operation of LAPD consists of the exchange of I-frames, S-frames, and U-frames between a subscriber TE and the

TABLE 9.2 LAPD Commands and Responses

Name	Control Field Encoding	C/R	Description
Information Transfer Format			
I (Information)	0-N(S)--P-N(R)--	C	Exchange user data
Supervisory Format			
RR (Receive Ready)	10000000*-N(R)--	C/R	Positive ack; ready to receive 1 frame
RNR (Receive Not Ready)	10100000*-N(R)--	C/R	Positive ack; not ready to receive
REJ (Reject)	10010000*-N(R)--	C/R	Negative ack; go back N
Unnumbered Format			
SABME (Set Asynchronous Balanced Mode)	1111P110	C	Request logical connection
DM (Disconnected Mode)	1111F000	R	Unable to establish or maintain logical connection
UI (Unnumbered Information)	1100P000	C	Used for unacknowledged information transfer service
DISC (Disconnect)	1100P010	C	Terminate logical connection
UA (Unnumbered Acknowledgment)	1100F110	R	Acknowledge SABME or DISC
FRMR (Frame Reject)	1110F001	R	Reports receipt of unacceptable frame
XID (Exchange Identification)	1111*101	C/R	Exchange identification information

* = P/F bit

network over the D channel. The various commands and responses defined for these frame types are listed in Table 9.2. In describing LAPD operation, we will discuss these three types of frames.

Connection Establishment. A logical connection may be requested by either the network or the subscriber by transmitting a SABME[3] frame. Generally, this will be in response to a request from a layer 3 entity.

---

[3] This stands for Set Asynchronous Balanced Mode (ABM) Extended. It is used in HDLC to choose the ABM mode, which involves two peer entities, as opposed to a primary and a secondary, and to select extended sequence number length of 7 bits, as opposed to the default value of 3 bits. Both ABM and 7-bit sequence numbers are mandatory in LAPD acknowledged operation. Thus, this is simply a connection request command, but the same terminology is retained for consistency.

The SABME frame contains the TEI and the SAPI of the layer 3 entity to which connection is requested. The peer LAPD entity receives the SABME frame and passes up a connection request indication to the appropriate layer 3 entity. If the layer 3 entity responds with an acceptance of the connection, then the LAPD entity transmits a UA frame back to the other side. When the UA is received, signifying acceptance, the LAPD entity passes a confirmation up to the requesting user. If the destination user rejects the connection request, its LAPD entity returns a DM frame, and the receiving LAPD entity informs its user of the rejection.

Data Transfer.   When the connection request has been accepted and confirmed, the connection is established. Both sides may begin to send user data in I-frames, starting with sequence number 0. The N(S) and N(R) fields of the I-frame are sequence numbers that support flow control and error control. A LAPD entity sending a sequence of I-frames will number them sequentially, modulo 128, and place the sequence number in N(S). N(R) is the piggybacked acknowledgment for I-frames received; it enables the LAPD entity to indicate which number I-frame it expects to receive next.

The S-frames are also used for flow control and error control. Sliding-window flow control and go-back-N ARQ error control are used. The Receive Ready (RR) frame is used to acknowledge the last I-frame received by indicating the next I-frame expected. The RR is used when there is no reverse user traffic to carry a piggybacked acknowledgment. Receive Not Ready (RNR) acknowledges an I-frame, as with RR, but also asks the peer entity to suspend transmission of I-frames. When the entity that issued RNR is again ready, it sends an RR. REJ initiates the go-back-N ARQ. It indicates that the last I-frame received has been rejected and that retransmission of all I-frames beginning with number N(R) is required.

Disconnect.   Either LAPD entity can initiate a disconnect, either on its own initiative if there is some sort of fault, or at the request of its layer 3 user. The LAPD entity issues a disconnect on a particular logical connection by sending a DISC frame to the peer entity on the connection. The remote entity must accept the disconnect by replying with a UA and informing its layer 3 user that the connection has been terminated. Any outstanding unacknowledged I-frames may be lost, and their recovery is the responsibility of higher layers.

Frame-reject Frame.   The frame reject (FRMR) frame is used to indicate that an improper frame has arrived—one that somehow violates the protocol (Figure 9.4). One or more of the following conditions have occurred:

1		17		25		33								40
Rejected frame control field	0	V(S)		C / R	V(R)	W	X	Y	Z	0	0	0	0	

V(S) = Current send sequence number
V(R) = Current receive sequence number
C/R = 1 if the rejected frame was a response
     = 0 if the rejected frame was a command
  W = 1 if control field is invalid
  X = 1 if frame contained an information field not permitted with this frame or is a
       supervisory or unnumbered frame with incorrect length
  Y = 1 information field exceeded maximum allowable length
  Z = 1 if received N(R) value invalid

FIGURE 9.4 Frame Reject (FRMR) Information Field

- The receipt of a control field that is undefined (not one of the control field encodings listed in Table 9.2) or not implemented.
- The receipt of an S-frame or U-frame with incorrect length.
- The receipt of an invalid N(R); the only valid N(R) is in the range from the sequence number of the last acknowledged frame to the sequence number of the last transmitted frame.
- The receipt of an I-frame with an information field that exceeds the maximum established length.

The effect of the FRMR is to abort the connection. Upon receipt of an FRMR, the receiving entity may try to reestablish the connection using the connection establishment procedure described earlier.

The exchange identification (XID) frame is used for two stations to exchange information relating to connection management. When a peer entity receives an XID command, it responds with an XID response. The actual information exchanged is beyond the scope of the standard.

Examples of Acknowledged Operation. In order to better understand the acknowledged operation, several examples are presented in Figure 9.5. The examples all make use of the vertical time sequence diagram [CARL80]. It has the advantages of showing time dependencies and illustrating the correct send-receive relationship. Each arrow represents a single frame transiting a data link between TE and NT. Each arrow includes a legend that specifies the frame name, the setting of the P/F bit, and, where appropriate, the values of N(R) and N(S). The setting of the P or F bit is 1 if the designation is present and 0 if absent.

Figure 9.5a shows the frames involved in link setup and disconnect. In the example, the TE is requesting the connection; a similar sequence occurs if the NT requests the connection. The data link entity for the TE issues an SABME command to the other side and starts a timer, T200 (see Table 9.3). The other LAPD entity, upon receiving the SABME,

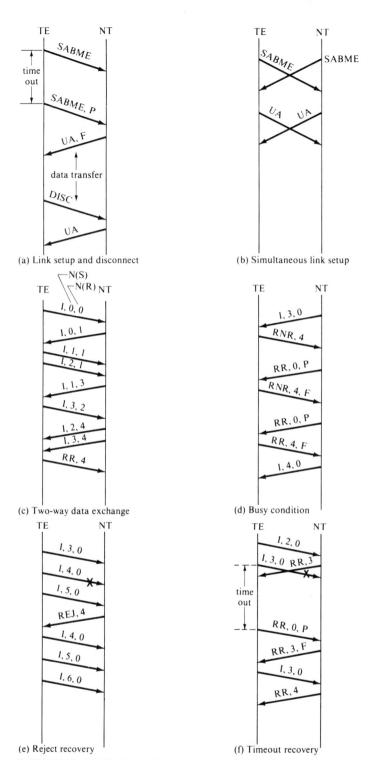

(a) Link setup and disconnect

(b) Simultaneous link setup

(c) Two-way data exchange

(d) Busy condition

(e) Reject recovery

(f) Timeout recovery

FIGURE 9.5 LAPD Operation

TABLE 9.3   LAPD System Parameters

Parameter	Default Value	Definition
T200	1 second	Time to wait for an acknowledgment to a frame before initiating recovery
T201	= T200	Minimum time between TEI identity check messages
T202	2 seconds	Minimum time between TEI identity request messages
T203	10 seconds	Maximum time with no frames exchanged
N200	3	Maximum number of retransmissions of a frame
N201	260 octets	Maximum length of information field
N202	3	Maximum number of retransmissions of TEI identity request message
k	1 for 16-kbps packet 3 for 16-kbps signaling 7 for 64 kbps	Maximum number of outstanding I-frames

returns a UA response and sets local variables and counters to their initial values. The initiating entity receives the UA response, sets its variables and counters, and stops the timer. The logical connection is now active, and both sides may begin transmitting frames. Should the T200 expire without a response, the originator will repeat the SABME, as illustrated. This would be repeated until a UA or DM is received or until, after a given number of tries (N200), the entity attempting initiation gives up and reports failure to a management entity. In this case, higher-layer intervention is necessary. The same figure (Figure 9.5a) shows the disconnect procedure. One side issues a DISC command, and the other responds with a UA response.

LAPD is a balanced mode of operation, meaning that the NT and TE entities have equal status. Thus it is possible that both sides may attempt to set up a logical connection to the same TEI/SAPI user at about the same time. Figure 9.5b illustrates that this situation is resolved by having both sides respond to the incoming SABME and then setting up the logical connection.

Figure 9.5c illustrates the full-duplex exchange of I-frames. When an entity sends a number of I-frames in a row with no incoming data, then the receive sequence number is simply repeated (e.g., I,1,1; I,2.1 in the TE-to-NT direction). When an entity receives a number of I-frames in a row with no outgoing frames, then the receive sequence number in the next outgoing frame must reflect the cumulative activity (e.g., I,1,3 in the NT-to-TE direction). Note that, in addition to I-frames, data exchange may involve supervisory frames.

Figure 9.5d shows an operation involving a busy condition. Such a condition may arise because an LAPD entity is not able to process I-frames as fast as they are arriving, or the intended user is not able to accept data as fast as they arrive in I-frames. In either case, the entity's receive buffer fills up and it must halt the incoming flow of I-frames using an RNR command. In this example, the TE issues an RNR, which requires the NT to halt transmission of I-frames. The station receiving the RNR will usually poll the busy station at some periodic interval by sending an RR with the P bit set. This requires the other side to respond with either an RR or an RNR. When the busy condition has cleared, the TE returns an RR, and I-frame transmission from NT can resume.

An example of error recovery using the REJ command is shown in Figure 9.5e. In this example, the TE transmits I-frames numbered 3, 4, and 5. Number 4 suffers an error. The NT detects the error and discards the frame. When the NT receives I-frame number 5, it discards this frame because it is out of order and sends an REJ with an N(R) of 4. This causes the TE entity to initiate retransmission of all I-frames sent, beginning with frame 4. It may continue to send additional frames after the retransmitted frames.

An example of error recovery using a timeout is shown in Figure 9.5f. In this example, the NT transmits I-frame number 3 as the last in a sequence of I-frames. The frame suffers an error. The NT detects the error and discards it. However, the NT cannot send an REJ. This is because there is no way to know on which logical connection the damaged frame was sent or, indeed, whether or not it was even an I-frame. If an error is detected in a frame, all of the bits of that frame are suspect, and the receiver has no way to act upon it. The transmitter, however, started a timer (T200) as the frame was transmitted. This timer has a duration long enough to span the expected response time. When the timer expires, the station initates recovery action. This is usually done by polling the other side with an RR command with the P bit set, to determine the status of the other side. Since the poll demands a response, the entity will receive a frame containing an N(R) field and be able to proceed. In this case, the response indicates that frame 3 was lost, which the TE retransmits.

These examples are not exhaustive. However, they should give the reader a good feel for the behavior of LAPD.

Unacknowledged Operation

Unacknowledged operation provides for the exchange of user data with no form of error control or flow control. The user information (UI) frame is used to transmit user data. When an LAPD user wishes to send data, it passes the data to its LAPD entity, which passes the data in the information field of a UI frame. When this frame is received, the information field is passed up to the destination user. There is no acknowledgment returned to the other side. However, error detection is performed and frames in error are discarded.

Management Functions

There are two functions related to link management that apply to the LAPD entity as a whole, rather than to a particular connection or user of LAPD. These are for TEI management and for parameter negotiation.

TEI Management.   The TEI management capability provides for automatic TEI assignment procedures. These procedures may be invoked for newly connected TE equipment at a specific user-network interface, so that no manual setting of a TEI value is necessary. The initiation of TEI assignment is triggered by one of two events. First, if equipment is connected to the user-network interface, and the user attempts either unacknowledged data transfer or the establishment of a logical connection, the LAPD entity suspends action on the request until a TEI assignment takes place. Or, second, the user-side layer management entity may initiate the TEI assignment procedures for its own reasons. In either case, the user LAPD entity transmits a UI frame with an SAPI of 63, a TEI of 127, and an information field that contains two subfields: message type and reference number. The message type is *identity request*. The reference number is a random number used to differentiate among a number of simultaneous identity requests by different user equipment. If the network side is able to assign an unused TEI value in the range 64 to 126, then it responds with a UI frame with an SAPI of 63, a TEI of 127, and an information field that contains three subfields: message type, reference number, and action indicator. The reference number is equal to the value received from the user, the message type is *identity assigned*, and the action indicator is the assigned TEI value. If the network is unable to assign a TEI, it returns a UI with a message type of identity denied.

In addition to automatic TEI assignment, there are procedures for checking the value of an existing TEI assignment and removing a TEI assignment. These procedures also make use of UI frames.

Parameter Negotiation.   Associated with LAPD operation are certain key parameters. Each parameter is assigned a default value in the standard, but provisions are made for the negotiation of other values. The parameters and their default values are listed in Table 9.3. If an LAPD entity wishes to use a different set of values for a particular logical connection, it may issue an XID frame, with the desired values contained in subfields of the information field. The other side responds with an XID containing the list of parameter values that the peer can support. Each value must be in the range between the default value and the requested value.

9.2

BEARER CHANNEL DATA LINK CONTROL USING I.465/V.120

In Chapter 7, we introduced I.465/V.120, which provided a technique for supporting non-ISDN terminals over an ISDN B channel using a data link control protocol that is a modified form of LAPD. I.465/V.120 provides a consistent method for carrying different types of data streams, including

- *Asynchronous protocol sensitive:* asynchronous terminal-computer traffic.
- *HDLC synchronous protocol sensitive:* synchronous transmission between devices using HDLC.
- *Bit transparent:* arbitrary synchronous data streams.

As described in Chapter 7, I.465/V.120 defines techniques for mapping from each of these data stream types into a common transmission technique using the I.465/V.120 data link control protocol. Thus two TE2s that share one of the preceding transmission techniques can communicate over ISDN via I.465/V.120. But more is implied in this Recommendation, as shown in Figure 9.6. A TE2 can also communicate with a TE1. In this case, the TA maps the TE2 traffic into I.465/V.120 traffic, and the TE1 must include logic for transmitting and receiving I.465/V.120 traffic. Finally, because this is a general-purpose data link control protocol, it can be used by two TE1s to communicate with each other. Thus, I.465/V.120 provides a flexible and useful data link control protocol for the B channel.

To explain I.465/V.120, we begin with an examination of the frame structure. Then connection control procedures are examined.

I.465/V.120 Frame Structure

Figure 9.7a shows the overall I.465/V.120 frame format. The flag, control, and frame check sequence (FCS) fields are the same as those of LAPD. The only differences are in the address and information fields.

Address Field.   The address field includes a 13-bit logical link identifier (LLI). The LLI makes it possible to simultaneously support multiple logical connections, or links, over the same B channel. This is analogous to the ability in X.25 level 3 to support multiple virtual circuits. The

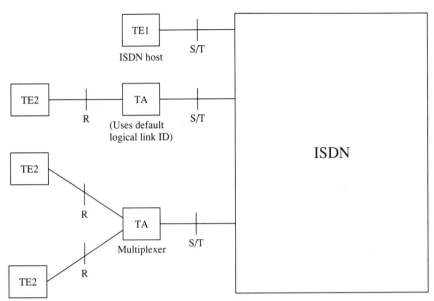

FIGURE 9.6 Types of I.465/V.120 TE Connections [WEIS89]

limitation here, compared to X.25, is that all of the communicating pairs must be on the two ends of a single B channel. One example of an application of this multiplexing capability is the support of multiple terminals through a TA that acts as a statistical multiplexer (Figure 9.8). All of the terminal traffic is multiplexed over a single B channel to a host computer. The data streams of the various terminals are individually identified by their LLI.

Table 9.4a shows the assignment of LLI values. A value of 0 is used for in-channel signaling. This has to do with setting up and managing logical link connections, as explained later. There is a default value of LLI = 256, which eliminates the LLI management procedure and thereby simplifies I.465/V.120 implementation for terminal adaptation of a single non-ISDN terminal. Values between 257 and 2047 are used for individual logical links; thus a total of 1791 logical links can be carried simultaneously on a single B channel. The value of 8191 is used for in-channel management procedures that are not part of the standard.

Information Field.   As usual, the information field is used to carry user information. In addition it may contain a one or two-octet header. The first header octet, referred to as the terminal adaptation header, is mandatory for protocol-sensitive modes (asynchronous and HDLC synchronous) and is optional for bit-transparent modes. The second header octet, referred to as the control state information octet, may be present if the first octet is present.

Flag	Address	Control	Information	FCS	Flag

←8→←——16——→←—8 or 16—→←————8 or 16————→←——16——→←8→
bits

(a) Frame format

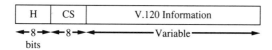

7	6	5	4	3	2	1	0
LLI0						C/R	EA0
LLI1							EA1

LLI0 = High order 6 bits of logical link identifier
LLI1 = Low order 7 bits of logical link identifier
C/R = Command/response
EAO = Octet 2 address extension bit—set to 0
EA1 = Octet 3 address extension bit—set to 1 (for 2-octet address field)

(b) Address field

H	CS	V.120 Information

←8→←8→←————Variable————→
bits

H = Terminal adaption header (optional for bit transparent mode)
CS = Optional header extension for control state information

(c) Information field

E	BR	res	res	C2	C1	B	F

E = Extension bit
BR = Break/HDLC idel bit
C1, C2 = Error control bits
B, F = Segmentation bits
res = reserved for future standardization

(d) Terminal adaption header

E	DR	SR	RR	res	res	res	res

E = Extension bit
DR = Data ready
SR = Send ready
RR = Receive ready
res = Reserved for future standardization

(e) Optional header extension

FIGURE 9.7　I.465/V.120 Formats

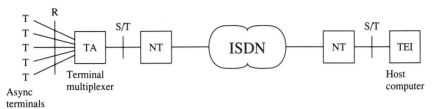

FIGURE 9.8 I.465/V.120 Scenario

TABLE 9.4   I.465/V.120 Assignments

(a) Reserved LLI values

LLI	Function
0	In-channel signaling
1–255	Reserved for future standardization
256	Default LLI
257–2047	For LLI assignment
2048–2190	Reserved for future standardization
8191	In-channel layer management

(b) Coding of C1 and C2 bits

C1	C2	Synchronous Mode	Asynchronous Mode	Bit Transparent Mode
0	0	No error detected	No error detected	No error detected
0	1	FCS error (interface at R)	Stop-bit error	Not applicable
1	0	Abort	Parity error on the last character in frame	Not applicable
1	1	TA overrun (interface at R)	Both stop-bit and parity error	Not applicable

(c) Coding of B and F bits

B	F	Synchronous Mode	Asynchronous Mode	Bit Transparent Mode
0	0	Begin frame	Not applicable	Not applicable
0	1	Middle frame	Not applicable	Not applicable
1	0	Final frame	Not applicable	Not applicable
1	1	Single frame	Required	Required

The bits of the terminal adaption header (Figure 9.7d) are as follows:

- *Extension bit (E):* Allows for extension of the header to provide additional control state information. A zero indicates that a control state octet follows.
- *Break/HDLC idle bit (BR):* In asynchronous mode, the bit indicates the invocation of the break function by the TE2. In HDLC mode, it indicates an HDLC idle condition at the R referent point.
- *Error-control bits (C1, C2):* Used for TA error detection and transmission. Table 9.4b indicates the coding of these bits.
- *Segmentation bits (B, F):* Used in HDLC synchronous mode for segmentation and reassembly. This allows the TA to segment a single HDLC frame into multiple segments, which are reassembled at the receiver. Table 9.4c indicates the coding of these bits.

The bits of the control state information octet (Figure 9.7e) are as follows:

- *Extension bit (E):* Allows for further extension of the header; currently, no such extension is defined.
- *Data Ready bit (DR):* Indicates whether the interface at the R reference point is activated.
- *Send Ready bit (SR):* This bit set to 1 indicates that the TE is ready to send data.
- *Receive Ready bit (RR):* This bit set to 1 indicates that the TE is ready to receive data.

The last three bits just listed correspond to leads commonly found on modem interfaces for terminals. This allows the setting of these leads to be transmitted across ISDN.

Connection Control

The first step in using the I.465/V.120 data link control protocol is to establish a B channel circuit across ISDN. This is done using the I.451/ Q.931 call-control protocol over the D channel, which is described in Chapter 10.

Once a circuit is established, the data link control protocol can be used in either connectionless or connection-oriented mode. For connectionless data transfer, an LLI of 256 is used and information is exchanged using UI frames, as in LAPD.

For connection-oriented data link control, it is necessary to proceed in three stages:

1. Establish a logical link between two peer entities at the two ends of the B channel circuit, and assign a unique LLI to the connection.

2. Exchange information in I-frames. The LLI field is used to allow multiplexing of a number of logical links.
3. Release the logical link.

Ultimately, when no more connections are active, one side or the other may choose to terminate the B channel circuit. Again, this is done using the I.451/Q.931 call-control protocol on the D channel. Now let us return to a consideration of the management of logical links on an existing B channel circuit.

The management of logical links is accomplished by an exchange of four messages (Table 9.5): SETUP, CONNect, RELease, and RELease COMPlete.[4] These messages can be exchanged between the peer data link control protocol entities in one of two ways:

1. In a B channel I.465/V.120 information frame with LLI = 0.
2. In a D channel I.451/Q.931 user-to-user information message, if provided by the network.

The choice of method is a terminal equipment option and is partially determined by the availability of end-to-end user signaling capability on the D channel. In both cases the message consists of a sequence of fields, as illustrated in Figure 9.9. If logical links are managed via the D channel, then these messages are embedded in an LAPD frame with an SAPI of 1 (see Table 9.1). If logical links are managed via the D channel, then these messages are embedded in an I.465/V.120 frame with an LLI of 0.

Three fields are common to all messages:

- *Protocol discriminator:* used to distinguish the protocol for I.465/V.120 logical link control from other protocols. Other protocols so far defined include I.451/Q.931, the X.25 packet level protocol, and the protocol for frame relay connection control.
- *Call reference:* identifies the B channel call to which this message refers. This parameter is discussed in Chapter 10.
- *Message type:* identifies which I.465/V.120 message is being sent. The contents of the remainder of the message depend on the message type.

Following these three common fields, the remainder of the message consists of a sequence of zero or more information elements, or parameters. These are described subsequently, as we consider the individual message types. Each of these information elements consists of three

---

[4] These message types are the same as four of the messages in I.451/Q.931, with roughly the same meaning. The parameters are different for the two protocols, and the semantics are somewhat different.

TABLE 9.5 I.465/V.120 Connection Control Messages

(a) SETUP Message Content

Information Element	Mandatory/Optional	Length
Protocol discriminator	M	1
Call reference	M	2
Message type	M	1
Low-layer compatibility	O (Note 1)	2–13
Logical link identifier	O (Note 2)	4

Note 1: Included when the calling user wants to pass low-layer compatibility information to the called user

Note 2: Included if the calling user has the responsibility for assigning LLI for that circuit

(b) CONNect Message Content

Information Element	Mandatory/Optional	Length
Protocol discriminator	M	1
Call reference	M	2
Message type	M	1
Low-layer compatibility	O (Note 1)	2–13
Logical link identifier	O (Note 2)	4

Note 1: Included to allow the called user to negotiate low-layer compatibility information with the calling user

Note 2: Included if the called user has the responsibility for assigning LLI for that circuit

(c) RELease Message Content

Information Element	Mandatory/Optional	Length
Protocol discriminator	M	1
Call reference	M	2
Message type	M	1
Cause	O	2–4

(d) RELease COMPlete Message Content

Information Element	Mandatory/Optional	Length
Protocol discriminator	M	1
Call reference	M	2
Message type	M	1
Cause	O	2–4

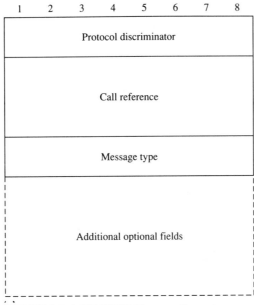

FIGURE 9.9 I.465/V.120 Message Format

fields: an identifier specifying which parameter this is, a length field, and a value.

Logical Link Establishment. Either side may request the establishment of a logical link by sending a SETUP message. The other side, upon receiving the SETUP message, must reply with a CONNect message if it accepts the connection; otherwise, it responds with a RELease COMPlete message.

If the side sending the SETUP message assigns the LLI, it chooses an unused value in the range 257–2047 and includes this value in the SETUP message. Otherwise, the LLI value is assigned by the accepting side in the CONNect message.

The two sides must agree on the type of terminal adaption support that is being provided. Unless this is arranged by prior agreement, the calling side should specify the relevant parameters in the low-layer compatibility element of the SETUP message. These parameters include the mode of operation (asynchronous protocol sensitive, HDLC synchronous protocol sensitive, bit transparent), the data rate in each direction, and other details of the terminals supported. The called side may alter any of these parameters by including a revised low-layer compatibility element in the CONNect message.

Logical Link Clearing. Either side may request to clear a logical link by sending a RELease message. The other side, upon receipt of this message, must respond with a RELease COMPlete message. The Cause parameter is currently used only to specify whether this is a normal clearing or a call-rejected action.

As an example of the use of these messages, consider the configuration of Figure 9.8. A terminal adapter (TA) acts as a multiplexer to support multiple terminals. In this scenario, a B channel circuit is set up between the TA and a host computer across ISDN. When any terminal is to be connected to the host, it is assigned a separate logical link. Figure 9.10 shows the sequence of steps involved.

9.3
FRAME-MODE BEARER SERVICE AND PROTOCOL

The 1988 I.122 recommendation, entitled *Framework for Providing Additional Packet Mode Bearer Services*, introduced a new form of packet transmission that has become one of the most significant contributions of the ISDN work reflected in the 1988 standards. This new technique is now generally referred to as frame-mode bearer service, or frame relay. The former term emphasizes the service being offered to the user, while the latter emphasizes the protocol that implements the service.

Since 1988, significant progress has been made on frame relay. In 1990, CCITT published two interim recommendations:

- I.2xy: ISDN Frame-mode Bearer Services (FMBS)
- I.3xx: Congestion Management for the Frame-relaying Bearer Service

The work on frame relay is more developed in the United States, where ANSI issued one standard and two draft standards in 1990:

- ANSI T1.606: Architectural Framework and Service Description for Frame-relaying Bearer Service
- Draft ANSI T1.6fr: Signaling Specification for Frame-relay Bearer Service
- Draft ANSI T1.6ca: Core Aspects of Frame Protocol for Use with Frame-relay Bearer Service

It is anticipated that the final CCITT Recommendations will be closely aligned with the current ANSI standard and draft standards. This section draws on all of these documents, using the ANSI specifications for details not provided by CCITT.

Motivation

The traditional approach to packet switching, as was discussed in Chapter 3, is X.25. Several key features of the X.25 approach:

• TA uses I.451/Q.931 on D channel to establish circuit on B channel to TE1; use of I.465/V.120 on B channel is specified.	• TA uses I.451/Q.931 on D channel to establish circuit on B channel to TE1; use of I.465/V.120 on B channel is specified.
• TA issues I.465/V.120 messages (SETUP, CONNect) on D channel to establish a logical connection from one of its terminals to the TE1. Protocol discriminator field distinguishes these messages from I.451/Q.931 messages. LLI field used to assign unique LLI to this logical connection.	• TA issues I.465/V.120 messages (SETUP, CONNect) on B channel to establish a logical connection from one of its terminals to the TE1. LLI field used to assign unique LLI to this logical connection.
• TA may establish logical connections for other terminals using D channel I.465/V.120 messages. Each connection is assigned a unique LLI.	• TA may establish logical connections for other terminals using B channel I.465/V.120 messages. Each connection is assigned a unique LLI.
• Information is exchanged on the B-channel using I.465/V.120 frames. The LLI field supports multiplexing.	• Information is exchanged on the B-channel using I.465/V.120 frames. The LLI field supports multiplexing.
• TA issues I.465/V.120 messages (RELease, RELease COMPlete) on D-channel to terminate a logical connection from one of its terminals to the TE1.	• TA issues I.465/V.120 messages (RELease, RELease COMPlete) on B-channel to terminate a logical connection from one of its terminals to the TE1.
• When all logical connections have been terminated, TA uses I.451/Q.931 on D channel to terminate circuit on B channel to TE1.	• When all logical connections have been terminated, TA uses I.451/Q.931 on D channel to terminate circuit on B channel to TE1.

(a) Logical link establishment via D channel   (b) Logical link establishment via B channel

FIGURE 9.10 Alternative Connection Control Procedures for Scenario of Figure 9.8

- Call-control packets, used for setting up and clearing virtual circuits, are carried on the same channel and same virtual circuit as data packets. In effect, inband signaling is used.
- Multiplexing of virtual circuits takes place at layer 3.
- Both layer 2 and layer 3 include flow-control and error-control mechanisms.

This approach results in considerable overhead. Figure 9.11a indicates the flow of data link frames required for the transmission of a single data packet from source end system to destination end system and the return of an acknowledgment packet. At each hop through the network, the data link control protocol involves the exchange of a data frame and an acknowledgment frame. Furthermore, at each intermediate node, state tables must be maintained for each virtual circuit to

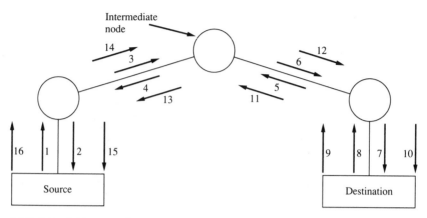

(a) Packet-switching network

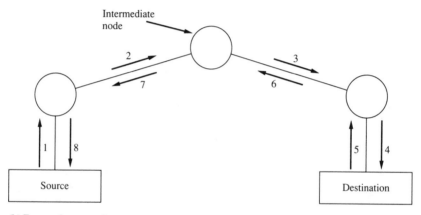

(b) Frame relay network

FIGURE 9.11 Packet Switching Versus Frame Relay: Source Sending, Destination Responding

deal with the call management and flow-control/error-control aspects of the X.25 protocol.

All of this overhead may be justified when there is a significant probability of error on any of the links in the network. This approach may not be the most appropriate for ISDN. On the one hand, ISDN employs reliable digital transmission technology over high-quality, reliable transmission links, many of which are optical fiber. On the other hand, with ISDN, high data rates can be achieved, especially with the use of H channels. In this environment, the overhead of X.25 is not only unnecessary, but degrades the effective utilization of the high data rates available with ISDN.

Frame relaying is designed to eliminate as much as possible of the overhead of X.25. The key differences of frame relaying from a conventional X.25 packet-switching service are

- Call-control signaling is carried on a separate logical connection from user data. Thus, intermediate nodes need not maintain state tables or process messages relating to call control on an individual per-connection basis.
- Multiplexing and switching of logical connections takes place at layer 2 instead of layer 3, eliminating one entire layer of processing.
- There is no hop-by-hop flow control and error control. End-to-end flow control and error control are the responsibility of a higher layer, if they are employed at all.

Figure 9.11b indicates the operation of frame relay, in which a single-user data frame is sent from source to destination, and an acknowledgment, generated at a higher layer, is carried back in a frame.

Let us consider the advantages and disadvantages of this approach. The principle potential disadvantage of frame relaying, compared to X.25, is that we have lost the ability to do link-by-link flow and error control. (Although frame relay does not provide end-to-end flow and error control, this is easily provided at a higher layer.) In X.25, multiple virtual circuits are carried on a single physical link, and LAPB is available at the link level for providing reliable transmission from the source to the packet-switching network and from the packet-switching network to the destination. In addition, at each hop through the network, the link control protocol can be used for reliability. With the use of frame relaying, this hop-by-hop link control is lost. However, with the increasing reliability of transmission and switching facilities, this is not a major disadvantage.

The advantage of frame relaying is that we have streamlined the communications process. The protocol functionality required at the user-network interface is reduced, as is the internal network processing. As a result, lower delay and higher throughput can be expected. Preliminary results indicate a reduction in frame processing time of an order of magnitude [BUSH89], and the CCITT recommendation (I.2xy) indicates that frame relay is to be used at access speeds up to 2 Mbps. Thus, we can expect to see frame relaying supplant X.25 as ISDN matures.

The ANSI standard T1.606 lists four examples of applications that would benefit from the frame relay service used over a high-speed H channel:

1. *Block-interactive data applications:* An example of a block-interactive application would be high-resolution graphics (e.g., high-resolution videotex, CAD/CAM). The pertinent characteristics of this type of application are low delays and high throughput.

2. *File transfer:* The file transfer application is intended to cater to large file transfer requirements. Transit delay is not as critical for this application as it is, for example, in the first application. High throughput might be necessary in order to produce reasonable transfer times for large files.

3. *Multiplexed low-bit rate:* The multiplexed low-bit-rate application exploits the multiplexing capability of the frame-relaying service in order to provide an economical access arrangement for a large group of low-bit-rate applications. An example of one such low-bit-rate application is given in (4) below. The low-bit-rate sources may be multiplexed onto a channel by an NT function.

4. *Character-interactive traffic:* An example of a character-interactive traffic application is text editing. The main characteristics of this type of application are short frames, low delays, and low throughput.

Frame relay can be viewed as a streamlined version of X.25, which accomplishes the key functions of X.25 using only two layers. Another way of viewing frame relay is that it is an enhanced version of I.465/V.120. That latter standard allows for multiple logical connections to be multiplexed on a single circuit between two subscribers. Frame relay supports not only multiplexing but switching: Multiple logical connections from one subscriber over one channel can be set up to multiple subscribers across the network.

Frame-relay Architecture

Figure 9.12 depicts the protocol architecture for frame relay. As in other areas of ISDN, we need to consider two separate planes of operation: a control (C) plane, which is involved in the establishment and termination of logical connections, and a user (U) plane, which is responsible for the transfer of user data between subscribers. Thus, C-plane protocols are between a subscriber and the network, while U-plane protocols provide end-to-end functionality.

For the actual transfer of information between end users, the U-plane protocol is Q.922. Q.922 is a new recommendation, issued for the first time on an interim basis in 1991, that is an enhanced version of LAPD (I.441/Q.921). Only the core functions of Q.922 are used for frame relay:

- Frame delimiting, alignment, and transparency.
- Frame multiplexing/demultiplexing using the address field.
- Inspection of the frame to ensure that it consists of an integer number of octets prior to zero bit insertion or following zero bit extraction.
- Inspection of the frame to ensure that it is neither too long nor too short.

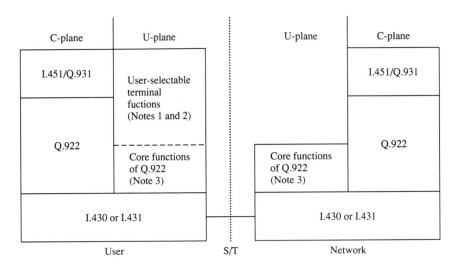

Note 1: Q.922 is one protocol that may be used. Other standard or proprietary protocols may be used.
Note 2: Additional requirements may be placed on terminals depending on the congestion control and
throughput enforcements used. One mechanism that can satisfy the congestion control
requirements is for the terminal to implement a dynamic window algorithm.
Note 3: Additional functions may be needed for throughput monitoring and enforcement.

FIGURE 9.12 Frame Relay Protocol Architecture

- Detection of transmission errors.
- Congestion control functions.

The last function just listed is new to Q.922 and is discussed in a later section. The remaining functions are also core functions of I.441/Q.921.

The core functions of Q.922 in the U plane constitute a sublayer of the data link layer. This provides the bare service of transferring data link frames from one subscriber to another, with no flow control or error control. Above this, the user may choose to select additional data link or network-layer end-to-end functions. These are not part of the ISDN service. Based on the core functions, ISDN offers frame relaying as a connection-oriented link layer service with the following properties:

- Preservation of the order of frame transfer from one edge of the network to the other.
- Nonduplication of frames.
- A small probability of frame loss.

In the control plane, Q.922 is used to provide a reliable data link control service, with error control and flow control, for the delivery of I.451/Q.931 messages.

As can be seen, this architecture reduces to the bare mininum the amount of work accomplished by the network. User data are transmitted in frames with virtually no processing by the intermediate network nodes, other than to check for errors and to route based on connection number. A frame in error is simply discarded, leaving error recovery to higher layers.

Figure 9.13 compares the protocol architecture of frame relay to that of X.25. The packet-handling functions of X.25 operate at layer 3 of the OSI model. At layer 2, either LAPB or LAPD is used, depending on whether the protocol is operating on a B channel or D channel. Table 9.6 provides a functional comparison of X.25 and frame relay. As can be seen, the processing burden on the network for X.25 is considerably higher than for frame relay.

Frame-relay Call Control

The call-control protocol for frame relay must deal with a number of alternatives. First, let us consider two cases for the provision of frame-handling services. For frame-relay operation, a user is not connected directly to another ISDN user, but rather to a frame handler in the network, just as for X.25, an ISDN user is connected to a packet handler. There are two cases (Figure 9.14):

Case A: The local exchange does not provide the frame-handling capability. In this case, switched access must be provided from the TE to the frame handler elsewhere in the network. This can either be a demand connection or a semipermanent connection. In either case, the frame-relay service is provided over a B or H channel.

Case B: The local exchange does provide the frame-handling ca-

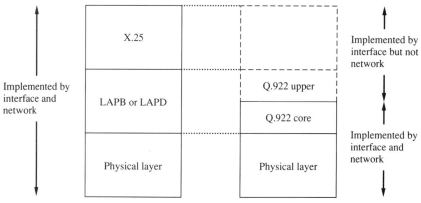

FIGURE 9.13 A Comparison of X.25 and Frame Relay Protocol Stacks

TABLE 9.6   Comparison of X.25/X.31 Packet Switching and Frame Relay

Function	X.25 in ISDN (X.31)	Frame Relay
Flag generation/recognition	X	X
Transparency	X	X
FCS generation/recognition	X	X
Recognize invalid frames	X	X
Discard incorrect frames	X	X
Address translation	X	X
Fill interframe time	X	X
Multiplexing of logical channels	X	X
Manage V(S) state variable	X	
Manage V(R) state variable	X	
Buffer packets awaiting acknowledgment	X	
Management retransmission timer T1	X	
Acknowledge received I-frames	X	
Check received N(S) against V(R)	X	
Generation of REJ (rejection message)	X	
Respond to P/F (poll/final) bit	X	
Keep track of number of retransmissions	X	
Act upon reception of REJ	X	
Respond to RNR (receiver not ready)	X	
Respond to RR (receiver ready)	X	
Management of D bit	X	
Management of M bit	X	
Management of Q bit	X	
Management of P(S)	X	
Management of P(R)	X	
Detection of out-of-sequence packets	X	
Management of network layer RR	X	
Management of network layer RNR	X	

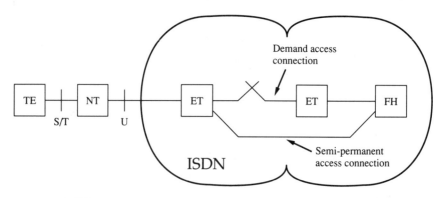

(a) Case A: Switched access

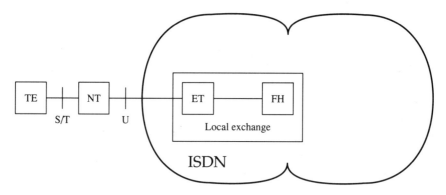

(b) Case B: Integrated access

FIGURE 9.14 Frame Relay Access Modes

pability. In this case, the frame-relay service may be provided on a B or H channel or on the D channel. For B or
H channel service, a demand connection must be used to
dedicate a B or H channel to frame relay unless a semipermanent assignment already exists. For D channel service, this point has not been finally specified, but it appears
that both a demand service and a semipermanent service
via the D channel may be options.

All of the previous considerations have to do with the connection
between the subscriber and the frame handler, which we refer to as the
access connection. Once this connection exists, it is possible to multiplex
multiple logical connections, referred to as **frame-relay connections,**
over this access connection. Such logical connections may be either on
demand or semipermanent.

Table 9.7 summarizes these call-control alternatives. First let consider

TABLE 9.7 Establishment of Connection for Frame-relay Services

		Access Connection/Frame-Relay Connection		
		Demand/Demand	**Semipermanent/ Demand**	**Semipermanent/ Semipermanent**
Case A: Switched access to frame handler	Establishment of access connection	I.451/Q.931 on D channel to set up connection on B or H channel	Semipermanent	
	Establishment of frame-relay connection	Inchannel frame-relay messages on B or H channel, DLCI = 0		Semipermanent
Case B: Integrated access to frame handler	Establishment of access connection	I.451/Q.931 on D channel to set up connection on D, B, or H channel	Semipermanent	
	Establishment of frame-relay connection	Frame-relay messages on D channel, SAPI = 0		Semipermanent

the establishment of an access connection. If the connection is semi-permanent, then no call-control protocol is required. If the connection is to be set up on demand, then there are two alternatives:

Case A: The access connection is to be set up on a B or H channel to a remote frame handler. The normal ISDN call-control protocol, I.451/Q.931, is used on the D channel to set up the access connection. This is the same strategy used to support X.25 on a B channel.

Case B: The access connection is to be set up to the local exchange. If the connection is to be set up on a B or H channel, then the normal ISDN call-control protocol, I.451/Q.931, is used on the D channel to set up the access connection. If the D channel is to be used and the access connection is on demand rather than semipermanent (for X.25, the connection is always semipermanent), then again I.451/Q.931 is used on the D channel to set up the access connection.

Now consider the establishment of a frame-relay connection. For this purpose an access connection must already exist. For a semipermanent frame-relay connection, no call-control protocol is required; note that this requires the existence of a semipermanent access connection. If the frame-relay connection is to be set up on demand over an existing access connection, there are again two alternatives:

Case A: It is possible to use call-control messages on frame-relay connection DLCI = 0. As with I.465/V.120, these messages are carred in the information field of the data link frame.

Case B: Alternatively, again as with I.465/V.120, it is possible to use the same call-control messages embedded in LAPD frames on the D channel. For this purpose SAPI 0 is used, as for I.451/Q.931 messages.

In either case, the call-control messages are actually a subset of the messages used in I.451/Q.931, with some new parameters tailored to the frame-relay application. Therefore, we defer a discussion until Chapter 10.

User Data Transfer

The operation of frame relay for user data transfer is best explained by beginning with the frame format, illustrated in Figure 9.15a. The format is similar to that of LAPD and LAPB with one obvious omission: There is no control field. This has the following implications:

• There is only one frame type, used for carrying user data. There are no control frames.

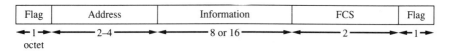

(a) Frame format

8	7	6	5	4	3	2	1
DLCI (high order)						C/R 0/1	EA0
DLCI (low order)				FECN	BECN	DE	EA1

(b) Address field—2 octets (default)

8	7	6	5	4	3	2	1
DLCI (high order)						C/R 0/1	EA0
DLCI				FECN	BECN	DE	EA1
DLCI (low order)							EA1

(c) Address field—3 octets

8	7	6	5	4	3	2	1
DLCI (high order)						C/R 0/1	EA0
DLCI				FECN	BECN	DE	EA0
DLCI							EA0
DLCI (low order)							EA1

(d) Address field—4 octets

C/R = Command/response; use is application-specific
EA = Address field extention
DE = Discard eligibility indicator
BECN = Backward explicit congestion notification
DLCI = Data link connection identifier

FIGURE 9.15   Frame Relay Formats

- It is not possible to use inband signaling; a logical connection can only carry user data.
- It is not possible to perform flow control and error control, since there are no sequence numbers.

The flag- and frame-check sequence (FCS) fields function as in LAPD and LAPB. The information field carries higher-layer data. If the user elects to implement additional data link control functions end-to-end, then a data link frame can be carried in this field. Specifically, a common selection will be to use enhanced LAPD, as defined in Q.922, to perform functions above the core functions of Q.922. Thus the entire LAPD frame would be carried in the information field. This is similar to the approach taken in I.465/V.120, in which an HDLC frame is carried in the information field of a I.465/V.120 frame. Note that the protocol implemented in this fashion is strictly between the end subscribers and is transparent to ISDN.

The address field has a default length of 2 octets and may be extended to 3 or 4 octets. It carries a data link connection identifier (DLCI) of 10, 17, or 24 bits. The DLCI serves the same function as the virtual circuit number in X.25: It allows multiple logical frame-relay connections to be multiplexed over a single channel. As in X.25, the connection identifier has only local significance: Each end of the logical connection assigns its own DLCI from the pool of locally unused numbers, and the network must map from one to the other. The alternative, using the same DLCI on both ends, would require some sort of global management of DLCI values.

For D channel frame relay, a 2-octet address field is assumed, and the DLCI values are limited to the range 480–1007. This is equivalent to a SAPI of 32–62. Thus frame-relay frames can be multiplexed with LAPD frames on the D channel, and the two types of frames are distinguished on the basis of bits 8 to 3 in the first octet of the address field.

The length of the address field, and hence of the DLCI, is determined by the address field extension (EA) bits. The C/R bit is application-specific and not used by the standard frame-relay protocol. The remaining bits in the address field have to do with congestion control and are discussed subsequently.

Network Function

The frame-relaying function performed by ISDN, or any network that supports frame relaying, consists of the routing of frames with the format of Figure 9.15a, based on their DLCI values.

Figure 9.16 suggests the operation of a frame handler in a situation in which a number of users are directly connected to the same frame handler over different physical channels. The operation could just as well involve relaying a frame through two or more frame handlers. In this figure, the decision-making logic is shown conceptually as a separate module, the frame relaying control point. This module is responsible for making routing decisions.

Typically, routing is controlled by entries in a connection table based on DLCI that map incoming frames from one channel to another. The frame handler switches a frame from an incoming channel to an outgoing channel based on the appropriate entry in the connection table and translates the DLCI in the frame before transmission. For example, incoming frames from TE B on logical connection 306 are retransmitted to TE D on logical connection 342. This technique has been referred to as chained-link path routing [LAI88]. The figure also shows the multi-

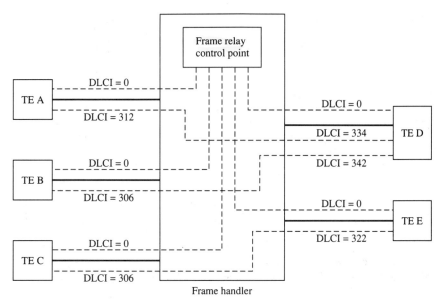

FIGURE 9.16 Frame Handler Operation

plexing function: Multiple logical connections to TE D are multiplexed over the same physical channel.

Note also that all of the TEs have a logical connection to the frame-relay control point with a value of DLCI = 0. These connections are reserved for in-channel call control, to be used when I.451/Q.931 on the D channel is not used for frame-relay call control.

As part of the frame-relay function, the FCS of each incoming frame is checked. When an error is detected, the frame is simply discarded. It is the responsibility of the end users to institute error recovery above the frame-relay protocol.

Figure 9.17 is another view of the protocols involved in frame relay, this time from the point of view of the individual frame-relay connections. There is a common physical layer and frame-relay sublayer. An optional layer 2 data link control protocol may be included above the frame-relay sublayer. This selection is application-dependent and may differ for different frame-relay connections (DLC-i). If frame-relay call control messages are carried in frame-relay frames, these are carried on DLCI 0, which provides a frame-relay connection between the user and the frame handler. DLCI 8191 is dedicated to management procedures.

Congestion Control

Background.   A frame-relay network is a form of packet-switching network in which the "packets" are layer 2 frames. As in any packet-

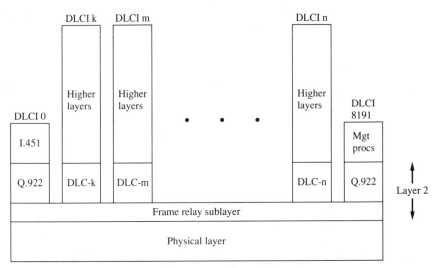

FIGURE 9.17 Multiplexing at the Frame Relay Sublayer

switching network, one of the key areas in the design of a frame-relay network is congestion control. To understand the issue involved in congestion control, we need to look at some results from queueing theory. In essence, a frame-relay network is a network of queues. At each frame handler, there is a queue of frames for each outgoing link. If the rate at which frames arrive and queue up exceeds the rate at which frames can be transmitted, the queue size grows without bound and the delay experienced by a frame goes to infinity. Even if the frame arrival rate is less than the frame transmission rate, queue length will grow dramatically as the arrival rate approaches the transmission rate. As a rule of thumb, when the line for which frames are queueing becomes more than 80 percent utilized, the queue length grows at an alarming rate.

Consider the queueing situation at a single frame handler, such as is illustrated in Figure 9.18. Any given node has a number of transmission links attached to it: one or more to other frame handlers and zero or more to ISDN subscribers. On each link, frames arrive and depart. We can consider that there are two buffers at each link, one to accept arriving frames and one to hold frames that are waiting to depart. In practice, there might be two fixed-size buffers associated with each link, or there might be a pool of memory available for all buffering activities. In the latter case, we can think of each link having two variable-size buffers associated with it, subject to the constraint that the sum of all buffer sizes is a constant.

In any case, as frames arrive, they are stored in the input buffer of

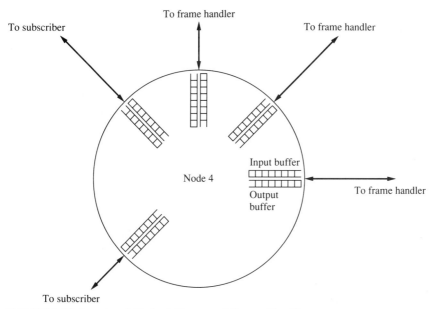

FIGURE 9.18 Input and Output Queues of Frame Handler

the corresponding link. The node examines each incoming frame to make a routing decision and then moves the frame to the appropriate output buffer. Frames queued up for output are transmitted as rapidly as possible. Now if frames arrive too fast for the node to process them (make routing decisions) or faster than frames can be cleared from the outgoing buffers, then eventually frames will arrive for which no memory is available.

When such a saturation point is reached, one of two general strategies can be adopted. The first such strategy is to simply discard any incoming frame for which there is no available buffer space. This approach is self-defeating, since the discarded frames will have to be retransmitted, adding to network congestion. The other alternative is for some mechanism to be used that restricts the rate at which new frames are inserted into the network. This latter approach is referred to as congestion control.

Figure 9.19 shows the effect of congestion in general terms. Figure 9.19a plots the throughput of a network (number of frames delivered to a destination station per unit time) versus the offered load (number of frames transmitted by all subscribers), while Figure 9.19b plots the average delay from entry to exit across the network. At light loads, throughput and hence network utilization increase as the offered load increases. As the load continues to increase, a point is reached (point

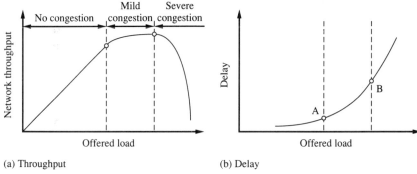

(a) Throughput   (b) Delay

FIGURE 9.19 The Effects of Congestion

A in the plot) beyond which the throughput of the network increases at a rate slower than the rate at which the offered load is increased. This is due to the network entry into a mild congestion state. In this region, the network continues to cope with the load, although with increased delays.

As the load on the network increases, the queue lengths of the various frame handlers grow. Eventually, a point is reached (point B in the plot) beyond which throughput actually drops with increased offered load. The reason for this is that the buffers at each node are of finite size. When the buffers at a frame handler become full, it must discard frames. Thus, the sources must retransmit the discarded frames in addition to new frames. This only exacerbates the situation: As more and more frames are retransmitted, the load on the system grows, and more buffers become saturated. While the system is trying desperately to clear the backlog, users are pumping old and new frames into the system. Even successfully delivered frames may be retransmitted because it takes too long, at a higher layer (e.g., transport layer), to acknowledge them: The sender assumes the frame did not get through. Under these circumstances, the effective capacity of the system is virtually zero.

It is clear that these catastrophic events must be avoided, which is the task of congestion control. The object of all congestion-control techniques is to limit queue lengths at the nodes so as to avoid throughput collapse.

Frame Relay and Congestion Control.   CCITT, in I.3xx, defines the objectives for frame-relay congestion control to be the following:

- Minimize frame discard.
- Maintain, with high probability and minimum variance, agreed-upon quality of service.

- Minimize the possibility that one end user can monopolize network resources at the expense of other end users.
- Be simple to implement and place little overhead on either end user or network.
- Create minimal additional network traffic.
- Distribute network resources fairly among end users.
- Limit spread of congestion to other networks and elements within the network.
- Operate effectively regardless of the traffic flow in either direction between end users.
- Have minimum interaction or impact on other systems in the frame-relaying network.
- Minimize the variance in quality of service delivered to individual frame-relay connections during congestion (e.g., individual logical connections should not experience sudden degradation when congestion approaches or has occurred).

The challenge of congestion control is particularly acute for a frame-relay network because of the limited tools available to the frame handlers. The frame-relay protocol has been streamlined in order to maximize throughput and efficiency. A consequence of this is that a frame handler cannot control the flow of frames coming from a subscriber or an adjacent node using the typical sliding-window flow-control protocol, such as is found in LAPD.

Congestion control is the joint responsibility of the network and the end users. The network (i.e., the collection of frame-handling nodes) is in the best position to monitor the degree of congestion, while the end users are in the best position to control congestion by limiting the flow of traffic. With the preceding in mind, we can consider two general congestion-control strategies: congestion avoidance and congestion recovery.

Congestion-avoidance procedures are used at the onset of congestion to minimize the effect on the network. Thus, these procedures would be initiated at or prior to point A in Figure 9.19, to prevent congestion from progressing to point B. Near point A, there would be little evidence available to end users that congestion is increasing. Thus, there must be some **explicit signaling** mechanism from the network that will trigger the congestion avoidance.

Congestion-recovery procedures are used to prevent network collapse in the face of severe congestion. These procedures are typically initiated when the network has begun to drop frames due to congestion. Such dropped frames will be reported by some higher layer of software (e.g., Q.922) and serve as an **implicit signaling** mechanism. Congestion recovery procedures operate around point B and within the region of severe congestion, as shown in Figure 9.19.

CCITT and ANSI consider congestion avoidance with explicit signaling and congestion recovery with implicit signaling to be complementary forms of congestion control in the frame-relaying bearer service.

Congestion Avoidance with Explicit Signaling.   For explicit signaling, two bits in the address field of each frame are provided. Either bit may be set by any frame handler that detects congestion. If a frame handler forwards a frame in which one or both of these bits are set, it must not clear the bits. Thus, the bits constitute signals from the network to the end user. The two bits are

- **Backward explicit congestion notification (BECN):** Notifies the user that congestion-avoidance procedures should be initiated where applicable for traffic in the opposite direction of the received frame. It indicates that the frames that the user transmits on this logical connection may encounter congested resources.
- **Forward explicit congestion notification (FECN):** Notifies the user that congestion-avoidance procedures should be initiated where applicable for traffic in the same direction as the received frame. It indicates that this frame, on this logical connection, has encountered congested resources.

Let us consider how these bits are used by the network and the user. First, for the **network response,** it is necessary for each frame handler to monitor its queueing behavior. If queue lengths begin to grow to a dangerous level, then either FECN or BECN bits, or a combination, should be set to try to reduce the flow of frames through that frame handler. The choice of FECN or BECN may be determined by whether the end users on a given logical connection are prepared to respond to one or the other of these bits. This may be determined at configuration time. In any case, the frame handler has some choice as to which logical connections should be alerted to congestion. If congestion is becoming quite serious, all logical connections through a frame handler might be notified. In the early stages of congestion, the frame handler might just notify users for those connections that are generating the most traffic.

In an appendix to ANSI T1.6ca, a procedure for monitoring queue lengths is suggested. The frame handler monitors the size of each of its queues. A cycle begins when the outgoing circuit goes from idle (queue empty) to busy (non-zero queue size, including the current frame). The average queue size over the previous cycle and the current cycle is calculated. If the average size exceeds a threshold value, then the circuit is in a state of incipient congestion, and the congestion-avoidance bits should be set on some or all logical connections that use that circuit. By averaging over two cycles instead of just monitoring current queue

The algorithm makes use of the following variables:

t = current time

t_i = time of ith arrival or departure event

f_{qi} = number of frames in the system after the event

T_0 = time at the beginning of the previous cycle

T_1 = time at the beginning of the current cycle

The algorithm consists of three components:

1. Queue Length Update: Beginning with $q_0 := 0$,
   If the ith event is an arrival event, $q_i := q_{i-1} + 1$
   If the ith event is a departure event, $q_i := q_{i-1} - 1$

2. Queue Area (integral) update:

Area of the previous cycle = $\displaystyle\sum_{t_i \, \varepsilon \, [T_0, T_1)} q_{i-1}(t_i - t_{i-1})$

Area of the current cycle = $\displaystyle\sum_{t_i \, \varepsilon \, [T_1, t)} q_{i-1}(t_i - t_{i-1})$

3. Average Queue Length Update

Average queue length over the two cycles

$$= \frac{\text{Area of the two cycles}}{\text{Time of the two cycles}} = \frac{\text{Area of the two cycles}}{t - T_0}$$

FIGURE 9.20 Queue Length Averaging Algorithm

length, the system avoids reacting to temporary surges that would not necessarily produce congestion.

The average queue length may be computed by determining the area (product of queue size and time interval) over the two cycles and dividing by the time of the two cycles. This algorithm is illustrated in Figure 9.20.

The **user response** is determined by the receipt of BECN or FECN signals. The simplest procedure is the response to a BECN signal: the user simply reduces the rate at which frames are transmitted until the signal ceases. The response to an FECN is more complex, since it requires the user to notify its peer user on this connection to restrict its flow of frames. The core functions used in the frame-relay protocol do not support this notification. Therefore, it must be done at a higher layer, such as the transport layer. The flow control could also be accomplished by Q.922 or some other link control protocol implemented above the frame-relay sublayer (Figure 9.17). Q.922 is particularly useful, since it includes an enhancement to LAPD that permits the user to adjust window size.

Congestion Recovery with Implicit Signaling. Implicit signaling occurs when the network discards a frame and this fact is detected by the end user at a higher layer, such as Q.922. For example, in a data link control protocol such as Q.922, when a frame is dropped because of buffer overflow in the network, the following frame will generate a REJECT frame from the receiving end point. Thus, a higher-layer procedure can be used to provide flow control to recover from congestion.

The ANSI standard suggests that a user that is capable of varying the flow-control window size uses this mechanism in response to implicit signaling. Let us assume that the layer 2 window size, W, can vary between the parameters W_{max} and W_{min} and is initially set to W_{max}. In general, we would like to reduce W as congestion increases to gradually throttle the transmission of frames. Three classes of adaptive window schemes, based on response to the receipt of a REJECT frame, have been suggested [CHEN89, DOSH88]:

     1.1   Set $W = \text{Max} [W - 1, W_{min}]$.
     1.2   Set $W = W_{min}$.
     1.3   Set $W = \text{Max} [\alpha W, W_{min}]$, where $0 < \alpha < 1$.

Successful transmissions (measured by receipt of acknowledgments) may indicate that the congestion has gone away and window size should be increased. Two possible approaches:

     2.1   Set $W = \text{Min} [W + 1, W_{max}]$ after N consecutive successful transmissions.
     2.2   Set $W = \text{Min} [W + 1, W_{max}]$ after W consecutive successful transmissions.

A study reported in [CHEN89] suggests that the use of strategy 1.3 with $\alpha = 0.5$ plus strategy 2.2 provides good performance over a wide range of network parameters and traffic patterns.

So far, we have talked about the user role in congestion recovery. The network role, of course, is to discard frames as necessary. One bit in the address field of each frame can be used to provide guidance:

- **Discard eligibility (DE):** Indicates a request that a frame should be discarded in preference to other frames in which this bit is not set, when it is necessary to discard frames.

The DE capability makes it possible for the user to temporarily send more frames than it is allowed to on average. In this case, the user sets the DE bit on the excess frames. The network will forward these frames if it has the capacity to do so. The DE bit also can be set by a frame handler. The network can monitor the influx of frames from the user and use the DE bit to protect the network with flexible "firewalls." That is, if the frame handler to which the user is directly connected decides that the input is potentially excessive, it sets the DE bit on each frame and then forwards it further into the network.

9.4

SUMMARY

Table 9.8 summarizes the four data link control protocols that are relevant to ISDN. The principal ISDN Recommendation in this area is LAPD, which defines the data link control protocol to be used on the D channel. This single protocol carries higher-layer protocol information for control signaling (I.451/Q.931) and for X.25 packet switching. LAPD is based on LAPB, which is part of the X.25 standard, with modifications to the address field.

LAPB constitutes layer 2 of the X.25 packet-switching interface standard. It is used in conjunction with X.25 layer 3 on B channels to provide packet-switching support for ISDN users. When X.25 is used over the D channel, LAPD replaces LAPB as the layer 2 protocol.

I.465/V.120 is a terminal adaption procedure that provides a general-purpose data link control protocol for use over B and H channels. The chief feature of this protocol is that it allows multiple logical connections to be set up on a single circuit between two end users.

Finally, CCITT and ANSI are in the process of standardizing an important new service known as the frame-mode bearer service. This is a streamlined data link control protocol that does not support flow-control and error-control functions. However, frame relay does provide a packet-switching type of service on D, B, and H channels.

9.5

RECOMMENDED READING

[LAI89], [CHER89], and [OPDE90] provide concise overviews of frame relay. Interesting examinations of frame-relay congestion-control issues are to be found in [DOSH88], [CHEN89a], and [CHEN89b]. A discussion of implementation approaches for the frame handler is found in [BIRM90]. [MARS91] discusses interworking issues related to frame relay.

9.6

PROBLEMS

9.1. It is clear that bit stuffing is needed for user data fields in LAPD frames, since we wish to accommodate arbitrary user data. Is it needed for the other fields? Specify which ones.

TABLE 9.8   Comparison of ISDN Data Link Layer Specifications

	I.441/Q.921 (LAP-D)	LAP-B (Layer 2 of X.25)	I.465/V.120	Frame-mode Bearer Service
User data channel	D	B	B + H	D + B + H
Call control for logical connections	N/A	N/A (X.25-3 uses in-channel call control)	I.451/Q.931 on D[1] or LLI = 0 on bearer channel	I.451/Q.931 on D[2] or DLCI = 0 on bearer channel
Multiplexing	Multiple TEs (TEI) Multiple layer 3 users (SAPI)	None (X.25-3 supports multiple virtual circuits)	Multiple users (LLI)	Multiple users (DLCI)
Logical connections	N/A	N/A (X.25-3 supports multiplexing and switching)	Multiplexing	Multiplexing and switching
Peer entities	Network	Multiple users on network	Multiple users on same circuit	Multiple users on network

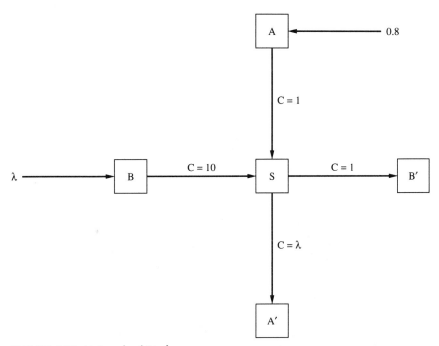

FIGURE 9.21 Network of Nodes

9.2. Suggest improvements to the bit-stuffing algorithm to overcome the problems of a single-bit error.

9.3. It was pointed out that some of the stuffed bits in Figure 9.2 were not strictly necessary. Consider the following rule: A 0 is stuffed by the transmitter only after the appearance of 011111.

   a. Describe the destuffing rule.

   b. Apply the rules to the bit stream in Figure 9.2.

9.4 Using the example bit string of Figure 9.2, show the signal pattern on the line using NRZL coding. Does this suggest a side benefit of bit stuffing?

9.5 Consider the frame-relay network depicted in Figure 9.21. C is the capacity of a link in frames per second. Node A presents a constant load of 0.8 frames per second destined for A'. Node B presents a load λ destined for B'. Node S has a common pool of buffers that it uses for traffic both to A' and B'. When the buffer is full, frames are discarded and are later retransmitted by the source user. Plot the total throughput (i.e., the sum of A-A' and B-B' delivered traffic) as a function of λ. What fraction of the throughput is A-A' traffic for $\lambda > 1$?

CHAPTER 10

ISDN Network Layer

For ISDN, a new network-layer protocol has been developed that provides out-of-band call control for B and H channel traffic. This protocol, I.451/Q.931, operates at the network level of the OSI model. It is used for both circuit-mode and packet-mode communication. In addition, a protocol based on I.451/Q.931 has been developed for use in frame-relay connection control. Both of these facilities are examined in this chapter.

10.1

ISDN CALL CONTROL

The ISDN specification for call control is contained in three Recommendations:

- I.450/Q.930: a general description of the layer 3 interface for call control.
- I.451/Q.931: a specification of the call-control protocol.
- I.452/Q.932: additional procedures for the control of ISDN supplementary service.

In what follows, we will simply refer to the protocol specified in these three documents as I.451/Q.931. This protocol specifies procedures for establishing connections on the B channels that share the

403

same interface to ISDN as the D channel. It also provides user-to-user control signaling over the D channel. In OSI terms, I.451/Q.931 is a layer 3, or network-layer, protocol. As Figure 10.1 indicates, this protocol relies on LAPD to transmit messages over the D channel. Each I.451/Q.931 message is encapsulated in a link-layer frame. This link-layer frame is transmitted on the D channel, which is multiplexed at the physical layer with other channels according to I.430 or I.431.

CCITT specifies the following as basic functions to be performed at the network layer for call control:

- Interacting with the data link layer (LAPD) to transmit and receive messages.
- Generation and interpretation of layer 3 messages.
- Administration of times and logical entities (e.g., call references) used in the call-control procedures.
- Administration of access resources, including B channels and packet-layer logical channels (X.25).
- Checking to ensure that services provided are consistent with user requirements (e.g., as expressed by bearer capability, addresses, low-layer and high-layer compatibilities).

In addition to these basic functions, a number of other functions may be required in certain network configurations to support certain services. CCITT cites the following:

- *Routing and relaying:* For end systems connected to different subnetworks, routing and relaying functions are required to establish an end-to-end network connection.
- *Network connection control:* Includes mechanisms for providing network connections making use of data link connections.
- *Conveying user-to-network and network-to-user information:* This function may be carried out with or without the establishment of a circuit-switched connection.

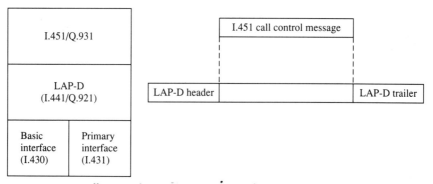

FIGURE 10.1 Call Control Communications Architecture

- *Network connection multiplexing:* Layer 3 provides multiplexing of call-control information for multiple calls onto a single data link (LAPD) connection.
- *Segmenting and reassembly:* It may be necessary to segment I.451/ Q.931 messages on transmission and reassemble these messages upon reception for transfer across particular local user-network interfaces.
- *Error detection:* Error-detection functions check for procedural errors in the layer 3 protocol.
- *Error recovery:* This function includes mechanisms for recovering from detected errors.
- *Sequencing:* This function provides mechanisms for sequenced delivery of layer 3 information when requested.
- *Congestion control and user data flow control:* Congestion control may dictate temporary denial of a connection establishment request. Flow control for user-to-user signaling may be provided.
- *Restart:* This function is used to return channels and interfaces to an idle condition to recover from certain abnormal conditions.

Terminal Types

Two basic types of user terminals are supported by ISDN: functional and stimulus. **Functional terminals** are considered to be intelligent devices and can employ the full range of I.451/Q.931 messages and parameters for call control. All signaling information is sent in a single control message (en bloc sending). **Stimulus terminals** are devices with a rudimentary signaling capability. A simple digital telephone is an example of a stimulus terminal. Messages sent to the network by a stimulus terminal are usually generated as a direct result of actions by the terminal user (e.g., handset lifted, key depression) and in general do little more than describe the event that has taken place at the man-machine interface. Thus, stimulus terminals transmit signaling information one event or one digit at a time (overlap sending). Signaling messages sent by the network to a stimulus terminal contain explicit instruction regarding the operations to be performed by the terminal (e.g., connect B channel, start alerting). For stimulus terminals, control functions are centralized in the exchange, and functional expansion, if any, will be realized by changes in the exchange.

Messages

The process of establishing, controlling, and terminating a call occurs as a result of control signaling messages exchanged between the user and the network over a D channel. A common format is used for all

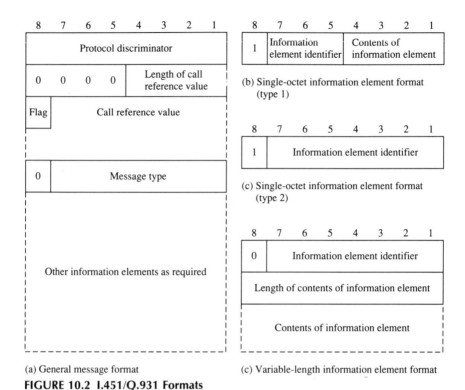

(a) General message format

(c) Variable-length information element format

FIGURE 10.2 I.451/Q.931 Formats

messages defined in I.451, illustrated in Figure 10.2a. Three fields are common to all messages:

- *Protocol discriminator:* Used to distinghish messages for user-network call control from other message types. Other sorts of protocols may share the D channel.
- *Call reference:* Identifies the B channel call to which this message refers. As with X.25 virtual circuit numbers, it has only local significance. The call reference field comprises three subfields. The length subfield specifies the length of the remainder of the field in octets. This length is one octet for a basic rate interface and two octets for a primary rate interface. The flag indicates which end of the LAPD logical connection initiated the call.
- *Message type:* Identifies which I.451 message is being sent. The contents of the remainder of the message depend on the message type.

There are two special cases of the call reference parameter to note. A dummy call reference has a length subfield value of 0 and hence is one octet long (all zeroes). This is reserved for Q.932 supplementary service procedures, discussed subsequently. The second case has a call reference value of zero (i.e., the length subfield has a value of 1, indicating the presence of the second octet in the call reference field, and the numerical value of the call reference value subfield is zero). This case is a global call reference, used for data link restart procedures; the messages are applicable to all call references associated with the data link connection identifier (DLCI).

Following these three common fields, the remainder of the message consists of a sequence of zero or more information elements, or parameters. These contain additional information to be conveyed with the message. Thus, the message type specifies a command or response, and the details are provided by the information elements. Some information elements must always be included with a given message (mandatory), and others are optional (additional). Three formats for information elements are used, as indicated in Figures 10.2b through d.

I.451/Q.931 messages can be grouped along two dimensions. Messages apply to one of four applications: circuit-mode connection control, packet-mode access connection control, user-to-user signaling not associated with circuit-switched calls, and messages used with the global call reference. In addition, messages perform functions in one of four categories: call establishment, call information, call clearing, and miscellaneous.

Circuit-mode connection control refers to the functions needed to set up, maintain, and clear a circuit-switched connection on a B channel. This function corresponds to call control in existing circuit-switching telecommuncations networks. **Packet-mode access connection control** refers to the functions needed to set up a circuit-switched connection (called an access connection in this context) to an ISDN packet-switching node; this connects the user to the packet-switching network provided by the ISDN provider. **User-to-user signaling messages** allow two users to communicate without setting up a circuit-switched connection. A temporary signaling connection is established and cleared in a manner similar to the control of a circuit-switched connection. Signaling takes place over the D channel and thus does not consume B channel resources. Finally, **global call reference** refers to the functions that enable user or network to return one or more channels to an idle condition.

Call establishment messages are used to initially set up a call. This group includes messages between the calling terminal and the network (SETUP, SETUP ACK, CALL PROC, CONN, PROGRESS) and between the network and the called terminal (SETUP, ALERT, CONN, CONN ACK, PROGRESS). These messages support the following services:

- Set up a B channel call in response to user request.
- Provide particular network facilities for this call.
- Inform calling user of the progress of the call establishment process.

TABLE 10.1   I.451/Q.931 Messages for Circuit-mode Connection Control

Message	Significance	Direction	Function
Call Establishment Messages			
ALERTING	global	both	Indicates that user alerting has begun
CALL PROCEEDING	local	both	Indicates that call establishment has been initiated
CONNECT	global	both	Indicates call acceptance by called TE
CONNECT ACKNOWLEDGE	local	both	Indicates that user has been awarded the call
PROGRESS	global	both	Reports progress of a call
SETUP	global	both	Initiates call establishment
SETUP ACKNOWLEDGE	local	both	Indicates that call establishment has been initiated but requests more information
Call Information Phase Messages			
RESUME	local	u → n	Requests resumption of previously suspended call
RESUME ACKNOWLEDGE	local	n → u	Indicates requested call has been reestablished
RESUME REJECT	local	n → u	Indicates failure to resume suspended call
SUSPEND	local	u → n	Requests suspension of a call
SUSPEND ACKNOWLEDGE	local	n → u	Indicates call has been suspended
SUSPEND REJECT	local	n → u	Indicates failure of requested call suspension
USER INFORMATION	access	both	Transfers information from one user to another
Call-clearing Messages			
DISCONNECT	global	both	Sent by user to request connection clearing; sent by network to indicate connection clearing
RELEASE	local	both	Indicates intent to release channel and call reference
RELEASE COMPLETE	local	both	Indicates release of channel and call reference

CONGESTION CONTROL	local	both	Sets or releases flow control on USER INFORMATION messages
FACILITY	local	both	Requests or acknowledges a supplementary service
INFORMATION	local	both	Provides additional information
NOTIFY	access	both	Indicates information pertaining to a call
STATUS	local	both	Sent in response to a STATUS ENQUIRY or at any time to report an error
STATUS ENQUIRY	local	both	Solicits STATUS message

Once a call has been set up, but prior to the disestablishment (termination) phase, **call information phase** messages are sent between user and network. One of the messages in this group allows the network to relay, without modification, information between the two users of the call. The nature of this information is beyond the scope of the standard, but it is assumed that it is control signaling information that can't or should not be sent directly over the B channel circuit. The remainder of the messages allow users to request the suspension and later resumption of a call. When a call is suspended, the network remembers the identity of the called parties and the network facilities supporting the call, but deactivates the call so that no additional charges are incurred and so that the corresponding B channel is freed up. Presumably, the resumption of a call is quicker and cheaper than the origination of a new call.

Call clearing messages are sent between user and network in order to terminate a call. Finally, there some **miscellaneous** messages that may be sent between user and network at various stages of the call. Some may be sent during call setup; others may be sent even though no calls exist. The primary function of these messages is to negotiate network features (supplementary services).

Circuit-mode Connection Control

Table 10.1 lists, with a brief definition, the messages used for circuit-mode connection control. Each entry includes an indication of the direction of the message:

- Only user to network (u → n).
- Only network to user (n → u).
- Both directions.

TABLE 10.2   Parameters for I.451/Q.931 Call Establishment Messages for Circuit-mode Connection Control

	Alerting	Call Proceeding	Connect	Connect Acknowledge	Progress	Setup	Setup Acknowledge
Sending complete						O	
Repeat indicator						O	
Bearer capability						M	
Facility	O		O			O	
Channel identification	O	O	O	O		O	O
Cause					O		
Progress indicator	O	O	O		M	O	O
Network-specific facilities						O	
Display	O	O	O	O	O	O	O
Keypad facility						O	
Signal	O	O	O	O		O	O

Switchhook		o		o	
Feature activation		o			o
Feature indication		o			o
Calling party number		o			
Calling party subaddress		o			
Called party number		o			
Called party subaddress		o			
Transit network selection		o			
Low-layer compatibility		o		o	
High-layer compatibility		o	o		
User-user		o		o	o

Each entry also specifies whether the message has

- *Local significance:* relevant only in the originating or terminating access (i.e., the user-network interface for the user that originated the call or the user that accepted the call) to the network by the user.
- *Access significance:* relevant in the originating and terminating access, but not in the network.
- *Global significance:* relevant in the originating and terminating access and in the network.

Tables 10.2 through 10.5 list the parameters associated with each circuit-mode connection control message for call establishment, call information phase, call clearing, and miscellaneous functions, respectively. Parameters are designated as mandatory (M) or optional (O). Finally, Table 10.6 provides a brief definition of these parameters.

Bearer Capability Information Element.   One key parameter, the bearer capability information element (Figure 10.3) warrants elaboration. This parameter is used in the SETUP message to request a bearer service as specified in I.231. Unlike many of the message parameters, which are passed through from source to destination, this one is used by the network in establishing the connection. The parameter actually carries two types of information:

- The selection of bearer service from the choice of bearer services offered by the network to which the calling user is connected. An example is unrestricted digital information. This information is coded in octets 3 and 4 of the bearer capability information element when circuit mode is requested and in octets 3, 4 (including 4a and 4b if necessary), 6, and 7 for packet mode.
- Information about the terminal or intended call that is used to decide destination terminal compatibility and possibly to facilitate interworking with other ISDNs or other non-ISDN networks. An example is A-law encoding. This information is encoded in octet 5 of the bearer capability information element.

Octet 3 includes an indication of whether the bearer capability is a CCITT standard or not. If it is, then the information transfer capability field specifies one of the following: speech, unrestricted digital information, restricted digital information, 3.1-kHz audio, 7-kHz audio, or video.

Octet 4 indicates whether circuit mode or packet mode is requested and the user channel data rate (64 kbps, 2 × 64 kbps, 384 kbps, 1.536 Mbps, 1.92 Mbps). In octet 4a, the structure field provides information on synchronization: 8-kHz integrity, service data unit integrity, unstructured. Currently, the remainder of octets 4a and 4b only supports point-

TABLE 10.3   Parameters for I.451/Q.931 Call Information Phase Messages for Circuit-mode Connection Control

	Resume	Resume Acknowledge	Resume Reject	Suspend	Suspend Acknowledge	Suspend Reject	User Information
Call identity	O			O			
Channel identification		M					
Cause			M			M	
Display		M	M		O	O	
More data							O
User-user							M

TABLE 10.4   Parameters for I.451/Q.931 Call-clearing Messages for Circuit-mode Connection Control

	Disconect	Release	Release Complete
Cause	M	O	O
Facility	O	O	O
Progress indicator	O		
Display	O	O	O
Signal	O	O	O
Feature indication	O	O	O
User-user	O	O	O

to-point configuration, demand circuit establishment, and bidirectional symmetric transfer. Since the traffic is symmetric, the information transfer rate in the destination-to-origination direction must be the same as in the other direction. Other options for these four fields are for further study.

Octet 5 is used to indicate the coding rule followed for the information transfer capability, for example: V.110 or V.120 rate adaption, X.31 flag stuffing, A-law, μ-law. Octet 5a includes an indication of synchronous or asynchronous transfer and a negotiation indication used with V.110. The user rate shows the base rate from which rate adaption occurs. Octet 5b deals with the details of the chosen rate-adaption technique and takes two forms, one used with V.110 and one used with V.120. For V.110 the fields are

- *Intermediate rate:* not used, 8 kbps, 16 kbps, 32 kbps.
- *Network independent clock on transmission:* required, not required.
- *Network independent clock on reception:* can be supported, cannot be supported.
- *Flow control on transmission:* required, not required.
- *Flow control on reception:* can be supported, cannot be supported.

For V.120, the fields are

- *Header:* rate adaption header included, not included.
- *Multiple frame establishment support:* supported, not supported.
- *Mode:* bit transparent, protocol sensitive.
- *Logical link identifier negotiation:* whether default LLI (256) will be used.
- *Assignor/assignee:* default assignee or assignee only.

TABLE 10.5 Parameters for I.451/Q.931 Miscellaneous Messages for Circuit-mode Connection Control

	Congestion Control	Facility	Information	Notify	Status	Status Enquiry
Congestion level	M					
Cause	O				M	
Facility		M				
Bearer capability				O		
Notification indicator				M		
Call state					M	
Display	O	O	O	O	O	O
Keypad facility			O			
Signal			O			
Switchhook			O			
Feature activation			O			
Feature indication			O			
Called party number			O			

TABLE 10.6   Parameters for I.451/U931 Messages

Bearer Capability

Indicates provision, by the network, of one of the bearer capabilities defined in I.231 and I.232. Contains detailed information on protocol options at each layer to construct the desired service.

Call Identity

Used to identify a suspended call. It is assigned at the start of call suspension.

Call State

Describes the current status of a call, such as active, detached, and disconnect request.

Called/Calling Party Number

Identifies the subnetwork address of the called or calling party.

Called/Calling Party Subaddress

Identifies the subaddress of the called or calling party.

Cause

Used to describe the reason for generating certain messages, to provide diagnostic information in the event of procedural errors, and to indicate the location of the cause originator. The location is specified in terms of which network originated the cause.

Channel Identification

Identifies channel/subchannel within the interface (e.g., which B channel).

Congestion Level

Describes the congestion status of the call. Currently, only receiver ready and receiver not ready values are defined.

Display

Supplies additional information coded in IA5 (International Alphabet 5, also known as ASCII) characters. Intended for display on user terminal.

Facility

Indicates the invocation and operation of supplementary services.

Feature Activation

Invokes a specific supplementary service.

Feature Indication

Allows the network to convey feature indications to the user regarding the status of a supplementary service.

High-layer Compatibility

Supplies the type terminal that is on the user side of an S/T interface. The network transports this information transparently end-to-end.

Keypad

Conveys IA5 characters entered by means of a terminal keypad.

Low-layer Compatibility

Used for compatibility checking. Includes information transfer capability, information transfer rate, and protocol identification at layers 1 through 3.

More Data

Transferred between users by the network. Its intended use is to permit one user to alert another that more data are coming in an additional USER INFORMATION message.

Network-Specific Facilities
Allows the specification of facilities peculiar to a particular network.

Notification Identifier
Indicates information pertaining to a call. User suspended, user resumed, and bearer service charge are the only values currently defined.

Progress Indicator
Describes an event that has occurred during the life of a call.

Repeat Indicator
Indicates that one possibility should be selected from repeated information elements.

Restart Indicator
Indicates whether channel or interface is to be restarted.

Segmented Message
Indicates that this transmission is part of a segmented message.

Sending Complete
Indicates completion of called party number.

Signal
Conveys indications causing a stimulus mode terminal to generate tones and alerting signals. Example values are dial tone on, ring back tone on, busy tone on, and tones off.

Switchhook
Indicates the state of the stimulus mode terminal switchhook to the network. Values are on-hook and off-hook.

Transit Network Selection
Identity of a network that connection should use to get to final destination. This parameter may be repeated within a message to select a sequence of networks through which a call must pass.

User-User Information
Used to transfer information between ISDN users that should not be interpreted by the network(s).

- *In-band/out-band negotiation:* negotiation with USER INFORMATION messages on D channel or in-band using LLI = 0.

Octets 5c and 5d contain additional physical layer characteristics.
Octet 6 covers layer 2 use (I.441/Q.921 or X.25 layer 2). Octet 7 covers layer 3 use (I.451/Q.931 or X.25 layer 3).

Circuit-mode-Example.   Figure 10.4 is an example of the use of the protocol to set up a B channel circuit-switched telephone call. We will follow this example through to give the reader an idea of the use of the I.451/Q.931 protocol. The example is for the placement of a telephone call, but the sequence would be similar for a computer-to-computer or terminal-to-computer data call.

8	7	6	5	4	3	2	1	Octets
			Bearer capability					
0	0	0	0	0	1	0	0	1
			Information element identifier					
			Length of the bearer capability contents					2
1 ext	Coding standard		Information transfer capability					
0/1 ext	Transfer mode		Information transfer rate					4
0/1 ext	Structure			Configuration		Establishment		4a* (Note 1)
1 ext	Symmetry		Information transfer rate (destination — origination)					4b* (Note 1)
0/1 ext	0 0 Layer 1 ident.		User information layer 1 protocol					5*
1 ext	Synch./ asynch.	Negot.	User rate					5a* (Note 4)
0/1 ext	Intermediate rate		NIC on Tx	NIC on Rx	Flow control on Tx	Flow control on Rx	0 Spare	5b* (Note 2)
0/1 ext	Hdr/ no Hdr	Multi frame support	Mode	LLI negot.	Assignor/ assignee	In-band/ out-band negot.	0 Spare	5b* (Note 3)
0/1 ext	Number of stop bits		Number of data bits		Parity			5c* (Note 4)
0/1 ext	Duplex mode	Modem type						5d* (Note 4)
1 ext	1 0 Layer 2 ident.		User inforation layer 2 protocol					6*
1 ext	1 1 Layer 3 ident.		User inforation layer 3 protocol					7*

Note 1—If default values are used for all fields of octets 4a and 4b, then these octets shall not be included. If default values are used for all fields of octet 4b, but not for one or more fields of octet 4a, then only octet 4a shall be included. Otherwise, both octets 4a and 4b shall be inlcuded.

Note 2—This octet may be present only if octet 5 indicates CCITT standardized rate adaption V.110[7]/X.30[8].

Note 3—This octet is present only if octet 5 indicates CCITT standardized rate adaption V.120 [9].

Note 4—This octet may be present if octet 5 indicates either of the CCITT standardized rate adoptions V.110/X.30 or V.120 [9].

FIGURE 10.3 Bearer Capacity Information Element

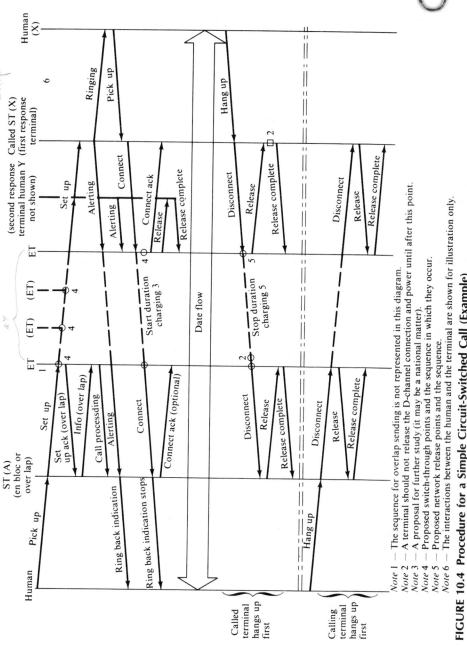

FIGURE 10.4 Procedure for a Simple Circuit-Switched Call (Example)

Note 1 — The sequence for overlap sending is not represented in this diagram.
Note 2 — A terminal should not release the D-channel connection and power until after this point.
Note 3 — A proposal for further study (it may be a national matter).
Note 4 — Proposed switch-through points and the sequence in which they occur.
Note 5 — Proposed network release points and the sequence.
Note 6 — The interactions between the human and the terminal are shown for illustration only.

The process begins when a calling subscriber lifts the handset. The ISDN-compatible telephone insures that the D channel is active before itself generating a dial tone (not shown). When the subscriber keys in the called number (not shown), the telephone set accumulates the digits and, when all are keyed in, sends a SETUP message over the D channel to the exchange. The SETUP message includes the destination number; a channel identification, which specifies which B channel is to be used; and any requested network services or facilities (e.g., reverse charging).

The SETUP message triggers two activities at the local exchange. First, using internal control signaling, the local exchange sends a message through the network that results in designating a route for the requested call and allocating resources for that call. Second, the exchange sends back a CALL PROC message, indicating that call setup is underway. The exchange may also request more information from the caller (via SETUP ACK and INFO). When the internal control message reaches the remote exchange, it sends a SETUP message to the called telephone. The called telephone accepts the call by sending an ALERT message to the network and generating a ringing tone. The ALERT message is transmitted all the way back to the calling telephone set. When the called party lifts the handset, the telephone sends a CONN message to the network. The local exchange sends a CONN ACK message to its subscriber and forwards the CONN message to the calling exchange, and it in turn forwards it to the calling telephone. The B channel circuit is now available for the called and calling telephones.

Because the call setup process makes use of common-channel signaling, other channels are undisturbed, and the fact that all of the B channels are engaged does not prevent the D channel dialogue. For example, even if all of a user's channels are assigned to circuits, an incoming call request will be presented to the user via the D channel; the user can, if desired, put a call in progress on hold in order to use the corresponding B channel for the new call.

Once the circuit is set up, full duplex 64-kbps data streams are exchanged via the B channel between the two end users. Additional signaling messages, such as call information phase messages, may be transmitted during this period.

Call termination begins when one of the telephone users hangs up. This causes a DISC message to be sent from the telephone to the exchange. The exchange responds with a REL message, and when the telephone sends REL COM, the B channel is released. The complementary action takes place at the other telephone-network interface.

Packet-mode Access Connection Control

Table 10.7 lists, with a brief definition, the messages used for packet-mode access connection control. As can be seen, these are a subset of

TABLE 10.7   I.451/Q.931 Messages for Packet-mode Access Connection Control

Message	Significance	Direction	Function
Access Connection Establishment Messages			
ALERTING	local	u → n	Indicates that user alerting has begun
CALL PROCEEDING	local	both	Indicates that access connection establishment has been initiated
CONNECT	local	both	Indicates access connection acceptance by called TE
CONNECT ACKNOWLEDGE	local	both	Indicates that user has been awarded the access connection
PROGRESS	local	u → n	Reports progress of an access connection in the event of interworking with a private network
SETUP	local	both	Initiates access connection establishment
Access Connection-clearing Messages			
DISCONNECT	local	both	Sent by user to request connection clearing; sent by network to indicate connection clearing
RELEASE	local	both	Indicates intent to release channel and call reference
RELEASE COMPLETE	local	both	Indicates release of channel and call reference
Miscellaneous Messages			
STATUS	local	both	Sent in response to a STATUS ENQUIRY or at any time to report an error
STATUS ENQUIRY	local	both	Solicits STATUS message

TABLE 10.8   **I.451/Q.931 Messages for User-to-User Signaling Not Associated with Circuit-switched Calls**

	Significance	Direction	Function
Call Establishment messages			
ALERTING	global	both	Indicates that user alerting has begun
CALL PROCEEDING	local	both	Indicates that call establishment has been initiated
CONNECT	global	both	Indicates call acceptance by called TE
CONNECT ACKNOWLEDGE	local	both	Indicates that user has been awarded the call
SETUP	global	both	Initiates call establishment
SETUP ACKNOWLEDGE	local	both	Indicates that call establishment has been initiated but requests more information
Call Information Phase Messages			
USER INFORMATION	access	both	Transfers information from one user to another
Call-clearing Messages			
RELEASE	local	both	Indicates intent to release channel and call reference
RELEASE COMPLETE	local	both	Indicates release of channel and call reference
Miscellaneous Messages			
CONGESTION CONTROL	local	both	Sets or releases flow control on USER INFORMATION messages
INFORMATION	local	both	Provides additional information
STATUS	local	both	Sent in response to a STATUS ENQUIRY or at any time to report an error
STATUS ENQUIRY	local	both	Solicits STATUS message

TABLE 10.9   I.451/Q.931 Messages Used with the Global Call Reference

Message	Significance	Direction	Function
RESTART	local	both	Requests the recipient to re-start the indicated chan-nel(s) or interface
RESTART ACKNOWLEDGE	local	both	Indicates that the requested restart is complete
STATUS	local	both	Reports an error condition

the messages used for circuit-mode connection control. A discussion of the use of control signaling for packet-mode service is contained in Chapter 7.

User-to-User Signaling Not Associated with Circuit-switched Calls

Table 10.8 lists, with a brief definition, the messages used for user-to-user signaling not associated with circuit-switched calls. This feature allows the users to communicate information without setting up a circuit-switched connection. A temporary signaling connection is established and cleared in a manner similar to the control of a circuit-switched call. The information exchanged is end-to-end, and no service descriptions for these connections are currently provided.

Global Call Reference

Table 10.9 lists, with a brief definition, the messages used for global call reference. Only three messages are used. The STATUS message is the same as that used in other contexts to report an error condition. The RESTART and RESTART ACKNOWLEDGE messages are only used for global call reference. These messages are used to return a given channel or all channels to a predefined state after a fault condition.

Supplementary Services Control

Recommendation I.452/Q.932, first issued in the 1988 Blue Book, defines the generic procedures applicable for the control of supplementary services. These procedures may be associated with a particular call or outside any existing call.

I.452/Q.392 identifies three major methods by which supplementary services may be controlled:

TABLE 10.10   Parameters for Frame-relay Call Establishment Messages

	Alerting	Call Proceeding	Connect	Connect Acknowledge	Progress	Setup
Protocol discriminator	M	M	M	M	M	M
Call reference	M	M	M	M	M	M
Message type	M	M	M	M	M	M
Channel identification	O	O	O			O
Data link connection identifier	O	O	O			O
Progress indicator	O	O	O		M	O
Display	O	O	O	O	O	O
User-user	O		O			O
End-to-end transit delay			O			O
Link-layer core parameters			O			O
Link-layer protocol parameters			O			O

Information element			
Connected number			O
Connected subaddress			O
Low-layer compatibility	O		O
Cause		O	
Bearer capability			M
Network-specific facilities			O
Calling party number			O
Calling party subaddress			O
Called party subaddress			O
Transit network selection			O
Repeat indicator			O
High-layer compatibility			O

- Keypad protocol.
- Feature key management protocol.
- Functional protocol.

The first two methods are appropriate for stimulus terminals, as defined earlier in this section, where individual keystrokes (Keypad) or button pressing (Feature key management) are used to trigger service operations.

The functional protocol allows more sophisticated use of supplementary services for functional terminals. It is based on the use of a FACILITY message for carrying explicit supplementary service requests. The following cases have been defined:

- The invocation of supplementary services during the establishment of a call.
- The invocation of supplementary services during the clearing of a call.
- The invocation of call-related supplementary services during the active state of a call.
- The invocation or registration of supplementary services independent from an active call.
- The invocation of multiple, different supplementary services within a single message.
- The invocation of supplementary services related to different calls.
- Cancellation of invoked supplementary services and notification to the initiator of the supplementary service.

The methods described in I.452/Q.932 are still evolving and are the subject of ongoing study.

10.2

FRAME-RELAY CONNECTION CONTROL

In Chapter 9, we examined the basic mechanisms for frame-relay call control. Recall that call control involves the exchange of messages between the user and a frame handler over a previously created connection. The messages are transmitted in one of two ways:

Case A: Messages are transmitted in frame-relay frames over the same channel (B or H) as the frame-relay connections, using the same frame structure, with a data link connection identifier of DLCI = 0.

Case B: Messages are transmitted in LAPD frames with SAPI = 0 over the D channel.

TABLE 10.11   Parameters for Frame-relay Call-clearing Messages

	Disconnect	Release	Release Complete
Protocol discriminator	M	M	M
Call reference	M	M	M
Message type	M	M	M
Cause	M	O	O
Display	O	O	O
Connected number	O	O	O
Connected subaddress	O	O	O
User-user	O	O	O

In either case, the set of messages is a subset of those used in I.451/Q.931. For frame relay, however, these messages are used to set up and manage logical frame-relay connections rather than actual circuits. Accordingly, some of the parameters used for frame-relay call control differ from those used in I.451/Q.931.

The set of messages used for frame-relay call control is, in fact, identical with that used for packet-mode access connection control. These messages were listed, with brief definitions, in Table 10.7. Tables 10.10 through 10.12 show the parameters used with these messages for frame-relay call control. Most of these parameters are defined in Table 10.6.

Several of the parameters are new and warrant further elaboration. The **data link connection identifier** (DLCI) is used to identify the logical connection that is the subject of the message. The DLCI allows multiple logical connections to be multiplexed over the same channel.

TABLE 10.12   Parameters for Miscellaneous Frame-relay Messages

	Status	Status Enquiry
Protocol discriminator	M	M
Call reference	M	M
Message type	M	M
Cause	M	
Call state	M	
Display	O	O

8	7	6	5	4	3	2	1	Octets
			Link layer protocol parameters					1
0	1	0	0	1	0	0	0	
			Information element identifier					
			Length of link layer core parameters contents					2
			Outgoing maximum frame size					3
0	1	0	0	1	0	0	0	
0 ext			Outgoing maximum frame size					3a (Note 2)
1 ext			Outgoing maximum frame size (cont)					3b
			Incoming maximum frame size					4
0	0	0	0	1	0	1	0	
0 ext			Incoming maximum frame size					4a (Note 2)
1 ext			Incoming maximum frame size (cont)					4b
			Requested/Agreed Throughput					5
0	0	0	0	1	0	1	1	
0 ext	Outgoing magnitude			Outgoing multiplier				5a
0/1 ext	Outgoing multiplier (cont.)							5b
0 ext	Incoming magnitude			Incoming multiplier				5c*
1 ext	Incoming multiplier (cont.)							5d*
			Minimum acceptable throughput					6 (Note 3)
0	0	0	0	1	1	0	0	
0 ext	Outgoing magnitude			Outgoing multiplier				6a
0/1 ext	Outgoing multiplier (cont.)							6b
0 ext	Incoming magnitude			Incoming multiplier				6c*
1 ext	Incoming multiplier (cont.)							6d*
			Outgoing burst size					7
0	0	0	0	1	1	0	1	
0 ext	Outgoing burst size value							7a
1 ext	Outgoing burst size value (cont.)							7b
			Incoming burst size					8
0	0	0	0	1	1	1	0	

FIGURE 10.5 Link Layer Core Parameters Information Element

0 ext	Incoming burst size value							8a
1 ext	Incoming burst size value (cont.)							8b
	Outgoing maximum frame rate							9
0	0	0	0	1	1	1	1	
1 ext	Outgoing maximum frame rate value							9a
	Incoming maximum frame rate							10
0	0	0	1	0	0	0	0	
1 ext	Incoming maximum frame rate value							10a

Note 1—The terms "incoming" and "outgoing" are defined with respect to the calling user. All the parameters are optional and postion independent. If certain parameters are not included, the network default value will be used.

Note 2—The size of a frame is the number of octets after address field and before the FCS held in the frame. The count is done either before zero-bit insertion or following zero-bit extraction.

Note 3—Included only in the SETUP message.

FIGURE 10.5 Link Layer Core Parameters Information Element (*continued*)

The **end-to-end transit delay** information element is used to request and indicate the nominal maximum permissible transit delay applicable on a per-call basis. The end-to-end delay is the time it takes to send a frame containing user data from one end user to another, including the total frame-relay processing time in the end-user systems.

The **link layer core parameters** information element indicates requested parameters related to the core data link service (see Figure 9.12). This information is exchanged between each end user and the network. The format of this information element is shown in Figure 10.5. Note that each parameter consists of a parameter identifier field followed by one or more octets of parameter value. The following parameters are included:

- *Maximum frame size:* The maximum size of a frame in octets, determined independently in each direction. The default value is 262 octets for the D channel and 4096 octets for the B and H channels. The two end users may negotiate a smaller maximum size.
- *Requested/agreed throughput:* The average number of frame-relay information field bits transferred per second. The value is expressed in the form $A \times 10^B$ bps, where A is the multiplier and B is the magnitude.
- *Minimum acceptable throughput:* The lowest throughput value that the calling user is willing to accept for the call. If the network or the called user is unable to sustain this throughput, the call shall be cleared.

8	7	6	5	4	3	2	1	Octets
			Link layer protocol parameters					
0	1	0	0	1	0	0	l	1
			Information element identifier					
		Length of link layer protocol parameters contents						2
			Forward window identifier					
0 Ext	0	0	0	0	0	1	0	1
1 Ext			Forward window value					3a
			Backward window identifier					
0 Ext	0	0	0	0	0	1	1	4
0 Ext			Backward window value					4a
			Forward acknowledgement timer identifier					5
0 Ext	0	0	0	0	1	1	0	(Note 1)
0 Ext			Forward acknowledgement timer value					5a
1 Ext			Forward acknowledgement timer value (cont.)					5b
			Backward acknowledgement timer identifier					
0 Ext	0	0	0	0	1	1	0	6
0 Ext			Backward acknowledgement timer value					6a
1 Ext			Backward acknowledgement timer value (cont.)					6b
			Mode of operation					7
0 Ext	0	0	0	1	0	0	0	(Note 2)
1 Ext			Spare				Mode Indication	7a

Note 1—In case of Frame Relay bearer service layer 2 elements of procedures are end-to-end. The acknowledgement timer value should be based on per-call cumulative transit delay. If included by the originating user, it will be based on the maximum end-to-end transit delay. The terminating user can adjust the value based on the cumulative transit delay.

Note 2—Mode of operation is only included when the LLC octet 6 "user information layer 2 protocol" is coded with one of the codepoints: CCITT Rec. X.25 link layer, CCITT Rec. X.25 multilink, Extended LAPB for half duplex operation (T71), and CCITT Rec. X.75 Single Link Procedure (SLP).

FIGURE 10.6 Link Layer Protocol Parameters Information Element

- *Burst size:* The maximum amount that the cumulative frames can exceed the value allowed by the mean throughput at any time.
- *Maximum frame rate value:* The maximum number of frames per second that may be sent in one direction across the user-network interface.

The **link-layer protocol parameters** information element indicates requested parameters related to the end-to-end data link service (see Figure 9.12). This information is exchanged between a pair of end users and is carried transparently by the network. The format of this information element is shown in Figure 10.6. The following parameters are included:

- *Window value:* The maximum size of the sliding-window flow-control window; may take on a value from 1 to 127.
- *Acknowledgment timer value:* The amount of time that a sender will wait for acknowledgment before retransmission, expressed in units of tenths of a second.
- *Mode of operation:* Indicates whether 3-bit or 7-bit sequence numbers will be used.

10.3

SUMMARY

For call-control signaling, the D channel layer 3 interface is defined in Recommendations I.450/Q.930 and I.451/Q.931. It specifies procedures for establishing a connection on the B and H channels that share the same interface to ISDN as the D channel. It also provides user-to-user control signaling over the D channel.

Connection control for frame relay can either be inchannel, on a different logical connection from user data connections, or on the D channel. In both cases, a subset of the message repertoire of I.451/Q.931 is used, with parameters tailored to frame relay.

10.4

RECOMMENDED READING

[HARM89] is a good survey of I.451/Q.931.

10.5

PROBLEMS

10.1. X.25 and most other layer 3 protocols provide techniques for flow control and error control. Why are such features not provided in I.451/Q.931?

10.2. Virtual X.25 circuits could be set up via a D channel protocol similar to the frame-relay connection-control protocol. Discuss the merits of this scheme relative to ordinary X.25 and relative to frame relay.

CHAPTER 11

Signaling System Number 7

In Chapter 2, we discussed the transition of network control signaling from an inchannel to a common-channel approach. Common-channel signaling is more flexible and powerful then inchannel signaling and is well suited to support the requirements of integrated digital networks. The culmination of this transition is Signaling System Number 7 (SS7), first issued by CCITT in 1980, with revisions in 1984 and 1988. SS7 is designed to be an open-ended common-channel signaling standard that can be used over a variety of digital circuit-switched networks. Furthermore, SS7 is specifically designed to be used in ISDNs. SS7 is the mechanism that provides the internal control and network intelligence essential to an ISDN.

The overall purpose of SS7 is to provide an internationally standardized general-purpose common-channel signaling system with the following primary characteristics:

- Optimized for use in digital telecommunication networks in conjunction with digital stored program-control exchanges, utilizing 64-kbps digital channels.
- Designed to meet present and future information transfer requirements for call control, remote control, management, and maintenance.
- Provides a reliable means for the transfer of information in the correct sequence without loss or duplication.

433

- Suitable for operation over analog channels and at speeds below 64 kbps.
- Suitable for use on point-to-point terrestrial and satellite links.

The scope of SS7 is immense, since it must cover all aspects of control signaling for complex digital networks, including the reliable routing and delivery of control messages and the application-oriented content of those messages. Appendix 5A, which lists the 39 CCITT Recommendations that comprise SS7, should give the reader some feel for the complexity of the standard. In this chapter, we provide an overview of SS7 and highlight key aspects of it.

11.1

SS7 ARCHITECTURE

Functional Architecture

With common-channel signaling, control messages are routed through the network to perform call management (setup, maintenance, termination) and network management functions. These messages are short blocks or packets that must be routed through the network. Thus, although the network being controlled is a circuit-switched network, the control signaling is implemented using packet-switching technology. In effect, a packet-switched network is overlaid on a circuit-switched network in order to operate and control the circuit-switched network.

SS7 defines the functions that are performed in the packet-switched network but does not dictate any particular hardware implementation. For example, all of the SS7 functions could be implemented in the circuit-switching nodes as additional functions; this approach is the associated signaling mode depicted in Figure 2.24a. Alternatively, separate switching points that carry only the control packets and are not used for carrying circuits can be used, as depicted in Figure 2.24b. Even in this case, the circuit-switching nodes would need to implement portions of SS7 so that they could receive control signals.

Signaling Network Elements. SS7 defines three functional entities: signaling points, signal transfer points, and signaling links. A **signaling point** (SP) is any point in the signaling network capable of handling SS7 control messages. It may be an endpoint for control messages and incapable of processing messages not directly addressed to itself. The circuit-switching nodes of the network, for example, could be endpoints. Another example is a network control center. A **signal transfer point** (STP) is a signaling point that is capable of routing control messages; that is, a message received on one signaling link is transferred to another link. An STP could be a pure routing node or could also include the functions of an endpoint. Finally, a **signaling link** is a data link that connects signaling points.

Figure 11.1 highlights the distinction between the packet-switching signaling function and the circuit-switching information transfer function, in the case of a nonassociated signaling architecture. We can

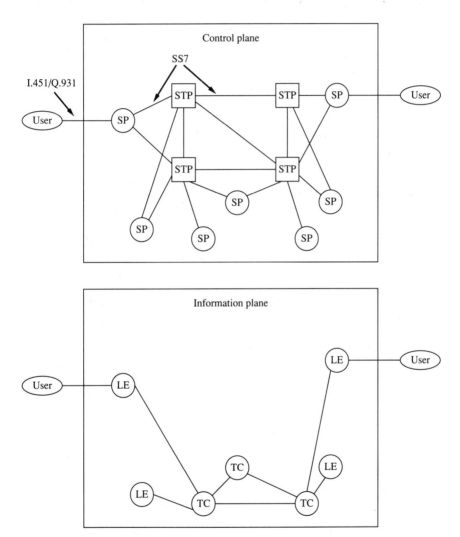

STP = Signaling transfer point
SP = Signaling point
TC = Transit center
LE = Local exchange

FIGURE 11.1 Signaling and Information Transfer Networks

consider that there are two planes of operation. The **control plane** is responsible for establishing and managing connections. These connections are requested by the user over the D channel using I.451/Q.931. The I.451/Q.931 dialogue is between the user and the local exchange. For this purpose, the local exchange acts as a signaling point, since it must convert between the dialogue with the user (I.451/Q.931) and the control messages inside the network that actually perform user-requested actions (SS7). Internal to the network, SS7 is used to establish and maintain a connection; this process may involve one or more signaling points and signal transfer points. Once a connection is set up, information is transferred from one user to another, end-to-end, in the **information plane.** A circuit is set up from the local exchange of one user to that of another, perhaps being routed through one or more other circuit-switching nodes, referred to as transit centers. All of these nodes (local exchanges, transit centers) are also signaling points, since they must be able to send and receive SS7 messages in order to establish and manage the connection.

Signaling Network Structures.   A complex network will typically have both signaling points (SP) and signal transfer points (STP). A signaling network that includes both SP and STP nodes could be considered as having a hierarchical structure in which the SPs constitute the lower level and the STPs represent the higher level. The latter may further be divided into several STP levels. Figure 11.1 is an example of a network with a single STP level.

Several parameters could influence the decisions concerning design of the network and the number of levels to be implemented:

- *STP capacities:* Includes the number of signaling links that can be handled by the STP, the signaling message transfer time, and the message throughput capacity.
- *Network performance:* Includes the number of SPs and the signaling delays.
- *Availability and reliability:* Measures the ability of the network to provide service in the face of STP failures.

When considering the network constraints in terms of performance, one STP level seems preferable. However, considerations of reliability and availability may dictate a solution with more than one level. The following guidelines are suggested by CCITT [CCIT90]:

- In a hierarchical signaling network with a single STP level:
  —Each SP that is not an STP at the same time is connected to at least two STPs.

—The meshing of STPs is as complete as possible (full mesh: every STP has a direct link to every other STP).
- In a hierarchical signaling network with two STP levels (e.g., Figure 11.2):
  —Each SP that is not an STP at the same time is connected to at least two STPs of the lower level.
  —Each STP in the lower level is connected to at least two STPs of the upper level.
  —The STPs in the upper level are fully meshed.

The two-level STP hierarchical design would be typically designed such that the lower level is dedicated to traffic in a particular geographic region of the network, and the higher level handles inter-region traffic.

One possible realization of an SS7 architecture is depicted in Figure 11.3, which shows the approach taken by AT&T [PHEL86, DONO86]. SPs and STPs are connected by links that are defined by function (Table 11.1). STPs are configured in pairs for redundancy and linked by cross (C) links. Circuit-switching nodes hook into the SS7 packet-switching network by means of access (A) links to paired STPs. Bridge (B) links are provided between STP pairs in different regions and D links between STP pairs at different hierarchical levels. The remaining link types (E and F) provide additional paths to and from circuit-swtiching nodes to reflect particular high traffic demands.

It can be seen that this design combines good performance with high availability. Between any pair of signaling points, messages must ordinarily traverse only one or two STPs. This provides low message transit delay. At the same time, the loss of a critical STP or signaling link does not prevent communication, although a somewhat longer route may need to be followed.

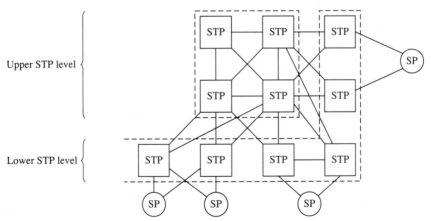

FIGURE 11.2 Example of a Hierarchical Signaling Network with Two STP Levels

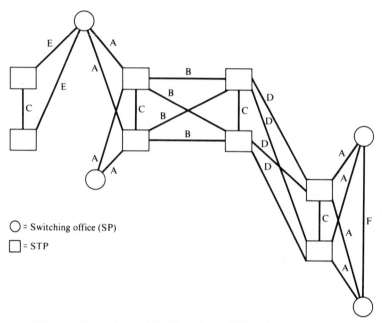

FIGURE 11.3 Example of Links Used in an SS7 Network

Protocol Architecture

So far, we have been discussing SS7 architecture in terms of the way in which functions are organized to create a packet-switching control network. The term *architecture* can also be used to refer to the structure of protocols that specify SS7. As with the open-systems interconnection (OSI) model, the SS7 standard is a layered architecture. Figure 11.4 shows the current structure of SS7 and relates it to OSI.

The SS7 architecture consists of four levels The lowest three levels of the SS7 architecture, referred to as the **message transfer part** (MTP), provide a reliable but connectionless (datagram style) service for routing messages through the SS7 network. The lowest level, **signaling data link,** corresponds to the physical layer of the OSI model and is concerned with the physical and electrical characteristics of the signaling links. These include links between STPs, between an STP and an SP, and control links between SPs. The **signaling link** level is a data link control protocol that provides for the reliable sequenced delivery of data across a signaling data link; it corresponds to layer 2 of the OSI model. The top level of the MTP, referred to as the **signaling network** level or function, provides for routing data across multiple STPs from control source to control destination. These three levels together do not provide the complete set of functions and services specified in the OSI layers 1–3, most notably in the areas of addressing and connection-oriented

TABLE 11.1   Signaling Links

Designation	Connection	Use
A	SP to STP	Provides access to the signaling network from a switching office.
B	STP to STP at same level of a hierarchy	Primary routing of messages from one SP to another via multiple STPs.
C	STP to mated STP	Communication between paired STPs; also provides alternate route around failed B links.
D	STP to STP at different levels of a hierarchy	Routing of messages up or down in a hierarchy.
E	SP to STP	Provides direct connection to non-home STP from a switching office.
F	SP to SP	Provides direct access between switching offices with a high community of interest.

service. In the 1984 version of SS7, an additional module was added, which resides in level 4, known as the **signaling connection control part** (SCCP). The SCCP and MTP together are referred to as the **network service part** (NSP). A variety of different network-layer services are defined in SCCP, to meet the needs of various users of NSP. The remainder of the modules of SS7 are considered to be at level four and comprise the various users of NSP. NSP is simply a message delivery system; the remaining parts deal with the actual contents of the messages. The **ISDN user part** (ISUP) provides for the control signaling needed in an ISDN to deal with ISDN subscriber calls and related functions. The **transaction capabilities application part** (TCAP), first introduced in 1988, provides the mechanisms for transaction-oriented (as opposed to connection-oriented) applications and functions. The **operations and maintenance application part** (O&MAP) specifies network management functions and messages related to operations and maintenance. This final area is in a preliminary state and will be expanded in future versions of the Recommendations. In addition, other modules, referred to as **application service elements** (ASE), may be defined to support other applications.

The MTP was developed prior to SCCP and was tailored to the real-time needs of telephony applications. The connectionless nature of MTP provides a low-overhead facility tailored to the requirements of telephony. In the context of ISDN, it became clear that there were other applications, such as network management, that needed the full ser-

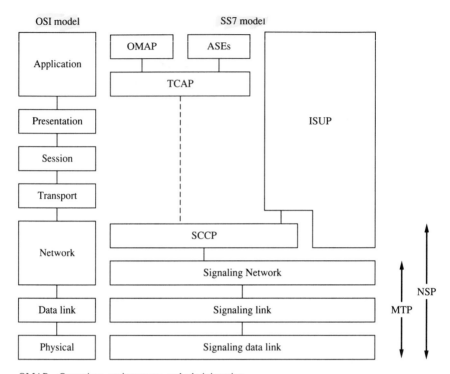

OMAP = Operations, maintenance, and administration
ASE = Application service element
TCAP = Transaction capabilities application part
ISUP = ISDN user part
SSCP = Signaling connection control part
MTP = Message transfer part
NSP = Network service part

FIGURE 11.4 SS7 Protocol Architecture

vices of the OSI network layer, such as expanded addressing capability
and reliable message transfer. SCCP was designed to meet these requirements. The resulting split in OSI network functions between the
signaling network layer and SCCP has the advantage that the higher-
overhead SCCP services can be used only when required, with the
more efficient MTP used for other applications.

11.2

SIGNALING-DATA-LINK LEVEL

The signaling data link is a full-duplex physical link dedicated to SS7
traffic. SS7 is optimized for use over 64-kbps digital links. However, the
recommendations allow for the use of circuit-switched connections to

the data link, lower speeds, and for the use of analog links with modems. The link can be routed via a satellite.

11.3
SIGNALING-LINK LEVEL

The signaling-link level corresponds to the data link control layer of the OSI model. Thus, its purpose is to turn a potentially unreliable physical link into a reliable data link. Reliability implies

- All transmitted blocks of data are delivered with no losses or duplications.
- Blocks of data are delivered in the same order in which they were transmitted.
- The receiver is capable of exercising flow control over the sender.

The last point assures that blocks of data are not lost after delivery because of buffer overflow.

Many of the techniques found in better-known data link control protocols, such as LAPD and LAPB, are used in the SS7 signaling link level. However, the formats and some of the procedures are different. The differences in some cases are matters of style rather than substance. In other cases, they arise from the performance needs of signaling that require the network to respond quickly to system- or component-failure events.

Signal Unit Formats

We begin our discussion of the signaling link protocol with a description of the formats of the basic elements of the protocol. The blocks of data transmitted at the signaling-link level are referred to as signal units. As Figure 11.5 illustrates, there are three types of signal units

- *Message signal unit (MSU):* Carries user data from level 4.
- *Level status signal unit (LSSU):* Carries control information needed at the signaling link level.
- *Fill-in signal unit (FISU):* Transmitted when no other signal units are available. This allows for a consistent error-monitoring method (described subsequently) so that faulty links can be quickly detected and removed from service even when traffic is low.

The MSU begins and ends with a **flag** field, which delimits the signal unit at both ends with the unique pattern 01111110. As with LAPB and LAPD, bit stuffing is used to avoid the appearance of the flag pattern in the body of the frame.

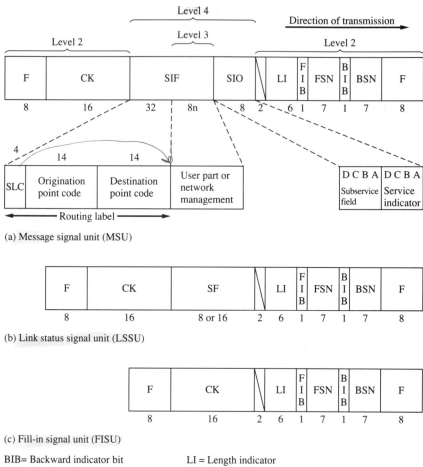

(a) Message signal unit (MSU)

(b) Link status signal unit (LSSU)

(c) Fill-in signal unit (FISU)

BIB= Backward indicator bit   LI = Length indicator
BSN = Backward sequence number   SF = Status field
CK = Check bits   SIF = Signaling information field
F = Flag   SIO = Service information octet
FIB = Forward indicator bit   SLC = Signaling link code
FSN = Forward sequence number

FIGURE 11.5 Signal Unit Formats

The next four fields are used to implement the typical flow-control and error-control mechanisms found in many layer 2 and layer 3 protocols. The flow control is the sliding-window mechanism, and error control is the go-back-N automatic-repeat-request (ARQ) mechanism. The basic operation of these mechanisms is explained in Appendix A. The **backward sequence number** (BSN) contains the number of the last MSU successfully received from the other side; this provides for piggybacked acknowledgment. Negative acknowledgment associated with this BSN is indicated by inverting the **backward indicator bit** (BIB). The new value of the BIB will be maintained in all subsequent signal units to indicate positive acknowledgment until another error is detected. When this occurs, the BIB is again inverted on the next outgoing signal unit. The **forward sequence number** (FSN) is used to uniquely number MSUs, modulo 128. The FSN of each new MSU is one more than the preceding MSU. The **forward indicator bit** (FIB) is used to indicate whether the MSU containing it is a new MSU or a retransmission due to receipt of a negative acknowledgment. For a retransmission, the FIB is inverted; all succeeding signal units maintain the same value of FIB until another negative acknowledgment is received.

The **length indicator** (LI) field specifies the length in octets of the following upper-level fields. This provides a cross-check on the closing flag. It also serves as a signal unit type indicator, since the three types of signal units carry upper-level data of different lengths. The FISU has no user data field; the LSSU has a single user data field of one octet; and the MSU has a data portion that is longer than 2 octets. Thus a value of 0 indicates an FISU; a value of 1 indicates an LSSU; and a value of 3 to 63 provides for various lengths of the MSU.

The next two fields contain information of use to higher levels and are simply treated as data to be transferred across the link. The **service information octet** (SIO) indicates the nature of the MSU. This octet consists of two subfields, the service indicator and the subservice field (Table 11.2). The service indicator specifies the user of the MTP: what type of message is being carried. The subservice field indicates whether the message relates to a national or international network. Some of the bits in the subservice field are either unused, reserved for future use, or available for national use. The **signaling information field** (SIF) contains information of interest to both the signaling network level and level 4 of SS7. This field consists of two subfields, the routing label and user data. The routing label is a 32-bit address field, containing 14-bit source and destination node addresses and a 4-bit signaling link selection field that is used to distribute the traffic among alternative routes. The second part of the SIF contains user data from some SS7 application or network management data. For example, an ISDN user part would be contained here.

The **check bits** (CK) field contains an error-detecting code used to enable the receiver to determine if there have been any transmission errors. The check bits are calculated from the remainder of the bits in the signal unit exclusive of flags, using a cyclic redundancy check (CRC). The CRC is calculated by the transmitter and inserted into the signal unit. The same calculation is performed by the receiver. If there is a discrepancy between the received CRC and the CRC calculated by the receiver, then an error is assumed. The 16-bit CRC-CCITT formula is used. This formula and the error-detection process are examined in Appendix A.

TABLE 11.2   Service Information Octet and Status Field Codes

(a) Service Information Octet

Service Indicator

DCBA	Indication
0000	Signaling network management messages
0001	Signaling network testing and maintenance messages
0010	Spare
0011	Signaling connection control part (SCCP)
0100	Telephone user part
0101	ISDN user part
0110	Data user part (call and circuit-related messages)
0111	Data user part (facility registration and cancellation)
1000 to 1111	Spare

Subservice Field

DCBA	Meaning
00XX	International network
01XX	Spare
10XX	National network
11XX	Reserved for national use

(b) Status Field

CBA	Indication
000	Out of alignment
001	Normal alignment
010	Emergency alignment
011	Out of service
100	Processor outage
101	Busy

The link status signal unit (LSSU) shares many of the same fields as the MSU. The only difference is that instead of the two user fields (SIO and SIF) in the MSU, there is a single **status field** (SF) that is carried as user data in the LSSU. Again, this field is simply treated as data to be transferred across the link. The field is used to indicate the sender's view of the actual status of the link. This information may be used for network management purposes.

Finally, the fill-in signal unit (FISU) contains no new fields. It has the same structure as the MSU and the LSSU, but with no user fields.

Operation

The key functions performed by the signaling-link protocol are flow control, error control, and error monitoring.

Flow Control.   Both flow control and error control employ a sliding-window technique (see Appendix A), in which each message signal unit (MSU) is numbered sequentially. Each new MSU is given a new forward sequence number (FSN) that is one more (modulo 128) than the preceding sequence number. Link status signal units (LSSU) and fill-in signal units (FISU) are not numbered separately but carry the FSN of the last transmitted MSU. All three types of signal units carry piggybacked acknowledgments and negative acknowledgments, in the form of backward sequence numbers (BSN). Figure 11.6 provides an example of an error-free exchange of signal units. Note that when both sides have data to send via the MSU, then the MSU is used to provide a piggybacked acknowledgment. When one side has no data to send, it transmits FISUs, which provide acknowledgment.

Flow control is provided by the LSSU. When one side is unable to keep up with the flow of data from the other side, it transmits an LSSU with a busy indication in the status field. When such an indication is received, all transmission of MSUs must cease; the busy side will notify the other side that it can resume transmission by means of another LSSU. This activity is generally invisible to the next higher level (signaling network level), which may simply notice that throughput has declined. However, if a congestion condition persists and is not reported to the signaling network level, then the performance of the entire signaling network may be degraded. If the network level is aware of a congestion problem, then control packets can be routed around the point of congestion. For this purpose, tight timer control on the allowable duration of the busy condition is imposed. Three rules specify the time constraints:

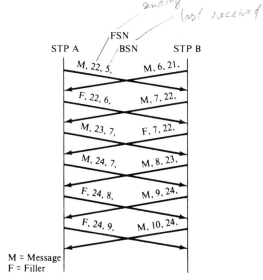

FIGURE 11.6 Error-Free Signal Unit Exchange

1. If a receiver becomes overloaded, it must send a busy signal to stop transmission from the other side. The receiver withholds acknowledgment of the MSU that triggered the congestion-control condition and of subsequent MSUs received during the busy condition. If the overload condition persists, the node must repeatedly send a busy indication at intervals of T5 time units (suggested value: 80–120 ms). The other side suspends transmission of MSUs while the busy condition persists.
2. When congestion abates at the receiver, it signals the end of the busy condition by resuming the positive acknowledgment of incoming MSUs.
3. Even if repeated busy indications are received every T5 time units, a node will report to the network level that a link is *out-of-service* after a time interval of T6 (suggested value: 3–6 seconds).

Error Control.   Two forms of error control are defined:

- *Basic method:* applies for signaling links where the one-way propagation delay is less than 15 ms.
- *Preventive cyclic retransmission method:* applies for signaling links with a one-way propagation delay greater than or equal to 15 ms; this would include signaling links established via satellite.

The **basic method** of error control is go-back-N ARQ (see Appendix A). If a node receives a negative acknowledgment in an MSU, LSSU, or FISU, it will retransmit the specified signal unit and all subsequent signal units. Figure 11.7 illustrates this algorithm.

The alternative to go-back-N for long-delay links is **preventive cyclic retransmission.** For a link with a relatively long propagation delay, each message unit is comparatively short, and the link may be idle most of the time. In such a circumstance, it is not efficient to wait for a negative acknowledgment before retransmitting. Instead, whenever a node has no MSUs to send, it automatically retransmits unacknowledged MSUs, without waiting for a positive or negative acknowledgment. Only positive acknowledgments are sent by the other side.

Because only positive acknowledgments are sent by the other side, there is a danger that a unit in error may go undetected and uncorrected for a considerable period of time. This is particularly true when the flow of traffic is heavy. In that case, one side may be so occupied sending new units that it rarely performs voluntary retransmission. Accordingly, when a predetermined number of outstanding, unacknowledged signal units exists, the transmission of new units is interrupted and the retained signal units are retransmitted cyclically until the number of unacknowledged signal units is reduced. This feature is known as the *forced retransmission procedure.*

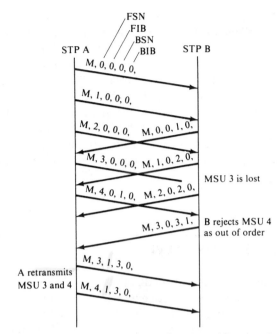

FIGURE 11.7 Transmission of MSUs with Error Correction

Error Monitoring. Two types of signaling-link error-rate monitoring are provided: signaling-unit error-rate monitor and alignment-error-rate monitor.

Signaling unit error-rate monitoring is employed while the signaling link is in service and provides a means for detecting when a link should be taken out of service due to excessive errors. A counter is maintained that is initialized to zero and manipulated based on two parameters:

T = threshold above which an error is signaled to level 3.

$1/D$ = the lowest error rate (ratio of signal unit errors to signal units) that will eventually cause an error to be signaled to level 3.

For each signal unit received in error, the counter is incremented by 1. The counter is decremented by 1 (but not below 0) for every sequence of D received signal units, whether in error or not. The link is considered unreliable whenever the count reaches the threshold T. For 64-kbps links, the parameter values are set at $T = 64$ and $D = 256$ (error rate = $1/D$ = 0.004). This technique is known as a "leaky bucket" algorithm. It will ultimately detect a consistent error rate at or above the rate of $1/D$, but it will not be triggered by an occasional surge of errors, such as might be caused by a noise burst.

Alignment error-rate monitoring is employed while the signaling link is being initialized and aligned. Alignment simply means that transmitter and receiver are aligned with respect to the opening flag field of each transmitted frame. The alignment error-rate monitoring procedure provides the criteria for rejecting a signaling link for service due to an excessive error rate. For this purpose a counter is used that is initialized to zero and is incremented by one for each signal unit received in error. If the counter exceeds a threshold before the end of an initial "proving period," the proving period is aborted. In the event of failure, the proving-period procedure may be tried up to five times. Five successive failures result in the link being declared unreliable.

11.4

SIGNALING NETWORK LEVEL

The signaling network level provides the functions and procedures for the transfer of SS7 messages between signaling points. As Figure 11.8 illustrates, the signaling network level includes functions related to message handling and functions related to network management.

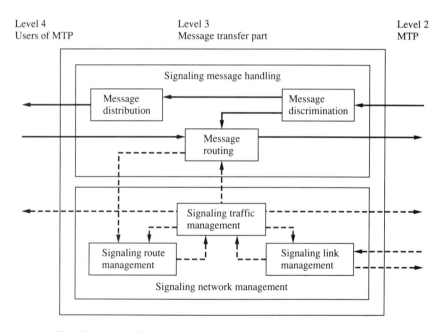

FIGURE 11.8 Message Transfer Part—Level 3

Signaling Message-handling Functions

The message-handling functions are performed at every signaling point (including signal transfer points). They are based on the parts of the message signal unit known as the routing label and the service information octet (Figure 11.5a).

The **message-handling functions** fall into three categories:

- *Discrimination:* Determines if a message is at its destination or is to be relayed to another node. This decision is based on analysis of the destination code in the routing label of the message. If this is the destination, the signal unit is delivered to the distribution function; otherwise, it is delivered to the routing function. The discrimination function is only needed in signal transfer points (STP).
- *Routing:* Determines the signaling link to be used in forwarding a message. The message may have been received from the discrimination function or from a local level 4 entity.
- *Distribution:* Determines the user part to which a message should be delivered. The decision is based on analysis of the service indicator portion of the service information octet.

The routing decision is based on the value of the signaling link selection (SLS) field, which is assigned by a user part in level 4. For a given source/destination pair, several alternate routes may be possible; the value of the SLS field specifies which particular route is to be followed. With a 4-bit field, a total of 16 different routes through the network may be defined. These different routes are, in effect, different internal virtual circuits. In general, all of the control signals associated with a single call will follow the same route; this guarantees that they will arrive in sequence. However, the MTP needs to distribute traffic uniformly. This requirement can be satisfied if the user part varies the route selection from one call to the next.

Signaling Network Management Functions

The other main component of the signaling network level is **signaling network management.** The main objective of this component is to overcome link degradations (failures or congestion). To meet this objective, the signaling management function is concerned with monitoring the status of each link, with dictating alternate routes to overcome link degradation and communicating the alternate routes to the affected nodes, and with recovering from the loss of messages due to link failure. The goal for SS7 is no more than 10 minutes of unavailability per year for any route. This goal is achieved through redundancy of links and dynamic rerouting.

This emphasis on the internal management of the network is rare; virtually all other network protocols make no mention of network management. In most cases, it is preterable to leave network management details to the provider, so that the provider can pursue the most cost-effective approach and be responsive to changes both in customer expectations and advances in technology. However, in the case of SS7, there are strong reasons for the emphasis on network management:

1. The function being specified is critical. The performance of a network's control signaling architecture affects all subscribers to the network.
2. The various networks involved must support international traffic. Degradations in one nation's signaling system will have repercussions beyond that nation's borders. Thus, some international agreement on the degree of reliability of national networks is indicated.
3. Recovery and restoration actions may involve multiple networks (e.g., in the case of international calls). If SS7 did not include failure and congestion recovery procedures, it would be necessary for the administration of each public network to enter into bilateral agreements with a number of other networks.

As Figure 11.8 indicates, signaling network management functions fall into three categories:

- Signaling traffic management.
- Signaling link management.
- Signaling route management.

Table 11.3 summarizes the functions performed in each category. As can be seen, the signaling network management component as a whole is quite complex. In the remainder of this section, we attempt only to give the reader a feel for the kinds of procedures contained within each category.

The functions listed in Table 11.3 are actually performed by the exchange of level 3 messages between signaling points. These messages are carried in the signaling information field (SIF) of an MSU (Figure 11.5a). Each message consists of an 8-bit field that identifies the particular message and a message value of 0, 8, 16, or 24 bits.

All of the procedures relating to signaling network management involve the monitoring and control of the status of various entities, including signaling links, signaling routes, signaling points, and signaling route sets. This latter entity refers to a collection of alternative routes between a source and destination. Table 11.4 summarizes the status values that each of these entities may have.

Signaling Traffic Management. Signaling traffic management is used to divert signaling traffic, without causing message loss or duplication,

TABLE 11.3 Signaling Network Management Procedures

Signaling Traffic Management

Changeover
Divert traffic to one or more alternative links in the event of a link unavailability.

Changeback
Reestablish traffic on a signaling link that becomes available.

Forced rerouting
Divert traffic to an alternate route when a route becomes unavailable.

Controlled rerouting
Divert traffic to a route that has been made available.

Signaling point restart
When a signaling point becomes available and when signaling traffic is diverted to or through this point, update the network routing status and control.

Management inhibiting
Link is made unavailable to user-part-generated traffic for maintenance or testing purposes.

Signaling traffic flow control
Limit signaling traffic at its source when the signaling network is not capable of transferring all signaling traffic offered by the user because of network failures or congestion.

Signaling Link Management

Signaling link activation, restoration, and deactivation
Restore failed links, activate new links, and deactivate links.

Link set activation
Activate a link set not having any links in service.

Automatic allocation of signaling terminals and signaling data links
Allocate terminals to links.

Signaling Route Management

Transfer-controlled procedure
Performed at an STP in the case of link congestion. Message sources are told to stop sending messages having a congestion priority less than the congestion level of the link.

Transfer-prohibited procedure
Performed at an STP to inform adjacent signaling points that they must no longer route to a particular destination via this STP.

Transfer-allowed procedure
Informs adjacent signaling points that routing to a given destination is now normal.

Transfer-restricted procedure
If possible, adjacent signaling points should no longer route to a particular destination via this STP.

Cont.

TABLE 11.3   **Signaling Network Management Procedures** *(continued)*

Signaling Route Management

Signaling-route-set test procedure

Used by signaling points receiving transfer-prohibited and transfer-restricted messages in order to recover the signaling route information that may not have been received due to some failure.

Signaling-route-set congestion test procedure

Used to update the congestion status associated with a route toward a particular destination.

from unavailable signaling links or routes to one or more alternative signaling links or routes, or to reduce traffic in the case of congestion.

As an example of the functions performed in the category of signaling traffic management, let us consider the changeover procedure. The objective of the changeover procedure is to ensure that signaling traffic carried by a link that becomes unavailable is diverted to the alternative signaling link(s) as quickly as possible while avoiding message loss, duplication, or missequencing.

Figure 11.9 shows an example of the changeover procedure for messages traveling along a route between signaling points A and D. Changeover is initiated when a signaling link is recognized as unavailable. This might occur, for example, if the link error-rate monitoring function of layer 2 reports the failure. The following actions are then performed:

1. Transmission and acceptance of MSUs on the concerned signaling link are terminated.
2. Alternative links are determined to construct an alternative route.
3. Those messages in the retransmission buffer of the unavailable link that have not been received by the far end are identified.
4. The identified messages are transferred to the transmission buffer of the alternate link.

Steps 3 and 4 are accomplished in the following way. A signaling point that recognizes the unavailability of a link sends a changeover order (COO) message to the remote signaling point over some available alternate route. The message value field contains the forward sequence number of the last message accepted from the unavailable signaling link. When the other side receives the COO, it responds with a changeover acknowledgment (COA) message, which contains the forward sequence number of its last accepted MSU. The two sides are now able to resume the exchange of MSUs containing user-part information over an alternate route, maintaining the proper sequence with no losses or

TABLE 11.4 Status Values for the Signaling Network Level

Signaling Link Status	
Available	Messages may be transmitted over this link.
Unavailable	
Failed	Unable to perform transmission function within acceptable performance parameters.
Deactivated	Removed from service by signaling link management or external management function.
Blocked	Processor outage exists at one end of the link.
Inhibited	Link unavailable to user-part-generated traffic.
Signaling Route Status	
Available	Signaling traffic toward a particular destination can be transferred via this signaling transfer point.
Restricted	Signaling traffic toward a particular destination is being transferred with some difficulty via this signaling transfer point.
Unavailable	Signaling traffic toward a particular destination cannot be transferred via this signaling transfer point.
Signaling Point Status	
Available	Signaling traffic may be transferred to this signaling point.
Unavailable	Signaling traffic may not be transferred to this signaling point.
Signaling Route Set Status	
Congested	Indicates that the buffer occupancy rate of a link exceeds a given threshold.
Uncongested	The buffer occupancy rate of a link is within predetermined limits.

duplications. The new route is decided by the signaling message-handling function of the two endpoints.

In our example, traffic between signaling points A and D is initially carried via signaling point B. When the link between A and B becomes unavailable, A sends a COO message to D via signal transfer point C. C responds along the same route with a COA. Subsequently, all MSUs follow the route through C.

Signaling Link Management. Signaling link management is used to restore failed signaling links, activate new signaling links, and deactivate aligned signaling links. There is a basic set of mandatory functions that perform signaling link management for links directly connected to a signaling point. There are additional, optional, functions that allow

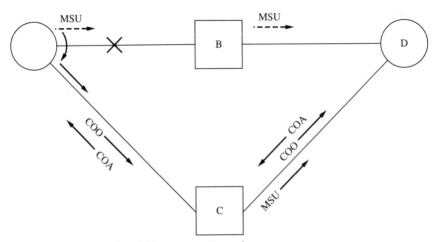

FIGURE 11.9 Example of Changeover Procedure

for more efficient use of signaling equipment when signaling terminal devices have switched access to signaling data links.

Signaling Route Management.   Signaling route management is used to distribute information about the signaling network status in order to block or unblock signaling routes.

As an example of the functions performed by signaling route management, we consider the signaling-route-set congestion procedure. This procedure is used by STPs to control congestion. Whereas congestion occurring between signaling points can easily be handled by flow control at level 2, when congestion occurs on a link emanating from an STP, the source SPs that send messages through that link must be controlled.

Each outgoing link of each signaling transfer point has a transmit buffer with three threshold levels: congestion onset (T), congestion abatement (A), and discard (D), where $A < T < D$. The discard threshold is equivalent to the buffer capacity. The set of routes through the link in question is either congested or uncongested, depending on the buffer occupancy history. When the link is uncongested and the arrival of incoming message units causes the portion of the buffer that is filled to exceed T, then the link is considered to be congested, and a choking message, the transfer controlled (TFC) message, is sent to the source of the node that caused the threshold to be reached and to the source of all subsequent messages while the link is congested. When the buffer occupancy level decreases below A, transmission of choking messages ceases and the link is considered uncongested. Thus, the status of the link when the occupancy of the buffer is between A and T can be in either state, depending on buffer occupancy history. This is a "hyster-esis" effect, which prevents frequent changes of the link status.

When a signaling point receives a choking message, it stops gener-ating messages for the route involved. Two timers are used to determine when to resume normal routing. When a node receives a choking message, it starts a timer with a duration of T_{15} seconds. When the timer expires, the node sends a signaling route set congestion test (RCT) message to the same destination along the normal route and waits for a time period T_{16} to see if another choking message is returned in response to this RCT message. If a choking message is received within T_{16}, the T_{15} timer is reset and the process begins again. If T_{16} expires, then the node assumes that the congestion has abated and resumes normal routing.

Figure 11.10 illustrates the operation of the algorithm at a signaling point. At time $t = 0$, the SP receives a TFC message. The SP stops generating user-part messages for the indicated destination and starts the T_{15} timer. When this timer expires, the SP sends an RCT message and prepares to wait for time T_{16}. Before this timer expires, another TFC message is received, and the process begins again. In this example, after the second RCT message, timer T_{16} expires and the SP resumes normal transmission.

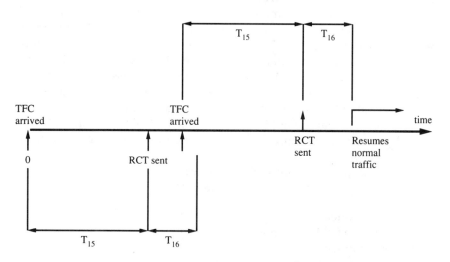

TFC = Transfer controlled message
RCT = Signaling route set congestion test message
T_{15} = Timer: waiting to start signaling route set congestion test
T_{16} = Timer: waiting for route set congestion status update

FIGURE 11.10   Example Behavior of an SP tor the SS7 Congestion Control Scheme [LEE89]

11.5

SIGNALING CONNECTION CONTROL PART

The signaling connection control part (SCCP) was developed as it became apparent that SS7 would have to support more than signaling and needed more explicit addressing and more sophisticated services between remote signaling points. The signaling network level does not provide all of the routing and addressing capabilities that the OSI model dictates for the network layer. As an example, the message distribution function provides only a limited addressing capability. For newer user-part applications, a more complex specification of the user of a message at a node is necessary; this can be provided by the signaling connection control part (SCCP). The SCCP enhances the connectionless sequenced transmission service provided by the MTP, to meet the needs of those user parts requiring enriched connectionless or connection-oriented service to transfer signaling information between nodes. Classic circuit-switched telephone call-related signaling does not use SCCP. For this application and those user parts for which MTP suffices, the extra overhead of SCCP can be avoided.

Thus, the enhancements provided by SCCP over those available in just the message transfer part are in the areas of addressing and message transfer services. The **addressing** capabilities of SCCP extend those found in MTP, which is limited to delivering a message to a specified node and using a four-bit service indicator (Table 11.2a) to distribute messages within a node. SCCP supplements this capability by providing addressing that uses destination point codes (DPC; see Figure 11.5) plus subsystem numbers (SSN). The SSN is local addressing information that identifies each of the SCCP users at a node. Another addressing enhancement is the ability to address messages with global titles, such as dialed digits, that are not in a form usable by MTP for routing. SCCP provides a mapping facility for translating global titles into an address of the form DPC + SSN.

SCCP also provides enhanced **message transfer services,** two connectionless and two connection-oriented. The four classes are

0—Basic connectionless.
1—Sequenced (MTP) connectionless class.
2—Basic connection-oriented.
3—Flow-control connection-oriented.

In Class 0 service, a user provides a block of data, referred to as a network service data unit (NSDU), to SCCP for delivery to a user at another node. The NSDUs are transported independently and may be delivered out of sequence. This is a pure connectionless or datagram service.

For Class 1 service, Class 0 is enhanced with the ability to specify that a particular stream of NSDUs should be delivered in sequence. SCCP does this by assigning a sequence number to each member NSDU and giving all messages in the stream the same signaling link code (Figure 11.5).

The remaining two classes of service operate over logical connections, called signaling connections. These connections are equivalent to virtual circuits through the signaling network. Each logical connection is given a unique signaling link code. Class 2 provides this basic connection-oriented service.

For Class 3 service, Class 2 is enhanced with the ability to perform flow control over a logical connection. Also, the detection of message loss and mis-sequencing is provided. In the event of lost or mis-sequenced messages, the signaling connection is reset and notification is given to higher layers.

As with most standards at the various layers of the OSI model, SCCP can be specified in terms of the services that it provides to higher layers and the protocol between peer SCCP entities in different nodes. Both of these aspects are summarized in Figure 11.11, which shows the internal structure of SCCP, which is implemented as a set of protocol elements, and the interface to upper and lower layers, which is defined by a service specification. The structure consists of four functional blocks:

1. *Connection-oriented control:* Controls the establishment and release of signaling connections and provides for data transfer on signaling connections.
2. *Connectionless control:* Provides for connectionless transfer of data units.
3. *Management:* Provides capabilities beyond those of MTP to handle the congestion or failure of either the SCCP user or the signaling route to the SCCP user. With this capability, SCCP can route messages to backup systems in the event failures prevent routing to the primary system.
4. *Routing control:* Upon receipt of a message from MTP or from functions (1) or (2), SCCP routing provides the necessary routing functions to either forward the message to MTP for transfer or pass the message to (1) or (2). A message whose "called party address" is a local user is passed to (1) or (2), while one destined for a remote user is forwarded to the MTP for transfer to a distant SCCP user.

We examine these two aspects of SCCP in turn.

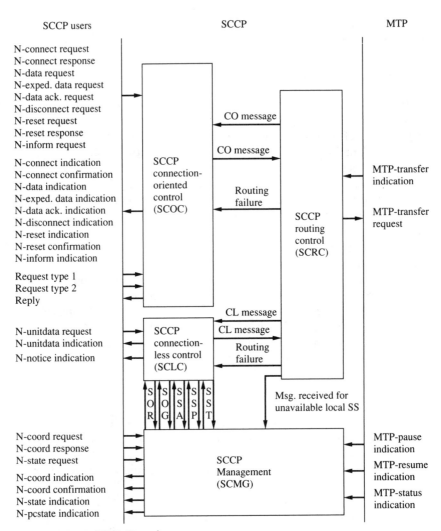

FIGURE 11.11 SCCP Overview

SCCP Services

As with any protocol service, SCCP can be expressed in terms of primitives, which can be viewed as commands or procedure calls, with parameters. Each type of primitive appears in one or more variations (request, indication, response, confirm), depending on the requirements of the service. See Appendix 11B for a discussion of the standard conventions used for primitives and parameters.

Connection-oriented Services. The connection-oriented service provided by SCCP is based on the OSI network service, which is defined in ISO 8348 and CCITT X.213.[1] Key characteristics of the network service, as listed in the standard, are

- *Independence of underlying communications facility:* Network service users need not be aware of the details of the subnetwork facilities used.
- *End-to-end transfer:* All routing and relaying are performed by the network layer and are not of concern to the network service user.
- *Transparency:* The network service does not restrict the content, format, or coding of the user data.
- *Quality-of-service selection:* The network service user has some ability to request a given quality of service.
- *User addressing:* A system of addressing is used that allows network service users to refer unambiguously to one another.

Table 11.5 lists the primitives and parameters for the connection-oriented service; the parameters are defined in Table 11.6. Figure 11.12 displays the sequences in which primitives may be used.

Connection establishment begins with a user request, contained in a N-CONNECT.request primitive. In addition to specifying the called and calling user, the primitive can request certain services to be provided for the requested connection:

- *Receipt confirmation selection:* Ordinarily, the network service will not confirm that data have been delivered to the other side; it is assumed that the data are delivered. However, the user may request that explicit confirmation be provided.
- *Expedited data selection:* The user may also request that an expedited data service be available.
- *Quality of service:* The user may specify two quality-of-service parameters. First, the user proposes one of the four classes to be used for the connection. If appropriate, the user also proposes a flow-control window size.

The remainder of the connection establishment process involves confirming the setup of a connection and the negotiation of quality-of-service parameters. The negotiation proceeds as follows:

1. The calling user specifies Class 3 or Class 2 in the quality-of-service parameter of the N-CONNECT.request. If Class 3 is selected, a flow-control window size is specified.
2. The SCCP at the calling user's node, at any intermediate STPs, or at the called user's node may downgrade a Class 3 request to a Class 2 request. If Class 3 was requested and is not downgraded, any of these nodes may reduce the window size.

---

[1] ISO 8348: Network Service Definition. The text of X.213 is virtually identical to that of ISO 8348.

TABLE 11.5   Network Service Primitives for Connection-Oriented Services

Primitives		Parameters
Generic Name	**Specific Name**	
N-CONNECT	Request Indication Response Confirmation	Called address Calling address Responding address Receipt confirmation selection Expedited data selection Quality of service parameter set User data Connection identification
N-DATA	Request Indication	Confirmation request User data Connection identification
N-EXPEDITED DATA	Request Indication	User data Connection identification
N-DATA ACKNOWLEDGE (for further study)	Request Indication	Connection identification
N-DISCONNECT	Request Indication	Originator Reason User data Responding address Connection identification
N-RESET	Request Indication Response Confirmation	Originator Reason Connection identification

TABLE 11.6   Parameters for SCCP Service Primitives

Affected DPC
  Identifies a signaling point that is failed, congested, or allowed.

Affected subsystem
  An address that identifies a user that is failed, withdrawn, congested, or allowed.

Called address
  Identifies the destination of a communication. Address may be a global title, subsystem number, or signaling point code.

Calling address
  Identifies the destination of a communication. Address may be a global title, subsystem number, or signaling point code.

Confirmation request
Used in an N-DATA primitive to indicate the need to confirm the receipt of the N-DATA primitive by the remote SCCP user.

Connection identification
Used to allocate a primitive to a certain connection.

Expedited data selection
May be used to indicate during setup whether expedited data can be transferred via the connection. A negotiation will be performed between SCCP users, local and remote.

Originator
Indicates the source of a reset or disconnect and can be any of the following:
- Network service provider.
- Network service user.
- Undefined.

Quality-of-service parameter set
Parameters used during call setup to negotiate the protocol class for the connection and, if applicable, the flow-control window size.

Reason
Gives information about the cause of a reset, disconnect, or connection refusal.

Reason for return
Identifies the reason why a message was not able to be delivered to its final destination.

Receipt confirmation selection
Indicates the use/availability of the receipt confirmation service. The need for such a service is a subject for further study.

Responding address
Indicates to which destination the connection has been established or refused.

Return option
Used in the connectionless service to determine the handling of messages encountering transport problems. The possible values are discard message on error and return message on error.

Signaling point status
Used to inform a user of the status of an affected DPC. Values are inaccessible, congested, and accessible.

Sequence control
For connectionless service, indicates to the SCCP whether the user wishes the service sequence guaranteed or sequence not guaranteed.

Subsystem multiplicity indicator
Identifies the number of replications of a subsystem.

User data
Data passed transparently by SCCP from one end user to the other.

User status
Used to inform an SCCP user of the status of an affected subsystem. Possible values are in service and out of service.

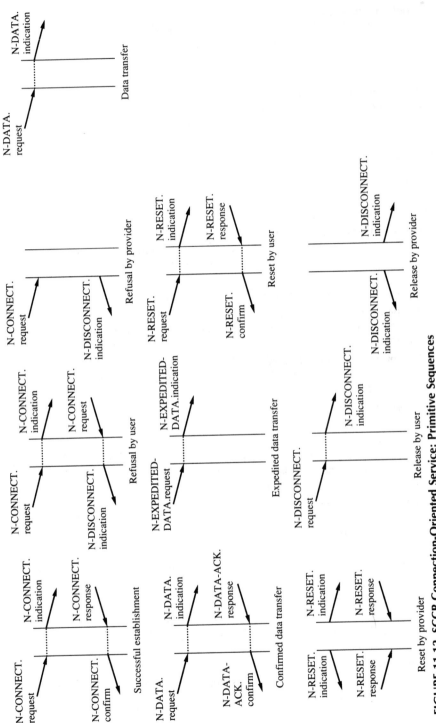

FIGURE 11.12 SCCP Connection-Oriented Service: Primitive Sequences

3. An N-CONNECT.indication is issued to the called user with the resulting quality of service.
4. The called user responds with an N-CONNECT.response. The called user may downgrade the class or reduce the flow-control window size.
5. The final quality of service is conveyed to the calling user in an N-CONNECT.confirm.

The preceding actions describe a successful connection establishment. A connection request may also be denied, in one of several ways. When the called user receives the N-CONNECT.indication, it may not have resources available for the call. In that case, the called user responds with an N-DISCONNECT.request. This result in an N-DISCONNECT.indication being passed to the calling user, which is a refusal of the request. Similarly, if the network cannot support the new connection, an N-DISCONNECT.indication is issued by SCCP to the calling user.

Once a logical connection is set up between two SCCP users, the **data transfer** phase is entered. User data are conveyed in an N-DATA primitive. Note that there are only request and indication primitives defined. The reason that there is no need for a confirmation back to the user that sent the data is that the connection-oriented service guarantees to deliver all data in the proper order, with no losses. However, if the user requires acknowledgment, then the N-DATA-ACKNOWLEDGE primitives are used.

The N-EXPEDITED-DATA primitive may be used if previously requested for this connection. The expedited data servive provides a means for expediting the delivery of occasional urgent data. Examples are an interrupt, an alarm, or an abrupt connection termination at a higher layer. The network service will endeavor to have the expedited data transmitted across the network as rapidly as possible, perhaps overtaking some previously transmitted ordinary data. Normal flow-control mechanisms are bypassed.

The N-RESET primitive can occur with Class 3 transfer. N-RESET overrides all other activities and causes SCCP to start a re-initialization procedure for sequence numbering. During this process, some outstanding data units may be lost. SCCP may need to perform a reset if for some reason it becomes out of synchronization with the other side. A user may need to perform a reset because it wishes to abort the current exchange without losing the connection.

The N-DISCONNECT primitive is used for the **connection release** phase and also for connection refusal during the connection establishment phase. Parameters are included to notify the reason for connection release/refusal and the initiator of the release/refusal procedure.

Connectionless Services. The connectionless service provided by SCCP is based on the OSI connectionless network service, which is defined in ISO 8348 and CCITT X.213. Table 11.7 lists the primitives and parameters for the connectionless service; the parameters are defined in Table 11.6.

The connectionless service provides the SCCP user with the ability to transfer signaling messages via the signaling network without the setup of a signaling connection. The basic enhancement provided over the MTP service is the ability to map the called address to the signaling point code of the MTP service.

The transfer of data is achieved with the N-UNITDATA primitives. Under certain conditions of congestion and unavailability of subsystems and/or signaling points, connectionless messages could be discarded instead of being delivered. If the user wishes to be informed of the nondelivery of messages, the return option parameter is set to "return message on error" in the N-UNITDATA.request. The sequence control parameter is used to select one of two data transfer modes:

- *With sequence control:* MTP guarantees an in-sequence delivery of messages that contain the same signaling link code (SLC). The SCCP user employs this service by including the sequence control parameter. SCCP will put the same SLC code into the primitive to MTP for all primitives from the SCCP user with the same sequence control value.
- *Without sequence control:* SCCP inserts SLCs randomly, or with respect to the load sharing within the signaling network.

If the user has selected the return message option, the SCCP will use the N-NOTICE primitive to notify the originating user of a failure to deliver a message.

TABLE 11.7   Primitives and Parameters of the Connectionless Service

Primitives		Parameters
Generic Name	**Specific Name**	
N-UNITDATA	Request Indication	Called address Calling address Sequence control* Return option* User data
N-NOTICE	Indication	Called address Calling address Reason for return User data

* An integration of the parameter sequence control/return option into the quality-of-service parameter set is for further study.

SCCP Management.   Table 11.8 lists the primitives and parameters for SCCP management; the parameters are defined in Table 11.6. SCCP management is used to maintain network performances by rerouting or throttling traffic in the event of failure or congestion in the network. These procedures apply to both connection-oriented and connectionless services of the SCCP.

The N-COORD primitive is used to coordinate the withdrawal of one of the SCCP users when multiple replications of a user at a node are employing SCCP. This informs SCCP that a particular user is no longer available.

The two N-STATE primitives allow a user and SCCP to exchange status information. The N-PCSTATE primitive is used to inform a user about the status of a signaling point.

SCCP Protocol

The SCCP protocol is subdivided into four protocol classes, one for each SCCP service class:

0—Basic connectionless.
1—Sequenced (MTP) connectionless class.
2—Basic connection-oriented.
3—Flow-control connection-oriented.

In effect, SCCP consists of four distinct services, each with its own protocol. The formats and many of the procedures are shared among the four protocol classes.

Protocol Formats.   The SCCP protocol makes use of 16 types of messages, which are listed and defined in Table 11.9. Table 11.10 shows the mandatory (M) and optional (O) parameters associated with each message, with the exception of management-related messages.

TABLE 11.8   Primitives and Parameters of the SCCP Management

| Primitives | | Parameters |
Generic Name	Specific Name	
R-COORD	Request Indication Response Confirmation	Affected subsystem Subsystem multiplicity indicator
N-STATE	Request Indication	Affected subsystem User status Subsystem multiplicity indicator
N-PCSTATE	Indication	Affected DPC Signaling point status

TABLE 11.9   SCCP Messages

Connection-Oriented (Protocol Classes 2 and 3)

Connection request (CR)
Sent by a calling SCCP to a called SCCP to request the setting up of a signaling connection between the two entities.

Connection confirm (CC)
Sent by the called SCCP to the calling SCCP to indicate to the calling SCCP that it has performed the setup of the signaling connection.

Connection refused (CREF)
Sent by the called SCCP or an intermediate node SCCP to indicate to the calling SCCP that the connection setup has been refused.

Data form 1 (DT1)
Sent by either end of a signaling connection to pass transparently SCCP user data between two SCCP nodes. Protocol class 2 only.

Data form 2 (DT2)
Sent by either end of a signaling connection to pass transparently SCCP user data between two SCCP nodes and to acknowledge messages flowing in the other direction. Protocol class 3 only.

Data acknowledgment (AK)
Controls the window flow-control mechanism. Protocol class 3 only.

Expedited data (ED)
Functions as a DT2 message but includes the ability to bypass the flow-control mechanism that has been selected for the data transfer phase. Protocol class 3 only.

Expedited data acknowledgment (EA)
Used to acknowledgment an EA message. Protocol class 3 only.

Inactivity test (IT)
May be sent periodically by either end of a signaling connection to check if this connection is active at both ends.

Protocol data unit error (ERR)
Sent on detection of any protocol errors.

Released (RLSD)
Indicates that the sending SCCP wants to release a signaling connection and that the associated resources at the sending SCCP have been brought into the disconnect pending condition. It also indicates that the receiving node should release the connection and any other associated resources as well.

Release complete (RLC)
Sent in response to a RLSD to acknowledge the RLSD and to indicate that the appropriate procedures have been completed.

Reset request (RSR)
Indicates that the sending SCCP wants to initiate a reset procedure (re-initialization of sequence numbers) with the receiving SCCP.

Reset confirm (RSC)
Sent in response to an RSR to acknowledge the RSRC and to indicate that the appropriate procedures have been completed.

Connectionless (Protocol Classes 0 and 1)

Unitdata (UDT)
Used by an SCCP to send data in connectionless mode.

Unitdata service (UDTS)
Indicates to the originating SCCP that a UDT it sent cannot be delivered to its destination.

Subsystem (User) Management

Subsystem allowed (SSA)
Sent to concerned destinations to inform those destinations that a subsystem that was formerly prohibited is now allowed.

Subsystem out-of-service request (SOR)
Allows subsystems to go out of service without degrading the performance of the network. When a subsystem wishes to go out of service, the request is transferred by means of an SOR between the SCCP at the subsystem's node and the SCCP at the duplicate subsystem's node.

Subsystem out-of-service grant (SOG)
Sent in response to an SOR to the requesting SCCP if both the requested SCCP and the backup of the affected subsystem agree to the request.

Subsystem prohibited (SSP)
Sent to concerned destinations to inform SCCP management at those destinations of the failure of a subsystem.

Subsystem status test (SST)
Sent to verify the status of a subsystem marked prohibited.

Figure 11.13 shows the format of an SCCP message. The routing label identifies a particular signaling connection for connection-oriented protocols (class 2 and 3) and may be used for sequencing and load leveling for connectionless protocols. The message type field identifies one of the 16 messages. The remainder of the message carries the parameters for the given message type. Some of these parameters are mandatory (must be included with every instance of the message) and some are optional. Of the mandatory parameters, some are of fixed length and can be represented in a compact form that consists of the value of the parameter. The remaining mandatory parameters and all of the optional parameters are of variable length. Hence, the length of each such parameter must also be included. In the case of optional parameters, each parameter must also be labeled, since it is not known ahead of time if the parameter is included.

Connectionless Data Transfer.   For Classes 0 and 1, only two message types are used: unitdata (UDT) and unitdata service (UDTS). SCCP constructs and sends a UDT in response to an N-UNITDATA.request

TABLE 11.10   Inclusion of Fields in Messages

Parameter Field	CR	CC	CREF	RLSD	RLC	DT1	DT2	AK	ED	EA	RSR	RSC	ERR	IT	UDT	UDTS
Destination local reference number		m	m	m	m	m	m	m	m	m	m	m	m	m		
Source local reference number	m	m		m	m						m	m	m	m		
Called party address	m	o	o												m	m
Calling party address	o														m	m
Protocol class	m	m												m	m	
Segmenting/reassembling						m										
Receive sequence number								m								
Sequencing/segmenting							m							m*		
Credit	o	o						m						m*		
Release cause				m												
Return cause																m
Reset cause											m					
Error cause													m			
User data	o	o	o	o		m	m		m						m	m
Refusal cause			m													
End of optional parameters	o	o	o	o												

* Information in these parameter fields is ignored if the protocol class parameter indicates class 2.

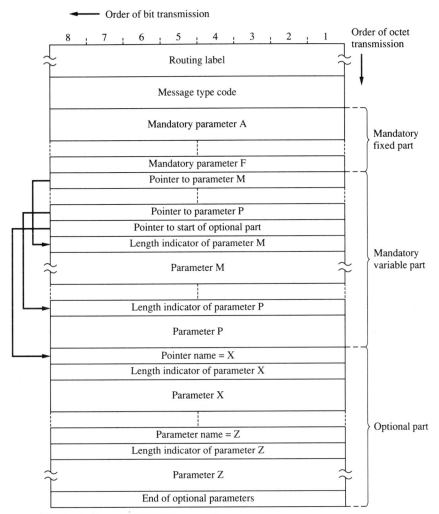

◄──── Order of bit transmission

FIGURE 11.13 General SCCP Message Format

from an SCCP user. The way in which the UDT is "sent" is to pass it down as MTP user data to MTP.

For Class 0 operation, SCCP translates the called address parameter in the N-UNITDATA.request into a destination point code (DPC) that can be understood by MTP. It selects a route through the network and requests that MTP transmit the message. If the message is successfully delivered to the called SCCP, this triggers an N-UNITDATA.indication up to the destination SCCP user. If the message is discarded, and if the return option has been selected, a UDTS message is returned to the calling SCCP, which in turn generates an N-NOTICE.indication.

For Class 1 operation, all of the procedures in the previous paragraph are followed. In addition, the sequence control parameter in the N-UNITDATA.request is used by SCCP. SCCP uses the same signaling link code for all messages that are to be sequenced.

Connection Establishment.   For connection-oriented service, the connection establishment phase requires, at minimum, the exchange of a CR and a CC message.

The purpose of this phase is to establish a signaling connection with an agreed protocol class, and if Class 3 is selected, an agreed flow-control window size.

The operation begins when an SCCP user issues an N-CONNECT.request. SCCP generates a corresponding CR message with the appropriate called party address. The protocol class parameter in the message indicates the requested protocol class (Class 2 or 3). If Class 3 is selected, the credit parameter indicates the requested flow-control window size. The source local reference number is the way in which this logical connection is to be identified at the calling end; it is equivalent to an X.25 virtual-circuit number.

At the called end, SCCP receives the CR message and issues an N-CONNECT.indication to the appropriate user. If the call is accepted, an N-CONNECT.response is issued back to SCCP. SCCP then returns a CC message with the appropriate protocol class and flow-control parameters. When this message is received at the calling SCCP, an N-CONNECT.confirm is issued to the calling user. If the call is not accepted, an N-DISCONNECT.request is issued by the called user, which generates a CREF message, which ultimately generates an N-DISCONNECT.indication to the calling user.

Connection-oriented Data Transfer.   Normal data transfer over a signaling connection is accomplished using data form 1 (DT1) or data form 2 (DT2) messages for Classes 2 and 3, respectively. Let us consider DT1 first.

Each DT1 may contain all of the user data, the NSDU, contained in an N-DATA.request. Alternatively, if the DT1 would exceed the maximum message size by transferring all of the NSDU, SCCP may segment the NSDU and send it out as a sequence of DT1 messages. In that case, each member of the sequence except the last has the segmenting/reassembly parameter set to one, to indicate that more data follow. The last message in the sequence has this parameter set to 0. When all of the data have arrived, the destination SCCP passes the NSDU up to the user in an N-DATA.indication.

For Class 3 operation, the DT2 message is used. In this case, the sequencing/segmenting parameter is used, which has the following components:

- P(S): a seven-bit send sequence number.
- P(R): a seven-bit receive sequence number.
- M: a one-bit more indicator.

The P(S) and P(R) fields operate the same way as send and receive sequence numbers in LAPD and X.25 to provide flow control. The M bit is used for segmentation and reassembly.

For Class 3, a flow-control scheme based on credit allocation is used. The initial credit is set in the CR and CC messages. Subsequent credit is granted in the AK message.

The credit allocation scheme decouples acknowledgment from flow control, in contrast to fixed sliding-window flow-control schemes, such as X.25 and LAPD, where the two mechanisms are coupled. The credit allocation scheme provides a greater degree of control over data flow. In a message scheme, a message may be acknowledged without granting new credit, and vice versa. Figure 11.14 illustrates the protocol (compare Figure A.3 in Appendix A). For simplicity, we show a data flow in one direction only. In this example, too, messages are numbered sequentially modulo 8 for simplicity. Initially, through the connection establishment process, the sending and receive sequence numbers are synchronized and A is granted a credit allocation of 7. A advances the trailing edge of its window each time that it transmits and advances the leading edge when it is granted additional credit.

Expedited data transfer uses the ED and EA messages. Only one ED may be outstanding at a time. The sender must receive an EA before sending another ED.

Connection Termination. A connection is terminated by the exchange of RLSD and RLC messages.

11.6

ISDN USER PART

The ISDN user part (ISUP) of Signaling System No. 7 defines the functions, procedures, and interexchange signaling information flows required to provide circuit-switched services and associated user facilities for voice and nonvoice calls over ISDN. We can state three requirements for the ISUP:

- It must rely on the message transfer part or network service part of SS7 for the transmission of messages.
- Its design must be flexible to accommodate future enhancements of ISDN capabilities.

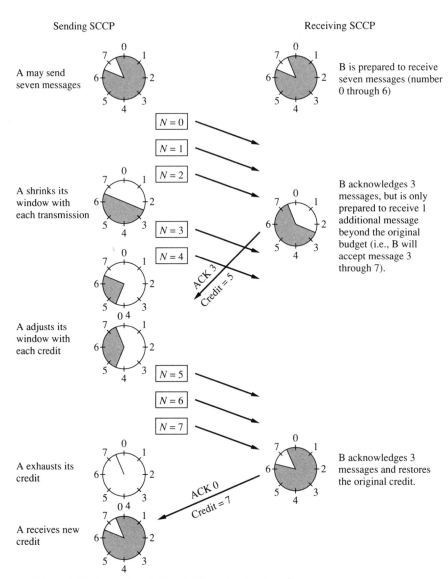

FIGURE 11.14 Example of Credit Allocation Protocol

- It must interwork with the user-network I.451/Q.931 call-control protocol.

This last point highlights the distinction between the ISUP, which is defined in CCITT Recommendations Q.761–Q.764, and I.451/Q.931. The call-control protocol defined in I.451/Q.931 refers to common-channel control-signaling facilities open to use by the ISDN subscriber. I.451/Q.931 is used by the subscriber to set up calls to other subscribers, with associated user facilities. ISUP refers to signaling facilities employed by the network provider on behalf of the ISDN user. Thus, ISDN communicates with the ISDN user (subscriber) via I.451/Q.931 for the purpose of call control and uses ISUP internal to the network to implement subscriber call-control requests. The term *user part* is unfortunate, since this does not refer to the ISDN user; rather, it refers to the fact that the ISUP is a user of the lower layers of SS7.

Messages

The network procedures for establishing, controlling, and terminating a call occur as a result of ISUP messages exchanged between exchanges and signal transfer points within the network. A common format is used for all messages defined in ISUP, illustrated in Figure 11.15. The message consists of fields organized into the following parts:

- *Routing label:* This is actually part of the MTP header, as shown in Figure 11.5a. This label indicates the source and destination points of the message. The label also includes a signaling link code field, used in load sharing across multiple physical links. This field is shown in Figure 11.15 to highlight the fact that for each individual circuit connection the same routing label must be used in all messages associated with that connection.
- *Circuit identification code:* Specifies the circuit to which this message relates.
- *Message type:* Identifies which ISUP message is being sent. The contents of the remainder of the message depend on the message type.
- *Mandatory fixed part:* Contains those parameters that are mandatory for a particular message type and of fixed length. The position, length, and order of the parameters are uniquely defined by the message type.
- *Mandatory variable part:* Contains those parameters that are mandatory for a particular message type and of variable length. Each parameter requires a pointer and a length indicator as well as a parameter value.
- *Optional part:* Contains those parameters that may or may not occur for a particular message type. Each parameter requires a name and length indicator as well as a parameter value.

Table 11.11 lists all of the ISUP messages, together with a brief definition. The messages can be divided into nine categories. **Forward setup messages** are used to set up a circuit. In addition to identifying the exchange endpoints, these messages allow for the specification of the desired characteristics of the call. These messages propagate in a forward direction, from the exchange originating the call to the ex-

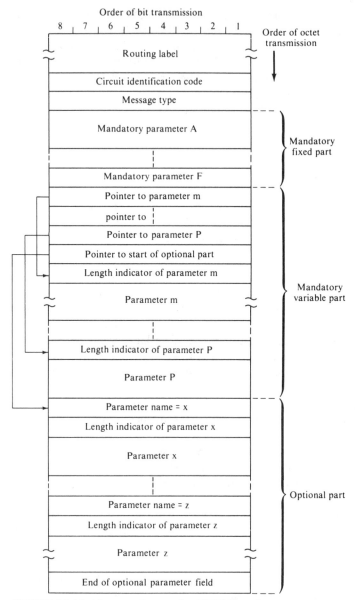

FIGURE 11.15 Message Format for ISDN User Part

change that is the destination point. **General setup messages** are used during the call establishment phase. They provide a means of transferring any additional information required during call setup, plus a means for checking that a circuit that straddles more than one ISDN maintains the desired characteristics across all networks. **Backward setup messages** support the call setup process and initiate accounting and charg-

TABLE 11.11 ISDN User-part Messages

Forward Setup

Initial address

Sent in forward direction to initiate seizure of an outgoing circuit and to transmit address and related information.

Subsequent address

May be sent following initial address message to convey additional calling party address information.

General Setup

Information request

Requests additional call-related information.

Information

Conveys additional call-related information.

Continuity

Sent in forward direction to indicate continuity of the preceding speech circuit to the following international exchange.

Backward Setup

Address complete

Sent in backward direction to indicate that all the address information required for routing the call to the called party has been received.

Connect

Sent in backward direction to indicate that all the address information required for routing the call to the called party has been received and that the call has been answered.

Call progress

Indicates that an event has occurred during call setup that should be relayed to the calling party.

Call Supervision

Answer

Sent in backward direction to indicate that the call has been answered.

Forward transfer

Sent in the forward direction on semiautomatic calls when the outgoing international exchange operator wants the help of an operator at the incoming international exchange.

Release

Indicates that the circuit identified in the message is being released.

Circuit Supervision

Delayed release

Indicates that the subscriber has disconnected but that the network is holding the connection.

Cont.

TABLE 11.11 ISDN User-part Messages *(continued)*

Circuit Supervision

Release complete
  Sent in response to a release message when the circuit concerned has been brought into the idle condition.

Continuity check request
  Sent by an exchange for a circuit on which a continuity check is to be performed to the exchange at the other end of the circuit, requesting that continuity checking equipment be attached.

Reset circuit
  Sent to release a circuit when, because of a fault, it is unknown whether a release or release complete message is appropriate. If, at the receiving end, the circuit is blocked, reception of this message should cause the condition to be removed.

Loop-back acknowledgment
  Sent in the backward direction in response to a continuity check request message, indicating that a loop has been connected.

Blocking
  Sent for maintenance purposes to the exchange at the other end of a circuit, to cause subsequent outgoing calls on that circuit to be blocked.

Unblocking
  Sent to the exchange at the other end of a circuit to cancel, in that exchange, the blocked condition caused by a previous blocking or circuit group blocking message.

Unequipped circuit identification code
  Sent from one exchange to another when it receives an unequipped circuit identification code.

Blocking acknowledgment
  Response to a blocking message, indicating that the circuit has been blocked.

Unblocking acknowledgment
  Response to an unblocking message, indicating that the circuit has been unblocked.

Overload
  Send in a backward direction, on nonpriority calls, in response to an initial address message, to invoke a temporary trunk blocking of the circuit concerned when the exchange generating the message is subject to load control.

Suspend
  Indicates that the subscriber's terminal has been temporarily disconnected.

Resume
  recomIndicates that the subscriber, after having sent a suspend message, is reconnected.

Confusion
  Sent in response to any message if the exchange does not recognize the message or a part of the message.

Circuit Group Supervision

Circuit group blocking

Sent for maintenance purposes to the exchange at the other end of a group of circuits to cause subsequent outgoing calls on that group of circuits to be blocked.

Circuit group unblocking

Sent to the exchange at the other end of a group of circuits to cancel, in that exchange, the blocked condition caused by a previous circuit group blocking message.

Circuit group blocking acknowledgment

Response to a circuit group blocking message, indicating that the group of circuits has been blocked.

Circuit group unblocking acknowledgment

Response to a circuit group unblocking message, indicating that the group of circuits has been unblocked.

Circuit group reset

Sent to release a group of circuits when, because of a fault, it is unknown which of the clearing signals is appropriate for each of the circuits in the group. Circuits that are blocked at the receiving end should be unblocked on receiving this message.

Circuit group reset acknowledgment

Response to a reset circuit group message, indicating either that the group of circuits has been reset or that resetting has been started and that the resulting status will be reported.

Circuit group query

Requests that the far-end exchange give the state of all circuits in a particular group.

Circuit group query response

Sent in response to a circuit group query message to indicate the state of all circuits in a particular range.

In-call Modification

Call modification request

Indicates a calling or called party request to modify the characteristics of an established call (e.g., from data to voice).

Call modification completed

Response to a call modification request message, indicating that the requested call modification has been completed.

Call modification reject

Response to a call modification request message, indicating that the request has been rejected.

Facility request

Sent from an exchange to another exchange or to a database to request activation of a facility.

Cont.

TABLE 11.11   ISDN User-part Messages (continued)

In-call Modification

Facility accepted
  Sent to an exchange from an exchange or database indicating that the requested facility has been invoked.

Facility reject
  Sent to an exchange from an exchange or database indicating that the facility
  request has been rejected.

End-to-End

Pass-along
  Sent to transfer information between two signaling points along the same signaling path as that used to establish a physical connection between those two
  points.

User-to-User Information
  Used for the transport of user-to-user signaling independent of call-control messages.

ing procedures. **Call supervision messages** are additional messages that
might be needed in the process of call establishment. This group includes indications of whether the call was answered or not and the
capability to support manual intervention between ISDNs that cross
national boundaries. **Circuit supervision messages** relate to an already
established circuit. Three key functions are supported. A circuit may be
released, which terminates the call. A circuit may be suspended and
later resumed. Finally, a circuit that is not currently being used for a
call may be established. In this case, it is possible to block the circuit
so that outgoing calls on the circuit are prevented, saving the circuit for
incoming calls. In the case of a group of circuits that is treated as a
single unit for control, **circuit group supervision messages** perform
similar functions. **In-call modification messages** are used to alter characteristics or associated network facilities of an active call, two quite
different facilities. Finally, the category of **end-to-end messages** includes
pass-along and end-to-end user information capabilities, explained subsequently.

Example

Figure 11.16 is an example of the use of the protocol to set up a B
channel circuit-switched telephone call. We will follow this example
through to give the reader an idea of the use of the ISUP protocol.

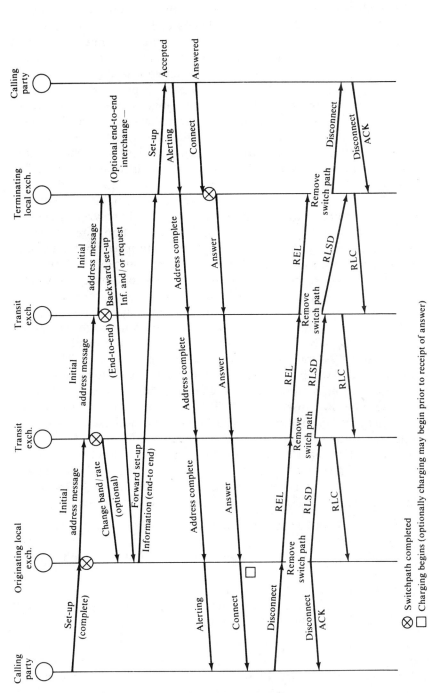

FIGURE 11.16 Successful Ordinary Call (En Bloc Operation)

Call Establishment. The process within the ISDN is triggered by an I.451/Q.931 SETUP message on the D channel between an ISDN user and an exchange, which becomes the originating exchange for this call. The SETUP message contains the information about the characteristics of the requested call and the associated network facilities required. If the exchange determines that the called party is on another exchange, then the first hop on the route to that exchange is determined, and an initial address message is sent to this intermediate exchange. This message contains the ISDN number of the called party, the type of connection required (e.g., 64-kbps transparent), the identity of the selected physical circuit to the succeeding exchange, and its characteristics. The initial address message is then sent to the exchange on which the selected outgoing link terminates. At each transit, or intermediate exchange, the initial address message is received and analyzed. Based on the destination address and other routing information, the transit exchange makes a routing decision, selects the appropriate outgoing link, and transmits the initial address message to the next exchange. A connection is set up between the incoming and outgoing paths. This process continues until the initial address message reaches the terminating, or destination, exchange. If the terminating exchange requires additional information, it sends a backward setup message. For example, the calling party address may be required at the destination exchange but not be included in the initial address message. The terminating exchange will determine the identity of the party to be connected. If the connection is allowed, the exchange notifies the called party of the incoming call with an I.451/Q.931 SETUP message on a D channel, containing any information received in the initial address message that is relevant to the called party.

When the terminal device begins alerting the user, it returns an I.451/Q.931 ALERT message. When this is received by the local exchange, it sends an address complete message back through the ISDN to the originating exchange. This message serves several purposes:

- It is an acknowledgment to the originating exchange that a connection has been established.
- It indicates that the called party was found to be idle and is being alerted.
- It may carry charging information.
- It may contain a request to the originating exchange to forward additional call-related information.

When the address complete message is received by the originating exchange, it sends an I.451/Q.931 ALERT message to the calling party.

When the called party answers, an I.451/Q.931 CONN message is sent to the terminating exchange, which sends an answer message back through the ISDN to the originating exchange, which issues an I.451/ Q.931 CONN to the calling party. At both ends, the user-network B channel is connected to the internal ISDN circuit. Charging, if applicable, begins.

Call Release. The release procedures are based on a three-message (release, released, release complete) approach in which the release message is transmitted through the network as quickly as possible. In this example we show a release initiated by the calling party. The same procedures are used whether the release is initiated by the called or calling party.

The process is triggered by an I.451/Q.931 DISC message on the D channel between the calling party and the local exchange. On receipt of this message, the exchange immediately starts the release of the switched path that supports the B channel circuit and, at the same time, sends a release message to the succeeding exchange. This message is passed through the network to all intermediate exchanges and the terminating exchange. The release message is intended to inform the exchanges involved in the call as quickly as possible that the call-related circuit connections are to be released.

Meanwhile, at the originating exchange, when the path has been fully disconnected, three actions are taken:

- Send an I.451/Q.931 REL message to the calling subscriber to indicate that the B channel circuit has been released.
- Send a released message to the succeeding exchange to indicate that the circuit has been released.
- Start a timer T_1 to ensure that a release complete message is received within a specified time.

At each intermediate exchange, the receipt of a release message causes the following actions:

- Start a timer T_{12} to ensure that a released message is received from the preceding exchange.
- Send a release message to the succeeding exchange.
- Disconnect the switched path.
- When the path has been fully disconnected, send a released message to the succeeding exchange.
- Start a timer T_1 to ensure receipt of a release complete message.
- When a released message is received from the preceding exchange, return a release complete message to the preceding exchange.

At the terminating exchange, the receipt of a release message causes the following actions:

- Issue an I.451/Q.931 DISC message to the called subscriber.
- Start a timer T_{12} to ensure receipt of a released message.
- Disconnect the switched path.
- When a released message is received from the preceding exchange, return a release complete message to the preceding exchange.

The timers are used in the following way. If a release complete message is not received within T_1, the exchange will repeat the released message. If repeated transmissions of released messages are not acknowledged, the exchange sends a reset circuit message and alerts maintenance personnel. If a released message is not received within T_{12}, the exchange sends a reset circuit message and alerts maintenance personnel.

The use of the three messages satisfies the requirements for both speed and reliability. The release message is sent through the network as quickly as possible so that all exchanges can begin to release the resources dedicated to the circuit. The released and release complete messages ensure that the circuit is in fact released throughout the network.

End-to-End Signaling

End-to-end signaling is defined as the capability to transfer signaling information directly between the endpoints of a circuit-switched connection or between signaling points that are not interconnected by a circuit-switched connection. End-to-end signaling is used typically between the ISUPs located in call originating and terminating exchanges. It can be used to request or respond to requests for additional call-related information or to transfer user-to-user information transparently through the network.

If the end-to-end signaling relates to an existing connection, it may be achieved by the **pass-along method.** With this method, signaling information is sent along the signaling path of a previously established physical connection. The message is passed along the route of transit exchanges that constitute the circuit path. No information processing occurs at a transit exchange, which simply forwards the information to the next exchange. With this method, the ISUP makes direct use of the message transfer part of SS7.

The pass-along method makes use of an end-to-end connection, which is set up whenever a circuit is established between two subscribers. The end-to-end connection consists of a number of connection sections, which run in parallel with and use the same identification code as the circuit sections that comprise the user's circuit. Thus, when a call is placed, two connections are established across ISDN. One is a circuit that supports the user's B channel traffic, and the other is an SS7 end-to-end connection. These two connections follow the same route through the network but are separate dedicated connections.

An alternative method for end-to-end signaling is the **signaling connection control part (SCCP) method.** This method, which makes use of the SCCP protocol of SS7, can be used whether or not there is a circuit established between the message originating and terminating exchanges. In this case, the route taken by end-to-end signaling messages is determined by SCCP and may not relate to any user circuit.

Services

The basic service provided by the ISDN user part is the setup and release of a simple circuit-switched call. In addition, the following supplementary services are supported:

- Calling line identification.
- Call forwarding.
- Closed user groups.
- Direct dialing in.
- User-to-user signaling.

Calling line identification consists of two related supplementary services: presentation and restriction. Calling line identification presentation is a service that enables a subscriber to be informed on incoming calls of the address of the calling party, unless the calling party restricts access to this information. The information may be contained in the initial address message. If not, the terminating exchange requests the information either by setting an appropriate indication in the address complete message or by generating an information request message. In either case, the originating exchange returns the requested information in an information message.

The **call forwarding** service redirects incoming calls addressed to a particular number to an alternate number. The redirection occurs only when the facility is activated by the subscriber at the called number. Three types of call forwarding have been defined:

- *Call forwarding busy:* Forward calls that encounter busy.
- *Call forwarding no reply:* Forward calls that meet no reply for a specified period of time.
- *Call forwarding unconditional:* Forward all calls.

The **closed user group** service enables a subscriber to belong to one or more closed user groups. In its basic form, a closed user group permits the subscribers belonging to the group to communicate with each other but precludes communication with all other subscribers. Thus, the members of the group are protected from unauthorized access (into or out of the group). A subscriber may belong to zero, one, or more closed user groups. In addition to the basic service, there are extensions that may be defined:

- *Closed user group with outgoing access:* This enables the subscriber in a closed user group to make outgoing calls to the open part of the network (i.e., subscribers not belonging to any closed user group) and to subscribers belonging to other closed user groups with the incoming access capability.
- *Closed user group with incoming access:* This enables the subscriber in a closed user group to receive incoming calls from the open part of the network and from subscribers belonging to other closed user groups with the outgoing access capability.
- *Incoming calls barred within a closed user group:* This enables the subscriber in a closed user group to originate calls to subscribers in the same group but precludes the reception of incoming calls from subscribers in the same group.
- *Outgoing calls barred within a closed user group:* This enables the subscriber in a closed user group to receive calls from subscribers in the same group but prevents the subscriber from originating calls to subscribers in the same group.

When this facility is in use, the originating and terminating exchanges must verify that a call is allowable before establishing that call, either by accessing information stored locally in the exchange or by access to some sort of centralized database. In the latter case, the closed user group selection and validation request and response messages are used to communicate with the database.

Direct dialing in enables a user to directly call another user on a digital PBX or other private system without attendant intervention.

User-to-user signaling provides a means of communication between two end users through the signaling network for the purpose of exchanging information of end-to-end significance. Three services are provided:

- *Service 1:* Allows the transfer of user-to-user information (UUI) during the setup and clearing phases of a call, with UUI embedded within ISUP call-control messages.
- *Service 2:* Allows the transfer of user-to-user information (UUI) during the setup phase of a call, transferred independently of call-control messages. The ISUP user-to-user information message is used.
- *Service 3:* Allows the transfer of user-to-user information (UUI)

during the active phase of a call. The ISUP user-to-user information message is used.

11.7
SUMMARY

Signaling System Number 7 is a set of specifications of services and protocols for use in the internal control and network intelligence of a digital network. It is based on the use of common-channel signaling and is designed specifically for ISDN.

The **signaling data link level** is the lowest level of SS7 and corresponds to OSI layer 1. It specifies a full-duplex physical link dedicated to SS7 traffic. The principal option is a 64-kbps digital link.

The **signaling link level** corresponds to OSI layer 2. This protocol uses the same principles as LAPD and LAPB. However, the formats and some of the procedures are different.

The **signaling network level** embodies some of the functions of OSI layer 3. It includes functions relating to message handling, such as discrimination, routing, and distribution, and functions relating to network management, such as traffic management, route management, and link management.

The **signaling connection control part (SCCP)** completes the set of functions normally associated with OSI layer 3. SCCP provides enhanced addressing capability over the signaling network level and supports reliable, connection-oriented data transfer.

The **ISDN user part (ISUP)** defines the functions, procedures, and interexchange signaling information flows required to provide user-channel services and associated user facilities for voice and nonvoice calls over ISDN.

11.8
RECOMMENDED READING

[MODA90a] is a special issue of the *IEEE Communications* magazine containing nine timely papers on SS7. [MODA90b] is an excellent tutorial on SS7, as is [JABB91]. A thorough treatment can also be found in [FREE89]. CCITT has published a handbook that provides a useful tutorial on the implementation of SS7 [CCIT90].

A detailed performance study of the two error-control methods of the signaling link level is provided in [FUJI90]. An analysis of congestion-control techniques is reported in [LEE89].

11.9

PROBLEMS

11.1. Would it be possible to provide a circuit-switched rather than a packet-switched implementation of SS7? What would be the relative merits of such an approach?

11.2. Is something like SS7 needed to provide control signaling in a packet-switched network? If so, why not use SS7?

11.3. A proposed refinement to the basic method of error control at the signaling link level is referred to as the basic method with double transmission (BDT). In this method, each unit is transmitted twice consecutively. A retransmission is requested by the receiver only when both copies of a unit are hit by errors, causing two identical copies to be sent again. Compare this method to the basic method and to the preventive cyclic retransmission method in terms of procedural complexity and performance.

11.4. Ignoring the effects of bit stuffing, calculate the message information capacity of an SS7 signaling link, assuming all messages consist of 2 octets and only MSUs are sent.

11.5. Figure 11.17 shows an example of the buffer occupancy history of a link. For the congestion-control strategy at the network signaling level, indicate the periods when the link is considered congested and uncongested.

11.6. Why is there not an N-DATA.response or an N-DATA.confirm primitive in Table 11.5?

11.7. In a credit flow-control scheme, what provision can be made for credit allocations that are lost in transit?

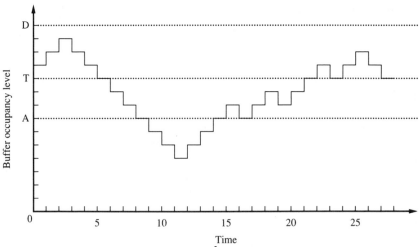

FIGURE 11.17 Example History of Buffer Occupancy Level

APPENDIX 11A

1988 CCITT Recommendations on CCITT

Number	Title	Description
Q.700	Introduction to CCITT SS7	Provides an overview of SS7.
Q.701	Functional Description of the Message Transfer Part (MTP) of SS7	An overview of MTP with its three levels and their functions, signaling network structure, services provided, and interworking issues.
Q.702	Signaling Data Link	Covers the physical layer characteristics of links used to convey MTP messages. Digital and analog channels operating between 4.8 and 64 kbps are specified.
Q.703	Signaling Link	Covers the layer 2 (data link control) characteristics of links used to convey MTP messages. Includes specification of frame format and technique for error detection and control.
Q.704	Signaling Network Functions and Messages	Covers the layer 3 characteristics of MTP. Relates to the transfer of messages between signaling points.
Q.705	Signaling Network Structure	Presents network architecture considerations and discusses aspects pertinent to the design of international signaling networks.
Q.706	Message Transfer Part Signaling Performance	Performance-related requirements are presented, including availability, errors, delays, and capacities.
Q.707	Testing and Maintenance	A limited capability for testing the signaling links and the network routing is provided. Covers testing, fault location, signaling network monitoring, and testing and maintenance messages.
Q.708	Numbering of International Signaling Point Codes	Describes the 14-bit code and allocations of signaling point codes in the international SS7 network. Networks may use larger codes nationally.

Cont.

Number	Title	Description
Q.709	Hypothetical Signaling Reference Connection	Defines a hypothetical connection in terms of mean and 95 percentile delays in message processing. Networks are defined in terms of distance from subscriber to signaling point and total subscribers as large or average-sized.
Q.710	Simplified MTP Version for Small Systems	Describes a simplified MTP version for PBXs or remote concentrators using the associated mode of signaling only.
Q.711	Function Description of the Signaling Connection Control Part (SCCP)	Contains a general description of the functions within the SCCP and the services provided to users.
Q.712	Definition and Functions of SCCP Messages	Defines the meaning of each SCCP message and of the information elements contained in each message.
Q.713	SCCP Formats and Codes	Defines the message formats and codes used in the SCCP.
Q.714	SCCP Procedures	Describes the control procedures of SCCP. Five protocol classes, from noncontrolled connectionless to fully controlled connection-oriented, are defined.
Q.716	SCCP Performances	Discusses SCCP performance, including definition of performance parameters and specified values for internal parameters.
Q.721	Functional Description of the SS7 Telephone User Part (TUP)	Describes functions of and services provided by TUP.
Q.722	General Function of Telephone Messages and Signals	Provides a description of TUP message types and nomenclature, plus a general description of the function of TUP messages.
Q.723	Formats and Codes	Specifies the encoding of TUP signaling information elements and the format of messages in which they are conveyed.
Q.724	Signaling Procedures	Details the procedures for basic call control.

Number	Title	Description
Q.725	Signaling Performance in the Telephone Application	Provides performance criteria for TUP message transfer over SS7 networks. Objectives for availability, dependability, and cross-exchange delay are presented.
Q.730	ISDN Supplementary Services	Describes signaling procedures for supplementary services to be used in conjunction with ISUP and TCAP.
Q.741	SS7—Data User Part	Defines the necessary call control, facility registration, and cancellation-related elements for international signaling using SS7 for circuit-switched data transmission services.
Q.761	Functional Description of the ISDN User Part of SS7	Describes functions of and services provided by ISUP.
Q.762	General Function of Messages and Signals	Provides a description of ISUP message types and nomenclature, plus a general description of the function of ISUP messages.
Q.763	Formats and Codes	Specifies the encoding of ISUP signaling information elements and the format of messages in which they are conveyed.
Q.764	Signaling Procedures	Details the procedures for basic call control and for providing a variety of other services with the ISUP.
Q.766	Performance Objectives in the ISDN Application	Provides performance criteria for ISUP message transfer over SS7. Objectives for availability, dependability, and cross-exchange delay are presented.
Q.771	Functional Description of Transaction Capabilities	Provides functional description of transaction capabilities, including TCAP plus supporting lower-level protocols.
Q.772	Transaction Capabilities Information Element Definitions	Defines terms used as information elements and parameters within TCAP messages.
Q.773	Transaction Capabilities Formats and Encoding	Provides the format and encoding of TCAP messages.

Cont.

Number	Title	Description
Q.774	Transaction Capabilities Procedures	Describes the procedures of the transaction capabilities based on a connectionless network service, including addressing.
Q.775	Guidelines for Using Transaction Capabilities	Provides guidelines to potential users of transaction capabilities, including operations, dialogues, application service elements, and application entities.
Q.780	SS7 Test Specification, General Description	Describes the principles and scope of the text specifications and their field and method of application.
Q.781	MTP Level 2 Test Specification	Specifies detailed tests of MTP level 2 protocols.
Q.782	MTP Level 3 Test Specification	Specifies detailed tests of MTP level 3 protocols.
Q.783	TUP Test Specification	Specifies detailed tests of TUP.
Q.791	Monitoring and Measurements for the SS7 Networks	Describes methods for monitoring and measuring performance for the MTP and SCCP. It specifies the set of parameters and the timing of measurements.
Q.795	Operations, Maintenance and Administration Part	Provides application-layer procedures and protocols related to accomplishing OA&M functions at signaling points.

APPENDIX 11B

SERVICE PRIMITIVES AND PARAMETERS

In a communications architecture, such as the OSI model or the SS7 protocol architecture, each layer is defined in two parts: the protocol between peer (at the same layer) entities in different systems, and the services provided by one layer to the next higher layer in the same system.

We have seen a number of examples of protocols, which are defined in terms of the formats of the protocol data units that are exchanged and the rules governing the use of those protocol data units. The services between adjacent layers are expressed in terms of primitives and parameters. A primitive specifies the function to be performed, and the parameters are used to pass data and control information. The actual form of a primitive is implementation-dependent. An example is a procedure call.

Four types of primitives are used in standards to define the interaction between adjacent layers in the architecture. These are defined in Table 11.12. The layout of Figure 11.18b suggests the time ordering of these events. For example, consider the transfer of a connection request from SCCP user A to a peer entity B in another system. The following steps occur:

1. A invokes the services of SCCP with an N-CONNECT.request primitive. Associated with the primitive are the parameters needed, such as the called address.
2. The SCCP entity in A's system prepares an SCCP message to be sent to its peer SCCP entity in B.
3. The destination SCCP entity delivers the data to B via an N-CONNECT.indication, which includes the calling address and other parameters.
4. B issues an N-CONNECT.response to its SCCP entity.
5. B's SCCP entity conveys the acknowledgment to A's SCCP entity in a message.
6. The acknowledgment is delivered to A via an N-CONNECT.confirm.

TABLE 11.12   Primitive Types

REQUEST	A primitive issued by a service user to invoke some service and to pass the parameters needed to fully specify the requested service.
INDICATION	A primitive issued by a service provider to either 1. Indicate that a procedure has been invoked by the peer service user on the connection and to provide the associated parameters, or 2. Notify the service user of a provider-initiated action.
RESPONSE	A primitive issued by a service user to acknowledge or complete some procedure previously invoked by an indication to that user.
CONFIRM	A primitive issued by a service provider to acknowledge or complete some procedure previously invoked by a request by the service user.

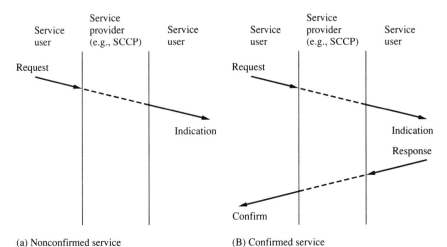

(a) Nonconfirmed service   (B) Confirmed service

FIGURE 11.18 Relationship Among Service Primitives

This sequence of events is referred to as a **confirmed service,** as the initiator receives confirmation that the requested service has had the desired effect at the other end. If only request and indication primitives are involved (corresponding to steps 1 through 3), then the service dialogue is a **nonconfirmed service;** the initiator receives no confirmation that the requested action has taken place.

PART THREE

Broadband ISDN

Although work continues on the Recommendations for ISDN, especially in the area of frame relay, the structure and most of the details for ISDN are now in final form. Since 1988, the attention of CCITT has focused on a far more ambitious undertaking, known as broadband ISDN.

Chapter 12 provides an overview of broadband ISDN (B-ISDN), beginning with an examination of the variety of services that this high-speed network is designed to support. The details of the functional architecture and protocol reference model for B-ISDN are also explored.

Chapter 13 focuses on the principal mechanism and major innovation of B-ISDN, the asynchronous transfer mode (ATM). The ATM specification is summarized. Next, the ATM adaptation layer, which is needed to provide a mapping between B-ISDN services and the ATM mechanism, is presented. The final aspect of ATM to explore is the way in which ATM cells are structured for transmission. One of these techniques involves the use of SONET/SDH, which is introduced first, before examining the ATM transmission alternatives.

CHAPTER 12

Broadband ISDN Overview

As we saw in Chapter 5, the planning for ISDN began as far back as 1976 and is only now moving from the planning stage to prototypes and actual implementations. It will be many years before the full spectrum of ISDN services is widely available, and there will continue to be refinements and improvements to ISDN services and network facilities. Nevertheless, with the publication of the 1988 "Blue Book" set of Recommendations from CCITT, the bulk of the work on ISDN is complete. To be sure, future versions of the CCITT standards will provide refinements and enhancements to ISDN. But, since 1988, much of the planning and design effort has become directed toward a network concept that will be far more revolutionary than ISDN itself. This new concept has been referred to as **broadband ISDN** (B-ISDN).

CCITT modestly defines B-ISDN as "a service requiring transmission channels capable of supporting rates greater than the primary rate." Behind this innocuous statement lie plans for a network and set of services that will have far more impact on business and residential customers than ISDN. With B-ISDN, services, especially video services, requiring data rates orders of magnitudes beyond those that can be delivered by ISDN will become available. These include support for image processing, video, and high-capacity workstations and local area networks (LANs). To contrast this new network and these new services to the original concept of ISDN, that original concept is now being referred to as **narrowband ISDN.**

The primary triggers for evolving toward the B-ISDN include an increasing demand for high bit-rate services, especially image and video services, and the evolution of technology to support those services. The key developments in technology are

- Optical fiber transmission systems that can offer low-cost, high data-rate transmission channels for network trunks and for subscriber lines.
- Microelectronic circuits that can offer high-speed, low-cost building blocks for switching, transmission, and subscriber equipment.
- High-quality video monitors and cameras that can, with sufficient production quantities, be offered at low cost.

These advances in technology will result in the integration of a wide range of communications facilities and the support of, in effect, universal communications with the following key characteristics:

- Worldwide exchange between any two subscribers in any medium or combination of media.
- Retrieval and sharing of massive amounts of information from multiple sources, in multiple media, among people in a shared electronic environment.
- Distribution, including switched distribution, of a wide variety of cultural, entertainment, and educational materials to home or office, virtually on demand.

In 1988, as part of its I series of recommendations on ISDN, CCITT issued the first two recommendations relating to B-ISDN: I.113, *Vocabulary of terms for broadband aspects of ISDN*, and I.121, *Broadband aspects of ISDN*. These documents represent the level of consensus reached among the participants concerning the nature of the future B-ISDN, as of late 1988. They provide a preliminary description and a basis for future standardization and development work. Some of the important notions developed in these documents are presented in Table 12.1. Table 12.2 lists the factors that are guiding CCITT work on B-ISDN.

With both demand (user interest) and supply (the technology for high-speed networking) evolving rapidly, the usual four-year cycle would be fatal to hopes of developing a standardized high-speed network utility. To head off the possibility of a fragmentation of effort and a proliferation of nonstandard products and services, CCITT has issued an interim set of 1990 draft Recommendations on B-ISDN. The set of fourteen documents (Appendix 12A) provides, for the first time, a detailed and specific master plan for the broadband revolution. This chapter provides an overview of this master plan.

TABLE 12.1 Noteworthy Statements in I.113 and I.121

Broadband: A service or a system requiring transmission channels capable of supporting rates greater than the primary rate.

The term B-ISDN is used for convenience in order to refer to and emphasize the broadband aspects of ISDN. The intent, however, is that there be one comprehensive notion of an ISDN which provides broadband and other ISDN services.

Asynchronous transfer mode (ATM) is the target transfer mode solution for implementing a B-ISDN. It will influence the standardization of digital hierarchies and multiplexing structures, switching, and interfaces for broadband signals.

B-ISDN will be based on the concepts developed for ISDN and may evolve by progressively incorporating additional functions and services (e.g., high-quality video applications).

The reference configuration defined in I.411 is considered sufficiently general to be applicable not only for a basic access and a primary rate access but also to a broadband access. Both reference points S and T are valid for broadband accesses.

12.1

BROADBAND SERVICES

When the capacity available to the ISDN user is increased substantially, then the range of services that it can support also increases substantially. CCITT classifies the services that could be provided by a B-ISDN into interactive services and distribution services (Figure 12.1). **Interactive services** are those in which there is a two-way exchange of information (other than control-signaling information) between two subscribers or

TABLE 12.2 Factors Guiding CCITT Work on B-ISDN

- The emerging demand for broadband services.
- The availability of high-speed transmission, switching, and signal-processing technologies.
- The improved data- and image-processing capabilities available to the user.
- The advances in software application processing in the computer and telecommunications industries.
- The need to integrate both interactive and distribution services.
- The need to integrate both circuit and packet transfer mode into one universal broadband network.
- The need to provide flexibility in satisfying the requirements of both user and operator.
- The need to cover broadband aspects of ISDN in CCITT Recommendations.

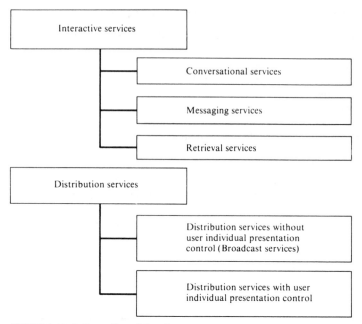

FIGURE 12.1 Broadband Services

between a subscriber and a service provider. These include conversational services, messaging services, and retrieval services. **Distribution services** are those in which the information transfer is primarily one way, from service provider to B-ISDN subscriber. These include broadcast services, for which the user has no control over the presentation of the information, and cyclical services (explained subsequently), which allow the user some measure of presentation control. Table 12.3, from interim CCITT Recommendation I.211, lists each of these five categories together with possible applications and characteristics. Let us look at each of these subcategories in turn.

Conversational Services

Conversational services provide the means for bidirectional dialogue communication with bidirectional, real-time (not store-and-forward) end-to-end information transfer between two users or between a user and a service provider host. These services support the general transfer of data specific to a given user application. That is, the information is generated by and exchanged between users; it is not "public" information.

This category encompasses a wide range of applications and data types. Table 12.3 divides these into moving pictures (video), data, and document. In the long run, perhaps the most important category of B-

TABLE 12.3   Possible Broadband Services in ISDN[a]

Service Classes	Type of Information	Examples of Broadband Services	Applications	Some Possible Attribute Values[b]
Conversational services	Moving pictures (video) and sound	Broadband[b,c] video telephony	Communication for the transfer of voice (sound), moving pictures, and video-scanned still images and documents between two locations (person-to-person)[c] —Tele-education —Tele-shopping —Tele-advertising	—Demand/reserved/permanent —Point-to-point/multipoint —Bidirectional symmetric/bidirectional asymmetric —(Value for information transfer rate is under study)
		Broadband[b,c] videoconference	Multipoint communication for the transfer of voice (sound), moving pictures, and video-scanned still images and documents between two or more locations (person-to-group, group-to-group)[c] —Tele-education —Tele-shopping —Tele-advertising	—Demand/reserved/permanent —Point-to-point/multipoint —Bidirectional symmetric/bidirectional asymmetric
		Video surveillance	—Building security —Traffic monitoring	—Demand/reserved/permanent —Point-to-point/multipoint —Bidirectional symmetric/unidirectional

Cont.

TABLE 12.3 Possible Broadband Services in ISDN[a] (continued)

Service Classes	Type of Information	Examples of Broadband Services	Applications	Some Possible Attribute Values[b]
		Video/audio information transmission service	—TV signal transfer —Video/audio dialogue —Contribution of information	—Demand/reserved/permanent —Point-to-point/multipoint —Bidirectional symmetric/bidirectional asymmetric
	Sound	Multiple sound-program signals	—Multilingual commentary channels —Multiple program transfers	—Demand/reserved/permanent —Point-to-point/multipoint —Bidirectional symmetric/bidirectional asymmetric
	Data	High-speed unrestricted digital information transmission service	—High-speed data transfer —LAN (local area network) interconnection —MAN (metropolitan area network) interconnection —Computer-computer interconnection —Transfer of video and other information types —Still image transfer —Multisite interactive CAD/CAM	—Demand/reserved/permanent —Point-to-point/multipoint —Bidirectional symmetric/bidirectional asymmetric —Connection-oriented/connectionless
		High-volume file transfer service	—Data file transfer	—Demand —Point-to-point/multipoint —Bidirectional symmetric/bidirectional asymmetric

Document	High-speed tele-action	—Real-time control —Telemetry —Alarms	—Demand —Point-to-point/multipoint —Bidirectional symmetric/bidirectional asymmetric
	High-speed tele-fax	User-to-user transfer of text, images, drawings, etc.	
	High-resolution image-communication service	—Professional images —Medical images —Remote games and game networks	
	Document communication service	User-to-user transfer of mixed documents[d]	—Demand —Point-to-point/multipoint —Bidirectional symmetric/bidirectional asymmetric
Messaging services	Moving pictures (video) and sound	Video mail service	Electronic mailbox service for the transfer of moving pictures and accompanying sound	—Demand —Point-to-point/multipoint —Bidirectional symmetric/unidirectional (for further study)
	Document	Document mail service	Electronic mailbox service for mixed documents[d]	—Demand —Point-to-point/multipoint —Bidirectional symmetric/unidirectional (for further study)
Retrieval services	Text, data, graphics,	Broadband videotex	—Videotex including moving pictures	—Demand —Point-to-point

Cont.

TABLE 12.3   Possible Broadband Services in ISDN[a] *(continued)*

Service Classes	Type of Information	Examples of Broadband Services	Applications	Some Possible Attribute Values[b]
	sound, still images, moving pictures		—Remote education and training —Telesoftware —Tele-shopping —Tele-advertising —News retrieval	—Bidirectional asymmetric
		Video retrieval service	—Entertainment purposes —Remote education and training	—Demand/reserved —Point-to-point/multipoint[f] —Bidirectional asymmetric
		High-resolution image-retrieval service	—Entertainment purposes —Remote education and training —Professional image communications —Medical image communications	—Demand/reserved —Point-to-point/multipoint[f] —Bidirectional asymmetric
		Document re-trieval service	"Mixed documents" retrieval from information centers, archives, etc.[d,e]	—Demand —Point-to-point/multipoint[f] —Bidirectional asymmetric
		Data retrieval service	Telesoftware	
Distribution services without user individual presentation control	Video	Existing quality TV distribution service (PAL, SECAM, NTSC)	TV program distribution	—Demand (selection)/permanent —Broadcast —Bidirectional asymmetric/unidi-rectional

	Service	Application	Attributes
	Extended quality TV distribution service —Enhanced definition TV distribution service —High-quality TV	TV program distribution	—Demand (selection)/permanent —Broadcast —Bidirectional asymmetric/unidirectional
	High-definition TV distribution service	TV program distribution	—Demand (selection)/permanent —Broadcast —Bidirectional asymmetric/unidirectional
	Pay TV (pay per view, pay per channel)	TV program distribution	—Demand (selection)/permanent —Broadcast/multipoint —Bidirectional asymmetric/unidirectional
Text, graphics, still images	Document distribution service	—Electronic newspaper —Electronic publishing	—Demand (selection)/permanent —Broadcast/multipoint[f] —Bidirectional asymmetric/unidirectional
Data	High-speed unrestricted digital information distribution service	—Distribution of unrestricted data	—Permanent —Broadcast —Unidirectional

Cont.

TABLE 12.3   Possible Broadband Services in ISDN[a] *(continued)*

Service Classes	Type of Information	Examples of Broadband Services	Applications	Some Possible Attribute Values[b]
	Moving pictures and sound	Video information distribution service	—Distribution of video/audio signals	—Permanent —Broadcast —Unidirectional
Distribution services with user individual presentation control	Text, graphics, sound, still images	Full-channel broadcast videography	—Remote education and training —Tele-advertising —News retrieval —Telesoftware	—Permanent —Broadcast —Unidirectional

[a] In this table only those broadband services are considered that may require higher transfer capacity than that of the H_1 capacity. Services for sound retrieval, main sound applications, and visual services with reduced or highly reduced resolutions are not listed.
[b] This terminology indicates that a redefinition regarding existing terms has taken place. The new terms may or may not exist for a transition period.
[c] The realization of the different applications may require the definition of different quality classes.
[d] "Mixed document" means that a document may contain text, graphic, and still and moving picture information, as well as voice annotation.
[e] Special high-layer functions are necessary if post-processing after retrieval is required.
[f] Further study is required to indicate whether the point-to-multipoint connection represents in this case a main application.
[g] For the moment this column merely highlights some possible attribute values to give a general indication of the characteristics of these services. The full specification of these services will require a listing of all attribute values that will be defined for broadband services in the Recommendations of the I.200 series.

ISDN service is video conversational services, and perhaps the most important of these services is video telephony. Video telephony simply means that the telephone instrument includes a video transmit and receive/display capability so that dial-up calls include both voice and live picture. The first use of this service is likely to be the office environment. It can be used in any situation where the visual component of a call is advantageous, including sales, consulting, instruction, negotiation, and the discussion of visual information, such as reports, charts, advertising layouts, and so on. As the cost of videophone terminals declines, it is likely that this will be a popular residential service as well.

Another video conversational service is videoconference. The simplest form of this service is a point-to-point capability, which can be used to connect conference rooms. This differs from videophone in the nature of the equipment used. Accordingly, the service must specify the interface and protocols to be used to assure compatible equipment between conference rooms. A point-to-point videoconference would specify additional features such as facsimile and document transfer and the use of special equipment such as electronic blackboards. A different sort of videoconference is a multipoint service. This would allow participants to tie together single videophones in a conference connection, without leaving their workplaces, using a video conference server within the network. Such a system would support a small number (e.g., five) of simultaneous users. Either one participant would appear on all screens at a time, as managed by the video conference server, or a split-screen technique could be used.

A third variant of video conversational service is video surveillance. This is not a distribution service, since the information delivery is limited to a specific intended subscriber. This form of service can be unidirectional; if the information is simple video images generated by a fixed camera, then the information flow is only from video source to subscriber. A reverse flow would come into play if the user had control over the camera (change orientation, zoom, etc.). The final example listed in the table is video/audio information transmission service. This is essentially the same capability as video telephony. The difference is that a higher-quality image may be required. For example, computer animation that represents a detailed engineering design may require much higher resolution than ordinary human-to-human conversation.

The next type of conversational service listed in Table 12.3 is for data. In this context, the term *data* means arbitrary information whose structure is not visible to ISDN. Examples of applications that would use this service:

- File transfer in a distributed architecture of computer and storage systems (load sharing, back-up systems, decentralized databases, etc.).

- Large-volume or high-speed transmission of measured values or control information.
- Program downloading.
- Computer-aided design and manufacturing (CAD/CAM).
- Connection of local area networks (LANs) at different locations.

Finally, there is a conversational transfer of documents. This could include very high-resolution facsimile or the transfer of mixed documents that might include text, facsimile images, voice annotation, and/or a video component. Two types of applications are likely here: a document transfer service for the exchange of documents between users at workstations and a document storage system, based on the document transfer service, which provides document servers for the filing, update, and access of documents by a community of users.

Messaging Services

Messaging services offer user-to-user communication between individual users via storage units with store-and-forward, mailbox, and/or message-handling (e.g., information editing, processing, and conversion) functions. In contrast to conversational services, messaging services are not in real time. Hence, they place lesser demands on the network and do not require that both users be available at the same time. Analogous narrowband services are X.400 and teletex.

One new form of messaging service that could be supported by ISDN is video mail, analogous to today's electronic mail (text/graphic mail), and voice mail. Just as electronic mail replaces the mailing of a letter, so video mail replaces mailing a video cassette. This may become one of the most powerful and useful forms of message communication. Similarly, a document mail service allows the transmission of mixed documents, containing text, graphics, voice, and/or video components.

Retrieval Services

Retrieval services provide the user with the capability to retrieve information stored in information centers that is, in general, available for public use. This information is sent to the user on demand only. The information can be retrieved on an individual basis; that is, the time at which an information sequence is to start is under the control of the user.

An analogous narrowband service is Videotex. This is an interactive system designed to service both home and business needs. It is a general-purpose database retrieval system that can use the public switched telephone network or an interactive metropolitan cable TV system. Figure 12.2 depicts a typical system. The Videotex provider maintains a variety of databases on a central computer. Some of these are public databases provided by the Videotex system. Others are vendor-supplied services, such as a stock market advisory. Information is provided in the form of pages of text and simple graphics.

Broadband videotex is an enhancement of the existing Videotex system [SUGI88]. The user would be able to select sound passages, high-resolution images of TV standard, and short video scenes, in addition to the current text and simplified graphics. Examples of broadband videotex services:

- Retrieval of encyclopedia entries.
- Results of quality tests on consumer goods.
- Computer-supported audiovisual entries.
- Electronic mail-order catalogs and travel brochures with the option of placing a direct order or making a direct booking.

Another retrievel service is video retrieval. With this service, a user could order full-length films or videos from a film/video library facility. Since the provider may have to satisfy many requests, bandwidth considerations dictate that only a small number of different video transmissions can be supported at any one time. A realistic service would offer perhaps 500 movies/videos for each two-hour period. Using a 50-Mbps video channel, this would require a manageable 25-Gbs transmission capacity from video suppliers to distribution points [WEIN87]. The user would be informed by the provider at what time the film will be available to be viewed or transmitted to the subscriber's video recorder.

Of greater interest to business, educational, and medical organizations, the envisioned broadband retrieval service would also allow the retrieval of high-resolution images such as X-ray or computerized axial tomography (CAT) scans, mixed-media documents, and large data files. This service could also be used for remote education and training.

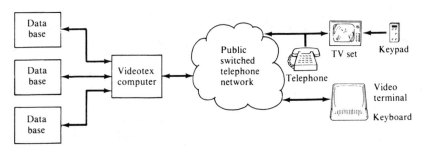

FIGURE 12.2 A Typical Videotex System

Distribution Services Without User Presentation Control

Services in this category are also referred to as broadcast services. They provide a continuous flow of information, which is distributed from a central source to an unlimited number of authorized receivers connected to the network. Each user can access this flow of information but has no control over it. In particular, the user cannot control the starting time or order of the presentation of the broadcasted information. All users simply tap into the flow of information.

The most common example of this service is broadcast television. Currently, broadcast television is available from network broadcast via radio waves and through cable television distribution systems. With the capacities planned for B-ISDN, this service can be integrated with the other telecommunications services. In addition, higher resolutions can now be achieved, and it is anticipated that these higher-quality services will also be available via B-ISDN.

An example of a nonvideo service is an electronic newspaper broadcast service. This would permit the transmission of facsimile images of newspaper pages to subscribers who had paid for the service.

Distribution Services with User Presentation Control

Services in this class also distribute information from a central source to a large number of users. However, the information is provided as a sequence of information entities (e.g, frames) with cyclical repetition. So the user has the ability of individual access to the cyclical distributed information and can control start and order of presentation. Due to the cyclical repetition, the information entities, selected by the user, will always be presented from the beginning.

An analogous narrowband service is Teletext (not to be confused with Teletex; see Chapter 6), which is depicted in Figure 12.3. Teletext is a simple one-way system that uses unallocated portions of the bandwidth of a broadcast TV signal. At the transmission end, a fixed set of pages of text is sent repeatedly in round-robin fashion. The receiver consists of a special decoder and storage unit, a keypad for user entry, and an ordinary TV set. The user keys in the number of the page desired. The decoder reads that page from the incoming signal, stores it, and displays it continuously until instructed to do otherwise. Typically, pages of Teletext form a tree pattern with higher-level pages containing menus that guide the selection of lower-level pages. Thus, although the system appears interactive to the user, it is actually a one-way broadcast of information. Since only a small portion of the TV signal bandwidth is used for this purpose, the number of pages is

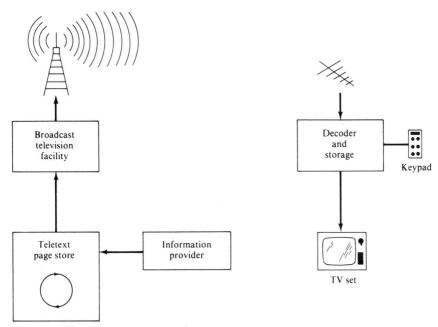

FIGURE 12.3 A Typical Teletext System

limited by a desire to reduce access time. A typical system will support a few hundred pages with a cycle time of a few tens of seconds.

Teletext is oriented primarily to the home market, with different sets of pages offered on different channels. Examples of information presented by such a system are stock market reports, weather reports, news, leisure information, and recipes.

With B-ISDN, an enhancement to Teletext known as cabletext can be provided. Whereas Teletext uses only a small portion of an analog TV channel, cabletext would use a full digital broadband channel for cyclical transmission of pages with text, images, and possible video and audio passages. As an electronic newspaper that uses public networks, or as an in-house information system for trade fairs, hotels, and hospitals, cabletext will provide low-cost access to timely and frequently requested information. A typical system might allow access to 10,000 pages with a cycle time of 1 second [ARMB87].

12.2

REQUIREMENTS

In order to get some sense of the functions and characteristics of a broadband ISDN, we need to look at the requirements it must satisfy.

As a first step, the B-ISDN services presented in Section 12.1 provide a qualitative description of requirements. To decide on the transmission structure, we need some ideas of the data rate requirements of the subscriber. Figure 12.4 [WEIN87] provides an estimate. As can be seen, the potential range of data rates is wide. The figure also gives estimated durations of calls, which is also a factor in network design.

Another estimate of data rate requirements is shown in Table 12.4 [CASA87]. Note that the values here differ from those in Figure 12.4. In both cases, the numbers can only be estimates for the projected services, and the differences point out the uncertainty in planning that will face B-ISDN designers. The table also includes the useful parameter of burstiness, which is the ratio between the time during which information is sent and the time for which the channel is occupied. This quantity provides guidance on the type of switching technology (circuit switching versus packet switching) appropriate for B-ISDN.

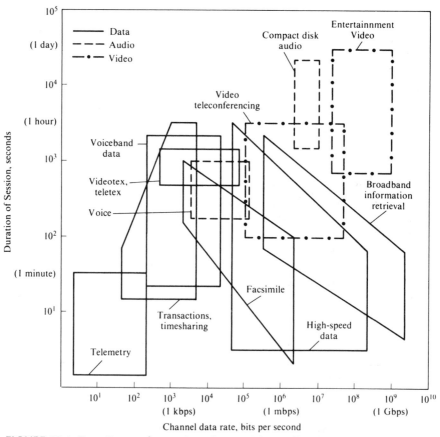

FIGURE 12.4 Data Rate and Duration of Potential Broadband ISDN Services

TABLE 12.4 Traffic Characteristics of B-ISDN

Services	Bit Rate (kbit/s)		Call Duration (secs)		Burstiness	
	Min	Max	Min	Max	Min	Max
Communicative services						
Dialog						
• Telephony	64		10^2		0.3	1
• Videotelephony	64	70.10^3	10^2		0.5	1
• Telemetry	10^{-2}	10	1	10	0.01	0.1
• Teletex	10		10^2		1	
• Facsimile (Group 4)	64		10	10^2	1	
• Videosurveillance	10	30.10^3	10^3	10^4	0.1	1
• Videoconference	10^3	70.10^3	10^3	10^4	0.5	1
Retrieval						
• Videotex	1	64	10^2	10^3	0.1	
• Broadband videotex	10^3	70.10^3	10^2	10^3	0.1	1
Messaging						
• Voice mail	16	64	10	10^2	0.3	0.5
• Video mail	10^3	70.10^3	10	10^3	0.1	0.5
• Electronic mail	10		10^2		0.5	
Distributive services						
• Hifi sound	768		10^3	10^4	1	
• TV	30.10^3	70.10^3	10^3	10^4	1	
• High-definition TV	140.10^3	565.10^3	10^3	10^4	1	

It is worth elaborating briefly on the data rate requirements for video transmission, since it is video that will drive the overall data rate requirement. The transmission of an analog video signal requires on the order of 6 MHz bandwidth. Using straightforward digitization techniques, the data rate required for digital video transmission can be as much as 1 Gbps. This is clearly too high even for a network based on optical fiber and high-speed switches. Two complementary approaches are used to reduce bit rate requirements:

- Use data-compression techniques that remove redundancy or unnecessary information.
- Allow for distortions that are least objectionable to the human eye.

Knowing what information is necessary and the types of acceptable distortion requires an in-depth understanding of the image source to be coded and of human vision. With this knowledge, one can apply various coding techniques and engineering tradeoffs to achieve the best image possible.

What is acceptable in terms of image quality and in terms of data rate is a function of application. For example, videophone and videoconferencing require both transmission and reception. To limit the engineering requirements at the subscriber site, we would like to drastically limit the video transmission data rate. Fortunately, in the case of videophone, the resolution required, especially for residential applications, is modest, and in the case of both videoconference and videophone, the rate of change of the picture is generally low. This latter property can be exploited with interframe redundancy-compression techniques, as opposed to merely the intraframe compression techniques used in systems such as facsimile.

CCITT has defined five levels of quality for video images, as shown in Table 12.5. The table also indicates the current state of the art for digital encoding of such images. The bottom two categories (D and E) are often referred to as low bit rate encoding systems, which are defined

TABLE 12.5   Bit Rates for Compressed Video Transmission

Service Quality	Description	Data Rate (Mbps)
A	High-definition television (HDTV)	92–200
B	Digital component-coding signal	30/45–145
C	Digitally coded NTSC, PAL, SE-CAM for distribution	20–45
D	Reduced spatial resolution and movement portrayal	0.384–1.92
E	Highly reduced spatial resolution and movement portrayal	0.064

as systems that transmit at data rates of about 2 Mbps or less [HASK87]. These quality levels are targeted at the videoconference and videophone applications. For quality level D, there is reduced resolution compared to broadcast television and reduced ability to track movement. In general, this produces acceptable quality. However, if there is rapid movement in the scene being televised, this will appear as jerky, discontinuous movement on the viewer's screen. Furthermore, if there is a desire to transmit a high-resolution graphics image (e.g., during a presentation at a videoconference), then the resolution on the screen may be inadequate. To overcome this latter problem, the transmitter should be capable of switching between a full-motion, lower-resolution transmission and a freeze-frame, higher-resolution transmission at the same data rate.

At the present time, a data rate of 64 kbps produces a noticeably inferior picture, designated quality level E. This data rate may be acceptable for videophone. However, the distinction between levels D and E may disappear as advances in coding technology continue. As an example of the pace of change, 64-kbps video codecs introduced in late 1986 were of equal quality to 1.544-Mbps codecs introduced in 1982 [KIM86]. By the time that B-ISDN is deployed, the need for the data rates of category D may disappear.

Quality level C corresponds to the quality of analog broadcast television today. Quality level B, known as digital component coding or extended-definition television, provides improved quality but retains the same number of lines and ratio of screen height to width of current analog broadcast television standards. In this technique, the analog television signal is broken up into components (usually the color components—red, green, blue). Each component is then separately digitally encoded and the resulting signals are time-division multiplexed. Traditional encoding techniques perform digitization on the original analog signal (known as the composite signal). It turns out that the component coding technique provides superior performance. The development of this system was undertaken with the direct-broadcast satellite application in mind, but it is certainly appropriate to B-ISDN.

Finally, the highest-quality standard is known as high-definition television (HDTV). This system is comparable in resolution to 35-mm film projection and will put the quality of TV reception in the home and office at the level of the cinema. With HDTV, not only is the resolution greater, but the system will support wider screens, more along the lines of cinema screens in height–width ratio.

You will note that Table 12.5 provides a rather large range of data rates within most of the categories. This is for two reasons. First, the technology of digital video coding is evolving rapidly, and this table attempts to predict the rates needed in the mid-1990s. Second, a distinction is made between two types of signals:

- *Contribution,* where the signal is transferred between studios and is subject to post-production studio processing.
- *Distribution,* where the signal is distributed for viewing and is not subject to such processing.

Generally, a higher degree of compression can be applied for distribution than for contribution signals.

The estimates in Figure 12.4 and Table 12.4 show that broadband services require the network to handle a wide range of call types, from those with short holding times (e.g., file transfer) to those with long holding times (e.g., distributive services), at a wide range of data rates. Also, it is to be expected that many of these services will show the same busy-hour characteristics of narrowband ISDN services, with peaks during business hours.

From a consideration of capacity, a more detailed list of requirements can be drawn up. Table 12.6, from [CASA87], suggests the requirements that B-ISDN must satisfy.

12.3

ARCHITECTURE

The B-ISDN will differ from a narrowband ISDN in a number of ways. To meet the requirements for high-resolution video, an upper channel rate of about 150 Mbps will be needed. To simultaneously support one or more interactive and distributive services, a total subscriber line rate of about 600 Mbps is needed. In terms of today's installed telephone plant, this is a stupendous data rate to sustain. The only appropriate technology for widespread support of such data rates is optical fiber. Hence, the introduction of B-ISDN depends on the pace of introduction of fiber subscriber loops.

Internal to the network, there is the issue of the switching technique to be used. The switching facility will have to be capable of handling a wide range of different bit rates and traffic parameters (e.g., burstiness). Despite the increasing power of digital circuit-switching hardware and the increasing use of optical fiber trunking, it may be difficult to handle the large and diverse requirements of B-ISDN with circuit-switching technology. For this reason, there is increasing interest in fast packet switching, described in Chapter 3, as the basic switching technique for B-ISDN. This form of switching readily supports a new user-network interface protocol known as asynchronous transfer mode (ATM), which is introduced in this chapter and examined in detail in the next chapter.

Table 12.7, taken from interim Recommendation I.121, lists the principles of B-ISDN and is suggestive of its architecture.

TABLE 12.6 Requirements for Broadband ISDN [CASA87]

Aspects	B-ISDN Requirements
Service	Support for narrowband and broadband signals, including full motion video of different service quality from high-definition TV to highly reduced resolution video Distributive and communicative service capability Point-to-point and point-to-multipoint connections
Network	Compliance with OSI network architecture reference model, including subnetworks and gateways Ability to accommodate different traffic patterns and different routing for the same multimedia communication (e.g., voice and video) Ability to be transparent or to provide value-added services (e.g., encryption, speed and format conversion) Smooth transition from narrowband ISDN Same numbering for all services to each subscriber access point Unique signaling channel for each subscriber access point
Switching	Ability to support multirate switched and nonswitched connections Network structure independent of switching mode
Transmission	Provision of a channel bandwidth up to 140 Mbit/s per service (e.g., compressed HDTV) Subscriber line bit rate range between 140 Mbit/s and 565 Mbit/s (at T reference point)
User	Dynamic allocation of access channels (bandwidth) from the user Attractive tariff structure
Operational	Simple operation and maintenance Simple extension and reconfiguration procedures Maximum use of existing infrastructures

Functional Architecture

Figure 12.5 depicts the functional architecture of B-ISDN (compare Figure 5.5). As with narrowband ISDN, control of B-ISDN is based on common-channel signaling. Within the network, an SS7, enhanced to support the expanded capabilities of a higher-speed network, will be used. Similarly, the user-network control signaling protocol will be an enhanced version of I.451/Q.931.

B-ISDN must of course support all of the 64-kbps transmission services, both circuit switching and packet switching, that are supported by narrowband ISDN. This protects the user's investment and facilitates

TABLE 12.7 Principles of B-ISDN

1. Asynchronous transfer mode (ATM) is the transfer mode for implementing B-ISDN and is independent of the means of transport at the physical layer.
2. B-ISDN supports switched, semipermanent, and permanent point-to-point and point-to-multipoint connections, and provides on demand reserved and permanent services. Connections in B-ISDN support both circuit-mode and packet-mode services of a mono- and/or multimedia type and of a connectionless or connection-oriented nature and in a bidirectional or unidirectional configuration.
3. The B-ISDN architecture is detailed in functional terms and is, therefore, technology- and implementation-independent.
4. A B-ISDN will contain intelligent capabilities for the purpose of providing advanced service characteristics and supporting powerful operation and maintenance tools, network control, and management. Further inclusion of additional intelligent features has to be considered in an overall context and may be allocated to different network/terminal elements.
5. Since the B-ISDN is based on overall ISDN concepts, the ISDN access reference configuration is also the basis for the B-ISDN access reference configuration.
6. A layered structure approach, as used in established ISDN protocol, is also appropriate for similar studies in B-ISDN. This approach should be used for studies on other overall aspects of B-ISDN, including information transfer, control, intelligence, and management.
7. Any extension of network capabilities or change in network performance parameters will not degrade the quality of service of existing services.
8. The evolution of B-ISDN should ensure the continued support of existing interfaces and services.
9. New network capabilities will be incorporated into B-ISDN in evolutionary steps to meet new user requirements and accommodate advances in network developments and progress in technology.
10. It is recognized that B-ISDN may be implemented in a variety of ways according to specific national situations.

migration from narrowband to broadband ISDN. In addition, broadband capabilities are provided for higher data rate transmission services. At the user-network interface, these capabilities will be provided with the connection-oriented asynchronous transfer mode (ATM) facility.

User-Network Interface

The reference configuration defined in I.411 is considered general enough to be used for B-ISDN. Figure 12.6, which is almost identical to Figure 7.2, shows the reference configuration for B-ISDN. In order

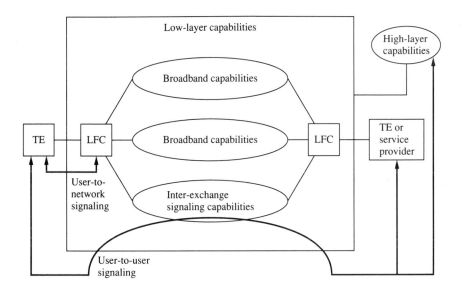

LFC = Local function capabilities
TE = Terminal equipment
FIGURE 12.5 B-ISDN Architecture

to clearly illustrate the broadband aspects, the notations for reference points and functional groupings are appended with the letter B (e.g., B-NT1, T_B). The broadband functional groups are equivalent to the functional groups defined in I.411 and discussed in Section 7-2 of this book. Interfaces at the R reference point may or may not have broadband capabilities.

Figure 12.7 is a general depiction of the B-ISDN user-access architec-

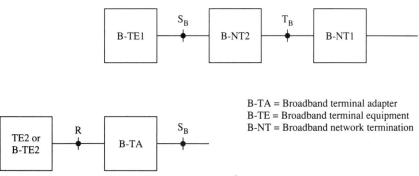

B-TA = Broadband terminal adapter
B-TE = Broadband terminal equipment
B-NT = Broadband network termination

FIGURE 12.6 B-ISDN Reference Configurations

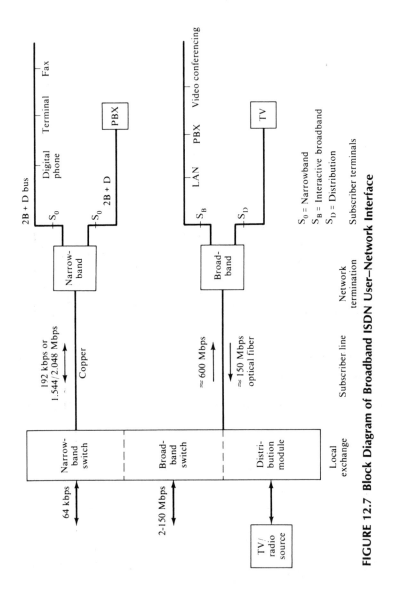

FIGURE 12.7 Block Diagram of Broadband ISDN User–Network Interface

ture. The local exchange to which subscribers attach must be able to handle both B-ISDN and ISDN subscribers. ISDN subscribers can be supported with twisted pair at the basic and primary access rates. For B-ISDN subscribers, optical fiber will be used. The data rate from network to subscriber will need to be on the order of 600 Mbps in order to handle multiple video distributions, such as might be required in an office environment. The data rate from subscriber to network would normally need to be much less, since the typical subscriber does not initiate distribution services. A rate of about 150 Mbps or less is probably adequate.

Transmission Structure

In terms of data rates available to B-ISDN subscribers, three new transmission services are defined. The first of these consists of a full-duplex 155.52-Mbps service. The second service defined is asymmetrical, providing transmission from the subscriber to the network at 155.52 Mbps and in the other direction at 622.08 Mbps. And the highest-capacity service yet defined is a full-duplex 622.08-Mbps service.

A data rate of 155.52 Mbps can certainly support all of the narrowband ISDN services. That is, it readily supports one or more basic or primary-rate interfaces. In addition, it can support most of the B-ISDN services. At that rate, one or several video channels can be supported, depending on the video resolution and the coding technique used. Thus, the full-duplex 155.52-Mbps service will probably be the most common B-ISDN service.

The higher data rate of 622.08 Mbps is needed to handle multiple video distribution, such as might be required when a business conducts multiple simultaneous videoconferences. This data rate makes sense in the network-to-subscriber direction. The typical subscriber will not initiate distribution services and thus would still be able to use the lower, 155.52-Mbps service. The full-duplex 622.08-Mbps service would be appropriate for a video distribution provider.

The 1988 document (I.121) discussed the need for a 150-Mbps and 600-Mbps data rate service. The specific rates chosen for the 1990 documents were designed to be compatible with defined digital transmission services.

The 1988 document also included a list of specific channel data rates to be supported within these services. The 1990 documents drop all reference to channel rates. This allows the user and the network to negotiate any channel capacity that can fit in the available capacity provided by the network. Thus, B-ISDN becomes considerably more flexible and can be tailored precisely to a wide variety of applications.

B-ISDN PROTOCOL REFERENCE MODEL

The protocol architecture for B-ISDN introduces some new elements not found in the ISDN architecture, as depicted in Figure 12.8. For B-ISDN, it is assumed that the transfer of information across the user-network interface will use what is referred to as asynchronous transfer mode (ATM). ATM is, in essence, a form of packet transmission across the user-network interface in the same way that X.25 is a form of packet transmission across the user-network interface. One difference between X.25 and ATM is that X.25 includes control signaling on the same channel as data transfer, whereas ATM makes use of common-channel signaling. Another difference is that X.25 packets may be of varying length, whereas ATM packets are of fixed size, referred to as cells.

The decision to use ATM for B-ISDN is a remarkable one. This implies that B-ISDN will be a packet-based network, certainly at the interface and almost certainly in terms of its internal switching. Although the recommendation also states that B-ISDN will support circuit-mode applications, this will be done over a packet-based transport mechanism. Thus, ISDN, which began as an evolution from the circuit-switching telephone networks, will transform itself into a packet-switching network as it takes on broadband services.

Two layers of the B-ISDN protocol architecture relate to ATM functions. There is an ATM layer common to all services, which provides packet transfer capabilities, and an ATM adaptation layer (AAL), which is service dependent. The AAL maps higher-layer information into ATM cells to be transported over B-ISDN, then collects information from ATM

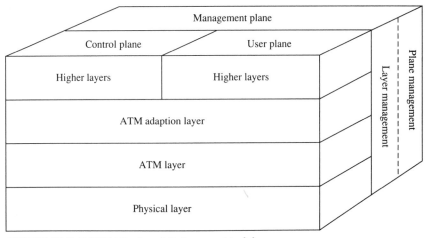

FIGURE 12.8 B-ISDN Protocol Reference Model

cells for delivery to higher layers. The use of ATM creates the need for an adaptation layer to support information-transfer protocols not based on ATM. Two examples listed in I.121 are PCM voice and LAP-D. PCM voice is an application that produces a stream of bits. To employ this application over ATM, it is necessary to assemble PCM bits into packets (called cells in the recommendation) for transmission and to read them out on reception in such a way as to produce a smooth, constant flow of bits to the receiver. For LAP-D, it is necessary to map LAP-D frames into ATM packets; this will probably mean segmenting one LAP-D frame into a number of packets on transmission and reassembling the frame from packets on reception. By allowing the use of LAP-D over ATM, all of the existing ISDN applications and control signaling protocols can be used on B-ISDN.

The protocol reference model makes reference to three separate planes:

- *User plane:* Provides for user information transfer, along with associated controls (e.g., flow control, error control).
- *Control plane:* Performs call-control and connection-control functions.
- *Management plane:* Includes plane management, which performs management functions related to a system as a whole and provides coordination between all the planes, and layer management, which performs management functions relating to resources and parameters residing in its protocol entities.

The 1988 I.121 Recommendation contains the protocol reference model depicted in Figure 12.8 but provides virtually no detail on the functions to be performed at each layer. The 1990 documents include a more detailed description of functions to be performed, as illustrated in Table 12.8. Let us examine each of these briefly.

Physical Layer

The physical layer consists of two sublayers: the physical medium sublayer and the transmission convergence sublayer.

Physical Medium Sublayer. This sublayer includes only physical medium-dependent functions. Its specification will therefore depend on the medium used. One function common to all medium types is bit timing. This sublayer is responsible for transmitting/receiving a continuous flow of bits with associated timing information to synchronize transmission and reception.

Transmission Convergence Sublayer. This sublayer is responsible for the following functions:

TABLE 12.8   Functions of the B-ISDN Layers

	Higher-layer Functions	Higher Layers		
		CS (AAL)	**SAR** (AAL)	
Layer Management	Convergence	CS		AAL
	Segmentation and reassembly		SAR	AAL
	Generic flow control			ATM
	Cell header generation/extraction			ATM
	Cell VPI/VCI translation			ATM
	Cell multiplex and demultiplex			ATM
	Cell rate decoupling			TC
	HEC header sequence generation/verification			TC (Physical Layer)
	Cell delineation			TC
	Transmission frame adaptation			TC
	Transmission frame generation/recovery			TC
	Bit timing			PM (Physical Layer)
	Physical medium			PM

CS = Convergence sublayer
SAR = Segmentation and reassembly sublayer
AAL = ATM adaptation layer
ATM = Asynchronous transfer mode
TC = Transmission control sublayer
PM = Physical medium sublayer

- *Transmission frame generation and recovery:* Transmission at the physical layer consists of frames, such as we saw in the basic and primary rate interfaces. This function is concerned with generating and maintaining the frame structure appropriate for a given data rate.
- *Transmission frame adaptation:* Information exchange at the ATM layer is a flow of ATM cells. This sublayer is responsible for packaging these cells into a frame. One option is to have no frame structure but to simply transmit and receive a flow of cells.
- *Cell delineation:* For transmission purposes, the bit flow may be scrambled (see Appendix 8A). This sublayer is responsible for maintaining the cell boundaries so that cells may be recovered after descrambling at the destination.
- *HEC sequence generation and cell header verification:* Each cell header is protected by a header error-control (HEC) code. This sublayer is responsible for generating and checking this code.
- *Cell rate decoupling:* This includes insertion and suppression of idle cells in order to adapt the rate of valid ATM cells to the payload capacity of the transmission system.

ATM Layer

The ATM layer is independent of the physical medium. The details of this layer will be examined in Chapter 13. Here we give a brief description of its principal functions:

- *Cell multiplexing and demultiplexing:* Multiple logical connections may be maintained across an interface, much like X.25 and frame relay.
- *Virtual path identifier (VPI) and virtual channel identifier (VCI) translation:* The VPI and VCI relate to logical connections and have local significance. Consequently, the values may need to be translated during switching.
- *Cell header generation/extraction:* In the transmit direction, a cell header is appended to user data from the AAL. All of the fields except the HEC code are generated. This function may also include translation from an address to a logical connection number (VPI and VCI).
- *Generic flow control:* This function generates flow-control information for placement in cell headers.

ATM Adaptation Layer

The ATM adaptation layer consists of two sublayers: the segmentation and reassembly sublayer and the convergence sublayer. The details of this layer will be examined in Chapter 13. Here we give a brief description of its principal functions.

The segmentation and reassembly sublayer is responsible for the segmentation of higher-layer information into a size suitable for the information field of an ATM cell on transmission and the reassembly of the contents of a sequence of ATM cell information fields into higher-layer information on reception.

The convergence sublayer is an interface specification. It defines the services that AAL provides to higher layers.

12.5

B-ISDN PHYSICAL LAYER

The 1988 document (I.121) does not address the issue of the physical medium on the subscriber's premises. In contrast, the 1990 documents provide preliminary specifications of the medium for the interface between the user and B-ISDN.

For the full-duplex 155.52-Mbps service, either coaxial cable or optical fiber may be used. The coaxial cable is to support connections up to a maximum distance of 100 to 200 meters, using one cable for transmission in each direction. The parameters defined in the 1988 Recommendation G.703 are to be used.

Optical fiber is to support connections up to a maximum distance of 800 to 2000 meters. The details of the optical media (e.g., single mode versus multimode, single full-duplex fiber versus dual fiber) have been postponed for further study.

For a service that includes the 622.08-Mbps rate in one or both directions, optical fiber is to be used. Again, the details of the fiber parameters are left for further study.

A final important issue at the physical layer is the transmission structure to be used to multiplex cells from various virtual channels. The 1988 document discussed this issue in general terms and proposed three alternatives. For the 155.52-Mbps data rate, the 1990 documents reduce the number of options to two and provide more detail. For the 622.08-Mbps data rate, the multiplex structure is left for further study.

The first of the two options for the 155.52-Mbps data rate is the use of a continuous stream of cells, with no multiplex frame structure imposed at the interface. Synchronization is on a cell-by-cell basis. That is, the receiver is responsible for assuring that it properly delineates cells on the 53-octet cell boundaries. This task is accomplished by using the header error-control (HEC) field. As long as the HEC calculation is indicating no errors, it is assumed that cell alignment is being properly maintained. An occasional error does not change this assumption. However, a string of error detections would indicate that the receiver is out of alignment, at which point it performs a hunting procedure to recover alignment.

The second option is to place the cells in a synchronous time-division multiplex envelope. In this case, the bit stream at the interface has an external frame based on the synchronous digital hierarchy (SDH) defined in Recommendation G.709. In the U.S., this frame structure is referred to as SONET (synchronous optical network). The SDH frame may be used exclusively for ATM cells or may also carry other bit streams not yet defined in B-ISDN.

The SDH standard defines a hierarchy of data rates, all of which are multiples of 51.84 Mbps, including 155.52 Mbps and 622.08 Mbps. Therefore, the SDH scheme could also be used to support the higher B-ISDN data rate. However, the 1990 specification does not address this possibility.

12.6

SUMMARY

Although the development and deployment of ISDN is still in its early stages, planners and designers are already looking toward a much more revolutionary change in telecommunications: the broadband ISDN. Advances in terminal technology, optical fiber transmission technology, and switching technology, together with a rising demand for information-rich services, are accelerating the telecommunications environment through ISDN to a B-ISDN before the end of the century. Just as the capacity of B-ISDN is several orders of magnitude greater than ISDN, its impact will also be greater.

12.7

RECOMMENDED READING

[COUD88] and [LEON89] are special issues devoted to broadband ISDN. [KIM89] and [BHAR91] are collections of papers on broadband ISDN. [PATT90] provides an interesting discussion of B-ISDN services. [MINZ89] examines the new requirements for user-network signaling for B-ISDN.

12.8

PROBLEMS

12.1. Is there a need to enhance or otherwise modify Signaling System Number 7 to support broadband ISDN?

12.2. Is there a need to enhance or otherwise modify the I.451 call-control protocol to support broadband ISDN?

12.3. In many developed countries, a substantial investment has been made in coaxial cable installation to support cable TV distribution to home and office.

    a. Can this installed plant, rather than optical fiber, become the subscriber loop for B-ISDN?

    b. If not, why not maintain this separate network for TV distribution rather than attempting to incorporate all communications services under B-ISDN?

APPENDIX 12A

1990 Interim CCITT Recommendations on Broadband ISDN

Number	Title	Description
I.113	Vocabulary of Terms for Broadband Aspects of ISDN	Defines terms considered essential to the understanding and application of the principles of B-ISDN.
I.121	Broadband Aspects of ISDN	States the basic principles of B-ISDN and indicates the evolution of ISDN required to support advanced services and applications.
I.150	B-ISDN ATM Functional Characteristics	Summarizes the functions of the ATM layer.
I.211	B-ISDN Service Aspects	Serves as a guideline for evolving Recommendations on B-ISDN services. Includes a classification of B-ISDN services and a consideration of necessary network aspects.
I.311	B-ISDN General Network Aspects	Describes networking techniques, signaling principles, traffic control, and resources management for B-ISDN. Introduces concepts of transmission path, virtual path, and virtual channel.
I.321	B-ISDN Protocol Reference Model and Its Application	Describes additions to the ISDN protocol reference model needed to accommodate B-ISDN services and functions.
I.327	B-ISDN Functional Architecture	Describes additions to the ISDN functional architecture needed to accommodate B-ISDN services and functions.

Number	Title	Description
I.35b	Broadband ISDN Performance	Defines the performance parameters and performance objectives for the ATM layer of a broadband ISDN.
I.361	B-ISDN ATM Layer Specification	Describes the ATM layer, including cell structure, cell coding, and ATM protocol.
I.362	B-ISDN ATM Adaptation Layer (AAL) Functional Description	Provides a service classification for AAL and indicates the relationship between AAL services and AAL protocols.
I.363	B-ISDN ATM Adaptation Layer (AAL) Specification	Describes the interactions between the AAL and the next higher layer, the AAL and the ATM layer, and AAL peer-to-peer operations.
I.413	B-ISDN User-Network Interface	Gives the reference configuration for the B-ISDN user-network interface and examples of physical realizations.
I.432	B-ISDN User-Network Interface Physical Layer Specification	Defines physical layer interface for B-ISDN. Includes physical medium specification, timing, and framing aspects, and header error control.
I.610	OAM Principles of B-ISDN Access	Describes the minimum functions required to maintain the physical layer and the ATM layer of the customer access.

CHAPTER 13

ATM and SONET/SDH

For B-ISDN, the transfer of information across the user-network interface will use what is referred to as asynchronous transfer mode (ATM). The use of ATM implies that B-ISDN will be a packet-based network, certainly at the interface and almost certainly in terms of its internal switching. Although the recommendation also states that B-ISDN will support circuit-mode applications, this will be done over a packet-based transport mechanism. Thus, ISDN, which began as an evolution from the circuit-switching telephone networks, will transform itself into a packet-switching network as it takes on broadband services.

We begin this chapter with an examination of the details of the ATM protocol and formats. Next, the requirement for mapping various applications onto ATM is examined with a consideration of the ATM adaptation layer (AAL). The remaining aspect of ATM to examine is the manner in which ATM cells are actually packaged for transmission across the user-network interface. Before addressing this topic, however, we need to look to one of the alternative transmission structures to be used: SONET/SDH.

13.1

ASYNCHRONOUS TRANSFER MODE

Synchronous Versus Asynchronous Transfer

When the standards work on broadband ISDN (B-ISDN) began in the mid-1980s, it was generally assumed by most participants that some

529

form of synchronous time-division multiplexing (TDM) technique would be used, as is the case with the basic and primary rate access methods for ISDN. Under this approach, the interface structure that was proposed was

$$j \times H4 + k \times H2 + 1 \times H1 + m \times H0 + n \times B + D$$

where D, B, H0, and H1 (H11 or H12) are narrowband ISDN channels and H2 and H4 are new B-ISDN fixed-rate channels. H2 would be in the range of 30 to 45 Mbps and H4 in the range of 120 to 140 Mbps.

Although the synchronous TDM approach is a natural extension of narrowband ISDN, it does not provide the best model for B-ISDN. There are two basic disadvantages of the synchronous approach [MINZ89b]. First, it does not provide a flexible interface for meeting a variety of needs. At the high data rates offered by B-ISDN, there could be a wide variety of applications, and many different data rates, that need to be switched. One or two fixed-rate channel types do not provide a structure that can easily accommodate this requirement. Furthermore, many data (as opposed to voice or video) applications are bursty in nature and can more efficiently be handled with some sort of packet-switching approach. A final aspect of the inflexibility of the synchronous approach is that it does not lend itself to rate adaptation. We have seen that rate adaptation within the 64-kbps channel is quite complex. One can imagine the complexity and inefficiency of extending this concept to channels in the tens and hundreds of megabits per second.

The second disadvantage of the synchronous approach for high-speed transmission is that the use of multiple high data rates (e.g., a number of H2 and H4 channels) complicates the switching system. We would require switches that can handle data streams of multiple high data rates. This is in contrast to narrowband ISDN, which has just the 64-kbps data stream to switch.

Thus, synchronous TDM has been rejected. However, it is still possible to multiplex several ATM streams using synchronous TDM techniques to achieve transmission interfaces that exceed the rate of operation of ATM switches and multiplexers. We examine this topic in Section 13-3.

ATM Overview

ATM is similar in concept to frame relay, which we examined in Chapters 9 and 10. Both frame relay and ATM take advantage of the reliability and fidelity of modern digital facilities to provide faster packet switching than X.25. ATM, at its higher data rate, is even more streamlined in its functionality than frame relay, as we shall see.

ATM is a packet-oriented transfer mode. Like frame relay and X.25, it allows multiple logical connections to be multiplexed over a single physical interface. The information flow on each logical connection is organized into fixed-size packets, called **cells.** As with frame relay, there is no link-by-link error control or flow control.

Figure 13.1 shows the overall hierarchy of function in an ATM-based network. This hierarchy is seen from the point of view of the internal network functions needed to support ATM as well as the user-network functions. The ATM layer consists of virtual channel and virtual path levels; these are discussed in the next subsection.

The physical layer can be divided into three functional levels:

- *Transmission path level:* Extends between network elements that assemble and disassemble the payload of a transmission system. For end-to-end communication, the payload is end-user information. For user-to-network communication, the payload may be signaling information. Cell delineation and header error-control functions are required at the endpoints of each transmission path.
- *Digital section:* Extends between network elements that assemble and disassemble a continuous bit or byte stream. This refers to the exchanges or signal transfer points in a network that are involved in switching data streams.
- *Regenerator section level:* A portion of a digital section. An example of this level is a repeater that is used to simply regenerate the digital signal along a transmission path that is too long to be used without such regeneration; no switching is involved.

Virtual Channels and Virtual Paths

Logical connections in ATM are referred to as **virtual channels.** A virtual channel is analogous to a virtual circuit in X.25 or a frame-relay logical connection. It is the basic unit of switching in B-ISDN. A virtual channel is set up between two end users through the network, and a variable-rate, full-duplex flow of fixed-size cells is exchanged over the connection. Virtual channels are also used for user-network exchange (control signaling) and network-network exchange (network management and routing).

Higher layers		
ATM layer	Virtual channel level	
	Virtual path level	
Physical layer	Transmission path level	
	Digital section level	
	Regenerator section level	

FIGURE 13.1 ATM Transport Hierarchy

For ATM, a second sublayer of processing has been introduced that deals with the concept of **virtual path** (Figure 13.2). A virtual path is a bundle of virtual channels that have the same endpoints. Thus all of the cells flowing over all of the virtual channels in a single virtual path are switched together.

Several advantages can be listed for the use of virtual paths:

- *Simplified network architecture:* Network transport functions can be separated into those related to an individual logical connection (virtual channel) and those related to a group of logical connections (virtual path).
- *Increased network performance and reliability:* The network deals with fewer, aggregated entities.
- *Reduced processing and short connection setup time:* Much of the work is done when the virtual path is set up. The addition of new virtual channels to an existing virtual path involves minimal processing.
- *Enhanced network services:* The virtual path is used internal to the network but is also visible to the end user. Thus, the user may define closed user groups or closed networks of virtual-channel bundles.

Virtual Path/Virtual Channel Characteristics.   As yet, many of the details of the virtual-path/virtual-channel concept have not been worked out. Interim Recommendation I.150 lists the following as characteristics of virtual channel connections:

- *Quality of service:* A user of a virtual channel is provided with a quality of service specified by parameters such as cell-loss ratio (ratio of cells lost to cells transmitted) and cell-delay variation.
- *Switched and semipermanent virtual-channel connections:* Both switched connections, which require call-control signaling, and dedicated channels can be provided.

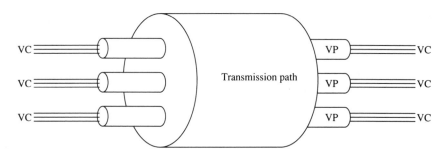

VP = Virtual path
VC = Virtual channel
FIGURE 13.2 ATM Connection Relationships

- *Cell sequence integrity:* The sequence of transmitted cells within a virtual channel is preserved.
- *Traffic parameter negotiation and usage monitoring:* Traffic parameters can be negotiated between a user and the network for each virtual channel. The input of cells to the virtual channel is monitored by the network to ensure that the negotiated parameters are not violated.

The types of traffic parameters that can be negotiated would include average rate, peak rate, burstiness, and peak duration. The network may need a number of strategies to deal with congestion and to manage existing and requested virtual channels. At the crudest level, the network may simply deny new requests for virtual channels to prevent congestion. Additionally, cells may be discarded if negotiated parameters are violated or if congestion becomes severe. In an extreme situation, existing connections might be terminated.

I.150 also lists characteristics of virtual paths. The first four characteristics listed are identical to those for virtual channels. That is, quality of service, switched and semipermanent virtual paths, cell sequence integrity, and traffic parameter negotiation and usage monitoring are also characteristics of a virtual path. There are a number of reasons for this duplication. First, this provides some flexibility in how the network manages the requirements placed upon it. Second, the network must be concerned with the overall requirements for a virtual path, and within a virtual path may negotiate the establishment of virtual circuits with given characteristics. Finally, once a virtual path is set up, it is possible for the end users to negotiate the creation of new virtual channels. The virtual path characteristics impose a discipline on the choices that the end users may make.

In addition, a fifth characteristic is listed for virtual paths:

- *Virtual channel identifier restriction within a virtual path:* One or more virtual channel identifiers, or numbers, may not be available to the user of the virtual path, but may be reserved for network use. Examples would be virtual channels used for network management.

Control Signaling. In narrowband ISDN, the D channel is provided for control signaling of calls on B and H channels. In B-ISDN, with its ATM interface, there is no simple fixed-rate structure of H, B, and D channels. Thus, a more flexible arrangement for control signaling is needed. The requirement is further complicated by the need for the establishment and release of two types of entities: virtual channels and virtual paths.

For virtual channels, I.150 specifies four methods for providing an establishment/release facility. One or a combination of these methods will be used in any particular network:

1. **A semipermanent virtual channel** may be used for control signaling.
2. If there is no preestablished call-control signaling channel, then one must be set up. For that purpose, a control-signaling exchange must take place between the user and the network on some channel. Hence we need a permanent channel, probably of low data rate, that can be used to set up a virtual channel that can be used for call control. Such a channel is called a **meta-signaling channel,** since the channel is used to set up signaling channels.
3. The meta-signaling channel can be used to set up a virtual channel between the user and the network for call-control signaling. This **user-to-network signaling virtual channel** can then be used to set up virtual channels to carry user data.
4. The meta-signaling channel can also be used to set up a **user-to-user signaling virtual channel.** Such a channel must be set up within a preestablished virtual path. It can then be used to allow the two end users, without network intervention, to establish and release user-to-user virtual channels to carry user data.

For virtual paths, three methods are defined in I.150:

1. A virtual path can be established on a **semipermanent** basis by prior agreement. In this case, no control signaling is required.
2. Virtual path establishment/release may be **customer-controlled.** In this case, the customer uses a signaling virtual channel to request the virtual path from the network.
3. Virtual path establishment/release may be **network-controlled.** In this case, the network establishes a virtual path for its own convenience. The path may be network-to-network, user-to-network, or user-to-user.

ATM Cells

The asynchronous transfer mode makes use of fixed-size cells, consisting of a 5-octet header and a 48-octet information field (Figure 13.3a). In the 1988 document (I.121), the header fields and header size are undefined, and it had not yet been decided to use fixed-size cells. The definitive decision to use fixed-size cells is documented in the 1990 Recommendations.

There are several advantages to the use of small, fixed-size cells. First, the use of small cells may reduce queueing delay for a high-priority cell, since it waits less if it arrives slightly behind a lower-priority cell that has gained access to a resource (e.g., the transmitter). Secondly, it appears that fixed-size cells can be switched more effi-

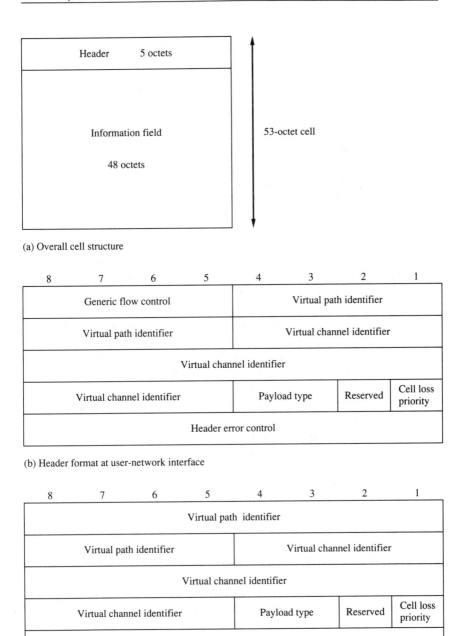

(a) Overall cell structure

(b) Header format at user-network interface

(c) Header format at network node interface

FIGURE 13.3 ATM Cell Format

ciently, which is important for the very high data rates of ATM. For a discussion of these issues, see [PARE88].

Header Format.   Figure 13.3b shows the header format at the user-network interface (S or T reference point).

Multiple terminals may share a single access link to the network. The **generic flow-control field** is to be used for end-to-end flow control. The details of its application are for further study. The field could be used to assist the customer in controlling the flow of traffic for different qualities of service. One candidate for the use of this field is a multiple-priority level indicator to control the flow of information in a service-dependent manner.

The virtual path identifier and virtual channel identifier fields constitute a routing field for the network. The **virtual path identifier** indicates a user-to-user or user-to-network virtual path. The **virtual channel identifier** indicates a user-to-user or user-to-network virtual channel. These identifiers have local significance (as with X.25 and frame relay) and may change as the cell traverses the network.

The **payload type** field indicates the type of information in the information field. A value of 00 indicates user information, that is, information from the next higher layer. Other values are for further study. Presumably, network management and maintenance values will be assigned. This field allows the insertion of network-management cells onto a user's virtual channel without impacting the user's data. Thus, it could provide inband control information.

The **cell-loss priority** is used to provide guidance to the network in the event of congestion. A value of 0 indicates a cell of relatively higher priority, which should not be discarded unless no other alternative is available. A value of 1 indicates that this cell is subject to discard within the network. The user might employ this field so that extra information may be inserted into the network, with a CLP of 1, and delivered to the destination if the network is not congested. The network sets this field to 1 for any data cell that is in violation of a traffic agreement. In this case, the switch that does the setting realizes that the cell exceeds the agreed traffic parameters but that that switch is capable of handling the cell. At a later point in the network, if congestion is encountered, this cell has been marked for discard in preference to cells that fall within agreed traffic limits.

The **header error-control (HEC)** field is an 8-bit error code that can be used to correct single-bit errors in the header and to detect double-bit errors. Its use is explained subsequently.

Figure 13.3c shows the cell header format internal to the network. The generic flow-control field, which performs end-to-end functions, is not retained. Instead, the virtual path identifier field is expanded from 8 to 12 bits. This allows support for an expanded number of virtual paths internal to the network, to include those supporting subscribers and those required for network management.

Header Error Control. In Appendix A-2, the use of a code for error detection is discussed. This code is commonly used in data communications protocols, such as LAPD and LAPB. The procedure is as follows:

1. The transmit side calculates an error-code value based on the contents of the transmitted data (e.g., an entire frame or the header of the frame).
2. The transmit side inserts the resulting code into the transmitted data as an additional field.
3. The receive side, using the same algorithm, calculates an error code value based on the contents of the received data.
4. The receive side compares the value that it has calculated with the contents of the error-code field that is received as part of the transmission. If the codes match, it is assumed that no error has occurred. If there is no match, then an error is detected.

A similar procedure is adopted in ATM, with the use of an 8-bit header error-control field (HEC) that is calculated based on the remaining 32 bits of the header. In this case, the polynomial used to generate the code is $X^8 + X^2 + X + 1$ (see Appendix A for a discussion of the use of polynomials to calculate an error code). There is, however, one significant difference. In the case of most existing protocols, such as LAPD and LAPB, the data that serve as input to the error-code calculation are in general much longer than the size of the resulting error code. This allows for error detection. In the case of ATM, the input to the calculation is only 32 bits, compared to 8 bits for the code. The fact that that input is relatively short allows the code to be used not only for error detection but, in some cases, for actual error correction. This is because there is sufficient redundancy in the code to recover from certain error patterns.

Figure 13.4 depicts the operation of the HEC algorithm at the receiver.

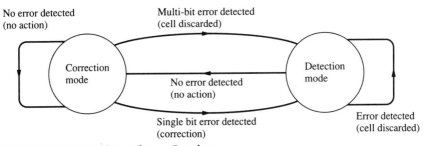

FIGURE 13.4 HEC Operation at Receiver

At initialization the receiver's error-correction algorithm is in the default mode for single-bit error correction. As each cell is received, the HEC calculation and comparison are performed. As long as no errors are detected, the receiver remains in error-correction mode. When an error is detected, the receiver will correct the error if it is a single-bit error or will detect that a multibit error has occurred. In either case, the receiver now moves to detection mode. In this mode, no attempt is made to correct errors. The reason for this change is to recognize that a noise burst or other event might cause a sequence of errors. The receiver remains in detection mode as long as errored cells are received. When a header is examined and found not to be in error, the receiver switches back to correction mode. The flowchart of Figure 13.5 shows the consequence of errors in the cell header.

The error-protection function provides both recovery from single-bit header errors and a low probability of the delivery of cells with errored headers under bursty error conditions. The error characteristics of fiber-based transmission systems appear to be a mix of single-bit errors and relatively large burst errors. For some transmission systems, the error-correction capability, which is more time-consuming, might not be invoked.

Figure 13.6, from I.432, indicates how random bit errors impact the probability of occurrence of discarded cells and valid cells with errored headers.

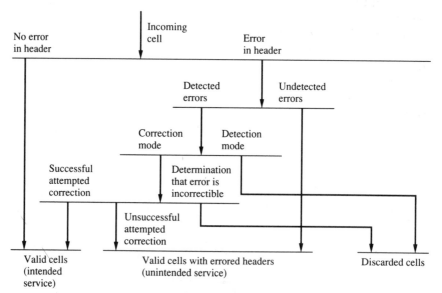

FIGURE 13.5 Effect of Error in Cell Header

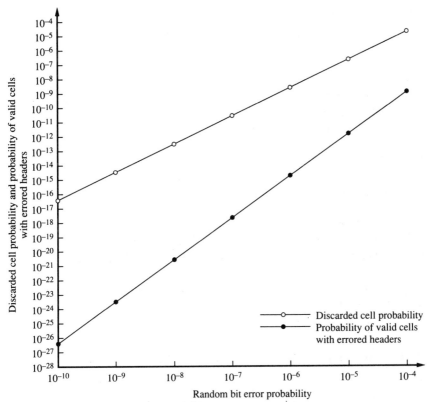

FIGURE 13.6 Impact of Random Bit Errors on HEC Performance

13.2

ATM ADAPTATION LAYER

The use of ATM creates the need for an adaptation layer to support information-transfer protocols not based on ATM. Two examples listed in the 1988 Recommendation are PCM (pulse code modulation) voice and LAPD. PCM voice is an application that produces a stream of bits from a voice signal. To employ this application over ATM, it is necessary to assemble PCM bits into cells for transmission and to read them out on reception in such a way as to produce a smooth, constant flow of bits to the receiver. LAPD is the standard data link control protocol for ISDN and B-ISDN. It is necessary to map LAPD frames into ATM cells; this will probably mean segmenting one LAPD frame into a number of cells on transmission and reassembling the frame from cells on reception. By allowing the use of LAPD over ATM, all of the existing ISDN applications and control-signaling protocols can be used on B-ISDN.

AAL Services

The 1988 Recommendation briefly mentions AAL and points out its functions of mapping information into cells and performing segmentation and reassembly. The 1990 documents provide greater detail of the functions and services of this layer. In the area of services, four classes of service are defined (Table 13.1). The classification is based on whether a timing relationship must be maintained between source and destination, whether the application requires a constant bit rate, and whether the transfer is connection-oriented or connectionless. An example of a Class A service is circuit emulation. In this case, a constant bit rate, which requires the maintenance of a timing relation, is used, and the transfer is connection-oriented. An example of a Class B service is variable-bit-rate video, such as might be used in a teleconference. Here, the application is connection-oriented and timing is important, but the bit rate varies, depending on the amount of activity in the scene. Classes C and D correspond to data transfer applications. In both cases, the bit rate may vary and no particular timing relationship is required; differences in data rate are handled by the end systems, using buffers. The data transfer may be either connection-oriented (Class C) or connectionless (Class D).

AAL Protocols

To support these various classes of service, a set of protocols at the AAL level is defined. In the 1990 version, a preliminary definiton is provided, which is primarily functional. However, the document does include some detail concerning header formats and procedures. The details of the AAL protocols remain to be worked out. An overview of the preliminary specification is provided in the remainder of this subsection.

The AAL layer is organized in two logical sublayers: the convergence sublayer (CS) and the segmentation and reassembly sublayer (SAR). The convergence sublayer provides the functions needed to support specific applications using AAL. Each application attaches to AAL at a service access point (SAP), which is simply the address of the applica-

TABLE 13.1   Service Classification for AAL

	Class A	Class B	Class C	Class D
Timing relation between source and destination	Required		Not Required	
Bit rate	Constant	Variable		
Connection mode	Connection-oriented			Connectionless

tion (see Appendix B for a discussion of SAPs). This sublayer is thus service-dependent.

The segmentation and reassembly sublayer is responsible for packaging information received from CS into cells for transmission and unpacking the information at the other end. As we have seen, at the ATM layer each cell consists of a 5-octet header and a 48-octet information field. Thus, SAR must pack any SAR headers and trailers plus CS information into 48-octet blocks.

Four AAL protocols have been defined by CCITT, one to support each of the four classes of service. The type 1 protocol supports Class A, type 2 supports Class B, and so on. Table 13.2 lists the currently defined functional details of the four types.

Figure 13.7 lists the format of the protocol data units (PDUs) at the SAR level for the four types; the PDU fields are defined in Table 13.3. PDUs for the CS level are not specified, since these are application-dependent. For type 1 operation, we are dealing with a constant bit-rate source. In this case, the only responsibility of the SAR protocol is to pack the bits into cells for transmission and unpack them at reception. Each block is accompanied by a sequence number so that errored PDUs can be tracked. The sequence number protection field is an error code for error detection and possibly correction on the sequence number field.

The remainder of the protocol types (2 through 4) deal with variable-bit-rate information. Type 2 is intended for analog applications, such as video and audio, that require timing information but do not require constant bit rate. Again, a sequence number is provided. In addition, an information type (IT) field and length indicator (LI) field are used to allow the segmentation and reassembly of bursts of information from higher levels. The IT field indicates whether this is the beginning, continuation, or end of a block from the application. If this is the last segment, the LI field indicates how many octets of information are included. This field is needed since each cell is of fixed size; therefore, the last cell is likely to be only partially filled. Note that segmentation and reassembly are also done in the type 1 protocol. However, since type 1 supports constant-bit-rate applications, there is no concept of bursts of information and therefore no need to mark beginning, middle, and end; there is simply a constant stream of bits to be packaged into cells. The information type of field can also be used to indicate whether the information is the video or audio component of a video signal.

Type 3 and type 4 protocols are intended for data transmission applications, so that the information received from a higher layer will be in the form of protocol data units or blocks of data. Type 3 provides a connection-oriented service. The reserved field can be used for multiplexing purposes. This would allow multiple user sessions to be multiplexed on a single ATM connection. All of the user sessions would

TABLE 13.2 ATM Adaptation Layer Protocol Types

	Services Provided	Overall Functions	SAR Functions	CS Functions
Type 1	• Transfer of SDUs with constant bit rate (CBR) • Transfer of timing information between source and destination • Indication of lost or errored information not recovered by type 1	• Segmentation and reassembly • Handling of cell delay variation • Handling of lost and misinserted cells • Source clock frequency recovery at destination • Monitoring and handling of PCI bit errors • Monitoring of user information for bit errors and possible corrective action	For further study	• Forward error correction for high-quality video and audio • For some services, clock recovery at the receiver • For services requiring explicit time indication, insertion of time-stamp pattern • Handling of lost and misinserted cells
Type 2	• Transfer of SDUs with variable bit rate (VBR) • Transfer of timing information between source and destination • Indication of lost or errored information not recovered by type 2	• Segmentation and reassembly • Handling of cell delay variation • Handling of lost and misinserted cells • Source clock frequency recovery at destination	For further study	• Forward error correction for high-quality video and audio • For some services, clock recovery at the receiver • Handling of lost and misinserted cells

Type 3	• Message-mode service • Streaming-mode service • Assured operation • Nonassured operation	• Monitoring and handling of header and trailer bit errors • Monitoring of user information for bit errors and possible corrective action	• Segmentation and reassembly • Error detection • Multiplexing	For further study
Type 4	• Message-mode service • Streaming-mode service • Assured operation • Nonassured operation		• Segmentation and reassembly • Error detection • Multiplexing	• Higher-layer PDU delineation and transparency • Mapping between AAL-SAPs and ATM layer connections • Error detection and handling • Message segmentation and reassembly • Identification of information • Buffer allocation size

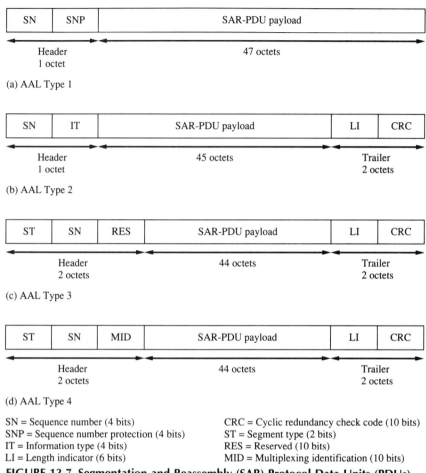

SN = Sequence number (4 bits)   CRC = Cyclic redundancy check code (10 bits)
SNP = Sequence number protection (4 bits)   ST = Segment type (2 bits)
IT = Information type (4 bits)   RES = Reserved (10 bits)
LI = Length indicator (6 bits)   MID = Multiplexing identification (10 bits)

FIGURE 13.7 Segmentation and Reassembly (SAR) Protocol Data Units (PDUs)

need to have the same quality-of-service parameters as the underlying ATM connection.

Type 4 provides a connectionless service. In this case, the concept of multiplexing takes on a different meaning than for type 3 operation. For type 4, if a single PDU at the CS level is divided into multiple PDUs at the SAR level, then all of the resulting SAR-PDUs will have the same multiplexing identification value. Thus, information from more than one CS-PDU can be interleaved over a single ATM connection without confusion.

For both type 3 and type 4 operation, two modes of service are defined:

- *Message-mode service:* Used for framed data. Thus, any of the OSI-related protocols and applications would fit into this category. In

TABLE 13.3   AAL Segmentation and Reassembly PDU Parameters

Cyclic Redundancy Check Code (10 bits)
Used to detect errors and correct up to two correlated bit errors in the SAR-PDU. The generating polynomial is $X^{10} + X^9 + X^5 + X^4 + X + 1$.

Information Type (4 bits)
Used in type 2 operation to indicate beginning of message, continuation of message, or end of message, and also component of the video or audio signal.

Length Indicator (6 bits)
Indicates the number of octets of the CS-PDU that are included in the SAR-PDU payload.

Multiplexing Identification (10 bits)
Provides for the multiplexing and demultiplexing of multiple CS-PDUs concurrently over a single ATM connection. All SAR-PDUs of a given CS-PDU will have the same MID value.

Segment Type
Used in type 3 and 4 operation to indicate beginning of message, continuation of message, end of message, or single-segment message.

Sequence Number (4 bits)
Used to detect lost or misinserted cells.

Sequence Number Protection (4 bits)
May be used to provide error-detection and correction capabilities for the sequence number field. For further study.

particular, LAPD or frame relay would be message mode. A single block of data from the layer above AAL is transferred in one or more cells.

- *Streaming-mode service:* Used for low-speed, continuous data with low delay requirements. The data are presented to AAL in fixed-size blocks, which may be as small as one octet. One block is transferred per cell.

Figure 13.8 gives an example of how the message-mode service could be implemented by AAL. The convergence sublayer accepts a block of information from a user and creates a CS protocol data unit. The PDU includes a header and trailer with protocol-control information and padding to make the PDU an integral multiple of 32 bits. This is then passed down to the SAR sublayer. The SAR sublayer accepts a CS-PDU from the CS sublayer and segments it into N 44-octet SAR-PDU payloads (see Figure 13.7c and d); thus, the last payload may have some unused portion.

For streaming-mode service, a CS-PDU may contain one or more blocks from the AAL user (Figure 13.9). This is in contrast to the message-mode service, where there is a one-to-one relationship. Fur-

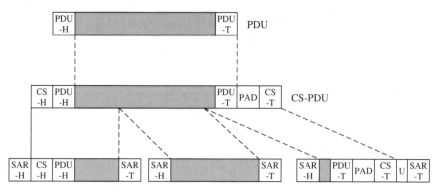

PDU-H = Protocol data unit header
PDU-T = Protocol data unit trailer
CS-H = Convergence sublayer header (4 octets)
CS-T = Convergence sublayer trailer (4 octets)
PAD = Padding (0-3 octets)
SAR-H = Segmentation and reassembly header (2 octets)
SAR-T = Segmentation and reassembly trailer (2 octets)
U = Unused

SAR-PDU
(each 48 octets)

FIGURE 13.8 Example of ATM Adaptation Layer (Message Mode Service) [JUNG91]

thermore, each block from the user ultimately travels in its own cell. Therefore, unlike message-mode service, where only the last segment may contain an unused portion, in streaming-mode service, any segment can have some unused portion.

13.3

SONET/SDH

SONET (synchronous optical network) is an optical transmission interface originally proposed by BellCore and standardized by ANSI. A compatible version, referred to as synchronous digital hierarchy (SDH), has been published by CCITT in Recommendations G.707, G.708, and G.709.[1] SONET is intended to provide a specification for taking advantage of the high-speed digital transmission capability of optical fiber.

The SONET standard addresses the following specific issues [BELL91]:

1. Establishes a standard multiplexing format using any number of 51.84-Mbps signals as building blocks. Because each building block can carry a DS3 signal, a standard rate is defined for any high-bandwidth transmission system that might be developed.

---

[1] In what follows, we will use the term SONET to refer to both specifications. Where differences exist, these will be addressed.

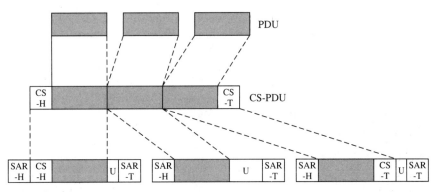

CS-H = Convergence sublayer header (4 octets)
CS-T = Convergence sublayer trailer (4 octets)
SAR-H = Segmentation and reassembly header (2 octets)
SAR-T = Segmentation and reassembly trailer (2 octets)
U = Unused

SAR-PDU
(each 48 octets)

FIGURE 13.9 Example of ATM Adaptation Layer (Streaming Mode Service) [JUNG91]

2. Establishes an optical signal standard for interconnecting equipment from different suppliers.
3. Establishes extensive operations, administration, and maintenance (OAM) capabilities as part of the standard.
4. Defines a synchronous multiplexing format for carrying lower-level digital signals (DS1, DS2, CCITT standards). The synchronous structure greatly simplifies the interface to digital switches, digital cross-connect switches, and add-drop multiplexers.
5. Establishes a flexible architecture capable of accommodating future applications such as broadband ISDN with a variety of transmission rates.

Three key requirements have driven the development of SONET. First was the need to push multiplexing standards beyond the existing DS-3 (44.736-Mbps) level. With the increasing use of optical transmission systems, a number of vendors have introduced their own proprietary schemes of combining anywhere from 2 to 12 DS-3s into an optical signal. In addition, the European schemes, based on the CCITT hierarchy, are incompatible with North American schemes. SONET provides a standardized hierarchy of multiplexed digital transmission rates that accommodates existing North American and CCITT rates.

A second requirement was to provide economic access to small amounts of traffic within the bulk payload of an optical signal. For this purpose, SONET introduces a new approach to time-division multiplexing. We address this issue subsequently when we examine the SONET frame format.

A third requirement is to prepare for future sophisticated service offerings, such as virtual private networking, time-of-day bandwidth allocation, and support of the broadband ISDN ATM transmission technique. To meet this requirement, a major increase in network management capabilities within the synchronous time-division signal was needed.

In this section, we provide an overview of SONET/SDH that shows how these requirements have been met.

Signal Hierarchy

The SONET specification defines a hierarchy of standardized digital data rates (Table 13.4). The lowest level, referred to as STS-1 (synchronous transport signal level 1), is 51.84 Mbps. This rate can be used to carry a single DS-3 signal or a group of lower-rate signals, such as DS1, DS1C, DS2, plus CCITT rates (e.g., 2.048 Mbps).

Multiple STS-1 signals can be combined to form an STS-*N* signal. The signal is created by interleaving bytes from *N* STS-1 signals that are mutually synchronized.

For the CCITT synchronous digital hierarchy, the lowest rate is 155.52 Mbps, which is designated STM-1. This corresponds to SONET STS-3. The reason for the discrepancy is that STM-1 is the lowest-rate signal that can accommodate a CCITT level 4 signal (139.264 Mbps).

System Hierarchy

SONET capabilities have been mapped into a four-layer hierarchy (Figure 13.10a):

- *Photonic:* This is the physical layer. It includes a specification of the type of optical fiber that may be used and details such as the required minimum powers and dispersion characteristics of the transmitting lasers and the required sensitivity of the receivers.
- *Section:* This layer creates the basic SONET frames, converts elec-

TABLE 13.4   SONET/SDH Signal Hierarchy

SONET Designation	CCITT Designation	Data Rate (MBPS)	Payload Rate
STS-1		51.84	50.112
STS-3	STM-1	155.52	150.336
STS-9	STM-3	466.56	451.008
STS-12	STM-4	622.08	601.344
STS-18	STM-6	933.12	902.016
STS-24	STM-8	1244.16	1202.688
STS-36	STM-12	1866.24	1804.032
STS-48	STM-16	2488.32	2405.376

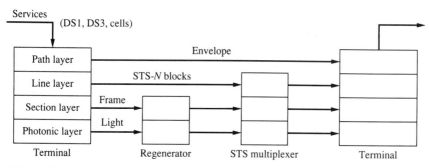

(a) Logical hierarchy

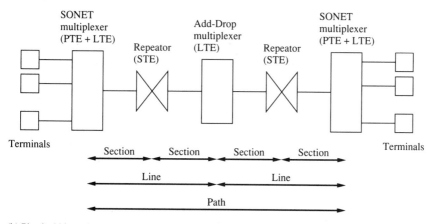

(b) Physical hierarchy

FIGURE 13.10 SONET System Hierarchy

tronic signals to photonic ones, and has some monitoring capabilities.

- *Line:* This layer is responsible for synchronization, multiplexing of data onto the SONET frames, protection and maintenance functions, and switching.
- *Path:* This layer is responsible for end-to-end transport of data at the appropriate signaling speed.

Figure 13.10b shows the physical realization of the logical layers. A section is the basic physical building block and represents a single run of optical cable between two optical fiber transmitter/receivers. For shorter runs, the cable may run directly between two end units. For longer distances, regenerating repeaters are needed. The repeater is a simple device that accepts a digital stream of data on one side and regenerates and repeats each bit out the other side. Issues of synchronization and timing need to be addressed. A line is a sequence of one or more sections such that the internal signal or channel structure of the signal remains constant. Endpoints and intermediate switches/multiplexers that may add or drop channels terminate a line. Finally, a path connects to end terminals; it corresponds to an end-to-end circuit. Data are assembled at the beginning of a path and are not accessed or modified until they are disassembled at the other end of the path.

Frame Format

The basic SONET building block is the STS-1 frame, which consists of 810 octets and is transmitted once every 125 μs, for an overall data rate of 51.84 Mbps (Figure 13.11a). The frame can logically be viewed as a matrix of 9 rows of 90 octets each, with transmission being one row at a time, from left to right and top to bottom.

The first three columns (3 octets × 9 rows = 27 octets) of the frame are devoted to overhead octets. Nine octets are devoted to section-related overhead, and 18 octets are devoted to line overhead. Figure 13.12a shows the arrangement of overhead octets, and Table 13.5 defines the various fields.

The remainder of the frame is payload, which is provided by the

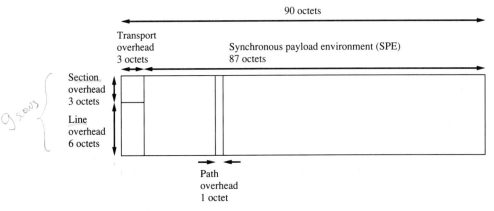

(a) STS-1 frame format

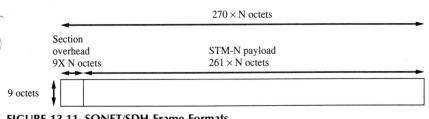

FIGURE 13.11 SONET/SDH Frame Formats

	Framing	Framing	STS-ID		Trace
	A1	A2	C1		J1
Section overhead	BIP-8	Orderwire	User		BIP-8
	B1	E1	F1		B3
	Data Com	Data Com	Data Com		Signal label
	D1	D2	D3		C2
	Pointer	Pointer	Pointer action		Path status
	H1	H2	H3		G1
	BIP-8	APS	APS		User
	B2	K1	K2		F2
	Data Com	Data Com	Data Com		Multiframe
Line overhead	D4	D5	D6		H4
	Data Com	Data Com	Data Com		Growth
	D7	D8	D9		Z3
	Data Com	Data Com	Data Com		Growth
	D10	D11	D12		Z4
	Growth	Growth	Orderwire		Growth
	Z1	Z2	E2		Z5

(a) Section overhead   (b) Path overhead

FIGURE 13.12 SONETS STS-1 Overhead Octets

path layer. The payload includes a column of path overhead, which is not necessarily in the first available column position; the line overhead contains a pointer that indicates where the path overhead starts. Figure 13.12b shows the arrangement of path overhead octets, and Table 13.5 defines these.

Figure 13.11b shows the general format for higher-rate frames, using the CCITT designation.

Pointer Adjustment

In conventional circuit-switched networks, most multiplexers and telephone company channel banks require the demultiplexing and remultiplexing of the entire signal just to access a piece of information that is addressed to a node. For example, consider that T-1 multiplexer B receives data on a single T-1 circuit from T-1 multiplexer A and passes the data on to multiplexer C. In the signal received, a single DS0 channel (64 kbps) is addressed to node B. The rest will pass on to node C and further on into the network. To remove that single DS0 channel, B must demultiplex every bit of the 1.544-Mbps signal, remove the data, and remultiplex every bit. A few proprietary T-1 multiplexers allow for drop-and-insert capability, meaning that only part of the signal has to be

TABLE 13.5   STS-1 Overhead Bits

Section Overhead	
A1, A2:	Framing bytes = F6,28 hex
C1:	STS-1 ID identifies the STS-1 number (1 to N) for each STS-1 within an STS-*N* multiplex
B1:	Bit-interleaved parity byte providing even parity over previous STS-*N* frame after scrambling
E1:	Section-level 64-kbps PCM orderwire (local orderwire)
F1:	64-kbps channel set aside for user purposes
D1–D3:	192-kbps data communications channel for alarms, maintenance, control, and administration between sections

Line Overhead	
H1–H3:	Pointer bytes used in frame alignment and frequency adjustment of payload data
B2:	Bit-interleaved parity for line-level error monitoring
K1, K2:	Two bytes allocated for signaling between line-level automatic protection switching equipment
D4–D12:	576-kbps data communications channel for alarms, maintenance, control, monitoring, and administration at the line level
Z1, Z2:	Reserved for future use
E2:	64-kbps PCM voice channel for line-level orderwire

Path Overhead	
J1:	64-kbps channel used to repetitively send a 64-byte fixed-length string so a receiving terminal can continuously verify the integrity of a path; the contents of the message are user-programmable
B3:	Bit-interleaved parity at the path level
C2:	STS path signal label to designate equipped versus unequipped STS signals and, for equipped signals, the specific STS payload mapping that might be needed in receiving terminals to interpret the payloads
G1:	Status byte sent from path-terminating equipment back to path-originating equipment to convey status of terminating equipment and path error performance
F2:	64-kbps channel for path user
H4:	Multiframe indicator for payloads needing frames that are longer than a single STS frame; multiframe indicators are used when packing lower-rate channels (virtual tributaries) into the SPE
Z3–Z5:	Reserved for future use

demultiplexed and remultiplexed, but this equipment will not communicate with that of other vendors.

SONET offers a standard drop-and-insert capability, and it applies not just to 64-kbps channels but to higher data rates as well. SONET makes use of a set of pointers that locate channels within a payload and the entire payload within a frame, so that information can be accessed, inserted, and removed with a simple adjustment of pointers. Pointer information is contained in the path overhead that refers to the multiplex structure of the channels contained within the payload. A pointer in the line overhead serves a similar function for the entire payload. We examine the use of this latter pointer in the remainder of this section.

The synchronous payload environment (SPE) of an STS-1 frame can float with respect to the frame. The actual payload (87 columns × 9 rows) can straddle two frames (Figure 13.13). The H1 and H2 octets in the line overhead indicate that start of the payload.

Because even the best atomic timing sources can differ by small amounts, SONET is faced with coping with the resulting timing differences. Each node must recalculate the pointer to alert the next receiving node of the exact location of the start of the payload. Thus, the payload is allowed to slip through an STS-1 frame, increasing or decreasing the pointer value at intervals by one byte position.

If the payload rate is higher than the local STS frame rate, the pointer is decreased by one octet position so that the next payload will begin one octet sooner than the earlier payload. To prevent the loss of an octet on the payload that is thus squeezed, the H3 octet is used to hold the extra octet for that one frame (Figure 13.14a). Similarly, if the payload rate lags behind the frame rate, the insertion of the next payload is delayed by one octet. In this case, the octet in the SPE that follows the H3 octet is left empty to allow for the movement of the payload (Figure 13.14b).

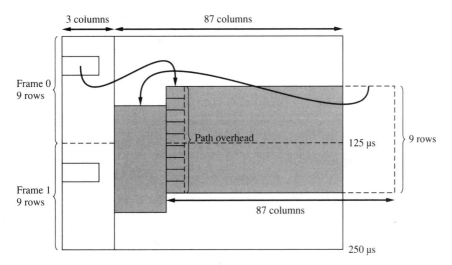

FIGURE 13.13 Representative Location of SPE in STS-1 Frame

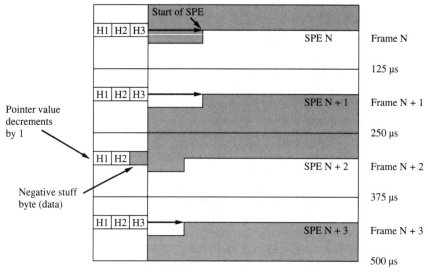

(a) Negative pointer adjustment

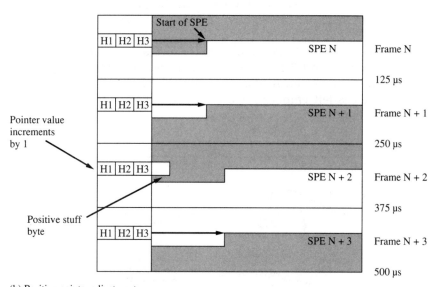

(b) Positive pointer adjustment

FIGURE 13.14 STS-1 Pointer Adjustment

13.4

TRANSMISSION OF ATM CELLS

The B-ISDN specifies that ATM cells are to be transmitted at a rate of
155.52 Mbps or 622.08 Mbps. As with ISDN, we need to specify the
transmission structure that will be used to carry this payload. For 622.08
Mbps, the matter has been left for further study. For the 155.52-Mbps
interface, two approaches are defined in I.413: a cell-based physical
layer and an SDH-based physical layer. We examine each of these
approaches in turn.

Cell-based Physical Layer

For the cell-based physical layer, no framing is imposed. The interface
structure consists of a continuous stream of 53-octet cells (Figure 13.15).

Since there is no external frame imposed in the cell-based approach,
some form of synchronization is needed. Synchronization is achieved
on the basis of the header error-control (HEC) field in the cell header.
The procedure is as follows (Figure 13.16):

1. In the HUNT state, a cell-delineation algorithm is performed bit
   by bit to determine if the HEC coding law is observed (i.e., match
   between received HEC and calculated HEC). Once a match is
   achieved, it is assumed that one header has been found, and the
   method enters the PRESYNCH state.
2. In the PRESYNCH state, a cell structure is now assumed. The cell-
   delineation algorithm is performed cell by cell until the encoding
   law has been confirmed *delta* times consecutively.
3. In the SYNCH state, the HEC is used for error detection and
   correction (see Figure 13.4). Cell delineation is assumed to be lost
   if the HEC coding law is recognized as incorrect *alpha* times consecutively.

Finally, ATM cells are used to convey operations, administration, and
maintenance (OAM) information. A virtual-path identifier of 0 and a
virtual-channel identifier of 9 identifies OAM cells.

The advantage of using a cell-based transmission scheme is the sim-

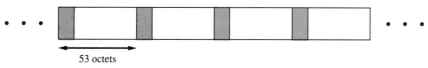

53 octets

FIGURE 13.15 Cell-Based Physical Interface for ATM Cell Transmission

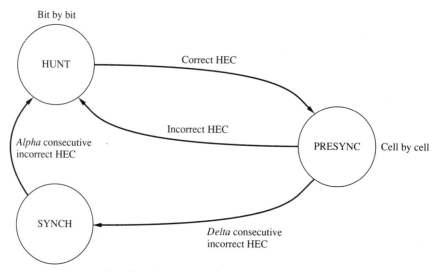

FIGURE 13.16 Cell Delineation State Diagram

plified interface that results when both transmission and transfer mode functions are based on a common structure.

SDH-based Physical Layer

For the SDH-based physical layer, framing is imposed using the STM-1 (STS-3) frame. Figure 13.17 shows the payload portion of an STM-1 frame. This payload may be offset from the beginning of the frame, as

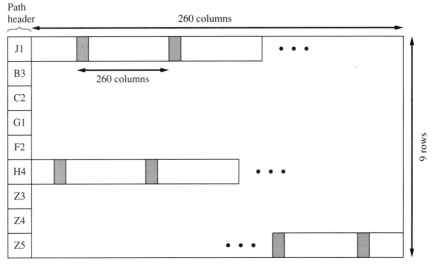

FIGURE 13.17 STM-1 Payload for SDH-Based ATM Cell Transmission

indicated by the pointer in the section overhead of the frame. As can be seen, the payload consists of a 9-octet path overhead portion and the remainder, which contains ATM cells. Since the payload capacity (2,340 octets) is not an integer multiple of the cell length (53 octets), a cell may cross a payload boundary.

The H4 octet in the path overhead is set at the sending side to indicate the next occurrence of a cell boundary. That is, the value in the H4 field indicates the number of octets to the first cell boundary following the H4 octet. The permissible range of values is 0 to 52.

The advantages of the SDH-based approach include [MINZ89]:

- It can be used to carry either ATM-based or STM-based (synchronous transfer mode) payloads, making it possible to initially deploy a high-capacity fiber-based transmission infrastructure for a variety of circuit-switched and dedicated applications and then to readily migrate to the support of B-ISDN.
- Some specific connection can be circuit-switched using an SDH channel. For example, a connection carrying constant-bit-rate video traffic can be mapped into its own exclusive payload envelope of the STM-1 signal, which can be circuit-switched. This may be more efficient than ATM switching.
- Using SDH synchronous multiplexing techniques, several ATM streams can be combined to build interfaces with higher bit rates than those supported by the ATM layer at a particular site. For example, four separate ATM streams, each with a bit rate of 155 Mbps (STM-1), can be combined to build a 622-Mbps (STM-4) interface. This arrangement may be more cost-effective than one using a single 622-Mbps ATM stream.

13.5

SUMMARY

For B-ISDN, the transfer of information across the user-network interface will use what is referred to as asynchronous transfer mode (ATM). The use of ATM implies that B-ISDN will be a packet-based network, certainly at the interface and almost certainly in terms of its internal switching. Although the recommendation also states that B-ISDN will support circuit-mode applications, this will be done over a packet-based transport mechanism. Thus, ISDN, which began as an evolution from the circuit-switching telephone networks, will transform itself into a packet-switching network as it takes on broadband services.

The use of ATM creates the need for an adaptation layer to support information-transfer protocols not based on ATM. The ATM adaptation layer (AAL) packages information from the AAL user into 48-octet packages to fit into the ATM cell. This may involve aggregating bits from a bit stream or segmenting a frame into smaller pieces.

Some form of transmission structure must be used to transport ATM cells. For the 155.52-Mbps interface, two options are specified. The first of the two options is the use of a continuous stream of cells, with no multiplex frame structure imposed at the interface. Synchronization is on a cell-by-cell basis. That is, it is the responsibility of the receiver to assure that it properly delineates cells on the 53-octet cell boundaries. The way that this is to be accomplished is by use of the header error-control (HEC) field. As long as the HEC calculation is indicating no errors, it is assumed that cell alignment is being properly maintained. An occasional error does not change this assumption. However, a string of error detections would indicate that the receiver is out of alignment, at which point it performs a hunting procedure to recover alignment.

The second option is to place the cells in a synchronous time-division multiplex envelope. In this case, the bit stream at the interface has an external frame based on the synchronous digital hierarchy (SDH) defined in Recommendation G.709. In the U.S., this frame structure is referred to as SONET (synchronous optical network). The standard defines a hierarchy of data rates, all of which are multiples of 51.84 Mbps, and including 155.52 Mbps and 622.08 Mbps. Therefore, the SDH scheme could also be used to support the higher B-ISDN data rate. However, the 1990 specifications do not address this possibility.

13.6

RECOMMENDED READING

Two interesting overviews of ATM are [YONE90] and [MINZ89b]. The virtual-path/virtual-channel approach of ATM is examined in [SATO90] and [BURG90]. [BAE91] discusses various approaches to flow control and congestion control in ATM networks; it also provides a brief but clear and up-to-date overview of ATM and AAL. [ZHAN91] discusses the use of ATM for video transmission.

A detailed example of the ATM adaptation layer is presented in [STAS90].

One of the best treatments of SONET/SDH is contained in [BELL91]. Another useful discussion is contained in [DAVI90]. The following survey articles are also worthwhile: [BALL89], [BOEH90], [LANE91], and [BORS91]. Finally, [HOLT90] examines the network-management aspects of SONET/SDH.

Discussions of the cell-based and SDH-based alternatives for ATM transmission can be found in [BAE91], [MINZ89b], and [HAC89].

Flow Control, Error Detection, and Error Control

Fundamental to the operation of a data communications facility are the mechanisms of flow control, error control, and error detection. These mechanisms are found in levels 2 and 3 of X.25, in the signaling link level of Signaling System Number 7, and in LAPD. They are also found in a number of other protocols, such as HDLC. This appendix examines the basic principles of these mechanisms. Their application in X.25, SS7, and ISDN is presented at the appropriate points in the main part of this book.

A.1

FLOW CONTROL

Flow control is a technique for assuring that a transmitting entity does not overwhelm a receiving entity with data. The receiver will typically allocate a data buffer of some maximum length. When data are received, the receiver must do a certain amount of processing (e.g., examine the header and remove it) before passing the data to a higher-level user. In the absence of flow control, the receiver's buffer may fill up and overflow while it is processing old data.

In this section, we examine mechanisms for flow control in the absence of errors. The model we will use is depicted in Figure A.1a. Data are sent as a sequence of blocks. We will refer to the block as a *protocol data unit* (PDU) to emphasize that the exact nature of the block depends

559

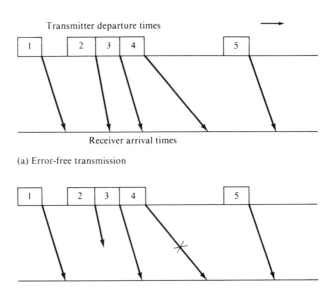

(a) Error-free transmission

(b) Transmission with losses and errors

FIGURE A.1 Model of Frame Transmission

on the protocol involved. In X.25 level 2 and in LAPD, the term *frame* is used; in the signaling link level of Signaling System Number 7, the term *signal unit* is used; and in X.25 level 3, the term *packet* is used. In any case, we assume that all PDUs that are transmitted are successfully received; no PDUs are lost and none arrive with errors. Furthermore, PDUs arrive in the same order in which they are sent. However, each transmitted PDU suffers an arbitrary and variable amount of delay before reception.

The simplest form of flow control, known as **stop-and-wait flow control,** works as follows. A source entity transmits a PDU. After reception, the destination entity indicates its willingness to accept another PDU by sending back an acknowledgment to the PDU just received. The source must wait until it receives the acknowledgment before sending the next PDU. The destination can thus stop the flow of data by simply withholding acknowledgment. This procedure works fine and, indeed, can hardly be improved upon when a message is sent as one continuous block of data. However, it is often the case that a source will break up a large block of data into smaller blocks and send these one at a time. This is done for one or more of the following reasons:

- The buffer size of the receiver may be limited.
- On a multipoint line (such as may be found using LAPD), it is usually desirable not to permit one station to occupy the line for very long, thus causing long delays at the other stations.

- On a shared network (such as an X.25 packet-switching network), the network may impose a maximum packet size.
- The longer the transmission, the more likely it is that there will be an error, necessitating retransmission of the entire block. With smaller blocks, errors are detected sooner, and a smaller amount of data needs to be retransmitted.

With the use of multiple PDUs for a single message, the stop-and-wait procedure may be inadequate. The essence of the problem is that only one PDU at a time can be in transit. In situations where the bit length of the link is greater than the PDU length, serious inefficiencies result. This is illustrated in Figure A.2; in the figure the transmission time (the time it takes for a station to transmit a PDU) is normalized to one, and the propagation delay (the time it takes for a bit to propagate from sender to receiver) is expressed as the variable a. Note that most of the time, most of the line is idle.

Efficiency can be greatly improved by allowing multiple PDUs to be in transit at the same time. Let us examine how this might work for two stations, A and B, connected via a full-duplex link. Station B allocates buffer space for n PDUs instead of the one just discussed. Thus B can accept n PDUs, and A is allowed to send n PDUs without waiting for an acknowledgment. To keep track of which PDUs have been acknowledged, each is labeled with a sequence number. B acknowledges a PDU by sending an acknowledgment that includes the sequence number of the next PDU expected. This acknowledgment also implicitly announces that B is prepared to receive the next n PDUs, beginning

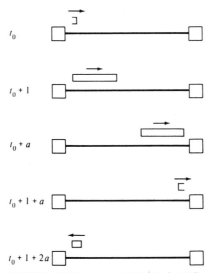

FIGURE A.2   Stop-and-Wait Link Utilization

with the number specified. This scheme can also be used to acknowledge multiple PDUs. For example, *B* could receive PDUs 2, 3, and 4,
but withhold acknowledgment until PDU 4 has arrived. By then returning an acknowledgment with sequence number 5, *B* acknowledges
PDUs 2, 3, and 4 at one time. *A* maintains a list of sequence numbers
that it is allowed to send and *B* maintains a list of sequence numbers
that it is prepared to receive. Each of these lists can be thought of as a
window of PDUs. The operation is referred to as **sliding-window flow
control.**

Several additional comments need to be made. First, since the sequence number to be used occupies a field in the PDU, it is clearly of
bounded size. For a *k*-bit field, the sequence number can range from 0
to $2^k - 1$. Accordingly, PDUs are numbered modulo 2^k; that is, after
sequence number $2^k - 1$, the next number is zero. Second, the maximum size of the window is some number $n \le 2^k - 1$. The limitation to
$2^k - 1$ rather than 2^k has to do with the error-control mechanism and
will be justified in due course.

An example of this mechanism is shown in Figure A.3. The example
assumes a 3-bit sequence number field and a maximum window size of

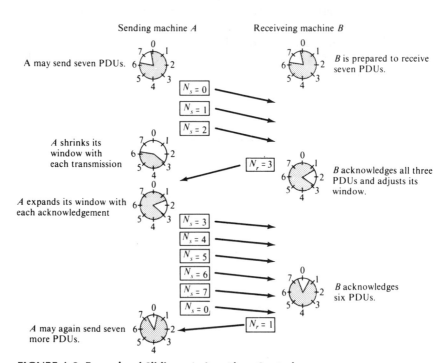

FIGURE A.3 Example of Sliding-window Flow Control

seven. Initially, A and B have windows indicating that A may transmit seven PDUs. After transmitting three PDUs without acknowledgment, A has shrunk its window to four PDUs. When PDU 2 is acknowledged, A is back up to permission to transmit seven PDUs.

Figure A.4, which shows the efficiency implications of this mechanism, is to be contrasted with the stop-and-wait mechanism illustrated in Figure A.3. If the maximum window size, n, is a little greater than twice the round-trip propagation delay ($n > 2a + 1$), then it is possible

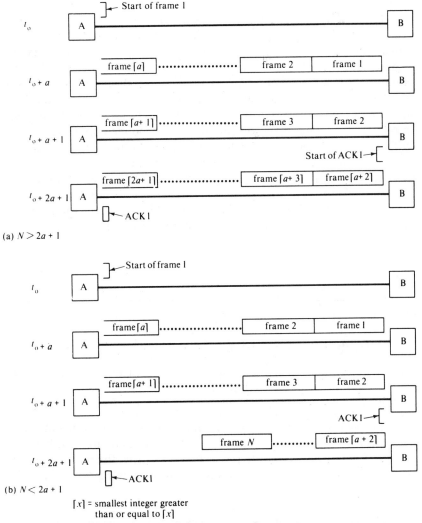

FIGURE A.4 Timing of a Sliding-window Protocol

to utilize the link to the fullest.[1] Even for smaller window sizes, the utilization of the link is clearly superior to that of stop-and-wait.

The mechanism so far described does indeed provide a form of flow control: The receiver must only be able to accommodate n PDUs beyond the one it has last acknowledged. To supplement this, most protocols also allow a station to completely cut off the flow of PDUs from the other side by sending a receive not ready (RNR) message, which acknowledges former PDUs but forbids transfer of future PDUs. Thus, RNR 5 means: "I have received all PDUs up through number 4 but am unable to accept any more." At some subsequent point, the station must send a normal acknowledgment to reopen the window.

So far, we have discussed transmission in one direction only. If two stations exchange data, each needs to maintain two windows: one for transmit and one for receive, and each side needs to send the data and acknowledgments to the other. To provide efficient support for this requirement, a feature known as *piggybacking* is typically provided. Each *data PDU* includes a field that holds the sequence number of that PDU plus a field that holds the sequence number used for acknowledgment. Thus, if a station has data to send and an acknowledgment to send, it sends both together in one PDU, saving communication capacity. Of course, if a station has an acknowledgment but no data to send, it sends a separate *acknowledgment PDU*. If a station has data to send but no new acknowledgment to send, it must repeat the last acknowledgment that it sent. This is because the data PDU includes a field for the acknowledgment number and some value must be put into that field. When a station receives a duplicate ACK, it simply ignores it.

A.2

ERROR DETECTION

The Error-detection Process

Any data transmission is subject to errors. In transmitting across a data link, signal impairments, such as the following, may alter the contents of a unit of data [STAL88a]:

- *Attenuation:* The strength of the signal decreases with distance over any transmission medium. With sufficient attenuation, it becomes difficult for the receiver to recover the data from the received signal.
- *Attenuation distortion:* Attenuation is an increasing function of fre-

---

[1] Recall that the time to transit one PDU is normalized to one time unit, and the propagation time is the variable a. Hence the time to transmit n PDUs in succession is n time units.

quency. Thus, frequency components of a signal are differentially affected, which introduces distortion into the signal.

- *Delay distortion:* The velocity of propagation of a signal through a wire medium varies with frequency; the velocity tends to be highest near the center frequency of the signal and fall off toward the two edges of the signal's bandwidth. This causes the signal energy from one bit time to spill into the time slots of neighboring bits, a phenomenon known as intersymbol interference.
- *Noise:* Noise is any unwanted signal that combines with, and hence distorts, the signal intended for reception. Varieties include thermal noise, intermodulation noise, crosstalk, and impulse noise.
- *Collisions:* In a multipoint link, if two stations transmit at the same time, their signals overlap and neither signal can be successfully received.

Because of these impairments, a protocol entity (e.g., LAPD, X.25 level 2, SS7 signaling-link level) may receive a PDU from the other side in which some bits have changed value. Accordingly, some form of error detection is needed to avoid delivering incorrect data to the user.

The error detection process is illustrated in Figure A.5. On transmission, a calculation is performed on the bits of the PDU to be transmitted; the result, called an **error-detecting code,** is inserted as an additional field in the frame. On reception, the same calculation is performed on the received bits and the calculated result is compared to the value stored in the incoming frame. If there is a discrepancy, the receiver assumes that an error has occurred and discards the PDU.

The Cyclic Redundancy Check

One of the most common, and one of the most powerful, of the error-detecting codes is the cyclic redundancy check (CRC). It is used in X.25

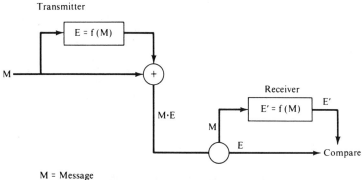

M = Message
E, E' = Error-detecting code
f = Error-detecting code function

FIGURE A.5 Error Detection

level 2, SS7 signaling-link level, and LAPD. We first examine the operation of this code and then look at its effectiveness.

CRC Operation.   Given a k-bit block of data, the transmitter generates an n-bit sequence, known as a *frame check sequence* (FCS) so that the resulting frame, consisting of $k + n$ bits, is exactly divisible by some predetermined number. The receiver then divides the incoming frame by the same number and, if there is no remainder, assumes that there was no error.

To clarify the preceding, we present the procedure in several ways:

- Modulo 2 arithmetic.
- Polynomials.
- Shift registers and exclusive-or gates.

First, we work with binary numbers and modulo 2 arithmetic. Modulo 2 arithmetic uses binary addition with no carries, which is just the exclusive-or operation.

Examples

$$
\begin{array}{r}
1111 \\
+\,1010 \\
\hline
0101
\end{array}
\qquad
\begin{array}{r}
11001 \\
\times\quad 11 \\
\hline
11001 \\
11001 \\
\hline
101011
\end{array}
$$

Now define:

$T = (k + n)$-bit PDU to be transmitted, with $n < k$.
$M = k$-bit message, the first k bits of T.
$F = n$-bit FCS, the last n bits of T.
$P =$ pattern of $n + 1$ bits; this is the predetermined divisor mentioned previously.

We would like T/P to have no remainder. It should be clear that

$$T = 2^n M + F$$

That is, by multiplying M by 2^n, we have in effect shifted it to the left by n bits and padded out the result with 0s. Adding F gives us the concatenation of M and F, which is T. Now we want T to be exactly divisible by P. Suppose that we divided $2^n M$ by P:

$$\frac{2^n M}{P} = Q + \frac{R}{P} \tag{A.1}$$

There is a quotient and a remainder. Since division is binary, the remainder is always one bit less than the divisor. We will use this remainder as our FCS. Then

$$T = 2^nM + R$$

Question: Does this R satisfy our condition? To see that it does, consider

$$\frac{T}{P} = \frac{2^nM + R}{P}$$

Substituting equation (A.1), we have

$$\frac{T}{P} = Q + \frac{R}{P} + \frac{R}{P}$$

However, any binary number added to itself modulo 2 yields zero. Thus,

$$\frac{T}{P} = Q + \frac{R + R}{P} = Q$$

There is no remainder, and therefore T is exactly divisible by P. Thus the FCS is easily generated. Simply divide 2^nM by P and use the remainder as the FCS. On reception, the receiver will divide T by P and will get no remainder if there have been no errors.

A simple example of the procedure is now presented:

1. Given

$$\begin{aligned} \text{Message } M &= 1010001101 \text{ (10 bits)} \\ \text{Pattern } P &= 110101 \text{ (6 bits)} \\ \text{FCS } R &= \text{to be calculated (5 bits)} \end{aligned}$$

2. The message is multiplied by 2^5, yielding 101000110100000.
3. This product is divided by P:

```
                      1101010110← Q
P → 110101|101000110100000← 2ⁿM
           110101
           111011
           110101
            111010
            110101
             111110
             110101
              101100
              110101
               110010
               110101
                1110← R
```

4. The remainder is added to 2^nM to give $T = 101000110101110$, which is transmitted.

5. If there are no errors, the receiver receives T intact. The received PDU is divided by P:

$$
\begin{array}{r}
1101010110 \\
110101\overline{)101000110101110} \\
\underline{110101} \\
111011 \\
\underline{110101} \\
111010 \\
\underline{110101} \\
111110 \\
\underline{110101} \\
101111 \\
\underline{110101} \\
110101 \\
\underline{110101} \\
00
\end{array}
$$

Since there is no remainder, it is assumed that there have been no errors.

The pattern P is chosen to be one bit longer than the desired FCS, and the exact bit pattern chosen depends on the type of errors expected. At minimum, both the high- and low-order bits of P must be 1.

The occurrence of an error is easily expressed. An error results in the reversal of a bit. Mathematically, this is equivalent to taking the exclusive-or of the bit and 1:0 + 1 = 1; 1 + 1 = 0. Thus the errors in an $(n + k)$-bit PDU can be represented by an $(n + k)$-bit field with 1s in each error position. The resulting frame T_r can be expressed as

$$T_r = T + E$$

where

T = transmitted frame

E = error pattern with 1s in positions where errors occur

T_r = received frame

The receiver will fail to detect an error if and only if T_r is divisible by P, that is, if and only if E is divisible by P. Intuitively, this seems an unlikely occurrence.

A second way of viewing the CRC process is to express all values as polynomials in a dummy variable X with binary coefficients. The coefficients correspond to the bits in the binary number. Thus for $M = 110011$, we have $M(X) = X^5 + X^4 + X + 1$, and for $P = 11001$, we have $P(X) = X^4 + X^3 + 1$. Arithmetic operations are again modulo 2. The CRC process can now be described as

$$1. \quad \frac{X^n M(X)}{P(X)} = Q(X) + \frac{R(X)}{P(X)}$$

$$2. \quad T(X) = X^n M(X) + R(X)$$

Four versions of $P(X)$ are widely used:

$$\text{CRC-12} = X^{12} + X^{11} + X^3 + X^2 + X + 1$$

$$\text{CRC-16} = X^{16} + X^{15} + X^2 + 1$$

$$\text{CRC-CCITT} = X^{16} + X^{12} + X^5 + 1$$

$$\text{CRC-32} = X^{32} + X^{26} + X^{23} + X^{22} + X^{16} + X^{12} + X^{11}$$

$$+ X^{10} + X^8 + X^7 + X^5 + X^4 + X^2 + X + 1$$

The CRC-12 system is used for transmission of streams of 6-bit characters and generates a 12-bit FCS. Both CRC-16 and CRC-CCITT are popular for 8-bit characters, in the United States and Europe respectively, and both result in a 16-bit FCS. This would seem adequate for most applications, although CRC-32 is specified as an option in some point-to-point synchronous transmission standards.

As a final representation, Figure A.6 shows that the CRC process can easily be implemented as a dividing circuit consisting of exclusive-or gates and a shift register. The circuit is implemented as follows:

1. The register contains n bits, equal to the length of the FCS.
2. There are up to n exclusive-or gates.
3. The presence or absence of a gate corresponds to the presence or absence of a term in the divisor polynomial, $P(X)$

In this example, we use

$$\text{Message } M = 1010001101; M(X) = X^9 + X^7 + X^3 + X^2 + 1$$

$$\text{Divisor } P = 110101; P(X) = X^5 + X^4 + X^2 + 1$$

which were used earlier in the discussion.

The process begins with the shift register cleared (all zeroes). The message, or dividend, is then entered, one bit at a time, starting with the most significant (leftmost) bit. Since no feedback occurs until a 1 dividend bit arrives at the most significant end of the register, the first four operations are simple shifts. Whenever a 1 bit arrives at the left end, a 1 is subtracted (exclusive-or) from the second and fifth bits on the next shift. This is identical to the binary long-division process illustrated earlier. The process continues through all the bits of the message, plus four zero bits. These latter bits account for shifting M to the left four positions to accommodate the FCS. After the last bit is processed, the shift register contains the remainder (FCS), which can then be transmitted.

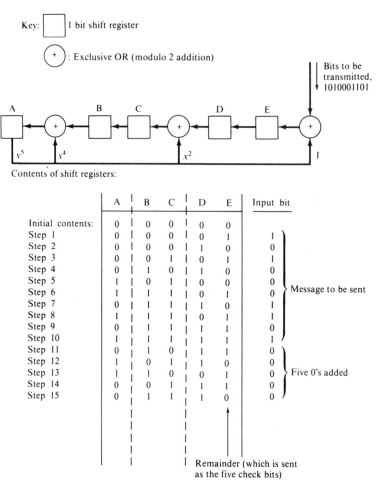

Key: ☐ } 1 bit shift register

⊕ : Exclusive OR (modulo 2 addition)

Bits to be transmitted, 1010001101

Contents of shift registers:

	A	B	C	D	E	Input bit
Initial contents:	0	0	0	0	0	
Step 1	0	0	0	0	1	1
Step 2	0	0	0	1	0	0
Step 3	0	0	1	0	1	1
Step 4	0	1	0	1	0	0
Step 5	1	0	1	0	0	0
Step 6	1	1	1	0	1	0
Step 7	0	1	1	1	0	1
Step 8	1	1	1	0	1	1
Step 9	0	1	1	1	1	0
Step 10	1	1	1	1	1	1
Step 11	0	1	0	1	1	0
Step 12	1	0	1	1	0	0
Step 13	1	1	0	0	1	0
Step 14	0	0	1	1	1	0
Step 15	0	1	1	1	0	0

Message to be sent (Steps 1–10)

Five 0's added (Steps 11–15)

Remainder (which is sent as the five check bits)

FIGURE A.6 Circuit with Shift Registers for Dividing by the Polynomial
$(X^5 + X^4 + X^2 + 1)$

At the receiver, the same logic is used. As each bit of M arrives, it is inserted into the shift register at A. If there have been no errors, the shift register should contain the bit pattern for R at the conclusion of M. The transmitted bits of R now begin to arrive, and the effect is to zero out the register so that, at the conclusion of reception, the register contains all 0s.

CRC Effectiveness. The measure of effectiveness of any error-detecting code is what percentage of errors it detects. In the case of CRC, effectiveness is most easily determined by using the polynomial representation. Consider, as before, that we are transmitting a block $T(X)$. When this block is transmitted, one or more bits may be altered by transmission impairments. The pattern of error bits may be represented by another polynomial $E(X)$. Thus the actual received pattern is $T(X) + E(X)$. Now, if this received pattern is divisible by $P(X)$, then the error will not be detected. We have:

$$\frac{T(X) + E(X)}{P(X)} = \frac{T(X)}{P(X)} + \frac{E(X)}{P(X)} = \frac{Q(X)\, E(X)}{P(X)}$$

Thus, the received pattern, when divided by $P(X)$, will produce a remainder only if $E(X)$ produces a remainder. Conversely, an error will remain undetected if $E(X)$ is divisible by $P(X)$. It can be shown that all of the following errors are not divisible by $P(X)$ and hence are detectable [MART73]:

- All single-bit errors.
- All double-bit errors, as long as $P(X)$ has at least three terms.
- Any odd number of errors, as long as $P(X)$ contains a factor $(X + 1)$.
- Any burst error for which the length of the burst is less than the length of the divisor polynomial $P(X)$; that is, less than or equal to the length of the FCS.
- Most larger burst errors.

Let us examine each of these assertions in turn.

1. *Single-bit Errors*
A single-bit error can be represented by $E(X) = X^i$ for some i less than the total message length ($i < k + n$). We have said that for $P(X)$, both the first and last terms must be nonzero. Thus $P(X)$ has at least two terms and cannot divide the one-term $E(X)$.

2. *Double-bit Errors*
A double-bit error can be represented by $E(X) = X^i + X^j = X^i(1 + X^{j-i})$ for some i and j with $i < j$. To avoid a remainder, $P(X)$ must exactly divide either X^i or $(1 + X^{j-i})$. We have shown that it does not divide X^i. If the polynomial has at least three terms, it cannot divide the two-term $(1 + X^{j-i})$ either. All of the CRC codes in common use have at least three terms.

3. *Odd Numbers of Errors*
Assume that $E(X)$ has an odd number of terms and is divisible by $(X + 1)$. Then we can express $E(X)$ as $E(X) = (X + 1)F(X)$. Then $E(1) = (1 + 1)F(x) = 0$, since $1 + 1 = 0$ in modulo 2 arithmetic. But any polynomial expression $E(X)$ will have the value $E(1) = 0$ if and only if it contains an even number of terms. Thus $E(X)$ with an odd number of terms is not divisible by $(X + 1)$ and any polynomial $P(X)$ with that factor will detect the error. Again, all of the CRC codes in common use have $(X + 1)$ as a factor.

4. *Burst Errors*
A burst error refers to a string of bits within a message in which at

least the first and last bits of the string are in error. Thus, a burst error of length j is a string of bits beginning and ending with 1 and containing intervening 1s and 0s. For example, if $E(X)$ represents the error pattern 0000010100110000, then there is a burst error of length 7.

A burst error can be expressed as $E(X) = X^i (X^{j-1} + \cdots + 1) = X^i G(X)$ where i expresses how far the burst is shifted from the right-hand end. For our example,

$$E(X) = X^{10} + X^8 + X^5 + X^4$$

$$= X^4(X^6 + X^4 + X + 1)$$

Since X^i is not divisible by $P(X)$, the error will go undetected only if the second factor, $G(X)$, is exactly divisible by $P(X)$. In the case of a burst error of length less than the length of the polynomial ($j < n + 1$), $P(X)$ will not divide the $G(X)$ since $P(X)$ is of higher order.

Now consider the case where the length of the burst error exactly equals the length of the polynomial ($j = n + 1$). In this case, the error will go undetected only if $G(X) = P(X)$. We already know that the first and last terms of both $G(X)$ and $P(X)$ are nonzero. Therefore, the remaining $n - 1$ bits of the two expressions must be equal. If we assume all bit errors are equally likely, then the probability that $G(X) = P(X)$ is $(1/2)^{n-1}$. Thus, for CRC-16 or CRC-CCITT, the probability of an undetected error is $(1/2)^{15} = 0.0000305$, given that the block contains a burst of length 17 bits (a very rare event).

Finally, when the number of bits in the burst is greater than the length of the polynomial ($j > n + 1$), then a number of different values of $G(X)$ will be divisible by $P(X)$. If $G(X)$ is exactly divisible by $P(X)$, we can write

$$\frac{G(X)}{P(X)} = Q(X)$$

where $Q(X)$ is the quotient obtained by dividing $G(X)$ by $P(X)$. Now, $G(X)$ is a polynomial of degree $j - 1$, and $P(X)$ is a polynomial of degree n. Thus the degree of $Q(X)$ is $(j - 1) - n$. The number of bits that correspond to $Q(X)$ is therefore $j - n$. We know that the first and last bits are one. The remaining $j - n - 2$ bits may take either binary value. This means that there are 2^{j-n-2} values of $G(X)$ that are exactly divisible by $P(X)$. Given a burst error of length j, then there are a total of 2^{j-2} possible values of $G(X)$. Thus the fraction of burst errors of length j that will go undetected is

$$\frac{2^{j-n-2}}{2^{j-2}} = (1/2)^n$$

Again, for CRC-16 and CRC-CCITT, the probability of an undetected error is $(1/2)^{16} = 0.0000153$, given that the block contains a burst of length greater than 17 bits.

These results are summarized in Table A.1.

A.3

ERROR CONTROL

Error control refers to mechanisms to detect and correct errors that occur in the transmission of protocol data units (PDUs). The model that we will use, which covers the typical case, is illustrated in Figure A.1b. As before, data are sent as a sequence of PDUs; PDUs arrive in the same order in which they are sent, and each transmitted PDU suffers an arbitrary and variable amount of delay before reception. In addition, we admit the possibility of two types of errors:

- *Lost PDU:* A PDU fails to arrive at the other side. In the case of a network, the network may simply fail to deliver a packet. In the case of a direct point-to-point data link, a noise burst may damage a frame to the extent that the receiver is not aware that a frame has been transmitted.
- *Damaged PDU:* A recognizable PDU does arrive but some of the bits are in error (have been altered during transmission).

The most common techniques for error control are based on some or all of the following ingredients:

- *Error detection:* The destination detects and discards PDUs that are in error, using the techniques described in the preceding section.
- *Positive acknowledgment:* The destination returns a positive acknowledgment to successfully received, error-free PDUs.
- *Retransmission after timeout:* The source retransmits a PDU that has not been acknowledged after a predetermined amount of time.

TABLE A.1   Effectiveness of the Cyclic Redundancy Check (CRC)

Type of Error	Probability of Detection
Single-bit errors	1.0
Two bits in error (separate or not)	1.0
Odd number of bits in error	1.0
Error burst of length less than $(n + 1)$ bits	1.0
Error burst of $(n + 1)$ bits	$1 - (1/2)^{n-1}$
Error burst of greater than $(n + 1)$ bits	$1 - (1/2)^n$

- *Negative acknowledgment and retransmission:* The destination returns a negative acknowledgment to PDUs in which an error is detected. The source retransmits such PDUs.

Collectively, these mechanisms are all referred to as **automatic repeat request** (ARQ). The two most common forms of ARQ are go-back-N ARQ and selective-repeat ARQ. Both of these forms are based on the use of the sliding-window flow-control technique described in Section A.1. We examine each of these in turn.

Go-back-N ARQ.   In go-back-N ARQ, a station may send a series of PDUs sequentially numbered modulo some maximum value. The number of unacknowledged PDUs outstanding is determined by window size, using the sliding-window flow-control technique. While no errors occur, the destination will acknowledge (ACK) incoming PDUs as usual. If the destination station detects an error in a PDU, it sends a negative acknowledgment (NAK) for that PDU. The destination station will discard that PDU and all future incoming PDUs until the PDU in error is correctly received. Thus the source station, when it receives a NAK, must retransmit the PDU in error plus all succeeding PDUs that had been transmitted in the interim.

Consider that station A is sending PDUs to station B. After each transmission, A sets an acknowledgment timer for the PDU just transmitted. The go-back-N technique takes into account the following contingencies:

1. Damaged PDU. There are three subcases:
   a. A transmits PDU i. B detects an error and has previously successfully received PDU $(i - 1)$. B sends a NAK i, indicating that frame i is rejected. When A receives this NAK, it must retransmit PDU i and all subsequent PDUs that it has transmitted.
   b. PDU i is lost in transit. A subsequently sends PDU $(i + 1)$. B receives PDU $(i + 1)$ out of order and sends a NAK i.
   c. PDU i is lost in transit and A does not soon send additional PDUs. B receives nothing and returns neither an ACK or a NAK. A will time out and retransmit PDU i.
2. Damaged ACK. There are two subcases:
   a. B receives PDU i and sends ACK $(i + 1)$, which is lost in transit. Since ACKs are cumulative (e.g., ACK 6 means that all PDUs through 5 are acknowledged), it may be that A will receive a subsequent ACK to a subsequent PDU that will do the job of the lost ACK before the associated timer expires.
   b. If A's timer expires, A retransmits PDU i and all subsequent PDUs.

3. Damaged NAK. If a NAK is lost, *A* will eventually time out on the associated PDU and retransmit that PDU and all subsequent PDUs.

Figure A.7 shows the PDU flow for go-back-N ARQ on a full-duplex line, assuming a 3-bit sequence number.

In the section of flow control, we mentioned that for a *k*-bit sequence number field, which provides a sequence number range of 2^k, the maximum window size is limited to 2^{k-1}. This has to do with the interaction between error control and acknowledgment. Consider that if data are being exchanged in both directions, station *B* must send a piggybacked acknowledgment to station *A*'s PDUs in the data PDUs being transmitted by *B*, even if the acknowledgment has already been sent. As we have mentioned, this is because *B* must put some number in the acknowledgment field of its data PDUs. As an example, assume a 3-bit sequence number size. Suppose a station sends PDU 0 and gets back an ACK 1, and then sends PDUs 1, 2, 3, 4, 5, 6, 7, 0 and gets another ACK 1. This could mean that all eight PDUs were received correctly and the ACK 1 is a cumulative acknowledgment. It could also mean that all eight PDUs were damaged in transit, and the receiving station is repeating its previous ACK 1. The problem is avoided if the maximum window size is limited to 7 ($2^3 - 1$).

Selective-repeat ARQ. With selective-repeat ARQ, the only PDUs retransmitted are those that receive a NAK or that time out. Figure A.8, which exhibits the same error pattern as Figure A.7, illustrates selective repeat. This would appear to be more efficient than the go-back-N approach, since it minimizes the amount of retransmission. On the other hand, the receiver must contain storage to save post-NAK PDUs until the PDU in error is retransmitted and must contain logic for reinserting the PDU in the proper sequence. The transmitter, too, will

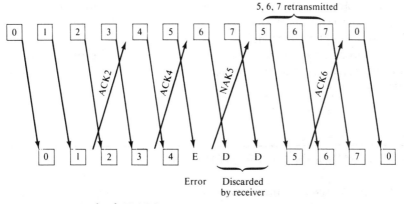

FIGURE A.7 Go-back-N ARQ

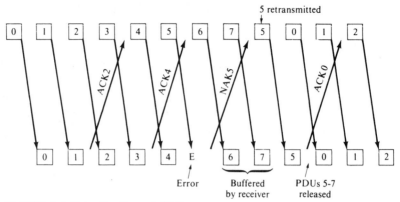

FIGURE A.8 Selective-Repeat ARQ

require more complex logic to be able to send PDUs out of sequence. Because of such complications, the selective-reject ARQ is rarely implemented.

The window size requirement is more restrictive for selective-repeat than for go-back-N. We have seen that for a sequence number space of 2^k, the maximum window size for go-back-N is 2^{k-1}. Now consider the case of a 3-bit sequence number size (sequence space is eight) using selective repeat. Allow a window size of seven, and consider the following scenario [TANE81]:

1. Station *A* sends PDUs 0 through 6 to station *B*.
2. Station *B* receives and acknowledges all seven PDUs.
3. Because of a long noise burst, all seven acknowledgments are lost.
4. Station *A* times out and retransmits PDU 0.
5. Station *B* has already advanced its receive window to accept PDUs 7, 0, 1, 2, 3, 4, and 5. Thus it assumes that PDU 7 has been lost and that this is a new PDU 0, which it accepts.

The problem with the foregoing scenario, for selective-repeat ARQ, is that there is an overlap between the sending and receiving windows. To overcome the problem, the maximum window size should be no more than half the range of sequence numbers. In the preceding scenario, if only four unacknowledged PDUs may be outstanding, no confusion can result.

A.4

A COMPARISON OF PROTOCOLS

In this book, we examine four protocols that make use of some or all of the flow- and error-control mechanisms described in this appendix:

- X.25 level 2 (LAPB).
- X.25 level 3.
- SS7 signaling link level.
- LAPD.

Table A.2 compares these protocols in terms of various aspects of flow control and error control. For flow control, SS7 and LAPD provide for the use of 7-bit sequence numbers and a maximum window size of 127 signal units. The other protocols in the table provide the option of 3-bit or 7-bit sequence numbers and the corresponding maximum window size of 7 or 127. The choice is made at the time of connection setup. All of the protocols employ piggybacking, when possible, for acknowledgment.

Note that no error detection is performed by X.25 level 3. The level-3 protocol relies on the level-2 protocol (LAPB) to assure that all received packets are free of bit errors. However, error-control mechanisms are still needed to account for lost packets. For the other three protocols, all at the link level, the CRC-CCITT divisor is used:

$$P(X) = X^{16} + X^{12} + X^5 + 1$$

Several refinements are added to the process described in Section A.2. Specifically, the 16-bit FCS is defined to be the ones complement of $R(X)$, where

$$R(X) = [X^{16}M(X) + X^kL(X)]/P(X)$$

with

$$L(X) = X^{15} + X^{14} + X^{13} + \cdots + X^2 + X + 1$$

TABLE A.2   A Comparison of Various Protocols

Feature	SS7 Signaling-link Level	LAPD	LAPB	X.25 Level 3
Sequence number field (bits)	7	7	3 or 7	3 or 7
Piggyback-ing	Yes	Yes	Yes	Yes
Maximum window size	127	127	7 or 127	7 or 127
CRC Code*	CRC-CCITT	CRC-CCITT	CRC-CCITT	None
ARQ type	Go-back-N, cyclic retransmission	Go-back-N	Go-back-N	Go-back-N
Bit stuffing	Yes	Yes	Yes	No
Address field	None	16 bits	8 bits	12 bits

* *Note:* The CRC calculation involves a bit inversion; see text.

and

$$k = \text{number of bits in } M$$

The addition of $X^kL(X)$ to $X^{16}M(X)$ is equivalent to inverting the first 16 bits of $M(X)$. It can be accomplished in a shift register implementation, such as Figure A.6, by presetting the register to all ones initially, instead of all zeros. This term is present to detect erroneous addition or deletion of zero bits at the leading end of $M(X)$. The procedure described in Section A.2 will produce the same result for two messages that differ only in the number of leading zeros. The complementing of $R(X)$ by the transmitter at the completion of the division insures that the transmitted sequence has a property that permits the receiver to detect addition or deletion of trailing zeros that may appear as a result of errors. Again, the procedure described in Section A.2 will produce the same result at the receiver for two transmissions that differ only in the number of trailing zeros.

At the receiver, the reverse operations must be done to perform error detection. Using a shift register implementation, the initial content of the receiver's register is set to all ones. If there have been no transmission errors, the final remainder after division of the incoming bits, including the FCS, by $P(X)$ will be the unique 16-bit sequence:

$$0001110100001111$$

Thus, instead of comparing the result to the received FCS, the receiver computes a value and compares it to this unique bit pattern.

Returning to Table A.2, we can see that all of the protocols use go-back-N ARQ for error control. In addition, SS7 signaling-link level employs a cyclic retransmission scheme.

Several other characteristics of the four protocols are worth comparison. All of the link-level protocols use bit stuffing. This is needed because all of these protocols use flags for marking the beginning and end of PDUs. For X.25 level 3, no flag is employed and bit stuffing is not required. Finally, the protocols differ in the manner in which addresses are handled. There is no address field in the SS7 signaling-link level protocol. Addressing usually serves no purpose on point-to-point links; a signal unit transmitted by one side is intended for the other side. LAPB also makes use of point-to-point links and could do without an address field. However, LAPB is intended to be compatible with HDLC, which allows multipoint configurations and which therefore requires an address field. LAPD provides a 16-bit address field that includes a service access-point identifier and a terminal endpoint identifier. Finally, X.25 level 3 employs a 12-bit virtual-circuit number for addressing purposes.

A.5

RECOMMENDED READING

A number of books cover the topic of error detection. [MCNA88], [MART73], and [BERT87] are especially readable. [PETE61] is also a good presentation. The CRC algorithm is usually implemented in hardware, but is sometimes implemented in software. In the latter case, an algorithm that treats data 8 bits at a time rather than one bit at a time is considerably more efficient. Two approaches are discussed in [PERE83] and [GRIF87].

Clear discussions of flow control and error control can be found in [MART81] and [BERT87]. The latter provides clear proofs that the various algorithms actually work as intended. Good survey articles on the subject are [LIN84] and [BERL87]. [STAL91a] provides a simple technique for calculating the efficiency of the various flow- and error-control techniques. More sophisticated analyses can be found in [BERT87] and [STUC85].

A.6

PROBLEMS

A.1. What is the purpose of using modulo 2 arithmetic in computing an FCS rather than binary arithmetic?

A.2. Using the CRC-CCITT polynomial, generate the 16-bit FCS for the message consisting of a one followed by 15 zeros.

A.3. Explain in words why the shift register implementation of CRC will result in all zeros at the receiver if there are no errors. Demonstrate by example.

A.4. For $P = 110011$ and $M = 11100011$, find the FCS.

A.5. In Section A.1, the variable a was defined to be the propagation time given that the transmission time is normalized to one. Another way of saying this is that a = (propagation time)/(transmission time).

　　a. Show that, for stop-and-wait flow control, the maximum utilization of the link is equal to $1/(1 + 2a)$.

　　b. Show that, for sliding-window flow control, the maximum utilization of the link is 1 if $n > (2a + 1)$ and is $n/(2a + 1)$ if $n < (2a + 1)$.

A.6. Explain how the procedure outlined in Section A-4 detects erroneous addition or deletion of zero bits at the beginning or end of a message.

A.7. An alternative to ARQ is the use of an error-correcting code. Such a code not only detects errors but enables the receiver to correct them. Does this accomplish the same thing as ARQ?

A.8. Selective-repeat ARQ has a major advantage and a major disadvantage compared to go-back-N ARQ. Discuss the tradeoffs involved.

A.9. In go-back-N ARQ, if a PDU is received out of order, it is discarded. However, such a PDU contains a piggybacked acknowledgment. Give an example in which the protocol will deadlock if each side ignores receive sequence numbers in discarded packets.

A.10. The following statement is made in the LAPB specification:

> If a DCE or DTE, due to a transmission error, does not receive (or receives and discards) a single I frame or the last I frame(s) in a sequence of I frames, it will not detect an $n(S)$ sequence error condition and therefore will not transmit a REJ frame.

An I frame is simply a data PDU. Explain this statement. Does it present a potential problem?

The OSI Reference Model

One of the most important concepts in data communications is the open-systems interconnection (OSI) reference model. This model serves as a framework within which communication protocol standards are developed. It also serves as a frame of reference for talking about data communications. Although the ISDN recommendations represent a separate effort from OSI and OSI-related standards, the ISDN protocols do fit within the OSI framework. This appendix provides an overview of the OSI model.

B.1

MOTIVATION

When work is done that involves more than one computer, additional elements must be added to the system: the hardware and software to support the communication between or among the systems. Communications hardware is reasonably standard and generally presents few problems. However, when communication is desired among heterogeneous (different vendors, different models of same vendor) machines, the software development effort can be a nightmare. Different vendors use different data formats and data exchange conventions. Even within one vendor's product line, different models of computers may communicate in unique ways.

As the use of computer communications and computer networking proliferates, a one-at-a-time special-purpose approach to communications software development is too costly to be acceptable. The only alternative is for computer vendors to adopt and implement a common set of conventions. For this to happen, a set of international or at least national standards must be promulgated by appropriate organizations. Such standards have two effects:

- Vendors feel encouraged to implement the standards because of an expectation that, because of wide usage of the standards, their products would be less marketable without them.
- Customers are in a position to require that the standards be implemented by any vendor wishing to propose equipment to them.

It should become clear from the ensuing discussion that no single standard will suffice. The task of communication in a truly cooperative way between applications on different computers is too complex to be handled as a unit. The problem must be decomposed into manageable parts. Hence, before one can develop standards, there should be a structure or *architecture* that defines the communications tasks.

This line of reasoning led the International Organization for Standardization (ISO) in 1977 to establish a subcommittee to develop such an architecture. The result was the *Open Systems Interconnection* reference model, which is a framework for defining standards for linking heterogeneous computers. The OSI model provides the basis for connecting *open* systems for distributed applications processing. The term *open* denotes the ability of any two systems conforming to the reference model and the associated standards to connect.

Box B.1, extracted from the basic OSI document [ISO84], summarizes the purpose of the model.

B.2

CONCEPTS

A widely accepted structuring technique, and the one chosen by ISO, is *layering*. The communications functions are partitioned into a vertical set of layers. Each layer performs a related subset of the functions required to communicate with another system. It relies on the next lower layer to perform more primitive functions and to conceal the details of those functions. It provides services to the next higher layer. Ideally, the layers should be defined so that changes in one layer do not require changes in the other layers. Thus, we have decomposed one problem into a number of more manageable subproblems.

The task of the ISO subcommittee was to define a set of layers and the services performed by each layer. The partitioning should group functions logically, should have enough layers to make each layer man-

> BOX B.1
>
> # Purpose of the OSI Model [ISO84]
>
> The purpose of this International Standard Reference Model of Open Systems Interconnection is to provide a common basis for the coordination of standards development for the purpose of systems interconnection, while allowing existing standards to be placed into perspective within the overall Reference Model.
>
> The term Open Systems Interconnection (OSI) qualifies standards for the exchange of information among systems that are "open" to one another for this purpose by virtue of their mutual use of the applicable standards.
>
> The fact that a system is open does not imply any particular systems implementation, technology, or means of interconnection, but refers to the mutual recognition and support of the applicable standards.
>
> It is also the purpose of this International Standard to identify areas for developing or improving standards and to provide a common reference for maintaining consistency of all related standards. It is not the intent of this International Standard either to serve as an implementation specification or to be a basis for appraising the conformance of actual implementations or to provide a sufficient level of detail to define precisely the services and protocols of the interconnection architecture. Rather, this International Standard provides a conceptual and functional framework which allows international teams of experts to work productively and independently on the development of standards for each layer of the Reference Model of OSI.

ageably small, but should not have so many layers that the processing overhead imposed by the collection of layers is burdensome. The principles by which ISO went about its task are summarized in Box B.2. The resulting OSI reference model has seven layers, which are listed with a brief definition in Table B.1. Box B.3 provides ISO's justification for the selection of these layers.

Table A.3 defines, in general terms, the functions that must be performed in a system for it to communicate. Of course, it takes two to communicate, so the same set of layered functions must exist in two systems. Communication is achieved by having the corresponding *(peer)* layers in two systems communicate. The peer layers communicate by means of a set of rules or conventions known as a *protocol*. The key elements of a protocol are

BOX B.2

Principles Used in Defining the OSI Layers [IS084]

1. Do not create so many layers as to make the system engineering task of describing and integrating the layers more difficult than necessary.
2. Create a boundary at a point where the description of services can be small and the number of interactions across the boundary are minimized.
3. Create separate layers to handle functions that are manifestly different in the process performed or the technology involved.
4. Collect similar functions into the same layer.
5. Select boundaries at a point that past experience has demonstrated to be successful.
6. Create a layer of easily localized functions so that the layer could be totally redesigned and its protocols changed in a major way to take advantage of new advances in architectural, hardware, or software technology without changing the services expected from and provided to the adjacent layers.
7. Create a boundary where it may be useful at some point in time to have the corresponding interface standardized.
8. Create a layer where there is a need for a different level of abstraction in the handling of data (e.g., morphology, syntax, semantics).
9. Allow changes of functions or protocols to be made within a layer without affecting other layers.
10. Create for each layer boundaries with its upper and lower layer only.

Similar principles have been applied to sublayering:

11. Create further subgrouping and organization of functions to form sublayers within a layer in cases where distinct communication services need it.
12. Create, where needed, two or more sublayers with a common and therefore minimal functionality to allow interface operation with adjacent layers.
13. Allow bypassing of sublayers.

TABLE B.1 The OSI Layers

Layer	Definition
1. Physical	Concerned with transmission of unstructured bit stream over physical link; involves such parameters as signal voltage swing and bit duration; deals with the mechanical, electrical, and procedural characteristics to establish, maintain, and deactivate the physical link.
2. Data link	Provides for the reliable transfer of data across the physical link; sends blocks of data (frames) with the necessary synchronization, error control, and flow control
3. Network	Provides upper layers with independence from the data-transmission and switching technologies used to connect systems; responsible for establishing, maintaining, and terminating connections
4. Transport	Provides reliable, transparent transfer of data between endpoints; provides end-to-end error recovery and flow control
5. Session	Provides the control structure for communication between applications; establishes, manages, and terminates connections (sessions) between cooperating applications
6. Presentation	Performs generally useful transformations on data to provide a standardized application interface and to provide common communications services; examples: encryption, text compression, reformatting
7. Application	Provides services to the users of the OSI environment; examples: transaction server, file transfer protocol, network management

- *Syntax:* Includes such things as data format and signal levels.
- *Semantics:* Includes control information for coordination and error handling.
- *Timing:* Includes speed matching and sequencing.

Figure B.1 illustrates the OSI model. Each system contains the seven layers. Communication is between applications in the systems, labeled AP X and AP Y in the figure. If AP X wishes to send a message to AP Y, it invokes the application layer (layer 7). Layer 7 establishes a peer relationship with layer 7 of the target machine, using a layer 7 protocol. This protocol requires services from layer 6, so the two layer 6 entities use a protocol of their own, and so on down to the physical layer, which actually passes the bits through a transmission medium.

Note that there is no direct communication between peer layers except at the physical layer. Even at that layer, the OSI model does not stipulate that two systems be directly connected. For example, a packet-switched or circuit-switched network may be used to provide the communications link. This point should become clearer subsequently, when we discuss the network layer.

Justification of the OSI Layers [ISO84]

a. It is essential that the architecture permit usage of a realistic variety of physical media for interconnection with different control procedures (e.g., V.24, V.25, X.21, etc.). Application of principles 3, 5, and 8 [Box B.2] leads to identification of a *physical layer* as the lowest layer in the architecture.

b. Some physical communications media (e.g., telephone line) require specific techniques to be used to transmit data between systems despite a relatively high error rate (i.e., an error rate not acceptable for the great majority of applications). These specific techniques are used in data-link control procedures, which have been studied and standardized for a number of years. It must also be recognized that new physical communication media (e.g., fiber optics) will require different data-link control procedures. Application of principles 3, 5, and 8 leads to identification of a *data link layer* on top of the physical layer in the architecture.

c. In the open-systems architecture, some systems will act as the final destination of data. Some systems may act only as intermediate nodes (forwarding data to other systems). Application of principles 3, 5, and 7 leads to identification of a *network layer* on top of the data link layer. Network-oriented protocols, such as routing, for example, will be grouped in this layer. Thus, the network layer will provide a connection path (network connection) between a pair of transport entities, including the case where intermediate nodes are involved.

d. Control of data transportation from source end system to destination end system (which is not performed in intermediate nodes) is the last function to be performed to provide the totality of the transport service. Thus, the upper layer in the transport-service part of the architecture is the *transport layer,* on top of the network layer. This transport layer relieves higher layer entities from any concern with the transportation of data between them.

e. There is a need to organize and synchronize dialogue and to manage the exchange of data. Application of principles 3 and 4 leads to the identification of a session layer on top of the transport layer.

f. The remaining set of general-interest functions is those related to representation and manipulation of structured data for the benefit of application programs. Application of principles 3 and 4 leads to identification of a *presentation layer* on top of the session layer.

g. Finally, there are applications consisting of application processes that perform information processing. An aspect of these applications processes and the protocols by which they communicate comprise the *application layer* as the highest layer of the architecture.

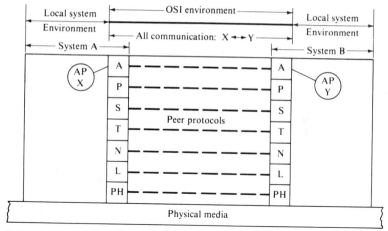

FIGURE B.1 The OSI Environment

The attractiveness of the OSI approach is that it promises to solve the heterogeneous computer communications problem. Two systems, no matter how different, can communicate effectively if they have the following in common:

- They implement the same set of communications functions.
- These functions are organized into the same set of layers. Peer layers must provide the same functions, but note that it is not necessary that they provide them in the same way.
- Peer layers must share a common protocol.

To assure the preceding, standards are needed. Standards must define the functions and services to be provided by a layer (but not how it is to be done—that may differ from system to system). Standards must also define the protocols between peer layers (each protocol must be identical for the two peer layers). The OSI model, by defining a 7-layer architecture, provides a framework for defining these standards.

Some useful OSI terminology is illustrated in Fig. B.2 For simplicity, any layer is referred to as the (N) *layer,* and names of constructs associated with that layer are also preceded by (N). Within a system, there are one or more active entities in each layer. An (N) *entity* implements functions of the (N) layer and also the protocol for communicating with (N) entities in other systems. An example of an entity is a process in a multiprocessing system. Or it could simply be a subroutine. There might be multiple identical (N) entities, if this is convenient or efficient for a given system. There might also be differing (N) entities, corresponding to different protocol standards at that level. Each (N) entity implements a protocol for communicating with (N) entities in other systems. Each entity communicates with entities in the layers above and below it across

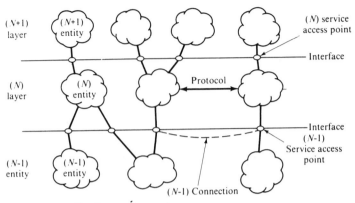

FIGURE B.2 The Layer Concept

an interface. The interface is realized as one or more *service access points* (SAPs).

To clarify these terms as well as some functions common to all layers, refer to Fig. B.3. The functions we wish to discuss are

- Encapsulation.
- Segmentation
- Connection establishment.
- Flow control.
- Error control.
- Multiplexing.

First, consider the most common way in which protocols are realized, which is by a process of *encapsulation*. When AP X has a message to send to AP Y, it transfers those data to a (7) entity in the application layer. A *header* is appended to the data that contain the required information for the peer layer 7 protocol; this is referred to as an encapsulation of the data. The original data, plus the header, are now passed as a unit to layer 6. The (6) entity treats the whole unit as data and appends its own header (a second encapsulation). This process continues down through layer 2, which generally adds both a header and a trailer, the function of which is explained later. This layer 2 unit, called a *frame*, is then transmitted by the physical layer onto the transmission medium. When the frame is received by the target system, the reverse process occurs. As the data ascend, each layer strips off the outermost header, acts on the protocol information contained therein, and passes the remainder up to the next layer.

At each stage of the process, a layer may segment the data unit it receives from the next higher layer into several parts, to accommodate its own requirements. These data units must then be reassembled by the corresponding peer layer before being passed up.

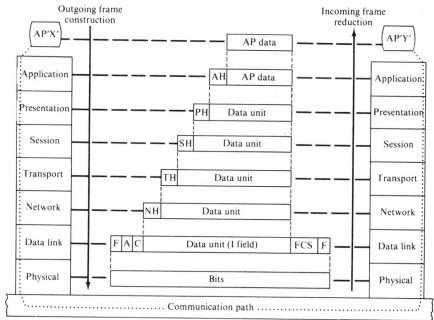

FIGURE B.3 OSI Operation

When two peer entities wish to exchange data, this may be done with or without a prior *connection*. A connection can exist at any layer of the hierarchy. In the abstract, a connection is established between two (N) entities by identifying a connection endpoint, (N − 1) CEP, within an (N − 1) SAP for each (N) entity. A connection facilitates flow control and error control. *Flow control* is a function performed by an (N) entity to limit the amount or rate of data it receives from another (N) entity. This function is needed to ensure that the receiving (N) entity does not experience overflow. *Error control* refers to mechanisms to detect and correct errors that occur in the transmission of data units between peer entities.

Multiplexing can occur in two directions. *Upward* multiplexing means that multiple (N) connections are multiplexed on, or share, a single (N − 1) connection. This may be needed to make more efficient use of the (N − 1) service or to provide several (N) connections in an environment where only a single (N − 1) connection exists. *Downward* multiplexing, or *splitting*, means that a single (N) connection is built on top of multiple (N − 1) connections, the traffic on the (N) connection being divided among the various (N − 1) connections. This technique may be used to improve reliability, performance, or efficiency.

B.3

LAYERS

Physical Layer

The *physical layer* covers the physical interface between devices and the rules by which bits are passed from one to another. The physical layer has four important characteristics:

- Mechanical.
- Electrical.
- Functional.
- Procedural.

Examples of standards at this layer are RS-232-C, RS-449/422/423, and portions of X.21.

Data Link Layer

Although the physical layer provides only a raw bit stream service, the *data link layer* attempts to make the physical link reliable and provides the means to activate, maintain, and deactivate the link. The principal service provided by the link layer to the higher layers is that of error detection and control. Thus, with a fully functional data link-layer protocol, the next higher layer may assume virtually error-free transmission over the link. If communication is between two systems that are not directly connected, however, the connection will comprise a number of data links in tandem, each functioning independently. Thus, the higher layers are not relieved of an error-control responsibility.

Examples of standards at this layer are HDLC, LAPB, LAPD, and LLC.

Network Layer

The basic service of the *network layer* is to provide for the transparent transfer of data between transport entities. It relieves the transport layer of the need to know anything about the underlying data transmission and switching technologies used to connect systems. The network service is responsible for establishing, maintaining, and terminating connections across the intervening communications facility.

It is at this layer that the concept of a protocol becomes a little fuzzy. This is best illustrated with reference to Fig. B.4, which shows two stations that are communicating, not via direct link, but via a packet-switched network. The stations have direct links to the network nodes. The layers 1 and 2 protocols are station-node protocols (local). Layers

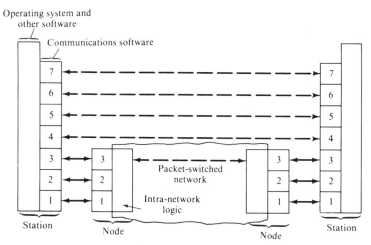

Operating system and
other software

Communications software

Packet-switched
network

Intra-network
logic

Station

Node

Node

Station

FIGURE B.4 Communication Across a Network

4 through 7 are clearly protocols between (N) entities in the two stations. Layer 3 is a little bit of both.

The principal dialogue is between the station and its node; the station sends addressed packets to the node for delivery across the network. It requests a virtual-circuit connection, uses the connection to transmit data, and terminates the connection. All of this is done by means of a station-node protocol. Because packets are exchanged and virtual circuits are set up between two stations, however, there are aspects of a station-station protocol as well.

There is a spectrum of possibilities for intervening communications facilities to be managed by the network layer. At one extreme, the simplest, there is a direct link between stations. In this case, there may be little or no need for a network layer, because the data link layer can perform the necessary functions of managing the link. Between extremes, the most common use of layer 3 is to handle the details of using a communication network. In this case, the network entity in the station must provide the network with sufficient information to switch and route data to another station. At the other extreme, two stations might wish to communicate but are not even connected to the same network. Rather, they are connected to networks that, directly or indirectly, are connected to each other. One approach to providing for data transfer in such a case is to use an internet protocol (IP), which sits on top of a network protocol and is used by a transport protocol. IP is responsible for internetwork routing and delivery and relies on a layer 3 at each network for intranetwork services. IP is sometimes referred to as "layer 3.5."

The best-known example of layer 3 is the X.25 layer 3 standard. The

X.25 standard refers to itself as an interface between a station and a node (using our terminology). In the context of the OSI model, it is actually a station-node protocol.

Transport Layer

The purpose of layer 4 is to provide a reliable mechanism for the exchange of data between processes in different systems. The *transport layer* ensures that data units are delivered error-free, in sequence, with no losses or duplications. The transport layer may also be concerned with optimizing the use of network services and providing a requested quality of service to session entities. For example, the session entity might specify acceptable error rates, maximum delay, priority, and security. In effect, the transport layer serves as the user's liaison with the communications facility.

The size and complexity of a transport protocol depend on the type of service it can get from layer 3. For a reliable layer 3 with a virtual-circuit capability, a minimal layer 4 is required. If layer 3 is unreliable, the layer 4 protocol should include extensive error detection and recovery. Accordingly, ISO has defined five classes of transport protocol, each oriented toward a different underlying service.

Session Layer

The *session layer* provides the mechanism for controlling the dialogue between presentation entities. At a minimum, the session layer provides a means for two presentation entities to establish and use a connection, called a *session*. In addition, it may provide some of the following services:

- *Dialogue type:* This can be two-way simultaneous, two-way alternate, or one-way.
- *Recovery:* The session layer can provide a checkpointing mechanism, so that if a failure of some sort occurs between checkpoints, the session entity can retransmit all data since the last checkpoint.

Presentation Layer

The presentation layer offers application programs and terminal-handler programs a set of data transformation services. Services that this layer would typically provide include

- *Data translation:* Code and character set translation.
- *Formatting:* Modification of data layout.
- *Syntax selection:* Initial selection and subsequent modification of the transformation used.

Examples of presentation protocols are data compression, encryption, and virtual-terminal protocol. A virtual-terminal protocol converts between specific terminal characteristics and a generic or virtual model used by application programs.

Application Layer

The *application layer* provides a means for application processes to access the OSI environment. This layer contains management functions and generally useful mechanisms to support distributed applications. Examples of protocols at this level are virtual-file protocol and job transfer and manipulation protocol.

B.4
PERSPECTIVES ON THE OPEN-SYSTEMS INTERCONNECTION MODEL

Figure B.5 provides two useful perspectives on the OSI architecture. The annotation along the right side suggests viewing the seven layers in three parts. The lower three layers contain the logic for a host to interact with a network. The host is attached physically to the network, uses a data link protocol to reliably communicate with the network, and uses a network protocol to request data exchange with another device on the network and to request network services (e.g., priority). The X.25 standard for packet-switched networks actually encompasses all three layers. Continuing from this perspective, the transport layer provides a reliable end-to-end connection regardless of the intervening network facility. Finally, the upper three layers, taken together, are involved in the exchange of data between end users, making use of a transport connection for reliable data transfer.

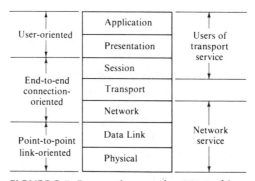

FIGURE B.5 Perspectives on the OSI Architecture

Another perspective is suggested by the annotation on the left. Again, consider host systems attached to a common network. The lower two layers deal with the link between the host system and the network. The next three layers are all involved in transfer data from one host to another. The network layer makes use of the communication network facilities to transfer data from one host to another; the transport layer assures that the transfer is reliable; and the session layer manages the flow of data over the logical connection. Finally, the upper two layers are oriented to the user's concerns, including considerations of the application to be performed and any formatting issues.

B.5

RECOMMENDED READING

[STAL90b] provides an in-depth examination of the OSI model, plus a discussion of protocol standards at each layer. [STAL91a] and [TANE88] also cover the OSI model, with more emphasis on the technology of protocols at each layer rather than the standards themselves. A more informal account can be found in [MART81]. Good articles on the subject are [VOEL86], [ASCH86], and [FOLT81]. [STAL91c] contains reprints of key articles covering OSI and the standards at each layer.

B.6

PROBLEMS

B.1. List the major disadvantages with the layered approach to protocols.

B.2. Based on the principles enunciated in Box B.2, design an architecture with eight layers and make a case for it. Design one with six layers and make a case for that.

B.3. Two blue armies are poised on opposite hills preparing to attack a single red army in the valley. The red army can defeat either of the blue armies separately but will fail to defeat both blue armies if they attack simultaneously. The blue armies communicate via an unreliable communication system (a foot soldier). The commander of one of the blue armies would like to attack at noon. His problem is this: If he sends a message ordering the attack, he cannot be sure it will get through. He could ask for acknowledgment, but the acknowledgment might not get through. Is there a protocol that the two blue armies can use to assure victory?

B.4. In Figure B.3, exactly one protocol data unit (PDU) in layer N is encapsulated in a PDU at layer $(N - 1)$. It is also possible to break one N-layer PDU into multiple $(N - 1)$-layer PDUs (segmentation) or to group multiple N-layer PDUs into one $(N - 1)$-layer PDU (blocking).

a. In the case of segmentation, is it necessary that each $(N - 1)$-layer PDU contain a copy of the N-layer header?

b. In the case of blocking, is it necessary that each N-layer PDU retain its own header, or can the data be consolidated into a single N-layer PDU with a single N-layer header?

B.5. A broadcast network is one in which a transmission from one station is automatically received by all other stations. An example is a local network. Discuss the need or lack of need for a network layer (OSI layer 3) in a broadcast network.

Glossary

Some of the definitions in this glossary are taken from CCITT Recommendation I.112, *Vocabulary of Terms for ISDN*, 1988; these are indicated by a "†" next to the term. Others are taken from U.S. Federal Standard 1037A, *Glossary of Telecommunication Terms*, 1986; these are indicated by a "*" next to the term.

Access Protocol.† A defined set of procedures that is adopted at an interface at a specified reference point between a user and a network to enable the user to employ the services and/or facilities of that network.

Analog Data.* Data represented by a physical quantity that is considered to be continuously variable and whose magnitude is made directly proportional to the data or to a suitable function of the data.

Analog Signal. A continuously varying electromagnetic wave that may be propagated over a variety of media.

Analog Transmission. The transmission of analog signals without regard to content. The signal may be amplified, but there is no intermediate attempt to recover the data from the signal.

Application Layer. Layer 7 of the OSI model. This layer determines the interface of the system with the user and provides useful application-oriented services.

Automatic Repeat Request (ARQ). A feature that automatically initiates a request for retransmission when an error in transmission is detected.

Bandwidth.* The difference between the limiting frequencies of a continuous frequency band.

Basic Access.† A term used to describe a simple standardized combination of access channels that constitute the access arrangements for the majority of ISDN users.

Bell Operating Company (BOC). Before the divestiture of AT&T, the 22 Bell Operating Companies were AT&T subsidiaries that built, operated, and maintained the local and intrastate networks and provided most of the day-to-day service for customers. After divestiture, the BOCs retain their identity within seven regional companies (RBOCs) and are responsible for local service as defined by local access and transport areas (LATAs).

Bit Stuffing. The insertion of extra bits into a data stream to avoid the appearance of unintended control sequences.

Broadband ISDN (BISDN). A second generation of ISDN. The key characteristic of broadband ISDN is that it provides transmission channels capable of supporting rates greater than the primary ISDN rate.

Centrex.† A service offered by operating telephone companies that provides, from the telephone company office, functions and features comparable to those provided by a PBX.

Circuit Switching. A method of communicating in which a dedicated communications path is established between two devices through one or more intermediate switching nodes. Unlike packet switching, digital data are sent as a continuous stream of bits. Data rate is guaranteed, and delay is essentially limited to propagation time.

Codec. Coder-decoder. Transforms analog data into a digital bit stream (coder), and digital signals into analog data (decoder).

Common Carrier. In the United States, companies that furnish long-distance telecommunication services to the public. Common carriers are subject to regulation by federal and state regulatory commissions.

Common-channel Signaling.† A method of signaling in which signaling information relating to a multiplicity of circuits, or function or for network management, is conveyed over a single channel by addressed messages.

Communications Architecture. The hardware and software structure that implements the communications function.

Cyclic Redundancy Check (CRC). An error-detecting code in which the code is the remainder resulting from dividing the bits to be checked by a predetermined binary number.

Data Circuit-terminating Equipment (DCE). In a data station, the equipment that provides the signal conversion and coding between the data terminal equipment (DTE) and the line. The DCE may be separate equipment or an integral part of the DTE or of intermediate equipment. The DCE may perform other functions that are normally performed at the network end of the line.

Datagram. In packet switching, a self-contained packet, independent of other packets, that does not require acknowledgment and that carries information sufficient for routing from the originating data terminal equipment (DTE), without relying on earlier exchanges between the DTEs and the network.

Data Link Layer. Layer 2 of the OSI model. Converts an unreliable transmission channel into a reliable one.

Data Terminal Equipment (DTE).* Equipment consisting of digital end instruments that convert the user information into data signals for transmission or reconvert the received data signals into user information.

Digital Data.* Data represented by discrete values or conditions.

Digital PBX. A private branch exchange (PBX) that operates internally on digital signals. Thus, voice signals must be digitized for use in the PBX.

Digital Signal. A discrete or discontinuous signal, such as a sequence of voltage pulses.

Digital Transmission. The transmission of digital data or analog data that have been digitized, using either an analog or digital signal, in which the digital content is recovered and repeated at intermediate points to reduce the effects of impairments, such as noise, distortion, and attenuation.

Digitize.* To convert an analog signal to a digital signal.

Encapsulation. The addition of control information by a protocol entity to data obtained from a protocol user.

Error-detecting Code.* A code in which each data signal conforms to specific rules of construction, so that departures from this construction in the received signal can be automatically detected.

Error Rate.* The ratio of the number of data units in error to the total number of data units.

Exchange Area. A geographical area within which there is a single uniform set of charges for telephone service. A call between any two points within an exchange area is a local call.

Facsimile. A system for the transmission of images. The image is scanned at the transmitter, reconstructed at the receiving station, and duplicated on some form of paper.

Fast Packet Switching. An approach to packet switching that attempts to exploit the high capacity of current digital transmission services. Formats and procedures are designed to minimize packet processing time.

Flow Control. A function performed by a receiving entity to limit the amount or rate of data sent by a transmitting entity.

Frame Check Sequence. An error-detecting code inserted as a field in a block of data to be transmitted. The code serves to check for errors upon reception of the data.

Frequency-division Multiplexing (FDM). Division of a transmission facility into two or more channels by splitting the frequency band transmitted by the facility into narrower bands, each of which is used to constitute a distinct channel.

Full-duplex Transmission. Transmission of data in both directions at the same time.

Functional Group.† A set of functions that may be performed by a single piece of equipment.

Half-duplex Transmission. Data transmitted in either direction, one direction at a time.

Header. System-defined control information that precedes user data.

Inchannel Signaling. A technique in which the same channel is used to carry network control signals as is used to carry the call to which the control signals relate.

Integrated Digital Network (IDN). The integration of transmission and switching functions using digital technology in a circuit-switched telecommunications network.

Integrated Services Digital Network (ISDN). Planned worldwide telecommunication service that will use digital transmission and switching technology to support voice and digital data communications.

Layer. A conceptual region that embodies one or more functions between an upper and a lower logical boundary.

Local Access and Transport Areas (LATA). A geographic area generally equivalent to a Standard Metropolitan Statistical Area. The territory served by the Bell system was divided into approximately 160 LATAs at divestiture. Intra-LATA services are provided by the Bell Operating Companies.

Local Loop. A transmission path, generally twisted pair, between the individual subscriber and the nearest switching center of a public telecommunications network. Also referred to as a subscriber loop.

Modem. Modulator/demodulator. Transforms a digital bit stream into an analog signal (modulator) and vice versa (demodulator).

Multiplexing.* In data transmission, a function that permits two or more data sources to share a common transmission medium such that each data source has its own channel.

Network Layer. Layer 3 of the OSI model. Responsible for routing data through a communication network.

Network Terminating Equipment (NTE). A grouping of ISDN functions at the boundary between the ISDN and the subscriber.

Open-systems Interconnection (OSI) Reference Model. A model of communications between cooperating devices. It defines a 7-layer architecture of communication functions.

Packet-Switching. A method of transmitting messages through a communications network, in which long messages are subdivided into short packets. Each packet is passed from source to destination through intermediate nodes. At each node, the entire message is received, stored briefly, and then passed on to the next node.

Physical Layer Layer 1 of the OSI model. Concerned with the electrical, mechanical, and timing aspects of signal transmission over a medium.

Picture Element (pel). The smallest discrete scanning line sample of a facsimile system, which contains only black/white information (no gray shading information is used).

Piggybacking. The inclusion of an acknowledgment of a previously received protocol data unit in an outgoing protocol data unit.

Ping-pong Transmission Technique See *Time-compression Multiplexing.*

Pixel.* A picture element that contains gray scale information.

Point-to-point. A configuration in which two stations share a transmission path.

Postal, Telegraph, and Telephone (PTT). A government organization that operates a nationalized public telecommunications network.

Presentation Layer. Layer 6 of the OSI model. Concerned with data format and display.

Private Branch Exchange (PBX). A telephone exchange on the user's premises. Provides a circuit-switching facility for telephones on extension lines within the building and access to the public telephone network.

Private Network. A facility in which the customer leases circuits and sometimes switching capacity for the customer's exclusive use. Access may be provided to a public switched telecommunication service.

Protocol.† A formal statement of the procedures that are adopted to ensure communication between two or more functions within the same layer of a hierarchy of functions.

Protocol Data Unit (PDU).* Information that is delivered as a unit between peer entities of a network and may contain control information, address information, or data.

Pseudoternary Coding. A form of digital signaling in which three signal levels are used to encode binary data. In ISDN, the form of pseudoternary is one in which binary one is represented by no line signal and binary zero is represented, alternately, by positive and negative voltage pulses.

Public Data Network (PDN). A packet-switched network that is publicly available to subscribers. Usually, the term connotes government control or national monopoly.

Pulse Code Modulation (PCM). A process in which a signal is sampled, and the magnitude of each sample with respect to a fixed reference is quantized and converted by coding to a digital signal.

Recognized Private Operating Agency (RPOA). A private or government-controlled corporation that provides telecommunications services (e.g., AT&T). RPOAs participate as nonvoting members of CCITT.

Reference Configuration.† A combination of functional groups and reference points that shows possible network arrangements.

Reference Point.† A conceptual point at the conjunction of two non-overlapping functional groupings.

Service Access Point (SAP). A means of identifying a user of the services of a protocol entity. A protocol entity provides one or more SAPs, for use by higher-level entities.

Session Layer. Layer 5 of the OSI model. Manages a logical connection (session) between two communicating processes or applications.

Signaling.† The exchange of information specifically concerned with the establishment and control of connections, and with management, in a telecommunication network.

Sliding-window Technique. A method of flow control in which a transmitting station may send numbered protocol data units (PDUs) within a window of numbers. The window changes dynamically to allow additional PDUs to be sent.

Software-defined Network (SDN). A facility based on a public circuit-switched network that gives the user the appearance of a private network. The network is "software defined" in the sense that the user provides the service supplier with entries to a database used by the supplier to configure, manage, monitor, and report on the operation of the network.

Space-division Switching. A circuit-switching technique in which each connection through the switch takes a physically separate and dedicated path.

Specialized Common Carrier. In the U.S., a telecommunications common carrier other than AT&T and the Bell Operating Companies, authorized to provide a variety of transmission services.

Spectrum. Refers to an absolute, contiguous range of frequencies.

Subscriber Loop. See *Local Loop*.

Synchronous Time-division Multiplexing. A method of TDM in which time slots on a shared transmission line are assigned to devices on a fixed, predetermined basis.

TDM Bus Switching. A form of time-division switching in which time slots are used to transfer data over a shared bus between transmitter and receiver.

Teleaction Service.† Telemetry service. A type of telecommunication service that uses short messages, requiring a very low transmission rate, between the user and the network.

Telecommunication Service.† That which is offered by an administration or RPOA to its customers in order to satisfy a specific telecommunications requirement. Bearer service, teleservice, and teleaction service are types of telecommunication service.

Telematics. User-oriented information-transfer services, including teletex, videotex, and facsimile.

Teleservice.† A type of telecommunication service that provides the complete capability, including terminal equipment functions, for communication between users according to protocols established by agreement between administrations and/or RPOAs.

Teletex. A text communications service that provides message preparation and transmission facilities.

Teletext. A one-way information-retrieval service. A fixed number of information pages are repetitively broadcast on unused portions of a TV channel bandwidth. A decoder at the TV set is used to select and display pages.

Time-compression Multiplexing. A means for providing full-duplex digital data transmission over a single twisted pair. Data are buffered at each end and are sent across the line at approximately double the subscriber data rate, with the two ends taking turns.

Time-division Multiplexing (TDM). The division of a transmission facility into multiple channels by allotting the facility to different channels, one at a time.

Time-division Switching. A circuit-switching technique in which time slots in a time-multiplexed stream of data are manipulated to pass data from an input to an output.

Time-multiplexed Switching (TMS). A form of space-division in which each input line is a TDM stream. The switching configuration may change for each time slot.

Time-slot Interchange (TSI). The interchange of time slots within a time-division multiplexed frame.

Transport Layer. Layer 4 of the OSI model. Provides reliable, sequenced transfer of data between endpoints.

User-User Protocol.† A protocol that is adopted between two or more users in order to ensure communication between them.

Value-added Network (VAN). A privately owned packet-switched network whose services are sold to the public.

Videotex. A two-way information-retrieval service accessible to terminals and TV sets equipped with a special decoder. Pages of information at a central resource are retrieved interactively over a switched telephone line connection.

Virtual Circuit. A packet-switching mechanism in which a logical connection (virtual circuit) is established between two stations at the start of transmission. All packets follow the same route, need not carry a complete address, and arrive in sequence.

References

ABBO84 Abbot, G. "Digital Space Division: A Technique for Switching High-Speed Data Signals." *IEEE Communications Magazine,* April 1984.

AHUJ83 Ahuja, V. *Design and Analysis of Computer Communication Networks.* New York: McGraw-Hill, 1983.

AMAN86 Amand, J. *A Guide to Packet-Switched, Valued-Added Networks.* New York: Macmillan, 1986.

AOYA88 Aoyama, T., W. Daumer, and G. Modena. eds. *Special Issue on Voice Coding for Communications. IEEE Journal on Selected Areas in Communications,* February 1988.

ASCH86 Aschenbrenner, J. *Open Systems Interconnection.* IBM Systems Journal, Nos. 3/4, 1986.

ASH89 Ash, G., et al. "Robust Design and Planning of a Worldwide Intelligent Network." *IEEE Journal on Selected Areas in Communications,* October 1989.

ASH90 Ash, G. "Design and Control of Networks with Dynamic Nonhierarchical Routing." *IEEE Communications Magazine,* October 1990.

ATT61 American Telephone and Telegraph Co. *Principles of Electricity Applied to Telephone and Telegraph Work,* 1961.

BAE91 Bae, J., and T. Suda. "Survey of Traffic Control Schemes and Protocols in ATM Networks." *Proceedings of the IEEE,* February 1991.

BALL89 Ballart, R., and Y. Ching. "SONET: Now It's the Standard Optical Network." *IEEE Communications Magazine,* March 1989.

BARC81 Barcomb, D. *Office Automation.* Bedford, MA: Digital Press, 1981.

BARR90 Barrett, M. "The Challenge of Fiber in the Loop." *IEEE LCS,* August 1990.

BART86 Bartee, T. *Digital Communications.* Indianapolis, IN: Sams, 1986.

BAUW87 Bauwens, J., and M. Prycker. "Broadband Experiment Using Asynchronous Time Division Techniques." *Electrical Communication,* No. 1, 1987.

603

BELL82 Bell Telephone Laboratories. *Transmission Systems for Communications.* Murray Hill, NJ, 1982.

BELL84 Bellchanbers, W., J. Francis, E. Hummel, and R. Nickelson. "The International Telecommunication Union and Development of Worldwide Telecommunications." *IEEE Communications Magazine,* May 1984.

BELL86 Bell, P., and K. Jabbour. "Review of Point-to-Point Routing Algorithms." *IEEE Communications Magazine,* January 1986.

BELL91 Bellamy, J. *Digital Telephony, Second Edition.* New York: Wiley, 1991.

BERL87 Berlekamp, E., R. Peile, and S. Pope. "The Application of Error Control to Communications." *IEEE Communications Magazine,* April 1987.

BERT87 Bertsekas, D., and R. Gallager. *Data Networks.* Englewood Cliffs, NJ: Prentice-Hall, 1987.

BEVA86 Bevan, M. "Image Processing May Cause Future Problems with Network Loading." *Data Communications,* March 1986.

BHAR91 Bhargava, A. *Integrated Broadband Networks.* Norwood, MA: Artech House, 1991.

BHUS83 Bhusri, G. "Optimum Implementation of Common Channel Signaling in Local Networks." *Proceedings of IEEE INFOCOM 83,* 1983.

BIRM90 Birman, A. "A High-Performance Switch with Applications to Frame Relay Networks." *Proceedings, IEEE INFOCOM '90,* June 1990.

BLAC87 Black, U. *Computer Networks: Protocols, Standards, and Interfaces.* Englewood Cliffs, NJ: Prentice-Hall, 1987.

BOCK88 Bocker, P. *ISDN: Concepts, Methods, and Systems.* New York: Springer-Verlag, 1988.

BODS86 Bodson, D., and N. Randall. "Analysis of Group 4 Facsimile Throughput." *IEEE Transactions on Communications,* September 1986.

BOEH90 Boehm, R. "Progress in Standardization of SONET." *IEEE LCS Magazine,* May 1990.

BORS91 Borsook, P. "SONET Technology Brings Solutions and Questions." *Network World,* January 14, 1991.

BRIE90 Briere, D. *Virtual Networks: A Buyer's Guide.* Norwood, MA: Artech House, 1990.

BROO83 Broomell, G., and J. Heath. "Classification Categories and Historical Development of Circuit Switching Topologies." *ACM Computing Surveys.* June 1983.

BROW86 Browne, T. "Network of the Future." *Proceedings of the IEEE.* September 1986.

BURG83 Burg, F. "Design Considerations for Using the X.25 Packet Layer on Data Terminal Equipment." *Proceedings, IEEE INFOCOM 83,* 1983.

BURG90 Burgin, J. "Broadband ISDN Resource Management." *Computer Networks and ISDN Systems,* December 1990.

BUSH89 Bush, J. "Frame-Relay Services Promise WAN Bandwidth on Demand." *Data Communications,* July 1989.

CARL80 Carlson, D. "Bit-Oriented Data Link Control Procedures." *IEEE Transactions on Communications,* April 1980.

CASA87 Casali, F., and S. Treves. "Towards the Integrated Broadband Communication Network." *Electrical Communication,* No. 1, 1987.

CCIT90 CCITT. *Guidelines for Implementing a Signaling System No. 7 Network.* Draft 4, July 1990.

CERN84 Cerni, D. *Standards in Process: Foundations and Profiles of ISDN and OSI Studies. National Telecommunications and Information Administration, Report 84–170.* December 1984.

CHEN89a Chen, K., and K. Rege. "A Comparative Performance Study of Various Congestion Controls for ISDN Frame-Relay Networks." *Proceedings, IEEE INFOCOM '89,* April 1989.

CHEN89b Chen, K., K. Ho, and V. Saksena. "Analysis and Design of a Highly Reliable Transport Architecture for ISDN Frame-Relay Networks." *IEEE Journal on Selected Areas in Communications,* October 1989.

CHER89 Cherukuri, R., and J. Derby. "Frame Relay: Protocols and Private Network Applications." *Proceedings, IEEE INFOCOM '89,* April 1989.

CHIL90 Chilton, P. *X. 400: The Messaging and Interconnection Medium for the Future.* Oxford, England: NCC Publications, 1990.

CHOU85 Chou, W., ed. *Computer Communications,* Volume II. *Systms and Applications.* Englewood Cliffs, NJ: Prentice-Hall, 1985.

COCH85 Cochrane, J., W. Falconer, V. Mummert, and W. Strich. "Latest Network Trends." *IEEE Communications Magazine,* October 1985.

COOK84 Cooke, R. "Intercity Limits: Looking Ahead to All-Digital Networks and No Bottlenecks." *Data Communications,* March 1984.

COOL87 Cooley, K., M. Goodman, H. Kerner, and D. Simmons. "Wideband Virtual Networks." *Telecommunications,* February 1987.

COUC90 Couch, L. *Digital and Analog Communication Systems, Third Edition.* New York: Macmillan, 1990.

COUD88 Coudreuse, J., W. Sincoskie, and J. Turner, editors. *Special Issue on Broadband Packet Communications. IEEE Journal on Selected Areas in Communications,* December 1988.

CRAI88 Craigie, J. "ISO 10021—X.400(88): A Tutorial for Those Familiar with X.400(84)." *Computer Networks and ISDN Systems,* September 1988.

DAVI73 Davies, D., and D. Barber. *Communication Networks for Computers.* New York: Wiley, 1973.

DAVI90 Davidson, R., and N. Muller. *LANs to WANs: Network Management in the 1990s.* Norwood, MA; Artech House, 1990.

DAYT89 Dayton, R. *Guide to Integrating Digital Services.* New York: McGraw-Hill, 1989.

DHAS86 Dhas, C., and U. Konangi. "X.25: An Interface to Public Packet Networks." *IEEE Communications Magazine,* September 1986.

DONO86 Donohoe, D., G. Johannessen, and R. Stone. "Realization of a Signaling System No. 7 Network for AT&T." *IEEE Journal on Selected Areas in Communications,* November 1986.

DORR83 Dorros, I. "Telephone Nets Go Digital." *IEEE Spectrum,* April 1983.

DOSH88 Doshi, B., and H. Nguyen. "Congestion Control in ISDN Frame-Relay Networks." *AT&T Technical Journal,* November/December 1988.

ERDE86 Erdelyi, B., and J. Batista. "Implementation and Verification of X.25 Packet Data Networks." *Proceedings, Fifth Annual International Phoenix Conference on Computers and Communications,* March 1986.

FALC82 Falconer, D. "Adaptive Reference Echo Cancellation." *IEEE Transactions on Communications,* September 1982.

FINN89 Finnie, G. "Lighting Up the Local Loop." *Telecommunications,* January 1989.

FOLT81 Folts, H. "Coming of Age: A Long-Awaited Standard for Heterogeneous Nets." *Data Communications,* January 1981.

FREE85 Freeman, R. *Telecommunications Engineering.* New York: Wiley, 1985.

FREE89 Freeman, R. *Telecomunication System Engineering, Second Edition.* New York: Wiley, 1989.

FUJI90 Fujioka, M., Y. Ikeda, and M. Norigoe. "Error Control Signaling in the Message Transfer Part of CCITT Signaling System No. 7." *IEEE Transactions on Communications,* September 1990.

GALL68 Gallager, R. *Information Theory and Reliable Communication.* New York: Wiley, 1968.

GAWD86 Gawdun, M. "Virtual Private Networks." *Telecommunications,* April 1986.

GERL80 Gerla, M., and L. Kleinrock. "Flow Control: A Comparative Survey." *IEEE Transactions on Communications,* April 1980.

GERL81 Gerla, M. "Routing and Flow Control." In [KUO81].

GERL84 Gerla, M. "Controlling Routes, Traffic Rates, and Buffer Allocation in Packet Networks." *IEEE Communications Magazine,* November 1984.

GERW84 Gerwen, P., N. Verhoeckx, and T. Claasen. "Design Considerations for a 144 kbit/s Digital Transmission Unit for the Local Telephone Network." *IEE Journal on Selected Areas in Communications,* March 1984.

GIFF86 Gifford, W. "ISDN User-Network Interfaces." *IEEE Journal on Selected Areas in Communications,* May 1986.

GILH87 Gilhooly, D. "Towards the Intelligent Network." *Telecommunications,* December 1987.

GLEN86 Glen, D. *Networks, Signaling, and Switching for Post-Divestiture and the ISDN. National Telecommunications and Information Administration Report 86–191,* February 1986.

GREE77 Greene, W., and U. Pooch. "A Review of Classification Schemes for Computer Communication Networks." *Computer,* November 1977.

GREE87 Green, P., and D. Godard. "Prospects and Design Choices for Integrated Private Networks." *IBM Systems Journal,* No. 1, 1987.

GRIF87 Griffiths, G., and C. Stones. "The Tea-Leaf Reader Algorithm: An Efficient Implementation of CRC-16 and CRC-32." *Communications of the ACM,* July 1987.

GRIF90 Griffiths, J. *ISDN Explained.* New York: Wiley, 1990.

HAC89 Hac, A., and H. Mutlu. "Synchronous Optical Network and Broadband ISDN Protocols." *Computer,* November 1989.

HARD89 Hardwick, S. *ISDN Design: A Practical Approach.* NewYork: Academic Press, 1989.

HARR86 Harrington, E., G. Cipriano, and V. Micheroni. "Public Switched 56-kbps Networks." *Telecommunications,* March 1986.

HASK81 Haskell, B., and R. Steele. "Audio and Video Bit-Rate Reduction." *Proceedings of the IEEE,* February 1981.

HASK87 Haskell, B., D. Pearson, and H. Yamamoto, eds. *Low Bit-Rate Coding of Moving Images. Special issue of IEEE Journal on Selected Areas in Communications,* August 1987.

HEAT91 Heath, D. "Virtual Networking/Telecommunications." *Telecommunications,* January 1991.

HELG91 Helgert, H. *Integrated Services Digital Networks: Architectures, Protocols, and Standards.* Reading, MA: Addison-Wesley, 1991.

HENS88 Henshall, J., and S. Shaw. *OSI Explained: End-to-End Computer Communication Standards.* New York: Wiley, 1988.

HELM92 Helmrich, H., and P. Bartuska. "Teletex: More Than a Speedy Alternative to Aging Telex." *Data Communications,* February 1982.

HIRS85 Hirschheim, R. *Office Automation.* Reading, MA: Addison-Wesley, 1985.

HOBE83 Hoberecht, W. "A Layered Network Protocol for Packet Voice and Data Integration." *IEEE Journal on Selected Areas in Communications,* December 1983.

HODG87 Hodges, P. "Three Decades by the Numbers." *Datamation,* September 15, 1987.

HOLM83 Holmes, E. "A Closer Look at AT&T's New High-Speed Digital Services." *Data Communications,* July 1983.

HOLT90 Holter, R. "SONET: A Network Management Viewpoint." *IEEE LCS Magazine,* November 1990.

HSIE84a Hsieh, W., and I. Gitman. "Routing Strategies in Computer Networks." *Computer,* June 1984.

HSIE84b Hsieh, W., and I. Gitman. "How to Prevent Congestion in Computer Networks." *Data Communications,* June 1984.

HUAN91 Huang, D., and C. Valenti. "Digital Subscriber Lines: Network Considerations for ISDN Basic Access Standard." *Proceedings of the IEEE,* February 1991.

HUI87 Hui, J., and E. Arthurs. "A Broadband Packet Switch for Integrated Transport." *IEEE Journal on Selected Areas in Communications,* October 1987.

HUMM85 Hummel, E. "The CCITT." *IEEE Communications Magazine,* January 1985.

HURL87 Hurley, B., C. Seid, and W. Sewell. "A Survey of Dynamic Routing Methods for Circuit-Switched Traffic." *IEEE Communications Magazine,* September 1987.

INOS79 Inose, H. *An Introduction to Digital Integrated Communications Systems.* University of Tokyo Press, 1979.

ISO84 International Organization for Standardization. *Basic Reference Model for Open Systems Interconnection.* ISO 7498, 1984.

JABB91 Jabbari, B. "Common Channel Signaling System Number 7 for ISDN and Intelligent Networks." *Proceedings of the IEEE,* February 1991.

JAYA84 Jayant, N., and P. Noll. *Digital Coding of Waveforms.* Englewood Cliffs, NJ: Prentice-Hall, 1984.

JAYA86 Jayant, N. "Coding Speech at Low Bits Rates." *IEEE Spectrum,* August 1986.

KANO91 Kano, S., K. Kitami, and M. Kawarasaki. "ISDN Standardization." *Proceedings of the IEEE,* February 1991.

KESS90 Kessler, G. *ISDN: Concepts, Facilities, and Services.* New York: McGraw-Hill, 1990.

KIM86 Kim, K., and P. Li. "Video Telephone: Gone Today, Here Tomorrow?" *Data Communications,* November 1986.

KIM89 Kim, B. *Current Advances in LANs, MANs, & ISDN.* Norwood, MA: Artech House, 1989.

KIMB75 Kimbleton, S., and F. Schneider. "Computer Communication Networks: Approaches, Objectives, and Performance Considerations." *ACM Computing Surveys,* September 1975.

KLEI76 Kleinrock, L. *Queuing Systems, Vol. II: Computer Applications.* New York: Wiley, 1976.

KLEI78 Kleinrock, L. "Principles and Lessons in Packet Communications." *Proceedings of the IEEE,* November 1978.

KOBA85 Kobayashi, K. "Advances in Facsimile Art." *IEEE Communications Magazine,* February 1985.

KUMM80 Kummede, K., and H. Rudin. "Packet and Circuit Switching: Cost/ Performance Boundaries." *Computer Networks,* No. 2, 1980.

KUO81 Kuo, F., ed. *Protocols and Techniques for Data Communication Networks.* Englewood Cliffs, NJ: Prentice-Hall, 1981.

LAI88 Lai, W. "Packet Forwarding." *IEEE Communications Magazine,* July 1988.

LAI89 Lai, W. "Frame Relaying Service: An Overview." *Proceedings, IEEE INFOCOM '89,* April 1989.

LANE91 Lane, J., and D. Upp. "SONET: The Next Premises Interface." *Telecommunications,* February 1991.

LECH86 Lechleider, J. "Loop Transmission Aspects of ISDN Basic Access." *IEEE Journal on Selected Areas in Communications,* November 1986.

LECH89 Lechleider, J. "Line Codes for Digital Subscriber Lines." *IEEE Communications Magazine,* September 1989.

LEE89 Lee, K., and Y. Lim. "Performance Analysis of the Congestion Control Scheme in Signaling System No. &." *Proceedings, INFOCOM '89,* April 1989.

LEON89 Leon-Garcia, A., editor. *Special Issue on Broadband Networks. IEEE Network,* January 1989.

LIN84 Lin, S., D. Costello, and M. Miller. "Automatic Repeat-Request Error-Control Schemes." *IEEE Communications Magazine,* December 1984.

LIN88 Lin, N., and C. Tzeng. "Full-Duplex Data Over Local Loops." *IEEE Communications Magazine,* February 1988.

LIN89 Lin, Y., D. Spears, and M. Yin. "Fiber-Based Local Access Network Architectures." *IEEE Communications Magazine,* October 1989.

LIN90 Lin, D. "Minimum Mean-Squared Error Echo Cancellation and Equalization for Digital Subscriber Line Transmission." *IEEE Transactions on Communications,* January 1990.

LU90 Lu, K., M. Eiger, and H. Lemberg. "System and Cost Analyses of Broad-Band Fiber Loop Architectures." *IEEE Journal on Selected Areas in Communications,* August 1990.

MANR89 Manros, C. *The X.400 Blue Book Companion.* Twickenham, England: Technology Appraisals, 1989.

MARI79 Marill, T. "Why the Telephone Is on Its Way Out and Electronic Mail is on Its Way In." *Datamation,* August 1979.

MARS91 Marsden, P. "Interworking IEEE 802/FDDI LANs Via the ISDN Frame Relay Bearer Service." *Proceedings of the IEEE,* February 1991.

MART73 Martin, J. *Security, Accuracy, and Privacy in Computer Systems.* Englewood Cliffs, NJ: Prentice-Hall, 1973.

MART81 Martin, J. *Computer Networks and Distributed Processing.* Englewood Cliffs, NJ: Prentice-Hall, 1981.

MART90 Martin, J. *Telecommunications and the Computer, Third Edition.* Englewood Cliffs, NJ: Prentice-Hall, 1990.

MARU83 Maruyama, K., and D. Shorter. "Dynamic Route Selection Algorithms for Session-Based Communication Networks." *Computer Communication Review,* April 1983.

MCNA88 McNamara, J. *Technical Aspects of Data Communication*, Third Edition. Bedford, MA: Digital Press, 1988.

MCQU80 McQuillan, J., L. Richer, and E. Rosen. "The New Routing Algorithm for the ARPANET." *IEEE Transactions on Communications*, May 1980.

MCQU85 McQuillan, J., and J. Herman. "Problems and Opportunities in Advanced Data Net Architectures." *Data Communications*, November 1985.

MESS84a Messerschmitt, D. "Echo Cancellation in Speech and Data Transmission." *IEEE Journal on Selected Areas in Communications*, March 1984.

MESS84b Messerschmitt, D. *Special Issue on Applications of Digital Signal Processing in Communications. IEEE Journal on Selected Areas in Communications*, March 1984.

MESS86 Messerschmitt, D. "Design Issues in the ISDN U-Interface Transceiver." *IEEE Journal on Selected Areas in Communications*, November 1986.

MINZ89a Minzer, S., and D. Spears. "New Directions in Signaling for Broadband ISDN." *IEEE Communications Magazine*, February 1989.

MINZ89b Minzer, S. "Broadband ISDN and Asynchronous Transfer Mode (ATM)." *IEEE Communications Magazine*, September 1989.

MITR91 Mitra, D., and J. Seery. "Comparative Evaluations of Randomized and Dynamic Routing Strategies for Circuit-Switched Networks." *IEEE Transactions on Communications*, January 1991.

MIYA75 Miyahura, H., T. Hasegawa, and Y. Teshigawara. "A Comparative Evaluation of Switching Methods in Computer Communication Networks." *Proceedings, International Communications Conference*, 1975.

MODA90a Modarressi, A., R. Skoog, and S. Boyles, editors. *Special Issue on Signaling System No. 7, IEEE Communications Magazine*, July 1990.

MODA90b Modarressi, A., and R. Skoog. "Signaling System No. 7: A Tutorial." *IEEE Communications Magazine*, July 1990.

MOOR83 Moore, D. "Teletex: A Worldwide Link Among Office Systems for Electronic Document Exchange." *IBM Systems Journal*, Nos. 1/2, 1983.

MULL87 Muller, N. "ADPCM Offers Practical Method for Doubling T1 Capacity." *Data Communications*, February 1987.

MURA87 Murakami, H., S. Matsumoto, Y. Hatori, and H. Yamamoto. "15/30 Mbit/s Universal Digital TV Codec Using a Median Adaptive Predictive Coding Method." *IEEE Transactions on Communications*, June 1987.

MURA90 Murano, K., S. Unagami, and F. Amano. "Echo Cancellation and Applications." *IEEE Communications Magazine*, January 1990.

NETR80 Netravati, A., and J. Limb. "Picture Coding: A Review." *Proceedings of the IEEE*, March 1980.

NETR88 Netravati, A., and B. Haskell. *Digital Pictures: Representation and Compression*. New York: Plenum, 1988.

NOJI86 Nojima, S., M. Hashimoto, H. Fuduka, and E. Tsutsui. "High Speed Packet Switching Network for Multi-Media Information." *Proceedings, Computer Networking Symposium*, November 1986.

NOJI87 Nojima, S., E. Tsutsui, H. Fuduka, and Hashimoto, M. "Integrated Services Packet Network Using Bus Matrix Switch." *IEEE Journal on Selected Areas in Communications*, October 1987.

NSPA79 National Standards Policy Advisory Committee. *National Policy on Standards for the United States*. 1979. Reprinted in [CERN84].

OPDE90 Opderbeck, H. "Frame Relay Networks: Not as Simple as They Seem." *Data Communications*, December 1990.

PAND87 Pandhi, S. "The Universal Data Connection." *IEEE Spectrum*, July 1987.

PAND90 Pandya, R., and M. Cullum. "Planning for Circuit-Switched Data Services in the ISDN Era: Interworking Solutions and Standards." *Computer Networks and ISDN Systems,* December 1990.

PARE88 Parekh, S., and K. Sohraby. "Some Performance Trade-Offs Associated with ATM Fixed-Length Vs. Variable-Length Cell Formats." *Proceedings, GlobeCom,* November 1988. Reprinted in [KIM89].

PATT90 Patterson, J., and C. Egido. "Three Keys to the Broadband Future: A View of Applications." *IEEE Network Magazine,* March 1990.

PEEB87 Peebles, P. *Digital Communication Systems.* Englewood Cliffs, NJ: Prentice-Hall, 1987.

PERE83 Perez, A. "Byte-wise CRC Calculations." *IEEE Micro,* June 1983.

PETE61 Peterson, W., and D. Brown. "Cyclic Codes for Error Detection." *Proceedings of the IRE,* January 1961.

PHEL86 Phelan, J. "Signaling System 7." *Telecommunications,* September 1986.

POTT77 Potter, R. "Electronic Mail." *Science,* March 19, 1977.

POUZ81 Pouzin, L. "Methods, Tools, and Observations on Flow Control in Packet-Switched Data Networks." *IEEE Transactions on Communications,* April 1981.

PRAT80 Pratt, W., et al. "Combined Symbol Matching Facsimile Data Compression Systems." *Proceedings of the IEEE,* July 1980.

QUAR86 Quarterman, J., and J. Hoskins. "Notable Computer Networks." *Communications of the ACM,* October 1986.

RAAC84 Raack, G., E. Sable, and R. Stewart. "Customer Control of Network Services." *IEEE Communications Magazine,* October 1984.

RAHN88 Rahnnema, M. "Smart Trunk Scheduling Strategies for Future Integrated Services Packet-Switched Networks." *IEEE Communications Magazine,* February 1988.

REGN90 Regnier, J., and W. Cameron. "State-Dependent Dynamic Traffic Management for Telephone Networks." *IEEE Communications Magazine,* October 1990.

REY83 Rey, R., editor. *Engineering and Operations in the Bell System,* Second Edition. Murray Hill, NJ: AT&T Bell Laboratories, 1983.

RIND79 Rinde, J., and A. Caisse. "Passive Flow Control Techniques for Distributed Networks." *Proceedings, IRIA Flow Control and Computer Networks Conference,* 1979.

ROBE78 Roberts, L. "The Evolution of Packet Switching." *Proceedings of the IEEE.* November 1978.

ROBI86 Robinson, R. "Digital Voice Compression." *Telecommunications,* February 1986.

ROBR91 Robrock, R. "The Intelligent Network—Changing the Face of Telecommunications." *Proceedings of the IEEE,* January 1991.

ROSN82 Rosner, R. *Packet Switching: Tomorrow's Communications Today.* Belmont, CA: Lifetime Learning, 1982.

RYAN87 Ryan, D. "Making Sense of Today's Image Communications Alternatives." *Data Communications,* April 1987.

SABR84 Sabri, S., and B. Prasada. "Coding of Broadcast TV Signals for Transmission Over Satellite Channels." *IEEE Transactions on Communications,* December 1984.

SAND80 Sanders, R. "Effects of Switching Technologies on Network Delay." *Data Communications,* April 1980.

SATO90 Sato, K., S. Ohta, and I. Tokizawa. "Broad-band ATM Network Architecture Based on Virtual Paths." *IEEE Transactions on Communications,* August 1990.

SCHW77 Schwartz, M. *Computer-Communication Network Design and Analysis.* Englewood Cliffs, NJ: Prentice-Hall, 1977.

SCHW80 Schwartz, M., and T. Stern. "Routing Techniques Used in Computer Communication Networks." *IEEE Transactions on Communications,* April 1980.

SHNE84 Shneiderman, B. "Response Time and Display Rate in Human Performance with Computers." *Computing Surveys,* September 1984.

SHUM89 Shumate, P. "Optical Fibers Reach into Homes." *IEEE Spectrum,* February 1989.

SILV87 Silver, D., and J. Williamson. "Data-Compression Chip Eases Document-Processing Design." *Computer Design,* November 15, 1987.

SIRB85 Sirbu, M., and L. Zwimpfer. "Standards Setting for Computer Communication: The Case of X.25." *IEEE Communications Magazine,* March 1985.

SKLA88 Sklar, B. *Digital Communications: Fundamentals and Applications.* Englewood Cliffs, NJ: Prentice-Hall, 1988.

STAI90 Stair, H., and J. Powers. *Megabit Data Communications.* Englewood Cliffs, NJ: Prentice-Hall, 1990.

STAL90a Stallings, W. *Computer Organization and Architecture, Second Edition.* New York: Macmillan, 1990.

STAL90b Stallings, W. *Handbook of Computer-Communications Standards, Volume I: The Open Systems Interconnections (OSI) Model and OSI-related Standards, Second Edition.* New York: Macmillan, 1990.

STAL90c Stallings, W. *Business Information Communications.* New York: Macmillan, 1990.

STAL91a Stallings, W. *Data and Computer Communications, Third Edition.* New York: Macmillan, 1991.

STAL91b Stallings, W. *Integrated Services Digital Networks (ISDN) and Broadband ISDN.* Los Alamitos, CA: IEEE Computer Society Press, 1991.

STAL91c Stallings, W. *Computer Communications: Architectures, Protocols, and Standards, Third Edition.* Los Alamitos, CA: IEEE Computer Society Press, 1991.

STAS90 Stassinopoulos, G. "ATM Adaptation Layer Protocols and IEEE LAN Interconnection." *Proceedings, 15th Conference on Local Computer Networks,* October 1990.

STUC85 Stuck, B., and E. A. Arthurs. *Computer Communications Network Performance Primer.* Englewood Cliffs, NJ: Prentice-Hall, 1985.

SUGI88 Sugimoto, M., M. Taniguchi, S. Yokoi, and H. Hata. "Videotex: Advancing to Higher Bandwidth." *IEEE Communications Magazine,* February 1988.

SZEC86 Szechenyi, K., F. Zapf, and D. Sallaerts. "Integrated Full Digital U-Interface Circuit for ISDN Subscriber Loops." *IEEE Journal on Selected Areas in Communications,* November 1986.

TAKE87 Takeuchi, T., T. Yamaguchi, H. Niwa, H. Suzuki, and S. Hayano. "Synchronous Composite Packet Switching: A Switching Architecture for Broadband ISDN." *IEEE Journal on Selected Areas in Communications,* October 1987.

TANE88 Tanebaum, A. *Computer Networks*. Englewood Cliffs, NJ: Prentice-Hall, 1988.

TAO84 Tao, Y., D. Kolwicz, C. Gritton, and D. Duttweiler. "A Cascadable VLSI Echo Canceller." *IEEE Journal on Selected Areas in Communications*, March 1984.

THAD81 Thadhani, A. "Interactive User Productivity." *IBM Systems Journal*, No. 4, 1981.

TURM88a Turman, B. "How Packet Terminals Will Work with ISDN." *Data Communications International*, June 1988.

TURM88b Turman, B. "Mixing Packets and ISDN." *Data Communications International*, July 1988.

TURN86 Turner, J. "Design of an Integrated Services Packet Network," *IEEE Journal on Selected Areas in Communications*, November 1986.

TYME81 Tymes, L. "Routing and Flow Control in TYMENET." *IEEE Transactions on Communications*, April 1981.

VAUG59 Vaughan, H. "Research Model for Time Separation Integrated Communication." *Bell System Technical Journal*, July 1959.

VERM90 Verma, P., ed. *ISDN Systems: Architecture, Technology, and Applications*. Englewood Cliffs, NJ: Prentice-Hall, 1990.

VOEL86 Voelcker, J. "Helping Computers Communicate." *IEEE Spectrum*, March 1986.

WAGN89 Wagner, S., and H. Kobrinski. "WDM Applications in Broadband Telecommunications Networks." *IEEE Communications Magazine*, March 1989.

WAKI91 Wakid, S., and K. Roberts. "Application Profile for ISDN." *Proceedings of the IEEE*, February 1991.

WATA90 Watanabe, Y., and T. Oda. "Dynamic Routing Schemes for International Networks." *IEEE Communications Magazine*, October 1990.

WEIN87 Weinstein, S. "Telecommunications in the Coming Decades." *IEEE Spectrum*, November 1987.

WEIS89 Weisberger, A. "The Evolving Versions of ISDN's Terminal Adapter." *Data Communications*, August 1989.

WOOD85 Wood, D. "Computer Networks." In [CHOU85].

WU91 Wu, W., and A. Livne. "ISDN: A Snapshot." *Proceedings of the IEEE*, February 1991.

WYND82 Wyndrum, R., ed. *Special Issue on Subscriber Loops. IEEE Transactions on Communications*, September 1982.

YASU80 Yasuda, Y. "Overview of Digital Facsimile Coding Techniques in Japan." *Proceedings of the IEEE*, July 1980.

YONE90 Yoneda, S. "Broadband ISDN ATM Layer Management: Operations, Administration, and Maintenance Considerations." *IEEE Network Magazine*, May 1990.

YUM87 Yum, T., and M. Schwartz. "Comparison of Routing Procedures for Circuit-Switched Traffic in Nonhierarchical Networks." *IEEE Transactions on Communications*, May 1987.

ZHAN91 Zhang, Y., et al. "Variable Bit-Rate Video Transmission in the Broadband ISDN Environment." *Proceedings of the IEEE*, February 1991.

Index

613

College Division
Macmillan Publishing Company
Front & Brown Streets
Riverside, NJ 08075

ORDER FORM

Ship To:
(Please print or type)

Name _____

Co. _____

Address _____

_____

City _____ St _____ Zip _____

Bill to:
(If different from shipping address)

Name _____

Co. _____

Address _____

_____

City _____ St _____ Zip _____

Mail your order to the above address or call 800-548-9939 (in New Jersey call 609-461-6500) or Fax 609-461-9265

Shipping Method **(select one)**
_____ UPS ground _____ 2nd Day Air _____ Book Rate

Payment Method **(select one)**	
_____ Check	_____ Visa
_____ Bill Me	_____ MasterCard
_____ Authorized Signature	
_____ Card Number	_____ Exp Date

(continued)

TEAR OUT THIS PAGE TO ORDER OTHER TITLES BY WILLIAM STALLINGS:

SEQ.	QTY.	ISBN NO.	TITLE	PRICE	TOTAL
1	_____	002-415491-1	Computer Organization & Architecture 2/e	$63.00	_____
2	_____	002-415454-7	Data and Computer Communications 3/e	$66.00	_____
3	_____	002-415531-4	Local Networks 3/e	$54.00	_____
4	_____	002-415431-8	Business Data Communications	$43.00	_____
5	_____	002-415475-X	ISDN and Broadband ISDN 2/e	$54.00	_____
6	_____	002-415481-4	Operating Systems	$42.00	_____

Handbooks of Computer Communications Standards

7	_____	002-415521-7	Volume 1, The Open Systems Interconnection (OSI) Model and OSI-Related Standards, 2/e	$43.00	_____
8	_____	002-415522-5	Volume 2, Local Area Network Standards, 2/e	$43.00	_____
9	_____	002-415523-3	Volume 3, The TCP/IP Protocol Suite, 2/e	$43.00	_____

GRAND TOTAL _____

A small shipping charge will be added. Prices subject to change without prior notification.

PSR-PSL 350-3500   FC# 1355

LIST OF ACRONYMS

AAL	ATM Adaptation Layer
AMI	Alternate Mark Inversion
ANSI	American National Standards Institute
ARQ	Automatic Repeat Request
ATM	Asynchronous Transfer Mode
B8ZS	Bipolar with 8-Zeros Substitution
BISDN	Broadband ISDN
BOC	Bell Operating Companies
CCITT	International Telegraph and Telephone Consultative Committee
CRC	Cyclic Redundancy Check
CSPDN	Circuit-Switched Public Data Network
DCE	Data Circuit-Terminating Equipment
DTE	Data Terminal Equipment
DNHR	Dynamic Nonhierarchical Routing
FCS	Frame Check Sequence
FDM	Frequency-Division Muliplexing
FMBS	Frame Mode Bearer Service
HDB3	High-Density Bipolar—3 Zones
HDLC	High-Level Data Link Control
IDN	Integrated Digital Network
ISDN	Integrated Services Digital Network
ISO	International Organization for Standardization
ISUP	ISDN User Part